key
BIBLE
VERSE
PARALLEL

key BIBLE VERSE PARALLEL

GEORGE W. KNIGHT
EDITOR

THOMAS NELSON PUBLISHERS
Nashville

Published in Nashville, Tennessee, by Thomas Nelson,
Inc. and distributed in Canada by Lawson Falle, Ltd., Cambridge, Ontario.

Printed in the United States of America.

Scripture quotations noted:

KJV are from the King James Version of the Bible.

NKJV are from the Holy Bible. New King James Version,
Copyright © Thomas Nelson, Inc., 1979, 1980, 1982.

TLB are from *The Living Bible*, copyright © 1971
by Tyndale House Publishers, Wheaton, IL. Used by permission.

NIV are from the HOLY BIBLE: NEW INTERNATIONAL VERSION.
Copyright © 1973, 1978, 1984 by the International Bible Society.
Used by permission of Zondervan Bible Publishers.

RSV are from the Revised Standard Version of the Bible,
Copyright © 1946, 1952, 1971 by the Division of Christian Education
of the National Council of Churches of Christ
in the USA, and are used by permission.

TEV are from the *Good News Bible*, the Bible in Today's English Version,
Copyright © American Bible Society 1966, 1971, 1976. Used by permission.

ISBN 0-8407-7562-8

1 2 3 4 5 6—92 91 90 89 88 87

──────── CONTENTS ────────

PREFACE

OLD TESTAMENT

NEW TESTAMENT

PREFACE

In recent years many new translations of God's Word have been published. While these new versions have kindled a renewed interest in study of the Scriptures, the typical reader of today is sometimes confused by such a varied menu in Bible translations. Is the King James Version the best translation because of its familiarity and wide acceptance? Or, do more modern versions—such as the New King James and the New International translations—give a more accurate and easier-to-understand rendering of the Bible's timeless message?

This book has been published to help Bible readers find the answers to practical questions such as these. The *Key Bible Verse Parallels* is exactly what its name implies—a handy comparison of hundreds of important Bible verses from several different translations. When boldface chapter and verse numbers appear, they signify that the verse—and the following verses, which only include the verse number—are taken from a new chapter. At a glance, the reader can compare a familiar verse from the Bible as rendered by the six most popular translations in use today: King James Version (KJV), New King James Version (NKJV), The Living Bible (TLB), New International Version (NIV), Revised Standard Version (RSV), and Today's English Version (TEV).

More than 1,800 key Bible verses are included in this sourcebook. Every book of the Bible is represented. This allows a reader to study parallel translations drawn from all types of literature in the Bible—history, poetry, drama, the prophetic writings, wisdom literature, and the gospels and epistles from the New Testament.

Careful comparison of the same verse in several different translations is an excellent habit to develop in Bible study. One translation will often throw new light on the meaning of a Bible passage by adding helpful information or by giving subtle shades of meaning not found in another version. For example, the King James Version renders Jesus' encouragement to His followers to watch expectantly for His return as a mild statement: "Take ye heed, watch and pray" (Mark 12:33). But the NIV translates these words as a strong command: "Be on guard! Be alert!" This stronger translation prods us to take the words of Jesus seriously and to be ready at all times for His return. The reader's understanding of this particular verse is enriched immeasurably by a careful comparison of the rendering from two different translations.

The six English translations of the Scriptures featured in this book were released across a period of more than three centuries by six different teams of translators. Following is a brief historical sketch of each version and how it came to be produced. With this information, the Bible reader should be able to compare these translations with greater precision and become more adept at the task of "rightly dividing the word of truth" (2 Tim. 2:15 KJV).

King James Version. Shortly after James VI of Scotland ascended the throne of England as James I, he convened a conference to settle several matters under dispute in the Church of England. The only important result of this conference was an approval to begin work on the King James Version of the English Bible.

A group of forty-seven scholars was appointed to undertake the work of preparing the new version. They used the 1602 edition of the Bishops' Bible as the basis of their revision, but they had access to many other versions and helps, as well as the texts in the original biblical languages. When the translators finished their task, the final draft was reviewed by a committee of twelve. The King James Version was published in 1611.

The new version won wide acceptance among the people of the English-speaking world. Nonsectarian in tone and approach, it did not favor one shade of theological or ecclesiastical opinion over another. The translators had an almost instinctive sense of good English style; the prose rhythms of the version gave it a secure place in the popular memory. Never was a version of the Bible more admirably suited for reading aloud in public.

Although there was some resistance to the King James Version at first, it quickly made a place for itself. For more than three centuries, it has remained "the Bible" throughout the English-speaking world.

New King James Version. During its long history, the King James Bible has been updated and revised several times to reflect changes in speech as well as growing knowledge of the original text of the Scriptures. Previous major revisions of this translation were issued in 1629, 1638, 1762, and 1769.

During the 1970s, Thomas Nelson Bible Publishers of Nashville, Tennessee, sensed the need for a fifth major revision. More than one hundred Bible scholars were selected to work on the New King James. The translators worked from the earliest and most trustworthy Hebrew and Greek texts available and also used the 1769 King James revision as a general guide to make sure the new edition preserved the majestic style and devotional quality of the original King James.

The most noticeable change in the New King James is replacement of the "thee's" and "thou's" and other archaic pronouns with their modern English equivalents. The "-est" and "-eth" verb endings also were eliminated in favor of more contemporary English idioms. The New Testament with Psalms was released in 1980, followed by the Old Testament in 1982.

The New King James Version is preferred by people who like the flowing style and familiar syntax of the original King James without many of the archaic words that have lost their meaning for modern readers.

The Living Bible. Although more of a paraphrase than a translation, *The Living Bible* has won wide acceptance across a broad spectrum of the evangelical world. This version of Scripture owes its genesis to publisher Kenneth Taylor's desire that his own children be able to understand the words of Scripture. He began putting the Bible into more contemporary renderings for the sake of his family's devotions. This led, eventually, to the publication of *Living Letters* in 1962, and the rest of the Bible followed at intervals after that.

Many users feel *The Living Bible* paraphrase speaks with an immediacy and an idiom that makes it more understandable than regular translations. Certainly, its colloquial style reminds us that the New Testament, at least, was written in the language of the people. *Koine* Greek was the *lingua franca* of the civilized, first-century world, the language in which God allowed His words to be inscripturated. Although not often used for Bible study, *The Living Bible* is one of the most popular Bible versions sold. Its devotional strength and clarity of expression have made it an enduring work.

New International Version. The New International Version is a completely new translation of the Bible, sponsored by the New York International Bible Society. It is the work of an interdenominational and international team of scholars, drawn mainly from the United States but also including scholars from Canada, Britain, Australia, and New Zealand. The NIV is written in clear and natural English, but its language is more literary than the "common English" of many modern translations.

The NIV strives to be faithful to the thought of the biblical writers and to produce a truly accurate translation. To do so, the translators occasionally moved away from a literal word-for-word translation, using the principle known as "dynamic equivalence." This concept of translation has as its goal to stimulate in the new reader in the new language the same reaction the original author wished to stimulate in his first readers.

The NIV has many helpful features, including a style and layout with verses running together in units of thought that invite extended reading of the Bible. It seeks to communicate the meaning of the original text in modern English. On the whole, it reads smoothly and is easy for the average reader to understand. Unlike the RSV, which retained "Thee," "Thou," and "Thy" when God was being addressed, the NIV uses "You" and "Your."

The New Testament of this version was published in 1973; the whole Bible appeared in 1978. It has been popular among general Bible readers because of its clear diction and readable style.

Revised Standard Version. In 1929, the International Council of Religious Education (an agency of the World Council of Churches) began work on a revision of the King James Version. After several false starts, the committee resolved on an entirely new translation, based on the latest scholarly texts. The New Testament of this new Bible was published in 1946, and the Old Testament in 1952.

The RSV met a mixed response. Many major denominations welcomed it as a more readable translation and supposedly a more reliable rendering of ancient texts. However, it has been criticized by many readers because it changed the wording of many classic passages that had far-reaching theological implications. This version is still the favored translation among several mainline Protestant denominations.

Today's English Version. In 1966 the American Bible Society issued this translation, also known as *Good News for Modern Man,* in the New Testament edition. Written in simple, contemporary English, this version was similar to basic English and plain English versions, but the *Good News Bible* used no limited vocabulary lists. In 1976 the entire Bible in Today's English Version was published.

The translators of the *Good News Bible* worked to achieve "dynamic equivalence." They wanted this translation to have the same effect on modern readers that the original text produced on those who first read it. However, some readers charge that the TEV pushed this principle too far, departing from the precise meaning of the original Hebrew and Greek texts at many points. In spite of these objections, this translation has gained wide acceptance among the Bible-reading public.

key
BIBLE
VERSE
PARALLEL

OLD TESTAMENT

Genesis

KJV	NKJV	TLB
1:1 In the beginning God created the heaven and the earth.	**1:1** In the beginning God created the heavens and the earth.	**1:1** When God began creating the heavens and the earth,
26 And God said, Let us make man in our image, after our likeness: and let them have dominion over the fish of the sea, and over the fowl of the air, and over the cattle, and over all the earth, and over every creeping thing that creepeth upon the earth.	26 Then God said, "Let Us make man in Our image, according to Our likeness; let them have dominion over the fish of the sea, over the birds of the air, and over the cattle, over all the earth and over every creeping thing that creeps on the earth."	26 Then God said, "Let us make a man—someone like ourselves, to be the master of all life upon the earth and in the skies and in the seas."
27 So God created man in his *own* image, in the image of God created he him; male and female created he them.	27 So God created man in His *own* image; in the image of God He created him; male and female He created them.	27 So God made man like his Maker. Like God did God make man; Man and maid did he make them.
2:1 Thus the heavens and the earth were finished, and all the host of them.	**2:1** Thus the heavens and the earth, and all the host of them, were finished.	**2:1** Now at last the heavens and earth were successfully completed, with all that they contained.
2 And on the seventh day God ended his work which he had made; and he rested on the seventh day from all his work which he had made.	2 And on the seventh day God ended His work which He had done, and He rested on the seventh day from all His work which He had done.	2 So on the seventh day, having finished his task, God ceased from this work he had been doing,
3 And God blessed the seventh day, and sanctified it: because that in it he had rested from all his work which God created and made.	3 Then God blessed the seventh day and sanctified it, because in it He rested from all His work which God had created and made.	3 and God blessed the seventh day and declared it holy, because it was the day when he ceased this work of creation.
3:7 And the eyes of them both were opened, and they knew that they *were* naked; and they sewed fig leaves together, and made themselves aprons.	**3:7** Then the eyes of both of them were opened, and they knew that they *were* naked; and they sewed fig leaves together and made themselves coverings.	**3:7** And as they ate it, suddenly they became aware of their nakedness, and were embarrassed. So they strung fig leaves together to cover themselves around the hips.
8 And they heard the voice of the LORD God walking in the garden in the cool of the day: and Adam and his wife hid themselves from the presence of the LORD God amongst the trees of the garden.	8 And they heard the sound of the LORD God walking in the garden in the cool of the day, and Adam and his wife hid themselves from the presence of the LORD God among the trees of the garden.	8 That evening they heard the sound of the Lord God walking in the garden; and they hid themselves among the trees.
14 And the LORD God said unto the serpent, Because thou hast done this, thou *art* cursed above all cattle, and above every beast of the field; upon thy belly shalt thou go, and dust shalt thou eat all the days of thy life:	14 So the LORD God said to the serpent: "Because you have done this, You *are* cursed more than all cattle, And more than every beast of the field; On your belly you shall go, And you shall eat dust All the days of your life.	14 So the Lord God said to the serpent, "This is your punishment: You are singled out from among all the domestic and wild animals of the whole earth—to be cursed. You shall grovel in the dust as long as you live, crawling along on your belly.
15 And I will put enmity between thee and the woman, and between thy seed and her seed; it shall bruise thy head, and thou shalt bruise his heel.	15 And I will put enmity Between you and the woman, And between your seed and her Seed; He shall bruise your head, And you shall bruise His heel."	15 From now on you and the woman will be enemies, as will all of your offspring and hers. And I will put the fear of you into the woman, and between your offspring and hers. He shall strike you on your head, while you will strike at his heel."
6:3 And the LORD said, My spirit shall not always strive with man, for that he also *is* flesh: yet his days shall be an hundred and twenty years.	**6:3** And the LORD said, "My Spirit shall not strive with man forever, for he *is* indeed flesh; yet his days shall be one hundred and twenty years."	**6:3** Then Jehovah said, "My Spirit must not forever be disgraced in man, wholly evil as he is. I will give him 120 years to mend his ways."
7 And the LORD said, I will destroy man whom I have created from the face of the earth; both man, and beast, and the creeping thing, and the fowls of the air; for it repenteth me that I have made them.	7 So the LORD said, "I will destroy man whom I have created from the face of the earth, both man and beast, creeping thing and birds of the air, for I am sorry that I have made them."	7 And he said, "I will blot out from the face of the earth all mankind that I created. Yes, and the animals too, and the reptiles and the birds. For I am sorry I made them."
8 But Noah found grace in the eyes of the LORD.	8 But Noah found grace in the eyes of the LORD.	8 But Noah was a pleasure to the Lord. Here is the story of Noah:

OLD TESTAMENT

NIV	RSV	TEV

Genesis

NIV	RSV	TEV
1:1 In the beginning God created the heavens and the earth.	**1:1** In the beginning God created the heavens and the earth.	**1:1** In the beginning, when God created the universe,
26 Then God said, "Let us make man in our image, in our likeness, and let them rule over the fish of the sea and the birds of the air, over the livestock, over all the earth, and over all the creatures that move along the ground."	26 Then God said, "Let us make man in our image, after our likeness; and let them have dominion over the fish of the sea, and over the birds of the air, and over the cattle, and over all the earth, and over every creeping thing that creeps upon the earth."	26 Then God said, "And now we will make human beings; they will be like us and resemble us. They will have power over the fish, the birds, and all animals, domestic and wild, large and small."
27 So God created man in his own image, in the image of God he created him; male and female he created them.	27 So God created man in his own image, in the image of God he created him; male and female he created them.	27 So God created human beings, making them to be like himself. He created them male and female,
2:1 Thus the heavens and the earth were completed in all their vast array.	**2:1** Thus the heavens and the earth were finished, and all the host of them.	**2:1** And so the whole universe was completed.
2 By the seventh day God had finished the work he had been doing; so on the seventh day he rested from all his work.	2 And on the seventh day God finished his work which he had done, and he rested on the seventh day from all his work which he had done.	2 By the seventh day God finished what he had been doing and stopped working.
3 And God blessed the seventh day and made it holy, because on it he rested from all the work of creating that he had done.	3 So God blessed the seventh day and hallowed it, because on it God rested from all his work which he had done in creation.	3 He blessed the seventh day and set it apart as a special day, because by that day he had completed his creation and stopped working.
3:7 Then the eyes of both of them were opened, and they realized they were naked; so they sewed fig leaves together and made coverings for themselves.	**3:7** Then the eyes of both were opened, and they knew that they were naked; and they sewed fig leaves together and made themselves aprons.	**3:7** As soon as they had eaten it, they were given understanding and realized that they were naked; so they sewed fig leaves together and covered themselves.
8 Then the man and his wife heard the sound of the LORD God as he was walking in the garden in the cool of the day, and they hid from the LORD God among the trees of the garden.	8 And they heard the sound of the LORD God walking in the garden in the cool of the day, and the man and his wife hid themselves from the presence of the LORD God among the trees of the garden.	8 That evening they heard the LORD God walking in the garden, and they hid from him among the trees.
14 So the LORD God said to the serpent, "Because you have done this, "Cursed are you above all the livestock and all of the wild animals! You will crawl on your belly and you will eat dust all the days of your life.	14 The LORD God said to the serpent, "Because you have done this, cursed are you above all cattle, and above all wild animals; upon your belly you shall go, and dust you shall eat all the days of your life.	14 Then the LORD God said to the snake, "You will be punished for this; you alone of all the animals must bear this curse: From now on you will crawl on your belly, and you will have to eat dust as long as you live.
15 And I will put enmity between you and the woman, and between your offspring and hers; he will crush your head, and you will strike his heel."	15 I will put enmity between you and the woman, and between your seed and her seed; he shall bruise your head, and you shall bruise his heel."	15 I will make you and the woman hate each other, her offspring and yours will always be enemies. Her offspring will crush your head, and you will bite their heel."
6:3 Then the LORD said, "My Spirit will not contend with man forever, for he is mortal; his days will be a hundred and twenty years."	**6:3** Then the LORD said, "My spirit shall not abide in man for ever, for he is flesh, but his days shall be a hundred and twenty years."	**6:3** Then the LORD said, "I will not allow people to live forever; they are mortal. From now on they will live no longer than 120 years."
7 So the LORD said, "I will wipe mankind, whom I have created, from the face of the earth—men and animals, and creatures that move along the ground, and birds of the air—for I am grieved that I have made them."	7 So the LORD said, "I will blot out man whom I have created from the face of the ground, man and beast and creeping things and birds of the air, for I am sorry that I have made them."	7 that he said, "I will wipe out these people I have created, and also the animals and the birds, because I am sorry that I made any of them."
8 But Noah found favor in the eyes of the LORD.	8 But Noah found favor in the eyes of the LORD.	8 But the LORD was pleased with Noah.

KJV	NKJV	TLB
9:6 Whoso sheddeth man's blood, by man shall his blood be shed: for in the image of God made he man.	**9:6** "Whoever sheds man's blood, By man his blood shall be shed; For in the image of God He made man.	**9:6** and any man who murders shall be killed; for to kill a man is to kill one made like God.
12 And God said, This *is* the token of the covenant which I make between me and you and every living creature that *is* with you, for perpetual generations:	**12** And God said: "This *is* the sign of the covenant which I make between Me and you, and every living creature that *is* with you, for perpetual generations:	**12** And I seal this promise with this sign:
13 I do set my bow in the cloud, and it shall be for a token of a covenant between me and the earth.	**13** "I set My rainbow in the cloud, and it shall be for the sign of the covenant between Me and the earth.	**13** I have placed my rainbow in the clouds as a sign of my promise until the end of time, to you and to all the earth.
25 And he said, Cursed *be* Canaan; a servant of servants shall he be unto his brethren.	**25** Then he said: "Cursed *be* Canaan; A servant of servants He shall be to his brethren."	**25** he cursed Ham's descendants: "A curse upon the Canaanites," he swore. "May they be the lowest of slaves to the descendants of Shem and Japheth."
26 And he said, Blessed *be* the LORD God of Shem; and Canaan shall be his servant.	**26** And he said: "Blessed *be* the LORD, The God of Shem, And may Canaan be his servant.	**26** Then he said, "God bless Shem, And may Canaan be his slave.
27 God shall enlarge Japheth, and he shall dwell in the tents of Shem; and Canaan shall be his servant.	**27** May God enlarge Japheth, And may he dwell in the tents of Shem; And may Canaan be his servant."	**27** God bless Japheth, And let him share the prosperity of Shem, And let Canaan be his slave."
11:5 And the LORD came down to see the city and the tower, which the children of men builded.	**11:5** But the LORD came down to see the city and the tower which the sons of men had built.	**11:5** But when God came down to see the city and the tower mankind was making,
6 And the LORD said, Behold, the people *is* one, and they have all one language; and this they begin to do: and now nothing will be restrained from them, which they have imagined to do.	**6** And the LORD said, "Indeed the people *are* one and they all have one language, and this is what they begin to do; now nothing that they propose to do will be withheld from them.	**6** he said, "Look! If they are able to accomplish all this when they have just *begun* to exploit their linguistic and political unity, just think of what they will do later! Nothing will be unattainable for them!
7 Go to, let us go down, and there confound their language, that they may not understand one another's speech.	**7** "Come, let Us go down and there confuse their language, that they may not understand one another's speech."	**7** Come, let us go down and give them different languages, so that they won't understand each other's words!"
12:1 Now the LORD had said unto Abram, Get thee out of thy country, and from thy kindred, and from thy father's house, unto a land that I will shew thee:	**12:1** Now the LORD had said to Abram: "Get out of your country, From your kindred and from your father's house, To a land that I will show you.	**12:1** After the death of Abram's father, God told him, "Leave your own country behind you, and your own people, and go to the land I will guide you to.
2 And I will make of thee a great nation, and I will bless thee, and make thy name great; and thou shalt be a blessing:	**2** I will make you a great nation; I will bless you And make your name great; And you shall be a blessing.	**2** If you do, I will cause you to become the father of a great nation; I will bless you and make your name famous, and you will be a blessing to many others.
3 And I will bless them that bless thee, and curse him that curseth thee: and in thee shall all families of the earth be blessed.	**3** I will bless those who bless you, And I will curse him who curses you; And in you all the families of the earth shall be blessed."	**3** I will bless those who bless you and curse those who curse you; and the entire world will be blessed because of you."
15:6 And he believed in the LORD; and he counted it to him for righteousness.	**15:6** And he believed in the LORD, and He accounted it to him for righteousness.	**15:6** And Abram believed God; then God considered him righteous on account of his faith.
17:1 And when Abram was ninety years old and nine, the LORD appeared to Abram, and said unto him, I *am* the Almighty God; walk before me, and be thou perfect.	**17:1** When Abram was ninety-nine years old, the LORD appeared to Abram and said to him, "I *am* Almighty God; walk before Me and be blameless.	**17:1** When Abram was ninety-nine years old, God appeared to him and told him, "I am the Almighty; obey me and live as you should.
2 And I will make my covenant between me and thee, and will multiply thee exceedingly.	**2** "And I will make My covenant between Me and you, and will multiply you exceedingly."	**2** I will prepare a contract between us, guaranteeing to make you into a mighty nation.
3 And Abram fell on his face: and God talked with him, saying,	**3** Then Abram fell on his face, and God talked with him, saying:	**3** Abram fell face downward in the dust as God talked with him.
4 As for me, behold, my covenant *is* with thee, and thou shalt be a father of many nations.	**4** "As for Me, behold, My covenant is with you, and you shall be a father of many nations.	**4** In fact you shall be the father of not only one nation, but a multitude of nations!"

NIV	RSV	TEV
9:6 "Whoever sheds the blood of man, by man shall his blood be shed; for in the image of God has God made man.	**9:6** Whoever sheds the blood of man, by man shall his blood be shed; for God made man in his own image.	**9:6** Man was made like God, so whoever murders a man will himself be killed by his fellowman.
12 And God said, "This is the sign of the covenant I am making between me and you and every living creature with you, a covenant for all generations to come:	**12** And God said, "This is the sign of the covenant which I make between me and you and every living creature that is with you, for all future generations:	**12** As a sign of this everlasting covenant which I am making with you and with all living beings,
13 I have set my rainbow in the clouds, and it will be the sign of the covenant between me and the earth.	**13** I set my bow in the cloud, and it shall be a sign of the covenant between me and the earth.	**13** I am putting my bow in the clouds. It will be the sign of my covenant with the world.
25 he said, "Cursed be Canaan! The lowest of slaves will he be to his brothers."	**25** he said, "Cursed by Canaan; a slave of slaves shall he be to his brothers."	**25** he said, "A curse on Canaan! He will be a slave to his brothers.
26 He also said, "Blessed be the LORD, the God of Shem! May Canaan be the slave of Shem.	**26** He also said, "Blessed by the LORD my God be Shem; and let Canaan be his slave.	**26** Give praise to the LORD, the God of Shem! Canaan will be the slave of Shem.
27 May God extend the territory of Japheth; may Japheth live in the tents of Shem, and may Canaan be his slave."	**27** God enlarge Japheth, and let him dwell in the tents of Shem; and let Canaan be his slave."	**27** May God cause Japheth to increase! May his descendants live with the people of Shem! Canaan will be the slave of Japheth."
11:5 But the LORD came down to see the city and the tower that the men were building.	**11:5** And the LORD came down to see the city and the tower, which the sons of men had built.	**11:5** Then the LORD came down to see the city and the tower which those men had built,
6 The LORD said, "If as one people speaking the same language they have begun to do this, then nothing they plan to do will be impossible for them.	**6** And the LORD said, "Behold, they are one people, and they have all one language; and this is only the beginning of what they will do; and nothing that they propose to do will now be impossible for them.	**6** and he said, "Now then, these are all one people and they speak one language; this is just the beginning of what they are going to do. Soon they will be able to do anything they want!
7 Come, let us go down and confuse their language so they will not understand each other."	**7** Come, let us go down, and there confuse their language, that they may not understand one another's speech."	**7** Let us go down and mix up their language so that they will not understand each other."
12:1 The LORD had said to Abram, "Leave your country, your people and your father's household and go to the land I will show you.	**12:1** Now the LORD said to Abram, "Go from your country and your kindred and your father's house to the land that I will show you.	**12:1** The LORD said to Abram, "Leave your country, your relatives, and your father's home, and go to a land that I am going to show you.
2 "I will make you a great nation and I will bless you; I will make your name great, and you will be a blessing.	**2** And I will make of you a great nation, and I will bless you, and make your name great, so that you will be a blessing.	**2** I will give you many descendants, and they will become a great nation. I will bless you and make your name famous, so that you will be a blessing.
3 I will bless those who bless you, and whoever curses you I will curse; and all peoples on earth will be blessed through you."	**3** I will bless those who bless you, and him who curses you I will curse; and by you all the families of the earth shall bless themselves."	**3** I will bless those who bless you, But I will curse those who curse you. And through you I will bless all the nations."
15:6 Abram believed the LORD, and he credited it to him as righteousness.	**15:6** And he believed the LORD; and he reckoned it to him as righteousness.	**15:6** Abram put his trust in the LORD, and because of this the LORD was pleased with him and accepted him.
17:1 When Abram was ninety-nine years old, the LORD appeared to him and said, "I am God Almighty; walk before me and be blameless.	**17:1** When Abram was ninety-nine years old the LORD appeared to Abram, and said to him, "I am God Almighty; walk before me, and be blameless.	**17:1** When Abram was ninety-nine years old, the LORD appeared to him and said, "I am the Almighty God. Obey me and always do what is right.
2 I will confirm my covenant between me and you and will greatly increase your numbers."	**2** And I will make my covenant between me and you, and will multiply you exceedingly."	**2** I will make my covenant with you and give you many descendants."
3 Abram fell facedown, and God said to him,	**3** Then Abram fell on his face; and God said to him,	**3** Abram bowed down with his face touching the ground, and God said,
4 "As for me, this is my covenant with you: You will be the father of many nations.	**4** "Behold, my covenant is with you, and you shall be the father of a multitude of nations.	**4** "I make this covenant with you: I promise that you will be the ancestor of many nations.

KJV	NKJV	TLB
5 Neither shall thy name any more be called Abram, but thy name shall be Abraham; for a father of many nations have I made thee.	5 "No longer shall your name be called Abram, but your name shall be Abraham; for I have made you a father of many nations.	5 "What's more," God told him, "I am changing your name. It is no longer 'Abram' ('Exalted Father'), but 'Abraham' ('Father of Nations')—for that is what you will be. I have declared it.
22:1 And it came to pass after these things, that God did tempt Abraham, and said unto him, Abraham: and he said, Behold, *here* I am.	22:1 Now it came to pass after these things that God tested Abraham, and said to him, "Abraham!" And he said, "Here I am."	22:1 Later on, God tested Abraham's [faith and obedience]. "Abraham!" God called. "Yes, Lord?" he replied.
2 And he said, Take now thy son, thine only *son* Isaac, whom thou lovest, and get thee into the land of Moriah; and offer him there for a burnt offering upon one of the mountains which I will tell thee of.	2 And He said, "Take now your son, your only *son* Isaac, whom you love, and go to the land of Moriah, and offer him there as a burnt offering on one of the mountains of which I shall tell you."	2 "Take with you your only son—yes, Isaac whom you love so much—and go to the land of Moriah and sacrifice him there as a burnt offering upon one of the mountains which I'll point out to you!"
12 And he said, Lay not thine hand upon the lad, neither do thou any thing unto him: for now I know that thou fearest God, seeing thou hast not withheld thy son, thine only *son* from me.	12 And He said, "Do not lay your hand on the lad, or do anything to him; for now I know that you fear God, seeing you have not withheld your son, your only *son*, from Me."	12 "Lay down the knife; don't hurt the lad in any way," the Angel said, "for I know that God is first in your life—you have not withheld even your beloved son from me."
15 And the angel of the LORD called unto Abraham out of heaven the second time,	15 And the Angel of the LORD called to Abraham a second time out of heaven,	15 Then the Angel of God called again to Abraham from heaven.
16 And said, By myself have I sworn, saith the LORD, for because thou hast done this thing, and hast not withheld thy son, thine only *son:*	16 and said: "By Myself I have sworn, says the LORD, because you have done this thing, and have not withheld your son, your only *son*,	16 "I, the Lord, have sworn by myself that because you have obeyed me and have not withheld even your beloved son from me,
17 That in blessing I will bless thee, and in multiplying I will multiply thy seed as the stars of the heaven, and as the sand which *is* upon the sea shore; and thy seed shall possess the gate of his enemies;	17 "in blessing I will bless you, and in multiplying I will multiply your descendants as the stars of the heaven and as the sand which *is* on the seashore; and your descendants shall possess the gate of their enemies.	17 I will bless you with incredible blessings and multiply your descendants into countless thousands and millions, like the stars above you in the sky, and like the sands along the seashore. These descendants of yours will conquer their enemies,
28:15 And, behold, I *am* with thee, and will keep thee in all *places* whither thou goest, and will bring thee again into this land; for I will not leave thee, until I have done *that* which I have spoken to thee of.	28:15 "Behold, I *am* with you and will keep you wherever you go, and will bring you back to this land; for I will not leave you until I have done what I have spoken to you."	28:15 What's more, I am with you, and will protect you wherever you go, and will bring you back safely to this land; I will be with you constantly until I have finished giving you all I am promising."
16 And Jacob awaked out of his sleep, and he said, Surely the LORD is in this place; and I knew *it* not.	16 Then Jacob awoke from his sleep and said, "Surely the LORD is in this place, and I did not know *it*."	16 Then Jacob woke up. "God lives here!"
17 And he was afraid, and said, How dreadful *is* this place! this *is* none other but the house of God, and this *is* the gate of heaven.	17 And he was afraid and said, "How awesome *is* this place! This *is* none other than the house of God, and this *is* the gate of heaven!"	17 he exclaimed in terror. "I've stumbled into his home! This is the awesome entrance to heaven!"
32:24 And Jacob was left alone; and there wrestled a man with him until the breaking of the day.	32:24 Then Jacob was left alone; and a Man wrestled with him until the breaking of day.	32:24 then returned again to the camp and was there alone; and a Man wrestled with him until dawn.
25 And when he saw that he prevailed not against him, he touched the hollow of his thigh; and the hollow of Jacob's thigh was out of joint, as he wrestled with him.	25 Now when He saw that He did not prevail against him, He touched the socket of his hip; and the socket of Jacob's hip was out of joint as He wrestled with him.	25 And when the Man saw that he couldn't win the match, he struck Jacob's hip, and knocked it out of joint at the socket.
26 And he said, Let me go, for the day breaketh. And he said, I will not let thee go, except thou bless me.	26 And He said, "Let Me go, for the day breaks." But he said, "I will not let You go unless You bless me!"	26 Then the Man said, "Let me go, for it is dawn." But Jacob panted, "I will not let you go until you bless me."
27 And he said unto him. What *is* thy name? And he said, Jacob.	27 So He said to him, "What *is* your name?" And he said, "Jacob."	27 "What is your name?" the Man asked. "Jacob," was the reply.
28 And he said, Thy name shall be called no more Jacob, but Israel: for as a prince hast thou power with God and with men, and hast prevailed.	28 And He said, "Your name shall no longer be called Jacob, but Israel; for you have struggled with God and with men, and have prevailed."	28 "It isn't anymore!" the Man told him. "It is Israel—one who has power with God. Because you have been strong with God, you shall prevail with men."
45:7 And God sent me before you to preserve you a posterity in the earth, and to save your lives by a great deliverance.	45:7 "And God sent me before you to preserve a posterity for you in the earth, and to save your lives by a great deliverance.	45:7 God has sent me here to keep you and your families alive, so that you will become a great nation.
8 So now *it was* not you *that* sent me hither, but God: and he hath made me a father to Pharaoh, and lord of all his house, and a ruler throughout all the land of Egypt.	8 "So now *it was* not you *who* sent me here, but God; and He has made me a father to Pharaoh, and lord of all his house, and a ruler throughout all the land of Egypt.	8 Yes, it was God who sent me here, not you! And he has made me a counselor to Pharaoh, and manager of this entire nation, ruler of all the land of Egypt.

NIV	RSV	TEV
5 No longer will you be called Abram; your name will be Abraham, for I have made you a father of many nations.	5 No longer shall your name be Abram, but your name shall be Abraham; for I have made you the father of a multitude of nations.	5 Your name will no longer be Abram, but Abraham, because I am making you the ancestor of many nations.
22:1 Some time later God tested Abraham. He said to him, "Abraham!" "Here I am," he replied.	22:1 After these things God tested Abraham, and said to him, "Abraham!" And he said, "Here am I."	22:1 Some time later God tested Abraham; he called to him, "Abraham!" And Abraham answered, "Yes, here I am!"
2 Then God said, "Take your son, your only son Isaac, whom you love, and go to the region of Moriah. Sacrifice him there as a burnt offering on one of the mountains I will tell you about."	2 He said, "Take your son, your only son Isaac, whom you love, and go to the land of Moriah, and offer him there as a burnt offering upon one of the mountains of which I shall tell you."	2 "Take your son," God said, "your only son, Isaac, whom you love so much, and go to the land of Moriah. There on a mountain that I will show you, offer him as a sacrifice to me."
12 "Do not lay a hand on the boy," he said. "Do not do anything to him. Now I know that you fear God, because you have not withheld from me your son, your only son."	12 He said, "Do not lay your hand on the lad or do anything to him; for now I know that you fear God, seeing you have not withheld your son, your only son, from me."	12 "Don't hurt the boy or do anything to him," he said. "Now I know that you honor and obey God, because you have not kept back your only son from him."
15 The angel of the LORD called to Abraham from heaven a second time	15 And the angel of the LORD called to Abraham a second time from heaven,	15 The angel of the LORD called to Abraham from heaven a second time,
16 and said, "I swear by myself, declares the LORD, that because you have done this and have not withheld your son, your only son,	16 and said, "By myself I have sworn, says the LORD because you have done this, and have not withheld your son, your only son,	16 "I make a vow by own name—the LORD is speaking—that I will richly bless you. Because you did this and did not keep back only son from me,
17 I will surely bless you and make your descendants as numerous as the stars in the sky and as the sand on the seashore. Your descendants will take possession of the cities of their enemies,	17 I will indeed bless you, and I will multiply your descendants as the stars of heaven and as the sand which is on the seashore. And your descendants shall possess the gate of their enemies,	17 I promise that I will give you as many descendants as there are stars in the sky or grains of sand along the seashore. Your descendants will conquer their enemies.
28:15 I am with you and will watch over you wherever you go, and I will bring you back to this land. I will not leave you until I have done what I have promised you."	28:15 Behold, I am with you and will keep you wherever you go, and will bring you back to this land; for I will not leave you until I have done that of which I have spoken to you."	28:15 Remember, I will be with you and protect you wherever you go, and I will bring you back to this land. I will not leave you until I have done all that I have promised you."
16 When Jacob awoke from his sleep, he thought, "Surely the LORD is in this place, and I was not aware of it."	16 Then Jacob awoke from his sleep and said, "Surely the LORD is in this place; and I did not know it."	16 Jacob woke up and said, "The LORD is here! He is in this place, and I didn't know it!"
17 He was afraid and said, "How awesome is this place! This is none other than the house of God; this is the gate of heaven."	17 And he was afraid, and said, "How awesome is this place! This is none other than the house of God, and this is the gate of heaven."	17 He was afraid and said, "What a terrifying place this is! It must be the house of God; it must be the gate that opens into heaven."
32:24 So Jacob was left alone, and a man wrestled with him till daybreak.	32:24 And Jacob was left alone; and a man wrestled with him until the breaking of the day.	32:24 but he stayed behind alone. Then a man came and wrestled with him until just before daybreak.
25 When the man saw that he could not overpower him, he touched the socket of Jacob's hip so that his hip was wrenched as he wrestled with the man.	25 When the man saw that he did not prevail against Jacob, he touched the hollow of his thigh; and Jacob's thigh was put out of joint as he wrestled with him.	25 When the man saw that he was not winning the struggle, he hit Jacob on the hip, and it was thrown out of joint.
26 Then the man said, "Let me go, for it is daybreak." But Jacob replied, "I will not let you go unless you bless me."	26 Then he said, "Let me go, for the day is breaking." But Jacob said, "I will not let you go, unless you bless me."	26 The man said, "Let me go; daylight is coming." "I won't, unless you bless me," Jacob answered.
27 The man asked him, "What is your name?" "Jacob," he answered.	27 And he said to him, "What is your name?" And he said, "Jacob."	27 "What is your name?" the man asked. "Jacob," he answered.
28 Then the man said, "Your name will no longer be Jacob, but Israel, because you have struggled with God and with men and have overcome."	28 Then he said, "Your name shall no more be called Jacob, but Israel, for you have striven with God and with men, and have prevailed."	28 The man said, "Your name will no longer be Jacob. You have struggled with God and with men, and you have won; so your name will be Israel."
45:7 But God sent me ahead of you to preserve for you a remnant on earth and to save your lives by a great deliverance.	45:7 And God sent me before you to preserve for you a remnant on earth, and to keep alive for you many survivors.	45:7 God sent me ahead of you to rescue you in this amazing way and to make sure that you and your descendants survive.
8 "So then, it was not you who set me here, but God. He made me father to Pharaoh, lord of his entire household and ruler of all Egypt.	8 So it was not you who sent me here, but God; and he has made me a father to Pharaoh, and lord of all his house and ruler over all the land of Egypt.	8 So it was not really you who sent me here, but God. He has made me the king's highest official. I am in charge of his whole country; I am the ruler of all Egypt.

KJV	NKJV	TLB
49:10 The sceptre shall not depart from Judah, nor a lawgiver from between his feet, until Shiloh come; and unto him *shall* the gathering of the people *be*.	**49:10** The scepter shall not depart from Judah, Nor a lawgiver from between his feet, Until Shiloh comes; And to Him *shall be* the obedience of the people.	**49:10** The scepter shall not depart from Judah until Shiloh comes, whom all people shall obey.

Exodus

KJV	NKJV	TLB
3:7 And the LORD said, I have surely seen the affliction of my people which *are* in Egypt, and have heard their cry by reason of their taskmasters; for I know their sorrows;	**3:7** And the LORD said: "I have surely seen the oppression of My people who *are* in Egypt, and have heard their cry because of their taskmasters, for I know their sorrows.	**3:7** Then the Lord told him, "I have seen the deep sorrows of my people in Egypt, and have heard their pleas for freedom from their harsh taskmasters.
8 And I am come down to deliver them out of the hand of the Egyptians, and to bring them up out of that land unto a good land and a large, unto a land flowing with milk and honey; unto the place of the Canaanites, and the Hittites, and the Amorites, and the Perizzites, and the Hivites, and the Jebusites.	**8** "So I have come down to deliver them out of the hand of the Egyptians, and to bring them up from that land to a good and large land, to a land flowing with milk and honey, to the place of the Canaanites and the Hittites and the Amorites and the Perizzites and the Hivites and the Jebusites.	**8** I have come to deliver them from the Egyptians and to take them out of Egypt into a good land, a large land, a land 'flowing with milk and honey'—the land where the Canaanites, Hittites, Amorites, Perizzites, Hivites, and Jebusites live.
12 And he said, Certainly I will be with thee; and this *shall be* a token unto thee, that I have sent thee: When thou hast brought forth the people out of Egypt, ye shall serve God upon this mountain.	**12** So He said, "I will certainly be with you. And this *shall be* a sign to you that I have sent you: When you have brought the people out of Egypt, you shall serve God on this mountain."	**12** Then God told him, "I will certainly be with you, and this is the proof that I am the one who is sending you: When you have led the people out of Egypt, you shall worship God here upon this mountain!"
13 And Moses said unto God, Behold, *when* I come unto the children of Israel, and shall say unto them, The God of your fathers hath sent me unto you; and they shall say to me, What *is* his name? what shall I say unto them?	**13** Then Moses said to God, "Indeed, *when* I come to the children of Israel and say to them, 'The God of your fathers has sent me to you,' and they say to me, 'What *is* His name?' what shall I say to them?"	**13** But Moses asked, "If I go to the people of Israel and tell them that their fathers' God has sent me, they will ask, 'Which God are you talking about?' What shall I tell them?"
14 And God said unto Moses, I AM THAT I AM: and he said, Thus shalt thou say unto the children of Israel, I AM hath sent me unto you.	**14** And God said to Moses, "I AM WHO I AM." And He said, "Thus you shall say to the children of Israel, 'I AM has sent me to you.'"	**14** "'The Sovereign God,'" was the reply. "Just say, 'I Am has sent me!'
6:6 Wherefore say unto the children of Israel, I *am* the LORD, and I will bring you out from under the burdens of the Egyptians, and I will rid you out of their bondage, and I will redeem you with a stretched out arm, and with great judgments:	**6:6** "Therefore say to the children of Israel: 'I *am* the LORD; I will bring you out from under the burdens of the Egyptians, I will rescue you from their bondage, and I will redeem you with an outstretched arm and with great judgments.	**6:6** "Therefore tell the descendants of Israel that I will use my mighty power and perform great miracles to deliver them from slavery, and make them free.
7 And I will take you to me for a people, and I will be to you a God: and ye shall know that I *am* the LORD your God, which bringeth you out from under the burdens of the Egyptians.	**7** 'I will take you as My people, and I will be your God. Then you shall know that I *am* the LORD your God who brings you out from under the burdens of the Egyptians.	**7** And I will accept them as my people and be their God. And they shall know that I am Jehovah their God who has rescued them from the Egyptians.
8 And I will bring you in unto the land, concerning the which I did swear to give it to Abraham, to Isaac, and to Jacob; and I will give it you for an heritage: I *am* the LORD.	**8** 'And I will bring you into the land which I swore to give to Abraham, Isaac, and Jacob; and I will give it to you *as* a heritage: I *am* the LORD.'"	**8** I will bring them into the land I promised to give to Abraham, Isaac, and Jacob. It shall belong to my people."
12:40 Now the sojourning of the children of Israel, who dwelt in Egypt, *was* four hundred and thirty years.	**12:40** Now the sojourn of the children of Israel who lived in Egypt *was* four hundred and thirty years.	**12:40** The sons of Jacob and their descendants had lived in Egypt 430 years,
41 And it came to pass at the end of the four hundred and thirty years, even the selfsame day it came to pass, that all the hosts of the LORD went out from the land of Egypt.	**41** And it came to pass at the end of the four hundred and thirty years—on that very same day—it came to pass that all the armies of the LORD went out from the land of Egypt.	**41** and it was on the last day of the 430th year that all of Jehovah's people left the land.
42 It *is* a night to be much observed unto the LORD for bringing them out from the land of Egypt: this *is* that night of the LORD to be observed of all the children of Israel in their generations.	**42** It *is* a night of solemn observance to the LORD for bringing them out of the land of Egypt. This *is* that night of the LORD, a solemn observance for all the children of Israel throughout their generations.	**42** This night was selected by the Lord to bring his people out from the land of Egypt; so the same night was selected as the date of the annual celebration of God's deliverance.
14:21 And Moses stretched out his hand over the sea; and the LORD caused the sea to go *back* by a strong east wind all that night, and made the sea dry *land*, and the waters were divided.	**14:21** Then Moses stretched out his hand over the sea; and the LORD caused the sea to go *back* by a strong east wind all that night, and made the sea into dry *land*, and the waters were divided.	**14:21** Meanwhile, Moses stretched his rod over the sea, and the Lord opened up a path through the sea, with walls of water on each side; and a strong east wind blew all that night, drying the sea bottom.
22 And the children of Israel went into the midst of the sea upon the dry *ground*: and the waters *were* a wall unto them on their right hand, and on their left.	**22** So the children of Israel went into the midst of the sea on the dry *ground*, and the waters *were* a wall to them on their right hand and on their left.	**22** So the people of Israel walked through the sea on dry ground!

NIV	RSV	TEV
49:10 The scepter will not depart from Judah, nor the ruler's staff from between his feet, until he comes to whom it belongs and the obedience of the nations is his.	**49:10** The scepter shall not depart from Judah, nor the ruler's staff from between his feet, until he comes to whom it belongs; and to him shall be the obedience of the peoples.	**49:10** Judah will hold the royal scepter, And his descendants will always rule. Nations will bring him tribute And bow in obedience before him.

Exodus

NIV	RSV	TEV
3:7 The LORD said, "I have indeed seen the misery of my people in Egypt. I have heard them crying out because of their slave drivers, and I am concerned about their suffering.	**3:7** Then the LORD said, "I have seen the affliction of my people who are in Egypt, and have heard their cry because of their taskmasters; I know their sufferings,	**3:7** Then the LORD said, "I have seen how cruelly my people are being treated in Egypt; I have heard them cry out to be rescued from their slave drivers. I know all about their sufferings,
8 So I have come down to rescue them from the hand of the Egyptians and to bring them up out of that land into a good and spacious land, a land flowing with milk and honey—the home of the Canaanites, Hittites, Amorites, Perizzites, Hivites and Jebusites.	8 and I have come down to deliver them out of the hand of the Egyptians, and to bring them up out of that land to a good and broad land, a land flowing with milk and honey, to the place of the Canaanites, the Hittites, the Amorites, the Perizzites, the Hivites, and the Jebusites.	8 and so I have come down to rescue them from the Egyptians and to bring them out of Egypt to a spacious land, one which is rich and fertile and in which the Canaanites, the Hittites, the Amorites, the Perizzites, the Hivites, and the Jebusites now live.
12 And God said, "I will be with you. And this will be the sign to you that it is I who have sent you: When you have brought the people out of Egypt, you will worship God on this mountain."	12 He said, "But I will be with you; and this shall be the sign for you, that I have sent you: when you have brought forth the people out of Egypt, you shall serve God upon this mountain."	12 God answered, "I will be with you, and when you bring the people out of Egypt, you will worship me on this mountain. That will be the proof that I have sent you."
13 Moses said to God, "Suppose I go to the Israelites and say to them, 'The God of your fathers has sent me to you,' and they ask me, 'What is his name?' Then what shall I tell them?"	13 Then Moses said to God, "If I come to the people of Israel and say to them, 'The God of your fathers has sent me to you,' and they ask me, 'What is his name?' what shall I say to them?"	13 But Moses replied, "When I go to the Israelites and say to them, 'The God of your ancestors sent me to you,' they will ask me, 'What is his name?' So what can I tell them?"
14 God said to Moses, "I am who I am. This is what you are to say to the Israelites: 'I AM has sent me to you.'"	14 God said to Moses, "I AM WHO I AM." And he said, "Say this to the people of Israel, 'I AM has sent me to you.'"	14 God said, "I am who I am. You must tell them: 'The one who is called I AM has sent me to you.'
6:6 Therefore, say to the Israelites: 'I am the LORD and I will bring you out from under the yoke of the Egyptians. I will free you from being slaves to them and will redeem you with an outstretched arm and with mighty acts of judgment.	**6:6** Say therefore to the people of Israel, 'I am the LORD, and I will bring you out from under the burdens of the Egyptians, and I will deliver you from their bondage, and I will redeem you with an outstretched arm and with great acts of judgment,	**6:6** So tell the Israelites that I say to them, 'I am the LORD; I will rescue you and set you free from your slavery to the Egyptians. I will raise my mighty arm to bring terrible punishment upon them, and I will save you.
7 I will take you as my own people, and I will be your God. Then you will know that I am the LORD your God, who brought you out from under the yoke of the Egyptians.	7 and I will take you for my people, and I will be your God; and you shall know that I am the LORD your God, who has brought you out from under the burdens of the Egyptians.	7 I will make you my own people, and I will be your God. You will know that I am the LORD your God when I set you free from slavery in Egypt.
8 And I will bring you to the land I swore with uplifted hand to give to Abraham, to Isaac and to Jacob. I will give it to you as a possession. I am the LORD.'"	8 And I will bring you into the land which I swore to give to Abraham, to Isaac, and to Jacob; I will give it to you for a possession. I am the LORD.'"	8 I will bring you to the land that I solemnly promised to give to Abraham, Isaac, and Jacob; and I will give it to you as your own possession. I am the LORD.'"
12:40 Now the length of time the Israelite people lived in Egypt was 430 years.	**12:40** The time that the people of Israel dwelt in Egypt was four hundred and thirty years.	**12:40** The Israelites had lived in Egypt for 430 years.
41 At the end of the 430 years, to the very day, all the LORD's divisions left Egypt.	41 And at the end of four hundred and thirty years, on that very day, all the hosts of the LORD went out from the land of Egypt.	41 On the day the 430 years ended, all the tribes of the LORD's people left Egypt.
42 Because the LORD kept vigil that night to bring them out of Egypt, on this night all the Israelites are to keep vigil to honor the LORD for the generations to come.	42 It was a night of watching by the LORD, to bring them out of the land of Egypt; so this same night is a night of watching kept to the LORD by all the people of Israel throughout their generations.	42 It was a night when the LORD kept watch to bring them out of Egypt; this same night is dedicated to the LORD for all time to come as a night when the Israelites must keep watch.
14:21 Then Moses stretched out his hand over the sea, and all that night the LORD drove the sea back with a strong east wind and turned it into dry land. The waters were divided,	**14:21** Then Moses stretched out his hand over the sea; and the LORD drove the sea back by a strong east wind all night, and made the sea dry land, and the waters were divided.	**14:21** Moses held out his hand over the sea, and the LORD drove the sea back with a strong east wind. It blew all night and turned the sea into dry land. The water was divided,
22 and the Israelites went through the sea on dry ground, with a wall of water on their right and on their left.	22 And the people of Israel went into the midst of the sea on dry ground, the waters being a wall to them on their right hand and on their left.	22 and the Israelites went through the sea on dry ground, with walls of water on both sides.

KEY VERSE COMPARISON CHART

KJV	NKJV	TLB
27 And Moses stretched forth his hand over the sea, and the sea returned to his strength when the morning appeared; and the Egyptians fled against it; and the LORD overthrew the Egyptians in the midst of the sea.	27 And Moses stretched out his hand over the sea; and when the morning appeared, the sea returned to its full depth, while the Egyptians were fleeing into it. So the LORD overthrew the Egyptians in the midst of the sea.	27 Moses did, and the sea returned to normal beneath the morning light. The Egyptians tried to flee, but the Lord drowned them in the sea.
20:2 I *am* the LORD thy God, which have brought thee out of the land of Egypt, out of the house of bondage.	20:2 "I *am* the LORD your God, who brought you out of the land of Egypt, out of the house of bondage.	20:2 "I am Jehovah your God who liberated you from your slavery in Egypt.
3 Thou shalt have no other gods before me.	3 "You shall have no other gods before Me.	3 "You may worship no other god than me.
4 Thou shalt not make unto thee any graven image, or any likeness *of any thing* that *is* in heaven above, or that *is* in the earth beneath, or that *is* in the water under the earth:	4 "You shall not make for yourself any carved image, or any likeness *of anything* that *is* in heaven above, or that *is* in the earth beneath, or that *is* in the water under the earth;	4 "You shall not make yourselves any idols: any images resembling animals, birds, or fish.
5 Thou shalt not bow down thyself to them, nor serve them: for I the LORD thy God *am* a jealous God, visiting the iniquity of the fathers upon the children unto the third and fourth *generation* of them that hate me;	5 you shall not bow down to them nor serve them. For I, the LORD your God, *am* a jealous God, visiting the iniquity of the fathers on the children to the third and fourth *generations* of those who hate Me,	5 You must never bow to an image or worship it in any way; for I, the Lord your God, am very possessive. I will not share your affection with any other god! And when I punish people for their sins, the punishment continues upon the children, grandchildren, and great-grandchildren of those who hate me;
6 And shewing mercy unto thousands of them that love me, and keep my commandments.	6 but showing mercy to thousands, to those who love Me and keep My commandments.	6 but I lavish my love upon thousands of those who love me and obey my commandments.
7 Thou shalt not take the name of the LORD thy God in vain; for the LORD will not hold him guiltless that taketh his name in vain.	7 "You shall not take the name of the LORD your God in vain, for the LORD will not hold guiltless who takes His name in vain.	7 "You shall not use the name of Jehovah your God irreverently, nor use it to swear to a falsehood. You will not escape punishment if you do.
8 Remember the sabbath day, to keep it holy.	8 "Remember the Sabbath day, to keep it holy.	8 "Remember to observe the Sabbath as a holy day.
9 "Six days shalt thou labour, and do all thy work:	9 Six days you shall labor and do all your work,	9 Six days a week are for your daily duties and your regular work,
10 But the seventh day *is* the sabbath of the LORD thy God: *in it* thou shalt not do any work, thou, nor thy son, nor thy daughter, thy manservant, nor thy maidservant, nor thy cattle, nor thy stranger that *is* within thy gates:	10 but the seventh day *is* the Sabbath of the LORD your God. *In it* you shall do no work: you, nor your son, nor your daughter, nor your manservant, nor your maidservant, nor your cattle, nor your stranger who *is* within your gates.	10 but the seventh day is a day of Sabbath rest before the Lord your God. On that day you are to do no work of any kind, nor shall your son, daughter, or slaves—whether men or women—or your cattle or your house guests.
11 For *in* six days the LORD made heaven and earth, the sea, and all that in them *is*, and rested the seventh day: wherefore the LORD blessed the sabbath day, and hallowed it.	11 For *in* six days the LORD made the heavens and the earth, the sea, and all that *is* in them, and rested the seventh day. Therefore the LORD blessed the Sabbath day and hallowed it.	11 For in six days the Lord made the heaven, earth, and sea, and everything in them, and rested the seventh day; so he blessed the Sabbath day and set it aside for rest.
12 Honour thy father and thy mother: that thy days may be long upon the land which the LORD thy God giveth thee.	12 "Honor your father and your mother, that your days may be long upon the land which the LORD your God is giving you.	12 "Honor your father and mother, that you may have a long, good life in the land the Lord your God will give you.
13 Thou shalt not kill.	13 "You shall not murder.	13 "You must not murder.
14 Thou shall not commit adultery.	14 "You shall not commit adultery.	14 "You must not commit adultery.
15 Thou shalt not steal.	14 "You shall not steal.	15 "You must not steal.
16 Thou shalt not bear false witness against thy neighbour.	16 "You shall not bear false witness against your neighbor.	16 "You must not lie.
17 Thou shalt not covet thy neighbour's house, thou shalt not covet thy neighbour's wife, nor his manservant, nor his maidservant, nor his ox, nor his ass, nor any thing that *is* thy neighbour's.	17 "You shall not covet your neighbor's house; you shall not covet your neighbor's wife, nor his manservant, nor his maidservant, nor his ox, nor his donkey, nor anything that *is* your neighbor's."	17 "You must not be envious of your neighbor's house, or want to sleep with his wife, or want to own his slaves, oxen, donkeys, or anything else he has."
32:31 And Moses returned unto the LORD, and said, Oh, this people have sinned a great sin, and have made them gods of gold.	32:31 Then Moses returned to the LORD and said, "Oh, these people have sinned a great sin, and have made for themselves a god of gold!	32:31 So Moses returned to the Lord and said, "Oh, these people have sinned a great sin, and have made themselves gods of gold.
32 Yet now, if thou wilt forgive their sin—; and if not, blot me, I pray thee, out of thy book which thou hast written.	32 "Yet now, if You will forgive their sin—but if not, I pray, blot me out of Your book which You have written."	32 Yet now if you will only forgive their sin—and if not, then blot *me* out of the book you have written."
33 And the LORD said unto Moses, Whosoever hath sinned against me, him will I blot out of my book.	33 And the LORD said to Moses, "Whoever has sinned against Me, I will blot him out of My book.	33 And the Lord replied to Moses, "Whoever has sinned against me will be blotted out of my book.
34 Therefore now go, lead the people unto *the place* of which I have spoken unto thee: behold, mine Angel shall go before thee: nevertheless in the day when I visit I will visit their sin upon them.	34 "Now therefore, go, lead the people to *the place* of which I have spoken to you. Behold, My Angel shall go before you. Nevertheless, in the day when I visit for punishment, I will visit punishment upon them for their sin."	34 And now go, lead the people to the place I told you about, and I assure you that my Angel shall travel on ahead of you; however, when I come to visit these people, I will punish them for their sins."

NIV	RSV	TEV
27 Moses stretched out his hand over the sea, and at daybreak the sea went back to its place. The Egyptians were fleeing toward it, and the LORD swept them into the sea.	27 So Moses stretched forth his hand over the sea, and the sea returned to its wonted flow when the morning appeared; and the Egyptians fled into it, and the LORD routed the Egyptians in the midst of the sea.	27 So Moses held out his hand over the sea, and at daybreak the water returned to its normal level. The Egyptians tried to escape from the water, but the LORD threw them into the sea.
20:2 "I am the LORD your God, who brought you out of Egypt, out of the land of slavery.	20:2 "I am the LORD your God, who brought you out of the land of Egypt, out of the house of bondage.	20:2 "I am the LORD your God who brought you out of Egypt, where you were slaves.
3 "You shall have no other gods before me.	3 "You shall have no other gods before me.	3 "Worship no god but me.
4 "You shall not make for yourself an idol in the form of anything in heaven above or on the earth beneath or in the waters below.	4 "You shall not make for yourself a graven image, or any likeness of anything that is in heaven above, or that is in the earth beneath, or that is in the water under the earth;	4 "Do not make for yourselves images of anything in heaven or on earth or in the water under the earth.
5 You shall not bow down to them or worship them; for I, the LORD your God, am a jealous God, punishing the children for the sin of the fathers to the third and fourth generation of those who hate me,	5 you shall not bow down to them or serve them; for I the LORD your God am a jealous God, visiting the iniquity of the fathers upon the children to the third and the fourth generation of those who hate me,	5 Do not bow down to any idol or worship it, because I am the LORD your God and I tolerate no rivals. I bring punishment on those who hate me and on their descendants down to the third and fourth generation.
6 but showing love to thousands who love me and keep my commandments.	6 but showing steadfast love to thousands of those who love me and keep my commandments.	6 But I show my love to thousands of generations of those who love me and obey my laws.
7 "You shall not misuse the name of the LORD your God, for the LORD will not hold anyone guiltless who misuses his name.	7 "You shall not take the name of the LORD your God in vain; for the LORD will not hold him guiltless who takes his name in vain.	7 "Do not use my name for evil purposes, for I, the LORD your God, will punish anyone who misuses my name.
8 "Remember the Sabbath day by keeping it holy.	8 "Remember the sabbath day, to keep it holy.	8 "Observe the Sabbath and keep it holy.
9 Six days you shall labor and do all your work,	9 Six days you shall labor, and do all your work;	9 You have six days in which to do your work,
10 but the seventh day is a Sabbath to the LORD your God. On it you shall not do any work, neither you, nor your son or daughter, nor your manservant or maidservant, nor your animals, nor the alien within your gates.	10 but the seventh day is a sabbath to the LORD your God; in it you shall not do any work, you, or your son, or your daughter, your manservant, or your maidservant, or your cattle, or the sojourner who is within your gates;	10 but the seventh day is a day of rest dedicated to me. On that day no one is to work—neither you, your children, your slaves, your animals, nor the foreigners who live in your country.
11 For in six days the LORD made the heavens and the earth, the sea, and all that is in them, but he rested on the seventh day. Therefore the LORD blessed the Sabbath day and made it holy.	11 for in six days the LORD made heaven and earth, the sea, and all that is in them, and rested the seventh day; therefore the LORD blessed the sabbath day and hallowed it.	11 In six days I, the LORD, made the earth, the sky, the sea, and everything in them, but on the seventh day I rested. That is why I, the LORD, blessed the Sabbath and made it holy.
12 "Honor your father and your mother, so that you may live long in the land the LORD your God is giving you.	12 "Honor your father and your mother, that your days may be long in the land which the LORD your God gives you.	12 "Respect your father and your mother, so that you may live a long time in the land that I am giving you.
13 "You shall not murder.	13 "You shall not kill.	13 "Do not commit murder.
14 "You shall not commit adultery.	14 "You shall not commit adultery.	14 "Do not commit adultery.
15 "You shall not steal.	15 "You shall not steal.	15 "Do not steal.
16 "You shall not give false testimony against your neighbor.	16 "You shall not bear false witness against your neighbor.	16 "Do not accuse anyone falsely.
17 "You shall not covet your neighbor's house. You shall not covet your neighbor's wife, or his manservant or maidservant, his ox or donkey, or anything that belongs to your neighbor."	17 "You shall not covet your neighbor's house; you shall not covet your neighbor's wife, or his manservant, or his maidservant, or his ox, or his ass, or anything that is your neighbor's."	17 "Do not desire another man's house; do not desire his wife, his slaves, his cattle, his donkeys, or anything else that he owns."
32:31 So Moses went back to the LORD and said, "Oh, what a great sin these people have committed! They have made themselves gods of gold.	32:31 So Moses returned to the LORD and said, "Alas, this people have sinned a great sin; they have made for themselves gods of gold.	32:31 Moses then returned to the LORD and said, "These people have committed a terrible sin. They have made a god out of gold and worshiped it.
32 But now, please forgive their sin—but if not, then blot me out of the book you have written."	32 But now, if thou wilt forgive their sin—and if not, blot me, I pray thee, out of thy book which thou hast written."	32 Please forgive their sin; but if you won't, then remove my name from the book in which you have written the names of your people."
33 The LORD replied to Moses, "Whoever has sinned against me I will blot out of my book,	33 But the LORD said to Moses, "Whoever has sinned against me, him will I blot out of my book.	33 The LORD answered, "It is those who have sinned against me whose names I will remove from my book.
34 Now go, lead the people to the place I spoke of, and my angel will go before you. However, when the time comes for me to punish, I will punish them for their sin."	34 But now go, lead the people to the place of which I have spoken to you; behold, my angel shall go before you. Nevertheless, in the day when I visit, I will visit their sin upon them."	34 Now go, lead the people to the place I told you about. Remember that my angel will guide you, but the time is coming when I will punish these people for their sin."

KJV	NKJV	TLB
34:5 And the LORD descended in the cloud, and stood with him there, and proclaimed the name of the LORD.	**34:5** Then the LORD descended in the cloud and stood with him there, and proclaimed the name of the LORD.	**34:5** Then the Lord descended in the form of a pillar of cloud and stood there with him, and passed in front of him and announced the meaning of his name.
6 And the LORD passed by before him, and proclaimed, The LORD, The LORD God, merciful and gracious, longsuffering, and abundant in goodness and truth,	**6** And the LORD passed before him and proclaimed, "The LORD, the LORD God, merciful and gracious, long-suffering, and abounding in goodness and truth,	**6** "I am Jehovah, the merciful and gracious God," he said, "slow to anger and rich in steadfast love and truth.
7 Keeping mercy for thousands, forgiving iniquity and transgression and sin, and that will by no means clear *the guilty;* visiting the iniquity of the fathers upon the children, and upon the children's children, unto the third and to the fourth *generation.*	**7** "keeping mercy for thousands, forgiving iniquity and transgression and sin, by no means clearing *the guilty,* visiting the iniquity of the fathers upon the children and the children's children to the third and the fourth generation."	**7** I, Jehovah, show this steadfast love to many thousands by forgiving their sins; or else I refuse to clear the guilty, and require that a father's sins be punished in the sons and grandsons, and even later generations."
40:34 Then a cloud covered the tent of the congregation, and the glory of the LORD filled the tabernacle.	**40:34** Then the cloud covered the tabernacle of meeting, and the glory of the LORD filled the tabernacle.	**40:34** Then the cloud covered the Tabernacle and the glory of the Lord filled it.

Leviticus

KJV	NKJV	TLB
16:34 And this shall be an everlasting statute unto you, to make an atonement for the children of Israel for all their sins once a year. And he did as the LORD commanded Moses.	**16:34** "This shall be an everlasting statute for you, to make atonement for the children of Israel, for all their sins, once a year." And he did as the LORD commanded Moses.	**16:34** This shall be an everlasting law for you, to make atonement for the people of Israel once each year, because of their sins."
17:11 For the life of the flesh *is* in the blood: and I have given it to you upon the altar to make an atonement for your souls: for it *is* the blood *that* maketh an atonement for the soul.	**17:11** 'For the life of the flesh *is* in the blood, and I have given it to you upon the altar to make atonement for your souls; for it *is* the blood *that* makes atonement for the soul.'	**17:11** For the life of the flesh is in the blood, and I have given you the blood to sprinkle upon the altar as an atonement for your souls; it is the blood that makes atonement, because it is the life.
25:10 And ye shall hallow the fiftieth year, and proclaim liberty throughout *all* the land unto all the inhabitants thereof: it shall be a jubile unto you; and ye shall return every man unto his possession, and ye shall return every man unto his family.	**25:10** 'And you shall consecrate the fiftieth year, and proclaim liberty throughout *all* the land to all its inhabitants. It shall be a Jubilee for you; and each of you shall return to his possession, and each of you shall return to his family.	**25:10** For the fiftieth year shall be holy, a time to proclaim liberty throughout the land to all enslaved debtors, and a time for the canceling of all public and private debts. It shall be a year when all the family estates sold to others shall be returned to the original owners or their heirs.
11 A jubile shall that fiftieth year be unto you: ye shall not sow, neither reap that which groweth of itself in it, nor gather *the grapes* in it of thy vine undressed.	**11** 'That fiftieth year shall be a Jubilee to you; in it you shall neither sow nor reap what grows of its own accord, nor gather *the grapes* of your untended vine.	**11** "What a happy year it will be! In it you shall not sow, nor gather crops nor grapes;
12 For it *is* the jubile; it shall be holy unto you: ye shall eat the increase thereof out of the field.	**12** 'For it *is* the Jubilee; it shall be holy to you; you shall eat its produce from the field.	**12** for it is a holy Year of Jubilee for you. That year your food shall be the volunteer crops that grow wild in the fields.
13 In the year of this jubile ye shall return every man unto his possession.	**13** 'In this Year of Jubilee, each of you shall return to his possession.	**13** Yes, during the Year of Jubilee everyone shall return home to his original family possession; if he has sold it, it shall be his again!
26:1 Ye shall make you no idols nor graven image, neither rear you up a standing image, neither shall ye set up *any* image of stone in your land, to bow down unto it: for I *am* the LORD your God.	**26:1** 'You shall not make idols for yourselves; neither a carved image nor a *sacred* pillar shall you rear up for yourselves; nor shall you set up an engraved stone in your land, to bow down to it; for I *am* the LORD your God.	**26:1** "You must have no idols; you must never worship carved images, obelisks, or shaped stones, for I am the Lord your God.
40 If they shall confess their iniquity, and the iniquity of their fathers, with their trespass which they trespassed against me, and that also they have walked contrary unto me;	**40** 'But if they confess their iniquity and the iniquity of their fathers, with their unfaithfulness in which they were unfaithful to Me, and that they also have walked contrary to Me,	**40** "But at last they shall confess their sins and their fathers' sins of treachery against me.
41 And *that* I also have walked contrary unto them, and have brought them into the land of their enemies; if then their uncircumcised hearts be humbled, and they then accept of the punishment of their iniquity:	**41** and *that* I also have walked contrary to them and have brought them into the land of their enemies; if their uncircumcised hearts are humbled, and they accept their guilt—	**41** (Because they were against me, I was against them, and brought them into the land of their enemies.) When at last their evil hearts are humbled and they accept the punishment I send them for their sins,
42 Then will I remember my covenant with Jacob, and also my covenant with Isaac, and also my covenant with Abraham will I remember; and I will remember the land.	**42** then I will remember My covenant with Jacob, and My covenant with Isaac and My covenant with Abraham I will remember; I will remember the land.	**42** then I will remember again my promises to Abraham, Isaac, and Jacob, and I will remember the land (and its desolation).

NIV	RSV	TEV
34:5 Then the LORD came down in the cloud and stood there with him and proclaimed his name, the LORD.	**34:5** And the LORD descended in the cloud and stood with him there, and proclaimed the name of the LORD.	**34:5** The LORD came down in a cloud, stood with him there, and pronounced his holy name, the LORD.
6 And he passed in front of Moses, proclaiming, "The LORD, the LORD, the compassionate and gracious God, slow to anger, abounding in love and faithfulness,	**6** The LORD passed before him, and proclaimed, "The LORD, the LORD, a God merciful and gracious, slow to anger, and abounding in steadfast love and faithfulness,	**6** The LORD then passed in front of him and called out, "I, the LORD, am a God who is full of compassion and pity, who is not easily angered and who shows great love and faithfulness.
7 maintaining love to thousands, and forgiving wickedness, rebellion and sin. Yet he does not leave the guilty unpunished; he punishes the children and their children for the sin of the fathers to the third and fourth generation."	**7** keeping steadfast love for thousands, forgiving iniquity and transgression and sin, but who will by no means clear the guilty, visiting the iniquity of the fathers upon the children and the children's children, to the third and the fourth generation."	**7** I keep my promise for thousands of generations and forgive evil and sin; but I will not fail to punish children and grandchildren to the third and fourth generation for the sins of their parents."
40:34 Then the cloud covered the Tent of Meeting, and the glory of the LORD filled the tabernacle.	**40:34** Then the cloud covered the tent of meeting, and the glory of the LORD filled the tabernacle.	**40:34** Then the cloud covered the Tent and the dazzling light of the LORD's presence filled it.

Leviticus

NIV	RSV	TEV
16:34 "This is to be a lasting ordinance for you: Atonement is to be made once a year for all the sins of the Israelites." And it was done, as the LORD commanded Moses.	**16:34** And this shall be an everlasting statute for you, that atonement may be made for the people of Israel once in the year because of all their sins." And Moses did as the LORD commanded him.	**16:34** These regulations are to be observed for all time to come. This ritual must be performed once a year to purify the people of Israel from all their sins. So Moses did as the LORD had commanded.
17:11 For the life of a creature is in the blood, and I have given it to you to make atonement for yourselves on the altar; it is the blood that makes atonement for one's life.	**17:11** For the life of the flesh is in the blood; and I have given it for you upon the altar to make atonement for your souls; for it is the blood that makes atonement, by reason of the life.	**17:11** The life of every living thing is in the blood, and that is why the LORD has commanded that all blood be poured out on the altar to take away the people's sins. Blood, which is life, takes away sins.
25:10 Consecrate the fiftieth year and proclaim liberty throughout the land to all its inhabitants. It shall be a jubilee for you; each one of you is to return to his family property and each to his own clan.	**25:10** And you shall hallow the fiftieth year, and proclaim liberty throughout the land to all its inhabitants; it shall be a jubilee for you, when each of you shall return to his property and each of you shall return to his family.	**25:10** In this way you shall set the fiftieth year apart and proclaim freedom to all the inhabitants of the land. During this year all property that has been sold shall be restored to the original owner or his descendants, and anyone who has been sold as a slave shall return to his family.
11 The fiftieth year shall be a jubilee for you; do not sow and do not reap what grows of itself or harvest the untended vines.	**11** A jubilee shall that fiftieth year be to you; in it you shall neither sow, nor reap what grows of itself, nor gather the grapes from the undressed vines.	**11** You shall not plant your fields or harvest the grain that grows by itself or gather the grapes in your unpruned vineyards.
12 For it is a jubilee and is to be holy for you; eat only what is taken directly from the fields.	**12** For it is a jubilee; it shall be holy to you; you shall eat what it yields out of the field.	**12** The whole year shall be sacred for you; you shall eat only what the fields produce of themselves.
13 "In this Year of Jubilee everyone is to return to his own property.	**13** "In this year of jubilee each of you shall return to his property.	**13** In this year all property that has been sold shall be restored to its original owner.
26:1 "Do not make idols or set up an image or a sacred stone for yourselves, and do not place a carved stone in your land to bow down before it. I am the LORD your God.	**26:1** "You shall make for yourselves no idols and erect no graven image or pillar, and you shall not set up a figured stone in your land, to bow down to them; for I am the LORD your God.	**26:1** The LORD said, "Do not make idols or set up statues, stone pillars, or carved stones to worship. I am the LORD your God.
40 "But if they will confess their sins and the sins of their fathers—their treachery against me and their hostility toward me,	**40** "But if they confess their iniquity and the iniquity of their fathers in their treachery which they committed against me, and also in walking contrary to me,	**40** "But your descendants will confess their sins and the sins of their ancestors, who resisted me and rebelled against me,
41 which made me hostile toward them so that I sent them into the land of their enemies—then when their uncircumcised hearts are humbled and they pay for their sin,	**41** so that I walked contrary to them and brought them into the land of their enemies; if then their uncircumcised heart is humbled and they make amends for their iniquity;	**41** and caused me to turn against them and send them into exile in the land of their enemies. At last, when your descendants are humbled and they have paid the penalty for their sin and rebellion,
42 I will remember my covenant with Jacob and my covenant with Isaac and my covenant with Abraham, and I will remember the land.	**42** then I will remember my covenant with Jacob, and I will remember my covenant with Isaac and my covenant with Abraham, and I will remember the land.	**42** I will remember my covenant with Jacob and with Isaac and with Abraham, and I will renew my promise to give my people the land.

KJV	NKJV	TLB

Numbers

KJV	NKJV	TLB
13:27 And they told him, and said, We came unto the land whither thou sentest us, and surely it floweth with milk and honey; and this *is* the fruit of it.	**13:27** Then they told him, and said: "We went to the land where you sent us. It truly flows with milk and honey, and this *is* its fruit.	**13:27** This was their report: "We arrived in the land you sent us to see, and it is indeed a magnificent country—a land 'flowing with milk and honey.' Here is some fruit we have brought as proof.
28 Nevertheless the people *be* strong that dwell in the land, and the cities *are* walled, *and* very great: and moreover we saw the children of Anak there.	**28** "Nevertheless the people who dwell in the land *are* strong; the cities *are* fortified *and* very large; moreover we saw the descendants of Anak there.	**28** But the people living there are powerful, and their cities are fortified and very large; and what's more, we saw Anakim giants there!
29 The Amalekites dwell in the land of the south: and the Hittites, and the Jebusites, and the Amorites, dwell in the mountains: and the Canaanites dwell by the sea, and by the coast of Jordan.	**29** "The Amalekites dwell in the land of the South; the Hittites, the Jebusites, and the Amorites dwell in the mountains; and the Canaanites dwell by the sea and along the banks of the Jordan."	**29** The Amalekites live in the south, while in the hill country there are the Hittites, Jebusites, and Amorites; down along the coast of the Mediterranean Sea and in the Jordan River valley are the Canaanites."
30 And Caleb stilled the people before Moses, and said, Let us go up at once, and possess it; for we are well able to overcome it.	**30** Then Caleb quieted the people before Moses, and said, "Let us go up at once and take possession, for we are well able to overcome it."	**30** But Caleb reassured the people as they stood before Moses. "Let us go up at once and possess it," he said, "for we are well able to conquer it!"
14:7 And they spake unto all the company of the children of Israel, saying, The land, which we passed through to search it, *is* an exceeding good land.	**14:7** and they spoke to all the congregation of the children of Israel, saying: "The land we passed through to spy out *is* an exceedingly good land.	**14:7** and said to all the people, "It is a wonderful country ahead,
8 If the LORD delight in us, then he will bring us into this land, and give it us; a land which floweth with milk and honey.	**8** "If the LORD delights in us, then He will bring us into this land and give it to us, 'a land which flows with milk and honey.'	**8** and the Lord loves us. He will bring us safely into the land and give it to us. It is *very* fertile, a land 'flowing with milk and honey'!
9 Only rebel not ye against the LORD, neither fear ye the people of the land; for they *are* bread for us: their defence is departed from them, and the LORD *is* with us: fear them not.	**9** "Only do not rebel against the LORD, nor fear the people of the land, for they *are* our bread; their protection has departed from them, and the LORD *is* with us. Do not fear them."	**9** Oh, do not rebel against the Lord, and do not fear the people of the land. For they are but bread for us to eat! The Lord is with us and he has removed his protection from them! Don't be afraid of them!"
10 But all the congregation bade stone them with stones. And the glory of the LORD appeared in the tabernacle of the congregation before all the children of Israel.	**10** And all the congregation said to stone them with stones. Now the glory of the LORD appeared in the tabernacle of meeting before all the children of Israel.	**10** But the only response of the people was to talk of stoning them. Then the glory of the Lord appeared,
28 Say unto them, *As truly as* I live, saith the LORD, as ye have spoken in mine ears, so will I do to you:	**28** "Say to them, 'As I live,' says the LORD, 'just as you have spoken in My hearing, so I will do to you:	**28** Tell them, 'The Lord vows to do to you what you feared:
29 Your carcases shall fall in this wilderness; and all that were numbered of you, according to your whole number, from twenty years old and upward, which have murmured against me,	**29** 'The carcasses of you who have murmured against Me shall fall in this wilderness, all of you who were numbered, according to your entire number, from twenty years old and above.	**29** You will all die here in this wilderness! Not a single one of you twenty years old and older, who has complained against me,
30 Doubtless ye shall not come into the land, *concerning* which I sware to make you dwell therein, save Caleb the son of Jephunneh, and Joshua the son of Nun.	**30** 'Except for Caleb the son of Jephunneh and Joshua the son of Nun, you shall by no means enter the land which I swore I would make you dwell in.	**30** shall enter the Promised Land. Only Caleb (son of Jephunneh) and Joshua (son of Nun) are permitted to enter it.
31 But your little ones, which ye said should be a prey, them will I bring in, and they shall know the land which ye have despised.	**31** 'But your little ones, whom you said would be victims, I will bring in, and they shall know the land which you have despised.	**31** "'You said your children would become slaves of the people of the land. Well, instead I will bring *them* safely into the land and they shall inherit what you have despised.
32 But *as for* you, your carcases, they shall fall in this wilderness.	**32** 'But *as for* you, your carcasses shall fall in this wilderness.	**32** But as for you, your dead bodies shall fall in this wilderness.
17:8 And it came to pass, that on the morrow Moses went into the tabernacle of witness; and, behold, the rod of Aaron for the house of Levi was budded, and brought forth buds, and bloomed blossoms, and yielded almonds.	**17:8** Now it came to pass on the next day that Moses went into the tabernacle of witness, and behold, the rod of Aaron, of the house of Levi, had sprouted and put forth buds, had produced blossoms and yielded ripe almonds.	**17:8** and when he went in the next day, he found that Aaron's rod, representing the tribe of Levi, had budded and was blossoming, and had ripe almonds hanging from it!
20:10 And Moses and Aaron gathered the congregation together before the rock, and he said unto them, Hear now, ye rebels; must we fetch you water out of this rock?	**20:10** And Moses and Aaron gathered the congregation together before the rock; and he said to them, "Hear now, you rebels! Must we bring water for you out of this rock?"	**20:10** then Moses and Aaron summoned the people to come and gather at the rock; and he said to them, "Listen, you rebels! Must we bring you water from this rock?"
11 And Moses lifted up his hand, and with his rod he smote the rock twice: and the water came out abundantly, and the congregation drank, and their beasts *also*.	**11** Then Moses lifted his hand and struck the rock twice with his rod; and water came out abundantly, and the congregation and their animals drank.	**11** Then Moses lifted the rod and struck the rock twice, and water gushed out; and the people and their cattle drank.

NIV   RSV   TEV

Numbers

NIV	RSV	TEV
13:27 They gave Moses this account: "We went into the land to which you sent us, and it does flow with milk and honey! Here is its fruit.	**13:27** And they told him, "We came to the land to which you sent us; it flows with milk and honey, and this is its fruit.	**13:27** They told Moses, "We explored the land and found it to be rich and fertile; and here is some of its fruit.
28 But the people who live there are powerful, and the cities are fortified and very large. We even saw descendants of Anak there.	28 Yet the people who dwell in the land are strong, and the cities are fortified and very large, and besides, we saw the descendants of Anak there.	28 But the people who live there are powerful, and their cities are very large and well fortified. Even worse, we saw the descendants of the giants there.
29 The Amalekites live in the Negev; the Hittites, Jebusites and Amorites live in the hill country; and the Canaanites live near the sea and along the Jordan."	29 The Amalekites dwell in the land of the Negeb; the Hittites, the Jebusites, and the Amorites dwell in the hill country; and the Canaanites dwell by the sea, and along the Jordan."	29 Amalekites live in the southern part of the land; Hittites, Jebusites, and Amorites live in the hill country; and Canaanites live by the Mediterranean Sea and along the Jordan River."
30 Then Caleb silenced the people before Moses and said, "We should go up and take possession of the land, for we can certainly do it."	30 But Caleb quieted the people before Moses, and said, "Let us go up at once, and occupy it; for we are well able to overcome it."	30 Caleb silenced the people who were complaining against Moses, and said, "We should attack now and take the land; we are strong enough to conquer it."
14:7 and said to the entire Israelite assembly, "The land we passed through and explored is exceedingly good.	**14:7** and said to all the congregation of the people of Israel, "The land, which we passed through to spy it out, is an exceedingly good land.	**14:7** and said to the people, "The land we explored is an excellent land.
8 If the LORD is pleased with us, he will lead us into that land, a land flowing with milk and honey, and will give it to us.	8 If the LORD delights in us, he will bring us into this land and give it to us, a land which flows with milk and honey.	8 If the LORD is pleased with us, he will take us there and give us that rich and fertile land.
9 Only do not rebel against the LORD. And do not be afraid of the people of the land, because we will swallow them up. Their protection is gone, but the LORD is with us. Do not be afraid of them."	9 Only, do not rebel against the LORD; and do not fear the people of the land, for they are bread for us; their protection is removed from them, and the LORD is with us; do not fear them."	9 Do not rebel against the LORD and don't be afraid of the people who live there. We will conquer them easily. The LORD is with us and has defeated the gods who protected them; so don't be afraid."
10 But the whole assembly talked about stoning them. Then the glory of the LORD appeared at the Tent of Meeting to all the Israelites.	10 But all the congregation said to stone them with stones. Then the glory of the LORD appeared at the tent of meeting to all the people of Israel.	10 The whole community was threatening to stone them to death, but suddenly the people saw the dazzling light of the LORD's presence appear over the Tent.
28 So tell them, 'As surely as I live, declares the LORD, I will do to you the very things I heard you say:	28 Say to them, 'As I live,' says the LORD, 'what you have said in my hearing I will do to you:	28 Now give them this answer: 'I swear that as surely as I live, I will do to you just what you have asked. I, the LORD, have spoken.
29 In this desert your bodies will fall—every one of you twenty years old or more who was counted in the census and who has grumbled against me,	29 your dead bodies shall fall in this wilderness; and of all your number, numbered from twenty years old and upward, who have murmured against me,	29 You will die and your corpses will be scattered across this wilderness. Because you have complained against me, none of you over twenty years of age will enter that land.
30 Not one of you will enter the land I swore with uplifted hand to make your home, except Caleb son of Jephunneh and Joshua son of Nun.	30 not one shall come into the land where I swore that I would make you dwell, except Caleb the son of Jephunneh and Joshua the son of Nun.	30 I promised to let you live there, but not one of you will, except Caleb and Joshua.
31 As for your children that you said would be taken as plunder, I will bring them in to enjoy the land you have rejected.	31 But your little ones, who you said would become a prey, I will bring in, and they shall know the land which you have despised.	31 You said that your children would be captured, but I will bring them into the land that you rejected, and it will be their home.
32 But you—your bodies will fall in this desert.	32 But as for you, your dead bodies shall fall in this wilderness.	32 You will die here in this wilderness.
17:8 The next day Moses entered the Tent of the Testimony and saw that Aaron's staff, which represented the house of Levi, had not only sprouted but had budded, blossomed and produced almonds.	**17:8** And on the morrow Moses went into the tent of the testimony; and behold, the rod of Aaron for the house of Levi had sprouted and put forth buds, and produced blossoms, and it bore ripe almonds.	**17:8** The next day, when Moses went into the Tent, he saw that Aaron's stick, representing the tribe of Levi, had sprouted. It had budded, blossomed, and produced ripe almonds!
20:10 He and Aaron gathered the assembly together in front of the rock and Moses said to them, "Listen, you rebels, must we bring you water out of this rock?"	**20:10** And Moses and Aaron gathered the assembly together before the rock, and he said to them, "Hear now, you rebels; shall we bring forth water for you out of this rock?"	**20:10** He and Aaron assembled the whole community in front of the rock, and Moses said, "Listen, you rebels! Do we have to get water out of this rock for you?"
11 Then Moses raised his arm and struck the rock twice with his staff. Water gushed out, and the community and their livestock drank.	11 And Moses lifted up his hand and struck the rock with his rod twice; and water came forth abundantly, and the congregation drank, and their cattle.	11 Then Moses raised the stick and struck the rock twice with it, and a great stream of water gushed out, and all the people and animals drank.

KJV	NKJV	TLB
12 And the LORD spake unto Moses and Aaron, Because ye believed me not, to sanctify me in the eyes of the children of Israel, therefore ye shall not bring this congregation into the land which I have given them.	12 Then the LORD spoke to Moses and Aaron, "Because you did not believe Me, to hallow Me in the eyes of the children of Israel, therefore you shall not bring this congregation into the land which I have given them."	12 But the Lord said to Moses and Aaron, "Because you did not believe me and did not sanctify me in the eyes of the people of Israel, you shall not bring them into the land I have promised them!"
21:8 And the LORD said unto Moses, Make thee a fiery serpent, and set it upon a pole: and it shall come to pass, that every one that is bitten, when he looketh upon it, shall live.	21:8 Then the LORD said to Moses, "Make a fiery *serpent*, and set it on a pole; and it shall be that everyone who is bitten, when he looks at it, shall live."	21:8 Then the Lord told him, "Make a bronze replica of one of these snakes and attach it to the top of a pole; anyone who is bitten shall live if he simply looks at it!"
9 And Moses made a serpent of brass, and put it upon a pole, and it came to pass, that if a serpent had bitten any man, when he beheld the serpent of brass, he lived.	9 So Moses made a bronze serpent, and put it on a pole; and so it was, if a serpent had bitten anyone, when he looked at the bronze serpent, he lived.	9 So Moses made the replica, and whenever anyone who had been bitten looked at the bronze snake, he recovered!
22:38 And Balaam said unto Balak, Lo, I am come unto thee: have I now any power at all to say any thing? the word that God putteth in my mouth, that shall I speak.	22:38 And Balaam said to Balak, "Look, I have come to you! Now, have I any power at all to say anything? The word that God puts in my mouth, that I must speak."	22:38 Balaam replied, "I have come, but I have no power to say anything except what God tells me to say; and that is what I shall speak."
23:19 God *is* not a man, that he should lie; neither the son of man, that he should repent: hath he said, and shall he not do *it?* or hath he spoken, and shall he not make it good?	23:19 "God *is* not a man, that He should lie, Nor a son of man, that He should repent. Has He said, and will He not do *it?* Or has He spoken, and will He not make it good?	23:19 God is not a man, that he should lie; He doesn't change his mind like humans do. Has he ever promised, Without doing what he said?
20 Behold, I have received *commandment* to bless: and he hath blessed; and I cannot reverse it.	20 Behold, I have received *a command* to bless; He has blessed, and I cannot reverse it.	20 Look! I have received a command to bless them, For God has blessed them, And I cannot reverse it!
24:17 I shall see him, but not now: I shall behold him, but not nigh: there shall come a Star out of Jacob, and a Sceptre shall rise out of Israel, and shall smite the corners of Moab, and destroy all the children of Sheth.	24:17 "I see Him, but not now; I behold Him, but not near; A Star shall come out of Jacob; A Scepter shall rise out of Israel, And batter the brow of Moab, And destroy all the sons of tumult.	24:17 I see in the future of Israel, Far down the distant trail, That there shall come a star from Jacob! This ruler of Israel Shall smite the people of Moab, And destroy the sons of Sheth.
18 And Edom shall be a possession, Seir also shall be a possession for his enemies; and Israel shall do valiantly.	18 "And Edom shall be a possession; Seir also, his enemies, shall be a possession, While Israel does valiantly.	18 Israel shall possess all Edom and Seir. They shall overcome their enemies.
19 Out of Jacob shall come he that shall have dominion, and shall destroy him that remaineth of the city.	19 Out of Jacob One shall have dominion, And destroy the remains of the city."	19 Jacob shall arise in power And shall destroy many cities."
33:51 Speak unto the children of Israel, and say unto them, When ye are passed over Jordan into the land of Canaan;	33:51 "Speak to the children of Israel, and say to them: 'When you have crossed the Jordan into the land of Canaan,	33:51 the Lord told Moses to tell the people of Israel, "When you pass across the Jordan River into the land of Canaan,
52 Then ye shall drive out all the inhabitants of the land from before you, and destroy all their pictures, and destroy all their molten images, and quite pluck down all their high places:	52 'then you shall drive out all the inhabitants of the land from before you, destroy all their engraved stones, destroy all their molded images, and demolish all their high places;	52 you must drive out all the people living there and destroy all their idols—their carved stones, molten images, and the open-air sanctuaries in the hills where they worship their idols.
53 And ye shall dispossess *the inhabitants of* the land, and dwell therein: for I have given you the land to possess it.	53 'you shall dispossess *the inhabitants of* the land and dwell in it, for I have given you the land to possess.	53 I have given the land to you; take it and live there.
54 And ye shall divide the land by lot for an inheritance among your families: *and* to the more ye shall give the more inheritance, and to the fewer ye shall give the less inheritance: every man's *inheritance* shall be in the place where his lot falleth; according to the tribes of your fathers ye shall inherit.	54 'And you shall divide the land by lot as an inheritance among your families; to the larger you shall give a larger inheritance, and to the smaller you shall give a smaller inheritance; there everyone's *inheritance* shall be whatever falls to him by lot. You shall inherit according to the tribes of your fathers.	54 You will be given land in proportion to the size of your tribes. The larger sections of land will be divided by lot among the larger tribes, and the smaller sections will be allotted to the smaller tribes.
55 But if ye will not drive out the inhabitants of the land from before you; then it shall come to pass, that those which ye let remain of them *shall be* pricks in your eyes, and thorns in your sides, and shall vex you in the land wherein ye dwell.	55 'But if you do not drive out the inhabitants of the land from before you, then it shall be that those whom you let remain *shall be* irritants in your eyes and thorns in your sides, and they shall harass you in the land where you dwell.	55 But if you refuse to drive out the people living there, those who remain will be as cinders in your eyes and thorns in your sides.
56 Moreover it shall come to pass, *that* I shall do unto you, as I thought to do unto them.	56 'Moreover it shall be *that* I will do to you as I thought to do to them.'"	56 And I will destroy you as I had planned for you to destroy them."

NIV	RSV	TEV
12 But the LORD said to Moses and Aaron, "Because you did not trust in me enough to honor me as holy in the sight of the Israelites, you will not bring this community into the land I give them."	**12** And the LORD said to Moses and Aaron, "Because you did not believe in me, to sanctify me in the eyes of the people of Israel, therefore you shall not bring this assembly into the land which I have given them."	**12** But the LORD reprimanded Moses and Aaron. He said, "Because you did not have enough faith to acknowledge my holy power before the people of Israel, you will not lead them into the land that I promised to give them."
21:8 The LORD said to Moses, "Make a snake and put it up on a pole; anyone who is bitten can look at it and live."	**21:8** And the LORD said to Moses, "Make a fiery serpent, and set it on a pole; and every one who is bitten, when he sees it, shall live."	**21:8** Then the LORD told Moses to make a metal snake and put it on a pole, so that anyone who was bitten could look at it and be healed.
9 So Moses made a bronze snake and put it up on a pole. Then when anyone was bitten by a snake and looked at the bronze snake, he lived.	**9** So Moses made a bronze serpent, and set it on a pole; and if a serpent bit any man, he would look at the bronze serpent and live.	**9** So Moses made a bronze snake and put it on a pole. Anyone who had been bitten would look at the bronze snake and be healed.
22:38 "Well, I have come to you now," Balaam replied. "But can I say just anything? I must speak only what God puts in my mouth."	**22:38** "Balaam said to Balak, "Lo, I have come to you! Have I now any power at all to speak anything? The word that God puts in my mouth, that must I speak."	**22:38** Balaam answered, "I came, didn't I? But now, what power do I have? I can say only what God tells me to say."
23:19 God is not a man, that he should lie, nor a son of man, that he should change his mind. Does he speak and then not act? Does he promise and not fulfill?	**23:19** God is not man, that he should lie, or a son of man, that he should repent. Has he said, and will he not do it? Or has he spoken, and will he not fulfil it?	**23:19** God is not like men, who lie; He is not a human who changes his mind. Whatever he promises, he does; He speaks, and it is done.
20 I have received a command to bless; he has blessed, and I cannot change it.	**20** Behold, I received a command to bless: he has blessed, and I cannot revoke it.	**20** I have been instructed to bless, And when God blesses, I cannot call it back.
24:17 "I see him, but not now; I behold him, but not near. A star will come out of Jacob; a scepter will rise out of Israel. He will crush the foreheads of Moab, the skulls of all the sons of Sheth.	**24:17** I see him, but not now; I behold him, but not nigh: a star shall come forth out of Jacob, and a scepter shall rise out of Israel; it shall crush the forehead of Moab, and break down all the sons of Sheth.	**24:17** I look into the future, And I see the nation of Israel. A king, like a bright star, will arise in that nation. Like a comet he will come from Israel. He will strike the leaders of Moab And beat down all the people of Seth.
18 Edom will be conquered; Seir, his enemy, will be conquered, but Israel will grow strong.	**18** Edom shall be dispossessed, Seir also, his enemies, shall be dispossessed, while Israel does valiantly.	**18** He will conquer his enemies in Edom And make their land his property, While Israel continues victorious.
19 A ruler will come out of Jacob and destroy the survivors of the city."	**19** By Jacob shall dominion be exercised, and the survivors of cities be destroyed!"	**19** The nation of Israel will trample them down And wipe out the last survivors."
33:51 "Speak to the Israelites and say to them: 'When you cross the Jordan into Canaan,	**33:51** "Say to the people of Israel, When you pass over the Jordan into the land of Canaan,	**33:51** the following instructions for Israel: "When you cross the Jordan into the land of Canaan,
52 drive out all the inhabitants of the land before you. Destroy all their carved images and their cast idols, and demolish all their high places.	**52** then you shall drive out all the inhabitants of the land from before you, and destroy all their figured stones, and destroy all their molten images, and demolish all their high places;	**52** you must drive out all the inhabitants of the land. Destroy all their stone and metal idols and all their places of worship.
53 Take possession of the land and settle in it, for I have given you the land to possess.	**53** and you shall take possession of the land and settle in it, for I have given the land to you to possess it.	**53** Occupy the land and settle in it, because I am giving it to you.
54 Distribute the land by lot, according to your clans. To a larger group give a larger inheritance, and to a smaller group a smaller one. Whatever falls to them by lot will be theirs. Distribute it according to your ancestral tribes.	**54** You shall inherit the land by lot according to your families; to a large tribe you shall give a large inheritance, and to a small tribe you shall give a small inheritance; wherever the lot falls to any man, that shall be his; according to the tribes of your fathers you shall inherit.	**54** Divide the land among the various tribes and clans by drawing lots, giving a large piece of property to a large clan and a small one to a small clan.
55 "'But if you do not drive out the inhabitants of the land, those you allow to remain will become barbs in your eyes and thorns in your sides. They will give you trouble in the land where you will live.	**55** But if you do not drive out the inhabitants of the land from before you, then those of them whom you let remain shall be as pricks in your eyes and thorns in your sides, and they shall trouble you in the land where you dwell.	**55** But if you do not drive out the inhabitants of the land, those that are left will be troublesome as splinters in your eyes and thorns in your sides, and they will fight against you.
56 And then I will do to you what I plan to do to them.'"	**56** And I will do to you as I thought to do to them."	**56** If you do not drive them out, I will destroy you, as I planned to destroy them."

Deuteronomy

KJV	NKJV	TLB
5:29 O that there were such an heart in them, that they would fear me, and keep all my commandments always, that it might be well with them, and with their children for ever!	**5:29** 'Oh, that they had such a heart in them that they would fear Me and always keep all My commandments, that it might be well with them and with their children forever!	**5:29** Oh, that they would always have such a heart for me, wanting to obey my commandments. Then all would go well with them in the future, and with their children throughout all generations!
33 Ye shall walk in all the ways which the LORD your God hath commanded you, that ye may live, and *that it may be* well with you, and *that ye* may prolong *your* days in the land which ye shall possess.	**33** "You shall walk in all the ways which the LORD your God has commanded you, that you may live and *that it may be* well with you, and *that* you may prolong *your* days in the land which you shall possess.	**33** only then will you live long and prosperous lives in the land you are to enter and possess.
6:6 And these words, which I command thee this day, shall be in thine heart:	**6:6** "And these words which I command you today shall be in your heart;	**6:6** And you must think constantly about these commandments I am giving you today.
7 And thou shalt teach them diligently unto thy children, and shalt talk of them when thou sittest in thine house, and when thou walkest by the way, and when thou liest down, and when thou risest up.	**7** "you shall teach them diligently to your children, and shall talk to them when you sit in your house, when you walk by the way, when you lie down, and when you rise up.	**7** You must teach them to your children and talk about them when you are at home or out for a walk; at bedtime and the first thing in the morning.
8 And thou shalt bind them for a sign upon thine hand, and they shall be as frontlets between thine eyes.	**8** "You shall bind them as a sign on your hand, and they shall be as frontlets between your eyes.	**8** Tie them on your finger, wear them on your forehead,
9 And thou shalt write them upon the posts of thy house, and on thy gates.	**9** "You shall write them on the doorposts of your house and on your gates.	**9** and write them on the doorposts of your house!
7:9 Know therefore that the LORD thy God, he *is* God, the faithful God, which keepeth covenant and mercy with them that love him and keep his commandments to a thousand generations;	**7:9** "Therefore know that the LORD your God, He *is* God, the faithful God who keeps covenant and mercy for a thousand generations with those who love Him and keep His commandments;	**7:9** "Understand, therefore, that the Lord your God is the faithful God who for a thousand generations keeps his promises and constantly loves those who love him and who obey his commands.
8:18 But thou shalt remember the LORD thy God: for *it is* he that giveth thee power to get wealth, that he may establish his covenant which he sware unto thy fathers, as *it is* this day.	**8:18** "And you shall remember the LORD your God, for *it is* He who gives you power to get wealth, that He may establish His covenant which He swore to your fathers, as *it is* this day.	**8:18** Always remember that it is the Lord your God who gives you power to become rich, and he does it to fulfill his promise to your ancestors.
10:18 He doth execute the judgment of the fatherless and widow, and loveth the stranger, in giving him food and raiment.	**10:18** "He administers justice for the fatherless and the widow, and loves the stranger, giving him food and clothing.	**10:18** He gives justice to the fatherless and widows. He loves foreigners and gives them food and clothing.
11:26 Behold, I set before you this day a blessing and a curse;	**11:26** "Behold, I set before you today a blessing and a curse:	**11:26** "I am giving you the choice today between God's blessing or God's curse!
27 A blessing, if ye obey the commandments of the LORD your God, which I command you this day;	**27** "the blessing, if you obey the commandments of the LORD your God which I command you today;	**27** There will be blessing if you obey the commandments of the Lord your God which I am giving you today,
28 And a curse, if ye will not obey the commandments of the LORD your God, but turn aside out of the way which I command you this day, to go after other gods, which ye have not known.	**28** "and the curse, if you do not obey the commandments of the LORD your God, but turn aside from the way which I command you today, to go after other gods which you have not known.	**28** and a curse if you refuse them and worship the gods of these other nations.
28:1 And it shall come to pass, if thou shalt hearken diligently unto the voice of the LORD thy God, to observe *and* to do all his commandments which I command thee this day, that the LORD thy God will set thee on high above all nations of the earth:	**28:1** "Now it shall come to pass, if you diligently obey the voice of the LORD your God, to observe carefully all His commandments which I command you today, that the LORD your God will set you high above all nations of the earth.	**28:1** "If you fully obey all of these commandments of the Lord your God, the laws I am declaring to you today, God will transform you into the greatest nation in the world.
2 And all these blessings shall come on thee, and overtake thee, if thou shalt harken unto the voice of the LORD thy God.	**2** "And all these blessings shall come upon you and overtake you, because you obey the voice of the LORD your God:	**2** These are the blessings that will come upon you:
3 Blessed *shalt* thou *be* in the city, and blessed *shalt* thou *be* in the field.	**3** "Blessed *shall* you *be* in the city, and blessed *shall* you *be* in the country.	**3** Blessings in the city, Blessings in the field;
4 Blessed *shall be* the fruit of thy body, and the fruit of thy ground, and the fruit of thy cattle, the increase of thy kine, and the flocks of thy sheep.	**4** "Blessed *shall be* the fruit of your body, the produce of your ground and the increase of your herds, the increase of your cattle and the offspring of your flocks.	**4** Many children, Ample crops, Large flocks and herds;
5 Blessed *shall be* thy basket and thy store.	**5** "Blessed *shall be* your basket and your kneading bowl.	**5** Blessings of fruit and bread;

NIV	RSV	TEV

Deuteronomy

NIV	RSV	TEV
5:29 Oh, that their hearts would be inclined to fear me and keep all my commands always, so that it might go well with them and their children forever!	**5:29** Oh that they had such a mind as this always, to fear me and to keep all my commandments, that it might go well with them and with their children for ever!	**5:29** If only they would always feel this way! If only they would always honor me and obey all my commands, so that everything would go well with them and their descendants forever.
33 Walk in all the way that the LORD your God has commanded you, so that you may live and prosper and prolong your days in the land that you will possess.	33 You shall walk in all the way which the LORD your God has commanded you, that you may live, and that it may go well with you, and that you may live long in the land which you shall possess.	33 Obey them all, so that everything will go well with you and so that you will continue to live in the land that you are going to occupy.
6:6 These commandments that I give you today are to be upon your hearts.	**6:6** And these words which I command you this day shall be upon your heart;	**6:6** Never forget these commands that I am giving you today.
7 Impress them on your children. Talk about them when you sit at home and when you walk along the road, when you lie down and when you get up.	7 and you shall teach them diligently to your children, and shall talk of them when you sit in your house, and when you walk by the way, and when you lie down, and when you rise.	7 Teach them to your children. Repeat them when you are at home and when you are away, when you are resting and when you are working.
8 Tie them as symbols on your hands and bind them on your foreheads.	8 And you shall bind them as a sign upon your hand, and they shall be as frontlets between your eyes.	8 Tie them on your arms and wear them on your foreheads as a reminder.
9 Write them on the doorframes of your houses and on your gates.	9 And you shall write them on the doorposts of your house and on your gates.	9 Write them on the doorposts of your houses and on your gates.
7:9 Know therefore that the LORD your God is God; he is the faithful God, keeping his covenant of love to a thousand generations of those who love him and keep his commands.	**7:9** Know therefore that the LORD your God is God, the faithful God who keeps covenant and steadfast love with those who love him and keep his commandments, to a thousand generations,	**7:9** Remember that the LORD your God is the only God and that he is faithful. He will keep his covenant and show his constant love to a thousand generations of those who love him and obey his commands,
8:18 But remember the LORD your God, for it is he who gives you the ability to produce wealth, and so confirms his covenant, which he swore to your forefathers, as it is today.	**8:18** You shall remember the LORD your God, for it is he who gives you power to get wealth; that he may confirm his covenant which he swore to your fathers, as at this day.	**8:18** Remember that it is the LORD your God who gives you the power to become rich. He does this because he is still faithful today to the covenant that he made with your ancestors.
10:18 He defends the cause of the fatherless and the widow, and loves the alien, giving him food and clothing.	**10:18** He executes justice for the fatherless and the widow, and loves the sojourner, giving him food and clothing.	**10:18** He makes sure that orphans and widows are treated fairly; he loves the foreigners who live with our people, and gives them food and clothes.
11:26 See, I am setting before you today a blessing and a curse—	**11:26** "Behold, I set before you this day a blessing and a curse:	**11:26** "Today I am giving you the choice between a blessing and a curse—
27 the blessing if you obey the commands of the LORD your God that I am giving you today;	27 the blessing, if you obey the commandments of the LORD your God, which I command you this day,	27 a blessing, if you obey the commands of the LORD your God that I am giving you today;
28 the curse if you disobey the commands of the LORD your God and turn from the way that I command you today by following other gods, which you have not known.	28 and the curse, if you do not obey the commandments of the LORD your God, but turn aside from the way which I command you this day, to go after other gods which you have not known.	28 but a curse, if you disobey these commands and turn away to worship other gods that you have never worshiped before.
28:1 If you fully obey the LORD your God and carefully follow all his commands I give you today, the LORD your God will set you high above all the nations on earth.	**28:1** "And if you obey the voice of the LORD your God, being careful to do all his commandments which I command you this day, the LORD your God will set you high above all the nations of the earth.	**28:1** "If you obey the LORD your God and faithfully keep all his commands that I am giving you today, he will make you greater than any other nation on earth.
2 All these blessings will come upon you and accompany you if you obey the LORD your God:	2 And all these blessings shall come upon you and overtake you, if you obey the voice of the LORD your God.	2 Obey the LORD your God and all these blessings will be yours:
3 You will be blessed in the city and blessed in the country.	3 Blessed shall you be in the city, and blessed shall you be in the field.	3 "The LORD will bless your towns and your fields.
4 The fruit of your womb will be blessed, and the crops of your land and the young of your livestock—the calves of your herds and the lambs of your flocks.	4 Blessed shall be the fruit of your body, and the fruit of your ground, and the fruit of your beasts, the increase of your cattle, and the young of your flock.	4 "The LORD will bless you with many children, with abundant crops, and with many cattle and sheep.
5 Your basket and your kneading trough will be blessed.	5 Blessed shall be your basket and your kneading-trough.	5 "The LORD will bless your grain crops and the food you prepare from them.

KJV	NKJV	TLB
6 Blessed *shalt* thou *be* when thou comest in, and blessed *shalt* thou *be* when thou goest out.	6 "Blessed *shall* you *be* when you come in, and blessed *shall* you *be* when you go out.	6 Blessings when you come in, Blessings when you go out.
7 The LORD shall cause thine enemies that rise up against thee to be smitten before thy face: they shall come out against thee one way, and flee before thee seven ways.	7 "The LORD will cause your enemies who rise against you to be defeated before your face; they shall come out against you one way and flee before you seven ways.	7 "The Lord will defeat your enemies before you; they will march out together against you but scatter before you in seven directions!
8 The LORD shall command the blessing upon thee in thy storehouses, and in all that thou settest thine hand unto; and he shall bless thee in the land which the LORD thy God giveth thee.	8 "The LORD will command the blessing on you in your storehouses and in all to which you set your hand, and He will bless you in the land which the LORD your God is giving you.	8 The Lord will bless you with good crops and healthy cattle, and prosper everything you do when you arrive in the land the Lord your God is giving you.
30:9 And the LORD thy God will make thee plenteous in every work of thine hand, in the fruit of thy body, and in the fruit of thy cattle, and in the fruit of thy land, for good: for the LORD will again rejoice over thee for good, as he rejoiced over thy fathers.	30:9 "The LORD your God will make you abound in all the work of your hand, in the fruit of your body, in the increase of your livestock, and in the produce of your land for good. For the LORD will again rejoice over you for good as He rejoiced over your fathers.	30:9 The Lord your God will prosper everything you do and give you many children and much cattle and wonderful crops; for the Lord will again rejoice over you as he did over your fathers.
31:6 Be strong and of a good courage, fear not, nor be afraid of them: for the LORD thy God, he *it is* that doth go with thee; he will not fail thee, nor forsake thee.	31:6 "Be strong and of good courage, do not fear nor be afraid of them; for the LORD your God, He *is* the One who goes with you. He will not leave you nor forsake you."	31:6 Be strong! Be courageous! Do not be afraid of them! For the Lord your God will be with you. He will neither fail you nor forsake you."
33:27 The eternal God *is thy* refuge, and underneath *are* the everlasting arms: and he shall thrust out the enemy from before thee; and shall say, Destroy *them*.	33:27 The eternal God *is your* refuge, And underneath *are* the everlasting arms; He will thrust out the enemy from before you, And will say, 'Destroy!'	33:27 The eternal God is your Refuge, And underneath are the everlasting arms. He thrusts out your enemies before you; It is he who cries, 'Destroy them!'

Joshua

KJV	NKJV	TLB
1:8 This book of the law shall not depart out of thy mouth; but thou shalt meditate therein day and night, that thou mayest observe to do according to all that is written therein: for then thou shalt make thy way prosperous, and then thou shalt have good success.	1:8 "This Book of the Law shall not depart from your mouth, but you shall meditate in it day and night, that you may observe to do according to all that is written in it. For then you will make your way prosperous, and then you will have good success.	1:8 Constantly remind the people about these laws, and you yourself must think about them every day and every night so that you will be sure to obey all of them. For only then will you succeed.
9 Have not I commanded thee? Be strong and of a good courage; be not afraid, neither be thou dismayed: for the LORD thy God *is* with thee whithersoever thou goest.	9 "Have I not commanded you? Be strong and of good courage; do not be afraid, nor be dismayed, for the LORD your God *is* with you wherever you go."	9 Yes, be bold and strong! Banish fear and doubt! For remember, the Lord your God is with you wherever you go."
4:21 And he spake unto the children of Israel, saying, When your children shall ask their fathers in time to come, saying, What *mean* these stones?	4:21 Then he spoke to the children of Israel, saying: "When your children ask their fathers in time to come, saying, 'What *are* these stones?'	4:21 Then Joshua explained again the purpose of the stones: "In the future," he said, "when your children ask you why these stones are here and what they mean,
22 Then ye shall let your children know, saying, Israel came over this Jordan on dry land.	22 "then you shall let your children know, saying, 'Israel crossed over this Jordan on dry land';	22 you are to tell them that these stones are a reminder of this amazing miracle—that the nation of Israel crossed the Jordan River on dry ground!
23 For the LORD your God dried up the waters of Jordan from before you, until ye were passed over, as the LORD your God did to the Red sea, which he dried up from before us, until we were gone over:	23 "for the LORD your God dried up the waters of the Jordan before you until you had crossed over, as the LORD your God did to the Red Sea, which He dried up before us until we had crossed over,	23 Tell them how the Lord our God dried up the river right before our eyes, and then kept it dry until we were all across! It is the same thing the Lord did forty years ago at the Red Sea!
24 That all the people of the earth might know the hand of the LORD, that it *is* mighty: that ye might fear the LORD your God for ever.	24 "that all the peoples of the earth may know the hand of the LORD, that it *is* mighty, that you may fear the LORD your God forever."	24 He did this so that all the nations of the earth will realize that Jehovah is the mighty God, and so that all of you will worship him forever."
5:13 And it came to pass, when Joshua was by Jericho, that he lifted up his eyes and looked, and, behold, there stood a man over against him with his sword drawn in his hand: and Joshua went unto him, and said unto him, *Art* thou for us, or for our adversaries?	5:13 And it came to pass, when Joshua was by Jericho, that he lifted his eyes and looked, and behold, a Man stood opposite him with His sword drawn in His hand. And Joshua went to Him and said to Him, "*Are* You for us or for our adversaries?"	5:13 As Joshua was sizing up the city of Jericho, a man appeared nearby with a drawn sword. Joshua strode over to him and demanded, "Are you friend or foe?"
14 And he said, Nay; but *as* captain of the host of the LORD am I now come. And Joshua fell on his face to the earth, and did worship, and said unto him, What saith my lord unto his servant?	14 So He said, "No, but *as* Commander of the army of the LORD I have now come." And Joshua fell on his face to the earth and worshiped, and said to Him, "What does my Lord say to His servant?"	14 "I am the Commander-in-Chief of the Lord's army," he replied. Joshua fell to the ground before him and worshiped him and said, "Give me your commands."

NIV	RSV	TEV
6 You will be blessed when you come in and blessed when you go out.	6 Blessed shall you be when you come in, and blessed shall you be when you go out.	6 "The LORD will bless everything you do.
7 The LORD will grant that the enemies who rise up against you will be defeated before you. They will come at you from one direction but flee from you in seven.	7 "The LORD will cause your enemies who rise against you to be defeated before you; they shall come out against you one way, and flee before you seven ways.	7 "The LORD will defeat your enemies when they attack you. They will attack from one direction, but they will run from you in all directions.
8 The LORD will send a blessing on your barns and on everything you put your hand to. The LORD your God will bless you in the land he is giving you.	8 The LORD will command the blessing upon you in your barns, and in all that you undertake; and he will bless you in the land which the LORD your God gives you.	8 "The LORD your God will bless your work and fill your barns with grain. He will bless you in the land that he is giving you.
30:9 Then the LORD your God will make you most prosperous in all the work of your hands and in the fruit of your womb, the young of your livestock and the crops of your land. The LORD will again delight in you and make you prosperous, just as he delighted in your fathers,	30:9 The LORD your God will make you abundantly prosperous in all the work of your hand, in the fruit of your body, and in the fruit of your cattle, and in the fruit of your ground; for the LORD will again take delight in prospering you, as he took delight in your fathers,	30:9 The LORD will make you prosperous in all that you do; you will have many children and a lot of livestock, and your fields will produce abundant crops. He will be as glad to make you prosperous as he was to make your ancestors prosperous.
31:6 Be strong and courageous. Do not be afraid or terrified because of them, for the LORD your God goes with you; he will never leave you nor forsake you."	31:6 Be strong and of good courage, do not fear or be in dread of them: for it is the LORD your God who goes with you; he will not fail you or forsake you."	31:6 Be determined and confident. Do not be afraid of them. Your God, the LORD himself, will be with you. He will not fail you or abandon you."
33:27 The eternal God is your refuge, and underneath are the everlasting arms. He will drive out your enemy before you, saying, 'Destroy him!'	33:27 The eternal God is your dwelling place, and underneath are the everlasting arms. And he thrust out the enemy before you, and said, Destroy.	33:27 God has always been your defense; his eternal arms are your support. He drove out your enemies as you advanced, and told you to destroy them all.

Joshua

NIV	RSV	TEV
1:8 Do not let this Book of the Law depart from your mouth; meditate on it day and night, so that you may be careful to do everything written in it. Then you will be prosperous and successful.	1:8 This book of the law shall not depart out of your mouth, but you shall meditate on it day and night, that you may be careful to do according to all that is written in it; for then you shall make your way prosperous, and then you shall have good success.	1:8 Be sure that the book of the Law is always read in your worship. Study it day and night, and make sure that you obey everything written in it. Then you will be prosperous and successful.
9 Have I not commanded you? Be strong and courageous. Do not be terrified; do not be discouraged, for the LORD your God will be with you wherever you go."	9 Have I not commanded you? Be strong and of good courage; be not frightened, neither be dismayed; for the LORD your God is with you wherever you go."	9 Remember that I have commanded you to be determined and confident! Do not be afraid or discouraged, for I, the LORD your God, am with you wherever you go."
4:21 He said to the Israelites, "In the future when your descendants ask their fathers, 'What do these stones mean?'	4:21 And he said to the people of Israel, "When your children ask their fathers in time to come, 'What do these stones mean?'	4:21 And he said to the people of Israel, "In the future, when your children ask you what these stones mean,
22 tell them, 'Israel crossed the Jordan on dry ground.'	22 then you shall let your children know, 'Israel passed over this Jordan on dry ground.'	22 you will tell them about the time when Israel crossed the Jordan on dry ground.
23 For the LORD your God dried up the Jordan before you until you had crossed over. The LORD your God did to the Jordan just what he had done to the Red Sea when he dried it up before us until we had crossed over.	23 For the LORD your God dried up the waters of the Jordan for you until you passed over, as the LORD your God did to the Red Sea, which he dried up for us until we passed over,	23 Tell them that the LORD your God dried up the water of the Jordan for you until you had crossed, just as he dried up the Red Sea for us.
24 He did this so that all the peoples of the earth might know that the hand of the LORD is powerful and so that you might always fear the LORD your God."	24 so that all the peoples of the earth may know that the hand of the LORD is mighty; that you may fear the LORD your God for ever."	24 Because of this everyone on earth will know how great the LORD's power is, and you will honor the LORD your God forever."
5:13 Now when Joshua was near Jericho, he looked up and saw a man standing in front of him with a drawn sword in his hand. Joshua went up to him and asked, "Are you for us or for our enemies?"	5:13 When Joshua was by Jericho, he lifted up his eyes and looked, and behold, a man stood before him with his drawn sword in his hand; and Joshua went to him and said to him, "Are you for us, or for our adversaries?"	5:13 While Joshua was near Jericho, he suddenly saw a man standing in front of him, holding a sword. Joshua went up to him and asked, "Are you one of our soldiers, or an enemy?"
14 "Neither," he replied, "but as commander of the army of the LORD I have now come." Then Joshua fell facedown to the ground in reverence, and asked him, "What message does my Lord have for his servant?"	14 And he said, "No; but as commander of the army of the LORD I have now come." And Joshua fell on his face to the earth, and worshiped, and said to him, "What does my lord bid his servant?"	14 "Neither," the man answered. "I am here as the commander of the LORD's army." Joshua threw himself on the ground in worship and said, "I am your servant, sir. What do you want me to do?"

KEY VERSE COMPARISON CHART

KJV	NKJV	TLB
15 And the captain of the LORD's host said unto Joshua, Loose thy shoe from off thy foot; for the place whereon thou standest is holy. And Joshua did so.	15 Then the Commander of the LORD's army said to Joshua, "Take your sandal off your foot, for the place where you stand is holy." And Joshua did so.	15 "Take off your shoes," the Commander told him, "for this is holy ground." And Joshua did.
7:8 O Lord, what shall I say, when Israel turneth their backs before their enemies!	7:8 "O Lord, what shall I say when Israel turns its back before its enemies?	7:8 O Lord, what am I to do now that Israel has fled from her enemies!
10 And the LORD said unto Joshua, Get thee up; wherefore liest thou thus upon thy face?	10 So the LORD said to Joshua: "Get up! Why do you lie thus on your face?	10 But the Lord said to Joshua, "Get up off your face!
11 Israel hath sinned, and they have also transgressed my covenant which I commanded them: for they have even taken of the accursed thing, and have also stolen, and dissembled also, and they have put it even among their own stuff.	11 "Israel has sinned, and they have also transgressed My covenant which I commanded them. For they have even taken some of the accursed things, and have both stolen and deceived; and they have also put it among their own stuff.	11 Israel has sinned and disobeyed my commandment and has taken loot when I said it was not to be taken; and they have not only taken it, they have lied about it and have hidden it among their belongings.
10:12 Then spake Joshua to the LORD in the day when the LORD delivered up the Amorites before the children of Israel, and he said in the sight of Israel, Sun, stand thou still upon Gibeon; and thou, Moon, in the valley of Ajalon.	10:12 Then Joshua spoke to the LORD in the day when the LORD delivered up the Amorites before the children of Israel, and he said in the sight of Israel: "Sun, stand still over Gibeon; And Moon, in the Valley of Aijalon."	10:12 As the men of Israel were pursuing and harassing the foe, Joshua prayed aloud, "Let the sun stand still over Gibeon, and let the moon stand in its place over the valley of Aijalon!"
13 And the sun stood still, and the moon stayed, until the people had avenged themselves upon their enemies. Is not this written in the book of Jasher? So the sun stood still in the midst of heaven, and hasted not to go down about a whole day.	13 So the sun stood still, And the moon stopped, Till the people had revenge Upon their enemies. Is this not written in the Book of Jasher? So the sun stood still in the midst of heaven, and did not hasten to go down for about a whole day.	13 And the sun and the moon didn't move until the Israeli army had finished the destruction of its enemies! This is described in greater detail in The Book of Jashar. So the sun stopped in the heavens and stayed there for almost twenty-four hours!
11:20 For it was of the LORD to harden their hearts, that they should come against Israel in battle, that he might destroy them utterly, and that they might have no favour, but that he might destroy them, as the LORD commanded Moses.	11:20 For it was the LORD to harden their hearts, that they should come against Israel in battle, that He might utterly destroy them, and that they might receive no mercy, but that He might destroy them, as the LORD had commanded Moses.	11:20 For the Lord made the enemy kings want to fight the Israelis instead of asking for peace; so they were mercilessly killed, as the Lord had commanded Moses.
21:43 And the LORD gave unto Israel all the land which he sware to give unto their fathers; and they possessed it, and dwelt therein.	21:43 So the LORD gave to Israel all the land of which He had sworn to give to their fathers, and they took possession of it and dwelt in it.	21:43 So in this way the Lord gave to Israel all the land he had promised to their ancestors, and they went in and conquered it and lived there.
45 There failed not ought of any good thing which the LORD had spoken unto the house of Israel; all came to pass.	45 Not a word failed of any good thing which the LORD had spoken to the house of Israel. All came to pass.	45 Every good thing the Lord had promised them came true.
23:16 When ye have transgressed the covenant of the LORD your God, which he commanded you, and have gone and served other gods, and bowed yourselves to them; then shall the anger of the LORD be kindled against you, and ye shall perish quickly from off the good land which he hath given unto you.	23:16 "When you have transgressed the covenant of the LORD your God, which He commanded you, and have gone and served other gods, and bowed down to them, then the anger of the LORD will burn against you, and you shall perish quickly from the good land which He has given you."	23:16 For if you worship other gods he will completely wipe you out from this good land which the Lord has given you. His anger will rise hot against you, and you will quickly perish."
24:15 And if it seem evil unto you to serve the LORD, choose you this day whom ye will serve; whether the gods which your fathers served that were on the other side of the flood, or the gods of the Amorites, in whose land ye dwell: but as for me and my house, we will serve the LORD.	24:15 "And if it seems evil to you to serve the LORD, choose for yourselves this day whom you will serve, whether the gods which your fathers served that were on the other side of the River, or the gods of the Amorites, in whose land you dwell. But as for me and my house, we will serve the LORD."	24:15 But if you are unwilling to obey the Lord, then decide today whom you will obey. Will it be the gods of your ancestors beyond the Euphrates or the gods of the Amorites here in this land? But as for me and my family, we will serve the Lord."

Judges

2:7 And the people served the LORD all the days of Joshua, and all the days of the elders that outlived Joshua, who had seen all the great works of the LORD, that he did for Israel.	2:7 So the people served the LORD all the days of Joshua, and all the days of the elders who outlived Joshua, who had seen all the great works of the LORD which He had done for Israel.	2:7 The people had remained true to the Lord throughout Joshua's lifetime, and as long afterward as the old men of his generation were still living—those who had seen the mighty miracles the Lord had done for Israel.

NIV	RSV	TEV
15 The commander of the LORD's army replied, "Take off your sandals, for the place where you are standing is holy." And Joshua did so.	15 And the commander of the LORD's army said to Joshua, "Put off your shoes from your feet; for the place where you stand is holy." And Joshua did so.	15 And the commander of the LORD's army told him, "Take your sandals off; you are standing on holy ground." And Joshua did as he was told.
7:8 O Lord, what can I say, now that Israel has been routed by its enemies?	7:8 O Lord, what can I say, when Israel has turned their backs before their enemies!	7:8 What can I say, O Lord, now that Israel has retreated from the enemy?
10 The LORD said to Joshua, "Stand up! What are you doing down on your face?	10 The LORD said to Joshua, "Arise, why have you thus fallen upon your face?	10 The LORD said to Joshua, "Get up! Why are you lying on the ground like this?
11 Israel has sinned; they have violated my covenant, which I commanded them to keep. They have taken some of the devoted things; they have stolen, they have lied, they have put them with their own possessions.	11 Israel has sinned; they have transgressed my covenant which I commanded them; they have taken some of the devoted things; they have stolen, and lied, and put them among their own stuff.	11 Israel has sinned! They have broken the agreement with me that I ordered them to keep. They have taken some of the things condemned to destruction. They stole them, lied about it, and put them with their own things.
10:12 On the day the LORD gave the Amorites over to Israel, Joshua said to the LORD in the presence of Israel: "O sun, stand still over Gibeon, O moon, over the Valley of Aijalon."	10:12 Then spoke Joshua to the LORD in the day when the LORD gave the Amorites over to the men of Israel; and he said in the sight of Israel, "Sun, stand thou still at Gibeon, and thou Moon in the valley of Aijalon."	10:12 On the day that the LORD gave the men of Israel victory over the Amorites, Joshua spoke to the LORD. In the presence of the Israelites he said, "Sun, stand still over Gibeon; Moon, stop over Aijalon Valley."
13 So the sun stood still, and the moon stopped, till the nation avenged itself on its enemies, as it is written in the Book of Jashar. The sun stopped in the middle of the sky and delayed going down about a full day.	13 And the sun stood still, and the moon stayed, until the nation took vengeance on their enemies. Is this not written in the Book of Jashar? The sun stayed in the midst of heaven, and did not hasten to go down for about a whole day.	13 The sun stood still and the moon did not move until the nation had conquered its enemies. This is written in *The Book of Jashar*. The sun stood still in the middle of the sky and did not go down for a whole day.
11:20 For it was the LORD himself who hardened their hearts to wage war against Israel, so that he might destroy them totally, exterminating them without mercy, as the LORD had commanded Moses.	11:20 For it was the LORD's doing to harden their hearts that they should come against Israel in battle, in order that they should be utterly destroyed, and should receive no mercy but be exterminated, as the LORD commanded Moses.	11:20 The LORD had made them determined to fight the Israelites, so that they would be condemned to total destruction and all be killed without mercy. This was what the LORD had commanded Moses.
21:43 So the LORD gave Israel all the land he had sworn to give their forefathers, and they took possession of it and settled there.	21:43 Thus the LORD gave to Israel all the land which he swore to give to their fathers; and having taken possession of it, they settled there.	21:43 So the LORD gave to Israel all the land that he had solemnly promised their ancestors he would give them. When they had taken possession of it, they settled down there.
45 Not one of all the LORD's good promises to the house of Israel failed; every one was fulfilled.	45 Not one of all the good promises which the LORD had made to the house of Israel had failed; all came to pass.	45 The LORD kept every one of the promises that he had made to the people of Israel.
23:16 If you violate the covenant of the LORD your God, which he commanded you, and go and serve other gods and bow down to them, the LORD's anger will burn against you, and you will quickly perish from the good land he has given you."	23:16 if you transgress the covenant of the LORD your God, which he commanded you, and go and serve other gods and bow down to them. Then the anger of the LORD will be kindled against you, and you shall perish quickly from off the good land which he has given to you."	23:16 If you do not keep the covenant which the LORD your God commanded you to keep and if you serve and worship other gods, then in his anger he will punish you, and soon none of you will be left in this good land that he has given you."
24:15 But if serving the LORD seems undesirable to you, then choose for yourselves this day whom you will serve, whether the gods your forefathers served beyond the River, or the gods of the Amorites, in whose land you are living. But as for me and my household, we will serve the LORD."	24:15 And if you be unwilling to serve the LORD, choose this day whom you will serve, whether the gods your fathers served in the region beyond the River, or the gods of the Amorites in whose land you dwell; but as for me and my house, we will serve the LORD."	24:15 If you are not willing to serve him, decide today whom you will serve, the gods your ancestors worshiped in Mesopotamia or the gods of the Amorites, in whose land you are now living. As for my family and me, we will serve the LORD."

Judges

2:7 The people served the LORD throughout the lifetime of Joshua and of the elders who outlived him and who had seen all the great things the LORD had done for Israel.	2:7 And the people served the LORD all the days of Joshua, and all the days of the elders who outlived Joshua, who had seen all the great work which the LORD had done for Israel.	2:7 As long as Joshua lived, the people of Israel served the LORD, and even after his death they continued to do so as long as the leaders were alive who had seen for themselves all the great things that the LORD had done for Israel.

KJV	NKJV	TLB
5:31 So let all thine enemies perish, O LORD: but *let* them that love him *be* as the sun when he goeth forth in his might. And the land had rest forty years.	**5:31** "Thus let all Your enemies perish, O LORD! But *let* those who love Him *be* like the sun When it comes out in full strength." So the land had rest for forty years.	**5:31** O Lord, may all your enemies Perish as Sisera did, But may those who love the Lord Shine as the sun!" After that there was peace in the land for forty years.
17:6 In those days *there was* no king in Israel, *but* every man did *that which was* right in his own eyes.	**17:6** In those days *there was* no king in Israel; everyone did *what was* right in his own eyes.	**17:6** (For in those days Israel had no king, so everyone did whatever he wanted to—whatever seemed right in his own eyes.)
21:25 In those days *there was* no king in Israel: every man did *that which was* right in his own eyes.	**21:25** In those days *there was* no king in Israel; everyone did *what was* right in his own eyes.	**21:25** (There was no king in Israel in those days, and every man did whatever he thought was right.)

Ruth

1:16 And Ruth said, Intreat me not to leave thee, *or* to return from following after thee: for whither thou goest, I will go; and where thou lodgest, I will lodge: thy people *shall be* my people, and thy God my God:	**1:16** But Ruth said: "Entreat me not to leave you, *Or* to turn back from following after you; For wherever you go, I will go; And wherever you lodge, I will lodge; Your people *shall be* my people, And your God, my God.	**1:16** But Ruth replied, "Don't make me leave you, for I want to go wherever you go, and to live wherever you live; your people shall be my people, and your God shall be my God;
17 Where thou diest, will I die, and there will I be buried: the LORD do so to me, and more also, *if ought* but death part thee and me.	**17** Where you die, I will die, And there will I be buried. The LORD do so to me, and more also, If *anything but* death parts you and me."	**17** I want to die where you die, and be buried there. May the Lord do terrible things to me if I allow anything but death to separate us."
4:14 And the women said unto Naomi, Blessed *be* the LORD, which hath not left thee this day without a kinsman, that his name may be famous in Israel.	**4:14** Then the women said to Naomi, "Blessed *be* the LORD, who has not left you this day without a near kinsman; and may his name be famous in Israel!	**4:14** And the women of the city said to Naomi, "Bless the Lord who has given you this little grandson; may he be famous in Israel.
15 And he shall be unto thee a restorer of *thy* life, and a nourisher of thine old age: for thy daughter in law, which loveth thee, which is better to thee than seven sons, hath born him.	**15** "And may he be to you a restorer of life and a nourisher of your old age; for your daughter-in-law, who loves you, who is better to you than seven sons, has borne him."	**15** May he restore your youth and take care of you in your old age; for he is the son of your daughter-in-law who loves you so much, and who has been kinder to you than seven sons!"

First Samuel

2:6 The LORD killeth, and maketh alive: he bringeth down to the grave, and bringeth up.	**2:6** "The LORD kills and makes alive; He brings down to the grave and brings up.	**2:6** The Lord kills, The Lord gives life.
7 The LORD maketh poor, and maketh rich: he bringeth low, and lifteth up.	**7** The LORD makes poor and makes rich; He brings low and lifts up.	**7** Some he causes to be poor and others to be rich. He cuts one down and lifts another up.
8 He raiseth up the poor out of the dust, *and* lifteth up the beggar from the dunghill, to set *them* among princes, and to make them inherit the throne of glory: for the pillars of the earth *are* the LORD's, and he hath set the world upon them.	**8** He raises the poor from the dust *And* lifts the beggar from the ash heap, To set *them* among princes And make them inherit the throne of glory. "For the pillars of the earth *are* the LORD's, And He has set the world upon them.	**8** He lifts the poor from the dust— Yes, from a pile of ashes— And treats them as princes Sitting in the seats of honor. For all the earth is the Lord's And he has set the world in order.
9 He will keep the feet of his saints, and the wicked shall be silent in darkness; for by strength shall no man prevail.	**9** He will guard the feet of His saints, But the wicked shall be silent in darkness. "For by strength no man shall prevail.	**9** He will protect his godly ones, But the wicked shall be silenced in darkness. No one shall succeed by strength alone.
10 The adversaries of the LORD shall be broken to pieces; out of heaven shall he thunder upon them: the LORD shall judge the ends of the earth; and he shall give strength unto his king, and exalt the horn of his anointed.	**10** The adversaries of the LORD shall be broken in pieces; From heaven He will thunder against them. The LORD will judge the ends of the earth. "He will give strength to His King, And exalt the horn of His anointed."	**10** Those who fight against the Lord shall be broken; He thunders against them from heaven. He judges throughout the earth. He gives mighty strength to his King, And gives great glory to his anointed one."

NIV	RSV	TEV
5:31 "So may all your enemies perish, O LORD! But may they who love you be like the sun when it rises in its strength." Then the land had peace forty years.	**5:31** "So perish all thine enemies, O LORD! But thy friends be like the sun as he rises in his might." And the land had rest for forty years.	**5:31** So may all your enemies die like that, O LORD, but may your friends shine like the rising sun! And there was peace in the land for forty years.
17:6 In those days Israel had no king; everyone did as he saw fit.	**17:6** In those days there was no king in Israel; every man did what was right in his own eyes.	**17:6** There was no king in Israel at that time; everyone did whatever he wanted.
21:25 In those days Israel had no king; everyone did as he saw fit.	**21:25** In those days there was no king in Israel; every man did what was right in his own eyes.	**21:25** There was no king in Israel at that time. Everyone did whatever he pleased.

Ruth

NIV	RSV	TEV
1:16 But Ruth replied, "Don't urge me to leave you or to turn back from you. Where you go I will go, and where you stay I will stay. Your people will be my people and your God my God.	**1:16** But Ruth said, "Entreat me not to leave you or to return from following you; for where you go I will go, and where you lodge I will lodge; your people shall be my people, and your God my God;	**1:16** But Ruth answered, "Don't ask me to leave you! Let me go with you. Wherever you go, I will go; wherever you live, I will live. Your people will be my people, and your God will be my God.
17 Where you die I will die, and there I will be buried. May the LORD deal with me, be it ever so severely, if anything but death separates you and me."	**17** where you die I will die, and there will I be buried. May the LORD do so to me and more also if even death parts me from you."	**17** Wherever you die, I will die, and that is where I will be buried. May the LORD's worst punishment come upon me if I let anything but death separate me from you!"
4:14 The women said to Naomi: "Praise be to the LORD, who this day has not left you without a kinsman-redeemer. May he become famous throughout Israel!	**4:14** Then the women said to Naomi, "Blessed be the LORD, who has not left you this day without next of kin; and may his name be renowned in Israel!	**4:14** The women said to Naomi, "Praise the LORD! He has given you a grandson today to take care of you. May the boy become famous in Israel!
15 He will renew your life and sustain you in your old age. For your daughter-in-law, who loves you and who is better to you than seven sons, has given him birth."	**15** He shall be to you a restorer of life and a nourisher of your old age; for your daughter-in-law who loves you, who is more to you than seven sons, has borne him."	**15** Your daughter-in-law loves you, and has done more for you than seven sons. And now she has given you a grandson, who will bring new life to you and give you security in your old age."

First Samuel

NIV	RSV	TEV
2:6 "The LORD brings death and makes alive; he brings down to the grave and raises up.	**2:6** The LORD kills and brings to life; he brings down to Sheol and raises up.	**2:6** The LORD kills and restores to life; he sends people to the world of the dead and brings them back again.
7 The LORD sends poverty and wealth; he humbles and he exalts.	**7** The LORD makes poor and makes rich; he brings low, he also exalts.	**7** He makes some men poor and others rich; he humbles some and makes others great.
8 He raises the poor from the dust and lifts the needy from the ash heap; he seats them with princes and has them inherit a throne of honor. "For the foundations of the earth are the LORD's; upon them he has set the world.	**8** He raises up the poor from the dust; he lifts the needy from the ash heap, to make them sit with princes and inherit a seat of honor. For the pillars of the earth are the LORD's, and on them he has set the world.	**8** He lifts the poor from the dust and raises the needy from their misery. He makes them companions of princes and puts them in places of honor. The foundations of the earth belong to the LORD; on them he has built the world.
9 He will guard the feet of his saints, but the wicked will be silenced in darkness. "It is not by strength that one prevails;	**9** "He will guard the feet of his faithful ones; but the wicked shall be cut off in darkness; for not by might shall a man prevail.	**9** "He protects the lives of his faithful people, but the wicked disappear in darkness; a man does not triumph by his own strength.
10 those who oppose the LORD will be shattered. He will thunder against them from heaven; the LORD will judge the ends of the earth. "He will give strength to his king and exalt the horn of his anointed."	**10** The adversaries of the LORD shall be broken to pieces; against them he will thunder in heaven. The LORD will judge the ends of the earth; he will give strength to his king, and exalt the power of his anointed."	**10** The LORD's enemies will be destroyed; he will thunder against them from heaven. The LORD will judge the whole world; he will give power to his king, he will make his chosen king victorious."

KJV	NKJV	TLB
10:17 And Samuel called the people together unto the LORD to Mizpeh;	**10:17** Then Samuel called the people together to the LORD at Mizpah,	**10:17** Samuel now called a convocation of all Israel at Mizpah,
18 And said unto the children of Israel, Thus saith the LORD God of Israel, I brought up Israel out of Egypt, and delivered you out of the hand of the Egyptians, and out of the hand of all kingdoms, *and* of them that oppressed you:	18 and said to the children of Israel, "Thus says the LORD God of Israel: 'I brought up Israel out of Egypt, and delivered you from the hand of the Egyptians *and* from the hand of all kingdoms and from those who oppressed you.'	18 and gave them this message from the Lord God: "I brought you from Egypt and rescued you from the Egyptians and from all of the nations that were torturing you.
19 And ye have this day rejected your God, who himself saved you out of all your adversities and your tribulations; and ye have said unto him, *Nay,* but set a king over us. Now therefore present yourselves before the LORD by your tribes, and by your thousands.	19 "But you have today rejected your God, who Himself saved you out of all your adversities and your tribulations; and you have said to Him, 'No, but set a king over us!' Now therefore, present yourselves before the LORD by your tribes and by your clans."	19 But although I have done so much for you, you have rejected me and have said, 'We want a king instead!' All right, then, present yourselves before the Lord by tribes and clans."
12:14 If ye will fear the LORD, and serve him, and obey his voice, and not rebel against the commandment of the LORD, then shall both ye and also the king that reigneth over you continue following the LORD your God:	**12:14** "If you fear the LORD and serve Him and obey His voice, and do not rebel against the commandment of the LORD, then both you and the king who reigns over you will continue following the LORD your God.	**12:14** "Now if you will fear and worship the Lord and listen to his commandments and not rebel against the Lord, and if both you and your king follow the Lord your God, then all will be well.
15 But if ye will not obey the voice of the LORD, but rebel against the commandment of the LORD, then shall the hand of the LORD be against you, as *it was* against your fathers.	15 "However, if you do not obey the voice of the LORD, but rebel against the commandment of the LORD, then the hand of the LORD will be against you, as *it was* against your fathers.	15 But if you rebel against the Lord's commandments and refuse to listen to him, then his hand will be as heavy upon you as it was upon your ancestors.
13:13 And Samuel said to Saul, Thou hast done foolishly: thou hast not kept the commandment of the LORD thy God, which he commanded thee: for now would the LORD have established thy kingdom upon Israel for ever.	**13:13** And Samuel said to Saul, "You have done foolishly. You have not kept the commandment of the LORD your God, which He commanded you. For now the LORD would have established your kingdom over Israel forever.	**13:13** "You fool!" Samuel exclaimed. "You have disobeyed the commandment of the Lord your God. He was planning to make you and your descendants kings of Israel forever,
14 But now thy kingdom shall not continue: the LORD hath sought him a man after his own heart, and the LORD hath commanded him *to be* captain over his people, because thou hast not kept *that* which the LORD commanded thee.	14 "But now your kingdom shall not continue. The LORD has sought for Himself a man after His own heart, and the LORD has commanded him *to be* commanded over His people, because you have not kept what the LORD commanded you."	14 but now your dynasty must end; for the Lord wants a man who will obey him. And he has discovered the man he wants and has already appointed him as king over his people; for you have not obeyed the Lord's commandment."
15:22 And Samuel said, Hath the LORD *as great* delight in burnt offerings and sacrifices, as in obeying the voice of the LORD? Behold, to obey *is* better than sacrifice, *and* to hearken than the fat of rams.	**15:22** Then Samuel said: "Has the LORD *as great* delight in burnt offerings and sacrifices, As in obeying the voice of the LORD? Behold, to obey is better than sacrifice, And to heed than the fat of rams.	**15:22** Samuel replied, "Has the Lord as much pleasure in your burnt offerings and sacrifices as in your obedience? Obedience is far better than sacrifice. He is much more interested in your listening to him than in your offering the fat of rams to him.
17:37 David said moreover, The LORD that delivered me out of the paw of the lion, and out of the paw of the bear, he will deliver me out of the hand of this Philistine. And Saul said unto David, Go, and the LORD be with thee.	**17:37** Moreover David said, "The LORD, who delivered me from the paw of the lion and from the paw of the bear, He will deliver me from the hand of this Philistine." And Saul said to David, "Go, and the LORD be with you!"	**17:37** The Lord who saved me from the claws and teeth of the lion and the bear will save me from this Philistine!" Saul finally consented, "All right, go ahead," he said, "and may the Lord be with you!"
24:17 And he said to David, Thou *art* more righteous than I: for thou hast rewarded me good, whereas I have rewarded thee evil.	**24:17** Then he said to David: "You *are* more righteous than I; for you have rewarded me with good, whereas I have rewarded you with evil.	**24:17** And he said to David, "You are a better man than I am, for you have repaid me good for evil.
18 And thou hast shewed this day how that thou hast dealt well with me: forasmuch as when the LORD had delivered me into thine hand, thou killedst me not.	18 "And you have shown this day how you have dealt well with me; for when the LORD delivered me into your hand, you did not kill me.	18 Yes, you have been wonderfully kind to me today, for when the Lord delivered me into your hand, you didn't kill me.

Second Samuel

KJV	NKJV	TLB
1:23 Saul and Jonathan *were* lovely and pleasant in their lives, and in their death they were not divided: they were swifter than eagles, they were stronger than lions.	**1:23** Saul and Jonathan *were* beloved and pleasant in their lives, And in their death they were not divided; They were swifter than eagles, They were stronger than lions.	**1:23** How much they were loved, how wonderful they were— Both Saul and Jonathan! They were together in life and in death. They were swifter than eagles, stronger than lions.
24 Ye daughters of Israel, weep over Saul, who clothed you in scarlet, with *other* delights, who put on ornaments of gold upon your apparel.	24 "O daughters of Israel, weep over Saul, Who clothed you in scarlet, with luxury; Who put ornaments of gold on your apparel.	24 But now, O women of Israel, weep for Saul; He enriched you With fine clothing and golden ornaments.

NIV	RSV	TEV
10:17 Samuel summoned the people of Israel to the LORD at Mizpah	**10:17** Now Samuel called the people together to the LORD at Mizpah;	**10:17** Samuel called the people together for a religious gathering at Mizpah
18 and said to them, "This is what the LORD, the God of Israel, says: 'I brought Israel up out of Egypt, and I delivered you from the power of Egypt and all the kingdoms that oppressed you.'	**18** and he said to the people of Israel, "Thus says the LORD, the God of Israel, 'I brought up Israel out of Egypt, and I delivered you from the hand of the Egyptians and from the hand of all the kingdoms that were oppressing you.'	**18** and said to them, "The LORD, the God of Israel, says, 'I brought you out of Egypt and rescued you from the Egyptians and all the other peoples who were oppressing you.
19 But you have now rejected your God, who saves you out of all your calamities and distresses. And you have said, 'No, set a king over us.' So now present yourselves before the LORD by your tribes and clans."	**19** But you have this day rejected your God, who saves you from all your calamities and your distresses; and you have said, 'No! but set a king over us.' Now therefore present yourselves before the LORD by your tribes and by your thousands."	**19** I am your God, the one who rescues you from all your troubles and difficulties, but today you have rejected me and have asked me to give you a king. Very well, then, gather yourselves before the LORD by tribes and by clans.'"
12:14 If you fear the LORD and serve and obey him and do not rebel against his commands, and if both you and the king who reigns over you follow the LORD your God—good!	**12:14** If you will fear the LORD and serve him and hearken to his voice and not rebel against the commandment of the LORD, and if both you and the king who reigns over you will follow the LORD your God, it will be well;	**12:14** All will go well with you if you honor the LORD your God, serve him, listen to him, and obey his commands, and if you and your king follow him.
15 But if you do not obey the LORD, and if you rebel against his commands, his hand will be against you, as it was against your fathers.	**15** but if you will not hearken to the voice of the LORD, but rebel against the commandment of the LORD, then the hand of the LORD will be against you and your king.	**15** But if you do not listen to the LORD but disobey his commands, he will be against you and your king.
13:13 "You acted foolishly," Samuel said. "You have not kept the command the LORD your God gave you; if you had, he would have established your kingdom over Israel for all time.	**13:13** And Samuel said to Saul, "You have done foolishly; you have not kept the commandment of the LORD your God, which he commanded you; for now the LORD would have established your kingdom over Israel for ever.	**13:13** "That was a foolish thing to do," Samuel answered. "You have not obeyed the command the LORD your God gave you. If you had obeyed, he would have let you and your descendants rule over Israel forever.
14 But now your kingdom will not endure; the LORD has sought out a man after his own heart and appointed him leader of his people, because you have not kept the LORD's command."	**14** But now your kingdom shall not continue; the LORD has sought out a man after his own heart; and the LORD has appointed him to be prince over his people, because you have not kept what the LORD commanded you."	**14** But now your rule will not continue. Because you have disobeyed him, the LORD will find the kind of man he wants and make him ruler of his people."
15:22 But Samuel replied: "Does the LORD delight in burnt offerings and sacrifices as much as in obeying the voice of the LORD? To obey is better than sacrifice, and to heed is better than the fat of rams.	**15:22** And Samuel said, "Has the LORD as great delight in burnt offerings and sacrifices, as in obeying the voice of the LORD? Behold, to obey is better than sacrifice, and to hearken than the fat of rams.	**15:22** Samuel said, "Which does the LORD prefer: obedience or offerings and sacrifices? It is better to obey him than to sacrifice the best sheep to him.
17:37 The LORD who delivered me from the paw of the lion and the paw of the bear will deliver me from the hand of this Philistine." Saul said to David, "Go, and the LORD be with you."	**17:37** And David said, "The LORD who delivered me from the paw of the lion and from the paw of the bear, will deliver me from the hand of this Philistine." And Saul said to David, "Go, and the LORD be with you!"	**17:37** The LORD has saved me from lions and bears; he will save me from this Philistine." "All right," Saul answered. "Go, and the LORD be with you."
24:17 "You are more righteous than I," he said. "You have treated me well, but I have treated you badly.	**24:17** He said to David, "You are more righteous than I; for you have repaid me good, whereas I have repaid you evil.	**24:17** Then he said to David, "You are right, and I am wrong. You have been so good to me, while I have done such wrong to you!
18 You have just now told me of the good you did to me; the LORD delivered me into your hands, but you did not kill me.	**18** And you have declared this day how you have dealt well with me, in that you did not kill me when the LORD put me into your hands.	**18** Today you have shown how good you are to me, because you did not kill me, even though the LORD put me in your power.

Second Samuel

NIV	RSV	TEV
1:23 "Saul and Jonathan— in life they were loved and gracious, and in death they were not parted. They were swifter than eagles, they were stronger than lions.	**1:23** "Saul and Jonathan, beloved and lovely! In life and in death they were not divided; they were swifter than eagles, they were stronger than lions.	**1:23** "Saul and Jonathan, so wonderful and dear; together in life, together in death; swifter than eagles, stronger than lions.
24 "O daughters of Israel, weep for Saul, who clothed you in scarlet and finery, who adorned your garments with ornaments of gold.	**24** "Ye daughters of Israel, weep over Saul, who clothed your daintily in scarlet, who put ornaments of gold upon your apparel.	**24** "Women of Israel, mourn for Saul! He clothed you in rich scarlet dresses and adorned you with jewels and gold.

KJV	NKJV	TLB
25 How are the mighty fallen in the midst of the battle! O Jonathan, *thou wast* slain in thine high places.	25 "How the mighty have fallen in the midst of the battle! Jonathan *was* slain in your high places	25 These mighty heroes have fallen in the midst of the battle. Jonathan is slain upon the hills.
26 I am distressed for thee, my brother Jonathan: very pleasant hast thou been unto me: thy love to me was wonderful, passing the love of women.	26 I am distressed for you, my brother Jonathan; You have been very pleasant to me; Your love to me was wonderful, Surpassing the love of women.	26 How I weep for you, my brother Jonathan; How much I loved you! And your love for me was deeper Than the love of women!
27 How are the mighty fallen, and the weapons of war perished!	27 "How the mighty have fallen, And the weapons of war perished!"	27 The mighty ones have fallen, Stripped of their weapons, and dead.
7:12 And when thy days be fulfilled, and thou shalt sleep with thy fathers, I will set up thy seed after thee, which shall proceed out of thy bowels, and I will establish his kingdom.	7:12 "When your days are fulfilled and you rest with your fathers, I will set up your seed after you, who will come from your body, and I will establish his kingdom.	7:12 For when you die, I will put one of your sons upon your throne and I will make his kingdom strong.
13 He shall build an house for my name, and I will stablish the throne of his kingdom for ever.	13 "He shall build a house for My name, and I will establish the throne of his kingdom forever.	13 He is the one who shall build me a temple. And I will continue his kingdom into eternity.
12:7 And Nathan said to David, Thou *art* the man. Thus saith the LORD God of Israel, I anointed thee king over Israel, and I delivered thee out of the hand of Saul;	12:7 Then Nathan said to David, "You *are* the man! Thus says the LORD God of Israel: 'I anointed you king over Israel, and I delivered you from the hand of Saul.	12:7 Then Nathan said to David, "*You* are that rich man! The Lord God of Israel says, 'I made you king of Israel and saved you from the power of Saul.
8 And I gave thee thy master's house, and thy master's wives into thy bosom, and gave thee the house of Israel and of Judah; and if *that had been* too little, I would moreover have given unto thee such and such things.	8 'I gave you your master's house and your master's wives into your keeping, and gave you the house of Israel and Judah. And if *that had been* too little, I also would have given you much more!	8 I gave you his palace and his wives and the kingdoms of Israel and Judah; and if that had not been enough, I would have given you much, much more.
9 Wherefore hast thou despised the commandment of the LORD, to do evil in his sight? thou hast killed Uriah the Hittite with the sword, and hast taken his wife *to be* thy wife, and hast slain him with the sword of the children of Ammon.	9 'Why have you despised the commandment of the LORD, to do evil in His sight? You have killed Uriah the Hittite with the sword; you have taken his wife *to be* your wife, and have killed him with the sword of the people of Ammon.	9 Why, then, have you despised the laws of God and done this horrible deed? For you have murdered Uriah and stolen his wife.
10 Now therefore the sword shall never depart from thine house; because thou hast despised me, and hast taken the wife of Uriah the Hittite to be thy wife.	10 'Now therefore, the sword shall never depart from your house, because you have despised Me, and have taken the wife of Uriah the Hittite to be your wife.'	10 Therefore murder shall be a constant threat in your family from this time on, because you have insulted me by taking Uriah's wife.
21 Then said his servants unto him, What thing *is* this that thou hast done? thou didst fast and weep for the child, *while it was* alive; but when the child was dead, thou didst rise and eat bread.	21 Then his servants said to him, "What *is* this that you have done? You fasted and wept for the child *while he was* alive, but when the child died, you arose and ate food."	21 His aides were amazed. "We don't understand you," they told him. "While the baby was still living, you wept and refused to eat; but now that the baby is dead, you have stopped your mourning and are eating again."
22 And he said, While the child was yet alive, I fasted and wept: for I said, Who can tell *whether* GOD will be gracious to me, that the child may live?	22 So he said, "While the child was *still* alive, I fasted and wept; for I said, 'Who can tell *whether* the LORD will be gracious to me, that the child may live?'	22 David replied, "I fasted and wept while the child was alive, for I said, 'Perhaps the Lord will be gracious to me and let the child live.'
23 But now he is dead, wherefore should I fast? can I bring him back again? I shall go to him, but he shall not return to me.	23 "But now he is dead; why should I fast? Can I bring him back again? I shall go to him, but he shall not return to me."	23 But why should I fast when he is dead? Can I bring him back again? I shall go to him, but he shall not return to me."
22:1 And David spake unto the LORD the words of this song in the day *that* the LORD had delivered him out of the hand of all his enemies, and out of the hand of Saul:	22:1 Then David spoke to the LORD the words of this song, on the day when the LORD had delivered him from the hands of all his enemies, and from the hand of Saul.	22:1 David sang this song to the Lord after he had rescued him from Saul and from all his other enemies:
2 And he said, The LORD *is* my rock, and my fortress, and my deliverer;	2 And he said: "The LORD *is* my rock, my fortress and my deliverer;	2 "Jehovah is my rock, My fortress and my Savior.
3 The God of my rock; in him will I trust: *he is* my shield, and the horn of my salvation, my high tower, and my refuge, my saviour; thou savest me from violence.	3 The God of my strength, in Him I will trust; My shield and the horn of my salvation, My stronghold and my refuge; My Savior, You save me from violence.	3 I will hide in God, Who is my rock and my refuge. He is my shield And my salvation, My refuge and high tower. Thank you, O my Savior, For saving me from all my enemies.

NIV	RSV	TEV
25 "How the mighty have fallen in battle! Jonathan lies slain on your heights.	25 "How are the mighty fallen in the midst of the battle! "Jonathan lies slain upon thy high places.	25 "The brave soldiers have fallen, they were killed in battle. Jonathan lies dead in the hills.
26 I grieve for you, Jonathan my brother; you were very dear to me. Your love for me was wonderful, more wonderful than that of women.	26 I am distressed for you, my brother Jonathan; very pleasant have you been to me; your love to me was wonderful, passing the love of women.	26 "I grieve for you, my brother Jonathan; how dear you were to me! How wonderful was your love for me, better even than the love of women.
27 "How the mighty have fallen! The weapons of war have perished!"	27 "How are the mighty fallen, and the weapons of war perished!"	27 "The brave soldiers have fallen, their weapons abandoned and useless."
7:12 When your days are over and you rest with your fathers, I will raise up your offspring to succeed you, who will come from your own body, and I will establish his kingdom.	7:12 When your days are fulfilled and you lie down with your fathers, I will raise up your off-spring after you, who shall come forth from your body, and I will establish his kingdom.	7:12 When you die and are buried with your ancestors, I will make one of your sons king and will keep his kingdom strong.
13 He is the one who will build a house for my Name, and I will establish the throne of his kingdom forever.	13 He shall build a house for my name, and I will establish the throne of his kingdom for ever.	13 He will be the one to build a temple for me, and I will make sure that his dynasty continues forever.
12:7 Then Nathan said to David, "You are the man! This is what the LORD, the God of Israel, says: 'I anointed you king over Israel, and I delivered you from the hand of Saul.	12:7 Nathan said to David, "You are the man. Thus says the LORD, the God of Israel, 'I anointed you king over Israel, and I delivered you out of the hand of Saul;	12:7 "You are that man," Nathan said to David. "And this is what the LORD God of Israel says: 'I made you king of Israel and rescued you from Saul.
8 I gave your master's house to you, and your master's wives into your arms. I gave you the house of Israel and Judah. And if all this had been too little, I would have given you even more.	8 and I gave you your master's house, and your master's wives into your bosom, and gave you the house of Israel and of Judah; and if this were too little, I would add to you as much more.	8 I gave you his kingdom and his wives; I made you king over Israel and Judah. If this had not been enough, I would have given you twice as much.
9 Why did you despise the word of the LORD by doing what is evil in his eyes? You struck down Uriah the Hittite with the sword and took his wife to be your own. You killed him with the sword of the Ammonites.	9 Why have you despised the word of the LORD, to do what is evil in his sight? You have smitten Uriah the Hittite with the sword, and have taken his wife to be your wife, and have slain him with the sword of the Ammonites.	9 Why, then, have you disobeyed my commands? Why did you do this evil thing? You had Uriah killed in battle; you let the Ammonites kill him, and then you took his wife!
10 Now, therefore, the sword will never depart from your house, because you despised me and took the wife of Uriah the Hittite to be your own.'	10 Now therefore the sword shall never depart from your house, because you have despised me, and have taken the wife of Uriah the Hittite to be your wife.'	10 Now, in every generation some of your descendants will die a violent death because you have disobeyed me and have taken Uriah's wife.
21 His servants asked him, "Why are you acting this way? While the child was alive, you fasted and wept, but now that the child is dead, you get up and eat!"	21 Then his servants said to him, "What is this thing that you have done? You fasted and wept for the child while it was alive; but when the child died, you arose and ate food."	21 "We don't understand this," his officials said to him. "While the child was alive, you wept for him and would not eat; but as soon as he died, you got up and ate!"
22 He answered, "While the child was still alive, I fasted and wept. I thought, 'Who knows? The LORD will be gracious to me and let the child live.'	22 He said, "While the child was still alive, I fasted and wept; for I said, 'Who knows whether the LORD will be gracious to me, that the child may live?'	22 "Yes," David answered, "I did fast and weep while he was still alive. I thought that the LORD might be merciful to me and not let the child die.
23 But now that he is dead, why should I fast? Can I bring him back again? I will go to him, but he will not return to me."	23 But now he is dead; why should I fast? Can I bring him back again? I shall go to him, but he will not return to me."	23 But now that he is dead, why should I fast? Could I bring the child back to life? I will some day go to where he is, but he can never come back to me."
22:1 David sang to the LORD the words of this song when the LORD delivered him from the hand of all his enemies and from the hand of Saul.	22:1 And David spoke to the LORD the words of this song on the day when the LORD delivered him from the hand of all his enemies, and from the hand of Saul.	22:1 When the LORD saved David from Saul and his other enemies, David sang this song to the LORD:
2 He said: "The LORD is my rock, my fortress and my deliverer;	2 He said, "The LORD is my rock, and my fortress, and my deliverer;	2 The LORD is my protector; he is my strong fortress.
3 my God is my rock, in whom I take refuge, my shield and the horn of my salvation. He is my stronghold, my refuge and my savior— from violent men you save me.	3 my God, my rock, in whom I take refuge, my shield and the horn of my salvation, my stronghold and my refuge; my savior; thou savest me from violence.	3 My God is my protection, and with him I am safe. He protects me like a shield; he defends me and keeps me safe. He is my savior; he protects me and saves me from violence.

KJV	NKJV	TLB
4 I will call on the LORD, *who is* worthy to be praised: so shall I be saved from mine enemies.	4 I will call upon the LORD, *who is* worthy to be praised; So shall I be saved from my enemies.	4 I will call upon the Lord, Who is worthy to be praised; He will save me from all my enemies.
23:3 The God of Israel said, the Rock of Israel spake to me, He that ruleth over men *must be* just, ruling in the fear of God.	**23:3** The God of Israel said, The Rock of Israel spoke to me: 'He who rules over men *must be* just,	**23:3** The Rock of Israel said to me: 'One shall come who rules righteously, Who rules in the fear of God.
4 And *he shall be* as the light of the morning, *when* the sun riseth, *even* a morning without clouds; *as* the tender grass *springing* out of the earth by clear shining after rain.	4 Ruling in the fear of God. And *he shall be* like the light of the morning *when* the sun rises, A morning without clouds, *Like* the tender grass *springing* out of the earth, By clear shining after rain.'	4 He shall be as the light of the morning; A cloudless sunrise When the tender grass Springs forth upon the earth; As sunshine after rain.'

First Kings

KJV	NKJV	TLB
2:2 I go the way of all the earth: be thou strong therefore, and shew thyself a man;	**2:2** "I go the way of all the earth; be strong, therefore, and prove yourself a man.	**2:2** "I am going where every man on earth must some day go. I am counting on you to be a strong and worthy successor.
3 And keep the charge of the LORD thy God, to walk in his ways, to keep his statutes, and his commandments, and his judgments, and his testimonies, as it is written in the law of Moses, that thou mayest prosper in all that thou doest, and whithersoever thou turnest thyself:	3 "And keep the charge of the LORD your God: to walk in His ways, to keep His statutes, His commandments, His judgments, and His testimonies, as it is written in the Law of Moses, that you may prosper in all that you do and wherever you turn;	3 Obey the laws of God and follow all his ways; keep each of his commands written in the law of Moses so that you will prosper in everything you do, wherever you turn.
3:23 Then said the king, The one saith, This *is* my son that liveth, and thy son *is* the dead: and the other saith, Nay; but thy son *is* the dead, and my son *is* the living.	**3:23** And the king said, "The one says, 'This *is* my son, who lives, and our son *is* the dead one'; and the other says, 'No! But your son *is* the dead one, and my son *is* the living one.'"	**3:23** Then the king said, "Let's get the facts straight: both of you claim the living child, and each says that the dead child belongs to the other.
24 And the king said, Bring me a sword. And they brought a sword before the king.	24 Then the king said, "Bring me a sword." So they brought a sword before the king.	24 All right, bring me a sword." So a sword was brought to the king.
25 And the king said, Divide the living child in two, and give half to the one, and half to the other.	25 And the king said, "Divide the living child in two, and give half to one, and half to the other."	25 Then he said, "Divide the living child in two and give half to each of these women!"
26 Then spake the woman whose the living child *was* unto the king, for her bowels yearned upon her son, and she said, O my lord, give her the living child, and in no wise slay it. But the other said, Let it be neither mine nor thine, *but* divide *it.*	26 Then the woman whose son *was* living spoke to the king, for she yearned with compassion for her son; and she said, "O my lord, give her the living child, and by no means kill him!" But the other said, "Let him be neither mine nor yours, *but* divide *him.*"	26 Then the woman who really was the mother of the child, and who loved him very much, cried out, "Oh, no, sir! Give her the child—don't kill him!" But the other woman said, "All right, it will be neither yours nor mine; divide it between us!"
27 Then the king answered and said, Give her the living child, and in no wise slay it: she *is* the mother thereof.	27 So the king answered and said, "Give the first woman the living child, and by no means kill him; she *is* his mother."	27 Then the king said, "Give the baby to the woman who wants him to live, for she is his mother!"
4:30 And Solomon's wisdom excelled the wisdom of all the children of the east country, and all the wisdom of Egypt.	**4:30** Thus Solomon's wisdom excelled the wisdom of all the men of the East and all the wisdom of Egypt.	**4:30** In fact, his wisdom excelled that of any of the wise men of the East, including those in Egypt.
34 And there came of all people to hear the wisdom of Solomon, from all kings of the earth, which had heard of his wisdom.	34 And men of all nations, from all the kings of the earth who had heard of his wisdom, came to hear the wisdom of Solomon.	34 And kings from many lands sent their ambassadors to him for his advice.
8:23 And he said, LORD God of Israel, *there is* no God like thee, in heaven above, or on earth beneath, who keepest covenant and mercy with thy servants that walk before thee with all their heart:	**8:23** and he said: "LORD God of Israel, *there is* no God in heaven above or on earth below like You, who keep Your covenant and mercy with Your servants who walk before You with all their heart.	**8:23** and said, "O Lord God of Israel, there is no god like you in heaven or earth, for you are loving and kind and you keep your promises to your people if they do their best to do your will.
24 Who hast kept with thy servant David my father that thou promisedst him: thou spakest also with thy mouth, and hast fulfilled *it* with thine hand, as *it is* this day.	24 "You have kept what You promised Your servant David my father; You have both spoken with Your mouth and fulfilled *it* with Your hand, as *it is* this day.	24 Today you have fulfilled your promise to my father David, who was your servant;
27 But will God indeed dwell on the earth? behold, the heaven and heaven of heavens cannot contain thee; how much less this house that I have builded?	27 "But will God indeed dwell on the earth? Behold, heaven and the heaven of heavens cannot contain You. How much less this temple which I have built!	27 "But is it possible that God would really live on earth? Why, even the skies and the highest heavens cannot contain you, much less this Temple I have built!

NIV	RSV	TEV
4 I call to the LORD, who is worthy of praise, and I am saved from my enemies.	4 I call upon the LORD, who is worthy to be praised, and I am saved from my enemies.	4 I call to the LORD, and he saves me from my enemies. Praise the LORD!
23:3 The God of Israel spoke, the Rock of Israel said to me: 'When one rules over men in righteousness, when he rules in the fear of God,	23:3 The God of Israel has spoken, the Rock of Israel has said to me: When one rules justly over men, ruling in the fear of God,	23:3 The God of Israel has spoken; the protector of Israel said to me: "The king who rules with justice, who rules in obedience to God,
4 he is like the light of morning at sunrise on a cloudless morning, like the brightness after rain that brings the grass from the earth.'	4 he dawns on them like the morning light, like the sun shining forth upon a cloudless morning, like rain that makes grass to sprout from the earth.	4 is like the sun shining on a cloudless dawn, the sun that makes the grass sparkle after rain."

First Kings

NIV	RSV	TEV
2:2 "I am about to go the way of all the earth," he said. "So be strong, show yourself a man,	2:2 "I am about to go the way of all the earth. Be strong, and show yourself a man,	2:2 "My time to die has come. Be confident and determined,
3 and observe what the LORD your God requires: Walk in his ways, and keep his decrees and commands, his laws and requirements, as written in the Law of Moses, so that you may prosper in all you do and wherever you go,	3 and keep the charge of the LORD your God, walking in his ways and keeping his statutes, his commandments, his ordinances, and his testimonies, as it is written in the law of Moses, that you may prosper in all that you do and wherever you turn;	3 and do what the LORD your God orders you to do. Obey all his laws and commands, as written in the Law of Moses, so that wherever you go you may prosper in everything you do.
3:23 The king said, "This one says, 'My son is alive and your son is dead,' while that one says, 'No! Your son is dead and mine is alive.'"	3:23 Then the king said, "The one says, 'This is my son that is alive, and your son is dead'; and the other says, 'No; but your son is dead, and my son is the living one.'"	3:23 Then King Solomon said, "Each of you claims that the living child is hers and that the dead child belongs to the other one."
24 Then the king said, "Bring me a sword." So they brought a sword for the king.	24 And the king said, "Bring me a sword." So a sword was brought before the king.	24 He sent for a sword, and when it was brought,
25 He then gave an order: "Cut the living child in two and give half to one and half to the other."	25 And the king said, "Divide the living child in two, and give half to the one, and half to the other."	25 he said, "Cut the living child in two and give each woman half of it."
26 The woman whose son was alive was filled with compassion for her son and said to the king, "Please, my lord, give her the living baby! Don't kill him!" But the other said, "Neither I nor you shall have him. Cut him in two!"	26 Then the woman whose son was alive said to the king, because her heart yearned for her son, "Oh, my lord, give her the living child, and by no means slay it." But the other said, "It shall be neither mine nor yours; divide it."	26 The real mother, her heart full of love for her son, said to the king, "Please, Your Majesty, don't kill the child! Give it to her!" But the other woman said, "Don't give it to either of us; go on and cut it in two."
27 Then the king gave his ruling: "Give the living baby to the first woman. Do not kill him; she is his mother."	27 Then the king answered and said, "Give the living child to the first woman, and by no means slay it; she is its mother."	27 Then Solomon said, "Don't kill the child! Give it to the first woman—she is its real mother."
4:30 Solomon's wisdom was greater than the wisdom of all the men of the East, and greater than all the wisdom of Egypt.	4:30 so that Solomon's wisdom surpassed the wisdom of all the people of the east, and all the wisdom of Egypt.	4:30 Solomon was wiser than the wise men of the East or the wise men of Egypt.
34 Men of all nations came to listen to Solomon's wisdom, sent by all the kings of the world, who had heard of his wisdom.	34 And men came from all peoples to hear the wisdom of Solomon, and from all the kings of the earth, who had heard of his wisdom.	34 Kings all over the world heard of his wisdom and sent people to listen to him.
8:23 and said: "O LORD, God of Israel, there is no God like you in heaven above or on earth below—you who keep your covenant of love with your servants who continue wholeheartedly in your way.	8:23 and said, "O LORD, God of Israel, there is no God like thee, in heaven above or on earth beneath, keeping covenant and showing steadfast love to thy servants who walk before thee with all their heart;	8:23 and prayed, "LORD God of Israel, there is no god like you in heaven above or on earth below! You keep your covenant with your people and show them your love when they live in wholehearted obedience to you.
24 You have kept your promise to your servant David my father; with your mouth you have promised and with your hand you have fulfilled it—as it is today.	24 who hast kept with thy servant David my father what thou didst declare to him; yea, thou didst speak with thy mouth, and with thy hand hast fulfilled it this day.	24 You have kept the promise you made to my father David; today every word has been fulfilled.
27 "But will God really dwell on earth? The heavens, even the highest heaven, cannot contain you. How much less this temple I have built!	27 "But will God indeed dwell on the earth? Behold, heaven and the highest heaven cannot contain thee; how much less this house which I have built!	27 "But can you, O God, really live on earth? Not even all of heaven is large enough to hold you, so how can this Temple that I have built be large enough?

KJV	NKJV	TLB
56 Blessed *be* the LORD, that hath given rest unto his people Israel, according to all that he promised: there hath not failed one word of all his good promise, which he promised by the hand of Moses his servant.	56 "Blessed *be* the LORD, who has given rest to His people Israel, according to all that He promised. There has not failed one word of all His good promise, which He promised through His servant Moses.	56 "Blessed be the Lord who has fulfilled his promise and given rest to his people Israel; not one word has failed of all the wonderful promises proclaimed by his servant Moses.
9:3 And the LORD said unto him, I have heard thy prayer and thy supplication, that thou hast made before me: I have hallowed this house, which thou hast built, to put my name there for ever; and mine eyes and mine heart shall be there perpetually.	9:3 And the LORD said to him: "I have heard your prayer and your supplication that you have made before Me; I have sanctified this house which you have built to put My name there forever, and My eyes and My heart will be there perpetually.	9:3 "I have heard your prayer. I have hallowed this Temple which you have built and have put my name here forever. I will constantly watch over it and rejoice in it.
4 And if thou wilt walk before me, as David thy father walked, in integrity of heart, and in uprightness, to do according to all that I have commanded thee, *and* wilt keep my statutes and my judgments:	4 "Now if you walk before Me as your father David walked, in integrity of heart and in uprightness, to do according to all that I have commanded you, *and* if you keep My statutes and My judgments,	4 And if you live in honesty and truth as your father David did, always obeying me,
5 Then I will establish the throne of thy kingdom upon Israel for ever, as I promised to David thy father, saying, There shall not fail thee a man upon the throne of Israel.	5 "then I will establish the throne of your kingdom over Israel forever, as I promised David your father, saying, 'You shall not fail to have a man on the throne of Israel.'	5 then I will cause your descendants to be the kings of Israel forever, just as I promised your father David when I told him, 'One of your sons shall always be upon the throne of Israel.'
11:4 For it came to pass, when Solomon was old, *that* his wives turned away his heart after other gods: and his heart was not perfect with the LORD his God, as *was* the heart of David his father.	11:4 For it was so, when Solomon was old, that his wives turned his heart after other gods; and his heart was not loyal to the LORD his God, as *was* the heart of his father David.	11:4 especially in his old age. They encouraged him to worship their gods instead of trusting completely in the Lord as his father David had done.
5 For Solomon went after Ashtoreth the goddess of the Zidonians, and after Milcom the abomination of the Ammonites.	5 For Solomon went after Ashtoreth the goddess of the Sidonians, and after Milcom the abomination of the Ammonites.	5 Solomon worshiped Ashtoreth, the goddess of the Sidonians, and Milcom, the horrible god of the Ammonites.
6 And Solomon did evil in the sight of the LORD, and went not fully after the LORD, as *did* David his father.	6 Solomon did evil in the sight of the LORD, and did not fully follow the LORD, as *did* his father David.	6 Thus Solomon did what was clearly wrong and refused to follow the Lord as his father David did.
17:1 And Elijah the Tishbite, *who was* of the inhabitants of Gilead, said unto Ahab, *As* the LORD God of Israel liveth, before whom I stand, there shall not be dew nor rain these years, but according to my word.	17:1 And Elijah the Tishbite, of the inhabitants of Gilead, said to Ahab, "*As* the LORD God of Israel lives, before whom I stand, there shall not be dew nor rain these years, except at my word."	17:1 Then Elijah, the prophet from Tishbe in Gilead, told King Ahab, "As surely as the Lord God of Israel lives—the God whom I worship and serve—there won't be any dew or rain for several years until I say the word!"
2 And the word of the LORD came unto him, saying,	2 Then the word of the LORD came to him, saying,	2 Then the Lord said to Elijah,
3 Get thee hence, and turn thee eastward, and hide thyself by the brook Cherith, that *is* before Jordan.	3 "Get away from here and turn eastward, and hide by the Brook Cherith, which flows into the Jordan.	3 "Go to the east and hide by Cherith Brook at a place east of where it enters the Jordan River.
4 And it shall be, *that* thou shalt drink of the brook; and I have commanded the ravens to feed thee there.	4 "And it will be *that* you shall drink from the brook, and I have commanded the ravens to feed you there."	4 Drink from the brook and eat what the ravens bring you, for I have commanded them to feed you."
5 So he went and did according unto the word of the LORD: for he went and dwelt by the brook Cherith, that *is* before Jordan.	5 So he went and did according to the word of the LORD, for he went and stayed by the Brook Cherith, which flows into the Jordan.	5 So he did as the Lord had told him to, and camped beside the brook.
6 And the ravens brought him bread and flesh in the morning, and bread and flesh in the evening; and he drank of the brook.	6 The ravens brought him bread and meat in the morning, and bread and meat in the evening; and he drank from the brook.	6 The ravens brought him bread and meat each morning and evening, and he drank from the brook.
18:21 And Elijah came unto all the people, and said, How long halt ye between two opinions? if the LORD *be* God, follow him: but if Baal, *then* follow him. And the people answered him not a word.	18:21 And Elijah came to all the people, and said, "How long will you falter between two opinions? If the LORD *is* God, follow Him; but if Baal, *then* follow him." But the people answered him not a word.	18:21 Then Elijah talked to them. "How long are you going to waver between two opinions?" he asked the people. "If the Lord is God, *follow* him! But if Baal is God, then follow *him!*"
22 Then said Elijah unto the people, I *even* I only, remain a prophet of the LORD; but Baal's prophets *are* four hundred and fifty men.	22 Then Elijah said to the people, "I alone am left a prophet of the LORD; but Baal's prophets *are* four hundred and fifty men.	22 Then Elijah spoke again. "I am the only prophet of the Lord who is left," he told them, "but Baal has 450 prophets.
23 Let them therefore give us two bullocks; and let them choose one bullock for themselves, and cut it in pieces, and lay *it* on wood, and put no fire *under:* and I will dress the other bullock, and lay *it* on wood, and put no fire *under:*	23 "Therefore let them give us two bulls; and let them choose one bull for themselves, cut it in pieces, and lay *it* on the wood, but put no fire *under it;* and I will prepare the other bull, and lay *it* on the wood, but put no fire *under it.*	23 Now bring two young bulls. The prophets of Baal may choose whichever one they wish and cut it into pieces and lay it on the wood of their altar, but without putting any fire under the wood; and I will prepare the other young bull and lay it on the wood on the Lord's altar, with no fire under it.

NIV	RSV	TEV
56 "Praise be to the LORD, who has given rest to his people Israel just as he promised. Not one word has failed of all the good promises he gave through his servant Moses.	56 "Blessed be the LORD who has given rest to his people Israel, according to all that he promised; not one word has failed of all his good promise, which he uttered by Moses his servant.	56 "Praise the LORD who has given his people peace, as he promised he would. He has kept all the generous promises he made through his servant Moses.
9:3 The LORD said to him: "I have heard the prayer and plea you have made before me; I have consecrated this temple, which you have built, by putting my Name there forever. My eyes and my heart will always be there.	9:3 And the LORD said to him, "I have heard your prayer and your supplication, which you have made before me; I have consecrated this house which you have built, and put my name there for ever; my eyes and my heart will be there for all time.	9:3 The LORD said to him, "I have heard your prayer. I consecrate this Temple which you have built as the place where I shall be worshiped forever. I will watch over it and protect it for all time.
4 "As for you, if you walk before me in integrity of heart and uprightness, as David your father did, and do all I command and observe my decrees and laws,	4 And as for you, if you will walk before me, as David your father walked, with integrity of heart and uprightness, doing according to all that I have commanded you, and keeping my statutes and my ordinances,	4 If you will serve me in honesty and integrity, as your father David did, and if you obey my laws and do everything I have commanded you,
5 I will establish your royal throne over Israel forever, as I promised David your father when I said, 'You shall never fail to have a man on the throne of Israel.'	5 then I will establish your royal throne over Israel for ever, as I promised David your father, saying, 'There shall not fail you a man upon the throne of Israel.'	5 I will keep the promise I made to your father David when I told him that Israel would always be ruled by his descendants.
11:4 As Solomon grew old, his wives turned his heart after other gods, and his heart was not fully devoted to the LORD his God, as the heart of David his father had been.	11:4 For when Solomon was old his wives turned away his heart after other gods; and his heart was not wholly true to the LORD his God, as was the heart of David his father.	11:4 and by the time he was old they had led him into the worship of foreign gods. He was not faithful to the LORD his God, as his father David had been.
5 He followed Ashtoreth the goddess of the Sidonians, and Molech the detestable god of the Ammonites.	5 For Solomon went after Ashtoreth the goddess of the Sidonians, and after Milcom the abomination of the Ammonites.	5 He worshiped Astarte, the goddess of Sidon, and Molech, the disgusting god of Ammon.
6 So Solomon did evil in the eyes of the LORD; he did not follow the LORD completely, as David his father had done.	6 So Solomon did what was evil in the sight of the LORD, and did not wholly follow the LORD, as David his father had done.	6 He sinned against the LORD and was not true to him as his father David had been.
17:1 Now Elijah the Tishbite, from Tishbe in Gilead, said to Ahab, "As the LORD, the God of Israel, lives, whom I serve, there will be neither dew nor rain in the next few years except at my word."	17:1 Now Elijah the Tishbite, of Tishbe in Gilead, said to Ahab, "As the LORD the God of Israel lives, before whom I stand, there shall be neither dew nor rain these years, except by my word."	17:1 A prophet named Elijah, from Tishbe in Gilead, said to King Ahab, "In the name of the LORD, the living God of Israel, whom I serve, I tell you that there will be no dew or rain for the next two or three years until I say so."
2 Then the word of the LORD came to Elijah:	2 And the word of the LORD came to him.	2 Then the LORD said to Elijah,
3 "Leave here, turn eastward and hide in the Kerith Ravine, east of the Jordan.	3 "Depart from here and turn eastward, and hide yourself by the brook Cherith, that is east of the Jordan.	3 "Leave this place and go east and hide yourself near Cherith Brook, east of the Jordan.
4 You will drink from the brook, and I have ordered the ravens to feed you there."	4 You shall drink from the brook, and I have commanded the ravens to feed you there."	4 The brook will supply you with water to drink, and I have commanded ravens to bring you food there."
5 So he did what the LORD had told him. He went to the Kerith Ravine, east of the Jordan, and stayed there.	5 So he went and did according to the word of the LORD; he went and dwelt by the brook Cherith that is east of the Jordan.	5 Elijah obeyed the LORD's command, and went and stayed by Cherith Brook.
6 The ravens brought him bread and meat in the morning and bread and meat in the evening, and he drank from the brook.	6 And the ravens brought him bread and meat in the morning, and bread and meat in the evening; and he drank from the brook.	6 He drank water from the brook, and ravens brought him bread and meat every morning and every evening.
18:21 Elijah went before the people and said, "How long will you waver between two opinions? If the LORD is God, follow him; but if Baal is God, follow him." But the people said nothing.	18:21 And Elijah came near to all the people, and said, "How long will you go limping with two different opinions? If the LORD is God, follow him; but if Baal, then follow him." And the people did not answer him a word.	18:21 Elijah went up to the people and said, "How much longer will it take you to make up your minds? If the LORD is God, worship him; but if Baal is God, worship him!" But the people didn't say a word.
22 Then Elijah said to them, "I am the only one of the LORD's prophets left, but Baal has four hundred and fifty prophets.	22 Then Elijah said to the people, "I, even I only, am left a prophet of the LORD; but Baal's prophets are four hundred and fifty men.	22 Then Elijah said, "I am the only prophet of the LORD still left, but there are 450 prophets of Baal.
23 Get two bulls for us. Let them choose one for themselves, and let them cut it into pieces and put it on the wood but not set fire to it. I will prepare the other bull and put it on the wood but not set fire to it.	23 Let two bulls be given to us; and let them choose one bull for themselves, and cut it in pieces and lay it on the wood, but put no fire to it; and I will prepare the other bull and lay it on the wood, and put no fire to it.	23 Bring two bulls; let the prophets of Baal take one, kill it, cut it in pieces, and put it on the wood—but don't light the fire. I will do the same with the other bull.

34   **First Kings 18:24**
Second Kings 2:11
    KEY VERSE COMPARISON CHART

KJV	NKJV	TLB
24 And call ye on the name of your gods, and I will call on the name of the LORD: and the God that answereth by fire, let him be God. And all the people answered and said, It is well spoken.	24 "Then you call on the name of your gods, and I will call on the name of the LORD; and the God who answers by fire, He is God." So all the people answered and said, "It is well spoken."	24 Then pray to your god, and I will pray to the Lord; and the god who answers by sending fire to light the wood is the true God!" And all the people agreed to this test.
29 And it came to pass, when midday was past, and they prophesied until the *time* of the offering of the *evening* sacrifice, that *there was* neither voice, nor any to answer, nor any that regarded.	29 And it was so, when midday was past, that they prophesied until the *time* of the offering of the *evening* sacrifice. But *there was* no voice; no one answered, no one paid attention.	29 They raved all afternoon until the time of the evening sacrifice, but there was no reply, no voice, no answer.
30 And Elijah said unto all the people, Come near unto me. And all the people came near unto him. And he repaired the altar of the LORD *that was* broken down.	30 Then Elijah said to all the people, "Come near to me." So all the people came near to him. And he repaired the altar of the LORD *that was* broken down.	30 Then Elijah called to the people, "Come over here." And they all crowded around him as he repaired the altar of the Lord which had been torn down.
37 Hear me. O LORD, hear me, that this people may know that thou *art* the LORD God, and *that* thou hast turned their heart back again.	37 "Hear me, O LORD, hear me, that this people may know that You *are* the LORD God, and *that* You have turned their hearts back *to* You again."	37 O Lord, answer me! Answer me so these people will know that you are God and that you have brought them back to yourself."
38 Then the fire of the LORD fell, and consumed the burnt sacrifice, and the wood, and the stones, and the dust, and licked up the water that *was* in the trench.	38 Then the fire of the LORD fell and consumed the burnt sacrifice, and the wood and the stones and the dust, and it licked up the water that *was* in the trench.	38 Then, suddenly, fire flashed down from heaven and burned up the young bull, the wood, the stones, the dust, and even evaporated all the water in the ditch!
39 And when all the people saw *it*, they fell on their faces: and they said, The LORD, he *is* the God; the LORD, he *is* the God.	39 Now when all the people saw *it*, they fell on their faces; and they said, "The LORD, He *is* God! The LORD, He *is* God!"	39 And when the people saw it, they fell to their faces upon the ground shouting, "Jehovah is God! Jehovah is God!"
19:9 And he came thither unto a cave, and lodged there; and, behold, the word of the LORD *came* to him, and he said unto him, What doest thou here, Elijah?	**19:9** And there he went into a cave, and spent the night in that place; and behold, the word of the LORD *came* to him, and He said to him, "What are you doing here, Elijah?"	**19:9** where he lived in a cave. But the Lord said to him, "What are you doing here, Elijah?"
10 And he said, I have been very jealous for the LORD God of hosts: for the children of Israel have forsaken thy covenant, thrown down thine altars, and slain thy prophets with the sword; and I, *even* I only, am left; and they seek my life, to take it away.	10 So he said, "I have been very zealous for the LORD God of hosts; for the children of Israel have forsaken Your covenant, torn down Your altars, and killed Your prophets with the sword. I alone am left; and they seek to take my life."	10 He replied, "I have worked very hard for the Lord God of the heavens; but the people of Israel have broken their covenant with you and torn down your altars and killed your prophets, and only I am left; and now they are trying to kill me, too."
11 And he said, Go forth, and stand upon the mount before the LORD. And, behold, the LORD passed by, and a great and strong wind rent the mountains, and brake in pieces the rocks before the LORD; *but* the LORD *was* not in the wind: and after the wind an earthquake; *but* the LORD *was* not in the earthquake:	11 Then He said, "Go out, and stand on the mountain before the LORD." And behold, the LORD passed by, and a great and strong wind tore into the mountains and broke the rocks in pieces before the LORD, *but* the LORD *was* not in the wind; and after the wind an earthquake, *but* the LORD *was* not in the earthquake;	11 "Go out and stand before me on the mountain," the Lord told him. And as Elijah stood there the Lord passed by, and a mighty windstorm hit the mountain; it was such a terrible blast that the rocks were torn loose, but the Lord was not in the wind. After the wind, there was an earthquake, but the Lord was not in the earthquake.
12 And after the earthquake a fire; *but* the LORD *was* not in the fire: and after the fire a still small voice.	12 and after the earthquake a fire, *but* the LORD *was* not in the fire; and after the fire a still small voice.	12 And after the earthquake, there was a fire, but the Lord was not in the fire. And after the fire, there was the sound of a gentle whisper.
18 Yet I have left *me* seven thousand in Israel, all the knees which have not bowed unto Baal, and every mouth which hath not kissed him.	18 "Yet I have reserved seven thousand in Israel, all whose knees have not bowed to Baal, and every mouth that has not kissed him."	18 And incidentally, there are 7,000 men in Israel who have never bowed to Baal nor kissed him!"

Second Kings

2:9 And it came to pass, when they were gone over, that Elijah said unto Elisha, Ask what I shall do for thee, before I be taken away from thee. And Elisha said, I pray thee, let a double portion of thy spirit be upon me.	**2:9** And so it was, when they had crossed over, that Elijah said to Elisha, "Ask! What may I do for you, before I am taken away from you?" And Elisha said, "Please let a double portion of your spirit be upon me."	**2:9** When they arrived on the other side Elijah said to Elisha, "What wish shall I grant you before I am taken away?" And Elisha replied, "Please grant me twice as much prophetic power as you have had."
10 And he said, Thou hast asked a hard thing: *nevertheless*, if thou see me *when I am* taken from thee, it shall be so unto thee; but if not, it shall not be *so*.	10 So he said, "You have asked a hard thing. *Nevertheless*, if you see me *when I am* taken from you, it shall be so for you; but if not, it shall not be *so*."	10 "You have asked a hard thing," Elijah replied. "If you see me when I am taken from you, then you will get your request. But if not, then you won't."
11 And it came to pass, as they still went on, and talked, that, behold, *there appeared* a chariot of fire, and horses of fire, and parted them both asunder; and Elijah went up by a whirlwind into heaven.	11 Then it happened, as they continued on and talked, that suddenly a chariot of fire *appeared* with horses of fire, and separated the two of them; and Elijah went up by a whirlwind into heaven.	11 As they were walking along, talking, suddenly a chariot of fire, drawn by horses of fire, appeared and drove between them, separating them, and Elijah was carried by a whirlwind into heaven.

NIV	RSV	TEV
24 Then you call on the name of your god, and I will call on the name of the LORD. The god who answers by fire—he is God." Then all the people said, "What you say is good."	24 And you call on the name of your god and I will call on the name of the LORD; and the God who answers by fire, he is God." And all the people answered, "It is well spoken."	24 Then let the prophets of Baal pray to their god, and I will pray to the LORD, and the one who answers by sending fire—he is God." The people shouted their approval.
29 Midday passed, and they continued their frantic prophesying until the time for the evening sacrifice. But there was no response, no one answered, no one paid attention.	29 And as midday passed, they raved on until the time of the offering of the oblation, but there was no voice; no one answered, no one heeded.	29 They kept on ranting and raving until the middle of the afternoon; but no answer came, not a sound was heard.
30 Then Elijah said to all the people, "Come here to me." They came to him, and he repaired the altar of the LORD, which was in ruins.	30 Then Elijah said to all the people, "Come near to me"; and all the people came near to him. And he repaired the altar of the LORD that had been thrown down;	30 Then Elijah said to the people, "Come closer to me," and they all gathered around him. He set about repairing the altar of the LORD which had been torn down.
37 Answer me, O LORD, answer me, so these people will know that you, O LORD, are God, and that you are turning their hearts back again."	37 Answer me, O LORD, answer me, that this people may know that thou, O LORD, art God, and that thou hast turned their hearts back."	37 Answer me, LORD, answer me, so that this people will know that you, the LORD, are God and that you are bringing them back to yourself."
38 Then the fire of the LORD fell and burned up the sacrifice, the wood, the stones and the soil, and also licked up the water in the trench.	38 Then the fire of the LORD fell, and consumed the burnt offering, and the wood, and the stones, and the dust, and licked up the water that was in the trench.	38 The LORD sent fire down, and it burned up the sacrifice, the wood, and the stones, scorched the earth and dried up the water in the trench.
39 When all the people saw this, they fell prostrate and cried, "The LORD—he is God! The LORD—he is God!"	39 And when all the people saw it, they fell on their faces; and they said, "The LORD, he is God; the LORD, he is God."	39 When the people saw this, they threw themselves on the ground and exclaimed, "The LORD is God; the LORD alone is God!"
19:9 There he went into a cave and spent the night. And the word of the LORD came to him: "What are you doing here, Elijah?"	19:9 And there he came to a cave, and lodged there; and behold, the word of the LORD came to him, and he said to him, "What are you doing here, Elijah?"	19:9 There he went into a cave to spend the night. Suddenly the LORD spoke to him, "Elijah, what are you doing here?"
10 He replied, "I have been very zealous for the LORD God Almighty. The Israelites have rejected your covenant, broken down your altars, and put your prophets to death with the sword. I am the only one left, and now they are trying to kill me too."	10 He said, "I have been very jealous for the LORD, the God of hosts; for the people of Israel have forsaken thy covenant, thrown down thy altars, and slain thy prophets with the sword; and I, even I only, am left; and they seek my life, to take it away."	10 He answered, "LORD God Almighty, I have always served you—you alone. But the people of Israel have broken their covenant with you, torn down your altars, and killed all your prophets. I am the only one left—and they are trying to kill me!"
11 The LORD said, "Go out and stand on the mountain in the presence of the LORD, for the LORD is about to pass by." Then a great and powerful wind tore the mountains apart and shattered the rocks before the LORD, but the LORD was not in the wind. After the wind there was an earthquake, but the LORD was not in the earthquake.	11 And he said, "Go forth, and stand upon the mount before the LORD." And behold, the LORD passed by, and a great and strong wind rent the mountains, and broke in pieces the rocks before the LORD, but the LORD was not in the wind; and after the wind an earthquake, but the LORD was not in the earthquake;	11 "Go out and stand before me on top of the mountain," the LORD said to him. Then the LORD passed by and sent a furious wind that split the hills and shattered the rocks—but the LORD was not in the wind. The wind stopped blowing, and then there was an earthquake—but the LORD was not in the earthquake.
12 After the earthquake came a fire, but the LORD was not in the fire. And after the fire came a gentle whisper.	12 and after the earthquake a fire, but the LORD was not in the fire; and after the fire a still small voice.	12 After the earthquake there was a fire—but the LORD was not in the fire. And after the fire there was the soft whisper of a voice.
18 Yet I reserve seven thousand in Israel—all whose knees have not bowed down to Baal and all whose mouths have not kissed him."	18 Yet I will leave seven thousand in Israel, all the knees that have not bowed to Baal, and every mouth that has not kissed him."	18 Yet I will leave seven thousand people alive in Israel—all those who are loyal to me and have not bowed to Baal or kissed his idol."

Second Kings

NIV	RSV	TEV
2:9 When they had crossed, Elijah said to Elisha, "Tell me, what can I do for you before I am taken from you?" "Let me inherit a double portion of your spirit," Elisha replied.	2:9 When they had crossed, Elijah said to Elisha, "Ask what I shall do for you, before I am taken from you." And Elisha said, "I pray you, let me inherit a double share of your spirit."	2:9 There, Elijah said to Elisha, "Tell me what you want me to do for you before I am taken away." "Let me receive the share of your power that will make me your successor," Elisha answered.
10 "You have asked a difficult thing," Elijah said, "yet if you see me when I am taken from you, it will be yours—otherwise not."	10 And he said, "You have asked a hard thing; yet, if you see me as I am being taken from you, it shall be so for you; but if you do not see me, it shall not be so."	10 "That is a difficult request to grant," Elijah replied. "But you will receive it if you see me as I am being taken away from you; if you don't see me, you won't receive it."
11 As they were walking along and talking together, suddenly a chariot of fire and horses of fire appeared and separated the two of them, and Elijah went up to heaven in a whirlwind.	11 And as they still went on and talked, behold, a chariot of fire and horses of fire separated the two of them. And Elijah went up by a whirlwind into heaven.	11 They kept talking as they walked on; then suddenly a chariot of fire pulled by horses of fire came between them, and Elijah was taken up to heaven by a whirlwind.

36   **Second Kings 4:32**
      First Chronicles 11:1
                 KEY VERSE COMPARISON CHART

KJV	NKJV	TLB
4:32 And when Elisha was come into the house, behold, the child was dead, *and* laid upon his bed.	**4:32** And when Elisha came into the house, there was the child, lying dead on his bed.	**4:32** When Elisha arrived, the child was indeed dead, lying there upon the prophet's bed.
33 He went in therefore, and shut the door upon them twain, and prayed unto the LORD.	33 He went in therefore, shut the door behind the two of them, and prayed to the LORD.	33 He went in and shut the door behind him and prayed to the Lord.
34 And he went up, and lay upon the child, and put his mouth upon his mouth, and his eyes upon his eyes, and his hands upon his hands: and he stretched himself upon the child; and the flesh of the child waxed warm.	34 And he went up and lay on the child, and put his mouth on his mouth, his eyes on his eyes, and his hands on his hands; and he stretched himself out on the child, and the flesh of the child became warm.	34 Then he lay upon the child's body, placing his mouth upon the child's mouth, and his eyes upon the child's eyes, and his hands upon the child's hands. And the child's body began to grow warm again!
35 Then he returned, and walked in the house to and fro; and went up, and stretched himself upon him: and the child sneezed seven times, and the child opened his eyes.	35 He returned and walked back and forth in the house, and again went up and stretched himself out on him; then the child sneezed seven times, and the child opened his eyes.	35 Then the prophet went down and walked back and forth in the house a few times; returning upstairs, he stretched himself again upon the child. This time the little boy sneezed seven times and opened his eyes!
36 And he called Gehazi, and said, Call this Shunammite. So he called her. And when she was come in unto him, he said, Take up thy son.	36 And he called Gehazi and said, "Call this Shunammite woman." So he called her. And when she came in to him, he said, "Pick up your son."	36 Then the prophet summoned Gehazi. "Call her!" he said. And when she came in, he said, "Here's your son!"
37 Then she went in, and fell at his feet, and bowed herself to the ground, and took up her son, and went out.	37 So she went in, fell at his feet, and bowed to the ground; then she picked up her son and went out.	37 She fell to the floor at his feet and then picked up her son and went out.
5:10 And Elisha sent a messenger unto him, saying, Go and wash in Jordan seven times, and thy flesh shall come again to thee, and thou shalt be clean.	**5:10** And Elisha sent a messenger to him, saying, "Go and wash in the Jordan seven times, and your flesh shall be restored to you, and *you shall* be clean."	**5:10** Elisha sent a messenger out to tell him to go and wash in the Jordan River seven times and he would be healed of every trace of his leprosy!
11 But Naaman was wroth, and went away, and said, Behold, I thought, He will surely come out to me, and stand, and call on the name of the LORD his God, and strike his hand over the place, and recover the leper.	11 But Naaman became furious, and went away and said, "Indeed, I said to myself, 'He will surely come out to me, and stand and call on the name of the LORD his God, and wave his hand over the place, and heal the leprosy.'	11 But Naaman was angry and stalked away. "Look," he said, "I thought at least he would come out and talk to me! I expected him to wave his hand over the leprosy and call upon the name of the Lord his God, and heal me!
12 *Are* not Abana and Pharpar, rivers of Damascus, better than all the waters of Israel? may I not wash in them, and be clean? So he turned and went away in a rage.	12 "*Are* not the Abanah and the Pharpar, the rivers of Damascus, better than all the waters of Israel? Could I not wash in them and be clean?" So he turned and went away in a rage.	12 Aren't the Abana River and Pharpar River of Damascus better than all the rivers of Israel put together? If it's rivers I need, I'll wash at home and get rid of my leprosy." So he went away in a rage.
13 And his servants came near, and spake unto him, and said, My father, *if* the prophet had bid thee *do some* great thing, wouldest thou not have done *it*? how much rather then, when he saith to thee, Wash, and be clean?	13 And his servants came near and spoke to him, and said, "My father, *if* the prophet had told you *to do* something great, would you not have done *it*? How much more then, when he says to you, 'Wash, and be clean'?"	13 But his officers tried to reason with him and said, "If the prophet had told you to do some great thing, wouldn't you have done it? So you should certainly obey him when he says simply to go and wash and be cured!"
14 Then went he down, and dipped himself seven times in Jordan, according to the saying of the man of God: and his flesh came again like unto the flesh of a little child, and he was clean.	14 So he went down and dipped seven times in the Jordan, according to the saying of the man of God; and his flesh was restored like the flesh of a little child, and he was clean.	14 So Naaman went down to the Jordan River and dipped himself seven times, as the prophet had told him to. And his flesh became as healthy as a little child's, and he was healed!
6:15 And when the servant of the man of God was risen early, and gone forth, behold, an host compassed the city both with horses and chariots. And his servant said unto him, Alas, my master! how shall we do?	**6:15** And when the servant of the man of God arose early and went out, there was an army, surrounding the city with horses and chariots. And his servant said to him, "Alas, my master! What shall we do?"	**6:15** When the prophet's servant got up early the next morning and went outside, there were troops, horses, and chariots everywhere. "Alas, my master, what shall we do now?" he cried out to Elisha.
16 And he answered, Fear not: for they that *be* with us *are* more than they that *be* with them.	16 So he answered, "Do not fear, for those who *are* with us *are* more than those who *are* with them."	16 "Don't be afraid!" Elisha told him. "For our army is bigger than theirs!"
17 And Elisha prayed, and said, LORD, I pray thee, open his eyes, that he may see. And the LORD opened the eyes of the young man; and he saw: and, behold, the mountain *was* full of horses and chariots of fire round about Elisha.	17 And Elisha prayed, and said, "LORD, I pray, open his eyes that he may see." Then the LORD opened the eyes of the young man, and he saw. And behold, the mountain *was* full of horses and chariots of fire all around Elisha.	17 Then Elisha prayed, "Lord, open his eyes and let him see!" And the Lord opened the young man's eyes so that he could see horses of fire and chariots of fire everywhere upon the mountain!

First Chronicles

11:1 Then all Israel gathered themselves to David unto Hebron, saying, Behold, we *are* thy bone and thy flesh.	**11:1** Then all Israel came together to David at Hebron, saying, "Indeed we *are* your bone and your flesh.	**11:1** Then the leaders of Israel went to David at Hebron and told him, "We are your relatives,

NIV	RSV	TEV
4:32 When Elisha reached the house, there was the boy lying dead on his couch.	**4:32** When Elisha came into the house, he saw the child lying dead on his bed.	**4:32** When Elisha arrived, he went alone into the room and saw the boy lying dead on the bed.
33 He went in, shut the door on the two of them and prayed to the LORD.	33 So he went in and shut the door upon the two of them, and prayed to the LORD.	33 He closed the door and prayed to the LORD.
34 Then he got on the bed and lay upon the boy, mouth to mouth, eyes to eyes, hands to hands. As he stretched himself out upon him, the boy's body grew warm.	34 Then he went up and lay upon the child, putting his mouth upon his mouth, his eyes upon his eyes, and his hands upon his hands; and as he stretched himself upon him, the flesh of the child became warm.	34 Then he lay down on the boy, placing his mouth, eyes, and hands on the boy's mouth, eyes, and hands. As he lay stretched out over the boy, the boy's body started to get warm.
35 Elisha turned away and walked back and forth in the room and then got on the bed and stretched out upon him once more. The boy sneezed seven times and opened his eyes.	35 Then he got up again, and walked once to and fro in the house, and went up, and stretched himself upon him; the child sneezed seven times, and the child opened his eyes.	35 Elisha got up, walked around the room, and then went back and again stretched himself over the boy. The boy sneezed seven times and then opened his eyes.
36 Elisha summoned Gehazi and said, "Call the Shunammite." And he did. When she came, he said, "Take your son."	36 Then he summoned Gehazi and said, "Call this Shunammite." So he called her. And when she came to him, he said, "Take up your son."	36 Elisha called Gehazi and told him to call the boy's mother. When she came in, he said to her, "Here's your son."
37 She came in, fell at his feet and bowed to the ground. Then she took her son and went out.	37 She came and fell at his feet, bowing to the ground; then she took up her son and went out.	37 She fell at Elisha's feet, with her face touching the ground; then she took her son and left.
5:10 Elisha sent a messenger to say to him, "Go, wash yourself seven times in the Jordan, and your flesh will be restored and you will be cleansed."	**5:10** And Elisha sent a messenger to him, saying, "Go and wash in the Jordan seven times, and your flesh shall be restored, and you shall be clean."	**5:10** Elisha sent a servant out to tell him to go and wash himself seven times in the Jordan River, and he would be completely cured of his disease.
11 But Naaman went away angry and said, "I thought that he would surely come out to me and stand and call on the name of the LORD his God, wave his hand over the spot and cure me of my leprosy.	11 But Naaman was angry, and went away, saying, "Behold, I thought that he would surely come out to me, and stand, and call on the name of the LORD his God, and wave his hand over the place, and cure the leper.	11 But Naaman left in a rage, saying, "I thought that he would at least come out to me, pray to the LORD his God, wave his hand over the diseased spot, and cure me!
12 Are not Abana and Pharpar, the rivers of Damascus, better than any of the waters of Israel? Couldn't I wash in them and be cleansed?" So he turned and went off in a rage.	12 Are not Abana and Pharpar, the rivers of Damascus, better than all the waters of Israel? Could I not wash in them, and be clean?" So he turned and went away in a rage.	12 Besides, aren't the rivers Abana and Pharpar, back in Damascus, better than any river in Israel? I could have washed in them and been cured!"
13 Naaman's servants went to him and said, "My father, if the prophet had told you to do some great thing, would you not have done it? How much more, then, when he tells you, 'Wash and be cleansed'!"	13 But his servants came near and said to him, "My father, if the prophet had commanded you to do some great thing, would you not have done it? How much rather, then, when he says to you, 'Wash, and be clean'?"	13 His servants went up to him and said, "Sir, if the prophet had told you to do something difficult, you would have done it. Now why can't you just wash yourself, as he said, and be cured?"
14 So he went down and dipped himself in the Jordan seven times, as the man of God had told him, and his flesh was restored and became clean like that of a young boy.	14 So he went down and dipped himself seven times in the Jordan, according to the word of the man of God; and his flesh was restored like the flesh of a little child, and he was clean.	14 So Naaman went down to the Jordan, dipped himself in it seven times, as Elisha had instructed, and he was completely cured. His flesh became firm and healthy like that of a child.
6:15 When the servant of the man of God got up and went out early the next morning, an army with horses and chariots had surrounded the city. "Oh, my lord, what shall we do?" the servant asked.	**6:15** When the servant of the man of God rose early in the morning and went out, behold, an army with horses and chariots was round about the city. And the servant said, "Alas, my master! What shall we do?"	**6:15** Early the next morning Elisha's servant got up, went out of the house, and saw the Syrian troops with their horses and chariots surrounding the town. He went back to Elisha and exclaimed, "We are doomed, sir! What shall we do?"
16 "Don't be afraid," the prophet answered. "Those who are with us are more than those who are with them."	16 He said, "Fear not, for those who are with us are more than those who are with them."	16 "Don't be afraid," Elisha answered. "We have more on our side than they have on theirs."
17 And Elisha prayed, "O LORD, open his eyes so he may see." Then the LORD opened the servant's eyes, and he looked and saw the hills full of horses and chariots of fire all around Elisha.	17 Then Elisha prayed, and said, "O LORD, I pray thee, open his eyes that he may see." So the LORD opened the eyes of the young man, and he saw; and behold, the mountain was full of horses and chariots of fire round about Elisha.	17 Then he prayed, "O LORD, open his eyes and let him see!" The LORD answered his prayer, and Elisha's servant looked up and say the hillside covered with horses and chariots of fire all around Elisha.

First Chronicles

11:1 All Israel came together to David at Hebron and said, "We are your own flesh and blood."	**11:1** Then all Israel gathered together to David at Hebron, and said, "Behold, we are your bone and flesh.	**11:1** All the people of Israel went to David at Hebron and said to him, "We are your own flesh and blood.

KJV	NKJV	TLB
2 And moreover in time past, even when Saul was king, thou *wast* he that leddest out and broughtest in Israel: and the LORD thy God said unto thee, Thou shalt feed my people Israel, and thou shalt be ruler over my people Israel.	2 "Also, in time past, even when Saul was king, you *were* the one who led Israel out and brought them in; and the LORD your God said to you, 'You shall shepherd My people Israel, and be ruler over My people Israel.'"	2 and even when Saul was king, you were the one who led our armies to battle and brought them safely back again. And the Lord your God has told you, 'You shall be the shepherd of my people Israel. You shall be their king.'"
3 Therefore came all the elders of Israel to the king to Hebron; and David made a covenant with them in Hebron before the LORD; and they anointed David king over Israel, according to the word of the LORD by Samuel.	3 Therefore all the elders of Israel came to the king at Hebron, and David made a covenant with them at Hebron before the LORD. Then they anointed David king over Israel, according to the word of the LORD by Samuel.	3 So David made a contract with them before the Lord, and they anointed him as king of Israel, just as the Lord had told Samuel.
16:8 Give thanks unto the Lord, call upon his name, make known his deeds among the people.	16:8 Oh, give thanks to the LORD! Call upon His name; Make known His deeds among the peoples!	16:8 "Oh, give thanks to the Lord and pray to him," they sang. "Tell the peoples of the world About his mighty doings.
9 Sing unto him, sing psalms unto him, talk ye of all his wondrous works.	9 Sing to Him, sing psalms to Him; Talk of all His wondrous works!	9 Sing to him; yes, sing his praises And tell of his marvelous works.
10 Glory ye in his holy name: let the heart of them rejoice that seek the LORD.	10 Glory in His holy name; Let the hearts of those rejoice who seek the LORD!	10 Glory in his holy name; Let all rejoice who seek the Lord.
11 Seek the LORD and his strength, seek his face continually.	11 Seek the LORD and His strength; Seek His face evermore!	11 Seek the Lord; yes, seek his strength And seek his face untiringly.
12 Remember his marvellous works that he hath done, his wonders, and the judgments of his mouth;	12 Remember His marvelous works which He has done, His wonders and the judgments of His mouth,	12-13 O descendants of his servant Abraham, O chosen sons of Jacob, Remember his mighty miracles And his marvelous miracles And his authority:
13 O ye seed of Israel his servant, ye children of Jacob, his chosen ones.	13 O seed of Israel His servant, You children of Jacob, His chosen ones!	
31 Let the heavens be glad, and let the earth rejoice: and let *men* say among the nations, The LORD reigneth.	31 Let the heavens rejoice, and let the earth be glad; And let them say among the nations, "The LORD reigns."	31 Let the heavens be glad, the earth rejoice; Let all the nations say, 'It is the Lord who reigns.'
32 Let the sea roar, and the fulness thereof: let the fields rejoice, and all that *is* therein.	32 Let the sea roar, and all its fullness; Let the field rejoice, and all that *is* in it.	32 Let the vast seas roar, Let the countryside and everything in it rejoice!
33 Then shall the trees of the wood sing out at the presence of the LORD, because he cometh to judge the earth.	33 Then the trees of the woods shall rejoice before the LORD, For He is coming to judge the earth.	33 Let the trees in the woods sing for joy before the Lord, For he comes to judge the earth.
34 O give thanks unto the LORD; for *he is* good; for his mercy *endureth* for ever.	34 Oh, give thanks to the LORD, for *He is* good! For His mercy *endures* forever.	34 Oh, give thanks to the Lord, for he is good; His love and his kindness go on forever.
35 And say ye, Save us, O God of our salvation, and gather us together, and deliver us from the heathen, that we may give thanks to thy holy name, *and* glory in thy praise.	35 And say, "Save us, O God of our salvation; Gather us together, and deliver us from the Gentiles, To give thanks to Your holy name, To triumph in Your praise."	35 Cry out to him, 'Oh, save us, God of our salvation; Bring us safely back from among the nations. Then we will thank your holy name, And triumph in your praise.'
36 Blessed *be* the LORD God of Israel for ever and ever. And all the people said, Amen, and praised the LORD.	36 Blessed *be* the LORD God of Israel From everlasting to everlasting! And all the people said, "Amen!" and praised the LORD.	36 Blessed be Jehovah, God of Israel, Forever and forevermore." And all the people shouted "Amen!" and praised the Lord.
17:11 And it shall come to pass, when thy days be expired that thou must go *to be* with thy fathers, that I will raise up thy seed after thee, which shall be of thy sons; and I will establish his kingdom.	17:11 "And it shall be, when your days are fulfilled, when you must go *to be* with your fathers, that I will set up your seed after you, who will be of your sons; and I will establish his kingdom.	17:11 "'When your time here on earth is over and you die, I will place one of your sons upon your throne; and I will make his kingdom strong.
12 He shall build me an house, and I will stablish his throne for ever.	12 "He shall build Me a house, and I will establish his throne forever.	12 He is the one who shall build me a temple, and I will establish his royal line of descent forever.
13 I will be his father, and he shall be my son: and I will not take my mercy away from him, as I took *it* from *him* that was before thee:	13 "I will be his Father, and he shall be My son; and I will not take My mercy away from him, as I took *it* from *him* who was before you.	13 I will be his father, and he shall be my son; I will never remove my mercy and love from him as I did from Saul.

NIV	RSV	TEV
2 In the past, even while Saul was king, you were the one who led Israel on their military campaigns. And the LORD your God said to you, 'You will shepherd my people Israel, and you will become their ruler.'"	2 In times past, even when Saul was king, it was you that led out and brought in Israel; and the LORD your God said to you, 'You shall be shepherd of my people Israel, and you shall be prince over my people Israel.'"	2 In the past, even when Saul was still our king, you led the people of Israel in battle, and the LORD your God promised you that you would lead his people and be their ruler."
3 When all the elders of Israel had come to King David at Hebron, he made a compact with them at Hebron before the LORD, and they anointed David king over Israel, as the LORD had promised through Samuel.	3 So all the elders of Israel came to the king at Hebron; and David made a covenant with them at Hebron before the LORD, and they anointed David king over Israel, according to the word of the LORD by Samuel.	3 So all the leaders of Israel came to King David at Hebron. He made a sacred alliance with them, they anointed him, and he became king of Israel, just as the LORD had promised through Samuel.
16:8 Give thanks to the LORD, call on his name; make known among the nations what he has done.	16:8 O give thanks to the LORD, call on his name, make known his deeds among the peoples!	16:8 Give thanks to the LORD, proclaim his greatness; tell the nations what he has done.
9 Sing to him, sing praise to him; tell of all his wonderful acts.	9 Sing to him, sing praises to him, tell of all his wonderful works!	9 Sing praise to the LORD; tell the wonderful things he has done.
10 Glory in his holy name; let the hearts of those who seek the LORD rejoice.	10 Glory in his holy name; let the hearts of those who seek the LORD rejoice!	10 Be glad that we belong to him; let all who worship him rejoice!
11 Look to the LORD and his strength; seek his face always.	11 Seek the LORD and his strength, seek his presence continually!	11 Go to the LORD for help, and worship him continually.
12 Remember the wonders he has done, his miracles, and the judgments he pronounced,	12 Remember the wonderful works that he has done, the wonders he wrought, the judgments he uttered,	12–13 You descendants of Jacob, God's servant, descendants of Israel, whom God chose, remember the miracles that God performed and the judgments that he gave.
13 O descendants of Israel his servant, O sons of Jacob, his chosen ones.	13 O offspring of Abraham his servant, sons of Jacob, his chosen ones!	
31 Let the heavens rejoice, let the earth be glad; let them say among the nations, "The LORD reigns!"	31 Let the heavens be glad, and let the earth rejoice, and let them say among the nations, "The LORD reigns!"	31 Be glad, earth and sky! Tell the nations that the LORD is king.
32 Let the sea resound, and all that is in it; let the fields be jubilant, and everything in them!	32 Let the sea roar, and all that fills it, let the field exult, and everything in it!	32 Roar, sea, and every creature in you; be glad, fields, and everything in you!
33 Then the trees of the forest will sing, they will sing for joy before the LORD, for he comes to judge the earth.	33 Then shall the trees of the wood sing for joy before the LORD, for he comes to judge the earth.	33 The trees in the woods will shout for joy when the LORD comes to rule the earth.
34 Give thanks to the LORD, for he is good; his love endures forever.	34 O give thanks to the LORD, for he is good; for his steadfast love endures for ever!	34 Give thanks to the LORD, because he is good; his love is eternal.
35 Cry out, "Save us, O God our Savior; gather us and deliver us from the nations, that we may give thanks to your holy name, that we may glory in your praise."	35 Say also: "Deliver us, O God of our salvation, and gather and save us from among the nations, that we may give thanks to thy holy name, and glory in thy praise.	35 Say to him, "Save us, O God our Savior; gather us together; rescue us from the nations, so that we may be thankful and praise your holy name."
36 Praise be to the LORD, the God of Israel, from everlasting to everlasting. Then all the people said "Amen" and "Praise the LORD."	36 Blessed be the LORD, the God of Israel, from everlasting to everlasting!" Then all the people said "Amen!" and praised the LORD.	36 Praise the LORD, the God of Israel! Praise him now and forever! Then all the people said, "Amen," and praised the LORD.
17:11 When your days are over and you go to be with your fathers, I will raise up your offspring to succeed you, one of your own sons, and I will establish his kingdom.	17:11 When your days are fulfilled to go to be with your fathers, I will raise up your offspring after you, one of your own sons, and I will establish his kingdom.	17:11 When you die and are buried with your ancestors, I will make one of your sons king and will keep his kingdom strong.
12 He is the one who will build a house for me, and I will establish his throne forever.	12 He shall build a house for me, and I will establish his throne for ever.	12 He will be the one to build a temple for me, and I will make sure that his dynasty continues forever.
13 I will be his father, and he will be my son. I will never take my love away from him, as I took it away from your predecessor.	13 I will be his father, and he shall be my son; I will not take my steadfast love from him, as I took it from him who was before you,	13 I will be his father, and he will be my son. I will not withdraw my support from him as I did from Saul, whom I removed so that you could be king.

KJV	NKJV	TLB
14 But I will settle him in mine house and in my kingdom for ever: and his throne shall be established for evermore.	14 "And I will establish him in My house and in My kingdom forever; and his throne shall be established forever." ' "	14 I will place him over my people and over the kingdom of Israel forever—and his descendants will always be kings." ' "
16 And David the king came and sat before the LORD, and said, Who *am* I, O LORD God, and what *is* mine house, that thou hast brought me hitherto?	16 Then King David went in and sat before the LORD; and he said: "Who *am* I, O LORD God? And what is my house, that You have brought me this far?	16 Then King David went in and sat before the Lord and said, "Who am I, O Lord God, and what is my family that you have given me all this?
17 And *yet* this was a small thing in thine eyes, O God; for thou hast *also* spoken of thy servant's house for a great while to come, and hast regarded me according to the estate of a man of high degree, O LORD God.	17 "And *yet* this was a small thing in Your sight, O God; and You have *also* spoken of Your servant's house for a great while to come, and have regarded me according to the estate of a man of high degree, O LORD God.	17 For all the great things you have already done for me are nothing in comparison to what you have promised to do in the future! For now, O Lord God, you are speaking of future generations of my children being kings too! You speak as though I were someone very great.
21:10 Go and tell David, saying, Thus saith the LORD, I offer thee three *things:* choose thee one of them, that I may do *it* unto thee.	21:10 "Go and tell David, saying, 'Thus says the LORD: "I offer you three *things;* choose one of them for yourself, that I may do *it* to you." ' "	21:10 "Go and tell David, 'The Lord has offered you three choices.
11 So Gad came to David, and said unto him, Thus saith the LORD, Choose thee	11 So Gad came to David and said to him, "Thus says the LORD: 'Choose for yourself,	11 Which will you choose?
12 Either three years' famine; or three months to be destroyed before thy foes, while that the sword of thine enemies overtaketh *thee;* or else three days the sword of the LORD, even the pestilence, in the land, and the angel of the LORD destroying throughout all the coasts of Israel. Now therefore advise thyself what word I shall bring again to him that sent me.	12 'either three years of famine, or three months to be defeated by your foes with the sword of your enemies overtaking *you,* or else for three days the sword of the LORD—the plague in the land, with the angel of the LORD destroying throughout all the territory of Israel.' Now consider what answer I should take back to Him who sent me."	12 You may have three years of famine, or three months of destruction by the enemies of Israel, or three days of deadly plague as the angel of the Lord brings destruction to the land. Think it over and let me know what answer to return to the one who sent me.' "
13 And David said unto Gad, I am in a great strait: let me fall now into the hand of the LORD; for very great *are* his mercies: but let me not fall into the hand of man.	13 And David said to Gad, "I am in great distress. Please let me fall into the hand of the LORD, for His mercies *are* very great; but do not let me fall into the hand of man."	13 "This is a terrible decision to make," David replied, "but let me fall into the hands of the Lord rather than into the power of men, for God's mercies are very great."
22:11 Now, my son, the LORD be with thee; and prosper thou, and build the house of the LORD thy God, as he hath said of thee.	22:11 "Now, my son, may the LORD be with you; and may you prosper, and build the house of the LORD your God, as He has said to you.	22:11 "So now, my son, may the Lord be with you and prosper you as you do what he told you to do and build the Temple of the Lord.
12 Only the LORD give thee wisdom and understanding, and give thee charge concerning Israel, that thou mayest keep the law of the LORD thy God.	12 "Only may the LORD give you wisdom and understanding, and give you charge concerning Israel, that you may keep the law of the LORD your God.	12 And may the Lord give you the good judgment to follow all his laws when he makes you king of Israel.
13 Then shalt thou prosper, if thou takest heed to fulfil the statutes and judgments which the LORD charged Moses with concerning Israel: be strong, and of good courage; dread not, nor be dismayed.	13 "Then you will prosper, if you take care to fulfill the statutes and judgments with which the LORD charged Moses concerning Israel. Be strong and of good courage; do not fear nor be dismayed.	13 For if you carefully obey the rules and regulations which he gave to Israel through Moses, you will prosper. Be strong and courageous, fearless and enthusiastic!
29:10 Wherefore David blessed the LORD before all the congregation: and David said, Blessed *be* thou, LORD God of Israel our father, for ever and ever.	29:10 Therefore David blessed the LORD before all the congregation; and David said: "Blessed are You, LORD God of Israel, our Father, forever and ever.	29:10 While still in the presence of the whole assembly, David expressed his praises to the Lord: "O Lord God of our father Israel, praise your name for ever and ever!
11 Thine, O LORD, *is* the greatness, and the power, and the glory, and the victory, and the majesty: for all *that is* in the heaven and in the earth *is thine;* thine *is* the kingdom, O LORD, and thou art exalted as head above all.	11 Yours, O LORD, *is* the greatness, The power and the glory, The victory and the majesty; For all *that is* in heaven and in earth *is Yours;* Yours *is* the kingdom, O LORD, And You are exalted as head over all.	11 Yours is the mighty power and glory and victory and majesty. Everything in the heavens and earth is yours, O Lord, and this is your kingdom. We adore you as being in control of everything.

Second Chronicles

1:11 And God said to Solomon, Because this was in thine heart, and thou hast not asked riches, wealth, or honour, nor the life of thine enemies, neither yet hast asked long life; but hast asked wisdom and knowledge for thyself, that thou mayest judge my people, over whom I have made thee king:	1:11 And God said to Solomon: "Because this was in your heart, and you have not asked riches or wealth or honor or the life of your enemies, nor have you asked long life—but have asked wisdom and knowledge for yourself, that you may judge My people over whom I have made you king—	1:11 God replied, "Because your greatest desire is to help your people, and you haven't asked for personal wealth and honor, and you haven't asked me to curse your enemies, and you haven't asked for a long life, but for wisdom and knowledge to properly guide my people—

NIV	RSV	TEV
14 I will set him over my house and my kingdom forever; his throne will be established forever.'"	14 but I will confirm him in my house and in my kingdom for ever and his throne shall be established for ever.'"	14 I will put him in charge of my people and my kingdom forever. His dynasty will never end.'"
16 Then King David went in and sat before the LORD, and he said: "Who am I, O LORD God, and what is my family, that you have brought me this far?	16 Then King David went in and sat before the LORD, and said, "Who am I, O LORD God, and what is my house, that thou hast brought me thus far?	16 Then King David went into the Tent of the LORD's presence, sat down, and prayed, "I am not worthy of what you have already done for me, LORD God, nor is my family.
17 And as if this were not enough in your sight, O God, you have spoken about the future of the house of your servant. You have looked on me as though I were the most exalted of men, O LORD God.	17 And this was a small thing in thy eyes, O God; thou hast also spoken of thy servant's house for a great while to come, and hast shown me future generations, O LORD God!	17 Yet now you are doing even more; you have made promises about my descendants in the years to come, and you, LORD God, are already treating me like a great man.
21:10 "Go and tell David, 'This is what the LORD says: I am giving you three options. Choose one of them for me to carry out against you.'"	21:10 "Go and say to David, 'Thus says the LORD, Three things I offer you; choose one of them, that I may do it to you.'"	21:10 "Go and tell David that I am giving him three choices. I will do whichever he chooses."
11 So Gad went to David and said to him, "This is what the LORD says: 'Take your choice:	11 So Gad came to David and said to him, "Thus says the LORD, 'Take which you will:	11 Gad went to David, told him what the LORD had said, and asked, "Which is it to be?
12 three years of famine, three months of being swept away before your enemies, with their swords overtaking you, or three days of the sword of the LORD—days of plague in the land, with the angel of the LORD ravaging every part of Israel.' Now then, decide how I should answer the one who sent me."	12 either three years of famine; or three months of devastation by your foes, while the sword of your enemies overtakes you; or else three days of the sword of the LORD, pestilence upon the land, and the angel of the LORD destroying throughout all the territory of Israel.' Now decide what answer I shall return to him who sent me."	12 Three years of famine? Or three months of running away from the armies of your enemies? Or three days during which the LORD attacks you with his sword and sends an epidemic on your land, using his angel to bring death throughout Israel? What answer shall I give the LORD?"
13 David said to Gad, "I am in deep distress. Let me fall into the hands of the LORD, for his mercy is very great; but do not let me fall into the hands of men."	13 Then David said to Gad, "I am in great distress; let me fall into the hand of the LORD, for his mercy is very great; but let me not fall into the hand of man."	13 David replied to Gad, "I am in a desperate situation! But I don't want to be punished by men. Let the LORD himself be the one to punish me, because he is merciful."
22:11 "Now, my son, the LORD be with you, and may you have success and build the house of the LORD your God, as he said you would.	22:11 Now, my son, the LORD be with you, so that you may succeed in building the house of the LORD your God, as he has spoken concerning you.	22:11 David continued, "Now, son, may the LORD your God be with you, and may he keep his promise to make you successful in building a temple for him.
12 May the LORD give you discretion and understanding when he puts you in command over Israel, so that you may keep the law of the LORD your God.	12 Only, may the LORD grant you discretion and understanding, that when he gives you charge over Israel you may keep the law of the LORD your God.	12 And may the LORD your God give you insight and wisdom so that you may govern Israel according to his Law.
13 Then you will have success if you are careful to observe the decrees and laws that the LORD gave Moses for Israel. Be strong and courageous. Do not be afraid or discouraged.	13 Then you will prosper if you are careful to observe the statutes and the ordinances which the LORD commanded Moses for Israel. Be strong, and of good courage. Fear not; be not dismayed.	13 If you obey all the laws which the LORD gave to Moses for Israel, you will be successful. Be determined and confident, and don't let anything make you afraid.
29:10 David praised the LORD in the presence of the whole assembly, saying, "Praise be to you, O LORD, God of our father Israel, from everlasting to everlasting.	29:10 Therefore David blessed the LORD in the presence of all the assembly; and David said: "Blessed art thou, O LORD, the God of Israel our father, for ever and ever.	29:10 There in front of the whole assembly King David praised the LORD. He said, "LORD God of our ancestor Jacob, may you be praised forever and ever!

11 Yours, O LORD, is the greatness and the power
  and the glory and the majesty and the splendor,
  for everything in heaven and earth is yours.
Yours, O LORD, is the kingdom;
  you are exalted as head over all.
	11 Thine, O LORD, is the greatness, and the power, and the glory, and the victory, and the majesty; for all that is in the heavens and in the earth is thine; thine is the kingdom, O LORD, and thou art exalted as head above all.	11 You are great and powerful, glorious, splendid, and majestic. Everything in heaven and earth is yours, and you are king, supreme ruler over all.

Second Chronicles

1:11 God said to Solomon, "Since this is your heart's desire and you have not asked for wealth, riches or honor, nor for the death of your enemies, and since you have not asked for a long life but for wisdom and knowledge to govern my people over whom I have made you king,	1:11 God answered Solomon, "Because this was in your heart, and you have not asked possessions, wealth, honor, or the life of those who hate you, and have not even asked long life, but have asked wisdom and knowledge for yourself that you may rule my people over whom I have made you king,	1:11 God replied to Solomon, "You have made the right choice. Instead of asking for wealth or treasure or fame or the death of your enemies or even for long life for yourself, you have asked for wisdom and knowledge so that you can rule my people, over whom I have made you king.

KJV	NKJV	TLB
12 Wisdom and knowledge *is* granted unto thee; and I will give thee riches, and wealth, and honour, such as none of the kings have had that *have been* before thee, neither shall there any after thee have the like.	12 "wisdom and knowledge *are* granted to you; and I will give you riches and wealth and honor, such as none of the kings have had who *have been* before you, nor shall any after you have the like."	12 yes, I am giving you the wisdom and knowledge you asked for! And I am also giving you such riches, wealth, and honor as no other king has ever had before you! And there will never again be so great a king in all the world!"
2:5 And the house which I build *is* great: for great *is* our God above all gods.	2:5 And the temple which I build *will be* great, for our God is greater than all gods.	2:5 It is going to be a wonderful temple because he is a great God, greater than any other.
6 But who is able to build him an house, seeing the heaven and heaven of heavens cannot contain him? who *am* I then, that I should build him an house, save only to burn sacrifice before him?	6 But who is able to build Him a temple, since heaven and the heaven of heavens cannot contain Him? Who *am* I then, that I should build Him a temple, except to burn sacrifice before Him?	6 But who can ever build him a worthy home? Not even the highest heaven would be beautiful enough! And who am I to be allowed to build a temple for God? But it will be a place to worship him.
6:14 And said, O Lᴏʀᴅ God of Israel, *there is* no God like thee in the heaven, nor in the earth; which keepest covenant, and *shewest* mercy unto thy servants, that walk before thee with all their hearts:	6:14 and said: "Lᴏʀᴅ God of Israel, *there is* no God in heaven or on earth like You, who keep *Your* covenant and mercy with Your servants who walk before You with all their hearts.	6:14 "O Lord God of Israel, there is no God like you in all of heaven and earth. You are the God who keeps his kind promises to all those who obey you, and who are anxious to do your will.
15 Thou which hast kept with thy servant David my father that which thou hast promised him; and spakest with thy mouth, and hast fulfilled *it* with thine hand, as *it is* this day.	15 "You have kept what You promised Your servant David my father; You have both spoken with Your mouth and fulfilled *it* with Your hand, as *it is* this day.	15 And you have kept your promise to my father David, as is evident today.
16 Now therefore, O Lᴏʀᴅ God of Israel, keep with thy servant David my father that which thou hast promised him, saying, There shall not fail thee a man in my sight to sit upon the throne of Israel; yet so that thy children take heed to their way to walk in my law, as thou hast walked before me.	16 "Therefore, Lᴏʀᴅ God of Israel, now keep what You promised Your servant David my father, saying, 'You shall not fail to have a man sit before Me on the throne of Israel, only if your sons take heed to their way, to walk in My law as you have walked before Me.'	16 And now, O God of Israel, carry out your further promise to him that 'your descendants shall always reign over Israel if they will obey my laws as you have.'
17 Now then, O Lᴏʀᴅ God of Israel, let thy word be verified, which thou hast spoken unto thy servant David.	17 "Now then, O Lᴏʀᴅ God of Israel, let Your word come true, which You have spoken to Your servant David.	17 Yes, Lord God of Israel, please fulfill this promise too.
18 But will God in very deed dwell with men on the earth? behold, heaven and the heaven of heavens cannot contain thee; how much less this house which I have built!	18 "But will God indeed dwell with men on the earth? Behold, heaven and the heaven of heavens cannot contain You; how much less this temple which I have built!	18 But will God really live upon the earth with men? Why, even the heaven and the heaven of heavens cannot contain you—how much less this Temple which I have built!
7:14 If my people, which are called by my name, shall humble themselves, and pray, and seek my face, and turn from their wicked ways; then will I hear from heaven, and will forgive their sin, and will heal their land.	7:14 "if My people who are called by My name will humble themselves, and pray and seek My face, and turn from their wicked ways, then I will hear from heaven, and will forgive their sin and heal their land.	7:14 then if my people will humble themselves and pray, and search for me, and turn from their wicked ways, I will hear them from heaven and forgive their sins and heal their land.
9:5 And she said to the king, *It was* a true report which I heard in mine own land of thine acts, and of thy wisdom:	9:5 Then she said to the king: "*It was* a true report which I heard in my own land about your words and your wisdom.	9:5 Finally she exclaimed to the king, "Everything I heard about you in my own country is true!
6 Howbeit I believed not their words, until I came, and mine eyes had seen *it:* and, behold, the one half of the greatness of thy wisdom was not told me: *for* thou exceedest the fame that I heard.	6 "However I did not believe their words until I came and saw with my own eyes; and indeed, the half of the greatness of your wisdom was not told me. You exceed the fame of which I heard.	6 I didn't believe it until I got here and saw it with my own eyes. Your wisdom is far greater than I could ever have imagined.
7 Happy *are* thy men, and happy *are* these thy servants, which stand continually before thee, and hear thy wisdom.	7 "Happy *are* your men and happy *are* these your servants, who stand continually before you and hear your wisdom!	7 What a privilege for these men of yours to stand here and listen to you talk!
8 Blessed be the Lᴏʀᴅ thy God, which delighted in thee to set thee on his throne, *to be* king for the Lᴏʀᴅ thy God: because thy God loved Israel, to establish them for ever, therefore made he thee king over them, to do judgment and justice.	8 "Blessed be the Lᴏʀᴅ your God, who delighted in you, setting you on His throne *to be* king for the Lᴏʀᴅ your God! Because your God has loved Israel, to establish them forever, therefore He made you king over them, to do justice and righteousness."	8 Blessed be the Lord your God! How he must love Israel to give them a just king like you! He wants them to be a great, strong nation forever."
10:13 And the king answered them roughly; and king Rehoboam forsook the counsel of the old men,	10:13 Then the king answered them roughly. King Rehoboam rejected the counsel of the elders,	10:13 he spoke roughly to them; for he refused the advice of the old men.
14 And answered them after the advice of the young men, saying, My father made your yoke heavy, but I will add thereto: my father chastised you with whips, but I *will chastise you* with scorpions.	14 and he spoke to them according to the counsel of the young men, saying, "My father made your yoke heavy, but I will add to it; my father chastised you with whips, but I *will chastise you* with scourges!"	14 and followed the counsel of the younger ones. "My father gave you heavy burdens but I will give you heavier!" he told them. "My father punished you with whips, but I will punish you with scorpions!"

NIV	RSV	TEV
12 therefore wisdom and knowledge will be given you. And I will also give you wealth, riches and honor, such as no king who was before you ever had and none after you will have."	12 wisdom and knowledge are granted to you. I will also give you riches, possessions, and honor, such as none of the kings had who were before you, and none after you shall have the like."	12 I will give you wisdom and knowledge. And in addition, I will give you more wealth, treasure, and fame than any king has ever had before or will ever have again."
2:5 "The temple I am going to build will be great, because our God is greater than all other gods.	2:5 The house which I am to build will be great, for our God is greater than all gods.	2:5 I intend to build a great temple, because our God is greater than any other god.
6 But who is able to build a temple for him, since the heavens, even the highest heavens, cannot contain him? Who then am I to build a temple for him, except as a place to burn sacrifices before him?	6 But who is able to build him a house, since heaven, even highest heaven, cannot contain him? Who am I to build a house for him, except as a place to burn incense before him?	6 Yet no one can really build a temple for God, because even all the vastness of heaven cannot contain him. How then can I build a temple that would be anything more than a place to burn incense to God?
6:14 He said: "O LORD, God of Israel, there is no God like you in heaven or on earth—you who keep your covenant of love with your servants who continue wholeheartedly in your way.	6:14 and said, "O LORD, God of Israel, there is no God like thee, in heaven or on earth, keeping covenant and showing steadfast love to thy servants who walk before thee with all their heart;	6:14 He prayed, "LORD God of Israel, in all heaven and earth there is no god like you. You keep your covenant with your people and show them your love when they live in wholehearted obedience to you.
15 You have kept your promise to your servant David my father; with your mouth you have promised and with your hand you have fulfilled it—as it is today.	15 who hast kept with thy servant David my father what thou didst declare to him; yea, thou didst speak with thy mouth, and with thy hand hast fulfilled it this day.	15 You have kept the promise you made to my father David; today every word has been fulfilled.
16 "Now LORD, God of Israel, keep for your servant David my father the promises you made to him when you said, 'You shall never fail to have a man to sit before me on the throne of Israel, if only your sons are careful in all they do to walk before me according to my law, as you have done.'	16 Now therefore, O LORD, God of Israel, keep with thy servant David my father what thou hast promised him, saying, 'There shall never fail you a man before me to sit upon the throne of Israel, if only your sons take heed to their way, to walk in my law as you have walked before me.'	16 Now, LORD God of Israel, keep the other promise you made to my father when you told him that there would always be one of his descendants ruling as king of Israel, provided that they carefully obeyed your Law just as he did.
17 And now, O LORD, God of Israel, let your word that you promised your servant David come true.	17 Now therefore, O LORD, God of Israel, let thy word be confirmed, which thou hast spoken to thy servant David.	17 So now, LORD God of Israel, let everything come true that you promised to your servant David.
18 "But will God really dwell on earth with men? The heavens, even the highest heavens, cannot contain you. How much less this temple I have built!	18 "But will God dwell indeed with man on the earth? Behold, heaven and the highest heaven cannot contain thee; how much less this house which I have built!	18 "But can you, O God, really live on earth among men and women? Not even all of heaven is large enough to hold you, so how can this Temple that I have built be large enough?
7:14 if my people, who are called by my name, will humble themselves and pray and seek my face and turn from their wicked ways, then will I hear from heaven and will forgive their sin and will heal their land.	7:14 if my people who are called by my name humble themselves, and pray, and seek my face, and turn from their wicked ways, then I will hear from heaven, and will forgive their sin and heal their land.	7:14 if they pray to me and repent and turn away from the evil they have been doing, then I will hear them in heaven, forgive their sins, and make their land prosperous again.
9:5 She said to the king, "The report I heard in my own country about your achievements and your wisdom is true.	9:5 And she said to the king, "The report was true which I heard in my own land of your affairs and of your wisdom,	9:5 She said to the king, "What I heard in my own country about you and your wisdom is true!
6 But I did not believe what they said until I came and saw with my own eyes. Indeed, not even half the greatness of your wisdom was told me; you have far exceeded the report I heard.	6 but I did not believe the reports until I came and my own eyes had seen it; and behold, half the greatness of your wisdom was not told me; you surpass the report which I heard.	6 I did not believe what they told me until I came and saw for myself. I had not heard of even half your wisdom. You are even wiser than people say.
7 How happy your men must be! How happy your officials, who continually stand before you and hear your wisdom!	7 Happy are your wives! Happy are these your servants, who continually stand before you and hear your wisdom!	7 How fortunate are the men who serve you, who are always in your presence and are privileged to hear your wise sayings!
8 Praise be to the LORD your God, who has delighted in you and placed you on his throne as king to rule for the LORD your God. Because of the love of your God for Israel and his desire to uphold them forever, he has made you king over them, to maintain justice and righteousness."	8 Blessed be the LORD your God, who has delighted in you and set you on his throne as king for the LORD your God! Because your God loved Israel and would establish them for ever, he has made you king over them, that you may execute justice and righteousness."	8 Praise the LORD your God! He has shown how pleased he is with you by making you king, to rule in his name. Because he loves his people Israel and wants to preserve them forever, he has made you their king so that you can maintain law and justice."
10:13 The king answered them harshly. Rejecting the advice of the elders,	10:13 And the king answered them harshly, and forsaking the counsel of the old men,	10:13 The king ignored the advice of the older men and spoke harshly to the people,
14 he followed the advice of the young men and said, "My father made your yoke heavy; I will make it even heavier. My father scourged you with whips; I will scourge you with scorpions."	14 King Rehoboam spoke to them according to the counsel of the young men, saying, "My father made your yoke heavy, but I will add to it; my father chastised you with whips, but I will chastise you with scorpions."	14 as the younger men had advised. He said, "My father placed heavy burdens on you; I will make them even heavier. He beat you with whips; I'll flog you with bullwhips!"

KEY VERSE COMPARISON CHART

KJV	NKJV	TLB
14:11 And Asa cried unto the LORD his God, and said, LORD, *it is* nothing with thee to help, whether with many, or with them that have no power: help us, O LORD our God; for we rest on thee, and in thy name we go against this multitude. O LORD thou *art* our God; let not man prevail against thee.	**14:11** And Asa cried out to the LORD his God, and said, "LORD, *it is* nothing for You to help, whether with many or with those who have no power; help us, O LORD our God, for we rest on You, and in Your name we go against this multitude. O LORD, You *are* our God; do not let man prevail against You!"	**14:11** "O Lord," he cried out to God, "no one else can help us! Here we are, powerless against this mighty army. Oh, help us, Lord our God! For we trust in you alone to rescue us, and in your name we attack this vast horde. Don't let mere men defeat you!"
15:1 And the Spirit of God came upon Azariah the son of Oded:	**15:1** Now the Spirit of God came upon Azariah the son of Oded.	**15:1** Then the Spirit of God came upon Azariah (son of Oded),
2 And he went out to meet Asa, and said unto him, Hear ye me, Asa, and all Judah and Benjamin; The LORD *is* with you, while ye be with him; and if ye seek him, he will be found of you; but if ye forsake him, he will forsake you.	**2** And he went out to meet Asa, and said to him: "Hear me, Asa, and all Judah and Benjamin. The LORD *is* with you while you are with Him. If you seek Him, He will be found by you; but if you forsake Him, He will forsake you.	**2** and he went out to meet King Asa as he was returning from the battle. "Listen to me, Asa! Listen, armies of Judah and Benjamin!" he shouted. "The Lord will stay with you as long as you stay with him! Whenever you look for him, you will find him. But if you forsake him, he will forsake you.
16:9 For the eyes of the LORD run to and fro throughout the whole earth, to shew himself strong in the behalf of *them* whose heart *is* perfect toward him. Herein thou hast done foolishly: therefore from henceforth thou shalt have wars.	**16:9** "For the eyes of the LORD run to and fro throughout the whole earth, to show Himself strong on behalf of *those* whose heart *is* loyal to Him. In this you have done foolishly; therefore from now on you shall have wars."	**16:9** For the eyes of the Lord search back and forth across the whole earth, looking for people whose hearts are perfect toward him, so that he can show his great power in helping them. What a fool you have been! From now on you shall have wars."
24:15 But Jehoiada waxed old, and was full of days when he died; an hundred and thirty years old *was he* when he died.	**24:15** But Jehoiada grew old and was full of days, and he died; *he was* one hundred and thirty years old when he died.	**24:15** He lived to a very old age, finally dying at 130.
16 And they buried him in the city of David among the kings, because he had done good in Israel, both toward God, and toward his house.	**16** And they buried him in the City of David among the kings, because he had done good in Israel, both toward God and His house.	**16** He was buried in the City of David among the kings, because he had done so much good for Israel, for God, and for the Temple.
17 Now after the death of Jehoiada came the princes of Judah, and made obeisance to the king. Then the king hearkened unto them.	**17** Now after the death of Jehoiada the leaders of Judah came and bowed down to the king. And the king listened to them.	**17** But after his death the leaders of Judah came to King Joash and induced him to
18 And they left the house of the LORD God of their fathers, and served groves and idols: and wrath came upon Judah and Jerusalem for this their trespass.	**18** Therefore they left the house of the LORD God of their fathers, and served wooden images and idols; and wrath came upon Judah and Jerusalem because of their trespass.	**18** abandon the Temple of the God of their ancestors, and to worship shame-idols instead! So the wrath of God came down upon Judah and Jerusalem again.
19 Yet he sent prophets to them, to bring them again unto the LORD; and they testified against them: but they would not give ear.	**19** Yet He sent prophets to them, to bring them back to the LORD; and they testified against them, but they would not listen.	**19** God sent prophets to bring them back to the Lord, but the people wouldn't listen.
30:9 For if ye turn again unto the LORD, your brethren and your children *shall find* compassion before them that lead them captive, so that they shall come again into this land: for the LORD your God *is* gracious and merciful, and will not turn away *his* face from you, if ye return unto him.	**30:9** "For if you return to the LORD, your brethren and your children *will be treated* with compassion by those who lead them captive, so that they may come back to this land; for the LORD your God *is* gracious and merciful, and will not turn *His* face from you if you return to Him."	**30:9** For if you turn to the Lord again, your brothers and your children will be treated mercifully by their captors, and they will be able to return to this land. For the Lord your God is full of kindness and mercy and will not continue to turn away his face from you if you return to him."
34:1 Josiah *was* eight years old when he began to reign, and he reigned in Jerusalem one and thirty years.	**34:1** Josiah *was* eight years old when he became king, and he reigned thirty-one years in Jerusalem.	**34:1** Josiah was only eight years old when he became king. He reigned thirty-one years, in Jerusalem.
2 And he did *that which was* right in the sight of the LORD, and walked in the ways of David his father, and declined *neither* to the right hand, nor to the left.	**2** And he did *what was* right in the sight of the LORD, and walked in the ways of his father David; *he* did *not* turn aside to the right hand or to the left.	**2** His was a good reign, as he carefully followed the good example of his ancestor King David.
3 For in the eighth year of his reign, while he was yet young, he began to seek after the God of David his father; and in the twelfth year he began to purge Judah and Jerusalem from the high places, and the groves, and the carved images, and the molten images.	**3** For in the eighth year of his reign, while he was still young, he began to seek the God of his father David; and in the twelfth year he began to purge Judah and Jerusalem of the high places, the wooden images, the carved images, and the molded images.	**3** For when he was sixteen years old, in the eighth year of his reign, he began to search for the God of his ancestor David; and four years later he began to clean up Judah and Jerusalem, destroying the heathen altars and the shame-idols on the hills.
4 And they brake down the altars of Baalim in his presence; and the images, that *were* on high above them, he cut down; and the groves, and the carved images, and the molten images, he brake in pieces, and made dust *of them*, and strowed *it* upon the graves of them that had sacrificed unto them.	**4** They broke down the altars of the Baals in his presence, and the incense altars which *were* above them he cut down; and the wooden images, the carved images, and the molded images he broke in pieces, and made dust of them and scattered *it* on the graves of those who had sacrificed to them.	**4** He went out personally to watch as the altars of Baal were knocked apart, the obelisks above the altars chopped down, and the shame-idols ground into dust and scattered over the graves of those who had sacrificed to them.

NIV	RSV	TEV
14:11 Then Asa called to the LORD his God and said, "LORD, there is no one like you to help the powerless against the mighty. Help us, O LORD our God, for we rely on you, and in your name we have come against this vast army. O LORD, you are our God; do not let man prevail against you."	**14:11** And Asa cried to the LORD his God, "O LORD, there is none like thee to help, between the mighty and the weak. Help us, O LORD our God, for we rely on thee, and in thy name we have come against this multitude. O LORD, thou art our God; let not man prevail against thee."	**14:11** Asa prayed to the LORD his God, "O LORD, you can help a weak army as easily as a powerful one. Help us now, O LORD our God, because we are relying on you, and in your name we have come out to fight against this huge army. LORD, you are our God; no one can hope to defeat you."
15:1 The Spirit of God came upon Azariah son of Oded.	**15:1** The Spirit of God came upon Azariah the son of Oded,	**15:1** The spirit of God came upon Azariah son of Oded,
2 He went out to meet Asa and said to him, "Listen to me, Asa and all Judah and Benjamin. The LORD is with you when you are with him. If you seek him, he will be found by you, but if you forsake him, he will forsake you.	**2** and he went out to meet Asa, and said to him, "Hear me, Asa, and all Judah and Benjamin: The LORD is with you, while you are with him. If you seek him, he will be found by you, but if you forsake him, he will forsake you.	**2** and he went to meet King Asa. He called out, "Listen to me, King Asa, and all you people of Judah and Benjamin! The LORD is with you as long as you are with him. If you look for him, he will let you find him, but if you turn away, he will abandon you.
16:9 For the eyes of the LORD range throughout the earth to strengthen those whose hearts are fully committed to him. You have done a foolish thing, and from now on you will be at war."	**16:9** For the eyes of the LORD run to and fro throughout the whole earth, to show his might in behalf of those whose heart is blameless toward him. You have done foolishly in this; for from now on you will have wars."	**16:9** The LORD keeps close watch over the whole world, to give strength to those whose hearts are loyal to him. You have acted foolishly, and so from now on you will always be at war."
24:15 Now Jehoiada was old and full of years, and he died at the age of a hundred and thirty.	**24:15** But Jehoiada grew old and full of days, and died; he was a hundred and thirty years old at his death.	**24:15** After reaching the very old age of a hundred and thirty, he died.
16 He was buried with the kings in the City of David, because of the good he had done in Israel for God and his temple.	**16** And they buried him in the city of David among the kings, because he had done good in Israel, and toward God and his house.	**16** They buried him in the royal tombs in David's City in recognition of the service he had done for the people of Israel, for God, and for the Temple.
17 After the death of Jehoiada, the officials of Judah came and paid homage to the king, and he listened to them.	**17** Now after the death of Jehoiada the princes of Judah came and did obeisance to the king; then the king hearkened to them.	**17** But once Jehoiada was dead, the leaders of Judah persuaded King Joash to listen to them instead.
18 They abandoned the temple of the LORD, the God of their fathers, and worshiped Asherah poles and idols. Because of their guilt, God's anger came upon Judah and Jerusalem.	**18** And they forsook the house of the LORD, the God of their fathers, and served the Asherim and the idols. And wrath came upon Judah and Jerusalem for this their guilt.	**18** And so the people stopped worshiping in the Temple of the LORD, the God of their ancestors, and began to worship idols and the images of the goddess Asherah. Their guilt for these sins brought the LORD's anger on Judah and Jerusalem.
19 Although the LORD sent prophets to the people to bring them back to him, and though they testified against them, they would not listen.	**19** Yet he sent prophets among them to bring them back to the LORD; these testified against them, but they would not give heed.	**19** The LORD sent prophets to warn them to return to him, but the people refused to listen.
30:9 If you return to the LORD, then your brothers and your children will be shown compassion by their captors and will come back to this land, for the LORD your God is gracious and compassionate. He will not turn his face from you if you return to him."	**30:9** For if you return to the LORD, your brethren and your children will find compassion with their captors, and return to this land. For the LORD your God is gracious and merciful, and will not turn away his face from you, if you return to him."	**30:9** If you return to the LORD, then those who have taken your relatives away as prisoners will take pity on them and let them come home. The LORD your God is kind and merciful, and if you return to him, he will accept you."
34:1 Josiah was eight years old when he became king, and he reigned in Jerusalem thirty-one years.	**34:1** Josiah was eight years old when he began to reign, and he reigned thirty-one years in Jerusalem.	**34:1** Josiah was eight years old when he became king of Judah, and he ruled in Jerusalem for thirty-one years.
2 He did what was right in the eyes of the LORD and walked in the ways of his father David, not turning aside to the right or to the left.	**2** He did what was right in the eyes of the LORD, and walked in the ways of David his father; and he did not turn aside to the right or to the left.	**2** He did what was pleasing to the LORD; he followed the example of his ancestor King David, strictly obeying all the laws of God.
3 In the eighth year of his reign, while he was still young, he began to seek the God of his father David. In his twelfth year he began to purge Judah and Jerusalem of high places, Asherah poles, carved idols and cast images.	**3** For in the eighth year of his reign, while he was yet a boy, he began to seek the God of David his father; and in the twelfth year he began to purge Judah and Jerusalem of the high places, the Asherim, and the graven and the molten images.	**3** In the eighth year that Josiah was king, while he was still very young, he began to worship the God of his ancestor King David. Four years later he began to destroy the pagan places of worship, the symbols of the goddess Asherah, and all the other idols.
4 Under his direction the altars of the Baals were torn down; he cut to pieces the incense altars that were above them, and smashed the Asherah poles, the idols and the images. These he broke to pieces and scattered over the graves of those who had sacrificed to them.	**4** And they broke down the altars of the Baals in his presence; and he hewed down the incense altars which stood above them; and he broke in pieces the Asherim and the graven and the molten images, and he made dust of them and strewed it over the graves of those who had sacrificed to them.	**4** Under his direction his men smashed the altars where Baal was worshiped and tore down the incense altars near them. They ground to dust the images of Asherah and all the other idols and then scattered the dust on the graves of the people who had sacrificed to them.

KJV	NKJV	TLB
18 Then Shaphan the scribe told the king, saying, Hilkiah the priest hath given me a book. And Shaphan read it before the king.	18 Then Shaphan the scribe told the king, saying, "Hilkiah the priest has given me a book." And Shaphan read it before the king.	18 Then he mentioned the scroll, and how Hilkiah had discovered it. So he read it to the king.
19 And it came to pass, when the king had heard the words of the law, that he rent his clothes.	19 Now it happened, when the king heard the words of the Law, that he tore his clothes.	19 When the king heard what these laws required of God's people, he ripped his clothing in despair,
31 And the king stood in his place, and made a covenant before the LORD, to walk after the LORD, and to keep his commandments, and his testimonies, and his statutes, with all his heart, and with all his soul, to perform the words of the covenant which are written in this book.	31 Then the king stood in his place and made a covenant before the LORD, to follow the LORD, and to keep His commandments and His testimonies and His statutes with all his heart and all his soul, to perform the words of the covenant that were written in this book.	31 As the king stood before them, he made a pledge to the Lord to follow his commandments with all his heart and soul, and to do what was written in the scroll.

Ezra

KJV	NKJV	TLB
1:1 Now in the first year of Cyrus king of Persia, that the word of the LORD by the mouth of Jeremiah might be fulfilled, the LORD stirred up the spirit of Cyrus king of Persia, that he made a proclamation throughout all his kingdom, and put it also in writing, saying,	1:1 Now in the first year of Cyrus king of Persia, that the word of the LORD spoken by the mouth of Jeremiah might be fulfilled, the LORD stirred up the spirit of Cyrus king of Persia, so that he made a proclamation throughout all his kingdom, and also put it in writing, saying,	1:1 During the first year of the reign of King Cyrus of Persia, the Lord fulfilled Jeremiah's prophecy by giving King Cyrus the desire to send this proclamation throughout his empire (he also put it into the permanent records of the realm):
2 Thus saith Cyrus king of Persia, The LORD God of heaven hath given me all the kingdoms of the earth; and he hath charged me to build him an house at Jerusalem, which is in Judah.	2 Thus says Cyrus king of Persia: All the kingdoms of the earth the LORD God of heaven has given me. And He has commanded me to build Him a house at Jerusalem which is in Judah.	2 "Cyrus, king of Persia, hereby announces that Jehovah, the God of heaven who gave me my vast empire, has now given me the responsibility of building him a Temple in Jerusalem, in the land of Judah.
3 Who is there among you of all his people? his God be with him, and let him go up to Jerusalem, which is in Judah, and build the house of the LORD God of Israel, (he is the God,) which is in Jerusalem.	3 Who is there among you of all His people? May his God be with him! Now let him go up to Jerusalem, which is in Judah, and build the house of the LORD God of Israel (He is God), which is in Jerusalem.	3 All Jews throughout the kingdom may now return to Jerusalem to rebuild this Temple of Jehovah, who is the God of Israel and of Jerusalem. May his blessings rest upon you.
4 And whosoever remaineth in any place where he sojourneth, let the men of his place help him with silver, and with gold, and with goods, and with beasts, beside the freewill offering for the house of God that is in Jerusalem.	4 And whoever remains in any place where he sojourns, let the men of his place help him with silver and gold, with goods and livestock, besides the freewill offerings for the house of God which is in Jerusalem.	4 Those Jews who do not go should contribute toward the expenses of those who do, and also supply them with clothing, transportation, supplies for the journey, and a freewill offering for the Temple."
3:10 And when the builders laid the foundation of the temple of the LORD, they set the priests in their apparel with trumpets, and the Levites the sons of Asaph with cymbals, to praise the LORD, after the ordinance of David king of Israel.	3:10 When the builders laid the foundation of the temple of the LORD, the priests stood in their apparel with trumpets, and the Levites, the sons of Asaph, with cymbals, to praise the LORD, according to the ordinance of David king of Israel.	3:10 When the builders completed the foundation of the Temple, the priests put on their priestly robes and blew their trumpets; and the descendants of Asaph crashed their cymbals to praise the Lord in the manner ordained by King David.
11 And they sang together by course in praising and giving thanks unto the LORD; because he is good, for his mercy endureth for ever toward Israel. And all the people shouted with a great shout, when they praised the LORD, because the foundation of the house of the LORD was laid.	11 And they sang responsively, praising and giving thanks to the LORD: "For He is good, For His mercy endures forever toward Israel." Then all the people shouted with a great shout, when they praised the LORD, because the foundation of the house of the LORD was laid.	11 They sang rounds of praise and thanks to God, singing this song: "He is good, and his love and mercy toward Israel will last forever." Then all the people gave a great shout, praising God because the foundation of the Temple had been laid.
7:8 And he came to Jerusalem in the fifth month, which was in the seventh year of the king.	7:8 And Ezra came to Jerusalem in the fifth month, which was in the seventh year of the king.	7:8-9 They left Babylon in the middle of March in the seventh year of the reign of Ar-ta-xerxes and arrived at Jerusalem in the month of August; for the Lord gave them a good trip.
9 For upon the first day of the first month began he to go up from Babylon, and on the first day of the fifth month came he to Jerusalem, according to the good hand of his God upon him.	9 On the first day of the first month he began his journey from Babylon, and on the first day of the fifth month he came to Jerusalem, according to the good hand of his God upon him.	
10 For Ezra had prepared his heart to seek the law of the LORD, and to do it, and to teach in Israel statutes and judgments.	10 For Ezra had prepared his heart to seek the Law of the LORD, and to do it, and to teach statutes and ordinances in Israel.	10 This was because Ezra had determined to study and obey the laws of the Lord and to become a Bible teacher, teaching those laws to the people of Israel.

NIV	RSV	TEV
18 Then Shaphan the secretary informed the king, "Hilkiah the priest has given me a book." And Shaphan read from it in the presence of the king.	18 Then Shaphan the secretary told the king, "Hilkiah the priest has given me a book." And Shaphan read it before the king.	18 Then he added, "I have here a book that Hilkiah gave me." And he read it aloud to the king.
19 When the king heard the words of the Law, he tore his robes.	19 When the king heard the words of the law he rent his clothes.	19 When the king heard the book being read, he tore his clothes in dismay.
31 The king stood by his pillar and renewed the covenant in the presence of the LORD—to follow the LORD and keep his commands, regulations and decrees with all his heart and all his soul, and to obey the words of the covenant written in this book.	31 And the king stood in his place and made a covenant before the LORD, to walk after the LORD and to keep his commandments and his testimonies and his statutes, with all his heart and all his soul, to perform the words of the covenant that were written in this book.	31 He stood by the royal column and made a covenant with the LORD to obey him, to keep his laws and commands with all his heart and soul, and to put into practice the demands attached to the covenant, as written in the book.

Ezra

NIV	RSV	TEV
1:1 In the first year of Cyrus king of Persia, in order to fulfill the word of the LORD spoken by Jeremiah, the LORD moved the heart of Cyrus king of Persia to make a proclamation throughout his realm and to put it in writing:	1:1 In the first year of Cyrus king of Persia, that the word of the LORD by the mouth of Jeremiah might be accomplished, the LORD stirred up the spirit of Cyrus king of Persia so that he made a proclamation throughout all his kingdom and also put it in writing:	1:1 In the first year that Cyrus of Persia was emperor, the LORD made what he had said through the prophet Jeremiah come true. He prompted Cyrus to issue the following command and send it out in writing to be read aloud everywhere in his empire:
2 "This is what Cyrus king of Persia says: "'The LORD, the God of heaven, has given me all the kingdoms of the earth and he has appointed me to build a temple for him at Jerusalem in Judah.	2 "Thus says Cyrus king of Persia: The LORD, the God of heaven, has given me all the kingdoms of the earth, and he has charged me to build him a house at Jerusalem, which is in Judah.	2 "This is the command of Cyrus, Emperor of Persia. The LORD, the God of Heaven, has made me ruler over the whole world and has given me the responsibility of building a temple for him in Jerusalem in Judah.
3 Anyone of his people among you—may his God be with him, and let him go up to Jerusalem in Judah and build the temple of the LORD, the God of Israel, the God who is in Jerusalem.	3 Whoever is among you of all his people, may his God be with him, and let him go up to Jerusalem, which is in Judah, and rebuild the house of the LORD, the God of Israel—he is the God who is in Jerusalem;	3 May God be with all of you who are his people. You are to go to Jerusalem and rebuild the Temple of the LORD, the God of Israel, the God who is worshiped in Jerusalem.
4 And the people of any place where survivors may now be living are to provide him with silver and gold, with goods and livestock, and with freewill offerings for the temple of God in Jerusalem.'"	4 and let each survivor, in whatever place he sojourns, be assisted by the men of his place with silver and gold, with goods and with beasts, besides freewill offerings for the house of God which is in Jerusalem."	4 If any of his people in exile need help to return, their neighbors are to give them this help. They are to provide them with silver and gold, supplies and pack animals, as well as offerings to present in the Temple of God in Jerusalem."
3:10 When the builders laid the foundation of the temple of the LORD, the priests in their vestments and with trumpets, and the Levites (the sons of Asaph) with cymbals, took their places to praise the LORD, as prescribed by David king of Israel.	3:10 And when the builders laid the foundation of the temple of the LORD, the priests in their vestments came forward with trumpets, and the Levites, the sons of Asaph, with cymbals, to praise the LORD, according to the directions of David king of Israel;	3:10 When the men started to lay the foundation of the Temple, the priests in their robes took their places with trumpets in their hands, and the Levites of the clan of Asaph stood there with cymbals. They praised the LORD according to the instructions handed down from the time of King David.
11 With praise and thanksgiving they sang to the LORD: "He is good; his love to Israel endures forever." And all the people gave a great shout of praise to the LORD, because the foundation of the house of the LORD was laid.	11 and they sang responsively, praising and giving thanks to the LORD, "For he is good, for his steadfast love endures for ever toward Israel." And all the people shouted with a great shout, when they praised the LORD, because the foundation of the house of the LORD was laid.	11 They sang the LORD's praises, repeating the refrain: "The LORD is good, and his love for Israel is eternal." Everyone shouted with all his might, praising the LORD, because the work on the foundation of the Temple had been started.
7:8 Ezra arrived in Jerusalem in the fifth month of the seventh year of the king.	7:8 And he came to Jerusalem in the fifth month, which was in the seventh year of the king;	7:8–9 They left Babylonia on the first day of the first month, and with God's help they arrived in Jerusalem on the first day of the fifth month.
9 He had begun his journey from Babylon on the first day of the first month, and he arrived in Jerusalem on the first day of the fifth month, for the good hand of his God was on him.	9 for on the first day of the first month he began to go up from Babylonia, and on the first day of the fifth month he came to Jerusalem, for the good hand of his God was upon him.	
10 For Ezra had devoted himself to the study and observance of the Law of the LORD, and to teaching its decrees and laws in Israel.	10 For Ezra had set his heart to study the law of the LORD, and to do it, and to teach his statutes and ordinances in Israel.	10 Ezra had devoted his life to studying the Law of the LORD, to practicing it, and to teaching all its laws and regulations to the people of Israel.

KJV	NKJV	TLB
8:22 For I was ashamed to require of the king a band of soldiers and horsemen to help us against the enemy in the way: because we had spoken unto the king, saying, The hand of our God *is* upon all them for good that seek him; but his power and his wrath *is* against all them that forsake him.	**8:22** For I was ashamed to request of the king an escort of soldiers and horsemen to help us against the enemy on the road, because we had spoken to the king, saying, "The hand of our God *is* upon all those for good who seek Him, but His power and His wrath *are* against all those who forsake Him."	**8:22** For I was ashamed to ask the king for soldiers and cavalry to accompany us and protect us from the enemies along the way. After all, we had told the king that our God would protect all those who worshiped him, and that disaster could come only to those who had forsaken him!
10:1 Now when Ezra had prayed, and when he had confessed, weeping and casting himself down before the house of God, there assembled unto him out of Israel a very great congregation of men and women and children: for the people wept very sore.	**10:1** Now while Ezra was praying, and while he was confessing, weeping, and bowing down before the house of God, a very large congregation of men, women, and children assembled to him from Israel; for the people wept very bitterly.	**10:1** As I lay on the ground in front of the Temple, weeping and praying and making this confession, a large crowd of men, women, and children gathered around and cried with me.
2 And Shechaniah the son of Jehiel, *one* of the sons of Elam, answered and said unto Ezra, We have trespassed against our God, and have taken strange wives of the people of the land: yet now there is hope in Israel concerning this thing.	**2** And Shechaniah the son of Jehiel, *one* of the sons of Elam, spoke up and said to Ezra, "We have trespassed against our God, and have taken pagan wives from the peoples of the land; yet now there is hope in Israel in spite of this.	**2** Then Shecaniah (the son of Jehiel of the clan of Elam) said to me, "We acknowledge our sin against our God, for we have married these heathen women. But there is hope for Israel in spite of this.
3 Now therefore let us make a covenant with our God to put away all the wives, and such as are born of them, according to the counsel of my lord, and of those that tremble at the commandment of our God; and let it be done according to the law.	**3** "Now therefore, let us make a covenant with our God to put away all these wives and those who have been born to them, according to the counsel of my master and of those who tremble at the commandment of our God; and let it be done according to the law.	**3** For we agree before our God to divorce our heathen wives and to send them away with our children; we will follow your commands, and the commands of the others who fear our God. We will obey the laws of God.
4 Arise; for *this* matter *belongeth* unto thee: we also *will be* with thee: be of good courage, and do *it*.	**4** "Arise, for *this* matter *is* your *responsibility*. We also *will be* with you. Be of good courage, and do *it*."	**4** Take courage and tell us how to proceed in setting things straight, and we will fully cooperate."
5 Then arose Ezra, and made the chief priests, the Levites, and all Israel, to swear that they should do according to this word. And they sware.	**5** Then Ezra arose, and made the leaders of the priests, the Levites, and all Israel swear an oath that they would do according to this word. So they swore an oath.	**5** So I stood up and demanded that the leaders of the priests and the Levites and all the people of Israel swear that they would do as Shecaniah had said; and they all agreed.

Nehemiah

KJV	NKJV	TLB
1:5 And said, I beseech thee, O Lᴏʀᴅ God of heaven, the great and terrible God, that keepeth covenant and mercy for them that love him and observe his commandments:	**1:5** And I said: "I pray, Lᴏʀᴅ God of heaven, O great and awesome God, *You* who keep Your covenant and mercy with those who love You and observe Your commandments,	**1:5** "O Lord God," I cried out; "O great and awesome God who keeps his promises and is so loving and kind to those who love and obey him! Hear my prayer!
6 Let thine ear now be attentive, and thine eyes open, that thou mayest hear the prayer of thy servant, which I pray before thee now, day and night, for the children of Israel thy servants, and confess the sins of the children of Israel, which we have sinned against thee: both I and my father's house have sinned.	**6** "please let Your ear be attentive and Your eyes open, that You may hear the prayer of Your servant which I pray before You now, day and night, for the children of Israel Your servants, and confess the sins of the children of Israel which we have sinned against You. Both my father's house and I have sinned.	**6** Listen carefully to what I say! Look down and see me praying night and day for your people Israel. I confess that we have sinned against you;
7 We have dealt very corruptly against thee, and have not kept the commandments, nor the statutes, nor the judgments, which thou commandest thy servant Moses.	**7** "We have acted very corruptly against You, and have not kept the commandments, the statutes, nor the ordinances which You commanded Your servant Moses.	**7** yes, I and my people have committed the horrible sin of not obeying the commandments you gave us through your servant Moses.
8 Remember, I beseech thee, the word that thou commandedst thy servant Moses, saying, *If ye transgress, I will scatter you abroad among the nations:*	**8** "Remember, I pray, the word that You commanded Your servant Moses, saying, '*If you are unfaithful, I will scatter you among the nations,*	**8** Oh, please remember what you told Moses! You said, "'*If you sin, I will scatter you among the nations;*
9 But *if* ye turn unto me, and keep my commandments, and do them; though there were of you cast out unto the uttermost part of heaven, *yet* will I gather them from thence, and will bring them unto the place that I have chosen to set my name there.	**9** 'but *if* you return to Me, and keep My commandments and do them, though some of you were cast out to the farthest part of the heavens, *yet* I will gather them from there, and bring them to the place which I have chosen as a dwelling for My name.'	**9** *but if you return to me and obey my laws, even though you are exiled to the farthest corners of the universe, I will bring you back to Jerusalem. For Jerusalem is the place in which I have chosen to live.'*
10 Now these *are* thy servants and thy people, whom thou hast redeemed by thy great power, and by thy strong hand.	**10** "Now these *are* Your servants and Your people, whom You have redeemed by Your great power, and by Your strong hand.	**10** "We are your servants, the people you rescued by your great power.

NIV	RSV	TEV
8:22 I was ashamed to ask the king for soldiers and horsemen to protect us from enemies on the road, because we had told the king, "The good hand of our God is on everyone who looks to him, but his great anger is against all who forsake him."	**8:22** For I was ashamed to ask the king for a band of soldiers and horsemen to protect us against the enemy on our way; since we had told the king, "The hand of our God is for good upon all that seek him, and the power of his wrath is against all that forsake him."	**8:22** I would have been ashamed to ask the emperor for a troop of cavalry to guard us from any enemies during our journey, because I had told him that our God blesses everyone who trusts him, but that he is displeased with and punishes anyone who turns away from him.
10:1 While Ezra was praying and confessing, weeping and throwing himself down before the house of God, a large crowd of Israelites—men, women and children—gathered around him. They too wept bitterly.	**10:1** While Ezra prayed and made confession, weeping and casting himself down before the house of God, a very great assembly of men, women, and children, gathered to him out of Israel; for the people wept bitterly.	**10:1** While Ezra was bowing in prayer in front of the Temple, weeping and confessing these sins, a large group of Israelites—men, women, and children—gathered around him, weeping bitterly.
2 Then Shecaniah son of Jehiel, one of the descendants of Elam, said to Ezra, "We have been unfaithful to our God by marrying foreign women from the peoples around us. But in spite of this, there is still hope for Israel.	**2** And Shecaniah the son of Jehiel, of the sons of Elam, addressed Ezra: "We have broken faith with our God and have married foreign women from the peoples of the land, but even now there is hope for Israel in spite of this.	**2** Then Shecaniah son of Jehiel, of the clan of Elam, said to Ezra, "We have broken faith with God by marrying foreign women, but even so there is still hope for Israel.
3 Now let us make a covenant before our God to send away all these women and their children, in accordance with the counsel of my lord and of those who fear the commands of our God. Let it be done according to the Law.	**3** Therefore let us make a covenant with our God to put away all these wives and their children, according to the counsel of my lord and of those who tremble at the commandment of our God; and let it be done according to the law.	**3** Now we must make a solemn promise to our God that we will send these women and their children away. We will do what you and the others who honor God's commands advise us to do. We will do what God's Law demands.
4 Rise up; this matter is in your hands. We will support you, so take courage and do it."	**4** Arise, for it is your task, and we are with you; be strong and do it."	**4** It is your responsibility to act. We are behind you, so go ahead and get it done."
5 So Ezra rose up and put the leading priests and Levites and all Israel under oath to do what had been suggested. And they took the oath.	**5** Then Ezra arose and made the leading priests and Levites and all Israel take oath that they would do as had been said. So they took the oath.	**5** So Ezra began by making the leaders of the priests, of the Levites, and of the rest of the people take an oath that they would do what Shecaniah had proposed.

Nehemiah

NIV	RSV	TEV
1:5 Then I said: "O LORD, God of heaven, the great and awesome God, who keeps his covenant of love with those who love him and obey his commands,	**1:5** And I said, "O LORD God of heaven, the great and terrible God who keeps covenant and steadfast love with those who love him and keep his commandments;	**1:5** "LORD God of Heaven! You are great, and we stand in fear of you. You faithfully keep your covenant with those who love you and do what you command.
6 let your ear be attentive and your eyes open to hear the prayer your servant is praying before you day and night for your servants, the people of Israel. I confess the sins we Israelites, including myself and my father's house, have committed against you.	**6** let thy ear be attentive, and thy eyes open, to hear the prayer of thy servant which I now pray before thee day and night for the people of Israel thy servants, confessing the sins of the people of Israel, which we have sinned against thee. Yea, I and my father's house have sinned.	**6** Look at me, LORD, and hear my prayer, as I pray day and night for your servants, the people of Israel. I confess that we, the people of Israel, have sinned. My ancestors and I have sinned.
7 We have acted very wickedly toward you. We have not obeyed the commands, decrees and laws you gave your servant Moses.	**7** We have acted very corruptly against thee, and have not kept the commandments, the statutes, and the ordinances which thou didst command thy servant Moses.	**7** We have acted wickedly against you and have not done what you commanded. We have not kept the laws which you gave us through Moses, your servant.
8 "Remember the instruction you gave your servant Moses, saying, 'If you are unfaithful, I will scatter you among the nations,	**8** Remember the word which thou didst command thy servant Moses, saying, 'If you are unfaithful, I will scatter you among the peoples;	**8** Remember now what you told Moses: 'If you people of Israel are unfaithful to me, I will scatter you among the other nations.
9 but if you return to me and obey my commands, then even if your exiled people are at the farthest horizon, I will gather them from there and bring them to the place I have chosen as a dwelling for my Name.'	**9** but if you return to me and keep my commandments and do them, though your dispersed be under the farthest skies, I will gather them thence and bring them to the place which I have chosen, to make my name dwell there.'	**9** But then if you turn back to me and do what I have commanded you, I will bring you back to the place where I have chosen to be worshiped, even though you are scattered to the ends of the earth.'
10 "They are your servants and your people, whom you redeemed by your great strength and your mighty hand.	**10** They are thy servants and thy people, whom thou hast redeemed by thy great power and by thy strong hand.	**10** "Lord, these are your servants, your own people. You rescued them by your great power and strength.

KJV	NKJV	TLB
11 O Lord, I beseech thee, let now thine ear be attentive to the prayer of thy servant, and to the prayer of thy servants, who desire to fear thy name: and prosper, I pray thee, thy servant this day, and grant him mercy in the sight of this man. For I was the king's cupbearer.	11 "O Lord, I pray, please let Your ear be attentive to the prayer of Your servant, and to the prayer of Your servants who desire to fear Your name; and let Your servant prosper this day, I pray, and grant him mercy in the sight of this man." For I was the king's cupbearer.	11 O Lord, please hear my prayer! Heed the prayers of those of us who delight to honor you. Please help me now as I go in and ask the king for a great favor—put it into his heart to be kind to me." (I was the king's cupbearer.)
2:2 Wherefore the king said unto me, Why *is* thy countenance sad, seeing thou *art* not sick? this *is* nothing *else* but sorrow of heart. Then I was very sore afraid.	2:2 Therefore the king said to me, "Why *is* your face sad, since you *are* not sick? This *is* nothing but sorrow of heart." Then I became dreadfully afraid,	2:2 he asked me, "Why so sad? You aren't sick, are you? You look like a man with deep troubles." (For until then I had always been cheerful when I was with him.) I was badly frightened,
3 And said unto the king, Let the king live for ever: why should not my countenance be sad, when the city, the place of my fathers' sepulchres, *lieth* waste, and the gates thereof are consumed with fire?	3 and said to the king, "May the king live forever! Why should my face not be sad, when the city, the place of my fathers' tombs, *lies* waste, and its gates are burned with fire?"	3 but I replied, "Sir, why shouldn't I be sad? For the city where my ancestors are buried is in ruins, and the gates have been burned down."
4 Then the king said unto me, For what dost thou make request? So I prayed to the God of heaven.	4 Then the king said to me, "What do you request?" So I prayed to the God of heaven.	4 "Well, what should be done?" the king asked. With a quick prayer to the God of heaven,
5 And I said unto the king, If it please the king, and if thy servant have found favour in thy sight, that thou wouldest send me unto Judah, unto the city of my fathers' sepulchres, that I may build it.	5 And I said to the king, "If it pleases the king, and if your servant has found favor in your sight, I ask that you send me to Judah, to the city of my fathers' tombs, that I may rebuild it."	5 I replied, "If it please Your Majesty and if you look upon me with your royal favor, send me to Judah to rebuild the city of my fathers!"
6 And the king said unto me, (the queen also sitting by him,) For how long shall thy journey be? and when wilt thou return? So it pleased the king to send me; and I set him a time.	6 So the king said to me (the queen also sitting beside him), "How long will your journey be? And when will you return?" So it pleased the king to send me; and I set him a time.	6 The king replied, with the queen sitting beside him, "How long will you be gone? When will you return?" So it was agreed! And I set a time for my departure!
4:3 Now Tobiah the Ammonite *was* by him, and he said, Even that which they build, if a fox go up, he shall even break down their stone wall.	4:3 Now Tobiah the Ammonite *was* beside him, and he said, "Whatever they build, if even a fox goes up *on it,* he will break down their stone wall."	4:3 Tobiah, who was standing beside him, remarked, "If even a fox walked along the top of their wall, it would collapse!"
4 Hear, O our God; for we are despised: and turn their reproach upon their own head, and give them for a prey in the land of captivity:	4 Hear, O our God, for we are despised; turn their reproach on their own heads, and give them as plunder to a land of captivity!	4 Then I prayed, "Hear us, O Lord God, for we are being mocked. May their scoffing fall back upon their own heads, and may they themselves become captives in a foreign land!
5 And cover not their iniquity, and let not their sin be blotted out from before thee: for they have provoked *thee* to anger before the builders.	5 Do not cover their iniquity, and do not let their sin be blotted out from before You; for they have provoked *You* to anger before the builders.	5 Do not ignore their sin. Do not blot it out, for they have despised you in despising us who are building your wall."
6 So built we the wall; and all the wall was joined together unto the half thereof: for the people had a mind to work.	6 So we built the wall, and the entire wall was joined together up to half its *height,* for the people had a mind to work.	6 At last the wall was completed to half its original height around the entire city—for the workers worked hard.
21 So we laboured in the work: and half of them held the spears from the rising of the morning till the stars appeared.	21 So we labored in the work, and half of the men held the spears from daybreak until the stars appeared.	21 We worked early and late, from sunrise to sunset; and half the men were always on guard.
22 Likewise at the same time said I unto the people, Let every one with his servant lodge within Jerusalem, that in the night they may be a guard to us, and labour on the day.	22 At the same time I also said to the people, "Let each man and his servant stay at night in Jerusalem, that they may be our guard by night and a working party by day."	22 I told everyone living outside the walls to move into Jerusalem so that their servants could go on guard duty as well as work during the day.
23 So neither I, nor my brethren, nor my servants, nor the men of the guard which followed me, none of us put off our clothes, *saving that* every one put them off for washing.	23 So neither I, my brethren, my servants, nor the men of the guard who followed me took off our clothes, *except* that everyone took them off for washing.	23 During this period none of us—I, nor my brothers, nor the servants, nor the guards who were with me—ever took off our clothes. And we carried our weapons with us at all times.
6:2 That Sanballat and Geshem sent unto me, saying, Come, let us meet together in *some one of* the villages in the plain of Ono. But they thought to do me mischief.	6:2 that Sanballat and Geshem sent to me, saying, "Come, let us meet together in *one of the* villages in the plain of Ono." But they thought to do me harm.	6:2 they sent me a message asking me to meet them in one of the villages in the Plain of Ono. But I realized they were plotting to kill me,
3 And I sent messengers unto them, saying, I *am* doing a great work, so that I cannot come down: why should the work cease, whilst I leave it, and come down to you?	3 So I sent messengers to them, saying, "I *am* doing a great work, so that I cannot come down. Why should the work cease while I leave it and go down to you?"	3 so I replied by sending back this message to them: "I am doing a great work! Why should I stop to come and visit with you?"

NIV	RSV	TEV
11 O Lord, let your ear be attentive to the prayer of this your servant and to the prayer of your servants who delight in revering your name. Give your servant success today by granting him favor in the presence of this man." I was cupbearer to the king.	11 O LORD, let thy ear be attentive to the prayer of thy servant, and to the prayer of thy servants who delight to fear thy name; and give success to thy servant today, and grant him mercy in the sight of this man." Now I was cupbearer to the king.	11 Listen now to my prayer and to the prayers of all your other servants who want to honor you. Give me success today and make the emperor merciful to me." In those days I was the emperor's wine steward.
2:2 so the king asked me, "Why does your face look so sad when you are not ill? This can be nothing but sadness of heart." I was very much afraid,	2:2 And the king said to me, "Why is your face sad, seeing you are not sick? This is nothing else but sadness of the heart." Then I was very much afraid.	2:2 so he asked, "Why are you looking so sad? You aren't sick, so it must be that you're unhappy." I was startled
3 but I said to the king, "May the king live forever! Why should my face not look sad when the city where my fathers are buried lies in ruins, and its gates have been destroyed by fire?"	3 I said to the king, "Let the king live for ever! Why should not my face be sad, when the city, the place of my fathers' sepulchres, lies waste, and its gates have been destroyed by fire?"	3 and answered, "May Your Majesty live forever! How can I keep from looking sad when the city where my ancestors are buried is in ruins and its gates have been destroyed by fire?"
4 The king said to me, "What is it you want?" Then I prayed to the God of heaven,	4 Then the king said to me, "For what do you make request?" So I prayed to the God of heaven.	4 The emperor asked, "What is it that you want?" I prayed to the God of Heaven,
5 and I answered the king, "If it pleases the king and if your servant has found favor in his sight, let him send me to the city in Judah where my fathers are buried so that I can rebuild it."	5 And I said to the king, "If it pleases the king, and if your servant has found favor in your sight, that you send me to Judah, to the city of my fathers' sepulchres, that I may rebuild it."	5 and then I said to the emperor, "If Your Majesty is pleased with me and is willing to grant my request, let me go to the land of Judah, to the city where my ancestors are buried, so that I can rebuild the city."
6 Then the king, with the queen sitting beside him, asked me, "How long will your journey take, and when will you get back?" It pleased the king to send me; so I set a time.	6 And the king said to me (the queen sitting beside him), "How long will you be gone, and when will you return?" So it pleased the king to send me; and I set him a time.	6 The emperor, with the empress sitting at his side, approved my request. He asked me how long I would be gone and when I would return, and I told him.
4:3 Tobiah the Ammonite, who was at his side, said, "What they are building—if even a fox climbed up on it, he would break down their wall of stones!"	4:3 Tobiah the Ammonite was by him, and he said, "Yes, what they are building—if a fox goes up on it he will break down their stone wall!"	4:3 Tobiah was standing there beside him, and he added, "What kind of wall could they ever build? Even a fox could knock it down!"
4 Hear us, O our God, for we are despised. Turn their insults back on their own heads. Give them over as plunder in a land of captivity.	4 Hear, O our God, for we are despised; turn back their taunt upon their own heads, and give them up to be plundered in a land where they are captives.	4 I prayed, "Hear how they make fun of us, O God! Let their ridicule fall on their own heads. Let them be robbed of everything they have, and let them be taken as prisoners to a foreign land.
5 Do not cover up their guilt or blot out their sins from your sight, for they have thrown insults in the face of the builders.	5 Do not cover their guilt, and let not their sin be blotted out from thy sight; for they have provoked thee to anger before the builders.	5 Don't forgive the evil they do and don't forget their sins, for they have insulted us who are building."
6 So we rebuilt the wall till all of it reached half its height, for the people worked with all their heart.	6 So we built the wall; and all the wall was joined together to half its height. For the people had a mind to work.	6 So we went on rebuilding the wall, and soon it was half its full height, because the people were eager to work.
21 So we continued the work with half the men holding spears, from the first light of dawn till the stars came out.	21 So we labored at the work, and half of them held the spears from the break of dawn till the stars came out.	21 So every day, from dawn until the stars came out at night, half of us worked on the wall, while the other half stood guard with spears.
22 At that time I also said to the people, "Have every man and his helper stay inside Jerusalem at night, so they can serve us as guards by night and workmen by day."	22 I also said to the people at that time, "Let every man and his servant pass the night within Jerusalem, that they may be a guard for us by night and may labor by day."	22 During this time I told the men in charge that they and all their helpers had to stay in Jerusalem at night, so that we could guard the city at night as well as work in the daytime.
23 Neither I nor my brothers nor my men nor the guards with me took off our clothes; each had his weapon, even when he went for water.	23 So neither I nor my brethren nor my servants nor the men of the guard who followed me, none of us took off our clothes; each kept his weapon in his hand.	23 I didn't take off my clothes even at night, neither did any of my companions nor my servants nor my bodyguards. And we all kept our weapons at hand.
6:2 Sanballat and Geshem sent me this message: "Come, let us meet together in one of the villages on the plain of Ono." But they were scheming to harm me;	6:2 Sanballat and Geshem sent to me, saying, "Come and let us meet together in one of the villages in the plain of Ono." But they intended to do me harm.	6:2 So Sanballat and Geshem sent me a message, suggesting that I meet with them in one of the villages in the Plain of Ono. This was a trick of theirs to try to harm me.
3 so I sent messengers to them with this reply: "I am carrying on a great project and cannot go down. Why should the work stop while I leave it and go down to you?"	3 And I sent messengers to them, saying, "I am doing a great work and I cannot come down. Why should the work stop while I leave it and come down to you?"	3 I sent messengers to say to them, "I am doing important work and can't go down there. I am not going to let the work stop just to go and see you."

KJV	NKJV	TLB
10 Afterward I came unto the house of Shemaiah the son of Delaiah the son of Mehetabeel, who *was* shut up; and he said, Let us meet together in the house of God, within the temple, and let us shut the doors of the temple: for they will come to slay thee; yea, in the night will they come to slay thee.	10 Afterward I came to the house of Shemaiah the son of Delaiah, the son of Mehetabeel, who *was* a secret informer; and he said, "Let us meet together in the house of God, within the temple, and let us close the doors of the temple, for they are coming to kill you; indeed, at night they will come to kill you."	10 A few days later I went to visit Shemaiah (son of Delaiah, who was the son of Mehetabel), for he said he was receiving a message from God. "Let us hide in the Temple and bolt the door," he exclaimed, "for they are coming tonight to kill you."
11 And I said, Should such a man as I flee? and who *is there*, that, *being* as I *am*, would go into the temple to save his life? I will not go in.	11 And I said, "Should such a man as I flee? And who *is there* such as I who would go into the temple to save his life? I will not go in!"	11 But I replied, "Should I, the governor, run away from danger? And if I go into the Temple, not being a priest, I would forfeit my life. No, I won't do it!"
15 So the wall was finished in the twenty and fifth *day* of *the month* Elul, in fifty and two days.	15 So the wall was finished on the twenty-fifth *day* of *the month* of Elul, in fifty-two days.	15 The wall was finally finished in early September—just fifty-two days after we had begun!
16 And it came to pass, that when all our enemies heard *thereof*, and all the heathen that *were* about us saw *these things*, they were much cast down in their own eyes: for they perceived that this work was wrought of our God.	16 And it happened, when all our enemies heard *of it*, and all the nations around us saw *these things*, that they were very disheartened in their own eyes; for they perceived that this work was done by our God.	16 When our enemies and the surrounding nations heard about it, they were frightened and humiliated, and they realized that the work had been done with the help of our God.
8:2 And Ezra the priest brought the law before the congregation both of men and women, and all that could hear with understanding, upon the first day of the seventh month.	8:2 So Ezra the priest brought the Law before the congregation, of men and women and all who *could* hear with understanding, on the first day of the seventh month.	8:2 So Ezra the priest brought out to them the scroll of Moses' laws.
3 And he read therein before the street that *was* before the water gate from the morning until midday, before the men and the women, and those that could understand; and the ears of all the people *were attentive* unto the book of the law.	3 Then he read from it in the open square that *was* in front of the Water Gate from morning until midday, before the men and women and those who could understand; and the ears of all the people *were attentive* to the Book of the Law.	3 He faced the square in front of the Water Gate, and read from early morning until noon. Everyone stood up as he opened the scroll. And all who were old enough to understand paid close attention.
8 So they read in the book in the law of God distinctly, and gave the sense, and caused *them* to understand the reading.	8 So they read distinctly from the book, in the Law of God; and they gave the sense, and helped *them* to understand the reading.	8 and explained the meaning of the passage that was being read.
9:3 And they stood up in their place, and read in the book of the law of the Lord their God one fourth part of the day; and *another* fourth part they confessed, and worshipped the Lord their God.	9:3 And they stood up in their place and read from the Book of the Law of the Lord their God *for* one-fourth of the day; and *for another* fourth they confessed and worshiped the Lord their God.	9:3 The laws of God were read aloud to them for two or three hours, and for several more hours they took turns confessing their own sins and those of their ancestors. And everyone worshiped the Lord their God.

Esther

2:2 Then said the king's servants that ministered unto him, Let there be fair young virgins sought for the king:	2:2 Then the king's servants who attended him said: "Let beautiful young virgins be sought for the king;	2:2 So his aides suggested, "Let us go and find the most beautiful girls in the empire and bring them to the king for his pleasure.
4 And let the maiden which pleaseth the king be queen instead of Vashti. And the thing pleased the king; and he did so.	4 "Then let the young woman who pleases the king be queen instead of Vashti." This thing pleased the king, and he did so.	4 and after that, the girl who pleases you most shall be the queen instead of Vashti." This suggestion naturally pleased the king very much, and he put the plan into immediate effect.
5 *Now* in Shushan the palace there was a certain Jew, whose name *was* Mordecai, the son of Jair, the son of Shimei, the son of Kish, a Benjamite:	5 *Now* in Shushan the citadel there was a certain Jew whose name *was* Mordecai the son of Jair, the son of Shimei, the son of Kish, a Benjamite.	5 Now there was a certain Jew at the palace named Mordecai (son of Jair, son of Shime-i, son of Kish, a Benjaminite).
6 Who had been carried away from Jerusalem with the captivity which had been carried away with Jeconiah king of Judah, whom Nebuchadnezzar the king of Babylon had carried away.	6 Kish had been carried away from Jerusalem with the captives who had been captured with Jeconiah king of Judah, whom Nebuchadnezzar the king of Babylon had carried away.	6 He had been captured when Jerusalem was destroyed by King Nebuchadnezzar, and had been exiled to Babylon along with King Jeconiah of Judah and many others.
7 And he brought up Hadassah, that *is*, Esther, his uncle's daughter: for she had neither father nor mother, and the maid *was* fair and beautiful; whom Mordecai, when her father and mother were dead, took for his own daughter.	7 And Mordecai had brought up Hadassah, that *is*, Esther, his uncle's daughter, for she had neither father nor mother. The young woman *was* lovely and beautiful. When her father and mother died, Mordecai took her as his own daughter.	7 This man had a beautiful and lovely young cousin, Hadassah (also called Esther), whose father and mother were dead, and whom he had adopted into his family and raised as his own daughter.
10 Esther had not shewed her people nor her kindred: for Mordecai had charged her that she should not shew *it*.	10 Esther had not revealed her people or kindred, for Mordecai had charged her not to reveal *it*.	10 Esther hadn't told anyone that she was a Jewess, for Mordecai had said not to.

NIV	RSV	TEV
10 One day I went to the house of Shemaiah son of Delaiah, the son of Mehetabel, who was shut in at his home. He said, "Let us meet in the house of God, inside the temple, and let us close the temple doors, because men are coming to kill you—by night they are coming to kill you."	10 Now when I went into the house of Shemaiah the son of Delaiah, son of Mehetabel, who was shut up, he said, "Let us meet together in the house of God, within the temple, and let us close the doors of the temple; for they are coming to kill you, at night they are coming to kill you."	10 About this time I went to visit Shemaiah, the son of Delaiah and grandson of Mehetabel, who was unable to leave his house. He said to me, "You and I must go and hide together in the Holy Place of the Temple and lock the doors, because they are coming to kill you. Any night now they will come to kill you."
11 But I said, "Should a man like me run away? Or should one like me go into the temple to save his life? I will not go!"	11 But I said, "Should such a man as I flee? And what man such as I could go into the temple and live? I will not go in."	11 I answered, "I'm not the kind of man that runs and and hides. Do you think I would try to save my life by hiding in the Temple? I won't do it."
15 So the wall was completed on the twenty-fifth of Elul, in fifty-two days.	15 So the wall was finished on the twenty-fifth day of the month Elul, in fifty-two days.	15 After fifty-two days of work the entire wall was finished on the twenty-fifth day of the month of Elul.
16 When all our enemies heard about this and all the surrounding nations saw it, our enemies lost their self-confidence, because they realized that this work had been done with the help of our God.	16 And when all our enemies heard of it, all the nations round about us were afraid and fell greatly in their own esteem; for they perceived that this work had been accomplished with the help of our God.	16 When our enemies in the surrounding nations heard this, they realized that they had lost face, since everyone knew that the work had been done with God's help.
8:2 So on the first day of the seventh month Ezra the priest brought the Law before the assembly, which was made up of men and women and all who were able to understand.	8:2 And Ezra the priest brought the law before the assembly, both men and women and all who could hear with understanding, on the first day of the seventh month.	8:2 So Ezra brought it to the place where the people had gathered—men, women, and the children who were old enough to understand.
3 He read it aloud from daybreak till noon as he faced the square before the Water Gate in the presence of the men, women and others who could understand. And all the people listened attentively to the Book of the Law.	3 And he read from it facing the square before the Water Gate from early morning until midday, in the presence of the men and the women and those who could understand; and the ears of all the people were attentive to the book of the law.	3 There in the square by the gate he read the Law to them from dawn until noon, and they all listened attentively.
8 They read from the Book of the Law of God, making it clear and giving the meaning so that the people could understand what was being read.	8 And they read from the book, from the law of God, clearly; and they gave the sense, so that the people understood the reading.	8 They gave an oral translation of God's Law and explained it so that the people could understand it.
9:3 They stood where they were and read from the Book of the Law of the LORD their God for a fourth of the day, and spent another fourth in confession and in worshiping the LORD their God.	9:3 And they stood up in their place and read from the book of the law of the LORD their God for a fourth of the day; for another fourth of it they made confession and worshiped the LORD their God.	9:3 For about three hours the Law of the LORD their God was read to them, and for the next three hours they confessed their sins and worshiped the LORD their God.

Esther

2:2 Then the king's personal attendants proposed, "Let a search be made for beautiful young virgins for the king.	2:2 Then the king's servants who attended him said, "Let beautiful young virgins be sought out for the king.	2:2 So some of the king's advisers who were close to him suggested, "Why don't you make a search to find some beautiful young virgins?
4 Then let the girl who pleases the king be queen instead of Vashti." This advice appealed to the king, and he followed it.	4 And let the maiden who pleases the king be queen instead of Vashti." This pleased the king, and he did so.	4 Then take the girl you like best and make her queen in Vashti's place." The king thought this was good advice, so he followed it.
5 Now there was in the citadel of Susa a Jew of the tribe of Benjamin, named Mordecai son of Jair, the son of Shimei, the son of Kish,	5 Now there was a Jew in Susa the capital whose name was Mordecai, the son of Jair, son of Shimei, son of Kish, a Benjaminite,	5 There in Susa lived a Jew named Mordecai son of Jair; he was from the tribe of Benjamin and was a descendant of Kish and Shimei.
6 who had been carried into exile from Jerusalem by Nebuchadnezzar king of Babylon, among those taken captive with Jehoiachin king of Judah.	6 who had been carried away from Jerusalem among the captives carried away with Jeconiah king of Judah, whom Nebuchadnezzar king of Babylon had carried away.	6 When King Nebuchadnezzar of Babylon took King Jehoiachin of Judah into exile from Jerusalem, along with a group of captives, Mordecai was among them.
7 Mordecai had a cousin named Hadassah, whom he had brought up because she had neither father nor mother. This girl, who was also known as Esther, was lovely in form and features, and Mordecai had taken her as his own daughter when her father and mother died.	7 He had brought up Hadassah, that is Esther, the daughter of his uncle, for she had neither father nor mother; the maiden was beautiful and lovely, and when her father and her mother died, Mordecai adopted her as his own daughter.	7 He had a cousin, Esther, whose Hebrew name was Hadassah; she was a beautiful girl, and had a good figure. At the death of her parents, Mordecai had adopted her and brought her up as his own daughter.
10 Esther had not revealed her nationality and family background, because Mordecai had forbidden her to do so.	10 Esther had not made known her people or kindred, for Mordecai had charged her not to make it known.	10 Now, on the advice of Mordecai, Esther had kept it secret that she was Jewish.

KJV	NKJV	TLB
11 And Mordecai walked every day before the court of the women's house, to know how Esther did, and what should become of her.	11 And every day Mordecai paced in front of the court of the women's quarters, to learn of Esther's welfare and what was happening to her.	11 He came daily to the court of the harem to ask about Esther and to find out what was happening to her.
15 Now when the turn of Esther, the daughter of Abihail the uncle of Mordecai, who had taken her for his daughter, was come to go in unto the king, she required nothing but what Hegai the king's chamberlain, the keeper of the women, appointed. And Esther obtained favour in the sight of all them that looked upon her.	15 Now when the turn came for Esther the daughter of Abihail the uncle of Mordecai, who had taken her as his daughter, to go in to the king, she requested nothing but what Hegai the king's eunuch, the custodian of the women, advised. And Esther obtained favor in the sight of all who saw her.	15 When it was Esther's turn to go to the king, she accepted the advice of Hegai, the eunuch in charge of the harem, dressing according to his instructions. And all the other girls exclaimed with delight when they saw her.
17 And the king loved Esther above all the women, and she obtained grace and favour in his sight more than all the virgins; so that he set the royal crown upon her head, and made her queen instead of Vashti.	17 The king loved Esther more than all the other women, and she obtained grace and favor in his sight more than all the virgins; so he set the royal crown upon her head and made her queen instead of Vashti.	17 Well, the king loved Esther more than any of the other girls. He was so delighted with her that he set the royal crown on her head and declared her queen instead of Vashti.
3:8 And Haman said unto king Ahasuerus, There is a certain people scattered abroad and dispersed among the people in all the provinces of thy kingdom; and their laws are diverse from all people; neither keep they the king's laws: therefore it is not for the king's profit to suffer them.	3:8 Then Haman said to King Ahasuerus, "There is a certain people scattered and dispersed among the people in all the provinces of your kingdom; their laws are different from all other people's, and they do not keep the king's laws. Therefore it is not fitting for the king to let them remain.	3:8 Haman now approached the king about the matter. "There is a certain race of people scattered through all the provinces of your kingdom," he began, "and their laws are different from those of any other nation, and they refuse to obey the king's laws; therefore, it is not in the king's interest to let them live.
9 If it please the king, let it be written that they may be destroyed: and I will pay ten thousand talents of silver to the hands of those that have the charge of the business, to bring it into the king's treasuries.	9 "If it pleases the king, let a decree be written that they be destroyed, and I will pay ten thousand talents of silver into the hands of those who do the work, to bring it into the king's treasuries."	9 If it please the king, issue a decree that they be destroyed, and I will pay $20,000,000 into the royal treasury for the expenses involved in this purge."
4:13 Then Mordecai commanded to answer Esther, Think not with thyself that thou shalt escape in the king's house, more than all the Jews.	4:13 Then Mordecai told them to answer Esther: "Do not think in your heart that you will escape in the king's palace any more than all the other Jews.	4:13 This was Mordecai's reply to Esther: "Do you think you will escape there in the palace, when all other Jews are killed?
14 For if thou altogether holdest thy peace at this time, then shall there enlargement and deliverance arise to the Jews from another place; but thou and thy father's house shall be destroyed: and who knoweth whether thou art come to the kingdom for such a time as this?	14 "For if you remain completely silent at this time, relief and deliverance will arise for the Jews from another place, but you and your father's house will perish. Yet who knows whether you have come to the kingdom for such a time as this?"	14 If you keep quiet at a time like this, God will deliver the Jews from some other source, but you and your relatives will die; what's more, who can say but that God has brought you into the palace for just such a time as this?"
5:2 And it was so, when the king saw Esther the queen standing in the court, that she obtained favour in his sight: and the king held out to Esther the golden sceptre that was in his hand. So Esther drew near, and touched the top of the sceptre.	5:2 So it was, when the king saw Queen Esther standing in the court, that she found favor in his sight, and the king held out to Esther the golden scepter that was in his hand. Then Esther went near and touched the top of the scepter.	5:2 And when he saw Queen Esther standing there in the inner court, he welcomed her, holding out the golden scepter to her. So Esther approached and touched its tip.
3 Then said the king unto her, What wilt thou, queen Esther? and what is thy request? it shall be even given thee to the half of the kingdom.	3 And the king said to her, "What do you wish, Queen Esther? What is your request? It shall be given to you—up to half my kingdom!"	3 Then the king asked her, "What do you wish, Queen Esther? What is your request? I will give it to you, even if it is half the kingdom!"
4 And Esther answered, If it seem good unto the king, let the king and Haman come this day unto the banquet that I have prepared for him.	4 So Esther answered, "If it pleases the king, let the king and Haman come today to the banquet that I have prepared for him."	4 And Esther replied, "If it please Your Majesty, I want you and Haman to come to a banquet I have prepared for you today."
9 Then went Haman forth that day joyful and with a glad heart: but when Haman saw Mordecai in the king's gate, that he stood not up, nor moved for him, he was full of indignation against Mordecai.	9 So Haman went out that day joyful and with a glad heart; but when Haman saw Mordecai in the king's gate, and that he did not stand or tremble before him, he was filled with indignation against Mordecai.	9 What a happy man was Haman as he left the banquet! But when he saw Mordecai there at the gate, not standing up or trembling before him, he was furious.
7:3 Then Esther the queen answered and said, If I have found favour in thy sight, O king, and if it please the king, let my life be given me at my petition, and my people at my request:	7:3 Then Queen Esther answered and said, "If I have found favor in your sight, O king, and if it pleases the king, let my life be given me at my petition, and my people at my request.	7:3 And at last Queen Esther replied, "If I have won your favor, O king, and if it please Your Majesty, save my life and the lives of my people.
4 For we are sold, I and my people, to be destroyed, to be slain, and to perish. But if we had been sold for bondmen and bondwomen, I had held my tongue, although the enemy could not countervail the king's damage.	4 "For we have been sold, my people and I, to be destroyed, to be killed, and to be annihilated. Had we been sold as male and female slaves, I would have held my tongue, although the enemy could never compensate for the king's loss."	4 For I and my people have been sold to those who will destroy us. We are doomed to destruction and slaughter. If we were only to be sold as slaves, perhaps I could remain quiet, though even then there would be incalculable damage to the king that no amount of money could begin to cover."

NIV	RSV	TEV
11 Every day he walked back and forth near the courtyard of the harem to find out how Esther was and what was happening to her.	11 And every day Mordecai walked in front of the court of the harem, to learn how Esther was and how she fared.	11 Every day Mordecai would walk back and forth in front of the courtyard of the harem, in order to find out how she was getting along and what was going to happen to her.
15 When the turn came for Esther (the girl Mordecai had adopted, the daughter of his uncle Abihail) to go to the king, she asked for nothing other than what Hegai, the king's eunuch who was in charge of the harem, suggested. And Esther won the favor of everyone who saw her.	15 When the turn came for Esther the daughter of Abihail the uncle of Mordecai, who had adopted her as his own daughter, to go in to the king, she asked for nothing except what Hegai the king's eunuch, who had charge of the women, advised. Now Esther found favor in the eyes of all who saw her.	15 The time came for Esther to go to the king. Esther—the daughter of Abihail and the cousin of Mordecai, who had adopted her as his daughter; Esther—admired by everyone who saw her. When her turn came, she wore just what Hegai, the eunuch in charge of the harem, advised her to wear.
17 Now the king was attracted to Esther more than to any of the other women, and she won his favor and approval more than any of the other virgins. So he set a royal crown on her head and made her queen instead of Vashti.	17 the king loved Esther more than all the women, and she found grace and favor in his sight more than all the virgins, so that he set the royal crown on her head and made her queen instead of Vashti.	17 The king liked her more than any of the other girls, and more than any of the others she won his favor and affection. He placed the royal crown on her head and made her queen in place of Vashti.
3:8 Then Haman said to King Xerxes, "There is a certain people dispersed and scattered among the peoples in all the provinces of your kingdom who keep themselves separate. Their customs are different from those of all other people, and they do not obey the king's laws; it is not in the king's best interest to tolerate them.	3:8 Then Haman said to King Ahasuerus, "There is a certain people scattered abroad and dispersed among the peoples in all the provinces of your kingdom; their laws are different from those of every other people, and they do not keep the king's laws, so that it is not for the king's profit to tolerate them.	3:8 So Haman told the king, "There is a certain race of people scattered all over your empire and found in every province. They observe customs that are not like those of any other people. Moreover, they do not obey the laws of the empire, so it is not in your best interests to tolerate them.
9 If it pleases the king, let a decree be issued to destroy them, and I will put ten thousand talents of silver into the royal treasury for the men who carry out this business."	9 If it please the king, let it be decreed that they be destroyed, and I will pay ten thousand talents of silver into the hands of those who have charge of the king's business, that they may put it into the king's treasuries."	9 If it please Your Majesty, issue a decree that they are to be put to death. If you do, I guarantee that I will be able to put 375 tons of silver into the royal treasury for the administration of the empire."
4:13 he sent back this answer: "Do not think that because you are in the king's house you alone of all the Jews will escape.	4:13 Then Mordecai told them to return answer to Esther, "Think not that in the king's palace you will escape any more than all the other Jews.	4:13 he sent her this warning: "Don't imagine that you are safer than any other Jew just because you are in the royal palace.
14 For if you remain silent at this time, relief and deliverance for the Jews will arise from another place, but you and your father's family will perish. And who knows but that you have come to royal position for such a time as this?"	14 For if you keep silence at such a time as this, relief and deliverance will rise for the Jews from another quarter, but you and your father's house will perish. And who knows whether you have not come to the kingdom for such a time as this?"	14 If you keep quiet at a time like this, help will come from heaven to the Jews, and they will be saved, but you will die and your father's family will come to an end. Yet who knows—maybe it was for a time like this that you were made queen!"
5:2 When he saw Queen Esther standing in the court, he was pleased with her and held out to her the gold scepter that was in his hand. So Esther approached and touched the tip of the scepter.	5:2 and when the king saw Queen Esther standing in the court, she found favor in his sight and he held out to Esther the golden scepter that was in his hand. Then Esther approached and touched the top of the scepter.	5:2 When the king saw Queen Esther standing outside, she won his favor, and he held out to her the gold scepter. She then came up and touched the tip of it.
3 Then the king asked, "What is it, Queen Esther? What is your request? Even up to half the kingdom, it will be given you."	3 And the king said to her, "What is it, Queen Esther? What is your request? It shall be given you, even to the half of my kingdom."	3 "What is it, Queen Esther?" the king asked. "Tell me what you want, and you shall have it—even if it is half my empire"
4 "If it pleases the king," replied Esther, "let the king, together with Haman, come today to a banquet I have prepared for him."	4 And Esther said, "If it please the king, let the king and Haman come this day to a dinner that I have prepared for the king."	4 Esther replied, "If it please Your Majesty, I would like you and Haman to be my guests tonight at a banquet I am preparing for you."
9 Haman went out that day happy and in high spirits. But when he saw Mordecai at the king's gate and observed that he neither rose nor showed fear in his presence, he was filled with rage against Mordecai.	9 And Haman went out that day joyful and glad of heart. But when Haman saw Mordecai in the king's gate, that he neither rose nor trembled before him, he was filled with wrath against Mordecai.	9 When Haman left the banquet he was happy and in a good mood. But then he saw Mordecai at the entrance of the palace, and when Mordecai did not rise or show any sign of respect as he passed, Haman was furious with him.
7:3 Then Queen Esther answered, "If I have found favor with you, O king, and if it pleases your majesty, grant me my life—this is my petition. And spare my people—this is my request.	7:3 Then Queen Esther answered, "If I have found favor in your sight, O king, and if it please the king, let my life be given me at my petition, and my people at my request.	7:3 Queen Esther answered, "If it please Your Majesty to grant my humble request, my wish is that I may live and that my people may live.
4 For I and my people have been sold for destruction and slaughter and annihilation. If we had merely been sold as male and female slaves, I would have kept quiet, because no such distress would justify disturbing the king."	4 For we are sold, I and my people, to be destroyed, to be slain, and to be annihilated. If we had been sold merely as slaves, men and women, I would have held my peace; for our affliction is not to be compared with the loss to the king."	4 My people and I have been sold for slaughter. If it were nothing more serious than being sold into slavery, I would have kept quiet and not bothered you about it, but we are about to be destroyed—exterminated!"

KJV	NKJV	TLB
5 Then the king Ahasuerus answered and said unto Esther the queen, Who is he, and where is he, that durst presume in his heart to do so?	5 Then King Ahasuerus answered and said to Queen Esther, "Who is he, and where is he, who would dare presume in his heart to do such a thing?"	5 "What are you talking about?" King Ahasuerus demanded. "Who would dare touch you?"
6 And Esther said, The adversary and enemy *is* this wicked Haman. Then Haman was afraid before the king and the queen.	6 And Esther said, "The adversary and enemy *is* this wicked Haman!" So Haman was terrified before the king and queen.	6 Esther replied, "This wicked Haman is our enemy." Then Haman grew pale with fright before the king and queen.
10 So they hanged Haman on the gallows that he had prepared for Mordecai. Then was the king's wrath pacified.	10 So they hanged Haman on the gallows that he had prepared for Mordecai. Then the king's wrath subsided.	10 "Hang Haman on it," the king ordered. So they did, and the king's wrath was pacified.
8:1 On that day did the king Ahasuerus give the house of Haman the Jews' enemy unto Esther the queen. And Mordecai came before the king; for Esther had told what he *was* unto her.	**8:1** On that day King Ahasuerus gave Queen Esther the house of Haman, the enemy of the Jews. And Mordecai came before the king, for Esther had told how he *was related* to her.	**8:1** On that same day King Ahasuerus gave the estate of Haman, the Jews' enemy, to Queen Esther. Then Mordecai was brought before the king, for Esther had told the king that he was her cousin and foster father.
2 And the king took off his ring, which he had taken from Haman, and gave it unto Mordecai. And Esther set Mordecai over the house of Haman.	2 So the king took off his signet ring, which he had taken from Haman, and gave it to Mordecai; and Esther appointed Mordecai over the house of Haman.	2 The king took off his ring—which he had taken back from Haman—and gave it to Mordecai, [appointing him Prime Minister]; and Esther appointed Mordecai to be in charge of Haman's estate.
11 Wherein the king granted the Jews which *were* in every city to gather themselves together, and to stand for their life, to destroy, to slay, and to cause to perish, all the power of the people and province that would assault them, *both* little ones and women, and *to take* the spoil of them for a prey,	11 By these letters the king permitted the Jews who *were* in every city to gather together and protect their lives—to destroy, kill, and annihilate all the forces of any people or province that would assault them, *both* little children and women, and to plunder their possessions,	11 This decree gave the Jews everywhere permission to unite in the defense of their lives and their families, to destroy all the forces opposed to them, and to take their property.
17 And in every province, and in every city, whithersoever the king's commandment and his decree came, the Jews had joy and gladness, a feast and a good day. And many of the people of the land became Jews; for the fear of the Jews fell upon them.	17 And in every province and city, wherever the king's command and decree came, the Jews had joy and gladness, a feast and a holiday. Then many of the people of the land became Jews, because fear of the Jews fell upon them.	17 And in every city and province, as the king's decree arrived, the Jews were filled with joy and had a great celebration and declared a holiday. And many of the people of the land pretended to be Jews, for they feared what the Jews might do to them.
9:20 And Mordecai wrote these things, and sent letters unto all the Jews that *were* in all the provinces of the king Ahasuerus, *both* nigh and far,	**9:20** And Mordecai wrote these things and sent letters to all the Jews who *were* in all the provinces of King Ahasuerus, *both* near and far,	**9:20** Mordecai wrote a history of all these events, and sent letters to the Jews near and far, throughout all the king's provinces,
21 To stablish *this* among them, that they should keep the fourteenth day of the month Adar, and the fifteenth day of the same, yearly.	21 to establish among them that they should celebrate yearly the fourteenth and fifteenth days of the month of Adar.	21 encouraging them to declare an annual holiday on the last days of the month,
22 As the days wherein the Jews rested from their enemies, and the month which was turned unto them from sorrow to joy, and from mourning into a good day: that they should make them days of feasting and joy, and of sending portions one to another, and gifts to the poor.	22 as the days on which the Jews had rest from their enemies, as the month which was turned from sorrow to joy for them, and from mourning to a holiday; that they should make them days of feasting and joy, of sending presents to one another and gifts to the poor.	22 to celebrate with feasting, gladness, and the giving of gifts this historic day when the Jews were saved from their enemies, when their sorrow was turned to gladness and their mourning into happiness.
26 Wherefore they called these days Purim after the name of Pur. Therefore for all the words of this letter, and *of that* which they had seen concerning this matter, and which had come unto them,	26 So they called these days Purim, after the name Pur. Therefore, because of all the words of this letter, what they had seen concerning this matter, and what had happened to them,	26 That is why this celebration is called "Purim," because the word for "throwing dice" in Persian is "pur."

Job

KJV	NKJV	TLB
1:20 Then Job arose, and rent his mantle, and shaved his head, and fell down upon the ground, and worshipped.	**1:20** Then Job arose and tore his robe and shaved his head, and he fell to the ground and worshiped.	**1:20** Then Job stood up and tore his robe in grief and fell down upon the ground before God.
21 And said, Naked came I out of my mother's womb, and naked shall I return thither: the LORD gave, and the LORD hath taken away; blessed be the name of the LORD.	21 And he said: "Naked I came from my mother's womb, And naked shall I return there. The LORD gave, and the LORD has taken away; Blessed be the name of the LORD."	21 "I came naked from my mother's womb," he said, "and I shall have nothing when I die. The Lord gave me everything I had, and they were his to take away. Blessed be the name of the Lord."

NIV	RSV	TEV
5 King Xerxes asked Queen Esther, "Who is he? Where is the man who has dared to do such a thing?"	5 Then King Ahasuerus said to Queen Esther, "Who is he, and where is he, that would presume to do this?"	5 Then King Xerxes asked Queen Esther, "Who dares to do such a thing? Where is this man?"
6 Esther said, "The adversary and enemy is this vile Haman." Then Haman was terrified before the king and queen.	6 And Esther said, "A foe and enemy! This wicked Haman!" Then Haman was in terror before the king and the queen.	6 Esther answered, "Our enemy, our persecutor, is this evil man Haman!" Haman faced the king and queen with terror.
10 So they hanged Haman on the gallows he had prepared for Mordecai. Then the king's fury subsided.	10 And the king said, "Hang him on that." So they hanged Haman on the gallows which he had prepared for Mordecai. Then the anger of the king abated.	10 So Haman was hanged on the gallows that he had built for Mordecai. Then the king's anger cooled down.
8:1 That same day King Xerxes gave Queen Esther the estate of Haman, the enemy of the Jews. And Mordecai came into the presence of the king, for Esther had told how he was related to her.	8:1 On that day King Ahasuerus gave to Queen Esther the house of Haman, the enemy of the Jews. And Mordecai came before the king, for Esther had told what he was to her;	8:1 That same day King Xerxes gave Queen Esther all the property of Haman, the enemy of the Jews. Esther told the king that Mordecai was related to her, and from then on Mordecai was allowed to enter the king's presence.
2 The king took off his signet ring, which he had reclaimed from Haman, and presented it to Mordecai. And Esther appointed him over Haman's estate.	2 and the king took off his signet ring, which he had taken from Haman, and gave it to Mordecai. And Esther set Mordecai over the house of Haman.	2 The king took off his ring with his seal on it (which he had taken back from Haman) and gave it to Mordecai. Esther put Mordecai in charge of Haman's property.
11 The king's edict granted the Jews in every city the right to assemble and protect themselves; to destroy, kill and annihilate any armed force of any nationality or province that might attack them and their women and children; and to plunder the property of their enemies.	11 By these the king allowed the Jews who were in every city to gather and defend their lives, to destroy, to slay, and to annihilate any armed force of any people or province that might attack them, with their children and women, and to plunder their goods,	11 These letters explained that the king would allow the Jews in every city to organize for self-defense. If armed men of any nationality in any province attacked the Jewish men, their children, or their women, the Jews could fight back and destroy the attackers; they could slaughter them to the last man and take their possessions.
17 In every province and in every city, wherever the edict of the king went, there was joy and gladness among the Jews, with feasting and celebrating. And many people of other nationalities became Jews because fear of the Jews had seized them.	17 And in every province and in every city, wherever the king's command and his edict came, there was gladness and joy among the Jews, a feast and a holiday. And many from the peoples of the country declared themselves Jews, for the fear of the Jews had fallen upon them.	17 In every city and province, wherever the king's proclamation was read, the Jews held a joyful holiday with feasting and happiness. In fact, many other people became Jews, because they were afraid of them now.
9:20 Mordecai recorded these events, and he sent letters to all the Jews throughout the provinces of King Xerxes, near and far,	9:20 And Mordecai recorded these things, and sent letters to all the Jews who were in all the provinces of King Ahasuerus, both near and far,	9:20 Mordecai had these events written down and sent letters to all the Jews, near and far, throughout the Persian Empire,
21 to have them celebrate annually the fourteenth and fifteenth days of the month of Adar	21 enjoining them that they should keep the fourteenth day of the month Adar and also the fifteenth day of the same, year by year,	21 telling them to observe the fourteenth and fifteenth days of Adar as holidays every year.
22 as the time when the Jews got relief from their enemies, and as the month when their sorrow was turned into joy and their mourning into a day of celebration. He wrote them to observe the days as days of feasting and joy and giving presents of food to one another and gifts to the poor.	22 as the days on which the Jews got relief from their enemies, and as the month that had been turned for them from sorrow into gladness and from mourning into a holiday; that they should make them days of feasting and gladness, days for sending choice portions to one another and gifts to the poor.	22 These were the days on which the Jews had rid themselves of their enemies; this was a month that had been turned from a time of grief and despair into a time of joy and happiness. They were told to observe these days with feasts and parties, giving gifts of food to one another and to the poor.
26 (Therefore these days were called Purim, from the word pur.) Because of everything written in this letter and because of what they had seen and what had happened to them,	26 Therefore they called these days Purim, after the term Pur. And therefore, because of all that was written in this letter, and of what they had faced in this matter, and of what had befallen them,	26 That is why the holidays are called Purim. Because of Mordecai's letter and because of all that had happened to them,

Job

NIV	RSV	TEV
1:20 At this, Job got up and tore his robe and shaved his head. Then he fell to the ground in worship	1:20 Then Job arose, and rent his robe, and shaved his head, and fell upon the ground, and worshiped.	1:20 Then Job got up and tore his clothes in grief. He shaved his head and threw himself face downward on the ground.
21 and said: "Naked I came from my mother's womb, and naked I will depart. The LORD gave and the LORD has taken away; may the name of the LORD be praised."	21 And he said, "Naked I came from my mother's womb, and naked shall I return; the LORD gave, and the LORD has taken away; blessed be the name of the LORD."	21 He said, "I was born with nothing, and I will die with nothing. The LORD gave, and now he has taken away. May his name be praised!"

KJV	NKJV	TLB
3:3 Let the day perish wherein I was born, and the night *in which* it was said, There is a man child conceived.	**3:3** "May the day perish on which I was born, And the night *in which* it was said, 'A male child is conceived.'	**3:2-3** "Let the day of my birth be cursed," he said, "and the night when I was conceived.
4:2 *If* we assay to commune with thee, wilt thou be grieved? but who can withhold himself from speaking?	**4:2** "If one attempts a word with you, will you become weary? But who can withhold himself from speaking?	**4:2** "Will you let me say a word? For who could keep from speaking out?
5:19 He shall deliver thee in six troubles: yea, in seven there shall no evil touch thee.	**5:19** He shall deliver you in six troubles, Yes, in seven no evil shall touch you.	**5:19** He will deliver you again and again, so that no evil can touch you.
26 Thou shalt come to *thy* grave in a full age, like as a shock of corn cometh in in his season.	26 You shall come to the grave at a full age, As a sheaf of grain ripens in its season.	26 You shall live a long, good life; like standing grain, you'll not be harvested until it's time!
6:8 Oh that I might have my request; and that God would grant *me* the thing that I long for!	**6:8** "Oh, that I might have my request, That God would grant *me* the thing that I long for!	**6:8** "Oh, that God would grant the thing I long for most—
9 Even that it would please God to destroy me; that he would let loose his hand, and cut me off!	9 That it would please God to crush me, That He would loose His hand and cut me off!	9 to die beneath his hand, and be freed from his painful grip.
8:20 Behold, God will not cast away a perfect *man,* neither will he help the evil doers:	**8:20** Behold, God will not cast away the blameless, Nor will He uphold the evildoers.	**8:20** "But look! God will not cast away a good man, nor prosper evildoers.
9:25 Now my days are swifter than a post: they flee away, they see no good.	**9:25** "Now my days are swifter than a runner; They flee away, they see no good.	**9:25** "My life passes swiftly away, filled with tragedy.
26 They are passed away as the swift ships: as the eagle *that* hasteth to the prey.	26 They pass by like swift ships, Like an eagle swooping on its prey.	26 My years disappear like swift ships, like the eagle that swoops upon its prey.
13:22 Then call thou, and I will answer: or let me speak, and answer thou me.	**13:22** Then call, and I will answer; Or let me speak, Then You respond to me.	**13:22** Call to me to come—how quickly I will answer! Or let me speak to you, and you reply.
23 How many *are* mine iniquities and sins? make me to know my transgression and my sin.	23 How many *are* my iniquities and sins? Make me know my transgression and my sin.	23 Tell me, what have I done wrong? Help me! Point out my sin to me.
17:9 The righteous also shall hold on his way, and he that hath clean hands shall be stronger and stronger.	**17:9** Yet the righteous will hold to his way, And he who has clean hands will be stronger and stronger.	**17:9** the righteous shall move onward and forward; those with pure hearts shall become stronger and stronger.
19:25 For I know *that* my redeemer liveth, and *that* he shall stand at the latter *day* upon the earth:	**19:25** For I know *that* my Redeemer lives, And He shall stand at last on the earth;	**19:25** "But as for me, I know that my Redeemer lives, and that he will stand upon the earth at last.
26 And *though* after my skin *worms* destroy this *body,* yet in my flesh shall I see God:	26 And after my skin is destroyed, this *I know,* That in my flesh I shall see God,	26 And I know that after this body has decayed, this body shall see God!
27 Whom I shall see for myself, and mine eyes shall behold, and not another; *though* my reins be consumed within me.	27 Whom I shall see for myself, And my eyes shall behold, and not another. *How* my heart yearns within me!	27 Then he will be on *my* side! Yes, I shall see him, not as a stranger, but as a friend! What a glorious hope!
36:11 If they obey and serve *him,* they shall spend their days in prosperity, and their years in pleasures.	**36:11** If they obey and serve *Him,* They shall spend their days in prosperity, And their years in pleasures.	**36:11** "If they listen and obey him, then they will be blessed with prosperity throughout their lives.
38:4 Where wast thou when I laid the foundations of the earth? declare, if thou hast understanding.	**38:4** "Where were you when I laid the foundations of the earth? Tell *Me,* if you have understanding.	**38:4** "Where were you when I laid the foundations of the earth? Tell me, if you know so much.
5 Who hath laid the measures thereof, if thou knowest? or who hath stretched the line upon it?	5 Who determined its measurements? Surely you know! Or who stretched the line upon it?	5 Do you know how its dimensions were determined, and who did the surveying?
6 Whereupon are the foundations thereof fastened? or who laid the corner stone thereof;	6 To what were its foundations fastened? Or who laid its cornerstone,	6 What supports its foundations, and who laid its cornerstone,

NIV	RSV	TEV
3:3 "May the day of my birth perish, and the night it was said, 'A boy is born!'	**3:3** "Let the day perish wherein I was born, and the night which said, 'A man-child is conceived.'	**3:2–3** O God, put a curse on the day I was born; put a curse on the night when I was conceived!
4:2 "If someone ventures a word with you, will you be impatient? But who can keep from speaking?	**4:2** "If one ventures a word with you, will you be offended? Yet who can keep from speaking?	**4:1–2** Job, will you be annoyed if I speak? I can't keep quiet any longer.
5:19 From six calamities he will rescue you; in seven no harm will befall you.	**5:19** He will deliver you from six troubles; in seven there shall no evil touch you.	**5:19** Time after time he will save you from harm;
26 You will come to the grave in full vigor, like sheaves gathered in season.	26 You shall come to your grave in ripe old age. as a shock of grain comes up to the threshing floor in its season.	26 Like wheat that ripens till harvest time, you will live to a ripe old age.
6:8 "Oh, that I might have my request, that God would grant what I hope for,	**6:8** "O that I might have my request, and that God would grant my desire;	**6:8** Why won't God give me what I ask? Why won't he answer my prayer?
9 that God would be willing to crush me, to let loose his hand and cut me off!	9 that it would please God to crush me, that he would let loose his hand and cut me off!	9 If only he would go ahead and kill me!
8:20 "Surely God does not reject a blameless man or strengthen the hands of evildoers.	**8:20** "Behold, God will not reject a blameless man, nor take the hand of evildoers.	**8:20** But God will never abandon the faithful or ever give help to evil men.
9:25 "My days are swifter than a runner; they fly away without a glimpse of joy.	**9:25** "My days are swifter than a runner; they flee away, they see no good.	**9:25** My days race by, not one of them good.
26 They skim past like boats of papyrus, like eagles swooping down on their prey.	26 They go by like skiffs of reed, like an eagle swooping on the prey.	26 My life passes like the swiftest boat, as fast as an eagle swooping down on a rabbit.
13:22 Then summon me and I will answer; or let me speak, and you reply.	**13:22** Then call, and I will answer; or let me speak, and do thou reply to me.	**13:22** Speak first, O God, and I will answer. Or let me speak, and you answer me.
23 How many wrongs and sins have I committed? Show me my offense and my sin.	23 How many are my iniquities and my sins? Make me know my transgression and my sin.	23 What are my sins? What wrongs have I done? What crimes am I charged with?
17:9 Nevertheless, the righteous will hold to their ways, and those with clean hands will grow stronger.	**17:9** Yet the righteous holds to his way, and he that has clean hands grows stronger and stronger.	**17:9** Those who claim to be respectable are more and more convinced they are right.
19:25 I know that my Redeemer lives, and that in the end he will stand upon the earth.	**19:25** For I know that my Redeemer lives, and at last he will stand upon the earth;	**19:25** But I know there is someone in heaven who will come at last to my defense.
26 And after my skin has been destroyed, yet in my flesh I will see God;	26 and after my skin has been thus destroyed, then from my flesh I shall see God,	26 Even after my skin is eaten by disease, while still in this body I will see God.
27 I myself will see him with my own eyes—I, and not another. How my heart yearns within me!	27 whom I shall see on my side, and my eyes shall behold, and not another. My heart faints within me!	27 I will see him with my own eyes, and he will not be a stranger. My courage failed because you said,
36:11 If they obey and serve him, they will spend the rest of their days in prosperity and their years in contentment.	**36:11** If they hearken and serve him, they complete their days in prosperity, and their years in pleasantness.	**36:11** If they obey God and serve him, they live out their lives in peace and prosperity.
38:4 "Where were you when I laid the earth's foundation? Tell me, if you understand.	**38:4** "Where were you when I laid the foundation of the earth? Tell me, if you have understanding.	**38:4** Were you there when I made the world? If you know so much, tell me about it.
5 Who marked off its dimensions? Surely you know! Who stretched a measuring line across it?	5 Who determined its measurements—surely you know! Or who stretched the line upon it?	5 Who decided how large it would be? Who stretched the measuring line over it? Do you know all the answers?
6 On what were its footings set, or who laid its cornerstone—	6 On what were its bases sunk, or who laid its cornerstone,	6 What holds up the pillars that support the earth? Who laid the cornerstone of the world?

60   **Job 38:7**
     Psalms 16:9
           KEY VERSE COMPARISON CHART

KJV	NKJV	TLB
7 When the morning stars sang together, and all the sons of God shouted for joy?	7 When the morning stars sang together, And all the sons of God shouted for joy?	7 as the morning stars sang together and all the angels shouted for joy?
40:4 Behold, I am vile; what shall I answer thee? I will lay mine hand upon my mouth.	**40:4** "Behold, I am vile; What shall I answer You? I lay my hand over my mouth.	**40:4** "I am nothing—how could I ever find the answers? I lay my hand upon my mouth in silence.
5 Once have I spoken; but I will not answer: yea, twice; but I will proceed no further.	5 Once I have spoken, but I will not answer; Yes, twice, but I will proceed no further."	5 I have said too much already."
42:2 I know that thou canst do every *thing*, and *that* no thought can be withholden from thee.	**42:2** "I know that You can do everything, And that no purpose *of* Yours can be withheld from You.	**42:2** "I know that you can do anything and that no one can stop you.
3 Who *is* he that hideth counsel without knowledge? therefore have I uttered that I understood not; things too wonderful for me, which I knew not.	3 *You asked*, 'Who *is* this who hides counsel without knowledge?' Therefore I have uttered what I did not understand, Things too wonderful for me, which I did not know.	3 You ask who it is who has so foolishly denied your providence. It is I. I was talking about things I knew nothing about and did not understand, things far too wonderful for me.
4 Hear, I beseech thee, and I will speak: I will demand of thee, and declare thou unto me.	4 Listen, please, and let me speak; *You said*, 'I will question you, and you shall answer Me.'	4 "[You said,] 'Listen and I will speak! Let me put the questions to you! See if you can answer them!'
5 I have heard of thee by the hearing of the ear: but now mine eye seeth thee.	5 "I have heard of You by the hearing of the ear, But now my eye sees You.	5 "[But now I say,] 'I had heard about you before, but now I have seen you,
6 Wherefore I abhor *myself*, and repent in dust and ashes.	6 Therefore I abhor *myself*, And repent in dust and ashes."	6 and I loathe myself and repent in dust and ashes.' "

Psalms

1:1 Blessed *is* the man that walketh not in the counsel of the ungodly, nor standeth in the way of sinners, nor sitteth in the seat of the scornful.	**1:1** Blessed *is* the man Who walks not in the counsel of the ungodly, Nor stands in the path of sinners, Nor sits in the seat of the scornful;	**1:1** Oh, the joys of those who do not follow evil men's advice, who do not hang around with sinners, scoffing at the things of God:
2 But his delight *is* in the law of the Lᴏʀᴅ; and in his law doth he meditate day and night.	2 But his delight *is* in the law of the Lᴏʀᴅ, And in His law he meditates day and night.	2 But they delight in doing everything God wants them to, and day and night are always meditating on his laws and thinking about ways to follow him more closely.
2:8 Ask of me, and I shall give *thee* the heathen *for* thine inheritance, and the uttermost parts of the earth *for* thy possession.	**2:8** Ask of Me, and I will give *You* The nations *for* Your inheritance, And the ends of the earth *for* Your possession.	**2:8** "Only ask, and I will give you all the nations of the world.
9 Thou shalt break them with a rod of iron; thou shalt dash them in pieces like a potter's vessel.	9 You shall break them with a rod of iron; You shall dash them in pieces like a potter's vessel.' "	9 Rule them with an iron rod; smash them like clay pots!"
4:3 But know that the Lᴏʀᴅ hath set apart him that is godly for himself: the Lᴏʀᴅ will hear when I call unto him.	**4:3** But know that the Lᴏʀᴅ has set apart for Himself him who is godly; The Lᴏʀᴅ will hear when I call to Him.	**4:3** Mark this well: The Lord has set apart the redeemed for himself. Therefore he will listen to me and answer when I call to him.
7 Thou hast put gladness in my heart, more than in the time *that* their corn and their wine increased.	7 You have put gladness in my heart, More than in the season that their grain and wine increased.	7 Yes, the gladness you have given me is far greater than their joys at harvest time as they gaze at their bountiful crops.
5:12 For thou, Lᴏʀᴅ, wilt bless the righteous; with favour wilt thou compass him as *with* a shield.	**5:12** For You, O Lᴏʀᴅ, will bless the righteous; With favor You will surround him as *with* a shield.	**5:12** For you bless the godly man, O Lord; you protect him with your shield of love.
9:9 The Lᴏʀᴅ also will be a refuge for the oppressed, a refuge in times of trouble.	**9:9** The Lᴏʀᴅ also will be a refuge for the oppressed, A refuge in times of trouble.	**9:9** All who are oppressed may come to him. He is a refuge for them in their times of trouble.
16:9 Therefore my heart is glad, and my glory rejoiceth: my flesh also shall rest in hope.	**16:9** Therefore my heart is glad, and my glory rejoices; My flesh also will rest in hope.	**16:9** Heart, body, and soul are filled with joy.

NIV	RSV	TEV
7 while the morning stars sang together; and all the angels shouted for joy?	7 when the morning stars sang together, and all the sons of God shouted for joy?	7 In the dawn of that day the stars sang together, and the heavenly beings shouted for joy.
40:4 "I am unworthy—how can I reply to you? I put my hand over my mouth.	40:4 "Behold, I am of small account; what shall I answer thee? I lay my hand on my mouth.	40:3–4 I spoke foolishly, LORD. What can I answer? I will not try to say anything else.
5 I spoke once, but I have no answer— twice, but I will say no more."	5 I have spoken once, and I will not answer; twice, but I will proceed no further."	5 I have already said more than I should.
42:2 "I know that you can do all things; no plan of yours can be thwarted.	42:2 "I know that thou canst do all things, and that no purpose of thine can be thwarted.	42:2 I know, LORD, that you are all-powerful; that you can do everything you want.
3 You asked, 'Who is this that obscures my counsel without knowledge?' Surely I spoke of things I did not understand, things too wonderful for me to know.	3 'Who is this that hides counsel without knowledge?' Therefore I have uttered what I did not understand, things too wonderful for me, which I did not know.	3 You ask how I dare question your wisdom when I am so very ignorant. I talked about things I did not understand, about marvels too great for me to know.
4 "You said, 'Listen now, and I will speak; I will question you, and you shall answer me.'	4 'Hear, and I will speak; I will question you, and you declare to me.'	4 You told me to listen while you spoke and to try to answer your questions.
5 My ears had heard of you but now my eyes have seen you.	5 I had heard of thee by the hearing of the ear, but now my eye sees thee;	5 In the past I knew only what others had told me, but now I have seen you with my own eyes.
6 Therefore I despise myself and repent in dust and ashes."	6 therefore I despise myself, and repent in dust and ashes."	6 So I am ashamed of all I have said and repent in dust and ashes.

Psalms

NIV	RSV	TEV
1:1 Blessed is the man who does not walk in the counsel of the wicked or stand in the way of sinners or sit in the seat of mockers.	1:1 Blessed is the man who walks not in the counsel of the wicked, nor stands in the way of sinners, nor sits in the seat of scoffers;	1:1 Happy are those who reject the advice of evil men, who do not follow the example of sinners or join those who have no use for God.
2 But his delight is in the law of the LORD, and on his law he meditates day and night.	2 but his delight is in the law of the LORD, and on his law he meditates day and night.	2 Instead, they find joy in obeying the Law of the LORD, and they study it day and night.
2:8 Ask of me, and I will make the nations your inheritance, the ends of the earth your possession.	2:8 Ask of me, and I will make the nations your heritage, and the ends of the earth your possession.	2:8 Ask, and I will give you all the nations; the whole earth will be yours.
9 You will rule them with an iron scepter; you will dash them to pieces like pottery."	9 You shall break them with a rod of iron, and dash them in pieces like a potter's vessel."	9 You will break them with an iron rod; you will shatter them in pieces like a clay pot.'"
4:3 Know that the LORD has set apart the godly for himself; the LORD will hear when I call to him.	4:3 But know that the LORD has set apart the godly for himself; the LORD hears when I call to him.	4:3 Remember that the LORD has chosen the righteous for his own, and he hears me when I call to him.
7 You have filled my heart with greater joy than when their grain and new wine abound.	7 Thou hast put more joy in my heart than they have when their grain and wine abound.	7 But the joy that you have given me is more than they will ever have with all their grain and wine.
5:12 For surely, O LORD, you bless the righteous; you surround them with your favor as with a shield.	5:12 For thou dost bless the righteous, O LORD; thou dost cover him with favor as with a shield.	5:12 You bless those who obey you, LORD; your love protects them like a shield.
9:9 The LORD is a refuge for the oppressed, a stronghold in times of trouble.	9:9 The LORD is a stronghold for the oppressed, a stronghold in times of trouble.	9:9 The LORD is a refuge for the oppressed, a place of safety in times of trouble.
16:9 Therefore my heart is glad and my tongue rejoices; my body also will rest secure,	16:9 Therefore my heart is glad, and my soul rejoices; my body also dwells secure.	16:9 And so I am thankful and glad, and I feel completely secure,

KEY VERSE COMPARISON CHART

KJV	NKJV	TLB
10 For thou wilt not leave my soul in hell; neither wilt thou suffer thine Holy One to see corruption.	10 For You will not leave my soul in Sheol, Nor will You allow Your Holy One to see corruption.	10 For you will not leave me among the dead; you will not allow your beloved one to rot in the grave.
11 Thou wilt shew me the path of life: in thy presence *is* fulness of joy; at thy right hand *there are* pleasures for evermore.	11 You will show me the path of life; In Your presence *is* fullness of joy; At Your right hand *are* pleasures forevermore.	11 You have let me experience the joys of life and the exquisite pleasures of your own eternal presence.
18:3 I will call upon the LORD, *who is worthy* to be praised: so shall I be saved from mine enemies.	18:3 I will call upon the LORD, *who is worthy* to be praised; So shall I be saved from my enemies.	18:3 All I need to do is cry to him—oh, praise the Lord—and I am saved from all my enemies!
30 *As for* God, his way *is* perfect: the word of the LORD is tried: he *is* a buckler to all those that trust in him.	30 *As for* God, His way *is* perfect; The word of the LORD is proven; He *is* a shield to all who trust in Him.	30 What a God he is! How perfect in every way! All his promises prove true. He is a shield for everyone who hides behind him.
19:7 The law of the LORD *is* perfect, converting the soul: the testimony of the LORD *is* sure, making wise the simple.	19:7 The law of the LORD *is* perfect, converting the soul; The testimony of the LORD *is* sure, making wise the simple;	19:7-8 God's laws are perfect. They protect us, make us wise, and give us joy and light.
8 The statutes of the LORD *are* right, rejoicing the heart: the commandment of the LORD *is* pure, enlightening the eyes.	8 The statutes of the LORD *are* right, rejoicing the heart; The commandment of the LORD *is* pure, enlightening the eyes;	
9 The fear of the LORD *is* clean, enduring for ever: the judgments of the LORD *are* true *and* righteous altogether.	9 The fear of the LORD *is* clean, enduring forever; The judgments of the LORD *are* true *and* righteous altogether.	9 God's laws are pure, eternal, just.
23:1 The LORD *is* my shepherd; I shall not want.	23:1 The LORD *is* my shepherd; I shall not want.	23:1 Because the Lord is my Shepherd, I have everything I need!
2 He maketh me to lie down in green pastures: he leadeth me beside the still waters.	2 He makes me to lie down in green pastures; He leads me beside the still waters.	2 He lets me rest in the meadow grass and leads me beside the quiet streams.
3 He restoreth my soul: he leadeth me in the paths of righteousness for his name's sake.	3 He restores my soul; He leads me in the paths of righteousness For His name's sake.	3 He restores my failing health. He helps me do what honors him the most.
4 Yea, though I walk through the valley of the shadow of death, I will fear no evil: for thou *art* with me; thy rod and thy staff they comfort me.	4 Yea, though I walk through the valley of the shadow of death, I will fear no evil; For You *are* with me; Your rod and Your staff, they comfort me.	4 Even when walking through the dark valley of death I will not be afraid, for you are close beside me, guarding, guiding all the way.
5 Thou preparest a table before me in the presence of mine enemies: thou anointest my head with oil; my cup runneth over.	5 You prepare a table before me in the presence of my enemies; You anoint my head with oil; My cup runs over.	5 You provide delicious food for me in the presence of my enemies. You have welcomed me as your guest; blessings overflow!
6 Surely goodness and mercy shall follow me all the days of my life: and I will dwell in the house of the LORD for ever.	6 Surely goodness and mercy shall follow me All the days of my life; And I will dwell in the house of the LORD Forever.	6 Your goodness and unfailing kindness shall be with me all of my life, and afterwards I will live with you forever in your home.
24:3 Who shall ascend into the hill of the LORD? or who shall stand in his holy place?	24:3 Who may ascend into the hill of the LORD? Or who may stand in His holy place?	24:3 Who may climb the mountain of the Lord and enter where he lives? Who may stand before the Lord?
4 He that hath clean hands, and a pure heart; who hath not lifted up his soul unto vanity, nor sworn deceitfully.	4 He who has clean hands and a pure heart, Who has not lifted up his soul to an idol, Nor sworn deceitfully.	4 Only those with pure hands and hearts, who do not practice dishonesty and lying.
7 Lift up your heads, O ye gates; and be ye lift up, ye everlasting doors; and the King of glory shall come in.	7 Lift up your heads, O you gates! And be lifted up, you everlasting doors! And the King of glory shall come in.	7 Open up, O ancient gates, and let the King of Glory in.

NIV	RSV	TEV
10 because you will not abandon me to the grave, nor will you let your Holy One see decay.	10 For thou dost not give me up to Sheol, or let thy godly one see the Pit.	10 because you protect me from the power of death. I have served you faithfully, and you will not abandon me to the world of the dead.
11 You have made known to me the path of life; you will fill me with joy in your presence, with eternal pleasures at your right hand.	11 Thou dost show me the path of life; in thy presence there is fullness of joy, in thy right hand are pleasures for evermore.	11 You will show me the path that leads to life; your presence fills me with joy and brings me pleasure forever.
18:3 I call to the LORD, who is worthy of praise, and I am saved from my enemies.	18:3 I call upon the LORD, who is worthy to be praised, and I am saved from my enemies.	18:3 I call to the LORD, and he saves me from my enemies. Praise the LORD!
30 As for God, his way is perfect; the word of the LORD is flawless. He is a shield for all who take refuge in him.	30 This God—his way is perfect; the promise of the LORD proves true; he is a shield for all those who take refuge in him.	30 This God—how perfect are his deeds! How dependable his words! He is like a shield for all who seek his protection.
19:7 The law of the LORD is perfect, reviving the soul. The statutes of the LORD are trustworthy, making wise the simple.	19:7 The law of the LORD is perfect, reviving the soul; the testimony of the LORD is sure, making wise the simple;	19:7 The law of the LORD is perfect; it gives new strength. The commands of the LORD are trustworthy, giving wisdom to those who lack it.
8 The precepts of the LORD are right, giving joy to the heart. The commands of the LORD are radiant, giving light to the eyes.	8 the precepts of the LORD are right, rejoicing the heart; the commandment of the LORD is pure, enlightening the eyes;	8 The laws of the LORD are right, and those who obey them are happy. The commands of the LORD are just and give understanding to the mind.
9 The fear of the LORD is pure, enduring forever. The ordinances of the LORD are sure and altogether righteous.	9 the fear of the LORD is clean, enduring for ever; the ordinances of the LORD are true, and righteous altogether.	9 Reverence for the LORD is good; it will continue forever. The judgments of the LORD are just; they are always fair.
23:1 The LORD is my shepherd, I shall lack nothing.	23:1 The LORD is my shepherd, I shall not want;	23:1 The LORD is my shepherd; I have everything I need.
2 He makes me lie down in green pastures, he leads me beside quiet waters,	2 he makes me lie down in green pastures. He leads me beside still waters;	2 He lets me rest in fields of green grass and leads me to quiet pools of fresh water.
3 he restores my soul. He guides me in paths of righteousness for his name's sake.	3 he restores my soul. He leads me in paths of righteousness for his name's sake.	3 He gives me new strength. He guides me in the right paths, as he has promised.
4 Even though I walk through the valley of the shadow of death, I will fear no evil, for you are with me; your rod and your staff, they comfort me.	4 Even though I walk through the valley of the shadow of death, I fear no evil; for thou art with me; thy rod and thy staff, they comfort me.	4 Even if I go through the deepest darkness, I will not be afraid, LORD, for you are with me. Your shepherd's rod and staff protect me.
5 You prepare a table before me in the presence of my enemies. You anoint my head with oil; my cup overflows.	5 Thou preparest a table before me in the presence of my enemies; thou anointest my head with oil, my cup overflows.	5 You prepare a banquet for me, where all my enemies can see me; you welcome me as an honored guest and fill my cup to the brim.
6 Surely goodness and love will follow me all the days of my life, and I will dwell in the house of the LORD forever.	6 Surely goodness and mercy shall follow me all the days of my life; and I shall dwell in the house of the LORD for ever.	6 I know that your goodness and love will be with me all my life; and your house will be my home as long as I live.
24:3 Who may ascend the hill of the Lord? Who may stand in his holy place?	24:3 Who shall ascend the hill of the LORD? And who shall stand in his holy place?	24:3 Who has the right to go up the LORD's hill? Who may enter his holy Temple?
4 He who has clean hands and a pure heart, who does not lift up his soul to an idol or swear by what is false.	4 He who has clean hands and a pure heart, who does not lift up his soul to what is false, and does not swear deceitfully.	4 Those who are pure in act and in thought, who do not worship idols or make false promises.
7 Lift up your heads, O you gates; be lifted up, you ancient doors, that the King of glory may come in.	7 Lift up your heads, O gates! and be lifted up, O ancient doors! that the King of glory may come in.	7 Fling wide the gates, open the ancient doors, and the great king will come in.

KJV	NKJV	TLB
27:1 The LORD *is* my light and my salvation; whom shall I fear? the LORD *is* the strength of my life; of whom shall I be afraid?	**27:1** The LORD *is* my light and my salvation; Whom shall I fear? The LORD *is* the strength of my life; Of whom shall I be afraid?	**27:1** The Lord is my light and my salvation; whom shall I fear?
10 When my father and my mother forsake me, then the LORD will take me up.	**10** When my father and my mother forsake me, Then the LORD will take care of me.	**10** For if my father and mother should abandon me, you would welcome and comfort me.
13 *I had fainted,* unless I had believed to see the goodness of the LORD in the land of the living.	**13** *I would have lost heart,* unless I had believed That I would see the goodness of the LORD In the land of the living.	**13** I am expecting the Lord to rescue me again, so that once again I will see his goodness to me here in the land of the living.
14 Wait on the LORD: be of good courage, and he shall strengthen thine heart: wait, I say, on the LORD.	**14** Wait on the LORD; Be of good courage, And He shall strengthen your heart; Wait, I say, on the LORD!	**14** Don't be impatient. Wait for the Lord, and he will come and save you! Be brave, stouthearted and courageous. Yes, wait and he will help you.
30:2 O LORD my God, I cried unto thee, and thou hast healed me.	**30:2** O LORD my God, I cried out to You, And You have healed me.	**30:2** O Lord my God, I pleaded with you, and you gave me my health again.
5 For his anger *endureth but* a moment; in his favour *is* life: weeping may endure for a night, but joy *cometh* in the morning.	**5** For His anger *is but for* a moment, His favor *is for* life; Weeping may endure for a night, But joy *comes* in the morning.	**5** His anger lasts a moment; his favor lasts for life! Weeping may go on all night, but in the morning there is joy.
31:3 For thou *art* my rock and my fortress; therefore for thy name's sake lead me, and guide me.	**31:3** For You *are* my rock and my fortress; Therefore, for Your name's sake, Lead me and guide me.	**31:3** Yes, you are my Rock and my fortress; honor your name by leading me out of this peril.
24 Be of good courage, and he shall strengthen your heart, all ye that hope in the LORD.	**24** Be of good courage, And He shall strengthen your heart, All you who hope in the LORD,	**24** So cheer up! Take courage if you are depending on the Lord.
32:1 Blessed *is* he whose transgression *is* forgiven, *whose* sin *is* covered.	**32:1** Blessed *is* he *whose* transgression *is* forgiven, *Whose* sin *is* covered.	**32:1** What happiness for those whose guilt has been forgiven! What joys when sins are covered over!
2 Blessed *is* the man unto whom the LORD imputeth not iniquity, and in whose spirit *there is* no guile.	**2** Blessed *is* the man to whom the LORD does not impute iniquity, And in whose spirit *there is* no guile.	**2** What relief for those who have confessed their sins and God has cleared their record.
8 I will instruct thee and teach thee in the way which thou shalt go: I will guide thee with mine eye.	**8** I will instruct you and teach you in the way you should go; I will guide you with My eye.	**8** I will instruct you (says the Lord) and guide you along the best pathway for your life; I will advise you and watch your progress.
33:6 By the word of the LORD were the heavens made; and all the host of them by the breath of his mouth.	**33:6** By the word of the LORD the heavens were made, And all the host of them by the breath of His mouth.	**33:6** He merely spoke, and the heavens were formed, and all the galaxies of stars.
11 The counsel of the LORD standeth for ever, the thoughts of his heart to all generations.	**11** The counsel of the LORD stands forever, The plans of His heart to all generations.	**11** but his own plan stands forever. His intentions are the same for every generation.
18 Behold, the eye of the LORD *is* upon them that fear him, upon them that hope in his mercy;	**18** Behold, the eye of the LORD *is* on those who fear Him, On those who hope in His mercy,	**18** But the eyes of the Lord are watching over those who fear him, who rely upon his steady love.
19 To deliver their soul from death, and to keep them alive in famine.	**19** To deliver their soul from death, And to keep them alive in famine.	**19** He will keep them from death even in times of famine!
34:1 I will bless the LORD at all times: his praise *shall* continually *be* in my mouth.	**34:1** I will bless the LORD at all times; His praise *shall* continually *be* in my mouth.	**34:1** I will praise the Lord no matter what happens. I will constantly speak of his glories and grace.
7 The angel of the LORD encampeth round about them that fear him, and delivereth them.	**7** The angel of the LORD encamps all around those who fear Him, And delivers them.	**7** For the Angel of the Lord guards and rescues all who reverence him.
10 The young lions do lack, and suffer hunger: but they that seek the LORD shall not want any good *thing.*	**10** The young lions lack and suffer hunger; But those who seek the LORD shall not lack any good *thing.*	**10** Even strong young lions sometimes go hungry, but those of us who reverence the Lord will never lack any good thing.
12 What man *is he that* desireth life, *and* loveth *many* days, that he may see good?	**12** Who is the man *who* desires life, And loves *many* days, that he may see good?	**12** Do you want a long, good life?

NIV	RSV	TEV
27:1 The LORD is my light and my salvation— whom shall I fear? The LORD is the stronghold of my life— of whom shall I be afraid?	**27:1** The LORD is my light and my salvation; whom shall I fear? The LORD is the stronghold of my life; of whom shall I be afraid?	**27:1** The LORD is my light and my salvation; I will fear no one. The LORD protects me from all danger; I will never be afraid.
10 Though my father and mother forsake me, the LORD will receive me.	**10** For my father and my mother have forsaken me, but the LORD will take me up.	**10** My father and mother may abandon me, but the LORD will take care of me.
13 I am still confident of this: I will see the goodness of the LORD in the land of the living.	**13** I believe that I shall see the goodness of the LORD in the land of the living!	**13** I know that I will live to see the LORD's goodness in this present life.
14 Wait for the LORD; be strong and take heart and wait for the LORD.	**14** Wait for the LORD; be strong, and let your heart take courage; yea, wait for the Lord!	**14** Trust in the LORD. Have faith, do not despair. Trust in the LORD.
30:2 O LORD my God, I called to you for help and you healed me.	**30:2** O LORD my God, I cried to thee for help, and thou hast healed me.	**30:2** I cried to you for help, O LORD my God, and you healed me;
5 For his anger lasts only a moment, but his favor lasts a lifetime; weeping may remain for a night, but rejoicing comes in the morning.	**5** For his anger is but for a moment, and his favor is for a lifetime. Weeping may tarry for the night, but joy comes with the morning.	**5** His anger lasts only a moment, his goodness for a lifetime. Tears may flow in the night, but joy comes in the morning.
31:3 Since you are my rock and my fortress, for the sake of your name lead and guide me.	**31:3** Yea, thou art my rock and my fortress; for thy name's sake lead me and guide me,	**31:3** You are my refuge and defense; guide me and lead me as you have promised.
24 Be strong and take heart, all you who hope in the LORD.	**24** Be strong, and let your heart take courage, all you who wait for the LORD!	**24** Be strong, be courageous, all you that hope in the LORD.
32:1 Blessed is he whose transgressions are forgiven, whose sins are covered.	**32:1** Blessed is he whose transgression is forgiven, whose sin is covered.	**32:1** Happy are those whose sins are forgiven, whose wrongs are pardoned.
2 Blessed is the man whose sin the LORD does not count against him and in whose spirit is no deceit.	**2** Blessed is the man to whom the LORD imputes no iniquity, and in whose spirit there is no deceit.	**2** Happy is the man whom the LORD does not accuse of doing wrong and who is free from all deceit.
8 I will instruct you and teach you in the way you should go; I will counsel you and watch over you.	**8** I will instruct you and teach you the way you should go; I will counsel you with my eye upon you.	**8** The LORD says, "I will teach you the way you should go; I will instruct you and advise you.
33:6 By the word of the LORD were the heavens made, their starry host by the breath of his mouth.	**33:6** By the word of the LORD the heavens were made, and all their host by the breath of his mouth.	**33:6** The LORD created the heavens by his command, the sun, moon, and stars by his spoken word.
11 But the plans of the LORD stand firm forever, the purposes of his heart through all generations.	**11** The counsel of the LORD stands for ever, the thoughts of his heart to all generations.	**11** But his plans endure forever; his purposes last eternally.
18 But the eyes of the LORD are on those who fear him, on those whose hope is in his unfailing love,	**18** Behold, the eye of the LORD is on those who fear him, on those who hope in his steadfast love,	**18** The LORD watches over those who obey him, those who trust in his constant love.
19 to deliver them from death and keep them alive in famine.	**19** that he may deliver their soul from death, and keep them alive in famine.	**19** He saves them from death; he keeps them alive in times of famine.
34:1 I will extol the LORD at all times; his praise will always be on my lips.	**34:1** I will bless the LORD at all times; his praise shall continually be in my mouth.	**34:1** I will always thank the LORD; I will never stop praising him.
7 The angel of the LORD encamps around those who fear him, and he delivers them.	**7** The angel of the LORD encamps around those who fear him, and delivers them.	**7** His angel guards those who honor the LORD and rescues them from danger.
10 The lions may grow weak and hungry, but those who seek the LORD lack no good thing.	**10** The young lions suffer want and hunger; but those who seek the LORD lack no good thing.	**10** Even lions go hungry for lack of food, but those who obey the LORD lack nothing good.
12 Whoever of you loves life and desires to see many good days.	**12** What man is there who desires life, and covets many days, that he may enjoy good?	**12** Would you like to enjoy life? Do you want long life and happiness?

KJV	NKJV	TLB
15 The eyes of the LORD *are* upon the righteous, and his ears *are* open unto their cry.	15 The eyes of the LORD *are* on the righteous, And His ears *are* open to their cry.	15 For the eyes of the Lord are intently watching all who live good lives, and he gives attention when they cry to him.
19 Many *are* the afflictions of the righteous: but the LORD delivereth him out of them all.	19 Many *are* the afflictions of the righteous, But the LORD delivers him out of them all.	19 The good man does not escape all troubles—he has them too. But the Lord helps him in each and every one.
36:5 Thy mercy, O LORD, *is* in the heavens; *and* thy faithfulness *reacheth* unto the clouds.	36:5 Your mercy, O LORD, *is* in the heavens, *And* Your faithfulness *reaches* to the clouds.	36:5 Your steadfast love, O Lord, is as great as all the heavens. Your faithfulness reaches beyond the clouds.
37:4 Delight thyself also in the LORD; and he shall give thee the desires of thine heart.	37:4 Delight yourself also in the LORD, And He shall give you the desires of your heart.	37:4 Be delighted with the Lord. Then he will give you all your heart's desires.
5 Commit thy way unto the LORD; trust also in him; and he shall bring *it* to pass.	5 Commit your way to the LORD, Trust also in Him, And He shall bring *it* to pass.	5 Commit everything you do to the Lord. Trust him to help you do it and he will.
7 Rest in the LORD, and wait patiently for him: fret not thyself because of him who prospereth in his way, because of the man who bringeth wicked devices to pass.	7 Rest in the LORD, and wait patiently for Him; Do not fret because of him who prospers in his way, Because of the man who brings wicked schemes to pass.	7 Rest in the Lord; wait patiently for him to act. Don't be envious of evil men who prosper.
8 Cease from anger, and forsake wrath: fret not thyself in any wise to do evil.	8 Cease from anger, and forsake wrath; Do not fret—*it* only *causes* harm.	8 Stop your anger! Turn off your wrath. Don't fret and worry—it only leads to harm.
9 for evildoers shall be cut off: but those that wait upon the LORD, they shall inherit the earth.	9 For evildoers shall be cut off; But those who wait on the LORD, They shall inherit the earth.	9 For the wicked shall be destroyed, but those who trust the Lord shall be given every blessing.
23 The steps of a *good* man are ordered by the LORD: and he delighteth in his way.	23 The steps of a *good* man are ordered by the LORD, And He delights in his way.	23 The steps of good men are directed by the Lord. He delights in each step they take.
24 Though he fall, he shall not be utterly cast down: for the LORD upholdeth *him with* his hand.	24 Though he fall, he shall not be utterly cast down; For the LORD upholds *him with* His hand.	24 If they fall it isn't fatal, for the Lord holds them with his hand.
25 I have been young, and *now* am old; yet have I not seen the righteous forsaken, nor his seed begging bread.	25 I have been young, and *now* am old; Yet I have not seen the righteous forsaken, Nor his descendants begging bread.	25 I have been young and now I am old. And in all my years I have never seen the Lord forsake a man who loves him; nor have I seen the children of the godly go hungry.
34 Wait on the LORD, and keep his way, and he shall exalt thee to inherit the land: when the wicked are cut off, thou shalt see *it*.	34 Wait on the LORD, And keep His way, And He shall exalt you to inherit the land; When the wicked are cut off, you shall see *it*.	34 Don't be impatient for the Lord to act! Keep traveling steadily along his pathway and in due season he will honor you with every blessing, and you will see the wicked destroyed.
39 But the salvation of the righteous *is* of the Lord: *he is* their strength in the time of trouble.	39 But the salvation of the righteous *is* from the LORD; *He is* their strength in the time of trouble.	39 The Lord saves the godly! He is their salvation and their refuge when trouble comes.
40:1 I waited patiently for the LORD; and he inclined unto me, and heard my cry.	40:1 I waited patiently for the LORD; And He inclined to me, And heard my cry.	40:1 I waited patiently for God to help me; then he listened and heard my cry.
41:1 Blessed *is* he that considereth the poor: the LORD will deliver him in time of trouble.	41:1 Blessed *is* he who considers the poor; The LORD will deliver him in time of trouble.	41:1 God blesses those who are kind to the poor. He helps them out of their troubles.
2 The LORD will preserve him, and keep him alive; *and* he shall be blessed upon the earth: and thou wilt not deliver him unto the will of his enemies.	2 The LORD will preserve him and keep him alive, *And* he will be blessed on the earth; You will not deliver him to the will of his enemies.	2 He protects them and keeps them alive; he publicly honors them and destroys the power of their enemies.
3 The LORD will strengthen him upon the bed of languishing: thou wilt make all his bed in his sickness.	3 The LORD will strengthen him on his bed of illness; You will sustain him on his sickbed.	3 He nurses them when they are sick, and soothes their pains and worries.

NIV	RSV	TEV
15 The eyes of the LORD are on the righteous and his ears are attentive to their cry;	15 The eyes of the LORD are toward the righteous, and his ears toward their cry.	15 The LORD watches over the righteous and listens to their cries;
19 A righteous man may have many troubles, but the LORD delivers him from them all;	19 Many are the afflictions of the righteous; but the LORD delivers him out of them all.	19 The good man suffers many troubles, but the LORD saves him from them all;
36:5 Your love, O LORD, reaches to the heavens, your faithfulness to the skies.	36:5 Thy steadfast love, O LORD, extends to the heavens, thy faithfulness to the clouds.	36:5 LORD, your constant love reaches the heavens; your faithfulness extends to the skies.
37:4 Delight yourself in the LORD and he will give you the desires of your heart.	37:4 Take delight in the LORD, and he will give you the desires of your heart.	37:4 Seek your happiness in the LORD, and he will give you your heart's desire.
5 Commit your way to the LORD; trust in him and he will do this:	5 Commit your way to the LORD; trust in him, and he will act.	5 Give yourself to the LORD; trust in him, and he will help you;
7 Be still before the LORD and wait patiently for him; do not fret when men succeed in their ways, when they carry out their wicked schemes.	7 Be still before the LORD, and wait patiently for him; fret not yourself over him who prospers in his way, over the man who carries out evil devices!	7 Be patient and wait for the LORD to act; don't be worried about those who prosper or those who succeed in their evil plans.
8 Refrain from anger and turn from wrath; do not fret—it leads only to evil.	8 Refrain from anger, and forsake wrath! Fret not yourself; it tends only to evil.	8 Don't give in to worry or anger; it only leads to trouble.
9 For evil men will be cut off, but those who hope in the LORD will inherit the land.	9 For the wicked shall be cut off; but those who wait for the LORD shall possess the land.	9 Those who trust in the LORD will possess the land, but the wicked will be driven out.
23 The LORD delights in the way of the man whose steps he has made firm;	23 The steps of a man are from the LORD, and he establishes him in whose way he delights;	23 The LORD guides a man in the way he should go and protects those who please him.
24 though he stumble, he will not fall, for the LORD upholds him with his hand.	24 though he fall, he shall not be cast headlong, for the LORD is the stay of his hand.	24 If they fall, they will not stay down, because the LORD will help them up.
25 I was young and now I am old, yet I have never seen the righteous forsaken or their children begging bread.	25 I have been young, and now am old; yet I have not seen the righteous forsaken or his children begging bread.	25 I am an old man now; I have lived a long time, but I have never seen a good man abandoned by the LORD or his children begging for food.
34 Wait for the LORD and keep his way. He will exalt you to possess the land; when the wicked are cut off, you will see it.	34 Wait for the LORD, and keep to his way, and he will exalt you to possess the land; you will look on the destruction of the wicked.	34 Put your hope in the LORD and obey his commands; he will honor you by giving you the land, and you will see the wicked driven out.
39 The salvation of the righteous comes from the LORD; he is their stronghold in time of trouble.	39 The salvation of the righteous is from the LORD; he is their refuge in the time of trouble.	39 The LORD saves righteous men and protects them in times of trouble.
40:1 I waited patiently for the LORD; he turned to me and heard my cry.	40:1 I waited patiently for the LORD; he inclined to me and heard my cry.	40:1 I waited patiently for the LORD's help; then he listened to me and heard my cry.
41:1 Blessed is he who has regard for the weak; the LORD delivers him in times of trouble.	41:1 Blessed is he who considers the poor! The LORD delivers him in the day of trouble;	41:1 Happy are those who are concerned for the poor; the LORD will help them when they are in trouble.
2 The LORD will protect him and preserve his life; he will bless him in the land and not surrender him to the desire of his foes.	2 the LORD protects him and keeps him alive; he is called blessed in the land; thou dost not give him up to the will of his enemies.	2 The LORD will protect them and preserve their lives; he will make them happy in the land; he will not abandon them to the power of their enemies.
3 The LORD will sustain him on his sickbed and restore him from his bed of illness.	3 The LORD sustains him on his sickbed; in his illness thou healest all his infirmities.	3 The LORD will help them when they are sick and will restore them to health.

KJV	NKJV	TLB
42:11 Why art thou cast down, O my soul? and why art thou disquieted within me? hope thou in God: for I shall yet praise him, *who is* the health of my countenance, and my God.	**42:11** Why are you cast down, O my soul? And why are you disquieted within me? Hope in God; For I shall yet praise Him, The help of my countenance and my God.	**42:11** But O my soul, don't be discouraged. Don't be upset. Expect God to act! For I know that I shall again have plenty of reason to praise him for all that he will do. He is my help! He is my God!
46:1 God *is* our refuge and strength, a very present help in trouble.	**46:1** God *is* our refuge and strength, A very present help in trouble.	**46:1** God is our refuge and strength, a tested help in times of trouble.
2 Therefore will not we fear, though the earth be removed, and though the mountains be carried into the midst of the sea;	2 Therefore we will not fear, Though the earth be removed, And though the mountains be carried into the midst of the sea;	2 And so we need not fear even if the world blows up, and the mountains crumble into the sea.
3 *Though* the waters thereof roar *and* be troubled, *though* the mountains shake with the swelling thereof. Selah.	3 *Though* its waters roar *and* be troubled, *Though* the mountains shake with its swelling. Selah	3 Let the oceans roar and foam; let the mountains tremble!
48:14 For this God *is* our God for ever and ever: he will be our guide *even* unto death.	**48:14** For this *is* God, Our God forever and ever; He will be our guide Even to death.	**48:14** For this great God is our God forever and ever. He will be our guide until we die.
49:15 But God will redeem my soul from the power of the grave: for he shall receive me. Selah.	**49:15** But God will redeem my soul from the power of the grave, For He shall receive me. Selah	**49:15** But as for me, God will redeem my soul from the power of death, for he will receive me.
51:3 For I acknowledge my transgressions: and my sin *is* ever before me.	**51:3** For I acknowledge my transgressions, And my sin *is* ever before me.	**51:3** For I admit my shameful deed—it haunts me day and night.
4 Against thee, thee only, have I sinned, and done *this* evil in thy sight: that thou mightest be justified when thou speakest, *and* be clear when thou judgest.	4 Against You, You only, have I sinned, And done *this* evil in Your sight— That You may be found just when You speak, *And* blameless when You judge.	4 It is against you and you alone I sinned, and did this terrible thing. You saw it all, and your sentence against me is just.
12 Restore unto me the joy of thy salvation; and uphold me *with thy* free spirit.	12 Restore to me the joy of Your salvation, And uphold me *with Your* generous Spirit	12 Restore to me again the joy of your salvation, and make me willing to obey you.
13 *Then* will I teach transgressors thy ways; and sinners shall be converted unto thee.	13 *Then* I will teach transgressors Your ways, And sinners shall be converted to You.	13 Then I will teach your ways to other sinners, and they—guilty like me—will repent and return to you.
14 Deliver me from bloodguiltiness, O God, thou God of my salvation: *and* my tongue shall sing aloud of thy righteousness.	14 Deliver me from bloodguiltiness, O God, The God of my salvation, *And* my tongue shall sing aloud of Your righteousness.	14 Don't sentence me to death. O my God, you alone can rescue me. Then I will sing of your forgiveness,
15 O Lord, open thou my lips; and my mouth shall shew forth thy praise.	15 O Lord, open my lips, And my mouth shall show forth Your praise.	15 for my lips will be unsealed—oh, how I will praise you.
17 The sacrifices of God *are* a broken spirit: a broken and a contrite heart, O God, thou wilt not despise.	17 The sacrifices of God *are* a broken spirit, A broken and a contrite heart— These, O God, You will not despise.	17 It is a broken spirit you want—remorse and penitence. A broken and a contrite heart, O God, you will not ignore.
55:22 Cast thy burden upon the LORD, and he shall sustain thee: he shall never suffer the righteous to be moved.	**55:22** Cast your burden on the LORD, And He shall sustain you; He shall never permit the righteous to be moved.	**55:22** Give your burdens to the Lord. He will carry them. He will not permit the godly to slip or fall.
63:3 Because thy lovingkindness *is* better than life, my lips shall praise thee.	**63:3** Because Your lovingkindness *is* better than life, My lips shall praise You.	**63:3** for your love and kindness are better to me than life itself. How I praise you!
68:5 A father of the fatherless, and a judge of the widows, *is* God in his holy habitation.	**68:5** A father of the fatherless, a defender of widows, *Is* God in His holy habitation.	**68:5** He is a father to the fatherless; he gives justice to the widows, for he is holy.
20 *He that is* our God *is* the God of salvation; and unto GOD the Lord *belong* the issues from death.	20 Our God is the God of salvation; And to GOD the Lord *belong* escapes from death.	20 He frees us! He rescues us from death.
69:1 Save me, O God; for the waters are come in unto *my* soul.	**69:1** Save me, O God! For the waters have come up to *my* neck.	**69:1** Save me, O my God. The floods have risen.

NIV	RSV	TEV
42:11 Why are you downcast, O my soul? Why so disturbed within me? Put your hope in God, for I will yet praise him, my Savior and my God.	**42:11** Why are you cast down, O my soul, and why are you disquieted within me? Hope in God; for I shall again praise him, my help and my God.	**42:11** Why am I so sad? Why am I so troubled? I will put my hope in God, and once again I will praise him, my savior and my God.
46:1 God is our refuge and strength, an ever present help in trouble.	**46:1** God is our refuge and strength, a very present help in trouble.	**46:1** God is our shelter and strength, always ready to help in times of trouble.
2 Therefore we will not fear, though the earth give way and the mountains fall into the heart of the sea,	**2** Therefore we will not fear though the earth should change, though the mountains shake in the heart of the sea;	**2** So we will not be afraid, even if the earth is shaken and mountains fall into the ocean depths;
3 though its waters roar and foam and the mountains quake with their surging. *Selah*	**3** though its waters roar and foam, though the mountains tremble with its tumult. *Selah*	**3** even if the seas roar and rage, and the hills are shaken by the violence.
48:14 For this God is our God for ever and ever; he will be our guide even to the end.	**48:14** that this is God, our God for ever and ever. He will be our guide for ever.	**48:14** "This God is our God forever and ever; he will lead us for all time to come."
49:15 But God will redeem my soul from the grave; he will surely take me to himself. *Selah*	**49:15** But God will ransom my soul from the power of Sheol, for he will receive me. *Selah*	**49:15** But God will rescue me; he will save me from the power of death.
51:3 For I know my transgressions, and my sin is always before me.	**51:3** For I know my transgressions, and my sin is ever before me.	**51:3** I recognize my faults; I am always conscious of my sins.
4 Against you, you only, have I sinned and done what is evil in your sight, so that you are proved right when you speak and justified when you judge.	**4** Against thee, thee only, have I sinned, and done that which is evil in thy sight, so that thou art justified in thy sentence and blameless in thy judgment.	**4** I have sinned against you—only against you— and done what you consider evil. So you are right in judging me; you are justified in condemning me.
12 Restore to me the joy of your salvation and grant me a willing spirit, to sustain me.	**12** Restore to me the joy of thy salvation, and uphold me with a willing spirit.	**12** Give me again the joy that comes from your salvation. and make me willing to obey you.
13 Then I will teach transgressors your ways. and sinners will turn back to you.	**13** Then I will teach transgressors thy ways, and sinners will return to thee.	**13** Then I will teach sinners your commands, and they will turn back to you.
14 Save me from bloodguilt, O God, the God who saves me, and my tongue will sing of your righteousness.	**14** Deliver me from bloodguiltiness, O God, thou God of my salvation, and my tongue will sing aloud of thy deliverance.	**14** Spare my life, O God, and save me, and I will gladly proclaim your righteousness.
15 O Lord, open my lips, and my mouth will declare your praise.	**15** O Lord, open thou my lips, and my mouth shall show forth thy praise.	**15** Help me to speak, Lord, and I will praise you.
17 The sacrifices of God are a broken spirit; a broken and contrite heart, O God, you will not despise.	**17** The sacrifice acceptable to God is a broken spirit; a broken and contrite heart, O God, thou wilt not despise.	**17** My sacrifice is a humble spirit, O God; you will not reject a humble and repentant heart.
55:22 Cast your cares on the LORD and he will sustain you; he will never let the righteous fall.	**55:22** Cast your burden on the LORD, and he will sustain you; he will never permit the righteous to be moved.	**55:22** Leave your troubles with the LORD, and he will defend you; he never lets honest men be defeated.
63:3 Because your love is better than life, my lips will glorify you.	**63:3** Because thy steadfast love is better than life, my lips will praise thee.	**63:3** Your constant love is better than life itself, and so I will praise you.
68:5 A father to the fatherless, a defender of widows, is God in his holy dwelling.	**68:5** Father of the fatherless and protector of widows is God in his holy habitation.	**68:5** God, who lives in his sacred Temple, cares for orphans and protects widows.
20 Our God is a God who saves; from the Sovereign LORD comes escape from death.	**20** Our God is a God of salvation; and to GOD, the Lord, belongs escape from death.	**20** Our God is a God who saves; he is the LORD, our Lord, who rescues us from death.
69:1 Save me, O God, for the waters have come up to my neck.	**69:1** Save me, O God! For the waters have come up to my neck.	**69:1** Save me, O God! The water is up to my neck;

KJV	NKJV	TLB
9 For the zeal of thine house hath eaten me up; and the reproaches of them that reproached thee are fallen upon me.	9 Because zeal for Your house has eaten me up, And the reproaches of those who reproach You have fallen on me.	9 My zeal for God and his work burns hot within me. And because I advocate your cause, your enemies insult me even as they insult you.
71:17 O God, thou hast taught me from my youth: and hitherto have I declared thy wondrous works.	**71:17** O God, You have taught me from my youth; And to this *day* I declare Your wondrous works.	**71:17** O God, you have helped me from my earliest childhood—and I have constantly testified to others of the wonderful things you do.
18 Now also when I am old and greyheaded, O God, forsake me not; until I have shewed thy strength unto *this* generation, *and* thy power to every one *that* is to come.	18 Now also when *I am* old and grayheaded, O God, do not forsake me, Until I declare Your strength to *this* generation, Your power to everyone *who* is to come.	18 And now that I am old and gray, don't forsake me. Give me time to tell this new generation (and their children too) about all your mighty miracles.
20 *Thou,* which hast shewed me great and sore troubles, shalt quicken me again, and shalt bring me up again from the depths of the earth.	20 *You,* who have shown me great and severe troubles, Shall revive me again, And bring me up again from the depths of the earth.	20 You have let me sink down deep in desperate problems. But you will bring me back to life again, up from the depths of the earth.
72:1 Give the king thy judgments, O God, and thy righteousness unto the king's son.	**72:1** Give the king Your judgments, O God, And Your righteousness to the king's Son.	**72:1** O God, help the king to judge as you would, and help his son to walk in godliness.
2 He shall judge thy people with righteousness, and thy poor with judgment.	2 He will judge Your people with righteousness, And Your poor with justice.	2 Help him to give justice to your people, even to the poor.
3 The mountains shall bring peace to the people, and the little hills, by righteousness.	3 The mountains will bring peace to the people, And the little hills, by righteousness.	3 May the mountains and hills flourish in prosperity because of his good reign.
4 He shall judge the poor of the people, he shall save the children of the needy, and shall break in pieces the oppressor.	4 He will bring justice to the poor of the people; He will save the children of the needy, And will break in pieces the oppressor.	4 Help him to defend the poor and needy and to crush their oppressors.
5 They shall fear thee as long as the sun and moon endure, throughout all generations	5 They shall fear You As long as the sun and moon endure, Throughout all generations.	5 May the poor and needy revere you constantly, as long as sun and moon continue in the skies! Yes, forever!
6 He shall come down like rain upon the mown grass: as showers *that* water the earth.	6 He shall come down like rain upon the mown grass, Like showers *that* water the earth.	6 May the reign of this son of mine be as gentle and fruitful as the springtime rains upon the grass—like showers that water the earth!
8 He shall have dominion also from sea to sea, and from the river unto the ends of the earth.	8 He shall have dominion also from sea to sea, And from the River to the ends of the earth.	8 Let him reign from sea to sea, and from the Euphrates River to the ends of the earth.
17 His name shall endure for ever: his name shall be continued as long as the sun: and *men* shall be blessed in him: all nations shall call him blessed.	17 His name shall endure forever; His name shall continue as long as the sun. And *men* shall be blessed in Him; All nations shall call Him blessed.	17 His name will be honored forever; it will continue as the sun; and all will be blessed in him; all nations will praise him.
73:24 Thou shalt guide me with thy counsel, and afterward receive me *to* glory.	**73:24** You will guide me with Your counsel, And afterward receive me *to* glory.	**73:24** You will keep on guiding me all my life with your wisdom and counsel; and afterwards receive me into the glories of heaven!
25 Whom have I in heaven *but thee?* and *there is* none upon earth *that* I desire beside thee.	25 Whom have I in heaven *but You?* And *there is* none upon earth *that* I desire besides You.	25 Whom have I in heaven but you? And I desire no one on earth as much as you!
84:11 For the LORD God *is* a sun and shield: the LORD will give grace and glory: no good *thing* will he withhold from them that walk uprightly.	**84:11** For the LORD God *is* a sun and shield; The LORD will give grace and glory; No good *thing* will He withhold From those who walk uprightly.	**84:11** For Jehovah God is our Light and our Protector. He gives us grace and glory. No good thing will he withhold from those who walk along his paths.
89:1 I will sing of the mercies of the LORD for ever: with my mouth will I make known thy faithfulness to all generations.	**89:1** I will sing of the mercies of the LORD forever; With my mouth will I make known Your faithfulness to all generations.	**89:1** Forever and ever I will sing about the tender kindness of the Lord! Young and old shall hear about your blessings.

NIV	RSV	TEV

9 for zeal for your house consumes me,
  and the insults of those who insult you
    fall on me.
	9 For zeal for thy house has consumed me,
	  and the insults of those who insult thee
	    have fallen on me.
		9 My devotion to your Temple burns in me
		  like a fire;
		  the insults which are hurled at you fall on
		    me.

71:17 Since my youth, O God, you have
    taught me,
  and to this day I declare your
    marvelous deeds.
	71:17 O God, from my youth thou hast taught
	  me,
	  and I still proclaim thy wondrous
	    deeds.
		71:17 You have taught me ever since I was
		    young,
		  and I still tell of your wonderful acts.

18 Even when I am old and gray,
  do not forsake me, O God,
  till I declare your power to the next
    generation,
  your might to all who are to come.
	18 So even to old age and gray hairs,
	  O God, do not forsake me,
	  till I proclaim thy might
	    to all the generations to come.
	  Thy power
		18 Now that I am old and my hair is gray,
		  do not abandon me, O God!
		  Be with me while I proclaim your power
		    and might
		  to all generations to come.

20 Though you have made me see troubles,
    many and bitter,
  you will restore my life again;
  from the depths of the earth
  you will again bring me up.
	20 Thou who hast made me see many sore
	    troubles
	  wilt revive me again;
	  from the depths of the earth
	  thou wilt bring me up again.
		20 You have sent troubles and suffering on
		    me,
		  but you will restore my strength;
		  you will keep me from the grave.

72:1 Endow the king with your justice, O
    God,
  the royal son with your righteousness.
	72:1 Give the king thy justice, O God,
	  and thy righteousness to the royal son!
		72:1 Teach the king to judge with your
		    righteousness, O God;
		  share with him your own justice,

2 He will judge your people in righteousness,
  your afflicted ones with justice.
	2 May he judge thy people with
	    righteousness,
	  and thy poor with justice!
		2 so that he will rule over your people with
		    justice
		  and govern the oppressed with
		    righteousness.

3 The mountains will bring prosperity to the
    people,
  the hills the fruit of righteousness.
	3 Let the mountains bear prosperity for the
	    people,
	  and the hills, in righteousness!
		3 May the land enjoy prosperity;
		  may it experience righteousness.

4 He will defend the afflicted among the
    people
  and save the children of the needy;
  he will crush the oppressor.
	4 May he defend the cause of the poor of the
	    people,
	  give deliverance to the needy,
	  and crush the oppressor!
		4 May the king judge the poor fairly;
		  may he help the needy
		  and defeat their oppressors.

5 He will endure as long as the sun,
  as long as the moon, through all
    generations.
	5 May he live while the sun endures,
	  and as long as the moon, throughout all
	    generations!
		5 May your people worship you as long as the
		    sun shines,
		  as long as the moon gives light, for ages
		    to come.

6 He will be like rain falling on a mown field,
  like showers watering the earth.
	6 May he be like rain that falls on the mown
	    grass,
	  like showers that water the earth!
		6 May the king be like rain on the fields,
		  like showers falling on the land.

8 He will rule from sea to sea
  and from the River to the ends of the
    earth.
	8 May he have dominion from sea to sea,
	  and from the River to the ends of the
	    earth!
		8 His kingdom will reach from sea to sea,
		  from the Euphrates to the ends of the
		    earth.

17 May his name endure forever;
  may it continue as long as the sun.
 	
All nations will be blessed through him,
  and they will call him blessed.
	17 May his name endure for ever,
	  his fame continue as long as the sun!
	May men bless themselves by him,
	  all nations call him blessed!
		17 May the king's name never be forgotten;
		  may his fame last as long as the sun.
		May all nations ask God to bless them
		  as he has blessed the king.

73:24 You guide me with your counsel,
  and afterward you will take me into
    glory.
	73:24 Thou dost guide me with thy counsel,
	  and afterward thou wilt receive me to
	    glory.
		73:24 You guide me with your instruction
		  and at the end you will receive me
		    with honor.

25 Whom have I in heaven but you?
  And being with you, I desire nothing on
    earth.
	25 Whom have I in heaven but thee?
	  And there is nothing upon earth that I
	    desire besides thee.
		25 What else do I have in heaven but you?
		  Since I have you, what else could I want
		    on earth?

84:11 For the LORD God is a sun and shield;
  the LORD bestows favor and honor;
  no good thing does he withhold
  from those whose walk is blameless.
	84:11 For the LORD God is a sun and shield;
	  he bestows favor and honor.
	  No good thing does the LORD withhold
	  from those who walk uprightly.
		84:11 The LORD is our protector and glorious
		    king,
		  blessing us with kindness and honor.
		  He does not refuse any good thing
		  to those who do what is right.

89:1 I will sing of the LORD's great love
    forever;
  with my mouth I will make your
  faithfulness known through all
    generations.
	89:1 I will sing of thy steadfast love,
	    O LORD, for ever;
	  with my mouth I will proclaim thy
	  faithfulness to all generations.
		89:1 O LORD, I will always sing of your
		    constant love;
		  I will proclaim your faithfulness
		    forever.

KJV	NKJV	TLB
2 For I have said, Mercy shall be built up for ever: thy faithfulness shalt thou establish in the very heavens.	2 For I have said, "Mercy shall be built up forever; Your faithfulness You shall establish in the very heavens."	2 Your love and kindness are forever; your truth is as enduring as the heavens.
16 In thy name shall they rejoice all the day: and in thy righteousness shall they be exalted.	16 In Your name they rejoice all day long, And in Your righteousness they are exalted.	16 They rejoice all day long in your wonderful reputation and in your perfect righteousness.
90:1 Lord, thou hast been our dwelling place in all generations.	90:1 Lord, You have been our dwelling place in all generations.	90:1 Lord, through all the generations you have been our home!
2 Before the mountains were brought forth, or ever thou hadst formed the earth and the world, even from everlasting to everlasting, thou *art* God.	2 Before the mountains were brought forth, Or ever You had formed the earth and the world, Even from everlasting to everlasting, You *are* God.	2 Before the mountains were created, before the earth was formed, you are God without beginning or end.
3 Thou turnest man to destruction; and sayest, Return, ye children of men.	3 You turn man to destruction, And say, "Return, O children of men."	3 You speak, and man turns back to dust.
4 For a thousand years in thy sight *are but* as yesterday when it is past, and *as* a watch in the night.	4 For a thousand years in Your sight *Are* like yesterday when it is past, And *like* a watch in the night.	4 A thousand years are but as yesterday to you! They are like a single hour!
9 For all our days are passed away in the wrath: we spend our years as a tale *that is told.*	9 For all our days have passed away in Your wrath; We finish our years like a sigh.	9 No wonder the years are long and heavy here beneath your wrath. All our days are filled with sighing.
10 The days of our years *are* threescore years and ten; and if by reason of strength *they be* fourscore years, yet *is* their strength labour and sorrow; for it is soon cut off, and we fly away.	10 The days of our lives *are* seventy years; And if by reason of strength *they are* eighty years, Yet their boast *is* only labor and sorrow; For it is soon cut off, and we fly away.	10 Seventy years are given us! And some may even live to eighty. But even the best of these years are often emptiness and pain; soon they disappear, and we are gone.
91:1 He that dwelleth in the secret place of the most High shall abide under the shadow of the Almighty.	91:1 He who dwells in the secret place of the Most High Shall abide under the shadow of the Almighty.	91:1 We live within the shadow of the Almighty, sheltered by the God who is above all gods.
2 I will say of the LORD, *He is* my refuge and my fortress: my God; in him will I trust.	2 I will say of the LORD, "*He is* my refuge and my fortress; My God, in Him I will trust."	2 This I declare, that he alone is my refuge, my place of safety; he is my God, and I am trusting him.
14 Because he hath set his love upon me, therefore will I deliver him: I will set him on high, because he hath known my name.	14 Because he has set his love upon Me, therefore I will deliver him; I will set him on high, because he has known My name.	14 For the Lord says, "Because he loves me, I will rescue him; I will make him great because he trusts in my name.
15 He shall call upon me, and I will answer him: I *will be* with him in trouble; I will deliver him, and honour him.	15 He shall call upon Me, and I will answer him; I *will be* with him in trouble; I will deliver him and honor him.	15 When he calls on me I will answer; I will be with him in trouble, and rescue him and honor him.
16 With long life wil! I satisfy him, and shew him my salvation.	16 With long life I will satisfy him, And show him My salvation.	16 I will satisfy him with a full life and give him my salvation."
92:1 *It is a* good *thing* to give thanks unto the LORD, and to sing praises unto thy name, O most High;	92:1 *It is* good to give thanks to the LORD, And to sing praises to Your name, O Most High;	92:1 It is good to say, "Thank you" to the Lord, to sing praises to the God who is above all gods.
2 To shew forth thy lovingkindness in the morning, and thy faithfulness every night,	2 To declare Your lovingkindness in the morning, And Your faithfulness every night.	2 Every morning tell him, "Thank you for your kindness," and every evening rejoice in all his faithfulness.
94:18 When I said, My foot slippeth; thy mercy, O LORD, held me up.	94:18 If I say, "My foot slips," Your mercy, O LORD, will hold me up.	94:18 I screamed, "I'm slipping, Lord!" and he was kind and saved me.
103:1 Bless the LORD, O my soul: and all that is within me, *bless* his holy name.	103:1 Bless the LORD, O my soul; And all that is within me, *bless* His holy name!	103:1 I bless the holy name of God with all my heart.
2 Bless the LORD, O my soul, and forget not all his benefits:	2 Bless the LORD, O my soul, And forget not all His benefits:	2 Yes, I will bless the Lord and not forget the glorious things he does for me.
3 Who forgiveth all thine iniquities; who healeth all thy diseases:	3 Who forgives all your iniquities, Who heals all your diseases,	3 He forgives all my sins. He heals me.
4 Who redeemeth thy life from destruction; who crowneth thee with lovingkindness and tender mercies;	4 Who redeems your life from destruction, Who crowns you with lovingkindness and tender mercies,	4 He ransoms me from hell. He surrounds me with lovingkindness and tender mercies.

NIV	RSV	TEV
2 I will declare that your love stands firm forever, that you established your faithfulness in heaven itself.	2 For thy steadfast love was established for ever, thy faithfulness is firm as the heavens.	2 I know that your love will last for all time, that your faithfulness is as permanent as the sky.
16 They rejoice in your name all day long; they exult in your righteousness.	16 who exult in thy name all the day, and extol thy righteousness.	16 Because of you they rejoice all day long, and they praise you for your goodness.
90:1 Lord, you have been our dwelling place throughout all generations.	90:1 Lord, thou hast been our dwelling place in all generations.	90:1 O Lord, you have always been our home.
2 Before the mountains were born or you brought forth the earth and the world, from everlasting to everlasting you are God.	2 Before the mountains were brought forth, or ever thou hadst formed the earth and the world, from everlasting to everlasting thou art God.	2 Before you created the hills or brought the world into being, you were eternally God, and will be God forever.
3 You turn men back to dust, saying, "Return to dust, O sons of men."	3 Thou turnest man back to the dust, and sayest, "Turn back, O children of men!"	3 You tell man to return to what he was; you change him back to dust.
4 For a thousand years in your sight are like a day that has just gone by, or like a watch in the night.	4 For a thousand years in thy sight are but as yesterday when it is past, or as a watch in the night.	4 A thousand years to you are like one day; they are like yesterday, already gone, like a short hour in the night.
9 All our days pass away under your wrath; we finish our years with a moan.	9 For all our days pass away under thy wrath, our years come to an end like a sigh.	9 Our life is cut short by your anger; it fades away like a whisper.
10 The length of our days is seventy years— or eighty, if we have the strength; yet their span is but trouble and sorrow, for they quickly pass, and we fly away.	10 The years of our life are threescore and ten, or even by reason of strength fourscore; yet their span is but toil and trouble; they are soon gone, and we fly away.	10 Seventy years is all we have— eighty years, if we are strong; yet all they bring us is trouble and sorrow; life is soon over, and we are gone.
91:1 He who dwells in the shelter of the Most High will rest in the shadow of the Almighty.	91:1 He who dwells in the shelter of the Most High, who abides in the shadow of the Almighty,	91:1 Whoever goes to the LORD for safety, whoever remains under the protection of the Almighty,
2 I will say of the LORD, "He is my refuge and my fortress, my God, in whom I trust."	2 I will say to the LORD, "My refuge and my fortress; my God, in whom I trust."	2 can say to him, "You are my defender and protector. You are my God; in you I trust."
14 "Because he loves me," says the LORD, "I will rescue him; I will protect him, for he acknowledges my name.	14 Because he cleaves to me in love, I will deliver him; I will protect him, because he knows my name.	14 God says, "I will save those who love me and will protect those who acknowledge me as LORD.
15 He will call upon me, and I will answer him; I will be with him in trouble, I will deliver him and honor him.	15 When he calls to me, I will answer him; I will be with him in trouble, I will rescue him and honor him.	15 When they call to me, I will answer them; when they are in trouble, I will be with them. I will rescue them and honor them.
16 With long life will I satisfy him and show him my salvation."	16 With long life I will satisfy him, and show him my salvation.	16 I will reward them with long life; I will save them."
92:1 It is good to praise the LORD and make music to your name, O Most High,	92:1 It is good to give thanks to the LORD, to sing praises to thy name, O Most High;	92:1 How good it is to give thanks to you, O LORD, to sing in your honor, O Most High God.
2 to proclaim your love in the morning and your faithfulness at night,	2 to declare thy steadfast love in the morning, and thy faithfulness by night,	2 to proclaim your constant love every morning and your faithfulness every night,
94:18 When I said, "My foot is slipping," your love, O LORD, supported me.	94:18 When I thought, "My foot slips," thy steadfast love, O LORD, held me up.	94:18 I said, "I am falling"; but your constant love, O LORD, held me up.
103:1 Praise the LORD, O my soul; all my inmost being, praise his holy name.	103:1 Bless the LORD, O my soul; and all that is within me, bless his holy name!	103:1 Praise the LORD, my soul! All my being, praise his holy name!
2 Praise the LORD, O my soul, and forget not all his benefits.	2 Bless the LORD, O my soul, and forget not all his benefits,	2 Praise the LORD, my soul, and do not forget how kind he is.
3 He forgives all my sins and heals all my diseases;	3 who forgives all your iniquity, who heals all your diseases,	3 He forgives all my sins and heals all my diseases.
4 he redeems my life from the pit and crowns me with love and compassion.	4 who redeems your life from the Pit, who crowns you with steadfast love and mercy,	4 He keeps me from the grave and blesses me with love and mercy.

KJV	NKJV	TLB
5 Who satisfieth thy mouth with good *things;* so *that* thy youth is renewed like the eagle's.	5 Who satisfies your mouth with good *things,* So *that* your youth is renewed like the eagle's.	5 He fills my life with good things! My youth is renewed like the eagle's!
12 As far as the east is from the west, *so far* hath he removed our transgressions from us.	12 As far as the east is from the west, So far has He removed our transgressions from us.	12 He has removed our sins as far away from us as the east is from the west.
13 Like as a father pitieth *his* children, *so* the LORD pitieth them that fear him.	13 As a father pities *his* children, So the LORD pities those who fear Him.	13 He is like a father to us, tender and sympathetic to those who reverence him.
14 For he knoweth our frame; he remembereth that we *are* dust.	14 For He knows our frame; He remembers that we *are* dust.	14 For he knows we are but dust,
107:8 Oh that *men* would praise the LORD *for* his goodness, and *for* his wonderful works to the children of men!	107:8 Oh, that *men* would give thanks to the LORD *for* His goodness, And *for* His wonderful works to the children of men!	107:8 Oh, that these men would praise the Lord for his lovingkindness, and for all of his wonderful deeds!
9 For he satisfieth the longing soul, and filleth the hungry soul with goodness.	9 For He satisfies the longing soul, And fills the hungry soul with goodness.	9 For he satisfies the thirsty soul and fills the hungry soul with good.
110:1 The LORD said unto my LORD, Sit thou at my right hand, until I make thine enemies thy footstool.	110:1 The LORD said to my Lord, "Sit at My right hand, Till I make Your enemies Your footstool."	110:1 Jehovah said to my Lord the Messiah, "Rule as my regent—I will subdue your enemies and make them bow low before you."
2 The LORD shall send the rod of thy strength out of Zion: rule thou in the midst of thine enemies.	2 The LORD shall send the rod of Your strength out of Zion. Rule in the midst of Your enemies!	2 Jehovah has established your throne in Jerusalem to rule over your enemies.
111:10 The fear of the LORD *is* the beginning of wisdom: a good understanding have all they that do *his commandments:* his praise endureth for ever.	111:10 The fear of the LORD *is* the beginning of wisdom; A good understanding have all those who do *His commandments.* His praise endures forever.	111:10 How can men be wise? The only way to begin is by reverence for God. For growth in wisdom comes from obeying his laws. Praise his name forever.
115:14 The LORD shall increase you more and more, you and your children.	115:14 May the LORD give you increase more and more, You and your children.	115:14 May the Lord richly bless both you and your children.
116:15 Precious in the sight of the LORD *is* the death of his saints.	116:15 Precious in the sight of the LORD *Is* the death of His saints.	116:15 His loved ones are very precious to him and he does not lightly let them die.
117:1 O Praise the LORD, all ye nations: praise him, all ye people.	117:1 Oh, praise the LORD, all you Gentiles! Laud Him, all you peoples!	117:1 Praise the Lord, all nations everywhere. Praise him, all the peoples of the earth.
2 For his merciful kindness is great toward us: and the truth of the LORD *endureth* for ever. Praise ye the LORD.	2 For His merciful kindness is great toward us, And the truth of the LORD *endures* forever. Praise the LORD!	2 For he loves us very dearly, and his truth endures. Praise the Lord.
119:1 Blessed *are* the undefiled in the way, who walk in the law of the LORD.	119:1 Blessed *are* the undefiled in the way, Who walk in the law of the LORD!	119:1 Happy are all who perfectly follow the laws of God.
2 Blessed *are* they that keep his testimonies, *and that* seek him with the whole heart.	2 Blessed *are* those who keep His testimonies, Who seek Him with the whole heart!	2 Happy are all who search for God, and always do his will,
9 Wherewithal shall a young man cleanse his way? by taking heed *thereto* according to thy word.	9 How can a young man cleanse his way? By taking heed according to Your word.	9 How can a young man stay pure? By reading your Word and following its rules.
11 Thy word have I hid in mine heart, that I might not sin against thee.	11 Your word I have hidden in my heart, That I might not sin against You.	11 I have thought much about your words, and stored them in my heart so that they would hold me back from sin.
24 Thy testimonies also *are* my delight *and* my counsellors.	24 Your testimonies also *are* my delight And my counselors.	24 Your laws are both my light and my counselors.
28 My soul melteth for heaviness: strengthen thou me according unto thy word.	28 My soul melts from heaviness; Strengthen me according to Your word.	28 I weep with grief; my heart is heavy with sorrow; encourage and cheer me with your words.
50 This *is* my comfort in my affliction: for thy word hath quickened me.	50 This *is* my comfort in my affliction, For Your word has given me life.	50 They give me strength in all my troubles; how they refresh and revive me!

NIV	RSV	TEV
5 He satisfies my desires with good things, so that my youth is renewed like the eagle's.	5 who satisfies you with good as long as you live so that your youth is renewed like the eagle's.	5 He fills my life with good things, so that I stay young and strong like an eagle.
12 as far as the east is from the west, so far has he removed our transgressions from us.	12 as far as the east is from the west, so far does he remove our transgressions from us.	12 As far as the east is from the west, so far does he remove our sins from us.
13 As a father has compassion on his children, so the LORD has compassion on those who fear him;	13 As a father pities his children, so the LORD pities those who fear him.	13 As a father is kind to his children, so the LORD is kind to those who honor him.
14 for he knows how we are formed, he remembers that we are dust.	14 For he knows our frame; he remembers that we are dust.	14 He knows what we are made of; he remembers that we are dust.
107:8 Let them give thanks to the LORD for his unfailing love and his wonderful deeds for men,	107:8 Let them thank the LORD for his steadfast love, for his wonderful works to the sons of men!	107:8 They must thank the LORD for his constant love, for the wonderful things he did for them.
9 for he satisfies the thirsty and fills the hungry with good things.	9 For he satisfies him who is thirsty, and the hungry he fills with good things.	9 He satisfies those who are thirsty and fills the hungry with good things.
110:1 The LORD says to my Lord: "Sit at my right hand until I make your enemies a footstool for your feet."	110:1 The LORD says to my lord: "Sit at my right hand, till I make your enemies your footstool."	110:1 The LORD said to my lord, the king, "Sit here at my right side until I put your enemies under your feet."
2 The LORD will extend your mighty scepter from Zion; you will rule in the midst of your enemies.	2 The LORD sends forth from Zion your mighty scepter. Rule in the midst of your foes!	2 From Zion the LORD will extend your royal power. "Rule over your enemies," he says.
111:10 The fear of the LORD is the beginning of wisdom; all who follow his precepts have good understanding. To him belongs eternal praise.	111:10 The fear of the LORD is the beginning of wisdom; a good understanding have all those who practice it. His praise endures for ever!	111:10 The way to become wise is to honor the LORD; he gives sound judgment to all who obey his commands. He is to be praised forever.
115:14 May the LORD make you increase, both you and your children.	115:14 May the LORD give you increase, you and your children!	115:14 May the LORD give you children— you and your descendants!
116:15 Precious in the sight of the LORD is the death of his saints.	116:15 Precious in the sight of the LORD is the death of his saints.	116:15 How painful it is to the LORD when one of his people dies!
117:1 Praise the LORD, all you nations; extol him, all you peoples.	117:1 Praise the LORD, all nations! Extol him, all peoples!	117:1 Praise the LORD, all nations! Praise him, all peoples!
2 For great is his love toward us, and the faithfulness of the LORD endures forever. Praise the LORD.	2 For great is his steadfast love toward us; and the faithfulness of the LORD endures for ever. Praise the LORD!	2 His love for us is strong, and his faithfulness is eternal. Praise the LORD!
119:1 Blessed are they whose ways are blameless, who walk according to the law of the LORD.	119:1 Blessed are those whose way is blameless, who walk in the law of the LORD!	119:1 Happy are those whose lives are faultless, who live according to the law of the LORD.
2 Blessed are they who keep his statutes and seek him with all their heart.	2 Blessed are those who keep his testimonies, who seek him with their whole heart,	2 Happy are those who follow his commands, who obey him with all their heart.
9 How can a young man keep his way pure? By living according to your word.	9 How can a young man keep his way pure? By guarding it according to thy word.	9 How can a young man keep his life pure? By obeying your commands.
11 I have hidden your word in my heart that I might not sin against you.	11 I have laid up thy word in my heart, that I might not sin against thee.	11 I keep your law in my heart, so that I will not sin against you.
24 Your statutes are my delight; they are my counselors.	24 Thy testimonies are my delight, they are my counselors.	24 Your instructions give me pleasure; they are my advisers.
28 My soul is weary with sorrow; strengthen me according to your word.	28 My soul melts away for sorrow; strengthen me according to thy word!	28 I am overcome by sorrow; strengthen me, as you have promised.
50 My comfort in my suffering is this: Your promise renews my life.	50 This is my comfort in my affliction that thy promise gives me life.	50 Even in my suffering I was comforted because your promise gave me life.

KJV	NKJV	TLB
80 Let my heart be sound in thy statutes; that I be not ashamed.	80 Let my heart be blameless regarding Your statutes, That I may not be ashamed.	80 Help me to love your every wish; then I will never have to be ashamed of myself.
89 For ever, O LORD, thy word is settled in heaven.	89 Forever, O LORD, Your word is settled in heaven.	89 Forever, O Lord, your Word stands firm in heaven.
93 I will never forget thy precepts: for with them thou hast quickened me.	93 I will never forget Your precepts, For by them You have given me life.	93 I will never lay aside your laws, for you have used them to restore my joy and health.
97 O how I love thy law! it is my meditation all the day.	97 Oh, how I love Your law! It is my meditation all the day.	97 Oh, how I love them. I think about them all day long.
105 Thy word is a lamp unto my feet, and a light unto my path.	105 Your word is a lamp to my feet And a light to my path.	105 Your words are a flashlight to light the path ahead of me, and keep me from stumbling.
130 The entrance of thy words giveth light; it giveth understanding unto the simple.	130 The entrance of Your words gives light; It gives understanding to the simple.	130 As your plan unfolds, even the simple can understand it.
165 Great peace have they which love thy law: and nothing shall offend them.	165 Great peace have those who love Your law, And nothing causes them to stumble.	165 Those who love your laws have great peace of heart and mind and do not stumble.
121:1 I will lift up mine eyes unto the hills, from whence cometh my help.	121:1 I will lift up my eyes to the hills— From whence comes my help?	121:1 Shall I look to the mountain gods for help?
2 My help cometh from the LORD, which made heaven and earth.	2 My help comes from the LORD, Who made heaven and earth.	2 No! My help is from Jehovah who made the mountains! And the heavens too!
3 He will not suffer thy foot to be moved: he that keepeth thee will not slumber.	3 He will not allow your foot to be moved; He who keeps you will not slumber.	3-4 He will never let me strumble, slip or fall. For he is always watching, never sleeping.
4 Behold, he that keepeth Israel shall neither slumber nor sleep.	4 Behold, He who keeps Israel Shall neither slumber nor sleep.	
5 The LORD is thy keeper: the LORD, is thy shade upon thy right hand.	5 The LORD is your keeper; The LORD is your shade at your right hand.	5 Jehovah himself is caring for you! He is your defender.
6 The sun shall not smite thee by day, nor the moon by night.	6 The sun shall not strike you by day, Nor the moon by night.	6 He protects you day and night.
7 The LORD shall preserve thee from all evil: he shall preserve thy soul.	7 The LORD shall preserve you from all evil; He shall preserve your soul.	7 He keeps you from all evil, and preserves your life.
8 The LORD shall preserve thy going out and thy coming in from this time forth, and even for evermore.	8 The LORD shall preserve your going out and your coming in From this time forth, and even forevermore.	8 He keeps his eye upon you as you come and go, and always guards you.
126:5 They that sow in tears shall reap in joy.	126:5 Those who sow in tears Shall reap in joy.	126:5 Those who sow tears shall reap joy.
6 He that goeth forth and weepeth, bearing precious seed, shall doubtless come again with rejoicing, bringing his sheaves with him.	6 He who continually goes forth weeping, Bearing seed for sowing, Shall doubtless come again with rejoicing, Bringing his sheaves with him.	6 Yes, they go out weeping, carrying seed for sowing, and return singing, carrying their sheaves.
127:1 Except the LORD build the house, they labour in vain that build it: except the LORD keep the city, the watchman waketh but in vain.	127:1 Unless the LORD builds the house, They labor in vain who build it; Unless the LORD guards the city, The watchman stays awake in vain.	127:1 Unless the Lord builds a house, the builders' work is useless. Unless the Lord protects a city, sentries do no good.
2 It is vain for you to rise up early, to sit up late, to eat the bread of sorrows: for so he giveth his beloved sleep.	2 It is vain for you to rise up early, To sit up late, To eat the bread of sorrows; For so He gives His beloved sleep.	2 It is senseless for you to work so hard from early morning until late at night, fearing you will starve to death; for God wants his loved ones to get their proper rest.
128:1 Blessed is every one that feareth the LORD; that walketh in his ways.	128:1 Blessed is every one who fears the LORD, Who walks in His ways.	128:1 Blessings on all who reverence and trust the Lord—on all who obey him!
6 Yea, thou shalt see thy children's children, and peace upon Israel.	6 Yes, may you see your children's children. Peace be upon Israel!	6 May you live to enjoy your grandchildren! And may God bless Israel!
133:1 Behold, how good and how pleasant it is for brethren to dwell together in unity!	133:1 Behold, how good and how pleasant it is For brethren to dwell together in unity!	133:1 How wonderful it is, how pleasant, when brothers live in harmony!

NIV	RSV	TEV
80 May my heart be blameless toward your decrees, that I may not be put to shame.	80 May my heart be blameless in thy statutes, that I may not be put to shame!	80 May I perfectly obey your commandments and be spared the shame of defeat.
89 Your word, O LORD, is eternal; it stands firm in the heavens.	89 For ever, O LORD, thy word is firmly fixed in the heavens.	89 Your word, O LORD, will last forever; it is eternal in heaven.
93 I will never forget your precepts, for by them you have renewed my life.	93 I will never forget thy precepts; for by them thou hast given me life.	93 I will never neglect your instructions, because by them you have kept me alive.
97 Oh, how I love your law! I meditate on it all day long.	97 Oh, how I love thy law! It is my meditation all the day.	97 How I love your law! I think about it all day long.
105 Your word is a lamp to my feet and a light for my path.	105 Thy word is a lamp to my feet and a light to my path.	105 Your word is a lamp to guide me and a light for my path.
130 The entrance of your words gives light; it gives understanding to the simple.	130 The unfolding of thy words gives light; it imparts understanding to the simple.	130 The explanation of your teachings gives light and brings wisdom to the ignorant.
165 Great peace have they who love your law, and nothing can make them stumble.	165 Great peace have those who love thy law; nothing can make them stumble.	165 Those who love your law have perfect security, and there is nothing that can make them fall.
121:1 I lift up my eyes to the hills— where does my help come from?	121:1 I lift up my eyes to the hills. From whence does my help come?	121:1 I look to the mountains; where will my help come from?
2 My help comes from the LORD, the Maker of heaven and earth.	2 My help comes from the LORD, who made heaven and earth.	2 My help will come from the LORD, who made heaven and earth.
3 He will not let your foot slip— he who watches over you will not slumber;	3 He will not let your foot be moved, he who keeps you will not slumber.	3 He will not let you fall; your protector is always awake.
4 indeed, he who watches over Israel will neither slumber nor sleep.	4 Behold, he who keeps Israel will neither slumber nor sleep.	4 The protector of Israel never dozes or sleeps.
5 The LORD watches over you— the LORD is your shade at your right hand;	5 The LORD is your keeper; the LORD is your shade on your right hand.	5 The LORD will guard you; he is by your side to protect you.
6 the sun will not harm you by day, nor the moon by night.	6 The sun shall not smite you by day, nor the moon by night.	6 The sun will not hurt you during the day, nor the moon during the night.
7 The LORD will keep you from all harm— he will watch over your life;	7 The LORD will keep you from all evil; he will keep your life.	7 The LORD will protect you from all danger; he will keep you safe.
8 the LORD will watch over your coming and going both now and forevermore.	8 The LORD will keep your going out and your coming in for this time forth and for evermore.	8 He will protect you as you come and go now and forever.
126:5 Those who sow in tears will reap with songs of joy.	126:5 May those who sow in tears reap with shouts of joy!	126:5 Let those who wept as they planted their crops, gather the harvest with joy!
6 He who goes out weeping, carrying seed to sow, will return with songs of joy, carrying sheaves with him.	6 He that goes forth weeping, bearing the seed for sowing, shall come home with shouts of joy, bringing his sheaves with him.	6 Those who wept as they went out carrying the seed will come back singing for joy, as they bring in the harvest.
127:1 Unless the LORD builds the house, its builders labor in vain. Unless the LORD watches over the city, the watchmen stand guard in vain.	127:1 Unless the LORD builds the house, those who build it labor in vain. Unless the LORD watches over the city, the watchman stays awake in vain.	127:1 If the LORD does not build the house, the work of the builders is useless; if the LORD does not protect the city, it does no good for the sentries to stand guard.
2 In vain you rise early and stay up late, toiling for food to eat— for he grants sleep to those he loves.	2 It is in vain that you rise up early and go late to rest, eating the bread of anxious toil; for he gives to his beloved sleep.	2 It is useless to work so hard for a living, getting up early and going to bed late. For the LORD provides for those he loves, while they are asleep.
128:1 Blessed are all who fear the LORD, who walk in his ways.	128:1 Blessed is every one who fears the LORD, who walks in his ways!	128:1 Happy are those who obey the LORD, who live by his commands.
6 and may you live to see your children's children. Peace be upon Israel.	6 May you see your children's children! Peace be upon Israel!	6 May you live to see your grandchildren! Peace be with Israel!
133:1 How good and pleasant it is when brothers live together in unity!	133:1 Behold, how good and pleasant it is when brothers dwell in unity!	133:1 How wonderful it is, how pleasant, for God's people to live together in harmony!

KJV	NKJV	TLB
2 *It is* like the precious ointment upon the head, that ran down upon the beard, *even* Aaron's beard: that went down to the skirts of his garments;	2 *It is* like the precious oil upon the head, Running down on the beard, The beard of Aaron, Running down on the edge of his garments.	2 For harmony is as precious as the fragrant anointing oil that was poured over Aaron's head, and ran down onto his beard, and onto the border of his robe.
3 As the dew of Hermon, *and as the dew* that descended upon the mountains of Zion: for there the LORD commanded the blessing, *even* life for evermore.	3 *It is* like the dew of Hermon, Descending upon the mountains of Zion; For there the LORD commanded the blessing— Life forevermore.	3 Harmony is as refreshing as the dew on Mount Hermon, on the mountains of Israel. And God has pronounced this eternal blessing on Jerusalem, even life forevermore.
138:8 The LORD will perfect *that which* concerneth me: thy mercy, O LORD, *endureth* for ever: forsake not the works of thine own hands.	138:8 The LORD will perfect *that which* concerns me; Your mercy, O LORD, *endures* forever; Do not forsake the works of Your hands.	138:8 The Lord will work out his plans for my life—for your lovingkindness, Lord, continues forever. Don't abandon me—for you made me.
145:18 The LORD *is* nigh unto all them that call upon him, to all that call upon him in truth.	145:18 The LORD *is* near to all who call upon Him, To all who call upon Him in truth.	145:18 He is close to all who call on him sincerely.
19 He will fulfil the desire of them that fear him: he also will hear their cry, and will save them.	19 He will fulfill the desire of those who fear Him; He also will hear their cry and save them.	19 He fulfills the desires of those who reverence and trust him; he hears their cries for help and rescues them.
20 The LORD preserveth all them that love him: but all the wicked will he destroy.	20 The LORD preserves all who love Him, But all the wicked He will destroy.	20 He protects all those who love him, but destroys the wicked.
147:1 Praise ye the LORD: for *it is* good to sing praises unto our God; for *it is* pleasant; *and* praise is comely.	147:1 Praise the LORD! For *it is* good to sing praises to our God; For *it is* pleasant, *and* praise is beautiful.	147:1 Hallelujah! Yes, praise the Lord! How good it is to sing his praises! How delightful, and how right!
3 He healeth the broken in heart, and bindeth up their wounds.	3 He heals the broken-hearted And binds up their wounds.	3 He heals the brokenhearted, binding up their wounds.
149:5 Let the saints be joyful in glory: let them sing aloud upon their beds.	149:5 Let the saints be joyful in glory; Let them sing aloud on their beds.	149:5 Let his people rejoice in this honor. Let them sing for joy as they lie upon their beds.
6 *Let* the high *praises* of God *be* in their mouth, and a two-edged sword in their hand;	6 *Let* the high praises of God *be* in their mouth, And a two-edged sword in their hand,	6 Adore him, O his people! And take a double-edged sword
150:1 Praise ye the LORD. Praise God in his sanctuary: praise him in the firmament of his power.	150:1 Praise the LORD! Praise God in His sanctuary; Praise Him in His mighty firmament!	150:1 Hallelujah! Yes, praise the Lord! Praise him in his Temple, and in the heavens he made with mighty power.
2 Praise him for his mighty acts: praise him according to his excellent greatness.	2 Praise Him for His mighty acts; Praise Him according to His excellent greatness!	2 Praise him for his mighty works. Praise his unequaled greatness.

Proverbs

KJV	NKJV	TLB
1:7 The fear of the LORD *is* the beginning of knowledge: *but* fools despise wisdom and instruction.	1:7 The fear of the LORD *is* the beginning of knowledge, *But* fools despise wisdom and instruction.	1:7 How does a man become wise? The first step is to trust and reverence the Lord! Only fools refuse to be taught.
8 My son, hear the instruction of thy father, and forsake not the law of thy mother:	8 My son, hear the instruction of your father, And do not forsake the law of your mother;	8 Listen to your father and mother.
9 For they *shall be* an ornament of grace unto thy head, and chains about thy neck.	9 For they *will be* graceful ornaments on your head, And chains about your neck.	9 What you learn from them will stand you in good stead; it will gain you many honors.
2:6 For the LORD giveth wisdom: out of his mouth *cometh* knowledge and understanding.	2:6 For the LORD gives wisdom; From His mouth *come* knowledge and understanding;	2:6 For the Lord grants wisdom! His every word is a treasure of knowledge and understanding.
7 He layeth up sound wisdom for the righteous: *he is* a buckler to them that walk uprightly.	7 He stores up sound wisdom for the upright; *He is* a shield to those who walk uprightly;	7 He grants good sense to the godly—his saints. He is their shield,
3:5 Trust in the LORD with all thine heart; and lean not unto thine own understanding.	3:5 Trust in the LORD with all your heart, And lean not on your own understanding;	3:5 then trust the Lord completely; don't ever trust yourself.

NIV	RSV	TEV
2 It is like precious oil poured on the head, running down on the beard, running down on Aaron's beard, down upon the collar of his robes.	2 It is like the precious oil upon the head, running down upon the beard, upon the beard of Aaron, running down on the collar of his robes!	2 It is like the precious anointing oil running down from Aaron's head and beard, down to the collar of his robes.
3 It is as if the dew of Hermon were falling on Mount Zion. For there the LORD bestows his blessing, even life forevermore.	3 It is like the dew of Hermon, which falls on the mountains of Zion! For there the LORD has commanded the blessing, life for evermore.	3 It is like the dew on Mount Hermon, falling on the hills of Zion. That is where the LORD has promised his blessing— life that never ends.
138:8 The LORD will fulfill his purpose for me; your love, O LORD, endures forever— do not abandon the works of your hands.	138:8 The LORD will fulfil his purpose for me; thy steadfast love, O LORD, endures for ever. Do not forsake the work of thy hands.	138:8 You will do everything you have promised; LORD, your love is eternal. Complete the work that you have begun.
145:18 The LORD is near to all who call on him, to all who call on him in truth.	145:18 The LORD is near to all who call upon him, to all who call upon him in truth.	145:18 He is near to those who call to him, who call to him with sincerity.
19 He fulfills the desires of those who fear him; he hears their cry and saves them.	19 He fulfils the desire of all who fear him, he also hears their cry, and saves them.	19 He supplies the needs of those who honor him; he hears their cries and saves them.
20 The LORD watches over all who love him, but all the wicked he will destroy.	20 The LORD preserves all who love him; but all the wicked he will destroy.	20 He protects everyone who loves him, but he will destroy the wicked.
147:1 Praise the LORD. How good it is to sing praises to our God, how pleasant and fitting to praise him!	147:1 Praise the LORD! For it is good to sing praises to our God; for he is gracious, and a song of praise is seemly.	147:1 Praise the LORD! It is good to sing praise to our God; it is pleasant and right to praise him.
3 He heals the brokenhearted and binds up their wounds.	3 He heals the brokenhearted, and binds up their wounds.	3 He heals the broken-hearted and bandages their wounds.
149:5 Let the saints rejoice in this honor and sing for joy on their beds.	149:5 Let the faithful exult in glory; let them sing for joy on their couches.	149:5 Let God's people rejoice in their triumph and sing joyfully all night long.
6 May the praise of God be in their mouths and a double-edged sword in their hands,	6 Let the high praises of God be in their throats and two-edged swords in their hands,	6 Let them shout aloud as they praise God, with their sharp swords in their hands
150:1 Praise the LORD. Praise God in his sanctuary; praise him in his mighty heavens.	150:1 Praise the LORD! Praise God in his sanctuary; praise him in his mighty firmament!	150:1 Praise the LORD! Praise God in his Temple! Praise his strength in heaven!
2 Praise him for his acts of power; praise him for his surpassing greatness.	2 Praise him for his mighty deeds; praise him according to his exceeding greatness!	2 Praise him for the mighty things he has done. Praise his supreme greatness.

Proverbs

NIV	RSV	TEV
1:7 The fear of the LORD is the beginning of knowledge, but fools despise wisdom and discipline.	1:7 The fear of the LORD is the beginning of knowledge; fools despise wisdom and instruction.	1:7 To have knowledge, you must first have reverence for the LORD. Stupid people have no respect for wisdom and refuse to learn.
8 Listen, my son, to your father's instruction and do not forsake your mother's teaching.	8 Hear, my son, your father's instruction, and reject not your mother's teaching;	8 Son, pay attention to what your father and mother tell you.
9 They will be a garland to grace your head and a chain to adorn your neck.	9 for they are a fair garland for your head, and pendants for your neck.	9 Their teaching will improve your character as a handsome turban or a necklace improves your appearance.
2:6 For the LORD gives wisdom, and from his mouth come knowledge and understanding.	2:6 For the LORD gives wisdom; from his mouth come knowledge and understanding;	2:6 It is the LORD who gives wisdom; from him come knowledge and understanding.
7 He holds victory in store for the upright, he is a shield to those whose walk is blameless,	7 he stores up sound wisdom for the upright; he is a shield to those who walk in integrity,	7 He provides help and protection for righ- teous, honest men.
3:5 Trust in the LORD with all your heart and lean not on your own understanding;	3:5 Trust in the LORD with all your heart, and do not rely on your own insight.	3:5 Trust in the LORD with all your heart. Never rely on what you think you know.

KJV	NKJV	TLB
6 In all thy ways acknowledge him, and he shall direct thy paths.	6 In all your ways acknowledge Him, And He shall direct your paths.	6 In everything you do, put God first, and he will direct you and crown your efforts with success.
9 Honour, the LORD with thy substance, and with the firstfruits of all thine increase:	9 Honor the LORD with your possessions, And with the firstfruits of all your increase;	9 Honor the Lord by giving him the first part of all your income,
10 So shall thy barns be filled with plenty, and thy presses shall burst out with new wine.	10 So your barns will be filled with plenty, And your vats will overflow with new wine.	10 and he will fill your barns with wheat and barley and overflow your wine vats with the finest wines.
25 Be not afraid of sudden fear, neither of the desolation of the wicked, when it cometh.	25 Do not be afraid of sudden terror, Nor of trouble from the wicked when it comes;	25 you need not be afraid of disaster or the plots of wicked men,
26 For the LORD shall be thy confidence, and shall keep thy foot from being taken.	26 For the LORD will be your confidence, And will keep your foot from being caught.	26 for the Lord is with you; he protects you.
4:20 My son, attend to my words; incline thine ear unto my sayings.	**4:20** My son, give attention to my words; Incline your ear to my sayings.	**4:20** Listen, son of mine, to what I say. Listen carefully.
21 Let them not depart from thine eyes; keep them in the midst of thine heart.	21 Do not let them depart from your eyes; Keep them in the midst of your heart;	21 Keep these thoughts ever in mind; let them penetrate deep within your heart,
22 For they *are* life unto those that find them, and health to all their flesh.	22 For they *are* life to those who find them, And health to all their flesh.	22 for they will mean real life for you, and radiant health.
5:18 Let thy fountain be blessed: and rejoice with the wife of thy youth.	**5:18** Let your fountain be blessed, And rejoice with the wife of your youth.	**5:18** Let your manhood be a blessing; rejoice in the wife of your youth.
19 *Let her be as* the loving hind and pleasant roe; let her breasts satisfy thee at all times; and be thou ravished always with her love.	19 *As a* loving deer and a graceful doe, Let her breasts satisfy you at all times; And always be enraptured with her love.	19 Let her charms and tender embrace satisfy you. Let her love alone fill you with delight.
6:20 My son, keep thy father's commandment, and forsake not the law of thy mother:	**6:20** My son, keep your father's command, And do not forsake the law of your mother.	**6:20** Young man, obey your father and your mother.
21 Bind them continually upon thine heart, *and* tie them about thy neck.	21 Bind them continually upon your heart; Tie them around your neck.	21 Tie their instructions around your finger so you won't forget. Take to heart all of their advice.
8:11 For wisdom *is* better than rubies; and all the things may be desired are not to be compared to it.	**8:11** For wisdom *is* better than rubies, And all the things one may desire cannot be compared with her.	**8:11** For the value of wisdom is far above rubies; nothing can be compared with it.
12 I wisdom dwell with prudence, and find out knowledge of witty inventions.	12 "I, wisdom, dwell with prudence, And find out knowledge *and* discretion.	12 Wisdom and good judgment live together, for wisdom knows where to discover knowledge and understanding.
13 The fear of the LORD *is* to hate evil: pride, and arrogancy, and the evil way, and the froward mouth, do I hate.	13 The fear of the LORD *is* to hate evil; Pride and arrogance and the evil way And the perverse mouth I hate.	13 If anyone respects and fears God, he will hate evil. For wisdom hates pride, arrogance, corruption and deceit of every kind.
9:10 The fear of the LORD *is* the beginning of wisdom: and the knowledge of the holy *is* understanding.	**9:10** "The fear of the LORD *is* the beginning of wisdom, And the knowledge of the Holy One *is* understanding.	**9:10** *For the reverence and fear of God are basic to all wisdom. Knowing God results in every other kind of understanding.*
10:27 The fear of the LORD prolongeth days: but the years of the wicked shall be shortened.	**10:27** The fear of the LORD prolongs days, But the years of the wicked will be shortened.	**10:27** Reverence for God adds hours to each day; so how can the wicked expect a long, good life?
12:4 A virtuous woman *is* a crown to her husband: but she that maketh ashamed *is* as rottenness in his bones.	**12:4** An excellent wife *is* the crown of her husband, But she who causes shame *is* like rottenness in his bones.	**12:4** A worthy wife is her husband's joy and crown; the other kind corrodes his strength and tears down everything he does.
13 The wicked is snared by the transgression of *his* lips: but the just shall come out of trouble.	13 The wicked is ensnared by the transgression of *his* lips, But the righteous will come through trouble.	13 Lies will get any man into trouble, but honesty is its own defense.
13:24 He that spareth his rod hateth his son: but he that loveth him chasteneth him betimes.	**13:24** He who spares his rod hates his son, But he who loves him disciplines him promptly.	**13:24** If you refuse to discipline your son, it proves you don't love him; for if you love him you will be prompt to punish him.
14:1 Every wise woman buildeth her house: but the foolish plucketh it down with her hands.	**14:1** *Every* wise woman builds her house, But the foolish pulls it down with her hands.	**14:1** A wise woman builds her house, while a foolish woman tears hers down by her own efforts.

NIV	RSV	TEV
6 in all your ways acknowledge him, and he will make your paths straight.	6 In all your ways acknowledge him, and he will make straight your paths.	6 Remember the LORD in everything you do, and he will show you the right way.
9 Honor the LORD with your wealth, with the firstfruits of all your crops;	9 Honor the LORD with your substance and with the first fruits of all your produce;	9 Honor the LORD by making him an offering from the best of all that your land produces.
10 then your barns will be filled to overflowing, and your vats will brim over with new wine.	10 then your barns will be filled with plenty, and your vats will be bursting with wine.	10 If you do, your barns will be filled with grain, and you will have too much wine to store it all.
25 Have no fear of sudden disaster or of the ruin that overtakes the wicked,	25 Do not be afraid of sudden panic, or of the ruin of the wicked, when it comes;	25 You will not have to worry about sudden disasters, such as come on the wicked like a storm.
26 for the LORD will be your confidence and will keep your foot from being snared.	26 for the LORD will be your confidence and will keep your foot from being caught.	26 The LORD will keep you safe. He will not let you fall into a trap.
4:20 My son, pay attention to what I say; listen closely to my words.	4:20 My son, be attentive to my words; incline your ear to my sayings.	4:20 Son, pay attention to what I say. Listen to my words.
21 Do not let them out of your sight, keep them within your heart;	21 Let them not escape from your sight; keep them within your heart.	21 Never let them get away from you. Remember them and keep them in your heart.
22 for they are life to those who find them and health to a man's whole body.	22 For they are life to him who finds them, and healing to all his flesh.	22 They will give life and health to anyone who understands them.
5:18 May your fountain be blessed, and may you rejoice in the wife of your youth.	5:18 Let your fountain be blessed, and rejoice in the wife of your youth,	5:18 So be happy with your wife and find your joy with the girl you married—
19 A loving doe, a graceful deer— may her breasts satisfy you always, may you ever be captivated by her love.	19 a lovely hind, a graceful doe. Let her affection fill you at all times with delight, be infatuated always with her love.	19 pretty and graceful as a deer. Let her charms keep you happy; let her surround you with her love.
6:20 My son, keep your father's commands and do not forsake your mother's teaching.	6:20 My son, keep your father's commandment, and forsake not your mother's teaching.	6:20 Son, do what your father tells you and never forget what your mother taught you.
21 Bind them upon your heart forever; fasten them around your neck.	21 Bind them upon your heart always; tie them about your neck.	21 Keep their words with you always, locked in your heart.
8:11 for wisdom is more precious than rubies, and nothing you desire can compare with her.	8:11 for wisdom is better than jewels, and all that you may desire cannot compare with her.	8:11 "I am Wisdom, I am better than jewels; nothing you want can compare with me.
12 "I, wisdom, dwell together with prudence; I possess knowledge and discretion.	12 I, wisdom, dwell in prudence, and I find knowledge and discretion.	12 I am Wisdom, and I have insight; I have knowledge and sound judgment.
13 To fear the LORD is to hate evil; I hate pride and arrogance, evil behavior and perverse speech.	13 The fear of the LORD is hatred of evil. Pride and arrogance and the way of evil and perverted speech I hate.	13 To honor the LORD is to hate evil; I hate pride and arrogance, evil ways and false words.
9:10 "The fear of the LORD is the beginning of wisdom, and knowledge of the Holy One is understanding.	9:10 The fear of the LORD is the beginning of wisdom, and the knowledge of the Holy One is insight.	9:10 To be wise you must first have reverence for the LORD. If you know the Holy One, you have understanding.
10:27 The fear of the LORD adds length to life, but the years of the wicked are cut short.	10:27 The fear of the LORD prolongs life, but the years of the wicked will be short.	10:27 Obey the LORD, and you will live longer. The wicked die before their time.
12:4 A wife of noble character is her husband's crown, but a disgraceful wife is like decay in his bones.	12:4 A good wife is the crown of her husband, but she who brings shame is like rottenness in his bones.	12:4 A good wife is her husband's pride and joy; but a wife who brings shame on her husband is like a cancer in his bones.
13 An evil man is trapped by his sinful talk, but a righteous man escapes trouble.	13 An evil man is ensnared by the transgression of his lips, but the righteous escapes from trouble.	13 A wicked man is trapped by his own words, but an honest man gets himself out of trouble.
13:24 He who spares the rod hates his son, but he who loves him is careful to discipline him.	13:24 He who spares the rod hates his son, but he who loves him is diligent to discipline him.	13:24 If you don't punish your son, you don't love him. If you do love him, you will correct him.
14:1 The wise woman builds her house, but with her own hands the foolish one tears hers down.	14:1 Wisdom builds her house, but folly with her own hands tears it down.	14:1 Homes are made by the wisdom of women, but are destroyed by foolishness.

KJV	NKJV	TLB
21 He that despiseth his neighbour sinneth: but he that hath mercy on the poor, happy *is* he.	21 He who despises his neighbor sins; But he who has mercy on the poor, happy *is* he.	21 To despise the poor is to sin. Blessed are those who pity them.
29 *He that is* slow to wrath *is* of great understanding: but *he that is* hasty of spirit exalteth folly.	29 *He who is* slow to wrath has great understanding, But *he who is* impulsive exalts folly.	29 A wise man controls his temper. He knows that anger causes mistakes.
15:1 A soft answer turneth away wrath: but grievous words stir up anger.	15:1 A soft answer turns away wrath, But a harsh word stirs up anger.	15:1 A soft answer turns away wrath, but harsh words cause quarrels.
20 A wise son maketh a glad father: but a foolish man despiseth his mother.	20 A wise son makes a father glad, But a foolish man despises his mother.	20 A sensible son gladdens his father. A rebellious son saddens his mother.
16:3 Commit thy works unto the LORD, and thy thoughts shall be established.	16:3 Commit your works to the LORD, And your thoughts will be established.	16:3 Commit your work to the Lord, then it will succeed.
9 A man's heart deviseth his way: but the LORD directeth his steps.	9 A man's heart plans his way, But the LORD directs his steps.	9 We should make plans—counting on God to direct us.
32 *He that is* slow to anger *is* better than the mighty; and he that ruleth his spirit than he that taketh a city.	32 *He who is* slow to anger *is* better than the mighty, And he who rules his spirit than he who takes a city.	32 It is better to be slow-tempered than famous; it is better to have self-control than to control an army.
18:22 *Whoso* findeth a wife findeth a good *thing,* and obtaineth favour of the LORD.	18:22 *He who* finds a wife finds a good *thing,* And obtains favor from the LORD.	18:22 The man who finds a wife finds a good thing; she is a blessing to him from the Lord.
24 A man *that hath* friends must shew himself friendly: and there is a friend *that* sticketh closer than a brother.	24 A man *who has* friends must himself be friendly, But there is a friend *who* sticks closer than a brother.	24 There are "friends" who pretend to be friends, but there is a friend who sticks closer than a brother.
19:11 The discretion of a man deferreth his anger; and *it is* his glory to pass over a transgression.	19:11 The discretion of a man makes him slow to anger, And *it is to* his glory to overlook a transgression.	19:11 A wise man restrains his anger and overlooks insults. This is to his credit.
14 House and riches *are* the inheritance of fathers: and a prudent wife *is* from the LORD.	14 Houses and riches *are* an inheritance from fathers, But a prudent wife *is* from the LORD.	14 A father can give his sons homes and riches, but only the Lord can give them understanding wives.
20:22 Say not thou, I will recompense evil; *but* wait on the LORD, and he shall save thee.	20:22 Do not say, "I will recompense evil"; Wait for the LORD, and He will save you.	20:22 Don't repay evil for evil. Wait for the Lord to handle the matter.
21:4 An high look, and a proud heart, *and* the plowing of the wicked, *is* sin.	21:4 A haughty look, a proud heart, *And* the plowing of the wicked *are* sin.	21:4 Pride, lust, and evil actions are all sin.
22:6 Train up a child in the way he should go: and when he is old, he will not depart from it.	22:6 Train up a child in the way he should go, And when he is old he will not depart from it.	22:6 Teach a child to choose the right path, and when he is older he will remain upon it.
9 He that hath a bountiful eye shall be blessed; for he giveth of his bread to the poor.	9 He who has a bountiful eye will be blessed, For he gives of his bread to the poor.	9 Happy is the generous man, the one who feeds the poor.
23:13 Withhold not correction from the child: for *if* thou beatest him with the rod, he shall not die.	23:13 Do not withhold correction from a child, For *if* you beat him with a rod, he will not die.	23:13 Don't fail to correct your children; discipline won't hurt them! They won't die if you use a stick on them!
14 Thou shalt beat him with the rod, and shalt deliver his soul from hell.	14 You shall beat him with a rod, And deliver his soul from hell.	14 Punishment will keep them out of hell.
22 Hearken unto thy father that begat thee, and despise not thy mother when she is old.	22 Listen to your father who begot you, And do not despise your mother when she is old.	22 Listen to your father's advice and don't despise an old mother's experience.
23 Buy the truth, and sell *it* not; *also* wisdom, and instruction, and understanding.	23 Buy the truth, and do not sell *it,* *Also* wisdom and instruction and understanding.	23 Get the facts at any price, and hold on tightly to all the good sense you can get.
24 The father of the righteous shall greatly rejoice: and he that begetteth a wise *child* shall have joy of him.	24 The father of the righteous will greatly rejoice, And he who begets a wise *child* will delight in him.	24 The father of a godly man has cause for joy—what pleasure a wise son is!
24:3 Through wisdom is an house builded; and by understanding it is established:	24:3 Through wisdom a house is built, And by understanding it is established;	24:3 Any enterprise is built by wise planning, becomes strong through common sense,

NIV	RSV	TEV
21 He who despises his neighbor sins, but blessed is he who is kind to the needy.	21 He who despises his neighbor is a sinner, but happy is he who is kind to the poor.	21 If you want to be happy, be kind to the poor; it is a sin to despise anyone.
29 A patient man has great understanding, but a quick-tempered man displays folly.	29 He who is slow to anger has great understanding, but he who has a hasty temper exalts folly.	29 If you stay calm, you are wise, but if you have a hot temper, you only show how stupid you are.
15:1 A gentle answer turns away wrath, but a harsh word stirs up anger.	15:1 A soft answer turns away wrath, but a harsh word stirs up anger.	15:1 A gentle answer quiets anger, but a harsh one stirs it up.
20 A wise son brings joy to his father, but a foolish man despises his mother.	20 A wise son makes a glad father, but a foolish man despises his mother.	20 A wise son makes his father happy. Only a fool despises his mother.
16:3 Commit to the LORD whatever you do, and your plans will succeed.	16:3 Commit your work to the LORD, and your plans will be established.	16:3 Ask the LORD to bless your plans, and you will be successful in carrying them out.
9 In his heart a man plans his course, but the LORD determines his steps.	9 A man's mind plans his way, but the LORD directs his steps.	9 You may make your plans, but God directs your actions.
32 Better a patient man than a warrior, a man who controls his temper than one who takes a city.	32 He who is slow to anger is better than the mighty, and he who rules his spirit than he who takes a city.	32 It is better to be patient than powerful. It is better to win control over yourself than over whole cities.
18:22 He who finds a wife finds what is good and receives favor from the LORD.	18:22 He who finds a wife finds a good thing, and obtains favor from the LORD.	18:22 Find a wife and you find a good thing; it shows that the LORD is good to you.
24 A man of many companions may come to ruin, but there is a friend who sticks closer than a brother.	24 There are friends who pretend to be friends, but there is a friend who sticks closer than a brother.	24 Some friendships do not last, but some friends are more loyal than brothers.
19:11 A man's wisdom gives him patience; it is to his glory to overlook an offense.	19:11 Good sense makes a man slow to anger, and it is his glory to overlook an offense.	19:11 If you are sensible, you will control your temper. When someone wrongs you, it is a great virtue to ignore it.
14 Houses and wealth are inherited from parents, but a prudent wife is from the LORD.	14 House and wealth are inherited from fathers, but a prudent wife is from the LORD.	14 A man can inherit a house and money from his parents, but only the LORD can give him a sensible wife.
20:22 Do not say, "I'll pay you back for this wrong!" Wait for the LORD, and he will deliver you.	20:22 Do not say, "I will repay evil"; wait for the LORD, and he will help you.	20:22 Don't take it on yourself to repay a wrong. Trust the LORD and he will make it right.
21:4 Haughty eyes and a proud heart, the lamp of the wicked, are sin!	21:4 Haughty eyes and a proud heart, the lamp of the wicked, are sin.	21:4 Wicked people are controlled by their conceit and arrogance, and this is sinful.
22:6 Train a child in the way he should go, and when he is old he will not turn from it.	22:6 Train up a child in the way he should go, and when he is old he will not depart from it.	22:6 Teach a child how he should live, and he will remember it all his life.
9 A generous man will himself be blessed, for he shares his food with the poor.	9 He who has a bountiful eye will be blessed, for he shares his bread with the poor.	9 Be generous and share your food with the poor. You will be blessed for it.
23:13 Do not withhold discipline from a child; if you punish him with the rod, he will not die.	23:13 Do not withhold discipline from a child; if you beat him with a rod, he will not die.	23:13 Don't hesitate to discipline a child. A good spanking won't kill him.
14 Punish him with the rod and save his soul from death.	14 If you beat him with the rod you will save his life from Sheol.	14 As a matter of fact, it may save his life.
22 Listen to your father, who gave you life, and do not despise your mother when she is old.	22 Hearken to your father who begot you, and do not despise your mother when she is old.	22 Listen to your father; without him you would not exist. When your mother is old, show her your appreciation.
23 Buy the truth and do not sell it; get wisdom, discipline and understanding.	23 Buy truth, and do not sell it; buy wisdom, instruction, and understanding.	23 Truth, wisdom, learning, and good sense— these are worth paying for, but too valuable for you to sell.
24 The father of a righteous man has great joy; he who has a wise son delights in him.	24 The father of the righteous will greatly rejoice; he who begets a wise son will be glad in him.	24 A righteous man's father has good reason to be happy. You can take pride in a wise son.
24:3 By wisdom a house is built, and through understanding it is established;	24:3 By wisdom a house is built, and by understanding it is established;	24:3 Homes are built on the foundation of wisdom and understanding.

KJV	NKJV	TLB
16 For a just *man* falleth seven times, and riseth up again: but the wicked shall fall into mischief.	16 For a righteous *man* may fall seven times And rise again, But the wicked shall fall by calamity.	16 Don't you know that this good man, though you trip him up seven times, will each time rise again! But one calamity is enough to lay you low.
27:1 Boast not thyself of to morrow; for thou knowest not what a day may bring forth.	**27:1** Do not boast about tomorrow, For you do not know what a day may bring forth.	**27:1** Don't brag about your plans for tomorrow—wait and see what happens.
17 Iron sharpeneth iron; so a man sharpeneth the countenance of his friend.	17 *As* iron sharpens iron, So a man sharpens the countenance of his friend.	17 A friendly discussion is as stimulating as the sparks that fly when iron strikes iron.
28:5 Evil men understand not judgment: but they that seek the LORD understand all *things*.	**28:5** Evil men do not understand justice, But those who seek the LORD understand all.	**28:5** Evil men don't understand the importance of justice, but those who follow the Lord are much concerned about it.
13 He that covereth his sins shall not prosper: but whoso confesseth and forsaketh *them* shall have mercy.	13 He who covers his sins will not prosper, But whoever confesses and forsakes *them* will have mercy.	13 A man who refuses to admit his mistakes can never be successful. But if he confesses and forsakes them, he gets another chance.
29:3 Whoso loveth wisdom rejoiceth his father: but he that keepeth company with harlots spendeth *his* substance.	**29:3** Whoever loves wisdom makes his father rejoice, But a companion of harlots wastes *his* wealth.	**29:3** A wise son makes his father happy, but a lad who hangs around with prostitutes disgraces him.
22 An angry man stirreth up strife, and a furious man aboundeth in transgression.	22 An angry man stirs up strife, And a furious man abounds in transgression.	22 A hot-tempered man starts fights and gets into all kinds of trouble.
25 The fear of man bringeth a snare: but whoso putteth his trust in the LORD shall be safe.	25 The fear of man brings a snare, But whoever trusts in the LORD shall be safe.	25 Fear of man is a dangerous trap, but to trust in God means safety.
30:5 Every word of God *is* pure: he *is* a shield unto them that put their trust in him.	**30:5** Every word of God *is* pure; He *is* a shield to those who put their trust in Him.	**30:5** Every word of God proves true. He defends all who come to him for protection.
6 Add thou not unto his words, lest he reprove thee, and thou be found a liar.	6 Do not add to His words, Lest He reprove you, and you be found a liar.	6 Do not add to his words, lest he rebuke you, and you be found a liar.
31:10 Who can find a virtuous woman? for her price *is* far above rubies.	**31:10** Who can find a virtuous wife? For her worth *is* far above rubies.	**31:10** If you can find a truly good wife, she is worth more than precious gems!
11 The heart of her husband doth safely trust in her, so that he shall have no need of spoil.	11 The heart of her husband safely trusts her; So he will have no lack of gain.	11 Her husband can trust her, and she will richly satisfy his needs.
12 She will do him good and not evil all the days of her life.	12 She does him good and not evil All the days of her life.	12 She will not hinder him, but help him all her life.
25 Strength and honour *are* her clothing; and she shall rejoice in time to come.	25 Strength and honor *are* her clothing; She shall rejoice in time to come.	25 She is a woman of strength and dignity, and has no fear of old age.
26 She openeth her mouth with wisdom; and in her tongue *is* the law of kindness.	26 She opens her mouth with wisdom, And on her tongue *is* the law of kindness.	26 When she speaks, her words are wise, and kindness is the rule for everything she says.
27 She looketh well to the ways of her household, and eateth not the bread of idleness.	27 She watches over the ways of her household, And does not eat the bread of idleness.	27 She watches carefully all that goes on throughout her household, and is never lazy.
28 Her children arise up, and call her blessed; her husband *also*, and he praiseth her.	28 Her children rise up and call her blessed; Her husband *also*, and he praises her:	28 Her children stand and bless her; so does her husband. He praises her with these words:
29 Many daughters have done virtuously, but thou excellest them all.	29 "Many daughters have done well, But you excel them all."	29 "There are many fine women in the world, but you are the best of them all!"
30 Favour *is* deceitful, and beauty *is* vain: *but* a woman *that* feareth the LORD, she shall be praised.	30 Charm *is* deceitful and beauty *is* vain, But a woman *who* fears the LORD, she shall be praised.	30 Charm can be deceptive and beauty doesn't last, but a woman who fears and reverences God shall be greatly praised.
31 Give her of the fruit of her hands; and let her own works praise her in the gates.	31 Give her of the fruit of her hands, And let her own works praise her in the gates.	31 Praise her for the many fine things she does. These good deeds of hers shall bring her honor and recognition from even the leaders of the nations.

Ecclesiastes

KJV	NKJV	TLB
1:2 Vanity of vanities, saith the Preacher, vanity of vanities; all *is* vanity.	**1:2** "Vanity of vanities," says the Preacher; "Vanity of vanities, all *is* vanity."	**1:2** In my opinion, nothing is worthwhile; everything is futile.

NIV	RSV	TEV
16 for though a righteous man falls seven times, he rises again, but the wicked are brought down by calamity.	**16** for a righteous man falls seven times, and rises again; but the wicked are overthrown by calamity.	**16** No matter how often an honest man falls, he always gets up again; but disaster destroys the wicked.
27:1 Do not boast about tomorrow, for you do not know what a day may bring forth.	**27:1** Do not boast about tomorrow, for you do not know what a day may bring forth.	**27:1** Never boast about tomorrow. You don't know what will happen between now and then.
17 As iron sharpens iron, so one man sharpens another.	**17** Iron sharpens iron, and one man sharpens another.	**17** People learn from one another, just as iron sharpens iron.
28:5 Evil men do not understand justice, but those who seek the LORD understand it fully.	**28:5** Evil men do not understand justice, but those who seek the LORD understand it completely.	**28:5** Evil people do not know what justice is, but those who worship the LORD understand it well.
13 He who conceals his sins does not prosper, but whoever confesses and renounces them finds mercy.	**13** He who conceals his transgressions will not prosper, but he who confesses and forsakes them will obtain mercy.	**13** You will never succeed in life if you try to hide your sins. Confess them and give them up; then God will show mercy to you.
29:3 A man who loves wisdom brings joy to his father, but a companion of prostitutes squanders his wealth.	**29:3** He who loves wisdom makes his father glad, but one who keeps company with harlots squanders his substance.	**29:3** If you appreciate wisdom, your father will be proud of you. It is a foolish waste to spend money on prostitutes.
22 An angry man stirs up dissension, and a hot-tempered one commits many sins.	**22** A man of wrath stirs up strife, and a man given to anger causes much transgression.	**22** People with quick tempers cause a lot of quarreling and trouble.
25 Fear of man will prove to be a snare, but whoever trusts in the LORD is kept safe.	**25** The fear of man lays a snare, but he who trusts in the LORD is safe.	**25** It is dangerous to be concerned with what others think of you, but if you trust the LORD, you are safe.
30:5 "Every word of God is flawless; he is a shield to those who take refuge in him.	**30:5** Every word of God proves true; he is a shield to those who take refuge in him.	**30:5** "God keeps every promise he makes. He is like a shield for all who seek his protection.
6 Do not add to his words, or he will rebuke you and prove you a liar.	**6** Do not add to his words, lest he rebuke you, and you be found a liar.	**6** If you claim that he said something that he never said, he will reprimand you and show that you are a liar."
31:10 A wife of noble character who can find? She is worth far more than rubies.	**31:10** A good wife who can find? She is far more precious than jewels.	**31:10** How hard it is to find a capable wife! She is worth far more than jewels!
11 Her husband has full confidence in her and lacks nothing of value.	**11** The heart of her husband trusts in her, and he will have no lack of gain.	**11** Her husband puts his confidence in her, and he will never be poor.
12 She brings him good, not harm, all the days of her life.	**12** She does him good, and not harm, all the days of her life.	**12** As long as she lives, she does him good and never harm.
25 She is clothed with strength and dignity; she can laugh at the days to come.	**25** Strength and dignity are her clothing, and she laughs at the time to come.	**25** She is strong and respected and not afraid of the future.
26 She speaks with wisdom, and faithful instruction is on her tongue.	**26** She opens her mouth with wisdom, and the teaching of kindness is on her tongue.	**26** She speaks with a gentle wisdom.
27 She watches over the affairs of her household and does not eat the bread of idleness.	**27** She looks well to the ways of her household, and does not eat the bread of idleness.	**27** She is always busy and looks after her family's needs.
28 Her children arise and call her blessed; her husband also, and he praises her:	**28** Her children rise up and call her blessed; her husband also, and he praises her:	**28** Her children show their appreciation, and her husband praises her.
29 "Many women do noble things, but you surpass them all."	**29** "Many women have done excellently, but you surpass them all."	**29** He says, "Many women are good wives, but you are the best of them all."
30 Charm is deceptive, and beauty is fleeting; but a woman who fears the LORD is to be praised.	**30** Charm is deceitful, and beauty is vain, but a woman who fears the LORD is to · be praised.	**30** Charm is deceptive and beauty disappears, but a woman who honors the LORD should be praised.
31 Give her the reward she has earned, and let her works bring her praise at the city gate.	**31** Give her of the fruit of her hands, and let her works praise her in the gates.	**31** Give her credit for all she does. She deserves the respect of everyone.

Ecclesiastes

1:2 "Meaningless! Meaningless!" says the Teacher. "Utterly meaningless! Everything is meaningless."	**1:2** Vanity of vanities, says the Preacher, vanity of vanities! All is vanity.	**1:2** It is useless, useless, said the Philosopher. Life is useless, all useless.

KJV	NKJV	TLB
3 What profit hath a man of all his labour which he taketh under the sun?	3 What profit has a man from all his labor In which he toils under the sun?	3 For what does a man get for all his hard work?
4 *One* generation passeth away, and *another* generation cometh: but the earth abideth for ever.	4 *One* generation passes away, and *another* generation comes; But the earth abides forever.	4 Generations come and go but it makes no difference.
5 The sun also ariseth, and the sun goeth down, and hasteth to his place where he arose.	5 The sun also rises, and the sun goes down, And hastens to the place where it arose.	5 The sun rises and sets and hurries around to rise again.
6 The wind goeth toward the south, and turneth about unto the north; it whirleth about continually, and the wind returneth again according to his circuits.	6 The wind goes toward the south, And turns around to the north; The wind whirls about continually, And comes again on its circuit.	6 The wind blows south and north, here and there, twisting back and forth, getting nowhere.
7 All the rivers run into the sea; yet the sea *is* not full; unto the place from whence the rivers come, thither they return again.	7 All the rivers run into the sea, Yet the sea *is* not full; To the place from which the rivers come, There they return again.	7 The rivers run into the sea but the sea is never full, and the water returns again to the rivers, and flows again to the sea . . .
8 All things *are* full of labour; man cannot utter *it:* the eye is not satisfied with seeing, nor the ear filled with hearing.	8 All things *are* full of labor; Man cannot express *it.* The eye is not satisfied with seeing, Nor the ear filled with hearing.	8 everything is unutterably weary and tiresome. No matter how much we see, we are never satisfied; no matter how much we hear, we are not content.
9 The thing that hath been, it *is that* which shall be; and that which is done *is* that which shall be done: and *there is* no new *thing* under the sun.	9 That which has been *is* what will be, That which *is* done is what will be done, And *there is* nothing new under the sun.	9 History merely repeats itself. Nothing is truly new; it has all been done or said before.
10 Is there *any* thing whereof it may be said, See, this *is* new? it hath been already of old time, which was before us.	10 Is there anything of which it may be said, "See, this *is* new"? It has already been in ancient times before us.	10 What can you point to that is new? How do you know it didn't exist long ages ago?
11 *There is* no remembrance of former *things;* neither shall there be *any* remembrance of *things* that are to come with *those* that shall come after.	11 *There is* no remembrance of former *things,* Nor will there be any remembrance of *things* that are to come By *those* who will come after.	11 We don't remember what happened in those former times, and in the future generations no one will remember what we have done back here.
2:11 Then I looked on all the works that my hands had wrought, and on the labour that I had laboured to do: and, behold, all *was* vanity and vexation of spirit, and *there was* no profit under the sun.	2:11 Then I looked on all the works that my hands had done And on the labor in which I had toiled; And indeed all *was* vanity and grasping for the wind. *There was* no profit under the sun.	2:11 But as I looked at everything I had tried, it was all so useless, a chasing of the wind, and there was nothing really worthwhile anywhere.
26 For *God* giveth to a man that *is* good in his sight wisdom, and knowledge, and joy: but to the sinner he giveth travail, to gather and to heap up, that he may give to *him that is* good before God. This also *is* vanity and vexation of spirit.	26 For *God* gives wisdom and knowledge and joy to a man who *is* good in His sight; but to the sinner He gives the work of gathering and collecting, that he may give to *him who is* good before God. This also *is* vanity and grasping for the wind.	26 For God gives those who please him wisdom, knowledge, and joy; but if a sinner becomes wealthy, God takes the wealth away from him and gives it to those who please him. So here, too, we see an example of foolishly chasing the wind.
3:1 To every *thing there is* a season, and a time to every purpose under the heaven:	3:1 To everything *there is* a season, A time for every purpose under heaven:	3:1 There is a right time for everything:
2 A time to be born, and a time to die; a time to plant, and a time to pluck up *that which is* planted;	2 A time to be born, And a time to die; A time to plant, And a time to pluck *what is* planted;	2 A time to be born, a time to die; A time to plant; A time to harvest;
3 A time to kill, and a time to heal; a time to break down, and a time to build up;	3 A time to kill, And a time to heal; A time to break down, And a time to build up;	3 A time to kill; A time to heal; A time to destroy; A time to rebuild;
4 A time to weep, and a time to laugh; a time to mourn, and a time to dance;	4 A time to weep, And a time to laugh; A time to mourn, And a time to dance;	4 A time to cry; A time to laugh; A time to grieve; A time to dance;
5 A time to cast away stones, and a time to gather stones together; a time to embrace, and a time to refrain from embracing;	5 A time to cast away stones, And a time to gather stones; A time to embrace, And a time to refrain from embracing;	5 A time for scattering stones; A time for gathering stones; A time to hug; A time not to hug;

NIV	RSV	TEV
3 What does man gain from all his labor at which he toils under the sun?	3 What does man gain by all the toil at which he toils under the sun?	3 You spend your life working, laboring, and what do you have to show for it?
4 Generations come and generations go, but the earth remains forever.	4 A generation goes, and a generation comes, but the earth remains for ever.	4 Generations come and generations go, but the world stays just the same.
5 The sun rises and the sun sets, and hurries back to where it rises.	5 The sun rises and the sun goes down, and hastens to the place where it rises.	5 The sun still rises, and it still goes down, going wearily back to where it must start all over again.
6 The wind blows to the south and turns to the north; round and round it goes, ever returning on its course.	6 The wind blows to the south, and goes round to the north; round and round goes the wind, and on its circuits the wind returns.	6 The wind blows south, the wind blows north—round and round and back again.
7 All streams flow into the sea, yet the sea is never full. To the place the streams come from, there they return again.	7 All streams run to the sea, but the sea is not full; to the place where the streams flow, there they flow again.	7 Every river flows into the sea, but the sea is not yet full. The water returns to where the rivers began, and starts all over again.
8 All things are wearisome, more than one can say. The eye never has enough of seeing, or the ear its fill of hearing.	8 All things are full of weariness; a man cannot utter it; the eye is not satisfied with seeing, nor the ear filled with hearing.	8 Everything leads to weariness—a weariness too great for words. Our eyes can never see enough to be satisfied; our ears can never hear enough.
9 What has been will be again, what has been done will be done again; there is nothing new under the sun.	9 What has been is what will be, and what has been done is what will be done; and there is nothing new under the sun.	9 What has happened before will happen again. What has been done before will be done again. There is nothing new in the whole world.
10 Is there anything of which one can say, "Look! This is something new"? It was here already, long ago; it was here before our time.	10 Is there a thing of which it is said, "See, this is new"? It has been already, in the ages before us.	10 "Look," they say, "here is something new!" But no, it has all happened before, long before we were born.
11 There is no remembrance of men of old, and even those who are yet to come will not be remembered by those who follow.	11 There is no remembrance of former things, nor will there be any remembrance of later things yet to happen among those who come after.	11 No one remembers what has happened in the past, and no one in days to come will remember what happens between now and then.
2:11 Yet when I surveyed all that my hands had done and what I had toiled to achieve, everything was meaningless, a chasing after the wind; nothing was gained under the sun.	2:11 Then I considered all that my hands had done and the toil I had spent in doing it, and behold, all was vanity and a striving after wind, and there was nothing to be gained under the sun.	2:11 Then I thought about all that I had done and how hard I had worked doing it, and I realized that it didn't mean a thing. It was like chasing the wind—of no use at all.
26 To the man who pleases him, God gives wisdom, knowledge and happiness, but to the sinner he gives the task of gathering and storing up wealth to hand it over to the one who pleases God. This too is meaningless, a chasing after the wind.	26 For to the man who pleases him God gives wisdom and knowledge and joy; but to the sinner he gives the work of gathering and heaping, only to give to one who pleases God. This also is vanity and a striving after wind.	26 God gives wisdom, knowledge, and happiness to those who please him, but he makes sinners work, earning and saving, so that what they get can be given to those who please him. It is all useless. It is like chasing the wind.
3:1 There is a time for everything, and a season for every activity under heaven:	3:1 For everything there is a season, and a time for every matter under heaven:	3:1 Everything that happens in this world happens at the time God chooses.
2 a time to be born and a time to die, a time to plant and a time to uproot,	2 a time to be born, and a time to die; a time to plant, and a time to pluck up what is planted;	2 He sets the time for birth and the time for death, the time for planting and the time for pulling up,
3 a time to kill and a time to heal, a time to tear down and a time to build,	3 a time to kill, and a time to heal; a time to break down, and a time to build up;	3 the time for killing and the time for healing, the time for tearing down and the time for building.
4 a time to weep and a time to laugh, a time to mourn and a time to dance,	4 a time to weep, and a time to laugh; a time to mourn, and a time to dance;	4 He sets the time for sorrow and the time for joy, the time for mourning and the time for dancing,
5 a time to scatter stones and a time to gather them, a time to embrace and a time to refrain,	5 a time to cast away stones, and a time to gather stones together; a time to embrace, and a time to refrain from embracing;	5 the time for making love and the time for not making love, the time for kissing and the time for not kissing.

KJV	NKJV	TLB
6 A time to get, and a time to lose; a time to keep, and a time to cast away;	6 A time to gain, And a time to lose; A time to keep, And a time to throw away;	6 A time to find; A time to lose; A time for keeping; A time for throwing away;
7 A time to rend, and a time to sew; a time to keep silence, and a time to speak;	7 A time to tear, And a time to sew; A time to keep silence, And a time to speak;	7 A time to tear; A time to repair; A time to be quiet; A time to speak up;
8 A time to love, and a time to hate; a time of war, and a time of peace.	8 A time to love, And a time to hate; A time of war, And a time of peace.	8 A time for loving; A time for hating; A time for war; A time for peace.
4:9 Two *are* better than one; because they have a good reward for their labour.	4:9 Two *are* better than one, Because they have a good reward for their labor.	4:9 Two can accomplish more than twice as much as one, for the results can be much better.
10 For if they fall, the one will lift up his fellow: but woe to him *that is* alone when he falleth; for *he hath* not another to help him up.	10 For if they fall, one will lift up his companion. But woe to him *who is* alone when he falls, For *he has* no one to help him up.	10 If one falls, the other pulls him up; but if a man falls when he is alone, he's in trouble.
5:10 He that loveth silver shall not be satisfied with silver; nor he that loveth abundance with increase: this *is* also vanity.	5:10 He who loves silver will not be satisfied with silver; Nor he who loves abundance, with increase. This also *is* vanity.	5:10 He who loves money shall never have enough. The foolishness of thinking that wealth brings happiness!
7:9 Be not hasty in thy spirit to be angry: for anger resteth in the bosom of fools.	7:9 Do not hasten in your spirit to be angry, For anger rests in the bosom of fools.	7:9 Don't be quick-tempered—that is being a fool.
8:12 Though a sinner do evil an hundred times, and his *days* be prolonged, yet surely I know that it shall be well with them that fear God, which fear before him:	8:12 Though a sinner does evil a hundred *times*, and his *days* are prolonged, yet I surely know that it will be well with those who fear God, who fear before Him.	8:12 But though a man sins a hundred times and still lives, I know very well that those who fear God will be better off,
9:9 Live joyfully with the wife whom thou lovest all the days of the life of thy vanity, which he hath given thee under the sun, all the days of thy vanity: for that *is* thy portion in *this* life, and in thy labour which thou takest under the sun.	9:9 Live joyfully with the wife whom you love all the days of your vain life which He has given you under the sun, all your days of vanity; for that *is* your portion in life, and in the labor which you perform under the sun.	9:9 Live happily with the woman you love through the fleeting days of life, for the wife God gives you is your best reward down here for all your earthly toil.
10:12 The words of a wise man's mouth *are* gracious; but the lips of a fool will swallow up himself.	10:12 The words of a wise man's mouth *are* gracious, But the lips of a fool shall swallow him up;	10:12 It is pleasant to listen to wise words, but a fool's speech brings him to ruin.
13 The beginning of the words of his mouth *is* foolishness: and the end of his talk *is* mischievous madness.	13 The words of his mouth begin with foolishness, And the end of his talk *is* raving madness.	13 Since he begins with a foolish premise, his conclusion is sheer madness.
14 A fool also is full of words: a man cannot tell what shall be; and what shall be after him, who can tell him?	14 A fool also multiplies words. No man knows what is to be; Who can tell him what will be after him?	14 A fool knows all about the future and tells everyone in detail! But who can really know what is going to happen?
11:9 Rejoice, O young man, in thy youth; and let thy heart cheer thee in the days of thy youth, and walk in the ways of thine heart, and in the sight of thine eyes: but know thou, that for all these *things* God will bring thee into judgment.	11:9 Rejoice, O young man, in your youth, And let your heart cheer you in the days of your youth; Walk in the ways of your heart, And in the sight of your eyes; But know that for all these God will bring you into judgment.	11:9 Young man, it's wonderful to be young! Enjoy every minute of it! Do all you want to; take in everything, but realize that you must account to God for everything you do.
12:1 Remember now thy Creator in the days of thy youth, while the evil days come not, nor the years draw nigh, when thou shalt say, I have no pleasure in them;	12:1 Remember *now* your Creator in the days of your youth, Before the difficult days come, And the years draw near when you say, "I have no pleasure in them":	12:1 Don't let the excitement of being young cause you to forget about your Creator. Honor him in your youth before the evil years come—when you'll no longer enjoy living.
13 Let us hear the conclusion of the whole matter: Fear God, and keep his commandments: for this is the whole *duty* of man.	13 Let us hear the conclusion of the whole matter: Fear God and keep His commandments, For this is the whole duty of man.	13 Here is my final conclusion: fear God and obey his commandments, for this is the entire duty of man.

NIV	RSV	TEV
6 a time to search and a time to give up, a time to keep and a time to throw away,	6 a time to seek, and a time to lose; a time to keep, and a time to cast away;	6 He sets the time for finding and the time for losing, the time for saving and the time for throwing away,
7 a time to tear and a time to mend, a time to be silent and a time to speak,	7 a time to rend, and a time to sew; a time to keep silence, and a time to speak;	7 the time for tearing and the time for mending, the time for silence and the time for talk.
8 a time to love and a time to hate, a time for war and a time for peace.	8 a time to love, and a time to hate; a time for war, and a time for peace.	8 He sets the time for love and the time for hate, the time for war and the time for peace.
4:9 Two are better than one, because they have a good return for their work:	4:9 Two are better than one, because they have a good reward for their toil.	4:9 Two are better off than one, because together they can work more effectively.
10 If one falls down, his friend can help him up. But pity the man who falls and has no one to help him up!	10 For if they fall, one will lift up his fellow; but woe to him who is alone when he falls and has not another to lift him up.	10 If one of them falls down, the other can help him up. But if someone is alone and falls, it's just too bad, because there is no one to help him.
5:10 Whoever loves money never has money enough; whoever loves wealth is never satisfied with his income. This too is meaningless.	5:10 He who loves money will not be satisfied with money; nor he who loves wealth, with gain: this also is vanity.	5:10 If you love money, you will never be satisfied; if you long to be rich, you will never get all you want. It is useless.
7:9 Do not be quickly provoked in your spirit, for anger resides in the lap of fools.	7:9 Be not quick to anger, for anger lodges in the bosom of fools.	7:9 Keep your temper under control; it is foolish to harbor a grudge.
8:12 Although a wicked man commits a hundred crimes and still lives a long time, I know that it will go better with God-fearing men, who are reverent before God.	8:12 Though a sinner does evil a hundred times and prolongs his life, yet I know that it will be well with those who fear God, because they fear before him;	8:12 A sinner may commit a hundred crimes and still live. Oh yes, I know what they say: "If you obey God, everything will be all right,
9:9 Enjoy life with your wife, whom you love, all the days of this meaningless life that God has given you under the sun—all your meaningless days. For this is your lot in life and in your toilsome labor under the sun.	9:9 Enjoy life with the wife whom you love, all the days of your vain life which he has given you under the sun, because that is your portion in life and in your toil at which you toil under the sun.	9:9 Enjoy life with the woman you love, as long as you live the useless life that God has given you in this world. Enjoy every useless day of it, because that is all you will get for all your trouble.
10:12 Words from a wise man's mouth are gracious, but a fool is consumed by his own lips.	10:12 The words of a wise man's mouth win him favor, but the lips of a fool consume him.	10:12 What a wise man says brings him honor, but a fool is destroyed by his own words.
13 At the beginning his words are folly; at the end they are wicked madness—	13 The beginning of the words of his mouth is foolishness, and the end of his talk is wicked madness.	13 He starts out with silly talk and ends up with pure madness.
14 and the fool multiplies words. No one knows what is coming— who can tell him what will happen after him?	14 A fool multiplies words, though no man knows what is to be, and who can tell him what will be after him?	14 A fool talks on and on. No one knows what is going to happen next, and no one can tell us what will happen after we die.
11:9 Be happy, young man, while you are young, and let your heart give you joy in the days of your youth. Follow the ways of your heart and whatever your eyes see, but know that for all these things God will bring you to judgment.	11:9 Rejoice, O young man, in your youth, and let your heart cheer you in the days of your youth; walk in the ways of your heart and the sight of your eyes. But know that for all these things God will bring you into judgment.	11:9 Young people, enjoy your youth. Be happy while you are still young. Do what you want to do, and follow your heart's desire. But remember that God is going to judge you for whatever you do.
12:1 Remember your Creator in the days of your youth, before the days of trouble come and the years approach when you will say, "I find no pleasure in them"—	12:1 Remember also your Creator in the days of your youth, before the evil days come, and the years draw nigh, when you will say, "I have no pleasure in them";	12:1 So remember your Creator while you are still young, before those dismal days and years come when you will say, "I don't enjoy life."
13 Now all has been heard; here is the conclusion of the matter: Fear God and keep his commandments, for this is the whole duty of man.	13 The end of the matter; all has been heard. Fear God, and keep his commandments; for this is the whole duty of man.	13 After all this, there is only one thing to say: Have reverence for God, and obey his commands, because this is all that man was created for.

KJV	NKJV	TLB
14 For God shall bring every work into judgment, with every secret thing, whether *it be* good, or whether *it be* evil.	14 For God will bring every work into judgment, Including every secret thing, Whether *it is* good or whether *it is* evil.	14 For God will judge us for everything we do, including every hidden thing, good or bad.

Song of Solomon

KJV	NKJV	TLB
2:10 My beloved spake, and said unto me, Rise up, my love, my fair one, and come away.	2:10 My beloved spoke, and said to me: "Rise up, my love, my fair one, And come away.	2:10 "My beloved said to me, 'Rise up, my love, my fair one, and come away.
11 For, lo, the winter is past, the rain is over *and* gone;	11 For lo, the winter is past, The rain is over *and* gone.	11 For the winter is past, the rain is over and gone.
12 The flowers appear on the earth; the time of the singing *of birds* is come, and the voice of the turtle is heard in our land;	12 The flowers appear on the earth; The time of singing has come, And the voice of the turtledove Is heard in our land.	12 The flowers are springing up and the time of the singing of birds has come. Yes, spring is here.
13 The fig tree putteth forth her green figs, and the vines *with* the tender grape give a *good* smell. Arise, my love, my fair one, and come away.	13 The fig tree puts forth her green figs, And the vines *with* the tender grapes Give a good smell. Rise up, my love, my fair one, And come away!	13 The leaves are coming out and the grape vines are in blossom. How delicious they smell! Arise, my love, my fair one, and come away.'
4:6 Until the day break, and the shadows flee away, I will get me to the mountain of myrrh, and to the hill of frankincense.	4:6 Until the day breaks And the shadows flee away, I will go my way to the mountain of myrrh And to the hill of frankincense.	4:6 Until the morning dawns and the shadows flee away, I will go to the mountain of myrrh and to the hill of frankincense.
7 Thou *art* all fair, my love; *there is* no spot in thee.	7 You *are* all fair, my love, And *there is* no spot in you.	7 You are so beautiful, my love, in every part of you.
5:8 I charge you, O daughters of Jerusalem, if ye find my beloved, that ye tell him, that I *am* sick of love.	5:8 I charge you, O daughters of Jerusalem, If you find my beloved, That you tell him I *am* lovesick!	5:8 I adjure you, O women of Jerusalem, if you find my beloved one, tell him that I am sick with love."
14 His hands *are as* gold rings set with the beryl: his belly *is as* bright ivory overlaid *with* sapphires.	14 His hands *are* rods of gold Set with beryl. His body *is* carved ivory Inlaid *with* sapphires.	14 His arms are round bars of gold set with topaz; his body is bright ivory encrusted with jewels.
15 His legs *are as* pillars of marble, set upon sockets of fine gold: his countenance *is* as Lebanon, excellent as the cedars.	15 His legs *are* pillars of marble Set on bases of fine gold. His countenance *is* like Lebanon, Excellent as the cedars.	15 His legs are as pillars of marble set in sockets of finest gold, like cedars of Lebanon; none can rival him.
16 His mouth *is* most sweet: yea, he *is* altogether lovely. This *is* my beloved, and this *is* my friend, O daughters of Jerusalem.	16 His mouth *is* most sweet, Yes, he *is* altogether lovely. This *is* my beloved, And this *is* my friend, O daughters of Jerusalem!	16 His mouth is altogether sweet, lovable in every way. Such, O women of Jerusalem, is my beloved, my friend."
6:1 Whither is thy beloved gone, O thou fairest among women? whither is thy beloved turned aside? that we may seek him with thee.	6:1 Where has your beloved gone, O fairest among women? Where has your beloved turned aside, That we may seek him with you?	6:1 "O rarest of beautiful women, where has your loved one gone? We will help you find him."
2 My beloved is gone down into his garden, to the beds of spices, to feed in the gardens, and to gather lilies.	2 My beloved has gone to his garden, To the beds of spices, To feed *his flock* in the gardens, And to gather lilies.	2 "He has gone down to his garden, to his spice beds, to pasture his flock and to gather the lilies.
3 I *am* my beloved's, and my beloved *is* mine: he feedeth among the lilies.	3 I *am* my beloved's, And my beloved *is* mine. He feeds *his flock* among the lilies.	3 I am my beloved's and my beloved is mine. He pastures his flock among the lilies!"
8:6 Set me as a seal upon thine heart, as a seal upon thine arm: for love *is* strong as death; jealousy *is* cruel as the grave: the coals thereof *are* coals of fire, *which hath* a most vehement flame.	8:6 Set me as a seal upon your heart, As a seal upon your arm; For love *is as* strong as death, Jealousy *as* cruel as the grave; Its flames *are* flames of fire, A most vehement flame.	8:6 "Seal me in your heart with permanent betrothal, for love is strong as death and jealousy is as cruel as Sheol. It flashes fire, the very flame of Jehovah.

NIV	RSV	TEV
14 For God will bring every deed into judgment, including every hidden thing, whether it is good or evil.	14 For God will bring every deed into judgment, with every secret thing, whether good or evil.	14 God is going to judge everything we do, whether good or bad, even things done in secret.

Song of Solomon

NIV	RSV	TEV
2:10 My lover spoke and said to me, "Arise, my darling, my beautiful one, and come with me.	2:10 My beloved speaks and says to me: "Arise, my love, my fair one, and come away;	2:10 My lover speaks to me. Come then, my love; my darling, come with me.
11 See! The winter is past; the rains are over and gone.	11 for lo, the winter is past, the rain is over and gone.	11 The winter is over; the rains have stopped;
12 Flowers appear on the earth; the season of singing has come, the cooing of doves is heard in our land.	12 The flowers appear on the earth, the time of singing has come, and the voice of the turtledove is heard in our land.	12 in the countryside the flowers are in bloom. This is the time for singing; the song of doves is heard in the fields.
13 The fig tree forms its early fruit; the blossoming vines spread their fragrance. Arise, come, my darling; my beautiful one, come with me."	13 The fig tree puts forth its figs, and the vines are in blossom; they give forth fragrance. Arise, my love, my fair one, and come away.	13 Figs are beginning to ripen; the air is fragrant with blossoming vines. Come then, my love; my darling, come with me.
4:6 Until the day breaks and the shadows flee, I will go to the mountain of myrrh and to the hill of incense.	4:6 Until the day breathes and the shadows flee, I will hie me to the mountain of myrrh and the hill of frankincense.	4:6 I will stay on the hill of myrrh, the hill of incense, until the morning breezes blow and the darkness disappears.
7 All beautiful you are, my darling; there is no flaw in you.	7 You are all fair, my love; there is no flaw in you.	7 How beautiful you are, my love; how perfect you are!
5:8 O daughters of Jerusalem, I charge you— if you find my lover, what will you tell him? Tell him I am faint with love.	5:8 I adjure you, O daughters of Jerusalem, if you find my beloved, that you tell him I am sick with love.	5:8 Promise me, women of Jerusalem, that if you find my lover, you will tell him I am weak from passion.
14 His arms are rods of gold set with chrysolite. His body is like polished ivory decorated with sapphires.	14 His arms are rounded gold, set with jewels. His body is ivory work, encrusted with sapphires.	14 His hands are well-formed, and he wears rings set with gems. His body is like smooth ivory, with sapphires set in it.
15 His legs are pillars of marble set on bases of pure gold. His appearance is like Lebanon, choice as its cedars.	15 His legs are alabaster columns, set upon bases of gold. His appearance is like Lebanon, choice as the cedars.	15 His thighs are columns of alabaster set in sockets of gold. He is majestic, like the Lebanon Mountains with their towering cedars.
16 His mouth is sweetness itself; he is altogether lovely. This is my lover, this my friend, O daughters of Jerusalem.	16 His speech is most sweet, and he is altogether desirable. This is my beloved and this is my friend, O daughters of Jerusalem.	16 His mouth is sweet to kiss; everything about him enchants me. This is what my lover is like, women of Jerusalem.
6:1 Where has your lover gone, most beautiful of women? Which way did your lover turn, that we may look for him with you?	6:1 Whither has your beloved gone, O fairest among women? Whither has your beloved turned, that we may seek him with you?	6:1 Most beautiful of women, where has your lover gone? Tell us which way your lover went, so that we can help you find him.
2 My lover has gone down to his garden, to the beds of spices, to browse in the gardens and to gather lilies.	2 My beloved has gone down to his garden, to the beds of spices, to pasture his flock in the gardens, and to gather lilies.	2 My lover has gone to his garden, where the balsam trees grow. He is feeding his flock in the garden and gathering lilies.
3 I am my lover's and my lover is mine; he browses among the lilies.	3 I am my beloved's and my beloved is mine; he pastures his flock among the lilies.	3 My lover is mine, and I am his; he feeds his flock among the lilies.
8:6 Place me like a seal over your heart, like a seal over your arm; for love is as strong as death, its jealousy unyielding as the grave. It burns like blazing fire, like a mighty flame.	8:6 Set me as a seal upon your heart, as a seal upon your arm; for love is strong as death, jealousy is cruel as the grave. Its flashes are flashes of fire, a most vehement flame.	8:6 Close your heart to every love but mine; hold no one in your arms but me. Love is as powerful as death; passion is as strong as death itself. It bursts into flame and burns like a raging fire.

KJV	NKJV	TLB
7 Many waters cannot quench love, neither can the floods drown it: if a man would give all the substance of his house for love, it would utterly be contemned.	7 Many waters cannot quench love, Nor can the floods drown it. If a man would give for love All the wealth of his house, It would be utterly despised.	7 Many waters cannot quench the flame of love, neither can the floods drown it. If a man tried to buy it with everything he owned, he couldn't do it."

Isaiah

KJV	NKJV	TLB
1:18 Come now, and let us reason together, saith the Lord: though your sins be as scarlet, they shall be as white as snow; though they be red like crimson, they shall be as wool.	1:18 "Come now, and let us reason together," Says the Lord, "Though your sins are like scarlet, They shall be as white as snow; Though they are red like crimson, They shall be as wool.	1:18 Come, let's talk this over! says the Lord; no matter how deep the stain of your sins, I can take it out and make you as clean as freshly fallen snow. Even if you are stained as red as crimson, I can make you white as wool!
2:2 And it shall come to pass in the last days, *that* the mountain of the Lord's house shall be established in the top of the mountains, and shall be exalted above the hills; and all nations shall flow unto it.	2:2 Now it shall come to pass in the latter days *That* the mountain of the Lord's house Shall be established on the top of the mountains, And shall be exalted above the hills; And all nations shall flow to it.	2:2 In the last days Jerusalem and the Temple of the Lord will become the world's greatest attraction,ᵃ and people from many lands will flow there to worship the Lord.
4 And he shall judge among the nations, and shall rebuke many people: and they shall beat their swords into plowshares, and their spears into pruninghooks: nation shall not lift up sword against nation, neither shall they learn war any more.	4 He shall judge between the nations, And shall rebuke many people; They shall beat their swords into plowshares, And their spears into pruning hooks; Nation shall not lift up sword against nation, Neither shall they learn war anymore.	4 The Lord will settle international disputes; all the nations will convert their weapons of war into implements of peace.ᵇ Then at the last all wars will stop and all military training will end.
6:3 And one cried unto another, and said, Holy, holy, holy, *is* the Lord of hosts: the whole earth *is* full of his glory.	6:3 And one cried to another and said: "Holy, holy, holy *is* the Lord of hosts; The whole earth *is* full of His glory!"	6:3 In a great antiphonal chorus they sang, "Holy, holy, holy is the Lord of Hosts; the whole earth is filled with his glory."
5 Then said I, Woe *is* me! for I am undone; because I *am* a man of unclean lips, and I dwell in the midst of a people of unclean lips; for mine eyes have seen the King, the Lord of hosts.	5 Then I said: "Woe *is* me, for I am undone! Because I *am* a man of unclean lips, And I dwell in the midst of a people of unclean lips; For my eyes have seen the King, The Lord of hosts."	5 Then I said, "My doom is sealed, for I am a foul-mouthed sinner, a member of a sinful, foul-mouthed race; and I have looked upon the King, the Lord of heaven's armies."
7:14 Therefore the Lord himself shall give you a sign; Behold, a virgin shall conceive, and bear a son, and shall call his name Immanuel.	7:14 "Therefore the Lord Himself will give you a sign: Behold, the virgin shall conceive and bear a Son, and shall call His name Immanuel.	7:14 All right then, the Lord himself will choose the sign—a child shall be born to a virgin!ᵈ And she shall call him Immanuel (meaning, "God is with us"):
9:2 The people that walked in darkness have seen a great light: they that dwell in the land of the shadow of death, upon them hath the light shined.	9:2 The people who walked in darkness Have seen a great light; Those who dwelt in the land of the shadow of death, Upon them a light has shined.	9:2 The people who walk in darkness shall see a great Light—a Light that will shine on all those who live in the land of the shadow of death.
6 For unto us a child is born, unto us a son is given: and the government shall be upon his shoulder: and his name shall be called Wonderful, Counsellor, The mighty God, The everlasting Father, The Prince of Peace.	6 For unto us a Child is born, Unto us a Son is given; And the government will be upon His shoulder. And His name will be called Wonderful, Counselor, Mighty God, Everlasting Father, Prince of Peace.	6 For unto us a Child is born; unto us a Son is given; and the government shall be upon his shoulder. These will be his royal titles: "Wonderful," "Counselor," "The Mighty God," "The Everlasting Father," "The Prince of Peace."
7 Of the increase of *his* government and peace *there shall be* no end, upon the throne of David, and upon his kingdom, to order it, and to establish it with judgment and with justice from henceforth even for ever. The zeal of the Lord of hosts will perform this.	7 Of the increase of *His* government and peace *There will be* no end, Upon the throne of David and over His kingdom, To order it and establish it with judgment and justice From that time forward, even forever. The zeal of the Lord of hosts will perform this.	7 His ever-expanding, peaceful government will never end. He will rule with perfect fairness and justice from the throne of his father David. He will bring true justice and peace to all the nations of the world. This is going to happen because the Lord of heaven's armies has dedicated himself to do it!

NIV	RSV	TEV
7 Many waters cannot quench love; rivers cannot wash it away. If one were to give all the wealth of his house for love, it would be utterly scorned.	7 Many waters cannot quench love, neither can floods drown it. If a man offered for love all the wealth of his house, it would be utterly scorned.	7 Water cannot put it out; no flood can drown it. But if anyone tried to buy love with his wealth, contempt is all he would get.

Isaiah

NIV	RSV	TEV
1:18 "Come now, let us reason together," says the LORD. "Though your sins are like scarlet, they shall be as white as snow; though they are red as crimson, they shall be like wool.	1:18 "Come now, let us reason together, says the LORD: though your sins are like scarlet, they shall be as white as snow; though they are red like crimson, they shall become like wool.	1:18 The LORD says, "Now, let's settle the matter. You are stained red with sin, but I will wash you as clean as snow. Although your stains are deep red, you will be as white as wool.
2:2 In the last days the mountain of the LORD's temple will be established as chief among the mountains; it will be raised above the hills, and all nations will stream to it.	2:2 It shall come to pass in the latter days that the mountain of the house of the LORD shall be established as the highest of the mountains, and shall be raised above the hills; and all the nations shall flow to it,	2:2 In days to come the mountain where the Temple stands will be the highest one of all, towering above all the hills. Many nations will come streaming to it,
4 He will judge between the nations and will settle disputes for many peoples. They will beat their swords into plowshares and their spears into pruning hooks. Nation will not take up sword against nation, nor will they train for war anymore.	4 He shall judge between the nations, and shall decide for many peoples; and they shall beat their swords into plowshares, and their spears into pruning hooks; nation shall not lift up sword against nation, neither shall they learn war any more.	4 He will settle disputes among great nations. They will hammer their swords into plows and their spears into pruning knives. Nations will never again go to war, never prepare for battle again.
6:3 And they were calling to one another: "Holy, holy, holy is the LORD Almighty; the whole earth is full of his glory."	6:3 And one called to another and said: "Holy, holy, holy is the LORD of hosts; the whole earth is full of his glory."	6:3 They were calling out to each other: "Holy holy, holy! The LORD Almighty is holy! His glory fills the world."
5 "Woe to me!" I cried. "I am ruined! For I am a man of unclean lips, and I live among a people of unclean lips, and my eyes have seen the King, the LORD Almighty."	5 And I said: "Woe is me! For I am lost; for I am a man of unclean lips, and I dwell in the midst of a people of unclean lips; for my eyes have seen the King, the LORD of hosts!"	5 I said, "There is no hope for me! I am doomed because every word that passes my lips is sinful, and I live among a people whose every word is sinful. And yet, with my own eyes I have seen the King, the LORD Almighty."
7:14 Therefore the Lord himself will give you a sign: The virgin will be with child and will give birth to a son, and will call him Immanuel.	7:14 Therefore the Lord himself will give you a sign. Behold, a young woman shall conceive and bear a son, and shall call his name Immanuel.	7:14 Well then, the Lord himself will give you a sign: a young woman who is pregnant will have a son and will name him 'Immanuel.'
9:2 The people walking in darkness have seen a great light; on those living in the land of the shadow of death a light has dawned.	9:2 The people who walked in darkness have seen a great light; those who dwelt in a land of deep darkness, on them has light shined.	9:2 The people who walked in darkness have seen a great light. They lived in a land of shadows, but now light is shining on them.
6 For to us a child is born, to us a son is given, and the government will be on his shoulders. And he will be called Wonderful Counselor, Mighty God, Everlasting Father, Prince of Peace.	6 For to us a child is born, to us a son is given; and the government will be upon his shoulder, and his name will be called "Wonderful Counselor, Mighty God, Everlasting Father, Prince of Peace."	6 A child is born to us! A son is give to us! And he will be our ruler. He will be called, "Wonderful Counselor," "Mighty God," "Eternal Father," "Prince of Peace."
7 Of the increase of his government and peace there will be no end. He will reign on David's throne and over his kingdom, establishing and upholding it with justice and righteousness from that time on and forever. The zeal of the LORD Almighty will accomplish this.	7 Of the increase of his government and of peace there will be no end, upon the throne of David, and over his kingdom, to establish it, and to uphold it with justice and with righteousness from this time forth and for evermore. The zeal of the LORD of hosts will do this.	7 His royal power will continue to grow; his kingdom will always be at peace. He will rule as King David's successor, basing his power on right and justice, from now until the end of time. The LORD Almighty is determined to do all this.

KJV	NKJV	TLB
11:1 And there shall come forth a rod out of the stem of Jesse, and a Branch shall grow out of his roots:	**11:1** There shall come forth a Rod from the stem of Jesse, And a Branch shall grow out of his roots.	**11:1** The royal line of David will be cut off, chopped down like a tree; but from the stump will grow a Shoot—yes, a new Branch from the old root.
2 And the spirit of the LORD shall rest upon him, the spirit of wisdom and understanding, the spirit of counsel and might, the spirit of knowledge and of the fear of the LORD;	**2** The Spirit of the LORD shall rest upon Him, The Spirit of wisdom and understanding, The Spirit of counsel and might, The Spirit of knowledge and of the fear of the LORD.	**2** And the Spirit of the Lord shall rest upon him, the Spirit of wisdom, understanding, counsel and might; the Spirit of knowledge and of the fear of the Lord.
3 And shall make him of quick understanding in the fear of the LORD: and he shall not judge after the sight of his eyes, neither reprove after the hearing of his ears:	**3** His delight *is* in the fear of the LORD, And He shall not judge by the sight of His eyes, Nor decide by the hearing of His ears;	**3** His delight will be obedience to the Lord. He will not judge by appearance, false evidence, or hearsay,
4 But with righteousness shall he judge the poor, and reprove with equity for the meek of the earth: and he shall smite the earth: with the rod of his mouth, and with the breath of his lips shall he slay the wicked.	**4** But with righteousness He shall judge the poor, And decide with equity for the meek of the earth; He shall strike the earth with the rod of His mouth, And with the breath of His lips He shall slay the wicked.	**4** but will defend the poor and the exploited. He will rule against the wicked who oppress them.
6 The wolf also shall dwell with the lamb, and the leopard shall lie down with the kid; and the calf and the young lion and the fatling together; and a little child shall lead them.	**6** "The wolf also shall dwell with the lamb, The leopard shall lie down with the young goat, The calf and the young lion and the fatling together; And a little child shall lead them.	**6** In that day the wolf and the lamb will lie down together, and the leopard and goats will be at peace. Calves and fat cattle will be safe among lions, and a little child shall lead them all.
10 And in that day there shall be a root of Jesse, which shall stand for an ensign of the people; to it shall the Gentiles seek: and his rest shall be glorious.	**10** "And in the day there shall be a Root of Jesse, Who shall stand as a banner to the people; For the Gentiles shall seek Him, And His resting place shall be glorious."	**10** In that day he who created the royal dynasty of David will be a banner of salvation to all the world. The nations will rally to him, for the land where he lives will be a glorious place.
14:12 How art thou fallen from heaven, O Lucifer, son of the morning! *how* art thou cut down to the ground, which didst weaken the nations!	**14:12** "How you are fallen from heaven, O Lucifer, son of the morning! *How* you are cut down to the ground, You who weakened the nations!	**14:12** How you are fallen from heaven, O Lucifer, son of the morning! How you are cut down to the ground—mighty though you were against the nations of the world.
25:9 And it shall be said in that day, Lo, this *is* our God; we have waited for him, and he will save us: this *is* the LORD; we have waited for him, we will be glad and rejoice in his salvation.	**25:9** And it will be said in that day: "Behold, this *is* our God; We have waited for Him, and He will save us. This *is* the LORD; We have waited for Him; We will be glad and rejoice in His salvation."	**25:9** In that day the people will proclaim, "This is our God, in whom we trust, for whom we waited. Now at last he is here." What a day of rejoicing!
26:3 Thou wilt keep *him* in perfect peace, *whose* mind *is* stayed *on thee:* because he trusteth in thee.	**26:3** You will keep *him* in perfect peace, *Whose* mind *is* stayed *on You,* Because he trusts in You.	**26:3** He will keep in perfect peace all those who trust in him, whose thoughts turn often to the Lord!
30:15 For thus saith the Lord GOD, the Holy One of Israel; In returning and rest shall ye be saved; in quietness and in confidence shall be your strength: and ye would not.	**30:15** For thus says the Lord GOD, the Holy One of Israel: "In returning and rest you shall be saved; In quietness and confidence shall be your strength." But you would not,	**30:15** For the Lord God, the Holy One of Israel, says: Only in returning to me and waiting for me will you be saved; in quietness and confidence is your strength; but you'll have none of this.
32:17 And the work of righteousness shall be peace; and the effect of righteousness quietness and assurance for ever.	**32:17** The work of righteousness will be peace, And the effect of righteousness, quietness and assurance forever.	**32:17** and out of justice, peace. Quietness and confidence will reign forever more.
35:6 Then shall the lame *man* leap as an hart, and the tongue of the dumb sing: for in the wilderness shall waters break out, and streams in the desert.	**35:6** Then the lame shall leap like a deer, And the tongue of the dumb sing. For waters shall burst forth in the wilderness, And streams in the desert.	**35:6** The lame man will leap up like a deer, and those who could not speak will shout and sing! Springs will burst forth in the wilderness, and streams in the desert.

NIV	RSV	TEV
11:1 A shoot will come up from the stump of Jesse; from his roots a Branch will bear fruit.	**11:1** There shall come forth a shoot from the stump of Jesse, and a branch shall grow out of his roots.	**11:1** The royal line of David is like a tree that has been cut down; but just as new branches sprout from a stump, so a new king will arise from among David's descendants.
2 The Spirit of the LORD will rest on him— the Spirit of wisdom and of understanding, the Spirit of counsel and of power, the Spirit of knowledge and of the fear of the LORD—	**2** And the Spirit of the LORD shall rest upon him, the spirit of wisdom and understanding, the spirit of counsel and might, the spirit of knowledge and the fear of the LORD.	**2** The spirit of the LORD will give him wisdom and the knowledge and skill to rule his people. He will know the LORD's will and honor him,
3 and he will delight in the fear of the LORD. He will not judge by what he sees with his eyes, or decide by what he hears with his ears;	**3** And his delight shall be in the fear of the LORD. He shall not judge by what his eyes see, or decide by what his ears hear;	**3** and find pleasure in obeying him. He will not judge by appearance or hearsay;
4 but with righteousness he will judge the needy, with justice he will give decisions for the poor of the earth. He will strike the earth with the rod of his mouth; with the breath of his lips he will slay the wicked.	**4** but with righteousness he shall judge the poor, and decide with equity for the meek of the earth; and he shall smite the earth with the rod of his mouth, and with the breath of his lips he shall slay the wicked.	**4** he will judge the poor fairly and defend the rights of the helpless. At his command the people will be punished, and evil persons will die.
6 The wolf will live with the lamb, the leopard will lie down with the goat, the calf and the lion and the yearling together; and a little child will lead them.	**6** The wolf shall dwell with the lamb, and the leopard shall lie down with the kid, and the calf and the lion and the fatling together, and a little child shall lead them.	**6** Wolves and sheep will live together in peace, and leopards will lie down with young goats. Calves and lion cubs will feed together, and little children will take care of them.
10 In that day the Root of Jesse will stand as a banner for the peoples; the nations will rally to him, and his place of rest will be glorious.	**10** In that day the root of Jesse shall stand as an ensign to the peoples; him shall the nations seek, and his dwellings shall be glorious.	**10** A day is coming when the new king from the royal line of David will be a symbol to the nations. They will gather in his royal city and give him honor.
14:12 How you have fallen from heaven, O morning star, son of the dawn! You have been cast down to the earth, you who once laid low the nations!	**14:12** "How you are fallen from heaven, O Day Star, son of Dawn! How you are cut down to the ground, you who laid the nations low!	**14:12** King of Babylon, bright morning star, you have fallen from heaven! In the past you conquered nations, but now you have been thrown to the ground.
25:9 In that day they will say, "Surely this is our God; we trusted in him, and he saved us. This is the LORD, we trusted in him; let us rejoice and be glad in his salvation."	**25:9** It will be said on that day, "Lo, this is our God; we have waited for him, that he might save us. This is the LORD; we have waited for him; let us be glad and rejoice in his salvation."	**25:9** When it happens, everyone will say, "He is our God! We have put our trust in him, and he has rescued us. He is the LORD! We have put our trust in him, and now we are happy and joyful because he has saved us."
26:3 You will keep in perfect peace him whose mind is steadfast, because he trusts in you.	**26:3** Thou dost keep him in perfect peace, whose mind is stayed on thee, because he trusts in thee.	**26:3** You, LORD, give perfect peace to those who keep their purpose firm and put their trust in you.
30:15 This is what the Sovereign LORD, the Holy One of Israel, says: "In repentance and rest is your salvation, in quietness and trust is your strength, but you would have none of it.	**30:15** For thus said the Lord GOD, the Holy One of Israel, "In returning and rest you shall be saved; in quietness and in trust shall be your strength." And you would not,	**30:15** The Sovereign LORD, the Holy One of Israel, says to the people, "Come back and quietly trust in me. Then you will be strong and secure." But you refuse to do it.
32:17 The fruit of righteousness will be peace; the effect of righteousness will be quietness and confidence forever.	**32:17** And the effect of righteousness will be peace, and the result of righteousness, quietness and trust for ever.	**32:17** Because everyone will do what is right, there will be peace and security forever.
35:6 Then will the lame leap like a deer, and the tongue of the dumb shout for joy. Water will gush forth in the wilderness and streams in the desert.	**35:6** then shall the lame man leap like a hart, and the tongue of the dumb sing for joy. For waters shall break forth in the wilderness, and streams in the desert;	**35:6** The lame will leap and dance, and those who cannot speak will shout for joy. Streams of water will flow through the desert;

KJV	NKJV	TLB
7 And the parched ground shall become a pool, and the thirsty land springs of water: in the habitation of dragons, where each lay, *shall be* grass with reeds and rushes.	7 The parched ground shall become a pool, And the thirsty land springs of water; In the habitation of jackals, where each lay, *There shall be* grass with reeds and rushes.	7 The parched ground will become a pool, with springs of water in the thirsty land. Where desert jackals lived, there will be reeds and rushes!
8 And an highway shall be there, and a way, and it shall be called They way of holiness; the unclean shall not pass over it; but it *shall be* for those: the wayfaring men, though fools, shall not err *therein.*	8 A highway shall be there, and a road, And it shall be called the Highway of Holiness. The unclean shall not pass over it, But it *shall be* for others. Whoever walks the road, although a fool, Shall not go astray.	8 And a main road will go through that once-deserted land; it will be named "The Holy Highway." No evil-hearted men may walk upon it. God will walk there with you; even the most stupid cannot miss the way.
9 No lion shall be there, nor *any* ravenous beast shall go up thereon, it shall not be found there; but the redeemed shall walk *there:*	9 No lion shall be there, Nor shall *any* ravenous beast go up on it; It shall not be found there. But the redeemed shall walk *there,*	9 No lion will lurk along its course, nor will there be any other dangers; only the redeemed will travel there.
10 And the ransomed of the LORD shall return, and come to Zion with songs and everlasting joy upon their heads: they shall obtain joy and gladness, and sorrow and sighing shall flee away.	10 And the ransomed of the LORD shall return, And come to Zion with singing, With everlasting joy on their heads. They shall obtain joy and gladness, And sorrow and sighing shall flee away.	10 These, the ransomed of the Lord, will go home along that road to Zion, singing the songs of everlasting joy. For them all sorrow and all sighing will be gone forever; only joy and gladness will be there.
40:3 The voice of him that crieth in the wilderness, Prepare ye the way of the LORD, make straight in the desert a highway for our God.	**40:3** The voice of one crying in the wilderness: "Prepare the way of the LORD; Make straight in the desert A highway for our God.	**40:3** Listen! I hear the voice of someone shouting, "Make a road for the Lord through the wilderness; make him a straight, smooth road through the desert.
4 Every valley shall be exalted, and every mountain and hill shall be made low: and the crooked shall be made straight, and the rough places plain:	4 Every valley shall be exalted, And every mountain and hill shall be made low; The crooked places shall be made straight, And the rough places smooth;	4 Fill the valleys; level the hills; straighten out the crooked paths and smooth off the rough spots in the road.
5 And the glory of the LORD shall be revealed, and all flesh shall see *it* together: for the mouth of the LORD hath spoken *it.*	5 The glory of the LORD shall be revealed, And all flesh shall see *it* together; For the mouth of the LORD has spoken."	5 The glory of the Lord will be seen by all mankind together." The Lord has spoken—it shall be.
30 Even the youths shall faint and be weary, and the young men shall utterly fall:	30 Even the youths shall faint and be weary, And the young men shall utterly fall,	30 Even the youths shall be exhausted, and the young men will all give up.
31 But they that wait upon the LORD shall renew their strength; they shall mount up with wings as eagles; they shall run, and not be weary *and* they shall walk, and not faint.	31 But those who wait on the LORD Shall renew *their* strength; They shall mount up with wings like eagles, They shall run and not be weary, They shall walk and not faint.	31 But they that wait upon the Lord shall renew their strength. They shall mount up with wings like eagles; they shall run and not be weary; they shall walk and not faint.
41:10 Fear thou not; for I *am* with thee: be not dismayed; for I *am* thy God: I will strengthen thee; yea, I will help thee; yea, I will uphold thee with the right hand of my righteousness.	**41:10** Fear not, for I *am* with you; Be not dismayed, for I *am* your God. I will strengthen you, Yes, I will help you, I will uphold you with My righteous right hand.'	**41:10** Fear not, for I am with you. Do not be dismayed. I am your God. I will strengthen you; I will help you; I will uphold you with my victorious right hand.
42:1 Behold my servant, whom I uphold; mine elect, *in whom* my soul delighteth; I have put my spirit upon him: he shall bring forth judgment to the Gentiles.	**42:1** "Behold! My Servant whom I uphold, My Elect One *in whom* My soul delights! I have put My Spirit upon Him; He will bring forth justice to the Gentiles	**42:1** See my servant, whom I uphold; my Chosen One, in whom I delight. I have put my Spirit upon him; he will reveal justice to the nations of the world.
2 He shall not cry, nor lift up, nor cause his voice to be heard in the street.	2 He will not cry out, nor raise *His voice,* Nor cause His voice to be heard in the street.	2 He will be gentle—he will not shout nor quarrel in the streets.
3 A bruised reed shall he not break, and the smoking flax shall he not quench: he shall bring forth judgment unto truth.	3 A bruised reed He will not break, And smoking flax He will not quench; He will bring forth justice for truth.	3 He will not break the bruised reed, nor quench the dimly burning flame. He will encourage the fainthearted, those tempted to despair. He will see full justice given to all who have been wronged.

NIV	RSV	TEV
7 The burning sand will become a pool, the thirsty ground bubbling springs. In the haunts where jackals once lay, grass and reeds and papyrus will grow.	7 the burning sand shall become a pool, and the thirsty ground springs of water; the haunt of jackals shall become a swamp, the grass shall become reeds and rushes.	7 the burning sand will become a lake, and dry land will be filled with springs. Where jackals used to live, marsh grass and reeds will grow.
8 And a highway will be there; it will be called the Way of Holiness. The unclean will not journey on it; it will be for those who walk in that Way; wicked fools will not go about on it.	8 And a highway shall be there, and it shall be called the Holy Way; the unclean shall not pass over it, and fools shall not err therein.	8 There will be a highway there, called "The Road of Holiness." No sinner will ever travel that road; no fools will mislead those who follow it.
9 No lion will be there, nor will any ferocious beast get up on it; they will not be found there. But only the redeemed will walk there,	9 No lion shall be there, nor shall any ravenous beast come up on it; they shall not be found there, but the redeemed shall walk there.	9 No lions will be there; no fierce animals will pass that way. Those whom the LORD has rescued will travel home by that road.
10 and the ransomed of the LORD will return. They will enter Zion with singing; everlasting joy will crown their heads. Gladness and joy will overtake them, and sorrow and sighing will flee away.	10 And the ransomed of the LORD shall return, and come to Zion with singing; everlasting joy shall be upon their heads; they shall obtain joy and gladness, and sorrow and sighing shall flee away.	10 They will reach Jerusalem with gladness, singing and shouting for joy. They will be happy forever, forever free from sorrow and grief.
40:3 A voice of one calling: "In the desert prepare the way for the LORD, make straight in the wilderness a highway for our God.	40:3 A voice cries: "In the wilderness prepare the way of the LORD, make straight in the desert a highway for our God.	40:3 A voice cries out, "Prepare in the wilderness a road for the LORD! Clear the way in the desert for our God!
4 Every valley shall be raised up, every mountain and hill made low; the rough ground shall become level, the rugged places a plain.	4 Every valley shall be lifted up, and every mountain and hill be made low; the uneven ground shall become level, and the rough places a plain.	4 Fill every valley; level every mountain. The hills will become a plain, and the rough country will be made smooth.
5 And the glory of the LORD will be revealed, and all mankind together will see it. For the mouth of the LORD has spoken."	5 And the glory of the LORD shall be revealed, and all flesh shall see it together, for the mouth of the LORD has spoken."	5 Then the glory of the LORD will be revealed, and all mankind will see it. The LORD himself has promised this."
30 Even youths grow tired and weary, and young men stumble and fall;	30 Even youths shall faint and be weary, and young men shall fall exhausted;	30 Even those who are young grow weak; young men can fall exhausted.
31 but those who hope in the LORD will renew their strength. They will soar on wings like eagles; they will run and not grow weary, they will walk and not be faint.	31 but they who wait for the LORD shall renew their strength, they shall mount up with wings like eagles, they shall run and not be weary, they shall walk and not faint.	31 But those who trust in the LORD for help will find their strength renewed. They will rise on wings like eagles; they will run and not get weary; they will walk and not grow weak.
41:10 So do not fear, for I am with you; do not be dismayed, for I am your God. I will strengthen you and help you; I will uphold you with my righteous right hand.	41:10 fear not, for I am with you, be not dismayed, for I am your God; I will strengthen you, I will help you, I will uphold you with my victorious right hand.	41:10 Do not be afraid—I am with you! I am your God—let nothing terrify you! I will make you strong and help you; I will protect you and save you.
42:1 "Here is my servant, whom I uphold, my chosen one in whom I delight; I will put my Spirit on him and he will bring justice to the nations.	42:1 Behold my servant, whom I uphold, my chosen, in whom my soul delights; I have put my Spirit upon him, he will bring forth justice to the nations.	42:1 The LORD says, "Here is my servant, whom I strengthen— the one I have chosen, with whom I am pleased. I have filled him with my spirit, and he will bring justice to every nation.
2 He will not shout or cry out, or raise his voice in the streets.	2 He will not cry or lift up his voice, or make it heard in the street;	2 He will not shout or raise his voice or make loud speeches in the streets.
3 A bruised reed he will not break, and a smoldering wick he will not snuff out. In faithfulness he will bring forth justice;	3 a bruised reed he will not break, and a dimly burning wick he will not quench; he will faithfully bring forth justice.	3 He will not break off a bent reed nor put out a flickering lamp. He will bring lasting justice to all.

KJV	NKJV	TLB
4 He shall not fail nor be discouraged, till he have set judgment in the earth: and the isles shall wait for his law.	4 He will not fail nor be discouraged, Till He has established justice in the earth;' And the coastlands shall wait for His law."	4 He won't be satisfied until truth and righteousness prevail throughout the earth, nor until even distant lands beyond the seas have put their trust in him.
43:2 When thou passest through the waters, I *will be* with thee; and through the rivers, they shall not overflow thee: when thou walkest through the fire, thou shalt not be burned; neither shall the flame kindle upon thee.	43:2 When you pass through the waters, I *will be* with you; And through the rivers, they shall not overflow you. When you walk through the fire, you shall not be burned, Nor shall the flame scorch you.	43:2 When you go through deep waters and great trouble, I will be with you. When you go through rivers of difficulty, you will not drown! When you walk through the fire of oppression, you will not be burned up—the flames will not consume you.
46:4 And *even* to *your* old age I *am* he; and *even* to hoar hairs will I carry *you:* I have made, and I will bear; even I will carry, and will deliver *you.*	46:4 Even to *your* old age, I *am* He, And *even* to gray hairs I will carry *you!* I have made, and I will bear; Even I will carry, and will deliver *you.*	46:4 I will be your God through all your lifetime, yes, even when your hair is white with age. I made you and I will care for you. I will carry you along and be your Savior.
50:7 For the Lord GOD will help me; therefore shall I not be confounded: therefore have I set my face like a flint, and I know that I shall not be ashamed.	50:7 "For the Lord GOD will help Me; Therefore I will not be disgraced; Therefore I have set My face like a flint, And I know that I will not be ashamed.	50:7 Because the Lord God helps me, I will not be dismayed; therefore, I have set my face like flint to do his will, and I know that I will triumph.
51:11 Therefore the redeemed of the LORD shall return, and come with singing unto Zion; and everlasting joy *shall be* upon their head: they shall obtain gladness and joy; *and* sorrow and mourning shall flee away.	51:11 So the ransomed of the LORD shall return. And come to Zion with singing, With everlasting joy on their heads; They shall obtain joy and gladness, *And* sorrow and sighing shall flee away.	51:11 The time will come when God's redeemed will all come home again. They shall come with singing to Jerusalem, filled with joy and everlasting gladness; sorrow and mourning will all disappear.
12 I, *even* I, *am* he that comforteth you: who *art* thou, that thou shouldest be afraid of a man *that* shall die, and of the son of man *which* shall be made *as* grass;	12 "I, *even* I, *am* He who comforts you. Who *are* you that you should be afraid Of a man *who* will die, And of the son of a man *who* will be made like grass?	12 I, even I, am he who comforts you and gives you all this joy. So what right have you to fear mere mortal men, who wither like the grass and disappear?
13 And forgettest the LORD thy maker, that hath stretched forth the heavens, and laid the foundations of the earth; and hast feared continually every day because of the fury of the oppressor, as if he were ready to destroy? and where *is* the fury of the oppressor?	13 And you forget the LORD your Maker, Who stretched out the heavens And laid the foundations of the earth; You have feared continually every day Because of the fury of the oppressor, When *he has* prepared to destroy. And where *is* the fury of the oppressor?	13 And yet you have no fear of God, your Maker—you have forgotten him, the one who spread the stars throughout the skies and made the earth. Will you be in constant dread of men's oppression, and fear their anger all day long?
52:7 How beautiful upon the mountains are the feet of him that bringeth good tidings, that publisheth peace; that bringeth good tidings of good, that publisheth salvation; that saith unto Zion. Thy God reigneth!	52:7 How beautiful upon the mountains Are the feet of him who brings good news, Who proclaims peace, Who brings glad tidings of good *things,* Who proclaims salvation, Who says to Zion, "Your God reigns!"	52:7 How beautiful upon the mountains are the feet of those who bring the happy news of peace and salvation, the news that the God of Israel reigns.
53:1 Who hath believed our report? and to whom is the arm of the LORD revealed?	53:1 Who has believed our report? And to whom has the arm of the LORD been revealed?	53:1 But, oh, how few believe it! Who will listen? To whom will God reveal his saving power?
2 For he shall grow up before him as a tender plant, and as a root out of a dry ground: he hath no form nor comeliness; and when we shall see him, *there is* no beauty that we should desire him.	2 For He shall grow up before Him as a tender plant, And as a root out of dry ground. He has no form or comeliness; And when we see Him, *There is* no beauty that we should desire Him.	2 In God's eyes he was like a tender green shoot, sprouting from a root in dry and sterile ground. But in our eyes there was no attractiveness at all, nothing to make us want him.
3 He is despised and rejected of men; a man of sorrows, and acquainted with grief: and we hid as it were *our* faces from him; he was despised, and we esteemed him not.	3 He is despised and rejected by men, A man of sorrows and acquainted with grief. And we hid, as it were, *our* faces from Him; He was despised, and we did not esteem Him.	3 We despised him and rejected him—a man of sorrows, acquainted with bitterest grief. We turned our backs on him and looked the other way when he went by. He was despised and we didn't care.

NIV	RSV	TEV
4　he will not falter or be discouraged 　　till he establishes justice on earth. 　In his law the islands will put their 　　hope."	4　He will not fail or be discouraged 　　till he has established justice in the earth; 　　and the coastlands wait for his law.	4　He will not lose hope or courage; 　　he will establish justice on the earth. 　Distant lands eagerly wait for his 　　teaching."
43:2　When you pass through the waters, 　　I will be with you; 　and when you pass through the rivers, 　　they will not sweep over you. 　When you walk through the fire, 　　you will not be burned; 　the flames will not set you ablaze.	43:2　When you pass through the waters I will 　　be with you; 　and through the rivers, they shall not 　　overwhelm you; 　when you walk through fire you shall not 　　be burned, 　and the flame shall not consume you.	43:2　When you pass through deep waters, I 　　will be with you; 　your troubles will not overwhelm you. 　When you pass through fire, you will not 　　be burned; 　the hard trials that come will not hurt 　　you.
46:4　Even to your old age and gray hairs 　　I am he, I am he who will sustain you. 　I have made you and I will carry you; 　　I will sustain you and I will rescue 　　you.	46:4　even to your old age I am He, 　　and to gray hairs I will carry you. 　I have made, and I will bear; 　　I will carry and will save.	46:4　I am your God and will take care of you 　　until you are old and your hair is gray. 　I made you and will care for you; 　　I will give you help and rescue you.
50:7　Because the Sovereign LORD helps me, 　　I will not be disgraced. 　Therefore have I set my face like flint, 　　and I know I will not be put to shame.	50:7　For the Lord GOD helps me; 　　therefore I have not been confounded; 　therefore I have set my face like a flint, 　　and I know that I shall not be put to 　　shame;	50:7　But their insults cannot hurt me 　　because the Sovereign LORD gives me 　　help. 　I brace myself to endure them. 　I know that I will not be disgraced,
51:11　The ransomed of the LORD will return. 　　They will enter Zion with singing; 　everlasting joy will crown their heads. 　Gladness and joy will overtake them, 　　and sorrow and sighing will flee away.	51:11　And the ransomed of the LORD shall 　　return, 　and come to Zion with singing; 　everlasting joy shall be upon their 　　heads; 　they shall obtain joy and gladness, 　　and sorrow and sighing shall flee 　　away.	51:11　Those whom you have rescued 　　will reach Jerusalem with gladness, 　singing and shouting for joy. 　They will be happy forever, 　　forever free from sorrow and grief.
12　"I, even I, am he who comforts you. 　　Who are you that you fear mortal men, 　　the sons of men, who are but grass,	12　"I, I am he that comforts you; 　　who are you that you are afraid of man 　　who dies, 　of the son of man who is made like 　　grass,	12　The LORD says, 　　"I am the one who strengthens you. 　Why should you fear mortal man, 　　who is no more enduring than grass?
13　that you forget the LORD your Maker, who 　　stretched out the heavens 　and laid the foundations of the earth, 　that you live in constant terror every day 　　because of the wrath of the oppressor, 　　who is bent on destruction? 　For where is the wrath of the oppressor?	13　and have forgotten the LORD, your Maker, 　　who stretched out the heavens 　and laid the foundations of the earth, 　and fear continually all the day 　　because of the fury of the oppressor, 　when he sets himself to destroy? 　And where is the fury of the oppressor?	13　Have you forgotten the LORD who made 　　you, 　who stretched out the heavens 　and laid the earth's foundations? 　Why should you live in constant fear 　　of the fury of those who oppress you, 　　of those who are ready to destroy you? 　Their fury can no longer touch you.
52:7　How beautiful on the mountains 　　are the feet of those who bring good 　　news, 　who proclaim peace, 　who bring good tidings, 　who proclaim salvation, 　who say to Zion, 　"Your God reigns!"	52:7　How beautiful upon the mountains 　　are the feet of him who brings good 　　tidings, 　who publishes peace, who brings good 　　tidings of good, 　who publishes salvation, 　who says to Zion, "Your God reigns."	52:7　How wonderful it is to see 　　a messenger coming across the 　　mountains, 　bringing good news, the news of peace! 　He announced victory and says to Zion, 　"Your God is king!"
53:1　Who has believed our message 　　and to whom has the arm of the LORD 　　been revealed?	53:1　Who has believed what we have heard? 　　And to whom has the arm of the LORD 　　been revealed?	53:1　The people reply, 　"Who would have believed what we now 　　report? 　Who could have seen the Lord's 　　hand in this?
2　He grew up before him like a tender shoot, 　　and like a root out of dry ground. 　He had no beauty or majesty to attract us 　　to him, 　nothing in his appearance that we should 　　desire him.	2　For he grew up before him like a young 　　plant, 　and like a root out of dry ground; 　he had no form or comeliness that we 　　should look at him, 　and no beauty that we should desire him.	2　It was the will of the LORD that his servant 　　grow like a plant taking root in dry 　　ground. 　He had no dignity or beauty 　　to make us take notice of him. 　There was nothing attractive about him, 　　nothing that would draw us to him.
3　He was despised and rejected by men, 　　a man of sorrows, and familiar with 　　suffering. 　Like one from whom men hide their faces 　　he was despised, and we esteemed him not.	3　He was despised and rejected by men; 　　a man of sorrows, and acquainted with 　　grief; 　and as one from whom men hide their faces 　　he was despised, and we esteemed him not.	3　We despised him and rejected him; 　　he endured suffering and pain. 　No one would even look at him— 　　we ignored him as if he were nothing.

KJV	NKJV	TLB
4 Surely he hath borne our griefs, and carried our sorrows: yet we did esteem him stricken, smitten of God, and afflicted.	4 Surely He has borne our griefs And carried our sorrows; Yet we esteemed Him stricken, Smitten by God, and afflicted.	4 Yet it was *our* grief he bore, *our* sorrows that weighed him down. And we thought his troubles were a punishment from God, for his *own* sins!
5 But he *was* wounded for our transgressions, *he was* bruised for our iniquities: the chastisement of our peace *was* upon him; and with his stripes we are healed.	5 But He *was* wounded for our transgressions, *He was* bruised for our iniquities; The chastisement for our peace *was* upon Him, And by His stripes we are healed.	5 But he was wounded and bruised for *our* sins. He was chastised that we might have peace; he was lashed—and we were healed!
6 All we like sheep have gone astray; we have turned every one to his own way; and the LORD hath laid on him the iniquity of us all.	6 All we like sheep have gone astray; We have turned, every one, to his own way; And the LORD has laid on Him the iniquity of us all.	6 *We* are the ones who strayed away like sheep! *We*, who left God's paths to follow our own. Yet God laid on *him* the guilt and sins of every one of us!
7 He was oppressed, and he was afflicted, yet he opened not his mouth: he is brought as a lamb to the slaughter, and as a sheep before her shearers is dumb, so he openeth not his mouth.	7 He was oppressed and He was afflicted, Yet He opened not His mouth; He was led as a lamb to the slaughter, And as a sheep before its shearers is silent, So He opened not His mouth.	7 He was oppressed and he was afflicted, yet he never said a word. He was brought as a lamb to the slaughter; and as a sheep before her shearers is dumb, so he stood silent before the ones condemning him.
8 He was taken from prison and from judgment: and who shall declare his generation? for he was cut off out of the land of the living: for the transgression of my people was he stricken.	8 He was taken from prison and from judgment, And who will declare His generation? For He was cut off from the land of the living; For the transgressions of My people He was stricken.	8 From prison and trial they led him away to his death. But who among the people of that day realized it was their sins that he was dying for— that he was suffering their punishment?
9 And he made his grave with the wicked, and with the rich in his death; because he had done no violence, neither *was any* deceit in his mouth.	9 And they made His grave with the wicked— But with the rich at His death, Because He had done no violence, Nor *was any* deceit in His mouth.	9 He was buried like a criminal in a rich man's grave; but he had done no wrong, and had never spoken an evil word.
10 Yet it pleased the LORD to bruise him; he hath put *him* to grief: when thou shalt make his soul an offering for sin, he shall see *his* seed, he shall prolong *his* days, and the pleasure of the LORD shall prosper in his hand.	10 Yet it pleased the LORD to bruise Him; He has put *Him* to grief. When You make His soul an offering for sin, He shall see *His* seed, He shall prolong *His* days, And the pleasure of the LORD shall prosper in His hand.	10 Yet it was the Lord's good plan to bruise him and fill him with grief. But when his soul has been made an offering for sin, then he shall have a multitude of children, many heirs. He shall live again and God's program shall prosper in his hands.
11 He shall see of the travail of his soul, *and* shall be satisfied: by his knowledge shall my righteous servant justify many; for he shall bear their iniquities.	11 He shall see the travail of His soul, *and* be satisfied. By His knowledge My righteous Servant shall justify many, For He shall bear their iniquities.	11 And when he sees all that is accomplished by the anguish of his soul, he shall be satisfied; and because of what he has experienced, my righteous Servant shall make many to be counted righteous before God, for he shall bear all their sins.
12 Therefore will I divide him a *portion* with the great, and he shall divide the spoil with the strong; because he hath poured out his soul unto death: and he was numbered with the transgressors; and he bare the sin of many, and made intercession for the transgressors.	12 Therefore I will divide Him a portion with the great, And He shall divide the spoil with the strong, Because He poured out His soul unto death, And He was numbered with the transgressors, And He bore the sin of many, And made intercession for the transgressors.	12 Therefore I will give him the honors of one who is mighty and great, because he has poured out his soul unto death. He was counted as a sinner, and he bore the sins of many, and he pled with God for sinners.
54:10 For the mountains shall depart, and the hills be removed; but my kindness shall not depart from thee, neither shall the covenant of my peace be removed, saith the LORD that hath mercy on thee.	54:10 For the mountains shall depart And the hills be removed, But My kindness shall not depart from you, Nor shall My covenant of peace be removed," Says the LORD, who has mercy on you.	54:10 For the mountains may depart and the hills disappear, but my kindness shall not leave you. My promise of peace for you will never be broken, says the Lord who has mercy upon you.

NIV	RSV	TEV
4 Surely he took up our infirmities and carried our sorrows, yet we considered him stricken by God, smitten by him, and afflicted.	4 Surely he has borne our griefs and carried our sorrows yet we esteemed him stricken, smitten by God, and afflicted.	4 "But he endured the suffering that should have been ours, the pain that we should have borne. All the while we thought that his suffering was punishment sent by God.
5 But he was pierced for our transgressions, he was crushed for our iniquities; the punishment that brought us peace was upon him, and by his wounds we are healed.	5 But he was wounded for our transgressions, he was bruised for our iniquities; upon him was the chastisement that made us whole, and with his stripes we are healed.	5 But because of our sins he was wounded, beaten because of the evil we did. We are healed by the punishment he suffered, made whole by the blows he received.
6 We all, like sheep, have gone astray, each of us has turned to his own way; and the LORD has laid on him the iniquity of us all.	6 All we like sheep have gone astray; we have turned every one to his own way; and the LORD has laid on him the iniquity of us all.	6 All of us were like sheep that were lost, each of us going his own way. But the LORD made the punishment fall on him, the punishment all of us deserved.
7 He was oppressed and afflicted, yet he did not open his mouth; he was led like a lamb to the slaughter, and as a sheep before her shearers is silent, so he did not open his mouth.	7 He was oppressed, and he was afflicted, yet he opened not his mouth; like a lamb that is led to the slaughter, and like a sheep that before its shearers is dumb, so he opened not his mouth.	7 "He was treated harshly, but endured it humbly; he never said a word. Like a lamb about to be slaughtered, like a sheep about to be sheared, he never said a word.
8 By oppression and judgment, he was taken away. And who can speak of his descendants? For he was cut off from the land of the living; for the transgression of my people he was stricken.	8 By oppression and judgment he was taken away; and as for his generation, who considered that he was cut off out of the land of the living, stricken for the transgression of my people?	8 He was arrested and sentenced and led off to die, and no one cared about his fate. He was put to death for the sins of our people.
9 He was assigned a grave with the wicked, and with the rich in his death, though he had done no violence, nor was any deceit in his mouth.	9 And they made his grave with the wicked and with a rich man in his death, although he had done no violence, and there was no deceit in his mouth.	9 He was placed in a grave with evil men, he was buried with the rich, even though he had never committed a crime or ever told a lie."
10 Yet it was the LORD's will to crush him and cause him to suffer, and though the LORD makes his life a guilt offering, he will see his offspring and prolong his days, and the will of the LORD will prosper in his hand.	10 Yet it was the will of the LORD to bruise him; he has put him to grief; when he makes himself an offering for sin, he shall see his offspring, he shall prolong his days; the will of the LORD sall prosper in his hand;	10 The LORD says, "It was my will that he should suffer; his death was a sacrifice to bring forgiveness. And so he will see his descendants; he will live a long life, and through him my purpose will succeed.
11 After the suffering of his soul, he will see the light of life, and be satisfied; by his knowledge my righteous servant will justify many, and he will bear their iniquities.	11 he shall see the fruit of the travail of his soul and be satisfied; by his knowledge shall the righteous one, my servant, make many to be accounted righteous; and he shall bear their iniquities.	11 After a life of suffering, he will again have joy; he will know that he did not suffer in vain. My devoted servant, with whom I am pleased, will bear the punishment of many and for his sake I will forgive them.
12 Therefore I will give him a portion among the great, and he will divide the spoils with the strong, because he poured out his life unto death, and was numbered with the transgressors. For he bore the sin of many, and made intercession for the transgressors.	12 Therefore I will divide him a portion with the great, and he shall divide the spoil with the strong; because he poured out his soul to death, and was numbered with the transgressors; yet he bore the sin of many, and made intercession for the transgressors.	12 And so I will give him a place of honor, a place among great and powerful men. He willingly gave his life and shared the fate of evil men. He took the place of many sinners and prayed that they might be forgiven."
54:10 Though the mountains be shaken and the hills be removed, yet my unfailing love for you will not be shaken nor my covenant of peace be removed," says the LORD, who has compassion on you.	54:10 For the mountains may depart and the hills be removed, but my steadfast love shall not depart from you, and my covenant of peace shall not be removed," says the LORD, who has compassion on you.	54:10 The mountains and hills may crumble, but my love for you will never end; I will keep forever my promise of peace." So says the LORD who loves you.

KJV	NKJV	TLB
13 And all thy children *shall be* taught of the LORD; and great *shall be* the peace of thy children.	13 All your children *shall be* taught by the LORD, And great *shall be* the peace of your children.	13 And all your citizens shall be taught by me, and their prosperity shall be great.
14 In righteousness shalt thou be established: thou shalt be far from oppression; for thou shalt not fear: and from terror; for it shall not come near thee.	14 In righteousness you shall be established; You shall be far from oppression, for you shall not fear; And from terror, for it shall not come near you.	14 You will live under a government that is just and fair. Your enemies will stay far away; you will live in peace. Terror shall not come near.
17 No weapon that is formed against thee shall prosper; and every tongue *that* shall rise against thee in judgment thou shalt condemn. This *is* the heritage of the servants of the LORD, and their righteousness *is* of me, saith the LORD.	17 No weapon formed against you shall prosper, And every tongue *which* rises against you in judgment You shall condemn. This *is* the heritage of the servants of the LORD, And their righteousness *is* from Me," Says the LORD.	17 But in that coming day, no weapon turned against you shall succeed, and you will have justice against every courtroom lie. This is the heritage of the servants of the Lord. This is the blessing I have given you, says the Lord.
55:1 Ho, every one that thirsteth, come ye to the waters, and he that hath no money; come ye, buy, and eat; yea, come, buy wine and milk without money and without price.	55:1 "Ho! Everyone who thirsts, Come to the waters; And you who have no money, Come, buy and eat. Yes, come, buy wine and milk Without money and without price.	55:1 Say there! is anyone thirsty? Come and drink—even if you have no money! Come, take your choice of wine and milk—it's all free!
2 Wherefore do ye spend money for *that which is* not bread? and your labour for *that which* satisfieth not? hearken diligently unto me, and eat ye *that which is* good, and let your soul delight itself in fatness.	2 Why do you spend money for *what is* not bread, And your wages for *what* does not satisfy? Listen diligently to Me, and eat *what is* good, And let your soul delight itself in abundance.	2 Why spend your money on foodstuffs that don't give you strength? Why pay for groceries that don't do you any good? Listen and I'll tell you where to get good food that fattens up the soul!
6 Seek ye the LORD while he may be found, call ye upon him while he is near:	6 Seek the LORD while He may be found, Call upon Him while He is near.	6 Seek the Lord while you can find him. Call upon him now while he is near.
7 Let the wicked forsake his way, and the unrighteous man his thoughts: and let him return unto the LORD, and he will have mercy upon him; and to our God, for he will abundantly pardon.	7 Let the wicked forsake his way, And the unrighteous man his thoughts; Let him return to the LORD, And He will have mercy on him; And to our God, For He will abundantly pardon.	7 Let men cast off their wicked deeds; let them banish from their minds the very thought of doing wrong! Let them turn to the Lord that he may have mercy upon them, and to our God, for he will abundantly pardon!
10 For as the rain cometh down, and the snow from heaven, and returneth not thither, but watereth the earth, and maketh it bring forth and bud, that it may give seed to the sower, and bread to the eater:	10 "For as the rain comes down, and the snow from heaven, And do not return there, But water the earth, And make it bring forth and bud, That it may give seed to the sower And bread to the eater,	10 As the rain and snow come down from heaven and stay upon the ground to water the earth, and cause the grain to grow and to produce seed for the farmer and bread for the hungry,
11 So shall my word be that goeth forth out of my mouth: it shall not return unto me void, but it shall accomplish that which I please, and it shall prosper *in the thing* whereto I sent it.	11 So shall My word be that goes forth from My mouth; It shall not return to Me void, But it shall accomplish what I please, And it shall prosper *in the thing* for which I sent it.	11 so also is my Word. I send it out and it always produces fruit. It shall accomplish all I want it to, and prosper everywhere I send it.
12 For ye shall go out with joy, and be led forth with peace: the mountains and the hills shall break forth before you into singing, and all the trees of the field shall clap *their* hands.	12 "For you shall go out with joy, And be led out with peace; The mountains and the hills Shall break forth into singing before you, And all the trees of the field shall clap *their* hands.	12 You will live in joy and peace. The mountains and hills, the trees of the field—all the world around you—will rejoice.
59:1 Behold, the LORD's hand is not shortened, that it cannot save; neither his ear heavy, that it cannot hear:	59:1 Behold, the LORD's hand is not shortened, That it cannot save; Nor His ear heavy, That it cannot hear.	59:1 Listen now! The Lord isn't too weak to save you. And he isn't getting deaf! He can hear you when you call!

NIV	RSV	TEV
13 All your sons will be taught by the LORD, and great will be your children's peace.	13 All your sons shall be taught by the LORD, and great shall be the prosperity of your sons.	13 "I myself will teach your people and give them prosperity and peace.
14 In righteousness you will be established: Tyranny will be far from you; you will have nothing to fear. Terror will be far removed; it will not come near you.	14 In righteousness you shall be established; you shall be far from oppression, for you shall not fear; and from terror, for it shall not come near you.	14 Justice and right will make you strong. You will be safe from oppression and terror.
17 no weapon forged against you will prevail, and you will refute every tongue that accuses you. This is the heritage of the servants of the LORD, and this is their vindication from me," declares the LORD.	17 no weapon that is fashioned against you shall prosper, and you shall confute every tongue that rises against you in judgment. This is the heritage of the servants of the LORD and their vindication from me, says the LORD."	17 But no weapon will be able to hurt you; you will have an answer for all who accuse you. I will defend my servants and give them victory." The LORD has spoken.
55:1 "Come, all you who are thirsty, come to the waters; and you who have no money, come, buy and eat! Come, buy wine and milk without money and without cost.	55:1 "Ho, every one who thirsts, come to the waters; and he who has no money, come, buy and eat! Come, buy wine and milk without money and without price.	55:1 The LORD says, "Come, everyone who is thirsty—here is water! Come, you that have no money— buy grain and eat! Come! Buy wine and milk— it will cost you nothing!
2 Why spend money on what is not bread, and your labor on what does not satisfy? Listen, listen to me, and eat what is good, and your soul will delight in the richest of fare.	2 Why do you spend your money for that which is not bread, and your labor for that which does not satisfy? Hearken diligently to me, and eat what is good, and delight yourselves in fatness.	2 Why spend money on what does not satisfy? Why spend your wages and still be hungry? Listen to me and do what I say, and you will enjoy the best food of all.
6 Seek the LORD while he may be found; call on him while he is near.	6 "Seek the LORD while he may be found, call upon him while he is near;	6 Turn to the LORD and pray to him, now that he is near.
7 Let the wicked forsake his way and the evil man his thoughts. Let him turn to the LORD, and he will have mercy on him, and to our God, for he will freely pardon.	7 let the wicked forsake his way, and the unrighteous man his thoughts; let him return to the LORD, that he may have mercy on him. and to our God, for he will abundantly pardon.	7 Let the wicked leave their way of life and change their way of thinking. Let them turn to the LORD, our God; he is merciful and quick to forgive.
10 As the rain and the snow come down from heaven, and do not return to it without watering the earth and making it bud and flourish, so that it yields seed for the sower and bread for the eater,	10 "For as the rain and the snow come down from heaven, and return not thither but water the earth, making it bring forth and sprout, giving seed to the sower and bread to the eater,	10 "My word is like the snow and the rain that come down from the sky to water the earth. They make the crops grow and provide seed for planting and food to eat.
11 so is my word that goes out from my mouth: It will not return to me empty, but will accomplish what I desire and achieve the purpose for which I sent it.	11 so shall my word be that goes forth from my mouth; it shall not return to me empty, but it shall accomplish that which I purpose, and prosper in the thing for which I sent it.	11 So also will be the word that I speak— it will not fail to do what I plan for it; it will do everything I send it to do.
12 You will go out in joy and be led forth in peace; the mountains and hills will burst into song before you, and all the trees of the field will clap their hands.	12 "For you shall go out in joy, and be led forth in peace; the mountains and the hills before you shall break forth into singing, and all the trees of the field shall clap their hands.	12 "You will leave Babylon with joy; you will be led out of the city in peace. The mountains and hills will burst into singing, and the trees will shout for joy.
59:1 Surely the arm of the LORD is not too short to save, nor his ear too dull to hear.	59:1 Behold, the LORD's hand is not shortened, that it cannot save, or his ear dull, that it cannot hear;	59:1 Don't think that the LORD is too weak to save you or too deaf to hear your call for help!

KJV	NKJV	TLB
2 But your iniquities have separated between you and your God, and your sins have hid *his* face from you, that he will not hear.	2 But your iniquities have separated you from your God; And your sins have hidden *His* face from you, So that He will not hear.	2 But the trouble is that your sins have cut you off from God. Because of sin he has turned his face away from you and will not listen anymore.
61:1 The Spirit of the Lord God *is* upon me; because the Lord hath anointed me to preach good tidings unto the meek; he hath sent me to bind up the brokenhearted, to proclaim liberty to the captives, and the opening of the prison to *them that are* bound;	61:1 "The Spirit of the Lord God *is* upon Me, Because the Lord has anointed Me To preach good tidings to the poor; He has sent Me to heal the brokenhearted, To proclaim liberty to the captives; And the opening of the prison to *those who are* bound;	61:1 The Spirit of the Lord God is upon me, because the Lord has anointed me to bring good news to the suffering and afflicted. He has sent me to comfort the broken-hearted, to announce liberty to captives and to open the eyes of the blind.
2 To proclaim the acceptable year of the Lord, and the day of vengeance of our God; to comfort all that mourn;	2 To proclaim the acceptable year of the Lord, And the day of vengeance of our God; To comfort all who mourn,	2 He has sent me to tell those who mourn that the time of God's favor to them has come, and the day of his wrath to their enemies.
3 To appoint unto them that mourn in Zion, to give unto them beauty for ashes, the oil of joy for mourning, the garment of praise for the spirit of heaviness; that they might be called trees of righteousness, the planting of the Lord, that he might be glorified.	3 To console those who mourn in Zion, To give them beauty for ashes, The oil of joy for mourning, The garment of praise for the spirit of heaviness; That they may be called trees of righteousness, The planting of the Lord, that He may be glorified."	3 To all who mourn in Israel he will give: Beauty for ashes; Joy instead of mourning; Praise instead of heaviness. For God has planted them like strong and graceful oaks for his own glory.
63:1 Who *is* this that cometh from Edom, with dyed garments from Bozrah? this *that is* glorious in his apparel, travelling in the greatness of his strength? I that speak in righteousness, mighty to save.	63:1 Who *is* this who comes from Edom, With dyed garments from Bozrah, This *One who is* glorious in His apparel, Traveling in the greatness of His strength?— "I who speak in righteousness, mighty to save."	63:1 Who is this who comes from Edom, from the city of Bozrah, with his magnificent garments of crimson? Who is this in kingly robes, marching in the greatness of his strength? "It is I, the Lord, announcing your salvation; I, the Lord, the one who is mighty to save!"
2 Wherefore *art thou* red in thine apparel, and thy garments like him that treadeth in the winefat?	2 Why *is* Your apparel red, And Your garments like one who treads in the winepress?	2 "Why are your clothes so red, as from treading out the grapes?"
3 I have trodden the winepress alone; and of the people *there was* none with me: for I will tread them in mine anger, and trample them in my fury; and their blood shall be sprinkled upon my garments, and I will stain all my raiment.	3 "I have trodden the winepress alone, And from the peoples no one *was* with Me. For I have trodden them in My anger, And trampled them in My fury; Their blood is sprinkled upon My garments, And I have stained all My robes.	3 "I have trodden the winepress alone. No one was there to help me. In my wrath I have trodden my enemies like grapes. In my fury I trampled my foes. It is their blood you see upon my clothes.
4 For the day of vengeance *is* in mine heart, and the year of my redeemed is come.	4 For the day of vengeance *is* in My heart, And the year of My redeemed has come.	4 For the time has come for me to avenge my people, to redeem them from the hands of their oppressors.
5 And I looked, and *there was* none to help; and I wondered that *there was* none to uphold: therefore mine own arm brought salvation unto me; and my fury, it upheld me.	5 I looked, but *there was* no one to help, And I wondered That *there was* no one to uphold; Therefore My own arm brought salvation for Me; And My own fury, it sustained Me.	5 I looked but no one came to help them; I was amazed and appalled. So I executed vengeance alone; unaided, I meted out judgment.
65:2 I have spread out my hands all the day unto a rebellious people, which walketh in a way *that was* not good, after their own thoughts;	65:2 I have stretched out My hands all day long to a rebellious people, Who walk in a way *that is* not good, According to their own thoughts;	65:2 But my own people—though I have been spreading out my arms to welcome them all day long—have rebelled; they follow their own evil paths and thoughts.
17 For, behold, I create new heavens and a new earth: and the former shall not be remembered, nor come into mind.	17 "For behold, I create new heavens and a new earth; And the former shall not be remembered or come to mind.	17 For see, I am creating new heavens and a new earth—so wonderful that no one will even think about the old ones anymore.

NIV	RSV	TEV
2 But your iniquities have separated you from your God; your sins have hidden his face from you, so that he will not hear.	2 but your iniquities have made a separation between you and your God, and your sins have hid his face from you so that he does not hear.	2 It is because of your sins that he doesn't hear you. It is your sins that separate you from God when you try to worship him.
61:1 The Spirit of the Sovereign LORD is on me, because the LORD has anointed me to preach good news to the poor. He has sent me to bind up the brokenhearted, to proclaim freedom for the captives and release for the prisoners,	61:1 The Spirit of the Lord GOD is upon me, because the LORD has anointed me to bring good tidings to the afflicted; he has sent me to bind up the brokenhearted, to proclaim liberty to the captives, and the opening of the prison to those who are bound;	61:1 The Sovereign LORD has filled me with his spirit. He has chosen me and sent me To bring good news to the poor, To heal the broken-hearted, To announce release to captives And freedom to those in prison.
2 to proclaim the year of the LORD's favor and the day of vengeance of our God, to comfort all who mourn,	2 to proclaim the year of the LORD's favor, and the day of vengeance of our God; to comfort all who mourn;	2 He has sent me to proclaim That the time has come When the LORD will save his people And defeat their enemies He has sent me to comfort all who mourn,
3 and provide for those who grieve in Zion— to bestow on them a crown of beauty instead of ashes, the oil of gladness instead of mourning, and a garment of praise instead of a spirit of despair. They will be called oaks of righteousness, a planting of the LORD for the display of his splendor.	3 to grant to those who mourn in Zion— to give them a garland instead of ashes, the oil of gladness instead of mourning, the mantle of praise instead of a faint spirit; that they may be called oaks of righteousness, the planting of the LORD, that he may be glorified.	3 To give to those who mourn in Zion Joy and gladness instead of grief, A song of praise instead of sorrow. They will be like trees That the LORD himself has planted. They will all do what is right, And God will be praised for what he has done.
63:1 Who is this coming from Edom, from Bozrah, with his garments stained crimson? Who is this, robed in splendor, striding forward in the greatness of his strength? "It is I, speaking in righteousness, mighty to save."	63:1 Who is this that comes from Edom, in crimsoned garments from Bozrah, he that is glorious in his apparel, marching in the greatness of his strength? "It is I, announcing vindication, mighty to save."	63:1 "Who is this coming from the city of Bozrah in Edom? Who is this so splendidly dressed in red, marching along in power and strength?" It is the LORD, powerful to save, coming to announce his victory.
2 Why are your garments red, like those of one treading the winepress?	2 Why is thy apparel red, and thy garments like his that treads in the wine press?	2 "Why is his clothing so red, like that of a man who tramples grapes to make wine?"
3 "I have trodden the winepress alone; from the nations no one was with me. I trampled them in my anger and trod them down in my wrath their blood spattered my garments, and I stained all my clothing.	3 "I have trodden the wine press alone, and from the peoples no one was with me; I trod them in my anger and trampled them in my wrath; their lifeblood is sprinkled upon my garments, and I have stained all my raiment.	3 The LORD answers, "I have trampled the nations like grapes, and no one came to help me. I trampled them in my anger, and their blood has stained all my clothing.
4 For the day of vengeance was in my heart, and the year of my redemption has come.	4 For the day of vengeance was in my heart, and my year of redemption has come.	4 I decided that the time to save my people had come; it was time to punish their enemies.
5 I looked, but there was no one to help, I was appalled that no one gave support; so my own arm worked salvation for me, and my own wrath sustained me.	5 I looked, but there was no one to help; I was appalled, but there was no one to uphold; so my own arm brought me victory, and my wrath upheld me.	5 I was amazed when I looked and saw that there was no one to help me. But my anger made me strong, and I won the victory myself.
65:2 All day long I have held out my hands to an obstinate people, who walk in ways not good, pursuing their own imaginations—	65:2 I spread out my hands all the day to a rebellious people, who walk in a way that is not good, following their own devices;	65:2 I have always been ready to welcome my people, who stubbornly do what is wrong and go their own way.
17 "Behold, I will create new heavens and a new earth. The former things will not be remembered, nor will they come to mind.	17 "For behold, I create new heavens and a new earth; and the former things shall not be remembered or come into mind.	17 The LORD says, "I am making a new earth and new heavens. The events of the past will be completely forgotten.

KJV	NKJV	TLB
18 But be ye glad and rejoice for ever *in that* which I create: for, behold, I create Jerusalem a rejoicing, and her people a joy.	18 But be glad and rejoice forever in what I create; For behold, I create Jerusalem *as* a rejoicing, And her people a joy.	18 Be glad; rejoice forever in my creation. Look! I will recreate Jerusalem as a place of happiness, and her people shall be a joy!
19 And I will rejoice in Jerusalem, and joy in my people: and the voice of weeping shall be no more heard in her, nor the voice of crying.	19 I will rejoice in Jerusalem, And joy in My people; The voice of weeping shall no longer be heard in her, Nor the voice of crying.	19 And I will rejoice in Jerusalem, and in my people; and the voice of weeping and crying shall not be heard there any more.
66:1 Thus saith the LORD, The heaven *is* my throne, and the earth *is* my footstool: where *is* the house that ye build unto me? and where *is* the place of my rest?	66:1 Thus says the LORD: "Heaven *is* My throne, And earth *is* My footstool. Where *is* the house that you will build Me? And where *is* the place of My rest?	66:1 Heaven is my throne and the earth is my footstool: What Temple can you build for me as good as that?
2 For all those *things* hath mine hand made, and all those *things* have been, saith the LORD: but to this *man* will I look, *even* to *him that is* poor and of a contrite spirit, and trembleth at my word.	2 For all those *things* My hand has made, And all those *things* exist," Says the LORD. "But on this *one* will I look: On *him who is* poor and of a contrite spirit, And who trembles at My word.	2 My hand has made both earth and skies, and they are mine. Yet I will look with pity on the man who has a humble and a contrite heart, who trembles at my word.

Jeremiah

KJV	NKJV	TLB
1:5 Before I formed thee in the belly I knew thee; and before thou camest forth out of the womb I sanctified thee, *and* I ordained thee a prophet unto the nations.	1:5 "Before I formed you in the womb I knew you; Before you were born I sanctified you; *And* I ordained you a prophet to the nations."	1:5 "I knew you before you were formed within your mother's womb; before you were born I sanctified you and appointed you as my spokesman to the world."
10 See, I have this day set thee over the nations and over the kingdoms, to root out, and to pull down, and to destroy, and to throw down, to build, and to plant.	10 See, I have this day set you over the nations and over the kingdoms, To root out and to pull down, To destroy and to throw down, To build and to plant."	10 Today your work begins, to warn the nations and the kingdoms of the world. In accord with my words spoken through your mouth I will tear down some and destroy them, and plant others and nuture them and make them strong and great."
3:1 They say, If a man put away his wife, and she go from him, and become another man's, shall he return unto her again? shall not that land be greatly polluted? but thou hast played the harlot with many lovers; yet return again to me saith the LORD.	3:1 "They say, 'If a man divorces his wife, And she goes from him And becomes another man's, May he return to her again?' Would not that land be greatly polluted? But you have played the harlot with many lovers; Yet return to Me," says the LORD.	3:1 There is a law that if a man divorces a woman who then remarries, he is not to take her back again, for she has become corrupted. But though you have left me and married many lovers, yet I have invited you to come to me again, the Lord says.
5:30 A wonderful and horrible thing is committed in the land;	5:30 "An astonishing and horrible thing Has been committed in the land:	5:30 A horrible thing has happened in this land—
31 The prophets prophesy falsely, and the priests bear rule by their means; and my people love *to have it* so: and what will ye do in the end thereof?	31 The prophets prophesy falsely And the priests rule by their *own* power; And My people love *to have it* so. But what will you do in the end?	31 the priests are ruled by false prophets, and my people like it so! But your doom is certain.
6:14 They have healed also the hurt *of the daughter* of my people slightly, saying, Peace, peace; when *there is* no peace.	6:14 They have also healed the hurt of My people slightly, Saying, 'Peace, peace!' When *there is* no peace.	6:14 You can't heal a wound by saying it's not there! Yet the priests and prophets give assurances of peace when all is war.
16 Thus saith the LORD, Stand ye in the ways, and see, and ask for the old paths, where *is* the good way, and walk therein, and ye shall find rest for your souls. But they said, We will not walk *therein.*	16 Thus says the LORD: "Stand in the ways and see, And ask for the old paths, where the good way *is,* And walk in it; Then you will find rest for your souls. But they said, 'We will not walk *in it.'*	16 Yet the Lord pleads with you still: Ask where the good road is, the godly paths you used to walk in, in the days of long ago. Travel there, and you will find rest for your souls. But you reply, "No, that is not the road we want!"

NIV	RSV	TEV

18 But be glad and rejoice forever
   in what I will create,
   for I will create Jerusalem to be a delight
   and its people a joy.
	18 But be glad and rejoice for ever
	   in that which I create;
	   for behold, I create Jerusalem a rejoicing,
	   and her people a joy.
		18 Be glad and rejoice forever in what I create. The new Jerusalem I make will be full of joy, and her people will be happy.

19 I will rejoice over Jerusalem
   and take delight in my people;
   the sound of weeping and of crying
   will be heard in it no more.
	19 I will rejoice in Jerusalem,
	   and be glad in my people;
	   no more shall be heard in it the sound of
	   weeping
	   and the cry of distress.
		19 I myself will be filled with joy because of Jerusalem and her people. There will be no weeping there, no calling for help.

66:1 This is what the LORD says:
 	
  "Heaven is my throne and the earth is my
   footstool.
  Where is the house you will build for
   me?
  Where will my resting place be?
	66:1 Thus says the LORD:
	  "Heaven is my throne
	   and the earth is my footstool;
	  what is the house which you would build
	   for me,
	  and what is the place of my rest?
		66:1 The LORD says, "Heaven is my throne, and the earth is my footstool. What kind of house, then, could you build for me, what kind of place for me to live in?

2 Has not my hand made all these things,
   and so they came into being?" declares
   the LORD.
 	
  "This is the one I esteem:
  he who is humble and contrite in spirit,
  and trembles at my word.
	2 All these things my hand has made,
	   and so all these things are mine, says the
	   LORD.
	  But this is the man to whom I will look,
	  he that is humble and contrite in spirit,
	  and trembles at my word.
		2 I myself created the whole universe! I am pleased with those who are humble and repentant, who fear me and obey me.

Jeremiah

NIV	RSV	TEV

1:5 "Before I formed you in the womb I knew
   you,
  before you were born I set you apart;
  I appointed you as a prophet to the
   nations."
	1:5 "Before I formed you in the womb I knew
	   you,
	  and before you were born I consecrated
	   you;
	  I appointed you a prophet to the
	   nations."
		1:5 "I chose you before I gave you life, and before you were born I selected you to be a prophet to the nations."

10 See, today I appoint you over nations and kingdoms to uproot and tear down, to destroy and overthrow, to build and to plant."	10 See, I have set you this day over nations
	   and over kingdoms,
	  to pluck up and to break down,
	  to destroy and to overthrow,
	  to build and to plant."
		10 Today I give you authority over nations and kingdoms to uproot and to pull down, to destroy and to overthrow, to build and to plant."

3:1 "If a man divorces his wife
   and she leaves him and marries
   another man,
  should he return to her again?
  Would not the land be completely
   defiled?
  But you have lived as a prostitute with
   many lovers—
  would you now return to me?"
  declares the LORD.
	3:1 "If a man divorces his wife
	   and she goes from him
	  and becomes another man's wife,
	   will he return to her?
	  Would not that land be greatly polluted?
	  You have played the harlot with many
	   lovers;
	  and would you return to me?
	  says the LORD.
		3:1 The LORD says, "If a man divorces his wife, and she leaves him and becomes another man's wife, he cannot take her back again. This would completely defile the land. But, Israel, you have had many lovers, and now you want to return to me!

5:30 "A horrible and shocking thing
   has happened in the land:
	5:30 An appalling and horrible thing
	   has happened in the land:
		5:30 A terrible and shocking thing has happened in the land:

31 The prophets prophesy lies,
   the priests rule by their own authority,
  and my people love it this way.
  But what will you do in the end?
	31 the prophets prophesy falsely,
	   and the priests rule at their direction;
	  my people love to have it so,
	  but what will you do when the end
	   comes?
		31 prophets speak nothing but lies; priests rule as the prophets command, and my people offer no objections. But what will they do when it all comes to an end?"

6:14 They dress the wound of my people
   as though it were not serious.
  'Peace, peace,' they say,
  when there is no peace.
	6:14 They have healed the wound of my
	   people lightly,
	  saying, 'Peace, peace,'
	  when there is no peace.
		6:14 They act as if my people's wounds were only scratches. 'All is well,' they say, when all is not well.

16 This is what the LORD says:
 	
  "Stand at the crossroads and look;
   ask for the ancient paths,
  ask where the good way is, and walk in
   it,
  and you will find rest for your souls.
  But you said, 'We will not walk in it.'
	16 Thus says the LORD:
	  "Stand by the roads, and look,
	   and ask for the ancient paths,
	  where the good way is; and walk in it,
	  and find rest for your souls.
	  But they said, 'We will not walk in it.'
		16 The LORD said to his people, "Stand at the crossroads and look. Ask for the ancient paths and where the best road is. Walk in it, and you will live in peace."
		But they said, "No, we will not!"

KJV	NKJV	TLB
7:4 Trust ye not in lying words, saying, The temple of the LORD, The temple of the LORD, The temple of the LORD, *are* these.	**7:4** "Do not trust in these lying words, saying, 'The temple of the LORD, the temple of the LORD, the temple of the LORD *are* these.'	**7:4** But don't be fooled by those who lie to you and say that since the Temple of the Lord is here, God will never let Jerusalem be destroyed.
5 For if ye throughly amend your ways and your doings; if ye thoroughly execute judgment between a man and his neighbour;	**5** "For if you thoroughly amend your ways and your doings, if you thoroughly execute judgment between a man and his neighbor,	**5** You may remain under these conditions only: If you stop your wicked thoughts and deeds, and are fair to others,
6 *If* ye oppress not the stranger, the fatherless, and the widow, and shed not innocent blood in this place, neither walk after other gods to your hurt:	**6** "*if* you do not oppress the stranger, the fatherless, and the widow, and do not shed innocent blood in this place, or walk after other gods to your hurt,	**6** and stop exploiting orphans, widows and foreigners. And stop your murdering. And stop worshiping idols as you do now to your hurt.
7 Then will I cause you to dwell in this place, in the land that I gave to your fathers, for ever and ever.	**7** "then I will cause you to dwell in this place, in the land that I gave to your fathers forever and ever.	**7** Then, and only then, will I let you stay in this land that I gave to your fathers to keep forever.

9:23 Thus saith the LORD, Let not the wise *man* glory in his wisdom, neither let the mighty *man* glory in his might, let not the rich *man* glory in his riches:	**9:23** Thus says the LORD:
	
	"Let not the wise *man*
	    glory in his wisdom,
	Let not the mighty *man*
	    glory in his might,
	Nor let the rich *man*
	    glory in his riches;
		9:23 The Lord says: Let not the wise man bask in his wisdom, nor the mighty man in his might, nor the rich man in his riches.

24 But let him that glorieth glory in this, that he understandeth and knoweth me, that I *am* the LORD which exercise lovingkindness, judgment, and righteousness, in the earth: for in these *things* I delight, saith the LORD.	**24** But let him who glories glory in this,
	    That he understands and knows Me,
	    That I *am* the LORD, exercising
	    lovingkindness, judgment, and
	    righteousness in the earth.
	For in these I delight," says the LORD.
		24 Let them boast in this alone: That they truly know me, and understand that I am the Lord of justice and of righteousness whose love is steadfast; and that I love to be this way.

12:5 If thou hast run with the footmen, and they have wearied thee, then how canst thou contend with horses? and *if* in the land of peace, *wherein* thou trustedst, *they* wearied *thee*, then how wilt thou do in the swelling of Jordan?	**12:5** "If you have run with the footmen, and
	    they have wearied you,
	Then how can you contend with
	    horses?
	And *if* in the land of peace,
	In which you trusted, *they wearied you,*
	Then how will you do in the flooding of
	    the Jordan?
		12:5 The Lord replied to me: If racing with mere men—these men of Anathoth—has wearied you, how will you race against horses, against the king, his court and all his evil priests? If you stumble and fall on open ground, what will you do in Jordan's jungles?

15:1 Then said the LORD unto me, Though Moses and Samuel stood before me, *yet* my mind *could* not *be* toward this people: cast *them* out of my sight, and let them go forth.	**15:1** Then the LORD said to me, "Though Moses and Samuel stood before Me, *yet* My mind *could* not *be* favorable toward this people. Cast *them* out of My sight, and let them go forth.	**15:1** Then the Lord said to me, Even if Moses and Samuel stood before me pleading for these people, even then I wouldn't help them—away with them! Get them out of my sight!

2 And it shall come to pass, if they say unto thee, Whither shall we go forth? then thou shalt tell them, Thus saith the LORD; Such as *are* for death, to death; and such as *are* for the sword, to the sword; and such as *are* for the famine, to the famine; and such as *are* for the captivity, to the captivity.	**2** "And it shall be, if they say to you, 'Where should we go?' then you shall tell them, 'Thus says the LORD:
	"Such as *are* for death, to death;
	And such as *are* for the sword, to the
	    sword;
	And such as *are* for the famine, to the
	    famine;
	And such as *are* for the captivity, to the
	    captivity.' "
		2 And if they say to you, But where can we go? tell them the Lord says: Those who are destined for death, to death; those who must die by the sword, to the sword; those doomed to starvation, to famine; and those for captivity, to captivity.

16:19 O LORD, my strength, and my fortress, and my refuge in the day of affliction, the Gentiles shall come unto thee from the ends of the earth, and shall say, Surely our fathers have inherited lies, vanity, and *things* wherein *there is* no profit.	**16:19** O LORD, my strength and my fortress,
	    My refuge in the day of affliction,
	The Gentiles shall come to You
	    From the ends of the earth and say,
	"Surely our fathers have inherited lies,
	    Worthlessness and unprofitable *things.*"
		16:19 O Lord, my Strength and Fortress, my Refuge in the day of trouble, nations from around the world will come to you saying, "Our fathers have been foolish, for they have worshiped worthless idols!

17:9 The heart *is* deceitful above all *things*, and desperately wicked: who can know it?	**17:9** "The heart *is* deceitful above all *things*,
	    And desperately wicked;
	    Who can know it?
		17:9 The heart is the most deceitful thing there is, and desperately wicked. No one can really know how bad it is!

10 I the LORD search the heart, *I* try the reins, even to give every man according to his ways, *and* according to the fruit of his doings.	**10** I, the LORD, search the heart,
	    I test the mind,
	Even to give every man according to his
	    ways,
	And according to the fruit of his doings.
		10 Only the Lord knows! He searches all hearts and examines deepest motives so he can give to each person his right reward, according to his deeds—how he has lived.

NIV	RSV	TEV
7:4 Do not trust in deceptive words and say, "This is the temple of the LORD, the temple of the LORD, the temple of the LORD!"	**7:4** Do not trust in these deceptive words: 'This is the temple of the LORD, the temple of the LORD, the temple of the LORD.'	**7:4** Stop believing those deceitful words, 'We are safe! This is the LORD's Temple, this is the LORD's Temple, this is the LORD's Temple!'
5 If you really change your ways and your actions and deal with each other justly,	**5** "For if you truly amend your ways and your doings, if you truly execute justice one with another,	**5** "Change the way you are living and stop doing the things you are doing. Be fair in your treatment of one another.
6 if you do not oppress the alien, the fatherless or the widow and do not shed innocent blood in this place, and if you do not follow other gods to your own harm,	**6** if you do not oppress the alien, the fatherless or the widow, or shed innocent blood in this place, and if you do not go after other gods to your own hurt,	**6** Stop taking advantage of aliens, orphans, and widows. Stop killing innocent people in this land. Stop worshiping other gods, for that will destroy you.
7 then I will let you live in this place, in the land I gave your forefathers for ever and ever.	**7** then I will let you dwell in this place, in the land that I gave of old to your fathers for ever.	**7** If you change, I will let you go on living here in the land which I gave your ancestors as a permanent possession.
9:23 This is what the LORD says: "Let not the wise man boast of his wisdom or the strong man boast of his strength or the rich man boast of his riches,	**9:23** Thus says the LORD: "Let not the wise man glory in his wisdom, let not the mighty man glory in his might, let not the rich man glory in his riches;	**9:23** The LORD says, "Wise men should not boast of their wisdom, nor strong men of their strength, nor rich men of their wealth.
24 but let him who boasts boast about this: that he understands and knows me, that I am the LORD, who exercises kindness, justice and righteousness on earth, for in these I delight," declares the LORD.	**24** but let him who glories glory in this, that he understands and knows me, that I am the LORD who practice steadfast love, justice, and righteousness in the earth; for in these things I delight says the LORD."	**24** If anyone wants to boast, he should boast that he knows and understands me, because my love is constant, and I do what is just and right. These are the things that please me. I, the LORD, have spoken."
12:5 "If you have raced with men on foot and they have worn you out, how can you compete with horses? If you stumble in safe country, how will you manage in the thickets by the Jordan?	**12:5** "If you have raced with men on foot, and they have wearied you, how will you compete with horses? And if in a safe land you fall down, how will you do in the jungle of the Jordan?	**12:5** The LORD said, "Jeremiah, if you get tired racing against men, how can you race against horses? If you can't even stand up in open country, how will you manage in the jungle by the Jordan?
15:1 Then the LORD said to me: "Even if Moses and Samuel were to stand before me, my heart would not go out to this people. Send them away from my presence! Let them go!	**15:1** Then the LORD said to me, "Though Moses and Samuel stood before me, yet my heart would not turn toward this people. Send them out of my sight, and let them go!	**15:1** Then the LORD said to me, "Even if Moses and Samuel were standing here pleading with me, I would not show these people any mercy. Make them go away; make them get out of my sight.
2 And if they ask you, 'Where shall we go?' tell them, 'This is what the LORD says: "'Those destined for death, to death; those for the sword, to the sword; those for starvation, to starvation; those for captivity, to captivity.'	**2** And when they ask you, 'Where shall we go?' you shall say to them, 'Thus says the LORD: "Those who are for pestilence, to pestilence, and those who are for the sword, to the sword; those who are for famine, to famine, and those who are for captivity, to captivity.'"	**2** When they ask you where they should go, tell them that I have said: Some are doomed to die by disease— that's where they will go! Others are doomed to die in war— that's where they will go! Some are doomed to die of starvation" that's where they will go! Others are doomed to be taken away as prisoners— that's where they will go!
16:19 O LORD, my strength and my fortress, my refuge in time of distress, to you the nations will come from the ends of the earth and say, "Our fathers possessed nothing but false gods, worthless idols that did them no good.	**16:19** O LORD, my strength and my stronghold, my refuge in the day of trouble, to thee shall the nations come from the ends of the earth and say: "Our fathers have inherited nought but lies, worthless things in which there is no profit.	**16:19** LORD, you are the one who protects me and gives me strength; you help me in times of trouble. Nations will come to you from the ends of the earth and say, "Our ancestors had nothing but false gods, nothing but useless idols.
17:9 The heart is deceitful above all things and beyond cure. Who can understand it?	**17:9** The heart is deceitful above all things, and desperately corrupt; who can understand it?	**17:9** "Who can understand the human heart? There is nothing else so deceitful; it is too sick to be healed.
10 "I the LORD search the heart and examine the mind, to reward a man according to his conduct, according to what his deeds deserve."	**10** "I the LORD search the mind and try the heart, to give to every man according to his ways, according to the fruit of his doings."	**10** I, the LORD, search the minds and test the hearts of men. I treat each one according to the way he lives, according to what he does."

KJV	NKJV	TLB

14 Heal me, O LORD, and I shall be healed; save me, and I shall be saved: for thou *art* my praise.	14 Heal me, O LORD,
	    and I shall be healed;
	Save me, and I shall be saved,
	    For You *are* my praise.
		14 Lord, you alone can heal me, you alone can save, and my praises are for you alone.

22:13 Woe unto him that buildeth his house by unrighteousness, and his chambers by wrong; *that* useth his neighbour's service without wages, and giveth him not for his work;	22:13 "Woe to him who builds his house by
	    unrighteousness
	And his chambers by injustice,
	Who uses his neighbor's service
	    without wages
	And gives him nothing for his work,
		22:13 And woe to you, King Jehoiakim, for you are building your great palace with forced labor. By not paying wages you are building injustice into its walls and oppression into its doorframes and ceilings.

23:5 Behold, the days come, saith the LORD, that I will raise unto David a righteous Branch, and a King shall reign and prosper, and shall execute judgment and justice in the earth.	23:5 "Behold, *the* days are coming," says the
	    LORD,
	"That I will raise to David a Branch of
	    righteousness;
	A King shall reign and prosper,
	And execute judgment and
	    righteousness in the earth.
		23:5 For the time is coming, says the Lord, when I will place a righteous Branch upon King David's throne. He shall be a King who shall rule with wisdom and justice and cause righteousness to prevail everywhere throughout the earth.

6 In his days Judah shall be saved, and Israel shall dwell safely: and this *is* his name whereby he shall be called, THE LORD OUR RIGHTEOUSNESS.	6 In His days Judah will be saved,
	And Israel will dwell safely;
	Now this *is* His name by which He will be
	    called:
	
	    THE LORD
	    OUR RIGHTEOUSNESS.
		6 And this is his name: *The Lord Our Righteousness.* At that time Judah will be saved and Israel will live in peace.

23 *Am* I a God at hand, saith the LORD, and not a God afar off?	23 "*Am* I a God near at hand," says the LORD, "And not a God afar off?"	23 Am I a God who is only in one place and cannot see what they are doing?

24 Can any hide himself in secret places that I shall not see him? saith the LORD. Do not I fill heaven and earth? saith the LORD.	24 Can anyone hide himself in secret places,
	    So I shall not see him?"
	    says the LORD;
	"Do I not fill heaven and earth?" says the
	    LORD.
		24 Can anyone hide from me? Am I not everywhere in all of heaven and earth?

24:7 And I will give them an heart to know me, That I *am* the LORD: and they shall be my people, and I will be their God: for they shall return unto me with their whole heart.	24:7 "Then I will give them a heart to know Me, that I *am* the LORD; and they shall be My people, and I will be their God, for they shall return to Me with their whole heart.	24:7 I will give them hearts that respond to me. They shall be my people and I will be their God, for they shall return to me with great joy.
31:34 And they shall teach no more every man his neighbour, and every man his brother, saying, Know the LORD: for they shall all know me, from the least of them unto the greatest of them, saith the LORD: for I will forgive their iniquity, and I will remember their sin no more.	31:34 "No more shall every man teach his neighbor, and every man his brother, saying, 'Know the LORD,' for they all shall know Me, from the least of them to the greatest of them," says the LORD. "For I will forgive their iniquity, and their sin I will remember no more."	31:34 At that time it will no longer be necessary to admonish one another to know the Lord. For everyone, both great and small, shall really know me then, says the Lord, and I will forgive and forget their sins.
33:3 Call unto me, and I will answer thee, and shew thee great and mighty things, which thou knowest not.	33:3 'Call to Me, and I will answer you, and show you great and mighty things, which you do not know.'	33:3 Ask me and I will tell you some remarkable secrets about what is going to happen here.

16 In those days shall Judah be saved, and Jerusalem shall dwell safely: and this *is the name* wherewith she shall be called, The LORD our righteousness.	16 In those days Judah will be saved,
	    And Jerusalem will dwell safely.
	And this *is the name* by which she will be
	    called:
	
	    THE LORD
	    OUR RIGHTEOUSNESS
		16 In that day the people of Judah and Jerusalem shall live in safety and their motto will be, "The Lord is our righteousness!"

17 For thus saith the LORD; David shall never want a man to sit upon the throne of the house of Israel;	17 "For thus says the LORD: 'David shall never lack a man to sit on the throne of the house of Israel;	17 For the Lord declares that from then on, David shall forever have an heir sitting on the throne of Israel.

46:28 Fear thou not, O Jacob my servant, saith the LORD: for I *am* with thee; for I will make a full end of all the nations whither I have driven thee: but I will not make a full end of thee, but correct thee in measure; yet will I not leave thee wholly unpunished.	46:28 Do not fear, O Jacob My servant,"
	    says the LORD,
	"For I *am* with you;
	For I will make a complete end of all
	    the nations
	To which I have driven you,
	But I will not make a complete end of you.
	I will rightly correct you,
	For I will not leave you wholly
	    unpunished."
		46:28 Fear not, O Jacob, my servant, says the Lord, for I am with you. I will destroy all the nations to which I have exiled you, but I will not destroy you. I will punish you, but only enough to correct you.

NIV	RSV	TEV
14 Heal me, O Lord, and I will be healed; save me and I will be saved, for you are the one I praise.	14 Heal me, O Lord, and I shall be healed; save me, and I shall be saved; for thou art my praise.	14 Lord, heal me and I will be completely well; rescue me and I will be perfectly safe. You are the one I praise!
22:13 "Woe to him who builds his palace by unrighteousness, his upper rooms by injustice, making his countrymen work for nothing, not paying them for their labor.	22:13 "Woe to him who builds his house by unrighteousness, and his upper rooms by injustice; who makes his neighbor serve him for nothing, and does not give him his wages;	22:13 Doomed is the man who builds his house by injustice and enlarges it by dishonesty; who makes his countrymen work for nothing and does not pay their wages.
23:5 "The days are coming," declares the Lord, "when I will raise up to David a righteous Branch, a King who will reign wisely and do what is just and right in the land.	23:5 "Behold, the days are coming, says the Lord, when I will raise up for David a righteous Branch, and he shall reign as king and deal wisely, and shall execute justice and righteousness in the land.	23:5 The Lord says, "The time is coming when I will choose as king a righteous descendant of David. That king will rule wisely and do what is right and just throughout the land.
6 In his days Judah will be saved and Israel will live in safety. This is the name by which he will be called: The Lord Our Righteousness.	6 In his days Judah will be saved, and Israel will dwell securely. And this is the name by which he will be called: 'The Lord is our righteousness.'	6 When he is king, the people of Judah will be safe, and the people of Israel will live in peace. He will be called 'The Lord Our Salvation.'
23 "Am I only a God nearby," declares the Lord, "and not a God far away?	23 "Am I a God at hand, says the Lord, and not a God afar off?	23 "I am a God who is everywhere and not in one place only.
24 Can anyone hide in secret places so that I cannot see him?" declares the Lord. "Do not I fill heaven and earth?" declares the Lord.	24 Can a man hide himself in secret places so that I cannot see him? says the Lord. Do I not fill heaven and earth? says the Lord.	24 Now one can hide where I cannot see him. Do you not know that I am everywhere in heaven and on earth?
24:7 I will give them a heart to know me, that I am the Lord. They will be my people, and I will be their God, for they will return to me with all their heart.	24:7 I will give them a heart to know that I am the Lord; and they shall be my people and I will be their God, for they shall return to me with their whole heart.	24:7 I will give them the desire to know that I am the Lord. Then they will be my people, and I will be their God, because they will return to me with all their heart.
31:34 No longer will a man teach his neighbor, or a man his brother, saying, 'Know the Lord,' because they will all know me, from the least of them to the greatest," declares the Lord. "For I will forgive their wickedness and will remember their sins no more."	31:34 And no longer shall each man teach his neighbor and each his brother, saying, 'Know the Lord,' for they shall all know me, from the least of them to the greatest, says the Lord; for I will forgive their iniquity, and I will remember their sin no more."	31:34 None of them will have to teach his fellow countryman to know the Lord, because all will know me, from the least to the greatest. I will forgive their sins and I will no longer remember their wrongs. I, the Lord, have spoken."
33:3 'Call to me and I will answer you and tell you great and unsearchable things you do not know.'	33:3 Call to me and I will answer you, and will tell you great and hidden things which you have not known.	33:3 "Call to me, and I will answer you; I will tell you wonderful and marvelous things that you know nothing about.
16 In those days Judah will be saved and Jerusalem will live in safety. This is the name by which it will be called: The Lord Our Righteousness.'	16 In those days Judah will be saved and Jerusalem will dwell securely. And this is the name by which it will be called: 'The Lord is our righteousness.'	16 The people of Judah and of Jerusalem will be rescued and will live in safety. The city will be called 'The Lord Our Salvation.'
17 For this is what the Lord says: 'David will never fail to have a man to sit on the throne of the house of Israel,	17 "For thus says the Lord: David shall never lack a man to sit on the throne of the house of Israel,	17 I, the Lord, promise that there will always be a descendant of David to be king of Israel
46:28 Do not fear, O Jacob my servant, for I am with you," declares the Lord. "Though I completely destroy all the nations among which I scatter you, I will not completely destroy you. I will discipline you but only with justice; I will not let you go entirely unpunished."	46:28 Fear not, O Jacob my servant, says the Lord, for I am with you. I will make a full end of all the nations to which I have driven you, but of you I will not make a full end. I will chasten you in just measure, and I will by no means leave you unpunished."	46:28 I will come to you and save you. I will destroy all the nations where I have scattered you, but I will not destroy you. I will not let you go unpunished; but when I punish you, I will be fair. I, the Lord, have spoken."

KJV	NKJV	TLB
52:12 Now in the fifth month, in the tenth *day* of the month, which *was* the nineteenth year of Nebuchadrezzar king of Babylon, came Nebuzaradan, captain of the guard, *which* served the king of Babylon, into Jerusalem,	**52:12** Now in the fifth month, on the tenth *day* of the month (which *was* the nineteenth year of King Nebuchadnezzar king of Babylon), Nebuzaradan, the captain of the guard, *who* served the king of Babylon, came to Jerusalem.	**52:12** On the tenth day of the fifth month during the nineteenth year of the reign of Nebuchadnezzar, king of Babylon, Nebuzaradan, captain of the guard, arrived in Jerusalem,
13 And burned the house of the LORD, and the king's house; and all the houses of Jerusalem, and all the houses of the great *men*, burned he with fire:	13 He burned the house of the LORD and the king's house; all the houses of Jerusalem, that is, all the houses of the great *men*, he burned with fire.	13 and burned the Temple and the palace and all the larger homes,
14 And all the army of the Chaldeans, that *were* with the captain of the guard, brake down all the walls of Jerusalem round about.	14 And all the army of the Chaldeans who *were* with the captain of the guard broke down all the walls of Jerusalem all around.	14 and set the Chaldean army to work tearing down the walls of the city.
15 Then Nebuzaradan the captain of the guard carried away captive *certain* of the poor of the people, and the residue of the people that remained in the city, and those that fell away, that fell to the king of Babylon, and the rest of the multitude.	15 Then Nebuzaradan the captain of the guard carried away captive *some* of the poor people, the rest of the people who remained in the city, the defectors who had deserted to the king of Babylon, and the rest of the craftsmen.	15 Then he took to Babylon, as captives, some of the poorest of the people—along with those who survived the city's destruction, and those who had deserted Zedekiah and had come over to the Babylonian army, and the tradesmen who were left.
16 But Nebuzaradan the captain of the guard left *certain* of the poor of the land of vinedressers and for husbandmen.	16 But Nebuzaradan the captain of the guard left *some* of the poor of the land as vinedressers and farmers.	16 But he left some of the poorest people to care for the crops as vinedressers and plowmen.

Lamentations

1:1 How doth the city sit solitary, *that was* full of people! *how* is she become as a widow! she *that was* great among the nations, *and* princess among the provinces, *how* is she become tributary!	**1:1** How lonely sits the city *That was* full of people! *How* like a widow is she, Who *was* great among the nations! The princess among the provinces Has become a slave!	**1:1** Jerusalem's streets, once thronged with people, are silent now. Like a widow broken with grief, she sits alone in her mourning. She, once queen of nations, is now a slave.
12 *Is it* nothing to you, all ye that pass by? behold, and see if there be any sorrow like unto my sorrow, which is done unto me, wherewith the LORD hath afflicted *me* in the day of his fierce anger.	12 "*Is it* nothing to you, all you who pass by? Behold and see If there is any sorrow like my sorrow, Which has been brought on me, Which the LORD has inflicted *on me* In the day of His fierce anger.	12 Is it nothing to you, all you who pass by? Look and see if there is any sorrow like my sorrow, because of all the Lord has done to me in the day of his fierce wrath.
20 Behold, O LORD; for I *am* in distress: my bowels are troubled; mine heart is turned within me; for I have grievously rebelled: abroad the sword bereaveth, at home *there is* as death.	20 "See, O LORD, that I *am* in distress; My soul is troubled; My heart is overturned within me, For I have been very rebellious. Outside the sword bereaves, At home *it is* like death.	20 *See, O Lord, my anguish;* my heart is broken and my soul despairs, for I have terribly rebelled. In the streets the sword awaits me; at home, disease and death.
3:22 *It is of* the LORD's mercies that we are not consumed, because his compassions fail not.	3:22 *Through* the LORD's mercies we are not consumed, Because His compassions fail not.	3:22 *his compassion never ends.* It is only the Lord's mercies that have kept us from complete destruction.
23 *They are* new every morning: great *is* thy faithfulness.	23 *They are* new every morning; Great *is* Your faithfulness.	23 Great is his faithfulness; his lovingkindness begins afresh each day.
26 *It is* good that *a man* should both hope and quietly wait for the salvation of the LORD.	26 *It is* good that *one* should hope and wait quietly For the salvation of the LORD.	26 It is good both to hope and wait quietly for the salvation of the Lord.
31 For the LORD will not cast off for ever:	31 For the LORD will not cast off forever.	31 for the Lord will not abandon him forever.
32 But though he cause grief, yet will he have compassion according to the multitude of his mercies.	32 Though He causes grief, Yet He will show compassion According to the multitude of His mercies.	32 Although God gives him grief, yet he will show compassion too, according to the greatness of his lovingkindness.
33 For he doth not afflict willingly nor grieve the children of men.	33 For He does not afflict willingly, Nor grieve the children of men.	33 For he does not enjoy afflicting men and causing sorrow.
5:19 Thou, O LORD, remainest for ever; thy throne from generation to generation.	5:19 You, O LORD, remain forever; Your throne from generation to generation.	5:19 O Lord, forever you remain the same! Your throne continues from generation to generation.

NIV	RSV	TEV
52:12 On the tenth day of the fifth month, in the nineteenth year of Nebuchadnezzar king of Babylon, Nebuzaradan commander of the imperial guard, who served the king of Babylon, came to Jerusalem.	**52:12** In the fifth month, on the tenth day of the month—which was the nineteenth year of King Nebuchadrezzar, king of Babylon—Nebuzaradan the captain of the bodyguard who served the king of Babylon, entered Jerusalem.	**52:12** On the tenth day of the fifth month of the nineteenth year of King Nebuchadnezzar of Babylonia, Nebuzaradan, adviser to the king and commander of his army, entered Jerusalem.
13 He set fire to the temple of the LORD, the royal palace and all the houses of Jerusalem. Every important building he burned down.	13 And he burned the house of the LORD, and the king's house and all the houses of Jerusalem; every great house he burned down.	13 He burned down the Temple, the palace, and the houses of all the important people in Jerusalem;
14 The whole Babylonian army under the commander of the imperial guard broke down all the walls around Jerusalem.	14 And all the army of the Chaldeans, who were with the captain of the guard, broke down all the walls round about Jerusalem.	14 and his soldiers tore down the city walls.
15 Nebuzaradan the commander of the guard carried into exile some of the poorest people and those who remained in the city, along with the rest of the craftsmen and those who had gone over to the king of Babylon.	15 And Nebuzaradan the captain of the guard carried away captive some of the poorest of the people and the rest of the people who were left in the city and the deserters who had deserted to the king of Babylon, together with the rest of the artisans.	15 Then Nebuzaradan took away to Babylonia the people who were left in the city, the remaining skilled workmen, and those who had deserted to the Babylonians.
16 But Nebuzaradan left behind the rest of the poorest people of the land to work the vineyards and fields.	16 But Nebuzaradan the captain of the guard left some of the poorest of the land of the vinedressers and plowmen.	16 But he left in Judah some of the poorest people, who owned no property, and he put them to work in the vineyards and fields.

Lamentations

NIV	RSV	TEV
1:1 How deserted lies the city, once so full of people! How like a widow is she, who once was great among the nations! She who was queen among the provinces has now become a slave.	**1:1** How lonely sits the city that was full of people! How like a widow has she become, she that was great among the nations! She that was a princess among the cities has become a vassal.	**1:1** How lonely lies Jerusalem, once so full of people! Once honored by the world, she is now like a widow; The noblest of cities has fallen into slavery.
12 "Is it nothing to you, all you who pass by? Look around and see. Is any suffering like my suffering that was inflicted on me, that the LORD brought on me in the day of his fierce anger?	12 "Is it nothing to you, all you who pass by? Look and see if there is any sorrow like my sorrow which was brought upon me, which the LORD inflicted on the day of his fierce anger.	12 "Look at me!" she cries to everyone who passes by. "No one has ever had pain like mine, Pain that the LORD brought on me in the time of his anger.
20 "See, O LORD, how distressed I am! I am in torment within, and in my heart I am disturbed, for I have been most rebellious. Outside, the sword bereaves; inside, there is only death.	20 "Behold, O LORD, for I am in distress, my soul is in tumult, my heart is wrung within me, because I have been very rebellious. In the street the sword bereaves; in the house it is like death.	20 "Look, O LORD, at my agony, at the anguish of my soul! My heart is broken in sorrow for my sins. There is murder in the streets; even indoors there is death.
3:22 Because of the LORD's great love we are not consumed, for his compassions never fail.	**3:22** The steadfast love of the LORD never ceases, his mercies never come to an end;	**3:22** The LORD's unfailing love and mercy still continue,
23 They are new every morning; great is your faithfulness.	23 they are new every morning; great is thy faithfulness.	23 Fresh as the morning, as sure as the sunrise.
26 it is good to wait quietly for the salvation of the LORD.	26 It is good that one should wait quietly for the salvation of the LORD.	26 So it is best for us to wait in patience—to wait for him to save us—
31 For men are not cast off by the Lord forever.	31 For the Lord will not cast off for ever,	31 The Lord is merciful and will not reject us forever.
32 Though he brings grief, he will show compassion, so great is his unfailing love.	32 but, though he cause grief, he will have compassion according to the abundance of his steadfast love;	32 He may bring us sorrow, but his love for us is sure and strong.
33 For he does not willingly bring affliction or grief to the children of men.	33 for he does not willingly afflict or grieve the sons of men.	33 He takes no pleasure in causing us grief or pain.
5:19 You, O LORD, reign forever; your throne endures from generation to generation.	**5:19** But thou, O LORD, dost reign for ever; thy throne endures to all generations.	**5:19** But you, O LORD, are king forever and will rule to the end of time.

KJV	NKJV	TLB

Ezekiel

KJV	NKJV	TLB
1:4 And I looked, and, behold, a whirlwind came out of the north, a great cloud, and a fire infolding itself, and a brightness *was* about it, and out of the midst thereof as the colour of amber, out of the midst of the fire.	**1:4** Then I looked, and behold, a whirlwind was coming out of the north, a great cloud with raging fire engulfing itself; and brightness *was* all around it and radiating out of its midst like the color of amber, out of the midst of the fire.	**1:4** I saw, in this vision, a great storm coming toward me from the north, driving before it a huge cloud glowing with fire, with a mass of fire inside that flashed continually; and in the fire there was something that shone like polished brass.
5 Also out of the midst thereof *came* the likeness of four living creatures. And this *was* their appearance; they had the likeness of a man.	5 Also from within it *came* the likeness of four living creatures. And this *was* their appearance: they had the likeness of a man.	5 Then from the center of the cloud, four strange forms appeared that looked like men,
6 And every one had four faces, and every one had four wings.	6 Each one had four faces, and each one had four wings.	6 except that each had four faces and two pairs of wings!
7 And their feet *were* straight feet; and the sole of their feet *was* like the sole of a calf's foot: and they sparkled like the colour of burnished brass.	7 Their legs *were* straight, and the soles of their feet *were* like the soles of calves' feet. They sparkled like the color of burnished bronze.	7 Their legs were like those of men, but their feet were cloven like calves' feet, and shone like burnished brass.
8 And *they had* the hands of a man under their wings on their four sides; and they four had their faces and their wings.	8 *They had* the hands of a man under their wings on their four sides; and each of the four had faces and wings.	8 And beneath each of their wings I could see human hands.
9 Their wings *were* joined one to another; they turned not when they went; they went every one straight forward.	9 Their wings touched one another. *The creatures* did not turn when they went, but each one went straight forward.	9 The four living beings were joined wing to wing, and they flew straight forward without turning.
15 Now as I beheld the living creatures, behold one wheel upon the earth by the living creatures, with his four faces.	15 Now as I looked at the living creatures, behold, a wheel *was* on the earth beside each living creature with its four faces.	15 As I stared at all of this, I saw four wheels on the ground beneath them, one wheel belonging to each.
16 The appearance of the wheels and their work *was* like unto the colour of a beryl: and they four had one likeness: and their appearance and their work *was* as it were a wheel in the middle of a wheel.	16 The appearance of the wheels and their words *was* like the color of beryl, and all four had the same likeness. The appearance of their works *was*, as it were, a wheel in the middle of a wheel.	16 The wheels looked as if they were made of polished amber and each wheel was constructed with a second wheel crosswise inside.
26 And above the firmament that *was* over their heads *was* the likeness of a throne, as the appearance of a sapphire stone: and upon the likeness of the throne *was* the likeness as the appearance of a man above upon it.	26 And above the firmament over their heads *was* the likeness of a throne, in appearance like a sapphire stone; on the likeness of the throne *was* a likeness with the appearance of a man high above it.	26 For high in the sky above them was what looked like a throne made of beautiful blue sapphire stones, and upon it sat someone who appeared to be a Man.
27 And I saw as the colour of amber, as the appearance of fire round about within it, from the appearance of his loins even upward, and from the appearance of his loins even downward, I saw as it were the appearance of fire, and it had brightness round about.	27 Also from the appearance of His waist and upward I saw, as it were, the color of amber with the appearance of fire all around within it; and from the appearance of His waist and downward I saw, as it were, the appearance of fire with brightness all around.	27 From his waist up, he seemed to be all glowing bronze, dazzling like fire; and from his waist down he seemed to be entirely flame,
28 As the appearance of the bow that is in the cloud in the day of rain, so *was* the appearance of the brightness round about. This *was* the appearance of the likeness of the glory of the LORD. And when I saw *it*, I fell upon my face, and I heard a voice of one that spake.	28 Like the appearance of a rainbow in a cloud on a rainy day, so *was* the appearance of the brightness all around it. This *was* the appearance of the likeness of the glory of the LORD. So when I saw *it*, I fell on my face, and I heard a voice of One speaking.	28 and there was a glowing halo like a rainbow all around him. That was the way the glory of the Lord appeared to me. And when I saw it, I fell face downward on the ground, and heard the voice of someone speaking to me:
2:3 And he said unto me, Son of man, I send thee to the children of Israel, to a rebellious nation that hath rebelled against me: they and their fathers have transgressed against me, *even* unto this very day.	**2:3** And He said to me: "Son of man, I am sending you to the children of Israel, to a rebellious nation that has rebelled against Me; they and their fathers have transgressed against Me to this very day.	**2:3** "Son of dust," he said, "I am sending you to the nation of Israel, to a nation rebelling against me. They and their fathers have kept on sinning against me until this very hour.
4 For *they are* impudent children and stiffhearted. I do send thee unto them; and thou shalt say unto them, Thus said the Lord GOD.	4 "For *they are* impudent and stubborn children. I am sending you to them, and you shall say to them, 'Thus says the Lord GOD.'	4 For they are a hardhearted, stiff-necked people. But I am sending you to give them my messages—the messages of the Lord God.
5 And they, whether they will hear, or whether they will forebear, (for they *are* a rebellious house,) yet shall know that there hath been a prophet among them.	5 "As for them, whether they hear or whether they refuse—for they *are* a rebellious house—yet they will know that a prophet has been among them.	5 And whether they listen or not (for remember, they are rebels), they will at least know they have had a prophet among them.

NIV	RSV	TEV

Ezekiel

NIV	RSV	TEV
1:4 I looked, and I saw a windstorm coming out of the north—an immense cloud with flashing lightning and surrounded by brilliant light. The center of the fire looked like glowing metal,	**1:4** As I looked, behold, a stormy wind came out of the north, and a great cloud, with brightness round about it, and fire flashing forth continually, and in the midst of the fire, as it were gleaming bronze.	**1:4** I looked up and saw a windstorm coming from the north. Lightning was flashing from a huge cloud, and the sky around it was glowing. Where the lightning was flashing, something shone like bronze.
5 and in the fire was what looked like four living creatures. In appearance their form was that of a man,	**5** And from the midst of it came the likeness of four living creatures. And this was their appearance: they had the form of men,	**5** At the center of the storm I saw what looked like four living creatures in human form,
6 but each of them had four faces and four wings.	**6** but each had four faces, and each of them had four wings.	**6** but each of them had four faces and four wings.
7 Their legs were straight; their feet were like those of a calf and gleamed like burnished bronze.	**7** Their legs were straight, and the soles of their feet were like the sole of a calf's foot; and they sparkled like burnished bronze.	**7** Their legs were straight, and they had hoofs like those of a bull. They shone like polished bronze.
8 Under their wings on their four sides they had the hands of a man. All four of them had faces and wings,	**8** Under their wings on their four sides they had human hands. And the four had their faces and their wings thus:	**8** In addition to their four faces and four wings, they each had four human hands, one under each wing.
9 and their wings touched one another. Each one went straight ahead; they did not turn as they moved.	**9** their wings touched one another; they went every one straight forward, without turning as they went.	**9** Two wings of each creature were spread out so that the creatures formed a square, with their wing tips touching. When they moved, they moved as a group without turning their bodies.
15 As I looked at the living creatures, I saw a wheel on the ground beside each creature with its four faces.	**15** Now as I looked at the living creatures, I saw a wheel upon the earth beside the living creatures, one for each of the four of them.	**15** As I was looking at the four creatures I saw four wheels touching the ground, one beside each of them.
16 This was the appearance and structure of the wheels: They sparkled like chrysolite, and all four looked alike. Each appeared to be made like a wheel intersecting a wheel.	**16** As for the appearance of the wheels and their construction: their appearance was like the gleaming of a chrysolite; and the four had the same likeness, their construction being as it were a wheel within a wheel.	**16** All four wheels were alike; each one shone like a precious stone, and each had another wheel intersecting it at right angles,
26 Above the expanse over their heads was what looked like a throne of sapphire, and high above on the throne was a figure like that of a man.	**26** And above the firmament over their heads there was the likeness of a throne, in appearance like sapphire; and seated above the likeness of a throne was a likeness as it were of a human form.	**26** Above the dome there was something that looked like a throne made of sapphire, and sitting on the throne was a figure that looked like a man.
27 I saw that from what appeared to be his waist up he looked like glowing metal, as if full of fire, and that from there down he looked like fire; and brilliant light surrounded him.	**27** And upward from what had the appearance of his loins I saw as it were gleaming bronze, like the appearance of fire enclosed round about; and downward from what had the appearance of his loins I saw as it were the appearance of fire, and there was brightness round about him.	**27** The figure seemed to be shining like bronze in the middle of a fire. It shone all over with a bright light
28 Like the appearance of a rainbow in the clouds on a rainy day, so was the radiance around him. This was the appearance of the likeness of the glory of the LORD. When I saw it, I fell facedown, and I heard the voice of one speaking.	**28** Like the appearance of the bow that is in the cloud on the day of rain, so was the appearance of the brightness round about. Such was the appearance of the likeness of the glory of the LORD. And when I saw it, I fell upon my face, and I heard the voice of one speaking.	**28** that had in it all the colors of the rainbow. This was the dazzling light which shows the presence of the LORD.
2:3 He said: "Son of man, I am sending you to the Israelites, to a rebellious nation that has rebelled against me; they and their fathers have been in revolt against me to this very day.	**2:3** And he said to me, "Son of man, I send you to the people of Israel, to a nation of rebels, who have rebelled against me; they and their fathers have transgressed against me to this very day.	**2:3** "Mortal man, I am sending you to the people of Israel. They have rebelled and turned against me and are still rebels, just as their ancestors were.
4 The people to whom I am sending you are obstinate and stubborn. Say to them, 'This is what the Sovereign LORD says.'	**4** The people also are impudent and stubborn: I send you to them; and you shall say to them, 'Thus says the Lord GOD.'	**4** They are stubborn and do not respect me, so I am sending you to tell them what I, the Sovereign LORD, am saying to them.
5 And whether they listen or fail to listen—for they are a rebellious house—they will know that a prophet has been among them.	**5** And whether they hear or refuse to hear (for they are a rebellious house) they will know that there has been a prophet among them.	**5** Whether those rebels listen to you or not, they will know that a prophet has been among them.

KJV	NKJV	TLB
4:4 Lie thou also upon thy left side, and lay the iniquity of the house of Israel upon it: *according* to the number of the days that thou shalt lie upon it thou shalt bear their iniquity.	**4:4** "Lie also on your left side, and lay the iniquity of the house of Israel upon it. *According* to the number of the days that you lie on it, you shall bear their iniquity.	**4:4-5** "Now lie on your left side for 390 days, to show that Israel will be punished for 390 years by captivity and doom. Each day you lie there represents a year of punishment ahead for Israel.
5 For I have laid upon thee the years of their iniquity, according to the number of the days, three hundred and ninety days: so shalt thou bear the iniquity of the house of Israel.	5 "For I have laid on you the years of their iniquity, according to the number of the days, three hundred and ninety days; so you shall bear the iniquity of the house of Israel.	
6 And when thou hast accomplished them, lie again on thy right side, and thou shalt bear the iniquity of the house of Judah forty days: I have appointed thee each day for a year.	6 "And when you have completed them, lie again on your right side; then you shall bear the iniquity of the house of Judah forty days. I have laid on you a day for each year.	6 Afterwards, turn over and lie on your right side for forty days, to signify the years of Judah's punishment. Each day will represent one year.
9 Take thou also unto thee wheat, and barley, and beans, and lentiles, and millet, and fitches, and put them in one vessel, and make thee bread thereof, *according* to the number of the days that thou shalt lie upon thy side, three hundred and ninety days shalt thou eat thereof.	9 "Also take for yourself wheat, barley, beans, lentils, millet, and spelt; put them into one vessel, and make bread of them for yourself. *During* the number of days that you lie on your side, three hundred and ninety days, you shall eat it.	9 "During the first 390 days eat bread made of flour mixed from wheat, barley, beans, lentils, and spelt. Mix the various kinds of flour together in a jar.
10 And thy meat which thou shalt eat *shall be* by weight, twenty shekels a day: from time to time shalt thou eat it.	10 "And your food which you eat *shall be* by weight, twenty shekels a day; from time to time you shall eat it.	10 You are to ration this out to yourself at the rate of eight ounces at a time, one meal a day.
11 Thou shalt drink also water by measure, the sixth part of an hin: from time to time shalt thou drink.	11 "You shall also drink water by measure, one-sixth of a hin; from time to time you shall drink.	11 And use one quart of water a day; don't use more than that.
12 And thou shalt eat it *as* barley cakes, and thou shalt bake it with dung that cometh out of man, in their sight.	12 "And you shall eat it *as* barley cakes; and bake it using fuel of human waste in their sight."	12 Each day take flour from the barrel and prepare it as you would barley cakes. While all the people are watching, bake it over a fire, using dried human dung as fuel, and eat it.
13 And the LORD said, Even thus shall the children of Israel eat their defiled bread among the Gentiles, whither I will drive them.	13 Then the LORD said, "So shall the children of Israel eat their defiled bread among the Gentiles, where I will drive them."	13 For the Lord declares, Israel shall eat defiled bread in the Gentile lands to which I exile them!"
10:1 Then I looked, and, behold, in the firmament that was above the head of the cherubims there appeared over them as it were a sapphire stone, as the appearance of the likeness of a throne.	**10:1** And I looked, and there in the firmament that was above the head of the cherubim, there appeared something like a sapphire stone, having the appearance of the likeness of a throne.	**10:1** Suddenly a throne of beautiful blue sapphire appeared in the sky above the heads of the cherubim.
2 And he spake unto the man clothed with linen, and said, Go in between the wheels, *even* under the cherub, and fill thine hand with coals of fire from between the cherubims, and scatter *them* over the city. And he went in in my sight.	2 And He spoke to the man clothed with linen, and said, "Go in among the wheels, under the cherub, fill your hands with coals of fire from among the cherubim, and scatter *them* over the city." And he went in as I watched.	2 Then the Lord spoke to the man in linen clothing and said: "Go in between the whirling wheels beneath the cherubim and take a handful of glowing coals and scatter them over the city." He did so while I watched.
3 Now the cherubims stood on the right side of the house, when the man went in; and the cloud filled the inner court.	3 Now the cherubim were standing on the south side of the temple when the man went in, and the cloud filled the inner court.	3 The cherubim were standing at the south end of the Temple when the man went in. And the cloud of glory filled the inner court.
4 Then the glory of the LORD went up from the cherub, *and stood* over the threshold of the house; and the house was filled with the cloud, and the court was full of the brightness of the LORD's glory.	4 Then the glory of the LORD went up from the cherub, *and paused* over the threshold of the temple; and the house was filled with the cloud, and the court was full of the brightness of the LORD's glory.	4 Then the glory of the Lord rose from above the cherubim and went over to the door of the Temple. The Temple was filled with the cloud of glory, and the court of the Temple was filled with the brightness of the glory of the Lord.
5 And the sound of the cherubims' wings was heard *even* to the oute.· court, as the voice of the Almighty God when he speaketh.	5 And the sound of the wings of the cherubim was heard *even* in the outer court, like the voice of Almighty God when He speaks.	5 And the sound of the wings of the cherubim was as the voice of Almighty God when he speaks and could be heard clear out in the outer court.
11:17 Therefore say, Thus saith the Lord GOD; I will even gather you from the people, and assemble you out of the countries where ye have been scattered, and I will give you the land of Israel.	**11:17** "Therefore say, 'Thus says the Lord GOD: "I will gather you from the peoples, assemble you from the countries where you have been scattered, and I will give you the land of Israel."'"	**11:17** and I will gather you back from the nations where you are scattered and give you the land of Israel again.
19 And I will give them one heart, and I will put a new spirit within you; and I will take the stony heart out of their flesh, and will give them an heart of flesh:	19 "Then I will give them one heart, and I will put a new spirit within them, and take the stony heart out of their flesh, and give them a heart of flesh,	19 I will give you one heart and a new spirit; I will take from you your hearts of stone and give you tender hearts of love for God,
20 That they may walk in my statutes, and keep mine ordinances, and do them: and they shall be my people, and I will be their God.	20 "that they may walk in My statutes and keep My judgments and do them; and they shall be My people, and I will be their God.	20 so that you can obey my laws and be my people, and I will be your God.

NIV	RSV	TEV
4:4 "Then lie on your left side and put the sin of the house of Israel upon yourself. You are to bear their sin for the number of days you lie on your side.	**4:4** "Then lie upon your left side, and I will lay the punishment of the house of Israel upon you; for the number of the days that you lie upon it, you shall bear the punishment.	**4:4–5** "Then lie down on your left side, and I will place on you the guilt of the nation of Israel. For 390 days you will stay there and suffer because of their guilt. I have sentenced you to one day for each year their punishment will last.
5 I have assigned you the same number of days as the years of their sin. So for 390 days you will bear the sin of the house of Israel.	5 For I assign to you a number of days, three hundred and ninety days, equal to the number of the years of their punishment; so long shall you bear the punishment of the house of Israel.	
6 "After you have finished this, lie down again, this time on your right side, and bear the sin of the house of Judah. I have assigned you 40 days, a day for each year.	6 And when you have completed these, you shall lie down a second time, but on your right side, and bear the punishment of the house of Judah; forty days I assign you, a day for each year.	6 When you finish that, turn over on your right side and suffer for the guilt of Judah for forty days—one day for each year of their punishment.
9 "Take wheat and barley, beans and lentils, millet and spelt; put them in a storage jar and use them to make bread for yourself. You are to eat it during the 390 days you lie on your side.	9 "And you, take wheat and barley, beans and lentils, millet and spelt, and put them into a single vessel, and make bread of them. During the number of days that you lie upon your side, three hundred and ninety days, you shall eat it.	9 "Now take some wheat, barley, beans, peas, millet, and spelt. Mix them all together and make bread. That is what you are to eat during the 390 days you are lying on your left side.
10 Weigh out twenty shekels of food to eat each day and eat it at set times.	10 And the food which you eat shall be by weight, twenty shekels a day; once a day you shall eat it.	10 You will be allowed eight ounces of bread a day, and it will have to last until the next day.
11 Also measure out a sixth of a hin of water and drink it at set times.	11 And water you shall drink by measure, the sixth part of a hin; once a day you shall drink.	11 You will also have a limited amount of water to drink, two cups a day.
12 Eat the food as you would a barley cake; bake it in the sight of the people, using human excrement for fuel."	12 And you shall eat it as a barley cake, baking it in their sight on human dung."	12 You are to build a fire out of dried human excrement, bake bread on the fire, and eat it where everyone can see you."
13 The LORD said, "In this way the people of Israel will eat defiled food among the nations where I will drive them."	13 And the LORD said, "Thus shall the people of Israel eat their bread unclean, among the nations whither I will drive them."	13 The LORD said, "This represents the way the Israelites will have to eat food which the Law forbids, when I scatter them to foreign countries."
10:1 I looked, and I saw the likeness of a throne of sapphire above the expanse that was over the heads of the cherubim.	**10:1** Then I looked, and behold, on the firmament that was over the heads of the cherubim there appeared above them something like a sapphire, in form resembling a throne.	**10:1** I looked at the dome over the heads of the living creatures and above them was something that seemed to be a throne made of sapphire.
2 The LORD said to the man clothed in linen, "Go in among the wheels beneath the cherubim. Fill your hands with burning coals from among the cherubim and scatter them over the city." And as I watched, he went in.	2 And he said to the man clothed in linen, "Go in among the whirling wheels underneath the cherubim; fill your hands with burning coals from between the cherubim, and scatter them over the city." And he went in before my eyes.	2 God said to the man wearing linen clothes, "Go between the wheels under the creatures and fill your hands with burning coals. Then scatter the coals over the city." I watched him go.
3 Now the cherubim were standing on the south side of the temple when the man went in, and a cloud filled the inner court.	3 Now the cherubim were standing on the south side of the house, when the man went in; and a cloud filled the inner court.	3 The creatures were standing to the south of the Temple when he went in, and a cloud filled the inner courtyard.
4 Then the glory of the LORD rose from above the cherubim and moved to the threshold of the temple. The cloud filled the temple, and the court was full of the radiance of the glory of the LORD.	4 And the glory of the LORD went up from the cherubim to the threshold of the house; and the house was filled with the cloud, and the court was full of the brightness of the glory of the LORD.	4 The dazzling light of the LORD's presence rose up from the creatures and moved to the entrance of the Temple. Then the cloud filled the Temple, and the courtyard was blazing with the light.
5 The sound of the wings of the cherubim could be heard as far away as the outer court, like the voice of God Almighty when he speaks.	5 And the sound of the wings of the cherubim was heard as far as the outer court, like the voice of God Almighty when he speaks.	5 The noise made by the creatures' wings was heard even in the outer courtyard. It sounded like the voice of Almighty God.
11:17 "Therefore say: 'This is what the Sovereign LORD says: I will gather you from the nations and bring you back from the countries where you have been scattered, and I will give you back the land of Israel again.'	**11:17** Therefore say, 'Thus says the Lord GOD: I will gather you from the peoples, and assemble you out of the countries where you have been scattered, and I will give you the land of Israel.'	**11:17** "So tell them what I, the Sovereign LORD, am saying. I will gather you out of the countries where I scattered them, and will give the land of Israel back to them.
19 I will give them an undivided heart and put a new spirit in them; I will remove from them their heart of stone and give them a heart of flesh.	19 And I will give them one heart, and put a new spirit within them; I will take the stony heart out of their flesh and give them a heart of flesh,	19 I will give them a new heart and a new mind. I will take away their stubborn heart of stone and will give them an obedient heart.
20 Then they will follow my decrees and be careful to keep my laws. They will be my people, and I will be their God.	20 that they may walk in my statutes and keep my ordinances and obey them; and they shall be my people, and I will be their God.	20 Then they will keep my laws and faithfully obey all my commands. They will be my people, and I will be their God.

KJV	NKJV	TLB
14:13 Son of man, when the land sinneth against me by trespassing grievously, then will I stretch out mine hand upon it, and will break the staff of the bread thereof, and will send famine upon it, and will cut off man and beast from it;	**14:13** "Son of man, when a land sins against Me by persistent unfaithfulness, I will stretch out My hand against it; I will cut off its supply of bread, send famine on it, and cut off man and beast from it.	**14:13** "Son of dust, when the people of this land sin against me, then I will crush them with my fist and break off their food supply and send famine to destroy both man and beast.
14 Though these three men, Noah, Daniel, and Job, were in it, they should deliver *but* their own souls by their righteousness, saith the Lord GOD.	**14** *"Though* these three men, Noah, Daniel, and Job, *were* in it, they would deliver *only* themselves by their righteousness," says the Lord GOD.	**14** If Noah, Daniel and Job were here today, they alone would be saved by their righteousness, and I would destroy the remainder of Israel, says the Lord God.
16:6 And when I passed by thee, and saw thee polluted in thine own blood, I said unto thee *when thou wast* in thy blood, Live; yea, I said unto thee *when thou wast* in thy blood, Live.	**16:6** "And when I passed by you and saw you struggling in your own blood, I said to you in your blood, 'Live!' Yes, I said to you in your blood, 'Live!'	**16:6** "But I came by and saw you there, covered with your own blood, and I said, 'Live!'
17:22 Thus saith the Lord GOD; I will also take of the highest branch of the high cedar, and will set *it;* I will crop off from the top of his young twigs a tender one, and will plant *it* upon an high mountain and eminent:	**17:22** Thus says the Lord GOD: "I will take also *one* of the highest branches of the high cedar and set *it* out. I will crop off from the topmost of its young twigs a tender one, and will plant *it* on a high and prominent mountain.	**17:22-23** "The Lord God says: I, myself, will take the finest and most tender twig from the top of the highest cedar, and I, myself, will plant it on the top of Israel's highest mountain. It shall become a noble cedar, bringing forth branches and bearing fruit. Animals of every sort will gather under it; its branches will shelter every kind of bird.
23 In the mountain of the height of Israel will I plant it: and it shall bring forth boughs, and bear fruit, and be a goodly cedar: and under it shall dwell all fowl of every wing; in the shadow of the branches thereof shall they dwell.	**23** "On the mountain height of Israel I will plant it; and it will bring forth boughs, and bear fruit, and be a majestic cedar. Under it will dwell birds of every sort; in the shadow of its branches they will dwell.	
18:2 What mean ye, that ye use this proverb concerning the land of Israel, saying, The fathers have eaten sour grapes, and the children's teeth are set on edge?	**18:2** "What do you mean when you use this proverb concerning the land of Israel, saying: 'The fathers have eaten sour grapes, And the children's teeth are set on edge'?	**18:2** "Why do people use this proverb about the land of Israel: The children are punished for their fathers' sins?
3 *As* I live, saith the Lord GOD, ye shall not have *occasion* any more to use this proverb in Israel.	**3** *"As* I live," says the Lord GOD, "you shall no longer use this proverb in Israel.	**3** As I live, says the Lord God, you will not use this proverb any more in Israel,
4 Behold, all souls are mine; as the soul of the father, so also the soul of the son is mine: the soul that sinneth, it shall die.	**4** "Behold, all souls are Mine; The soul of the father As well as the soul of the son is Mine; The soul who sins shall die.	**4** for all souls are mine to judge—fathers and sons alike—and my rule is this: It is for a man's own sins that he will die.
28:12 Son of man, take up a lamentation upon the king of Tyrus, and say unto him, Thus saith the Lord GOD; Thou sealest up the sum, full of wisdom, and perfect in beauty.	**28:12** "Son of man, take up a lamentation for the king of Tyre, and say to him, 'Thus says the Lord GOD: "You *were* the seal of perfection, Full of wisdom and perfect in beauty.	**28:12** "Son of dust, weep for the king of Tyre. Tell him, the Lord God says: You were the perfection of wisdom and beauty.
13 Thou hast been in Eden the garden of God; every precious stone *was* thy covering, the sardius, topaz, and the diamond, the beryl, the onyx, and the jasper, the sapphire, the emerald, and the carbuncle, and gold: the workmanship of thy tabrets and of thy pipes was prepared in thee in the day that thou wast created.	**13** You were in Eden, the garden of God; Every precious stone *was* your covering: The sardius, topaz, and diamond, Beryl, onyx, and jasper, Sapphire, turquoise, and emerald with gold. The workmanship of your timbrels and pipes Was prepared for you on the day you were created.	**13** You were in Eden, the garden of God; your clothing was bejeweled with every precious stone—ruby, topaz, diamond, chrysolite, onyx, jasper, sapphire, carbuncle, and emerald—all in beautiful settings of finest gold. They were given to you on the day you were created.
14 Thou *art* the anointed cherub that covereth; and I have set thee *so:* thou wast upon the holy mountain of God; thou hast walked up and down in the midst of the stones of fire.	**14** "You *were* the anointed cherub who covers; I established you; You were on the holy mountain of God; You walked back and forth in the midst of fiery stones.	**14** I appointed you to be the anointed guardian cherub. You had access to the holy mountain of God. You walked among the stones of fire.
15 Thou *wast* perfect in thy ways from the day that thou wast created, till iniquity was found in thee.	**15** You *were* perfect in your ways from the day you were created, Till iniquity was found in you.	**15** "You were perfect in all you did from the day you were created until that time when wrong was found in you.
33:8 When I say unto the wicked, O wicked *man,* thou shalt surely die; if thou dost not speak to warn the wicked from his way, that wicked *man* shall die in his iniquity; but his blood will I require at thine hand.	**33:8** "When I say to the wicked, 'O wicked *man,* you shall surely die!' and you do not speak to warn the wicked from his way, that wicked *man* shall die in his iniquity; but his blood I will require at your hand.	**33:8** When I say to the wicked, 'O wicked man, you will die!' and you don't tell him what I say, so that he does not repent—that wicked person will die in his sins, but I will hold you responsible for his death.

NIV	RSV	TEV
14:13 "Son of man, if a country sins against me by being unfaithful and I stretch out my hand against it to cut off its food supply and send famine upon it and kill its men and their animals,	**14:13** "Son of man, when a land sins against me by acting faithlessly, and I stretch out my hand against it, and break its staff of bread and send famine upon it, and cut off from it man and beast,	**14:13** "Mortal man," he said, "if a country sins and is unfaithful to me, I will reach out and destroy its supply of food. I will send a famine and kill people and animals alike.
14 even if these three men—Noah, Daniel and Job—were in it, they could save only themselves by their righteousness, declares the Sovereign LORD.	14 even if these three men, Noah, Daniel, and Job, were in it, they would deliver but their own lives by their righteousness, says the Lord GOD.	14 Even if those three men, Noah, Danel, and Job, were living there, their goodness would save only their own lives." The Sovereign LORD has spoken.
16:6 "'Then I passed by and saw you kicking about in your blood, and as you lay there in your blood I said to you, "Live!"	**16:6** "And when I passed by you, and saw you weltering in your blood, I said to you in your blood, 'Live,	**16:6** "Then I passed by and saw you squirming in your own blood. You were covered with blood, but I wouldn't let you die.
17:22 "'This is what the Sovereign LORD says: I myself will take a shoot from the very top of a cedar and plant it; I will break off a tender sprig from its topmost shoots and plant it on a high and lofty mountain.	**17:22** Thus says the Lord GOD: "I myself will take a sprig from the lofty top of the cedar, and will set it out; I will break off from the topmost of its young twigs a tender one, and I myself will plant it upon a high and lofty mountain;	**17:22** This is what the Sovereign LORD says: "I will take the top of a tall cedar and break off a tender sprout; I will plant it on a high mountain,
23 On the mountain heights of Israel I will plant it; it will produce branches and bear fruit and become a splendid cedar. Birds of every kind will nest in it; they will find shelter in the shade of its branches.	23 on the mountain height of Israel will I plant it, that it may bring forth boughs and bear fruit, and become a noble cedar; and under it will dwell all kinds of beasts; in the shade of its branches birds of every sort will nest.	23 on Israel's highest mountain. It will grow branches and bear seed and become a magnificent cedar. Birds of every kind will live there and find shelter in its shade.
18:2 "What do you people mean by quoting this proverb about the land of Israel: "'The fathers eat sour grapes, and the children's teeth are set on edge'?	**18:2** "What do you mean by repeating this proverb concerning the land of Israel, 'The fathers have eaten sour grapes, and the children's teeth are set on edge'?	**18:2** and said, "What is this proverb people keep repeating in the land of Israel? 'The parents ate the sour grapes, But the children got the sour taste.'
3 "As surely as I live, declares the Sovereign LORD, you will no longer quote this proverb in Israel.	3 As I live, says the Lord GOD, this proverb shall no more be used by you in Israel.	3 "As surely as I am the living God," says the Sovereign LORD, "you will not repeat this proverb in Israel any more.
4 For every living soul belongs to me, the father as well as the son—both alike belong to me. The soul who sins is the one who will die.	4 Behold, all souls are mine; the soul of the father as well as the soul of the son is mine: the soul that sins shall die.	4 The life of every person belongs to me, the life of the parent as well as that of the child. The person who sins is the one who will die.
28:12 "Son of man, take up a lament concerning the king of Tyre and say to him: 'This is what the Sovereign LORD says: "'You were the model of perfection, full of wisdom and perfect in beauty.	**28:12** "Son of man, raise a lamentation over the king of Tyre, and say to him, Thus says the Lord GOD: "You were the signet of perfection, full of wisdom and perfect in beauty.	**28:12** "Mortal man," he said, "grieve for the fate that is waiting for the king of Tyre. Tell him what I, the Sovereign LORD, am saying: You were once an example of perfection. How wise and handsome you were!
13 You were in Eden, the garden of God; every precious stone adorned you: ruby, topaz and emerald, chrysolite, onyx and jasper, sapphire, turquoise and beryl. Your settings and mountings were made of gold; on the day you were prepared.	13 You were in Eden, the garden of God; every precious stone was your covering, carnelian, topaz, and jasper, chrysolite, beryl, and onyx, sapphire, carbuncle, and emerald; and wrought in gold were your settings and your engravings. On the day that you were created they were prepared.	13 You lived in Eden, the garden of God, and wore gems of every kind: rubies and diamonds; topaz, beryl, carnelian, and jasper; sapphires, emeralds, and garnets. You had ornaments of gold. They were made for you on the day you were created.
14 You were anointed as a guardian cherub, for so I ordained you. You were on the holy mount of God; you walked among the fiery stones.	14 With an anointed guardian cherub I placed you; you were on the holy mountain of God; in the midst of the stones of fire you walked.	14 I put a terrifying angel there to guard you. You lived on my holy mountain and walked among sparkling gems.
15 You were blameless in your ways from the day you were created till wickedness was found in you.	15 You were blameless in your ways from the day you were created, till iniquity was found in you.	15 Your conduct was perfect from the day you were created until you began to do evil.
33:8 When I say to the wicked, 'O wicked man, you will surely die,' and you do not speak out to dissuade him from his ways, that wicked man will die for his sin, and I will hold you accountable for his blood.	**33:8** If I say to the wicked, O wicked man, you shall surely die, and you do not speak to warn the wicked to turn from his way, that wicked man shall die in his iniquity, but his blood I will require at your hand.	**33:8** If I announce that an evil man is going to die but you do not warn him to change his ways so that he can save his life, then he will die, still a sinner, and I will hold you responsible for his death.

KJV	NKJV	TLB
9 Nevertheless, if thou warn the wicked of his way to turn from it; if he do not turn from his way, he shall die in his iniquity; but thou has delivered thy soul.	9 "Nevertheless if you warn the wicked to turn from his way, and he does not turn from his way, he shall die in his iniquity; but you have delivered your soul.	9 But if you warn him to repent and he doesn't, he will die in his sin, and you will not be responsible.
18 When the righteous turneth from his righteousness, and committeth iniquity, he shall even die thereby.	18 "When the righteous turns from his righteousness and commits iniquity, he shall die because of it.	18 For again I say, when the good man turns to evil, he shall die.
19 But if the wicked turn from his wickedness, and do that which is lawful and right, he shall live thereby.	19 "But when the wicked turns from his wickedness and does what is lawful and right, he shall live because of it.	19 But if the wicked turns from his wickedness and does what's fair and just, he shall live.
34:2 Son of man, prophesy against the shepherds of Israel, prophesy, and say unto them, Thus saith the Lord GOD unto the shepherds; Woe be to the shepherds of Israel that do feed themselves! should not the shepherds feed the flocks?	34:2 "Son of man, prophesy against the shepherds of Israel, prophesy and say to them, 'Thus says the Lord GOD to the shepherds: "Woe to the shepherds of Israel who feed themselves! Should not the shepherds feed the flocks?	34:2 "Son of dust, prophesy against the shepherds, the leaders of Israel, and say to them: The Lord God says to you: Woe to the shepherds who feed themselves instead of their flocks. Shouldn't shepherds feed the sheep?
3 Ye eat the fat, and ye clothe you with the wool, ye kill them that are fed: but ye feed not the flock.	3 "You eat the fat and clothe yourselves with the wool; you slaughter the fatlings, but you do not feed the flock.	3 You eat the best food and wear the finest clothes, but you let your flocks starve.
22 Therefore will I save my flock, and they shall no more be a prey; and I will judge between cattle and cattle.	22 "therefore I will save My flock, and they shall no longer be a prey; and I will judge between sheep and sheep.	22 So I myself will save my flock; no more will they be picked on and destroyed. And I will notice which is plump and which is thin, and why!
23 And I will set up one shepherd over them, and he shall feed them, even my servant David; he shall feed them, and he shall be their shepherd.	23 "I will establish one shepherd over them, and he shall feed them—My servant David. He shall feed them and be their shepherd.	23 And I will set one Shepherd over all my people, even my Servant, David. He shall feed them and be a Shepherd to them.
24 And I the LORD will be their God, and my servant David a prince among them; I the LORD have spoken it.	24 "And I, the LORD, will be their God, and My servant David a prince among them; I, the LORD, have spoken.	24 "And I, the Lord, will be their God, and my Servant David shall be a Prince among my people. I, the Lord, have spoken it.
36:24 For I will take you from among the heathen, and gather you out of all countries, and will bring you into your own land.	36:24 "For I will take you from among the nations, gather you out of all countries, and bring you into your own land.	36:24 For I will bring you back home again to the land of Israel.
37:4 Again he said unto me, Prophesy upon these bones, and say unto them, O ye dry bones, hear the word of the LORD.	37:4 Again He said to me, "Prophesy to these bones, and say to them, 'O dry bones, hear the word of the LORD!	37:4 Then he told me to speak to the bones and say: "O dry bones, listen to the words of God,
5 Thus saith the Lord GOD unto these bones; Behold, I will cause breath to enter into you, and ye shall live:	5 'Thus says the Lord GOD to these bones: "Surely I will cause breath to enter into you, and you shall live.	5 for the Lord God says, See! I am going to make you live and breathe again!
6 And I will lay sinews upon you, and will bring up flesh upon you, and cover you with skin, and put breath in you, and ye shall live; and ye shall know that I am the LORD.	6 "I will put sinews on you and bring flesh upon you, cover you with skin and put breath in you; and you shall live. Then you shall know that I am the LORD."'"	6 I will replace the flesh and muscles on you and cover you with skin. I will put breath into you, and you shall live and know I am the Lord."
7 So I prophesied as I was commanded: and as I prophesied, there was a noise, and behold a shaking, and the bones came together, bone to his bone.	7 So I prophesied as I was commanded; and as I prophesied, there was a noise, and suddenly a rattling; and the bones came together, bone to bone.	7 So I spoke these words from God, just as he told me to; and suddenly there was a rattling noise from all across the valley, and the bones of each body came together and attached to each other as they used to be.
8 And when I beheld, lo, the sinews and the flesh came up upon them, and the skin covered them above: but there was no breath in them.	8 Indeed, as I looked, the sinews and the flesh came upon them, and the skin covered them over; but there was no breath in them.	8 Then, as I watched, the muscles and flesh formed over the bones, and skin covered them, but the bodies had no breath.
9 Then said he unto me, Prophesy unto the wind, prophesy, son of man, and say to the wind, thus saith the Lord GOD; Come from the four winds, O breath, and breathe upon these slain, that they may live.	9 Then He said to me, "Prophesy to the breath, prophesy, son of man, and say to the breath, 'Thus says the Lord GOD: "Come from the four winds, O breath, and breathe on these slain, that they may live."'"	9 Then he told me to call to the wind and say: "The Lord God says: Come from the four winds, O Spirit, and breathe upon these slain bodies, that they may live again."
10 So I prophesied as he commanded me, and the breath came into them, and they lived, and stood up upon their feet, an exceeding great army.	10 So I prophesied as He commanded me, and breath came into them, and they lived, and stood upon their feet, an exceedingly great army.	10 So I spoke to the winds as he commanded me and the bodies began breathing; they lived, and stood up—a very great army.
38:3 And say, Thus saith the Lord GOD; Behold, I am against thee, O Gog, the chief prince of Meshech and Tubal:	38:3 "and say, 'Thus says the Lord GOD: "Behold, I am against you, O Gog, the prince of Rosh, Meshech, and Tubal.	38:3 Tell him that the Lord God says: I am against you, Gog.
4 And I will turn thee back, and put hooks into thy jaws, and I will bring thee forth, and all thine army, horses and horsemen, all of them clothed with all sorts of armour, even a great company with bucklers and shields, all of them handling swords:	4 "I will turn you around, put hooks into your jaws, and lead you out, with all your army, horses, and horsemen, all splendidly clothed, a great company with bucklers and shields, all of them handling swords.	4 I will put hooks into your jaws and pull you to your doom. I will mobilize your troops and armored cavalry, and make you a mighty host, all fully armed.

NIV	RSV	TEV
9 But if you do warn the wicked man to turn from his ways and he does not do so, he will die for his sin, but you will have saved yourself.	9 But if you warn the wicked to turn from his way, and he does not turn from his way; he shall die in his iniquity, but you will have saved your life.	9 If you do warn an evil man and he doesn't stop sinning, he will die, still a sinner, but your life will be spared."
18 If a righteous man turns from his righteousness and does evil, he will die for it.	18 When the righteous turns from his righteousness, and commits iniquity, he shall die for it.	18 When a righteous man stops doing good and starts doing evil, he will die for it.
19 And if a wicked man turns away from his wickedness and does what is just and right, he will live by doing so.	19 And when the wicked turns from his wickedness, and does what is lawful and right, he shall live by it.	19 When an evil man quits sinning and does what is right and good, he has saved his life.
34:2 "Son of man, prophesy against the shepherds of Israel; prophesy and say to them: 'This is what the Sovereign LORD says: Woe to the shepherds of Israel who only take care of themselves! Should not shepherds take care of the flock?	34:2 "Son of man, prophesy against the shepherds of Israel, prophesy, and say to them, even to the shepherds, Thus says the Lord GOD: Ho, shepherds of Israel who have been feeding yourselves! Should not shepherds feed the sheep?	34:2 "Mortal man," he said, "denounce the rulers of Israel. Prophesy to them, and tell them what I, the Sovereign LORD, say to them: You are doomed, you shepherds of Israel! You take care of yourselves, but never tend the sheep.
3 You eat the curds, clothe yourselves with the wool and slaughter the choice animals, but you do not take care of the flock.	3 You eat the fat, you clothe yourselves with the wool, you slaughter the fatlings; but you do not feed the sheep.	3 You drink the milk, wear clothes made from the wool, and kill and eat the finest sheep. But you never tend the sheep.
22 I will save my flock, and they will no longer be plundered. I will judge between one sheep and another.	22 I will save my flock, they shall no longer be a prey; and I will judge between sheep and sheep.	22 But I will rescue my sheep and not let them be mistreated any more. I will judge each of my sheep and separate the good from the bad.
23 I will place over them one shepherd, my servant David, and he will tend them; he will tend them and be their shepherd.	23 And I will set up over them one shepherd, my servant David, and he shall feed them: he shall feed them and be their shepherd.	23 I will give them a king like my servant David to be their one shepherd, and he will take care of them.
24 I the LORD will be their God, and my servant David will be prince among them. I the LORD have spoken.	24 And I, the LORD, will be their God, and my servant David shall be prince among them; I, the LORD, have spoken.	24 I, the LORD, will be their God, and a king like my servant David will be their ruler. I have spoken.
36:24 "'For I will take you out of the nations; I will gather you from all the countries and bring you back into your own land.	36:24 For I will take you from the nations, and gather you from all the countries, and bring you into your own land.	36:24 I will take you from every nation and country and bring you back to your own land.
37:4 Then he said to me, "Prophesy to these bones and say to them, 'Dry bones, hear the word of the LORD!	37:4 Again he said to me, "Prophesy to these bones, and say to them, O dry bones, hear the word of the LORD.	37:4 He said, "Prophesy to the bones. Tell these dry bones to listen to the word of the LORD.
5 This is what the Sovereign LORD says to these bones: I will make breath enter you, and you will come to life.	5 Thus says the Lord GOD to these bones: Behold, I will cause breath to enter you, and you shall live.	5 Tell them that I, the Sovereign LORD, am saying to them: I am going to put breath into you and bring you back to life.
6 I will attach tendons to you and make flesh come upon you and cover you with skin; I will put breath in you, and you will come to life. Then you will know that I am the LORD.'"	6 And I will lay sinews upon you, and will cause flesh to come upon you, and cover you with skin, and put breath in you, and you shall live; and you shall know that I am the LORD."	6 I will give you sinews and muscles, and cover you with skin. I will put breath into you and bring you back to life. Then you will know that I am the LORD."
7 So I prophesied as I was commanded. And as I was prophesying, there was a noise, a rattling sound, and the bones came together, bone to bone.	7 So I prophesied as I was commanded; and as I prophesied, there was a noise, and behold, a rattling; and the bones came together, bone to its bone.	7 So I prophesied as I had been told. While I was speaking, I heard a rattling noise, and the bones began to join together.
8 I looked, and tendons and flesh appeared on them and skin covered them, but there was no breath in them.	8 And as I looked, there were sinews on them, and flesh had come upon them, and skin had covered them; but there was no breath in them.	8 While I watched, the bones were covered with sinews and muscles, and then with skin. But there was no breath in the bodies.
9 Then he said to me, "Prophesy to the breath; prophesy, son of man, and say to it, 'This is what the Sovereign LORD says: Come from the four winds, O breath, and breathe into these slain, that they may live.'"	9 Then he said to me, "Prophesy to the breath, prophesy, son of man, and say to the breath, Thus says the Lord GOD: Come from the four winds, O breath, and breathe upon these slain, that they may live."	9 God said to me, "Mortal man, prophesy to the wind. Tell the wind that the Sovereign LORD commands it to come from every direction, to breathe into these dead bodies, and to bring them back to life."
10 So I prophesied as he commanded me, and breath entered them; they came to life and stood up on their feet—a vast army.	10 So I prophesied as he commanded me, and the breath came into them, and they lived, and stood upon their feet, an exceedingly great host.	10 So I prophesied as I had been told. Breath entered the bodies, and they came to life and stood up. There were enough of them to form an army.
38:3 and says: 'This is what the Sovereign LORD says: I am against you, O Gog, chief prince of Meshech and Tubal.	38:3 and say, Thus says the Lord GOD: Behold, I am against you, O Gog, chief prince of Meshech and Tubal;	38:3 and tell him that I, the Sovereign LORD, am his enemy.
4 I will turn you around, put hooks in your jaws and bring you out with your whole army—your horses, your horsemen fully armed, and a great horde with large and small shields, all of them brandishing their swords.	4 and I will turn you about, and put hooks into your jaws, and I will bring you forth, and all your army, horses and horsemen, all of them clothed in full armor, a great company, all of them with buckler and shield, wielding swords;	4 I will turn him around, put hooks in his jaws, and drag him and all his troops away. His army, with its horses and uniformed riders, is enormous, and every soldier carries a shield and is armed with a sword.

KJV	NKJV	TLB
5 Persia, Ethiopia, and Libya with them; all of them with shield and helmet:	5 "Persia, Ethiopia, and Libya are with them, all of them *with* shield and helmet;	5 Peras, Cush and Put shall join you too with all their weaponry,
6 Gomer, and all his bands; the house of Togarmah of the north quarters, and all his bands: *and* many people with thee.	6 "Gomer and all its troops; the house of Togarmah *from* the far north and all its troops— many people *are* with you.	6 and so shall Gomer and all his hordes and the armies of Togarmah from the distant north, as well as many others.
7 Be thou prepared, and prepare for thyself, thou, and all thy company that are assembled unto thee, and be thou a guard unto them.	7 "Prepare yourself and be ready, you and all your companies that are gathered about you; and be a guard for them.	7 Be prepared! Stay mobilized. You are their leader, Gog!
8 After many days thou shalt be visited: in the latter years thou shalt come into the land *that is* brought back from the sword, *and is* gathered out of many people, against the mountains of Israel, which have been always waste: but it is brought forth out of the nations, and they shall dwell safely all of them.	8 "After many days you will be visited. In the later years you will come into the land of those brought back from the sword *and* gathered from many people on the mountains of Israel, which had long been desolate; they were brought out of the nations, and now all of them dwell safely.	8 "A long time from now you will be called to action. In distant years you will swoop down onto the land of Israel, that will be lying in peace after the return of its people from many lands.
10 Thus saith the Lord GOD; It shall also come to pass, *that* at the same time shall things come into thy mind, and thou shalt think an evil thought:	10 'Thus says the Lord GOD: "On that day it shall come to pass *that* thoughts will arise in your mind, and you will make an evil plan:	10 For at that time an evil thought will have come to your mind.
11 And thou shalt say, I will go up to the land of unwalled villages; I will go to them that are at rest that dwell safely, all of them dwelling without walls, and having neither bars nor gates'	11 "You will say, 'I will go up against a land of unwalled villages; I will go to a peaceful people, who dwell safely, all of them dwelling without walls, and having neither bars nor gates'—	11 You will have said, 'Israel is an unprotected land of unwalled villages! I will march against her and destroy these people living in such confidence!
39:1 Therefore, thou son of man, prophesy against Gog, and say, Thus saith the Lord GOD; behold, I *am* against thee, O Gog, the chief prince of Meshech and Tubal:	39:1 "And you, son of man, prophesy against Gog, and say, 'Thus says the Lord GOD: "Behold, I *am* against you, O Gog, prince of Rosh, Meshech, and Tubal;	39:1 "Son of dust, prophesy this also against Gog. Tell him:
I stand against you, Gog, leader of Meshech and Tubal.
2 And I will turn thee back, and leave but the sixth part of thee, and will cause thee to come up from the north parts, and will bring thee upon the mountains of Israel:	2 "and I will turn you around and lead you on, bringing you up from the far north, and bring you against the mountains of Israel.	2 I will turn you and drive you toward the mountains of Israel, bringing you from the distant north. And I will destroy 85 percent of your army in the mountains.
3 And I will smite thy bow out of thy left hand, and will cause thine arrows to fall out of thy right hand.	3 "Then I will knock the bow out of your left hand, and cause the arrows to fall out of your right hand.	3 I will knock your weapons from your hands and leave you helpless.
48:35 *It was* round about eighteen thousand *measures:* and the name of the city from *that* day *shall be,* The LORD *is* there.	48:35 "All the way around *shall be* eighteen thousand cubits; and the name of the city from *that* day *shall be:* THE LORD IS THERE."	48:35 "The entire circumference of the city is six miles. And the name of the city will be 'The City of God.'"

Daniel

1:3 And the king spake unto Ashpenaz the master of his eunuchs, that he should bring *certain* of the children of Israel, and of the king's seed, and of the princes;	1:3 Then the king instructed Ashpenaz, the master of his eunuchs, to bring some of the children of Israel and some of the king's descendants and some of the nobles,	1:3 Then he ordered Ashpenaz, who was in charge of his palace personnel, to select some of the Jewish youths brought back as captives—young men of the royal family and nobility of Judah—
4 Children in whom *was* no blemish, but well favoured, and skilful in all wisdom, and cunning in knowledge, and understanding science, and such as *had* ability in them to stand in the king's palace, and whom they might teach the learning and the tongue of the Chaldeans.	4 young men in whom *there was* no blemish, but good-looking, gifted in all wisdom, possessing knowledge and quick to understand, who *had* ability to serve in the king's palace, and whom they might teach the language and literature of the Chaldeans.	4 and to teach them the Chaldean language and literature. "Pick strong, healthy, good-looking lads," he said; "those who have read widely in many fields, are well informed, alert and sensible, and have enough poise to look good around the palace."
16 Thus Melzar took away the portion of their meat, and the wine that they should drink; and gave them pulse.	16 Thus the steward took away their portion of delicacies and the wine that they were to drink, and gave them vegetables.	16 So after that the steward fed them only vegetables and water, without the rich foods and wines!
17 As for these four children, God gave them knowledge and skill in all learning and wisdom: and Daniel had understanding in all visions and dreams.	17 As for these four young men, God gave them knowledge and skill in all literature and wisdom; and Daniel had understanding in all visions and dreams.	17 God gave these four youths great ability to learn and they soon mastered all the literature and science of the time, and God gave to Daniel special ability in understanding the meanings of dreams and visions.
2:20 Daniel answered and said, Blessed be the name of God for ever and ever: for wisdom and might are his:	2:20 Daniel answered and said: "Blessed be the name of God forever and ever, For wisdom and might are His.	2:20 saying, "Blessed be the name of God forever and ever, for he alone has all wisdom and all power.

NIV	RSV	TEV
5 Persia, Cush and Put will be with them, all with shields and helmets,	5 Persia, Cush, and Put are with them, all of them with shield and helmet;	5 Men from Persia, Sudan, and Libya are with him, and all have shields and helmets.
6 also Gomer with all its troops, and Beth Togarmah from the far north with all its troops—the many nations with you.	6 Gomer and all his hordes; Beth-togarmah from the uttermost parts of the north with all his hordes—many peoples are with you.	6 All the fighting men of the lands of Gomer and Beth Togarmah in the north are with him, and so are men from many other nations.
7 "'Get ready; be prepared, you and all the hordes gathered about you, and take command of them.	7 "Be ready and keep ready, you and all the hosts that are assembled about you, and be a guard for them.	7 Tell him to get ready and have all his troops ready at his command.
8 After many days you will be called to arms. In future years you will invade a land that has recovered from war, whose people were gathered from many nations to the mountains of Israel, which had long been desolate. They had been brought out from the nations, and now all of them live in safety.	8 After many days you will be mustered; in the latter years you will go against the land that is restored from war, the land where people were gathered from many nations upon the mountains of Israel, which had been a continual waste; its people were brought out from the nations and now dwell securely, all of them.	8 After many years I will order him to invade a country where the people were brought back together from many nations and have lived without fear of war. He will invade the mountains of Israel, which were desolate and deserted so long, but where all the people now live in safety.
10 "'This is what the Sovereign LORD says: On that day thoughts will come into your mind and you will devise an evil scheme.	10 "Thus says the Lord GOD: On that day thoughts will come into your mind, and you will devise an evil scheme	10 This is what the Sovereign LORD says to Gog: "When that time comes, you will start thinking up an evil plan.
11 You will say, "I will invade a land of unwalled villages; I will attack a peaceful and unsuspecting people—all of them living without walls and without gates and bars.	11 and say, 'I will go up against the land of unwalled villages; I will fall upon the quiet people who dwell securely, all of them dwelling without walls, and having no bars or gates';	11 You will decide to invade a helpless country where the people live in peace and security in unwalled towns that have no defenses.
39:1 "Son of man, prophesy against Gog and say: 'This is what the Sovereign LORD says: I am against you, O Gog, chief prince of Meshech and Tubal.	39:1 "And you, son of man, prophesy against Gog, and say, Thus says the Lord GOD: Behold, I am against you, O Gog, chief prince of Meshech and Tubal;	39:1 The Sovereign LORD said, "Mortal man, denounce Gog, the chief ruler of the nations of Meshech and Tubal, and tell him that I am his enemy.
2 I will turn you around and drag you along. I will bring you from the far north and send you against the mountains of Israel.	2 and I will turn you about and drive you forward, and bring you up from the uttermost parts of the north, and lead you against the mountains of Israel.	2 I will turn him in a new direction and lead him out of the far north until he comes to the mountains of Israel.
3 Then I will strike your bow from your left hand and make your arrows drop from your right hand.	3 then I will strike your bow from your left hand, and will make your arrows drop out of your right hand.	3 Then I will knock his bow out of his left hand and his arrows out of his right hand.
48:35 "The distance all around will be 18,000 cubits. "And the name of the city from that time on will be: THE LORD IS THERE."	48:35 The circumference of the city shall be eighteen thousand cubits. And the name of the city henceforth shall be, The LORD is there."	48:35 The total length of the wall on all four sides of the city is 10,080 yards. The name of the city from now on will be "The-LORD-Is-Here!"

Daniel

1:3 Then the king ordered Ashpenaz, chief of his court officials, to bring in some of the Israelites from the royal family and the nobility—	1:3 Then the king commanded Ashpenaz, his chief eunuch, to bring some of the people of Israel, both of the royal family and of the nobility,	1:3 The king ordered Ashpenaz, his chief official, to select from among the Israelite exiles some young men of the royal family and of the noble families.
4 young men without any physical defect, handsome, showing aptitude for every kind of learning, well informed, quick to understand, and qualified to serve in the king's palace. He was to teach them the language and literature of the Babylonians.	4 youths without blemish, handsome and skilful in all wisdom, endowed with knowledge, understanding learning, and competent to serve in the king's palace, and to teach them the letters and language of the Chaldeans.	4 They had to be handsome, intelligent, well-trained, quick to learn, and free from physical defects, so that they would be qualified to serve in the royal court. Ashpenaz was to teach them to read and write the Babylonian language.
16 So the guard took away their choice food and the wine they were to drink and gave them vegetables instead.	16 So the steward took away their rich food and the wine they were to drink, and gave them vegetables.	16 So from then on the guard let them continue to eat vegetables instead of what the king provided.
17 To these four young men God gave knowledge and understanding of all kinds of literature and learning. And Daniel could understand visions and dreams of all kinds.	17 As for these four youths, God gave them learning and skill in all letters and wisdom; and Daniel had understanding in all visions and dreams.	17 God gave the four young men knowledge and skill in literature and philosophy. In addition, he gave Daniel skill in interpreting visions and dreams.
2:20 and said: "Praise be to the name of God for ever and ever; wisdom and power are his.	2:20 Daniel said: "Blessed be the name of God for ever and ever, to whom belong wisdom and might.	2:20 "God is wise and powerful! Praise him forever and ever.

KJV	NKJV	TLB
21 And he changeth the times and the seasons: he removeth kings, and setteth up kings: he giveth wisdom unto the wise, and knowledge to them that know understanding:	21 And He changes the times and the seasons; He removes kings and raises up kings; He gives wisdom to the wise And knowledge to those who have understanding.	21 World events are under his control. He removes kings and sets others on their thrones. He gives wise men their wisdom, and scholars their intelligence.
44 And in the days of these kings shall the God of heaven set up a kingdom, which shall never be destroyed: and the kingdom shall not be left to other people, *but* it shall break in pieces and consume all these kingdoms, and it shall stand for ever.	44 "And in the days of these kings the God of heaven will set up a kingdom which shall never be destroyed; and the kingdom shall not be left to other people; it shall break in pieces and consume all these kingdoms, and it shall stand forever.	44 "During the reigns of those kings, the God of heaven will set up a kingdom that will never be destroyed; no one will ever conquer it. It will shatter all these kingdoms into nothingness, but it shall stand forever, indestructible.
3:16 Shadrach, Meshach, and Abednego, answered and said to the king, O Nebuchadnezzar, we *are* not careful to answer thee in this matter.	3:16 Shadrach, Meshach, and Abed-Nego answered and said to the king, "O Nebuchadnezzar, we have no need to answer you in this matter.	3:16 Shadrach, Meshach, and Abednego replied, "O Nebuchadnezzar, we are not worried about what will happen to us.
17 If it be *so*, our God whom we serve is able to deliver us from the burning fiery furnace, and he will deliver *us* out of thine hand, O king.	17 "If that *is the case,* our God whom we serve is able to deliver us from the burning fiery furnace, and He will deliver *us* from your hand, O king.	17 If we are thrown into the flaming furnace, our God is able to deliver us; and he will deliver us out of your hand, Your Majesty.
18 But if not, be it known unto thee, O king, that we will not serve thy gods, nor worship the golden image which thou hast set up.	18 "But if not, let it be known to you, O king, that we do not serve your gods, nor will we worship the gold image which you have set up."	18 But if he doesn't, please understand, sir, that even then we will never under any circumstance serve your gods or worship the golden statue you have erected."
4:3 How great *are* his signs! and how mighty *are* his wonders! his kingdom *is* an everlasting kingdom, and his dominion *is* from generation to generation.	4:3 How great *are* His signs, And how mighty His wonders! His kingdom *is* an everlasting kingdom, And His dominion *is* from generation to generation.	4:3 It was incredible—a mighty miracle! And now I know for sure that his kingdom is everlasting; he reigns forever and ever.
34 And at the end of the days I Nebuchadnezzar lifted up mine eyes unto heaven, and mine understanding returned unto me, and I blessed the most High, and I praised and honoured him that liveth for ever, whose dominion *is* an everlasting dominion, and his kingdom *is* from generation to generation:	34 And at the end of the time I, Nebuchadnezzar, lifted my eyes to heaven, and my understanding returned to me; and I blessed the Most High and praised and honored Him who lives forever: For His dominion *is* an everlasting dominion, And His kingdom *is* from generation to generation.	34 "At the end of seven years I, Nebuchadnezzar, looked up to heaven, and my sanity returned, and I praised and worshiped the Most High God and honored him who lives forever, whose rule is everlasting, his kingdom evermore.
35 And all the inhabitants of the earth *are* reputed as nothing: and he doeth according to his will in the army of heaven, and *among* the inhabitants of the earth: and none can stay his hand, or say unto him, What doest thou?	35 All the inhabitants of the earth *are* reputed as nothing; He does according to His will in the army of heaven And *among* the inhabitants of the earth. No one can restrain His hand Or say to Him, "What have You done?"	35 All the people of the earth are nothing when compared to him; he does whatever he thinks best among the hosts of heaven, as well as here among the inhabitants of earth. No one can stop him or challenge him, saying, 'What do you mean by doing these things?'
5:5 In the same hour came forth fingers of a man's hand, and wrote over against the candlestick upon the plaister of the wall of the king's palace: and the king saw the part of the hand that wrote.	5:5 In the same hour the fingers of a man's hand appeared and wrote opposite the lampstand on the plaster of the wall of the king's palace; and the king saw the part of the hand that wrote.	5:5 Suddenly, as they were drinking from these cups, they saw the fingers of a man's hand writing on the plaster of the wall opposite the lampstand. The king himself saw the fingers as they wrote.
26 This *is* the interpretation of the thing: MENE; God hath numbered thy kingdom, and finished it.	26 "This *is* the interpretation of *each* word. MENE: God has numbered your kingdom, and finished it;	26 "This is what it means: "*Mene* means 'numbered'—God has numbered the days of your reign, and they are ended.
27 TEKEL; Thou art weighed in the balances, and art found wanting.	27 "TEKEL: You have been weighed in the balances, and found wanting;	27 "*Tekel* means 'weighed'—you have been weighed in God's balances and have failed the test.
28 PERES; Thy kingdom is divided, and given to the Medes and Persians.	28 "PERES: Your kingdom has been divided, and given to the Medes and Persians."	28 "*Parsin* means 'divided'—your kingdom will be divided and given to the Medes and Persians."
29 Then commanded Belshazzar, and they clothed Daniel with scarlet, and *put* a chain of gold about his neck, and made a proclamation concerning him, that he should be the third ruler in the kingdom.	29 Then Belshazzar gave the command, and they clothed Daniel with purple and *put* a chain of gold around his neck, and made a proclamation concerning him that he should be the third ruler in the kingdom.	29 Then at Belshazzar's command, Daniel was robed in purple, and a golden chain was hung around his neck, and he was proclaimed third ruler in the kingdom.
30 In that night was Belshazzar the king of the Chaldeans slain.	30 That very night Belshazzar, king of the Chaldeans, was slain.	30 That very night Belshazzar, the Chaldean king, was killed,

NIV	RSV	TEV
21 He changes times and seasons; he sets up kings and deposes them. He gives wisdom to the wise and knowledge to the discerning.	21 He changes times and seasons; he removes kings and sets up kings; he gives wisdom to the wise and knowledge to those who have understanding;	21 He controls the times and the seasons; he makes and unmakes kings; it is he who gives wisdom and understanding.
44 "In the time of those kings, the God of heaven will set up a kingdom that will never be destroyed, nor will it be left to another people. It will crush all those kingdoms and bring them to an end, but it will itself endure forever.	44 And in the days of those kings the God of heaven will set up a kingdom which shall never be destroyed, nor shall its sovereignty be left to another people. It shall break in pieces all these kingdoms and bring them to an end, and it shall stand for ever;	44 At the time of those rulers the God of heaven will establish a kingdom that will never end. It will never be conquered, but will completely destroy all those empires and then last forever.
3:16 Shadrach, Meshach and Abednego replied to the king, "O Nebuchadnezzar, we do not need to defend ourselves before you in this matter.	3:16 Shadrach, Meshach, and Abed-nego answered the king, "O Nebuchadnezzar, we have no need to answer you in this matter.	3:16 Shadrach, Meshach, and Abednego answered, "Your Majesty, we will not try to defend ourselves.
17 If we are thrown into the blazing furnace, the God we serve is able to save us from it, and he will rescue us from your hand, O king.	17 If it be so, our God whom we serve is able to deliver us from the burning fiery furnace; and he will deliver us out of your hand, O king.	17 If the God whom we serve is able to save us from the blazing furnace and from your power, then he will.
18 But even if he does not, we want you to know, O king, that we will not serve your gods or worship the image of gold you have set up."	18 But if not, be it known to you, O king, that we will not serve your gods or worship the golden image which you have set up."	18 But even if he doesn't, Your Majesty may be sure that we will not worship your god, and we will not bow down to the gold statue that you have set up."
4:3 How great are his signs, how mighty his wonders! His kingdom is an eternal kingdom; his dominion endures from generation to generation.	4:3 How great are his signs, how mighty his wonders! His kingdom is an everlasting kingdom, and his dominion is from generation to generation.	4:3 "How great are the wonders God shows us! How powerful are the miracles he performs! God is king forever; he will rule for all time.
34 At the end of that time, I, Nebuchadnezzar, raised my eyes toward heaven, and my sanity was restored. Then I praised the Most High; I honored and glorified him who lives forever. His dominion is an eternal dominion; his kingdom endures from generation to generation.	34 At the end of the days I, Nebuchadnezzar, lifted my eyes to heaven, and my reason returned to me, and I blessed the Most High, and praised and honored him who lives for ever; for his dominion is an everlasting dominion, and his kingdom endures from generation to generation;	34 "When the seven years had passed," said the king, "I looked up at the sky, and my sanity returned. I praised the Supreme God and gave honor and glory to the one who lives forever. "He will rule forever, and his kingdom will last for all time.
35 All the peoples of the earth are regarded as nothing. He does as he pleases with the powers of heaven and the peoples of the earth. No one can hold back his hand or say to him: "What have you done?"	35 all the inhabitants of the earth are accounted as nothing; and he does according to his will in the host of heaven and among the inhabitants of the earth; and none can stay his hand or say to him, "What doest thou?"	35 He looks on the people of the earth as nothing; angels in heaven and people on earth are under his control. No one can oppose his will or question what he does.
5:5 Suddenly the fingers of a human hand appeared and wrote on the plaster of the wall, near the lampstand in the royal palace. The king watched the hand as it wrote.	5:5 Immediately the fingers of a man's hand appeared and wrote on the plaster of the wall of the king's palace, opposite the lampstand; and the king saw the hand as it wrote.	5:5 Suddenly a human hand appeared and began writing on the plaster wall of the palace, where the light from the lamps was shining most brightly. And the king saw the hand as it was writing.
26 "This is what these words mean: Mene: God has numbered the days of your reign and brought it to an end.	26 This is the interpretation of the matter: MENE, God has numbered the days of your kingdom and brought it to an end;	26 And this is what it means: number, God has numbered the days of your kingdom and brought it to an end;
27 Tekel: You have been weighed on the scales and found wanting.	27 TEKEL, you have been weighed in the balances and found wanting;	27 weight, you have been weighed on the scales and found to be too light;
28 Peres: Your kingdom is divided and given to the Medes and Persians."	28 PERES, your kingdom is divided and given to the Medes, and Persians."	28 divisions, your kingdom is divided up and given to the Medes and Persians."
29 Then at Belshazzar's command, Daniel was clothed in purple, a gold chain was placed around his neck, and he was proclaimed the third highest ruler in the kingdom.	29 Then Belshazzar commanded, and Daniel was clothed with purple, a chain of gold was put about his neck, and proclamation was made concerning him, that he should be the third ruler in the kingdom.	29 Immediately Belshazzar ordered his servants to dress Daniel in a robe of royal purple and to hang a gold chain of honor around his neck. And he made him the third in power in the kingdom.
30 That very night Belshazzar, king of the Babylonians, was slain,	30 That very night Belshazzar the Chaldean king was slain.	30 That same night Belshazzar, the king of Babylonia, was killed;

KJV	NKJV	TLB
31 And Darius the Median took the kingdom, *being* about threescore and two years old.	31 And Darius the Mede received the kingdom, *being* about sixty-two years old.	31 and Darius the Mede entered the city and began reigning at the age of sixty-two.
6:16 Then the king commanded, and they brought Daniel, and cast *him* into the den of lions. *Now* the king spake and said unto Daniel, Thy God whom thou servest continually, he will deliver thee.	6:16 So the king gave the command, and they brought Daniel and cast *him* into the den of lions. *But* the king spoke, saying to Daniel, "Your God, whom you serve continually, He will deliver you."	6:16 So at last the king gave the order for Daniel's arrest, and he was taken to the den of lions. The king said to him, "May your God, whom you worship continually, deliver you." And then they threw him in.
17 And a stone was brought, and laid upon the mouth of the den; and the king sealed it with his own signet, and with the signet of his lords; that the purpose might not be changed concerning Daniel.	17 Then a stone was brought and laid on the mouth of the den, and the king sealed it with his own signet ring and with the signets of his lords, that the purpose concerning Daniel might not be changed.	17 A stone was brought and placed over the mouth of the den; and the king sealed it with his own signet ring, and that of his government, so that no one could rescue Daniel from the lions.
21 Then said Daniel unto the king, O king, live for ever.	21 Then Daniel said to the king, "O king, live forever!	21 Then he heard a voice! "Your Majesty, live forever!" It was Daniel!
22 My God hath sent his angel, and hath shut the lions' mouths, that they have not hurt me: forasmuch as before him innocency was found in me; and also before thee, O king, have I done no hurt.	22 "My God sent His angel and shut the lions' mouths, so that they have not hurt me, because I was found innocent before Him; and also, O king, I have done no wrong before you."	22 "My God has sent his angel," he said, "to shut the lions' mouths so that they can't touch me; for I am innocent before God, nor, sir, have I wronged you."
7:13 I saw in the night visions, and, behold, *one* like the Son of man came with the clouds of heaven, and came to the Ancient of days, and they brought him near before him.	7:13 "I was watching in the night visions, And behold, *One* like the Son of Man, Coming with the clouds of heaven! He came to the Ancient of Days, And they brought Him near before Him.	7:13 Next I saw the arrival of a Man—or so he seemed to be—brought there on clouds from heaven; he approached the Ancient of Days and was presented to him.
14 And there was given him dominion, and glory, and a kingdom, that all people, nations, and languages, should serve him: his dominion *is* an everlasting dominion, which shall not pass away, and his kingdom *that* which shall not be destroyed.	14 Then to Him was given dominion and glory and a kingdom, That all peoples, nations, and languages should serve Him. His dominion *is* an everlasting dominion, Which shall not pass away, And His kingdom *the one* Which shall not be destroyed.	14 He was given the ruling power and glory over all the nations of the world, so that all people of every language must obey him. His power is eternal—it will never end; his government shall never fall.
27 And the kingdom and dominion, and the greatness of the kingdom under the whole heaven, shall be given to the people of the saints of the most High, whose kingdom *is* an everlasting kingdom, and all dominions shall serve and obey him.	27 Then the kingdom and dominion, And the greatness of the kingdoms under the whole heaven, Shall be given to the people, the saints of the Most High. His kingdom *is* an everlasting kingdom, And all dominions shall serve and obey Him.'	27 Then every nation under heaven, and all their power, shall be given to the people of God; they shall rule all things forever, and all rulers shall serve and obey them."
9:24 Seventy weeks are determined upon thy people and upon thy holy city, to finish the transgression, and to make an end of sins, and to make reconciliation for iniquity, and to bring in everlasting righteousness, and to seal up the vision and prophecy, and to anoint the most Holy.	9:24 "Seventy weeks are determined For your people and for your holy city, To finish the transgression, To make an end of sins, To make reconciliation for iniquity, To bring in everlasting righteousness, To seal up vision and prophecy, And to anoint the Most Holy.	9:24 "The Lord has commanded 490 years of further punishment upon Jerusalem and your people. Then at last they will learn to stay away from sin, and their guilt will be cleansed; then the kingdom of everlasting righteousness will begin, and the Most Holy Place (in the Temple) will be rededicated, as the prophets have declared.
25 Know therefore and understand, *that* from the going forth of the commandment to restore and to build Jerusalem unto the Messiah the Prince *shall be* seven weeks, and threescore and two weeks: the street shall be built again, and the wall, even in troublous times.	25 "Know therefore and understand, *That* from the going forth of the command To restore and build Jerusalem Until Messiah the Prince, *There shall be* seven weeks and sixty-two weeks; The street shall be built again, and the wall, Even in troublesome times.	25 Now listen! It will be forty-nine years plus 434 years from the time the command is given to rebuild Jerusalem, until the Anointed One comes! Jerusalem's streets and walls will be rebuilt despite the perilous times.
26 And after threescore and two weeks shall Messiah be cut off, but not for himself: and the people of the prince that shall come shall destroy the city and the sanctuary; and the end thereof *shall be* with a flood, and unto the end of the war desolations are determined.	26 "And after the sixty-two weeks Messiah shall be cut off, but not for Himself; And the people of the prince who is to come Shall destroy the city and the sanctuary. The end of it *shall be* with a flood, And till the end of the war desolations are determined.	26 "After this period of 434 years, the Anointed One will be killed, his kingdom still unrealized . . . and a king will arise whose armies will destroy the city and the Temple. They will be overwhelmed as with a flood, and war and its miseries are decreed from that time to the very end."

NIV	RSV	TEV
31 and Darius the Mede took over the kingdom, at the age of sixty-two.	31 And Darius the Mede received the kingdom, being about sixty-two years old.	31 and Darius the Mede, who was then sixty-two years old, seized the royal power.
6:16 So the king gave the order, and they brought Daniel and threw him into the lions's den. The king said to Daniel, "May your God, whom you serve continually, rescue you!"	6:16 Then the king commanded, and Daniel was brought and cast into the den of lions. The king said to Daniel, "May your God, whom you serve continually, deliver you!"	6:16 So the king gave orders for Daniel to be taken and thrown into the pit filled with lions. He said to Daniel, "May your God, whom you serve so loyally, rescue you."
17 A stone was brought and placed over the mouth of the den, and the king sealed it with his own signet ring and with the rings of his nobles, so that Daniel's situation might not be changed.	17 And a stone was brought and laid upon the mouth of the den, and the king sealed it with his own signet and with the signet of his lords, that nothing might be changed concerning Daniel.	17 A stone was put over the mouth of the pit, and the king placed his own royal seal and the seal of his noblemen on the stone, so that no one could rescue Daniel.
21 Daniel answered, "O king, live forever!	21 Then Daniel said to the king, "O king, live for ever!	21 Daniel answered, "May Your Majesty live forever!
22 My God sent his angel, and he shut the mouths of the lions. They have not hurt me, because I was found innocent in his sight. Nor have I ever done any wrong before you, O king."	22 My God sent his angel and shut the lions' mouths, and they have not hurt me, because I was found blameless before him; and also before you, O king, I have done no wrong."	22 God sent his angel to shut the mouths of the lions so that they would not hurt me. He did this because he knew that I was innocent and because I have not wronged you, Your Majesty."
7:13 "In my vision at night I looked, and there before me was one like a son of man, coming with the clouds of heaven. He approached the Ancient of Days and was led into his presence.	7:13 I saw in the night visions, and behold, with the clouds of heaven there came one like a son of man, and he came to the Ancient of Days and was presented before him.	7:13 During this vision in the night, I saw what looked like a human being. He was approaching me, surrounded by clouds, and he went to the one who had been living forever and was presented to him.
14 He was given authority, glory and sovereign power; all peoples, nations and men of every language worshiped him. His dominion is an everlasting dominion that will not pass away, and his kingdom is one that will never be destroyed.	14 And to him was given dominion and glory and kingdom, that all peoples, nations, and languages should serve him; his dominion is an everlasting dominion, which shall not pass away, and his kingdom one that shall not be destroyed.	14 He was given authority, honor, and royal power, so that the people of all nations, races, and languages would serve him. His authority would last forever, and his kingdom would never end.
27 Then the sovereignty, power and greatness of the kingdoms under the whole heaven will be handed over to the saints, the people of the Most High. His kingdom will be an everlasting kingdom, and all rulers will worship and obey him.'	27 And the kingdom and the dominion and the greatness of the kingdoms under the whole heaven shall be given to the people of the saints of the Most High their kingdom shall be an everlasting kingdom, and all dominions shall serve and obey them.'	27 The power and greatness of all the kingdoms on earth will be given to the people of the Supreme God. Their royal power will never end, and all rulers on earth will serve and obey them."
9:24 "Seventy 'sevens' are decreed for your people and your holy city to finish transgression, to put an end to sin, to atone for wickedness, to bring in everlasting righteousness, to seal up vision and prophecy and to anoint the most holy.	9:24 "Seventy weeks of years are decreed concerning your people and your holy city, to finish the transgression, to put an end to sin, and to atone for iniquity, to bring in everlasting righteousness, to seal both vision and prophet, and to anoint a most holy place.	9:24 "Seven times seventy years is the length of time God has set for freeing your people and your holy city from sin and evil. Sin will be forgiven and eternal justice established, so that the vision and the prophecy will come true, and the holy Temple will be rededicated.
25 "Know and understand this: From the issuing of the decree to restore and rebuild Jerusalem until the Anointed One, the ruler, comes, there will be seven 'sevens,' and sixty-two 'sevens.' It will be rebuilt with streets and a trench, but in times of trouble.	25 Know therefore and understand that from the going forth of the word to restore and build Jerusalem to the coming of an anointed one, a prince, there shall be seven weeks. Then for sixty-two weeks it shall be built again with squares and moat, but in a troubled time.	25 Note this and understand it: From the time the command is given to rebuild Jerusalem until God's chosen leader comes, seven times seven years will pass. Jerusalem will be rebuilt with streets and strong defenses, and will stand for seven times sixty-two years, but this will be a time of troubles.
26 After the sixty-two 'sevens,' the Anointed One will be cut off and will have nothing. The people of the ruler who will come will destroy the city and the sanctuary. The end will come like a flood: War will continue until the end, and desolations have been decreed.	26 And after the sixty-two weeks, an anointed one shall be cut off, and shall have nothing; and the people of the prince who is to come shall destroy the city and the sanctuary. Its end shall come with a flood, and to the end there shall be war; desolations are decreed.	26 And at the end of that time God's chosen leader will be killed unjustly. The city and the Temple will be destroyed by the invading army of a powerful ruler. The end will come like a flood, bringing the war and destruction which God has prepared.

KJV	NKJV	TLB
27 And he shall confirm the covenant with many for one week: and in the midst of the week he shall cause the sacrifice and the oblation to cease, and for the overspreading of abominations he shall make *it* desolate, even until the consummation, and that determined shall be poured upon the desolate.	27 Then he shall confirm a covenant with many for one week; But in the middle of the week He shall bring an end to sacrifice and offering. And on the wing of abominations shall be one who makes desolate, Even until the consummation, which is determined, Is poured out on the desolate."	27 This king will make a seven-year treaty with the people, but after half that time, he will break his pledge and stop the Jews from all their sacrifices and their offerings; then, as a climax to all his terrible deeds, the Enemy shall utterly defile the sanctuary of God. But in God's time and plan, his judgment will be poured out upon this Evil One."
12:2 And many of them that sleep in the dust of the earth shall awake, some to everlasting life, and some to shame *and* everlasting contempt.	12:2 And many of those who sleep in the dust of the earth shall awake, Some to everlasting life, Some to shame *and* everlasting contempt.	12:2 "And many of those whose bodies lie dead and buried will rise up, some to everlasting life and some to shame and everlasting contempt.
3 And they that be wise shall shine as the brightness of the firmament; and they that turn many to righteousness as the stars for ever and ever.	3 Those who are wise shall shine Like the brightness of the firmament, And those who turn many to righteousness Like the stars forever and ever.	3 "And those who are wise—the people of God—shall shine as brightly as the sun's brilliance, and those who turn many to righteousness will glitter like stars forever.
4 But thou, O Daniel, shut up the words, and seal the book, *even* to the time of the end: many shall run to and fro, and knowledge shall be increased.	4 "But you, Daniel, shut up the words, and seal the book until the time of the end; many shall run to and fro, and knowledge shall increase."	4 "But Daniel, keep this prophecy a secret; seal it up so that it will not be understood until the end times, when travel and education shall be vastly increased!"
9 And he said, Go thy way, Daniel: for the words *are* closed up and sealed till the time of the end.	9 And he said, "Go *your way*, Daniel, for the words *are* closed up and sealed till the time of the end.	9 But he said, "Go now, Daniel, for what I have said is not to be understood until the time of the end.
10 Many shall be purified, and made white, and tried; but the wicked shall do wickedly: and none of the wicked shall understand; but the wise shall understand.	10 "Many shall be purified, made white, and refined, but the wicked shall do wickedly; and none of the wicked shall understand, but the wise shall understand.	10 Many shall be purified by great trials and persecutions. But the wicked shall continue in their wickedness, and none of them will understand. Only those who are willing to learn will know what it means.
13 But go thou thy way till the end *be:* for thou shalt rest; and stand in thy lot at the end of the days.	13 "But you, go *your way* till the end; for you shall rest, and will arise to your inheritance at the end of the days."	13 "But go on now to the end of your life and your rest; for you will rise again and have your full share of those last days."

Hosea

KJV	NKJV	TLB
1:2 The beginning of the word of the LORD by Hosea. And the LORD said to Hosea, Go, take unto thee a wife of whoredoms and children of whoredoms: for the land hath committed great whoredom, *departing* from the LORD.	1:2 *When* the LORD began to speak by Hosea, the LORD said to Hosea: "Go, take yourself a wife of harlotry And children of harlotry, For the land has committed great harlotry *By departing* from the LORD."	1:2 Here is the first message: The Lord said to Hosea, "Go and marry a girl who is a prostitute, so that some of her children will be born to you from other men. This will illustrate the way my people have been untrue to me, committing open adultery against me by worshiping other gods."
3 So he went and took Gomer the daughter of Diblaim; which conceived, and bare him a son.	3 So he went and took Gomer the daughter of Diblaim, and she conceived and bore him a son.	3 So Hosea married Gomer, daughter of Diblaim, and she conceived and bore him a son.
4 And the LORD said unto him, Call his name Jezreel; for yet a little *while,* and I will avenge the blood of Jezreel upon the house of Jehu, and will cause to cease the kingdom of the house of Israel.	4 Then the LORD said to him: "Call his name Jezreel, For in a little *while* I will avenge the bloodshed of Jezreel on the house of Jehu, And bring an end to the kingdom of the house of Israel.	4 And the Lord said, "Name the child Jezreel, for in the Valley of Jezreel I am about to punish King Jehu's dynasty to avenge the murders he committed; in fact, I will put an end to Israel as an independent kingdom,
5 And it shall come to pass at that day, that I will break the bow of Israel in the valley of Jezreel.	5 It shall come to pass in that day That I will break the bow of Israel in the Valley of Jezreel."	5 breaking the power of the nation in the Valley of Jezreel."
6 And she conceived again, and bare a daughter. And *God* said unto him, Call her name Loruhamah: for I will no more have mercy upon the house of Israel; but I will utterly take them away.	6 And she conceived again and bore a daughter. Then *God* said to him: "Call her name Lo-Ruhamah, For I will no longer have mercy on the house of Israel, But I will utterly take them away.	6 Soon Gomer had another child—this one a daughter. And God said to Hosea, "Name her Lo-ruhamah (meaning 'No more mercy') for I will have no more mercy upon Israel, to forgive her again.

NIV	RSV	TEV
27 He will confirm a covenant with many for one 'seven,' but in the middle of that 'seven' he will put an end to sacrifice and offering. And one who causes desolation will place abominations on a wing of the temple until the end that is decreed is poured out on him."	27 And he shall make a strong covenant with many for one week; and for half of the week he shall cause sacrifice and offering to cease; and upon the wing of abominations shall come one who makes desolate, until the decreed end is poured out on the desolator."	27 That ruler will have a firm agreement with many people for seven years, and when half this time is past, he will put an end to sacrifices and offerings. The Awful Horror will be placed on the highest point of the Temple and will remain there until the one who put it there meets the end which God has prepared for him."
12:2 Multitudes who sleep in the dust of the earth will awake: some to everlasting life, others to shame and everlasting contempt.	12:2 And many of those who sleep in the dust of the earth shall awake, some to everlasting life, and some to shame and everlasting contempt.	12:2 Many of those who have already died will live again: some will enjoy eternal life, and some will suffer eternal disgrace.
3 Those who are wise will shine like the brightness of the heavens, and those who lead many to righteousness, like the stars for ever and ever.	3 And those who are wise shall shine like the brightness of the firmament; and those who turn many to righteousness, like the stars for ever and ever.	3 The wise leaders will shine with all the brightness of the sky. And those who have taught many people to do what is right will shine like the stars forever."
4 But you, Daniel, close up and seal the words of the scroll until the time of the end. Many will go here and there to increase knowledge."	4 But you, Daniel, shut up the words, and seal the book, until the time of the end. Many shall run to and fro, and knowledge shall increase."	4 He said to me, "And now, Daniel, close the book and put a seal on it until the end of the world. Meanwhile, many people will waste their efforts trying to understand what is happening."
9 He replied, "Go your way, Daniel, because the words are closed up and sealed until the time of the end.	9 He said, "Go your way, Daniel, for the words are shut up and sealed until the time of the end.	9 He answered, "You must go now, Daniel, because these words are to be kept secret and hidden until the end comes.
10 Many will be purified, made spotless and refined, but the wicked will continue to be wicked. None of the wicked will understand, but those who are wise will understand.	10 Many shall purify themselves, and make themselves white, and be refined; but the wicked shall do wickedly; and none of the wicked shall understand; but those who are wise shall understand.	10 Many people will be purified. Those who are wicked will not understand but will go on being wicked; only those who are wise will understand.
13 "As for you, go your way till the end. You will rest; and then at the end of the days you will rise to receive your allotted inheritance."	13 But go your way till the end; and you shall rest, and shall stand in your allotted place at the end of the days."	13 "And you, Daniel, be faithful to the end. Then you will die, but you will rise to receive your reward at the end of time."

Hosea

NIV	RSV	TEV
1:2 When the LORD began to speak through Hosea, the LORD said to him, "Go, take to yourself an adulterous wife and children of unfaithfulness, because the land is guilty of the vilest adultery in departing from the LORD."	1:2 When the LORD first spoke through Hosea, the LORD said to Hosea, "Go, take to yourself a wife of harlotry and have children of harlotry, for the land commits great harlotry by forsaking the LORD."	1:2 When the LORD first spoke to Israel through Hosea, he said to Hosea, "Go and get married; your wife will be unfaithful, and your children will be just like her. In the same way my people have left me and become unfaithful."
3 So he married Gomer daughter of Diblaim, and she conceived and bore him a son.	3 So he went and took Gomer the daughter of Diblaim, and she conceived and bore him a son.	3 So Hosea married a woman named Gomer, the daughter of Diblaim. After the birth of their first child, a son.
4 Then the LORD said to Hosea, "Call him Jezreel, because I will soon punish the house of Jehu for the massacre at Jezreel, and I will put an end to the kingdom of Israel.	4 And the LORD said to him, "Call his name Jezreel; for yet a little while, and I will punish the house of Jehu for the blood of Jezreel, and I will put an end to the kingdom of the house of Israel.	4 the LORD said to Hosea, "Name him 'Jezreel,' because it will not be long before I punish the king of Israel for the murders that his ancestor Jehu committed at Jezreel. I am going to put an end to Jehu's dynasty.
5 In that day I will break Israel's bow in the Valley of Jezreel."	5 And on that day, I will break the bow of Israel in the valley of Jezreel."	5 And in Jezreel Valley I will at that time destroy Israel's military power."
6 Gomer conceived again and gave birth to a daughter. Then the LORD said to Hosea, "Call her Lo-Ruhamah, for I will no longer show love to the house of Israel, that I should at all forgive them.	6 She conceived again and bore a daughter. And the LORD said to him, "Call her name Not pitied, for I will no more have pity on the house of Israel, to forgive them at all.	6 Gomer had a second child—this time it was a girl. The LORD said to Hosea, "Name her 'Unloved,' because I will no longer show love to the people of Israel or forgive them.

130   Hosea 1:7
            Hosea 11:9
            KEY VERSE COMPARISON CHART

KJV	NKJV	TLB
7 But I will have mercy upon the house of Judah, and will save them by the LORD their God, and will not save them by bow, nor by sword, nor by battle, by horses, nor by horsemen.	7 Yet I will have mercy on the house of Judah, Will save them by the LORD their God, And will not save them by bow, Nor by sword or battle, By horses or horsemen."	7 But I *will* have mercy on the tribe of Judah. I will personally free her from her enemies without any help from her armies or her weapons."
8 Now when she had weaned Loruhamah, she conceived, and bare a son.	8 Now when she had weaned Lo-Ruhamah, she conceived and bore a son.	8 After Gomer had weaned Lo-ruhamah, she again conceived and this time gave birth to a son.
9 Then said *God*, Call his name Loammi: for ye *are* not my people, and I will not be your *God*.	9 Then *God* said: "Call his name Lo-Ammi, For you *are* not My people, And I will not be your *God*.	9 And God said, "Call him Lo-ammi (meaning 'Not mine'), for Israel is not mine and I am not her God.
10 Yet the number of the children of Israel shall be as the sand of the sea, which cannot be measured nor numbered; and it shall come to pass, *that* in the place where it was said unto them, Ye *are* not my people, *there* it shall be said unto them, Ye *are* the sons of the living God.	10 "Yet the number of the children of Israel Shall be as the sand of the sea, Which cannot be measured or numbered. And it shall come to pass In the place where it was said to them, 'You *are* not My people,' *There* it shall be said to them, 'You *are* the sons of the living God.'	10 "Yet the time will come when Israel shall prosper and become a great nation; in that day her people will be too numerous to count—like sand along a seashore! Then, instead of saying to them, 'You are not my people,' I will tell them, 'You are my sons, children of the Living God.'
11 Then shall the children of Judah and the children of Israel be gathered together, and appoint themselves one head, and they shall come up out of the land: for great *shall be* the day of Jezreel.	11 Then the children of Judah and the children of Israel Shall be gathered together, And appoint for themselves one head; And they shall come up out of the land, For great *will be* the day of Jezreel!	11 Then the people of Judah and Israel will unite and have one leader; they will return from exile together; what a day that will be—the day when God will sow his people in the fertile soil of their own land again."
3:4 For the children of Israel shall abide many days without a king, and without a prince, and without a sacrifice, and without an image, and without an ephod, and *without* teraphim:	3:4 For the children of Israel shall abide many days without king or prince, without sacrifice or sacred pillar, without ephod or teraphim.	3:4 This illustrates the fact that Israel will be a long time without a king or prince, and without an altar, temple, priests, or even idols!
5 Afterward shall the children of Israel return, and seek the LORD their God, and David their king; and shall fear the LORD and his goodness in the latter days.	5 Afterward the children of Israel shall return, seek the LORD their God and David their king, and fear the LORD and His goodness in the latter days.	5 Afterward they will return to the Lord their God, and to the Messiah, their King, and they shall come trembling, submissive to the Lord and to his blessings, in the end times.
6:1 Come, and let us return unto the LORD: for he hath torn, and he will heal us; he hath smitten, and he will bind us up.	6:1 Come, and let us return to the LORD; For He has torn, but He will heal us; He has stricken, but He will bind us up.	6:1 "Come, let us return to the Lord; it is he who has torn us—he will heal us. He has wounded—he will bind us up.
6 For I desired mercy, and not sacarifice; and the knowledge of God more than burnt offerings.	6 For I desire mercy and not sacrifice, And the knowledge of God more than burnt offerings.	6 I don't want your sacrifices—I want your love; I don't want your offerings—I want you to know me.
8:7 For they have sown the wind, and they shall reap the whirlwind: it hath no stalk: the bud shall yield no meal: if so be it yield, the strangers shall swallow it up.	8:7 "They sow the wind, And reap the whirlwind. The stalk has no bud; It shall never produce meal. If it should produce, Aliens would swallow it up.	8:7 They have sown the wind and they will reap the whirlwind. Their cornstalks stand there barren, withered, sickly, with no grain; if it has any, foreigners will eat it.
9:17 My God will cast them away, because they did not hearken unto him: and they shall be wanderers among the nations.	9:17 My God will cast them away, Because they did not obey Him; And they shall be wanderers among the nations.	9:17 My God will destroy the people of Israel because they will not listen or obey. They will be wandering Jews, homeless among the nations.
11:1 When Israel *was* a child, then I loved him, and called my son out of Egypt.	11:1 "When Israel *was* a child, I loved him, And out of Egypt I called My son.	11:1 When Israel was a child I loved him as a son and brought him out of Egypt.
8 How shall I give thee up, Ephraim? how shall I deliver thee, Israel? how shall I make thee as Admah? how shall I set thee as Zeboim? mine heart is turned within me, my repentings are kindled together.	8 "How can I give you up, Ephraim? *How* can I hand you over, Israel? How can I make you like Admah? *How* can I set you like Zeboiim? My heart churns within Me; My sympathy is stirred.	8 Oh, how can I give you up, my Ephraim? How can I let you go? How can I forsake you like Admah and Zeboiim? My heart cries out within me; how I long to help you!
9 I will not execute the fierceness of mine anger, I will not return to destroy Ephraim: for I *am* God, and not man; the Holy One in the midst of thee: and I will not enter into the city.	9 I will not execute the fierceness of My anger; I will not again destroy Ephraim. For I *am* God, and not man, The Holy One in your midst; And I will not come with terror.	9 No, I will not punish you as much as my fierce anger tells me to. This is the last time I will destroy Ephraim. For I am God and not man; I am the Holy One living among you, and I did not come to destroy.

NIV	RSV	TEV
7 Yet I will show love to the house of Judah; and I will save them—not by bow, sword or battle, or by horses and horsemen, but by the LORD their God."	7 But I will have pity on the house of Judah, and I will deliver them by the LORD their God; I will not deliver them by bow, nor by sword, nor by war, nor by horses, nor by horsemen."	7 But to the people of Judah I will show love. I, the LORD their God, will save them, but I will not do it by war—with swords or bows and arrows or with horses and horsemen."
8 After she had weaned Lo-Ruhamah, Gomer had another son.	8 When she had weaned Not pitied, she conceived and bore a son.	8 After Gomer had weaned her daughter, she became pregnant again and had another son.
9 Then the LORD said, "Call him Lo-Ammi, for you are not my people, and I am not your God.	9 And the LORD said, "Call his name Not my people, for you are not my people and I am not your God."	9 The LORD said to Hosea, "Name him 'Not-My-People,' because the people of Israel are not my people, and I am not their God."
10 "Yet the Israelites will be like the sand on the seashore, which cannot be measured or counted. In the place where it was said to them, 'You are not my people,' they will be called 'sons of the living God.'	10 Yet the number of the people of Israel shall be like the sand of the sea, which can be neither measured nor numbered; and in the place where it was said to them, "You are not my people," it shall be said to them, "Sons of the living God."	10 The people of Israel will become like the sand of the sea, more than can be counted or measured. Now God says to them, "You are not my people," but the day is coming when he will say to them, "You are the children of the living God!"
11 The people of Judah and the people of Israel will be reunited, and they will appoint one leader and will come up out of the land, for great will be the day of Jezreel.	11 And the people of Judah and the people of Israel shall be gathered together, and they shall appoint for themselves one head; and they shall go up from the land, for great shall be the day of Jezreel.	11 The people of Judah and the people of Israel will be reunited. They will choose for themselves a single leader, and once again they will grow and prosper in their land. Yes, the day of Jezreel will be a great day!
3:4 For the Israelites will live many days without king or prince, without sacrifice or sacred stones, without ephod or idol.	3:4 For the children of Israel shall dwell many days without king or prince, without sacrifice or pillar, without ephod or teraphim.	3:4 In this way the people of Israel will have to live for a long time without kings or leaders, without sacrifices or sacred stone pillars, without idols or images to use for divination.
5 Afterward the Israelites will return and seek the LORD their God and David their king. They will come trembling to the LORD and to his blessings in the last days.	5 Afterward the children of Israel shall return and seek the LORD their God, and David their king; and they shall come in fear to the LORD and to his goodness in the latter days.	5 But the time will come when the people of Israel will once again turn to the LORD their God and to a descendant of David their king. Then they will fear the LORD and will receive his good gifts.
6:1 "Come, let us return to the LORD. He has torn us to pieces but he will heal us; he has injured us but he will bind up our wounds.	6:1 "Come, let us return to the LORD; for he has torn, that he may heal us; He has stricken and he will bind us up.	6:1 The people say, "Let's return to the LORD! He has hurt us, but he will be sure to heal us; he has wounded us, but he will bandage our wounds, won't he?
6 For I desire mercy, not sacrifice, and acknowledgment of God rather than burnt offerings.	6 For I desire steadfast love and not sacrifice, the knowledge of God, rather than burnt offerings.	6 I want your constant love, not your animal sacrifices. I would rather have my people know me than burn offerings to me.
8:7 "They sow the wind and reap the whirlwind. The stalk has no head; it will produce no flour. Were it to yield grain, foreigners would swallow it up.	8:7 For they sow the wind, and they shall reap the whirlwind. The standing grain has no heads, it shall yield no meal; if it were to yield, aliens would devour it.	8:7 When they sow the wind, they will reap a storm! A field of grain that doesn't ripen can never produce any bread. But even if it did, foreigners would eat it up.
9:17 My God will reject them because they have not obeyed him; they will be wanderers among the nations.	9:17 My God will cast them off, because they have not hearkened to him; they shall be wanderers among the nations.	9:17 The God I serve will reject his people, because they have not listened to him. They will become wanderers among the nations.
11:1 "When Israel was a child, I loved him, and out of Egypt I called my son.	11:1 When Israel was a child, I loved him, and out of Egypt I called my son.	11:1 The LORD says, "When Israel was a child, I loved him and called him out of Egypt as my son.
8 "How can I give you up, Ephraim? How can I hand you over, Israel? How can I treat you like Admah? How can I make you like Zeboiim? My heart is changed within me; all my compassion is aroused.	8 How can I give you up, O Ephraim! How can I hand you over, O Israel! How can I make you like Admah! How can I treat you like Zeboiim! My heart recoils within me, my compassion grows warm and tender.	8 "How can I give you up, Israel? How can I abandon you? Could I ever destroy you as I did Admah, or treat you as I did Zeboiim? My heart will not let me do it! My love for you is too strong.
9 I will not carry out my fierce anger, nor devastate Ephraim again. For I am God, and not man— the Holy One among you. I will not come in wrath.	9 I will not execute my fierce anger, I will not again destroy Ephraim; for I am God and not man, the Holy One in your midst, and I will not come to destroy.	9 I will not punish you in my anger; I will not destroy Israel again. For I am God and not man. I, the Holy One, am with you. I will not come to you in anger.

KJV	NKJV	TLB
13:14 I will ransom them from the power of the grave; I will redeem them from death: O death, I will be thy plagues; O grave, I will be thy destruction: repentance shall be hid from mine eyes.	**13:14** "I will ransom them from the power of the grave; I will redeem them from death. O Death, I will be your plagues! O Grave, I will be your destruction! Pity is hidden from My eyes.	**13:14** Shall I ransom him from hell? Shall I redeem him from Death? O Death, bring forth your terrors for his tasting! O Grave, demonstrate your plagues! For I will not relent!
14:3 Asshur shall not save us; we will not ride upon horses: neither will we say any more to the work of our hands, *Ye are* our gods: for in thee the fatherless findeth mercy.	**14:3** Assyria shall not save us, We will not ride on horses, Nor will we say anymore to the work of our hands, '*You are* our gods.' For in You the fatherless finds mercy."	**14:3** Assyria cannot save us, nor can our strength in battle; never again will we call the idols we have made 'our gods'; for in you alone, O Lord, the fatherless find mercy."
4 I will heal their backsliding, I will love them freely; for mine anger is turned away from him.	**4** "I will heal their backsliding, I will love them freely, For My anger has turned away from him.	**4** Then I will cure you of idolatry and faithlessness, and my love will know no bounds, for my anger will be forever gone!

Joel

1:4 That which the palmerworm hath left hath the locust eaten; and that which the locust hath left hath the cankerworm eaten; and that which the cankerworm hath left hath the caterpiller eaten.	**1:4** What the chewing locust left, the swarming locust has eaten; What the swarming locust left, the crawling locust has eaten; And what the crawling locust left, the consuming locust has eaten.	**1:4** After the cutter-locusts finish eating your crops, the swarmer-locusts will take what's left! After them will come the hopper-locusts! And then the stripper-locusts, too!
15 Alas for the day! for the day of the LORD *is* at hand, and as a destruction from the Almighty shall it come.	**15** Alas for the day! For the day of the LORD *is* at hand; It shall come as destruction from the Almighty.	**15** Alas, this terrible day of punishment is on the way. Destruction from the Almighty is almost here!
2:1 Blow ye the trumpet in Zion, and sound an alarm in my holy mountain: let all the inhabitants of the land tremble: for the day of the LORD cometh, for *it is* nigh at hand;	**2:1** Blow the trumpet in Zion, And sound an alarm in My holy mountain! Let all the inhabitants of the land tremble; For the day of the LORD is coming, For it is at hand:	**2:1** Sound the alarm in Jerusalem! Let the blast of the warning trumpet be heard upon my holy mountain! Let everyone tremble in fear, for the day of the Lord's judgment approaches.
2 A day of darkness and of gloominess, a day of clouds and of thick darkness, as the morning spread upon the mountains: a great people and a strong; there hath not been ever the like, neither shall be any more after it, *even* to the years of many generations.	**2** A day of darkness and gloominess, A day of clouds and thick darkness, Like the morning *clouds* spread over the mountains. A people *come*, great and strong, The like of whom has never been; Nor will there ever be any *such* after them, Even for many successive generations.	**2** It is a day of darkness and gloom, of black clouds and thick darkness. What a mighty army! It covers the mountains like night! How great, how powerful these "people" are! The likes of them have not been seen before, and never will again throughout the generations of the world!
12 Therefore also now, saith the LORD, Turn ye *even* to me with all your heart, and with fasting, and with weeping, and with mourning:	**12** "Now, therefore," says the LORD, "Turn to me with all your heart, With fasting, with weeping, and with mourning."	**12** That is why the Lord says, "Turn to me now, while there is time. Give me all your hearts. Come with fasting, weeping, mourning.
13 And rend your heart, and not your garments, and turn unto the LORD your God: for he *is* gracious and merciful, slow to anger, and of great kindness, and repenteth him of the evil.	**13** So rend your heart, and not your garments; Return to the LORD your God, For He *is* gracious and merciful, Slow to anger, and of great kindness; And He relents from doing harm.	**13** Let your remorse tear at your hearts and not your garments." Return to the Lord your God, for he is gracious and merciful. He is not easily angered; he is full of kindness, and anxious not to punish you.
25 And I will restore to you the years that the locust hath eaten, the cankerworm, and the caterpiller, and the palmerworm, my great army which I sent among you.	**25** "So I will restore to you the years that the swarming locust has eaten, The crawling locust, The consuming locust, And the chewing locust, My great army which I sent among you.	**25** And I will give you back the crops the locusts ate!—my great destroying army that I sent against you.
3:1 For, behold, in those days, and in that time, when I shall bring again the captivity of Judah and Jerusalem,	**3:1** "For behold, in those days and at that time, When I bring back the captives of Judah and Jerusalem,	**3:1** "At that time, when I restore the prosperity of Judah and Jerusalem," says the Lord,

NIV	RSV	TEV
13:14 "I will ransom them from the power of the grave; I will redeem them from death. Where, O death, are your plagues? Where, O grave, is your destruction?" "I will have no compassion,	**13:14** Shall I ransom them from the power of Sheol? Shall I redeem them from Death? O Death, where are your plagues? O Sheol, where is your destruction? Compassion is hid from my eyes.	**13:14** I will not save this people from the world of the dead or rescue them from the power of death. Bring on your plagues, death! Bring on your destruction, world of the dead! I will no longer have pity for this people.
14:3 Assyria cannot save us; we will not mount war-horses. We will never again say 'Our gods' to what our own hands have made, for in you the fatherless find compassion."	**14:3** Assyria shall not save us, we will not ride upon horses; and we will say no more, 'Our God,' to the work of our hands. In thee the orphan finds mercy."	**14:3** Assyria can never save us, and war horses cannot protect us. We will never again say to our idols that they are our God. O LORD, you show mercy to those who have no one else to turn to."
4 "I will heal their waywardness and love them freely, for my anger has turned away from them.	**4** I will heal their faithlessness; I will love them freely, for my anger has turned from them.	**4** The LORD says, "I will bring my people back to me. I will love them with all my heart; no longer am I angry with them.

Joel

NIV	RSV	TEV
1:4 What the locust swarm has left the great locusts have eaten; what the great locusts have left the young locusts have eaten; what the young locusts have left other locusts have eaten.	**1:4** What the cutting locust left, the swarming locust has eaten. What the swarming locust left, the hopping locust has eaten, and what the hopping locust left, the destroying locust has eaten.	**1:4** Swarm after swarm of locusts settled on the crops; what one swarm left, the next swarm devoured.
15 What a dreadful day! For the day of the LORD is near; it will come like destruction from the Almighty.	**15** Alas for the day! For the day of the LORD is near, and as destruction from the Almighty it comes.	**15** The day of the LORD is near, the day when the Almighty brings destruction. What terror that day will bring!
2:1 Blow the trumpet in Zion; sound the alarm on my holy hill. Let all who live in the land tremble, for the day of the LORD is coming. It is close at hand—	**2:1** Blow the trumpet in Zion; sound the alarm on my holy mountain! Let all the inhabitants of the land tremble, for the day of the LORD is coming, it is near,	**2:1** Blow the trumpet; sound the alarm on Zion, God's sacred hill. Tremble, people of Judah! The day of the LORD is coming soon.
2 a day of darkness and gloom, a day of clouds and blackness. Like dawn spreading across the mountains a large and mighty army comes, such as never was of old nor ever will be in ages to come.	**2** a day of darkness and gloom, a day of clouds and thick darkness! Like blackness there is spread upon the mountains a great and powerful people; their like has never been from of old, nor will be again after them through the years of all generations.	**2** It will be a dark and gloomy day, a black and cloudy day. The great army of locusts advances like darkness spreaking over the mountains. There has never been anything like it, and there never will be again.
12 "Even now," declares the LORD, "return to me with all your heart, with fasting and weeping and mourning."	**12** "Yet even now," says the LORD, "return to me with all your heart, with fasting, with weeping, and with mourning;	**12** "But even now," says the LORD, "repent sincerely and return to me with fasting and weeping and mourning.
13 Rend your heart and not your garments. Return to the LORD your God, for he is gracious and compassionate, slow to anger and abounding in love, and he relents from sending calamity.	**13** and rend your hearts and not your garments." Return to the LORD, your God, for he is gracious and merciful, slow to anger, and abounding in steadfast love, and repents of evil.	**13** Let your broken heart show your sorrow; tearing your clothes is not enough." Come back to the LORD your God. He is kind and full of mercy; he is patient and keeps his promise; he is always ready to forgive and not punish.
25 "I will repay you for the years the locusts have eaten— the great locust and the young locust, the other locusts and the locust swarm" my great army that I sent among you.	**25** I will restore to you the years which the swarming locust has eaten, the hopper, the destroyer, and the cutter, my great army, which I sent among you.	**25** I will give you back what you lost in the years when swarms of locusts are your crops. It was I who sent this army against you.
3:1 "In those days and at that time, when I restore the fortunes of Judah and Jerusalem,	**3:1** "For behold, in those days and at that time, when I restore the fortunes of Judah and Jerusalem,	**3:1** The LORD says, "At that time I will restore the prosperity of Judah and Jerusalem.

KJV	NKJV	TLB
2 I will also gather all nations, and will bring them down into the valley of Jehoshaphat, and will plead with them there for my people and *for* my heritage Israel, whom they have scattered among the nations, and parted my land.	2 I will also gather all nations, And bring them down to the Valley of Jehoshaphat; And I will enter into judgment with them there On account of My people, My heritage Israel, Whom they have scattered among the nations; They have also divided up My land.	2 "I will gather the armies of the world into the "Valley Where Jehovah Judges" and punish them there for harming my people, for scattering my inheritance among the nations and dividing up my land.
10 Beat your plowshares into swords, and your pruninghooks into spears: let the weak say, I *am* strong.	10 Beat your plowshares into swords And your pruninghooks into spears; Let the weak say, 'I *am* strong.'"	10 Melt your plowshares into swords and beat your pruning hooks into spears. Let the weak be strong.
18 And it shall come to pass in that day, *That* the mountains shall drop down new wine, and the hills shall flow with milk, and all the rivers of Judah shall flow with waters, and a fountain shall come forth of the house of the LORD, and shall water the valley of Shittim.	18 And it will come to pass in that day *That* the mountains shall drip with new wine, The hills shall flow with milk, And all the brooks of Judah shall be flooded with water; A fountain shall flow from the house of the LORD And water the Valley of Acacias.	18 "Sweet wine will drip from the mountains, and the hills shall flow with milk. Water will fill the dry stream beds of Judah, and a fountain will burst forth from the Temple of the Lord to water Acacia Valley.

Amos

KJV	NKJV	TLB
1:3 Thus saith the LORD; For three transgressions of Damascus, and for four, I will not turn away *the punishment* thereof; because they have threshed Gilead with threshing instruments of iron:	**1:3** Thus says the LORD: "For three transgressions of Damascus, and for four, I will not turn away its *punishment*, Because they have threshed Gilead with implements of iron.	**1:3** The Lord says, "The people of Damascus have sinned again and again, and I will not forget it. I will not leave her unpunished any more. For they have threshed my people in Gilead as grain is threshed with iron rods.
2:4 Thus saith the LORD; For three transgressions of Judah, and for four, I will not turn away *the punishment* thereof; because they have despised the law of the LORD, and have not kept his commandments, and their lies caused them to err, after the which their fathers have walked:	**2:4** Thus says the LORD: "For three transgressions of Judah, and for four, I will not turn away its *punishment*, Because they have despised the law of the LORD, And have not kept His commandments. Their lies lead them astray, *Lies* after which their fathers walked.	**2:4** The Lord says, "The people of Judah have sinned again and again, and I will not forget it. I will not leave them unpunished any more. For they have rejected the laws of God, refusing to obey him. They have hardened their hearts and sinned as their fathers did.
3:2 You only have I known of all the families of the earth: therefore I will punish you for all your iniquities.	**3:2** "You only have I known of all the families of the earth; Therefore I will punish you for all your iniquities."	**3:2** "Of all the peoples of the earth, I have chosen you alone. That is why I must punish you the more for all your sins.
3 Can two walk together, except they be agreed?	3 Can two walk together, unless they are agreed?	3 For how can we walk together with your sins between us?
4:12 Therefore thus will I do unto thee, O Israel: *and* because I will do this unto thee, prepare to meet thy God, O Israel.	**4:12** "Therefore thus will I do to you, O Israel; *And* because I will do this to you, Prepare to meet your God, O Israel!"	**4:12** "Therefore I will bring upon you all these further evils I have spoken of. Prepare to meet your God in judgment, Israel.
5:14 Seek good, and not evil, that ye may live: and so the LORD, the God of hosts, shall be with you, as ye have spoken.	**5:14** Seek good and not evil, That you may live; So the LORD God of hosts will be with you, As you have spoken.	**5:14** Be good, flee evil—and live! Then the Lord God of Hosts will truly be your Helper, as you have claimed he is.
21 I hate, I despise your feast days, and I will not smell in your solemn assemblies.	21 "I hate, I despise your feast days, And I do not savor your sacred assemblies.	21 "I hate your show and pretense—your hypocrisy of 'honoring' me with your religious feasts and solemn assemblies.
22 Though ye offer me burnt offerings and your meat offerings, I will not accept *them*: neither will I regard the peace offerings of your fat beasts.	22 Though you offer Me burnt offerings and your grain offerings, I will not accept *them*, Nor will I regard your fattened peace offerings.	22 I will not accept your burnt offerings and thank offerings. I will not look at your offerings of peace.

NIV	RSV	TEV

2 I will gather all nations
  and bring them down to the Valley of
  Jehoshaphat.
There I will enter into judgment against
  them
  concerning my inheritance, my people
  Israel,
for they scattered my people among the
  nations
  and divided up my land.
	2 I will gather all the nations and bring them
	down to the valley of Jehoshaphat, and I will
	enter into judgment with them there, on account
	of my people and my heritage Israel, because
	they have scattered them among the nations, and
	have divided up my land.
		2 I will gather all the nations
		  and bring them to the Valley of Judgment.
		There I will judge them
		  for all they have done to my people.
		They have scattered the Israelites in foreign
		  countries
		  and divided Israel, my land.

10 Beat your plowshares into swords
  and your pruning hooks into spears.
Let the weakling say,
  "I am strong!"
	10 Beat your plowshares into swords,
	  and your pruning hooks into spears;
	  let the weak say, "I am a warrior."
		10 Hammer the points of your plows into
		  swords
		  and your pruning knives into spears.
		Even the weak must fight.

18 "In that day the mountains will drip new
  wine,
  and the hills will flow with milk;
all the ravines of Judah will run with
  water.
A fountain will flow out of the LORD's
  house
  and will water the valley of acacias.
	18 "And in that day
	  the mountains shall drip sweet wine,
	  and the hills shall flow with milk,
	and all the stream beds of Judah
	  shall flow with water;
	and a fountain shall come forth from the
	  house of the LORD
	  and water the valley of Shittim.
		18 At that time the mountains will be covered
		  with vineyards,
		  and cattle will be found on every hill;
		  there will be plenty of water for all of
		  Judah.
		A stream will flow from the Temple of the
		  LORD,
		  and it will water Acacia Valley.

Amos

NIV	RSV	TEV

1:3 This is what the LORD says:
 	
"For three sins of Damascus,
  even for four, I will not turn back my
  wrath.
Because she threshed Gilead
  with sledges having iron teeth,
	1:3 Thus says the LORD:
	"For three transgressions of Damascus,
	  and for four, I will not revoke the
	  punishment;
	because they have threshed Gilead
	  with threshing sledges of iron.
		1:3 The LORD says, "The people of Damascus
		have sinned again and again, and for this I will
		certainly punish them. They treated the people
		of Gilead with savage cruelty.

2:4 This is what the LORD says:
 	
"For three sins of Judah,
  even for four, I will not turn back my
  wrath.
Because they have rejected the law of the
  LORD
  and have not kept his decrees,
because they have been led astray by
  false gods,
  the gods their ancestors followed,
	2:4 Thus says the LORD:
	"For three transgressions of Judah,
	  and for four, I will not revoke the
	  punishment;
	because they have rejected the law of the
	  LORD,
	  and have not kept his statutes,
	but their lies have led them astray,
	  after which their fathers walked.
		2:4 The LORD says, "The people of Judah
		have sinned again and again, and for this I will
		certainly punish them. They have despised my
		teachings and have not kept my commands.
		They have been led astray by the same false gods
		that their ancestors served.

3:2 "You only have I chosen
  of all the families of the earth;
therefore I will punish you
  for all your sins."
	3:2 "You only have I known
	  of all the families of the earth;
	therefore I will punish you
	  for all your iniquities.
		3:2 "Of all the nations on earth, you are the
		only one I have known and cared for. That is what
		makes your sins so terrible, and that is why I
		must punish you for them."

3 Do two walk together
  unless they have agreed to do so?
	3 "Do two walk together,
	  unless they have made an appointment?
		3 Do two men start traveling together without
		arranging to meet?

4:12 "Therefore this is what I will do to you,
  Israel,
  and because I will do this to you,
  prepare to meet your God, O Israel."
	4:12 "Therefore thus I will do to you, O
	  Israel;
	  because I will do this to you,
	  prepare to meet your God, O Israel!"
		4:12 "So then, people of Israel, I am going to
		punish you. And because I am going to do this,
		get ready to face my judgment!"

5:14 Seek good, not evil,
  that you may live.
Then the LORD God Almighty will be
  with you,
  just as you say he is.
	5:14 Seek good, and not evil,
	  that you may live;
	  and so the LORD, the God of hosts, will
	  be with you,
	  as you have said.
		5:14 Make it your aim to do what is right, not
		what is evil, so that you may live. Then the LORD
		God Almighty really will be with you, as you
		claim he is.

21 "I hate, I despise your religious feasts;
  I cannot stand your assemblies.
	21 "I hate, I despise your feasts,
	  and I take no delight in your solemn
	  assemblies.
		21 The LORD says, "I hate your religious fes-
		tivals; I cannot stand them!

22 Even though you bring me burnt offerings
  and grain offerings,
I will not accept them.
Though you bring choice fellowship
  offerings,
  I will have no regard for them.
	22 Even though you offer me your burnt
	  offerings and cereal offerings,
	  I will not accept them,
	and the peace offerings of your fatted
	  beasts
	  I will not look upon.
		22 When you bring me burnt offerings and
		grain offerings, I will not accept them; I will not
		accept the animals you have fattened to bring me
		as offerings.

KJV	NKJV	TLB
23 Take thou away from me the noise of thy songs; for I will not hear the melody of thy viols.	23 Take away from Me the noise of your songs, For I will not hear the melody of your stringed instruments.	23 Away with your hymns of praise—they are mere noise to my ears. I will not listen to your music, no matter how lovely it is.
24 But let judgment run down as waters, and righteousness as a mighty stream.	24 But let justice run down like water, And righteousness like a mighty stream.	24 "I want to see a mighty flood of justice—a torrent of doing good.
6:3 Ye that put far away the evil day, and cause the seat of violence to come near;	6:3 Woe to you who put far off the day of doom, Who cause the seat of violence to come near;	6:3 You push away all thought of punishment awaiting you, but by your deeds you bring the Day of Judgment near.
4 That lie upon beds of ivory, and stretch themselves upon their couches, and eat the lambs out of the flock, and the calves out of the midst of the stall;	4 Who lie on beds of ivory, Stretch out on your couches, Eat lambs from the flock And calves from the midst of the stall;	4 You lie on ivory beds surrounded with luxury, eating the meat of the tenderest lambs and the choicest calves.
5 That chant to the sound of the viol, and invent to themselves instruments of music, like David;	5 Who chant to the sound of stringed instruments, And invent for yourselves musical instruments like David;	5 You sing idle songs to the sound of the harp, and fancy yourselves to be as great musicians as King David was.
6 That drink wine in bowls, and anoint themselves with the chief ointments: but they are not grieved for the affliction of Joseph.	6 Who drink wine from bowls, And anoint yourselves with the best ointments, But are not grieved for the affliction of Joseph.	6 You drink wine by the bucketful and perfume yourselves with sweet ointments, caring nothing at all that your brothers need your help.
7 Therefore now shall they go captive with the first that go captive, and the banquet of them that stretched themselves shall be removed.	7 Therefore they shall now go captive as the first of the captives, And those who recline at banquets shall be removed.	7 Therefore you will be the first to be taken as slaves; suddenly your revelry will end.
7:7 Thus he shewed me: and, behold, the Lord stood upon a wall made by a plumbline, with a plumbline in his hand.	7:7 Thus He showed me: Behold, the Lord stood on a wall made with a plumb line, with a plumb line in His hand.	7:7 Then he showed me this: The Lord was standing beside a wall built with a plumbline, checking it with a plumbline to see if it was straight.
8 And the LORD said unto me, Amos, what seest thou? And I said, A plumbline. Then said the LORD, Behold, I will set a plumbline in the midst of my people Israel: I will not again pass by them any more:	8 And the LORD said to me, "Amos, what do you see?" And I said, "A plumb line." Then the Lord said: "Behold, I am setting a plumb line In the midst of My people Israel; I will not pass by them anymore.	8 And the Lord said to me, "Amos, what do you see?" I answered, "A plumbline." And he replied, "I will test my people with a plumbline. I will no longer turn away from punishing.
14 Then answered Amos, and said to Amaziah, I was no prophet, neither was I a prophet's son; but I was an herdman, and a gatherer of sycamore fruit:	14 Then Amos answered, and said to Amaziah: "I was no prophet, Nor was I a son of a prophet, But I was a herdsman And a tender of sycamore fruit.	14 But Amos replied, "I am not really one of the prophets. I do not come from a family of prophets. I am just a herdsman and fruit picker.
15 And the LORD took me as I followed the flock, and the LORD said unto me, Go, prophesy unto my people Israel.	15 Then the LORD took me as I followed the flock, And the LORD said to me, 'Go, prophesy to My people Israel.'	15 But the Lord took me from caring for the flocks and told me, 'Go and prophesy to my people Israel.'
8:11 Behold, the days come, saith the Lord GOD, that I will send a famine in the land, not a famine of bread, nor a thirst for water, but of hearing the words of the LORD:	8:11 "Behold, the days are coming" says the Lord GOD, "That I will send a famine on the land, Not a famine of bread, Nor a thirst for water, But of hearing the words of the LORD.	8:11 The time is surely coming," says the Lord God, "when I will send a famine on the land—not a famine of bread or water, but of hearing the words of the Lord.
12 And they shall wander from sea to sea, and from the north even to the east, they shall run to and fro to seek the word of the LORD, and shall not find it.	12 They shall wander from sea to sea, And from north to east; They shall run to and fro, seeking the word of the LORD, But shall not find it.	12 Men will wander everywhere from sea to sea, seeking the Word of the Lord, searching, running here and going there, but will not find it.
9:11 In that day will I raise up the tabernacle of David that is fallen, and close up the breaches thereof; and I will raise up his ruins, and I will build it as in the days of old:	9:11 "On that day I will raise up The tabernacle of David, which has fallen down, And repair its damages; I will raise up its ruins, And rebuild it as in the days of old;	9:11 "Then, at that time, I will rebuild the City of David, which is now lying in ruins, and return it to its former glory,

NIV	RSV	TEV
23 Away with the noise of your songs! I will not listen to the music of your harps.	23 Take away from me the noise of your songs; to the melody of your harps I will not listen.	23 Stop your noisy songs; I do not want to listen to your harps.
24 But let justice roll on like a river, righteousness like a never-failing stream!	24 But let justice roll down like waters, and righteousness like an everflowing stream.	24 Instead, let justice flow like a stream, and righteousness like a river that never goes dry.
6:3 You put off the evil day and bring near a reign of terror.	6:3 O you who put far away the evil day, and bring near the seat of violence?	6:3 You refuse to admit that a day of disaster is coming, but what you do only brings that day closer.
4 You lie on beds inlaid with ivory and lounge on your couches. You dine on choice lambs and fattened calves.	4 "Woe to those who lie upon beds of ivory, and stretch themselves upon their couches, and eat lambs from the flock, and calves from the midst of the stall;	4 How terrible it will be for you that stretch out on your luxurious couches, feasting on veal and lamb!
5 You strum away on your harps like David and improvise on musical instruments.	5 who sing idle songs to the sound of the harp, and like David invent for themselves instruments of music;	5 You like to compose songs, as David did, and play them on harps.
6 You drink wine by the bowlful and use the finest lotions, but you do not grieve over the ruin of Joseph.	6 who drink wine in bowls, and anoint themselves with the finest oils, but are not grieved over the ruin of Joseph!	6 You drink wine by the bowlful and use the finest perfumes, but you do not mourn over the ruin of Israel.
7 Therefore you will be among the first to go into exile; your feasting and lounging will end.	7 Therefore they shall now be the first of those to go into exile, and the revelry of those who stretch themselves shall pass away."	7 So you will be the first to go into exile. Your feasts and banquets will come to an end.
7:7 This is what he showed me: The Lord was standing by a wall that had been built true to plumb, with a plumb line in his hand.	7:7 He showed me: behold, the Lord was standing beside a wall built with a plumb line, with a plumb line in his hand.	7:7 I had another vision from the Lord. In it I saw him standing beside a wall that had been built with the use of a plumb line, and there was a plumb line in his hand.
8 And the Lord asked me, "What do you see, Amos?" "A plumb line," I replied. Then the Lord said, "Look, I am setting a plumb line among my people Israel; I will spare them no longer.	8 And the Lord said to me, "Amos, what do you see?" And I said, "A plumb line." Then the Lord said, "Behold, I am setting a plumb line in the midst of my people Israel; I will never again pass by them;	8 He asked me, "Amos, what do you see?" "A plumb line," I answered. Then he said, "I am using it to show that my people are like a wall that is out of line. I will not change my mind again about punishing them.
14 Amos answered Amaziah, "I was neither a prophet nor a prophet's son, but I was a shepherd, and I also took care of sycamore-fig trees.	14 Then Amos answered Amaziah, "I am no prophet, nor a prophet's son; but I am a herdsman, and a dresser of sycamore trees,	14 Amos answered, "I am not the kind of prophet who prophesies for pay. I am a herdsman, and I take care of fig trees.
15 But the Lord took me from tending the flock and said to me, 'Go, prophesy to my people Israel.'	15 and the Lord took me, from following the flock, and the Lord said to me, 'Go, prophesy to my people Israel.'	15 But the Lord took me from my work as a shepherd and ordered me to come and prophesy to his people Israel.
8:11 "The days are coming," declares the Sovereign Lord, "when I will send a famine through the land— not a famine of food or a thirst for water, but a famine of hearing the words of the Lord.	8:11 "Behold, the days are coming," says the Lord God, "when I will send a famine on the land; not a famine of bread, nor a thirst for water, but of hearing the words of the Lord.	8:11 "The time is coming when I will send famine on the land. People will be hungry, but not for bread; they will be thirsty, but not for water. They will hunger and thirst for a message from the Lord. I, Sovereign Lord, have spoken.
12 Men will stagger from sea to sea and wander from north to east, searching for the word of the Lord, but they will not find it.	12 They shall wander from sea to sea, and from north to east; they shall run to and fro, to seek the word of the Lord, but they shall not find it.	12 People will wander from the Dead Sea to the Mediterranean and then on around from the north to the east. They will look everywhere for a message from the Lord, but they will not find it.
9:11 "In that day I will restore David's fallen tent. I will repair its broken places, restore its ruins, and build it as it used to be,	9:11 "In that day I will raise up the booth of David that is fallen and repair its breaches, and raise up its ruins, and rebuild it as in the days of old;	9:11 The Lord says, "A day is coming when I will restore the kingdom of David, which is like a house fallen into ruins. I will repair its walls and restore it. I will rebuild it and make it as it was long ago.

KJV	NKJV	TLB
12 That they may possess the remnant of Edom, and of all the heathen, which are called by my name, saith the LORD that doeth this.	12 That they may possess the remnant of Edom, And all the Gentiles who are called by My name," Says the LORD who does this thing.	12 and Israel will possess what is left of Edom, and of all the nations that belong to me." For so the Lord, who plans it all, has said.
13 Behold, the days come, saith the LORD, that the plowman shall overtake the reaper, and the treader of grapes him that soweth seed; and the mountains shall drop sweet wine, and all the hills shall melt.	13 "Behold, the days are coming," says the LORD, "When the plowman shall overtake the reaper, And the treader of grapes him who sows seed; The mountains shall drip with sweet wine, And all the hills shall flow *with it*.	13 "The time will come when there will be such abundance of crops, that the harvest time will scarcely end before the farmer starts again to sow another crop, and the terraces of grapes upon the hills of Israel will drip sweet wine!

Obadiah

KJV	NKJV	TLB
4 Though thou exalt *thyself* as the eagle, and though thou set thy nest among the stars, thence will I bring thee down, saith the LORD.	4 Though you exalt *yourself as* high as the eagle, And though you set your nest among the stars, From there I will bring you down," says the LORD.	4 Though you soar as high as eagles, and build your nest among the stars, I will bring you plummeting down, says the Lord.
17 But upon mount Zion shall be deliverance, and there shall be holiness; and the house of Jacob shall possess their possessions.	17 "But on Mount Zion there shall be deliverance, And there shall be holiness; The house of Jacob shall possess their possessions.	17 But Jerusalem will become a refuge, a way of escape. Israel will reoccupy the land.
21 And saviours shall come up on mount Zion to judge the mount of Esau; and the kingdom shall be the LORD's.	21 Then saviors shall come to Mount Zion To judge the mountains of Esau, And the kingdom shall be the LORD's.	21 For deliverers will come to Jerusalem and rule all Edom. And the Lord shall be King!

Jonah

KJV	NKJV	TLB
1:1 Now the word of the LORD came unto Jonah the son of Amittai, saying,	1:1 Now the word of the LORD came to Jonah the son of Amittai, saying,	1:1 *The Lord sent this message to Jonah, the son of Amittai:*
2 Arise, go to Nineveh, that great city, and cry against it; for their wickedness is come up before me.	2 "Arise, go to Nineveh, that great city, and cry out against it; for their wickedness has come up before Me."	2 "Go to the great city of Nineveh, and give them this announcement from the Lord: 'I am going to destroy you, for your wickedness rises before me; it smells to highest heaven.'"
3 But Jonah rose up to flee unto Tarshish from the presence of the LORD, and went down to Joppa; and he found a ship going to Tarshish: so he paid the fare thereof, and went down into it, to go with them unto Tarshish from the presence of the LORD.	3 But Jonah arose to flee to Tarshish from the presence of the LORD. He went down to Joppa, and found a ship going to Tarshish; so he paid the fare, and went down into it, to go with them to Tarshish from the presence of the LORD.	3 But Jonah was afraid to go and ran away from the Lord. He went down to the seacoast, to the port of Joppa, where he found a ship leaving for Tarshish. He bought a ticket, went on board, and climbed down into the dark hold of the ship to hide there from the Lord.
15 So they took up Jonah, and cast him forth into the sea: and the sea ceased from her raging.	15 So they picked up Jonah and threw him into the sea, and the sea ceased from its raging.	15 Then they picked up Jonah and threw him overboard into the raging sea—and the storm stopped!
2:1 Then Jonah prayed unto the LORD his God out of the fish's belly,	2:1 Then Jonah prayed to the LORD his God from the fish's belly.	2:1 Then Jonah prayed to the Lord his God from inside the fish:
2 And said, I cried by reason of mine affliction unto the LORD, and he heard me; out of the belly of hell cried I, *and* thou heardest my voice.	2 And he said: "I cried out to the LORD because of my affliction, And He answered me. "Out of the belly of Sheol I cried, *And* You heard my voice.	2 "In my great trouble I cried to the Lord and he answered me; from the depths of death I called, and Lord, you heard me!
3 For thou hadst cast me into the deep, in the midst of the seas; and the floods compassed me about: all thy billows and thy waves passed over me.	3 For You cast me into the deep, Into the heart of the seas, And the floods surrounded me; All Your billows and Your waves passed over me.	3 You threw me into the ocean depths; I sank down into the floods of waters and was covered by your wild and stormy waves.
9 But I will sacrifice unto thee with the voice of thanksgiving; I will pay *that* that I have vowed. Salvation *is* of the LORD.	9 But I will sacrifice to You With the voice of thanksgiving; I will pay what I have vowed. Salvation *is* of the LORD."	9 "I will never worship anyone but you! For how can I thank you enough for all you have done? I will surely fulfill my promises. For my deliverance comes from the Lord alone."

NIV	RSV	TEV
12 so that they may possess the remnant of Edom and all the nations that bear my name, declares the LORD, who will do these things.	12 that they may possess the remnant of Edom and all the nations who are called by my name," says the LORD who does this.	12 And so the people of Israel will conquer what is left of the land of Edom and all the nations that were once mine," says the LORD, who will cause this to happen.
13 "The days are coming," declares the LORD, "when the reaper will be overtaken by the plowman and the planter by the one treading grapes. New wine will drip from the mountains and flow from all the hills.	13 "Behold, the days are coming," says the LORD, "when the plowman shall overtake the reaper and the treader of grapes him who sows the seed; the mountains shall drip sweet wine, and all the hills shall flow with it.	13 "The days are coming," says the LORD, when grain will grow faster than it can be harvested, and grapes will grow faster than the wine can be made. The mountains will drip with sweet wine, and the hills will flow with it.

Obadiah

4 Though you soar like the eagle and make your nest among the stars, from there I will bring you down," declares the LORD.	4 Though you soar aloft like the eagle, though your nest is set among the stars, thence I will bring you down, says the LORD.	4 Even though you make your home as high as an eagle's nest, so that it seems to be among the stars, yet I will pull you down.
17 But on Mount Zion will be deliverance; it will be holy, and the house of Jacob will possess its inheritance.	17 But in Mount Zion there shall be those that escape, and it shall be holy; and the house of Jacob shall possess their own possessions.	17 "But on Mount Zion some will escape, and it will be a sacred place. The people of Jacob will possess the land that is theirs by right.
21 Deliverers will go up on Mount Zion to govern the mountains of Esau. And the kingdom will be the LORD's.	21 Saviors shall go up to Mount Zion to rule Mount Esau; and the kingdom shall be the LORD's.	21 The victorious men of Jerusalem will attack Edom and rule over it. And the LORD himself will be king."

Jonah

1:1 The word of the LORD came to Jonah son of Amittai:	1:1 Now the word of the LORD came to Jonah the son of Amittai, saying,	1:1 One day the LORD spoke to Jonah son of Amittai.
2 "Go to the great city of Nineveh and preach against it, because its wickedness has come up before me."	2 "Arise, go to Nineveh, that great city, and cry against it; for their wickedness has come up before me."	2 He said, "Go to Nineveh, that great city, and speak out against it; I am aware of how wicked its people are."
3 But Jonah ran away from the LORD and headed for Tarshish. He went down to Joppa, where he found a ship bound for that port. After paying the fare, he went aboard and sailed for Tarshish to flee from the LORD.	3 But Jonah rose to flee to Tarshish from the presence of the LORD. He went down to Joppa and found a ship going to Tarshish; so he paid the fare, and went on board, to go with them to Tarshish, away from the presence of the LORD.	3 Jonah, however, set out in the opposite direction in order to get away from the LORD. He went to Joppa, where he found a ship about to go to Spain. He paid his fare and went aboard with the crew to sail to Spain, where he would be away from the LORD.
15 Then they took Jonah and threw him overboard, and the raging sea grew calm.	15 So they took up Jonah and threw him into the sea; and the sea ceased from its raging.	15 Then they picked Jonah up and threw him into the sea, and it calmed down at once.
2:1 From inside the fish Jonah prayed to the LORD his God.	2:1 Then Jonah prayed to the LORD his God from the belly of the fish,	2:1 From deep inside the fish Jonah prayed to the LORD his God:
2 He said: "In my distress I called to the LORD, and he answered me. From the depths of the grave I called for help, and you listened to my cry.	2 saying, "I called to the LORD, out of my distress, and he answered me; out of the belly of Sheol I cried, and thou didst hear my voice.	2 "In my distress, O LORD, I called to you, and you answered me. From deep in the world of the dead I cried for help, and you heard me.
3 You hurled me into the deep, into the very heart of the seas, and the currents swirled about me; all your waves and breakers swept over me.	3 For thou didst cast me into the deep, into the heart of the seas, and the flood was round about me; all thy waves and thy billows passed over me.	3 You threw me down into the depths, to the very bottom of the sea, where the waters were all around me, and all your mighty waves rolled over me.
9 But I, with a song of thanksgiving, will sacrifice to you. What I have vowed I will make good. Salvation comes from the LORD."	9 But I with the voice of thanksgiving will sacrifice to thee; what I have vowed I will pay. Deliverance belongs to the LORD!"	9 But I will sing praises to you; I will offer you a sacrifice and do what I have promised. Salvation comes from the LORD!"

KJV	NKJV	TLB
3:4 And Jonah began to enter into the city a day's journey, and he cried, and said, Yet forty days, and Nineveh shall be overthrown.	**3:4** And Jonah began to enter the city on the first day's walk. Then he cried out and said, "Yet forty days, and Nineveh shall be overthrown!"	**3:4** But the very first day when Jonah entered the city and began to preach, the people repented. Jonah shouted to the crowds that gathered around him, "Forty days from now Nineveh will be destroyed!"
10 And God saw their works, that they turned from their evil way; and God repented of the evil, that he had said that he would do unto them; and he did *it* not.	**10** Then God saw their works, that they turned from their evil way; and God relented from the disaster that He had said He would bring upon them, and He did not do it.	**10** And when God saw that they had put a stop to their evil ways, he abandoned his plan to destroy them, and didn't carry it through.
4:1 But it displeased Jonah exceedingly, and he was very angry.	**4:1** But it displeased Jonah exceedingly, and he became angry.	**4:1** This change of plans made Jonah very angry.
9 And God said to Jonah, Doest thou well to be angry for the gourd? And he said, I do well to be angry, *even* unto death.	**9** Then God said to Jonah, "*Is it* right for you to be angry about the plant?" And he said, "*It is* right for me to be angry, even to death!"	**9** And God said to Jonah, "Is it right for you to be angry because the plant died?" "Yes," Jonah said, "it is; it is right for me to be angry enough to die!"
10 Then said the Lord, Thou hast had pity on the gourd, for the which thou hast not laboured, neither madest it grow; which came up in a night, and perished in a night:	**10** But the Lord said, "You have had pity on the plant for which you have not labored, nor made it grow, which came up in a night and perished in a night.	**10** Then the Lord said, "You feel sorry for yourself when your shelter is destroyed, though you did no work to put it there, and it is, at best, short-lived.
11 And should not I spare Nineveh, that great city, wherein are more than sixscore thousand persons that cannot discern between their right hand and their left hand; and *also* much cattle?	**11** "And should I not pity Nineveh, that great city, in which are more than one hundred and twenty thousand persons who cannot discern between their right hand and their left, and *also* much livestock?"	**11** And why shouldn't I feel sorry for a great city like Nineveh with its 120,000 people in utter spiritual darkness, and all its cattle?"

Micah

KJV	NKJV	TLB
2:12 I will surely assemble, O Jacob, all of thee; I will surely gather the remnant of Israel; I will put them together as the sheep of Bozrah, as the flock in the midst of their fold: they shall make great noise by reason of *the multitude of men.*	**2:12** "I will surely assemble all of you, O Jacob, I will surely gather the remnant of Israel; I will put them together like sheep of the fold, Like a flock in the midst of their pasture; They shall make a loud noise because of *so many* men.	**2:12** The time will come, O Israel, when I will gather you—all that are left—and bring you together again like sheep in a fold, like a flock in a pasture—a noisy, happy crowd.
13 The breaker is come up before them: they have broken up, and have passed through the gate, and are gone out by it: and their king shall pass before them, and the Lord on the head of them.	**13** The one who breaks open will come up before them; They will break out, Pass through the gate, And go out by it; Their king will pass before them, With the Lord at their head."	**13** The Messiah will lead you out of exile and bring you through the gates of your cities of captivity, back to your own land. Your King will go before you—the Lord leads on.
4:1 But in the last days it shall come to pass, *that* the mountain of the house of the Lord shall be established in the top of the mountains, and it shall be exalted above the hills; and people shall flow unto it.	**4:1** Now it shall come to pass in the latter days *That* the mountain of the Lord's house Shall be established on the top of the mountains, And shall be exalted above the hills; And peoples shall flow to it.	**4:1** But in the last days Mount Zion will be the most renowned of all the mountains of the world, praised by all nations; people from all over the world will make pilgrimages there.
2 And many nations shall come, and say, Come, and let us go up to the mountain of the Lord, and to the house of the God of Jacob; and he will teach us of his ways, and we will walk in his paths: for the law shall go forth of Zion, and the word of the Lord from Jerusalem.	**2** Many nations shall come and say, "Come, and let us go up to the mountain of the Lord, To the house of the God of Jacob; He will teach us His ways, And we shall walk in His paths." For out of Zion the law shall go forth, And the word of the Lord from Jerusalem.	**2** "Come," they will say to one another, "let us visit the mountain of the Lord, and see the Temple of the God of Israel; he will tell us what to do, and we will do it." For in those days the whole world will be ruled by the Lord from Jerusalem! He will issue his laws and announce his decrees from there.
3 And he shall judge among many people, and rebuke strong nations afar off; and they shall beat their swords into plowshares, and their spears into pruninghooks: nation shall not lift up a sword against nation, neither shall they learn war any more.	**3** He shall judge between many peoples, And rebuke strong nations afar off; They shall beat their swords into plowshares, And their spears into pruning hooks; Nation shall not lift up sword against nation, Neither shall they learn war any more.	**3** He will arbitrate among the nations, and dictate to strong nations far away. They will beat their swords into plowshares and their spears into pruning-hooks; nations shall no longer fight each other, for all war will end. There will be universal peace, and all the military academies and training camps will be closed down.

NIV	RSV	TEV
3:4 Jonah started into the city, going a day's journey, and he proclaimed: "Forty more days and Nineveh will be destroyed."	**3:4** Jonah began to go into the city, going a day's journey. And he cried, "Yet forty days, and Nineveh shall be overthrown!"	**3:4** Jonah started through the city, and after walking a whole day, he proclaimed, "In forty days Nineveh will be destroyed!"
10 When God saw what they did and how they turned from their evil ways, he had compassion and did not bring upon them the destruction he had threatened.	**10** When God saw what they did, how they turned from their evil way, God repented of the evil which he had said he would do to them; and he did not do it.	**10** God saw what they did; he saw that they had given up their wicked behavior. So he changed his mind and did not punish them as he had said he would.
4:1 But Jonah was greatly displeased and became angry.	**4:1** But it displeased Jonah exceedingly, and he was angry.	**4:1** Jonah was very unhappy about this and became angry.
9 But God said to Jonah, "Do you have a right to be angry about the vine?" "I do," he said. "I am angry enough to die."	**9** But God said to Jonah, "Do you do well to be angry for the plant?" And he said, "I do well to be angry, angry enough to die."	**9** But God said to him, "What right do you have to be angry about the plant?" Jonah replied, "I have every right to be angry—angry enough to die!"
10 But the LORD said, "You have been concerned about this vine, though you did not tend it or make it grow. It sprang up overnight and died overnight.	**10** And the LORD said, "You pity the plant, for which you did not labor, nor did you make it grow, which came into being in a night, and perished in a night.	**10** The LORD said to him, "This plant grew up in one night and disappeared the next; you didn't do anything for it and you didn't make it grow—yet you feel sorry for it!
11 But Nineveh has more than a hundred and twenty thousand people who cannot tell their right hand from their left, and many cattle as well. Should I not be concerned about that great city?"	**11** And should not I pity Nineveh, that great city, in which there are more than a hundred and twenty thousand persons who do not know their right hand from their left, and also much cattle?"	**11** How much more, then, should I have pity on Nineveh, that great city. After all, it has more than 120,000 innocent children in it, as well as many animals!"

Micah

NIV	RSV	TEV
2:12 "I will surely gather all of you, O Jacob; I will surely bring together the remnant of Israel. I will bring them together like sheep in a pen, like a flock in its pasture; the place will throng with people.	**2:12** I will surely gather all of you, O Jacob, I will gather the remnant of Israel; I will set them together like sheep in a fold, like a flock in its pasture, a noisy multitude of men.	**2:12** "But I will gather you together, all you people of Israel that are left. I will bring you together like sheep returning to the fold. Like a pasture full of sheep, your land will once again be filled with many people."
13 One who breaks open the way will go up before them; they will break through the gate and go out. Their king will pass through before them, the LORD at their head."	**13** He who opens the breach will go up before them; they will break through and pass the gate, going out by it. Their king will pass on before them, the LORD at their head.	**13** God will open the way for them and lead them out of exile. They will break out of the city gates and go free. Their king, the LORD himself, will lead them out.
4:1 In the last days the mountain of the LORD's temple will be established as chief among the mountains; it will be raised above the hills, and peoples will stream to it.	**4:1** It shall come to pass in the latter days that the mountain of the house of the LORD shall be established as the highest of the mountains, and shall be raised up above the hills; and peoples shall flow to it,	**4:1** In days to come the mountain where the Temple stands will be the highest one of all, towering above all the hills. Many nations will come streaming to it,
2 Many nations will come and say, "Come, let us go up to the mountain of the LORD, to the house of the God of Jacob. He will teach us his ways, so that we may walk in his paths." The law will go out from Zion, the word of the LORD from Jerusalem.	**2** and many nations shall come, and say: "Come let us go up to the mountain of the LORD, to the house of the God of Jacob; that he may teach us his ways and we may walk in his paths." For out of Zion shall go forth the law, and the word of the LORD from Jerusalem.	**2** and their people will say, "Let us go up the hill of the LORD, to the Temple of Israel's God. For he will teach us what he wants us to do; we will walk in the paths he has chosen. For the LORD's teaching comes from Jerusalem; from Zion he speaks to his people."
3 He will judge between many peoples and will settle disputes for strong nations far and wide. They will beat their swords into plowshares and their spears into pruning hooks. Nation will not take up sword against nation, nor will they train for war anymore.	**3** He shall judge between many peoples, and shall decide for strong nations afar off; and they shall beat their swords into plowshares, and their spears into pruning hooks; nation shall not lift up sword against nation, neither shall they learn war any more;	**3** He will settle disputes among the nations, among the great powers near and far. They will hammer their swords into plows and their spears into pruning knives. Nations will never again go to war, never prepare for battle again.

KJV	NKJV	TLB
4 But they shall sit every man under his vine and under his fig tree; and none shall make *them* afraid: for the mouth of the LORD of hosts hath spoken *it*.	4 But everyone shall sit under his vine and under his fig tree, And no one shall make *them* afraid; For the mouth of the LORD of hosts has spoken.	4 Everyone will live quietly in his own home in peace and prosperity, for there will be nothing to fear. The Lord himself has promised this.
5:2 But thou, Bethlehem Ephratah, *though* thou be little among the thousands of Judah, *yet* out of thee shall he come forth unto me *that is* to be ruler in Israel; whose goings forth *have been* from of old, from everlasting.	5:2 "But you, Bethlehem Ephrathah, *Though* you are little among the thousands of Judah, *Yet* out of you shall come forth to Me The One to be ruler in Israel, Whose goings forth *have been* from of old, From everlasting."	5:2 O Bethlehem Ephrathah, you are but a small Judean village, yet you will be the birthplace of my King who is alive from everlasting ages past!
6:8 He hath shewed thee, O man, what *is* good; and what doth the LORD require of thee, but to do justly, and to love mercy, and to walk humbly with thy God?	6:8 He has shown you, O man, what *is* good; And what does the LORD require of you But to do justly, To love mercy, And to walk humbly with your God?	6:8 No, he has told you what he wants, and this is all it is: *to be fair and just and merciful, and to walk humbly with your God.*
7:5 Trust ye not in a friend, put ye not confidence in a guide: keep the doors of thy mouth from her that lieth in thy bosom.	7:5 Do not trust in a friend; Do not put your confidence in a companion; Guard the doors of your mouth From her who lies in your bosom.	7:5 Don't trust anyone, not your best friend—not even your wife!
6 For the son dishonoureth the father, the daughter riseth up against her mother, the daughter in law against her mother in law; a man's enemies *are* the men of his own house.	6 For son dishonors father, Daughter rises against her mother, Daughter-in-law against her mother-in-law; A man's enemies *are* the men of his own house.	6 For the son despises his father; the daughter defies her mother; the bride curses her mother-in-law. Yes, a man's enemies will be found in his own home.
7 Therefore I will look unto the LORD; I will wait for the God of my salvation: my God will hear me.	7 Therefore I will look to the LORD; I will wait for the God of my salvation; My God will hear me.	7 As for me, I look to the Lord for his help; I wait for God to save me; he will hear me.
19 He will turn again, he will have compassion upon us; he will subdue our iniquities; and thou wilt cast all their sins into the depths of the sea.	19 He will again have compassion on us, And will subdue our iniquities. You will cast all our sins Into the depths of the sea.	19 Once again you will have compassion on us. You will tread our sins beneath your feet; you will throw them into the depths of the ocean!

Nahum

KJV	NKJV	TLB
1:7 The LORD *is* good, a strong hold in the day of trouble; and he knoweth them that trust in him.	1:7 The LORD *is* good, A stronghold in the day of trouble; And He knows those who trust in Him.	1:7 The Lord is good. When trouble comes, he is the place to go! And he knows everyone who trusts in him!
3:1 Woe to the bloody city! it *is* all full of lies *and* robbery; the prey departeth not;	3:1 Woe to the bloody city! It *is* all full of lies *and* robbery. *Its* victim never departs.	3:1 Woe to Nineveh, City of Blood, full of lies, crammed with plunder.

Habakkuk

KJV	NKJV	TLB
1:2 O LORD, how long shall I cry, and thou wilt not hear! *even* cry out unto thee *of* violence, and thou wilt not save!	1:2 O LORD, how long shall I cry, And You will not hear? Even cry out to You, "Violence!" And You will not save.	1:2 O Lord, how long must I call for help before you will listen? I shout to you in vain; there is no answer. "Help! Murder!" I cry, but no one comes to save.
3 Why dost thou shew me iniquity, and cause *me* to behold grievance? for spoiling and violence *are* before me: and there are *that* raise up strife and contention.	3 Why do You show me iniquity, And cause *me* to see trouble? For plundering and violence *are* before me; There is strife, and contention arises.	3 Must I forever see this sin and sadness all around me? Wherever I look there is oppression and bribery and men who love to argue and to fight.
4 Therefore the law is slacked, and judgment doth never go forth: for the wicked doth compass about the righteous; therefore wrong judgment proceedeth.	4 Therefore the law is powerless, And justice never goes forth, For the wicked surround the righteous; Therefore perverse judgment proceeds.	4 The law is not enforced and there is no justice given in the courts, for the wicked far outnumber the righteous, and bribes and trickery prevail.

NIV	RSV	TEV
4 Every man will sit under his own vine and under his own fig tree, and no one will make them afraid, for the LORD Almighty has spoken.	4 but they shall sit every man under his vine and under his fig tree, and none shall make them afraid; for the mouth of the LORD of hosts has spoken.	4 Everyone will live in peace among his own vineyards and fig trees, and no one will make him afraid. The LORD Almighty has promised this.
5:2 "But you, Bethlehem Ephrathah, though you are small among the clans of Judah, out of you will come for me one who will be ruler over Israel, whose origins are from of old, from ancient times."	5:2 But you, O Bethlehem Ephrathah, who are little to be among the clans of Judah, from you shall come forth for me one who is to be ruler in Israel, whose origin is from of old, from ancient days.	5:2 The LORD says, "Bethlehem Ephrathah, you are one of the smallest towns in Judah, but out of you I will bring a ruler of Israel, whose family line goes back to ancient times."
6:8 He has showed you, O man, what is good. And what does the LORD require of you? To act justly and to love mercy and to walk humbly with your God.	6:8 He has showed you, O man, what is good; and what does the LORD require of you but to do justice, and to love kindness, and to walk humbly with your God?	6:8 No, the LORD has told us what is good. What he requires of us is this: to do what is just, to show constant love, and to live in humble fel- lowship with our God.
7:5 Do not trust a neighbor; put no confidence in a friend. Even with her who lies in your embrace be careful of your words.	7:5 Put no trust in a neighbor, have no confidence in a friend; guard the doors of your mouth from her who lies in your bosom;	7:5 Don't believe your neighbor or trust your friend. Be careful what you say even to your wife.
6 For a son dishonors his father, a daughter rises up against her mother, a daughter-in-law against her mother-in- law— a man's enemies are the members of his own household.	6 for the son treats the father with contempt, the daughter rises up against her mother, the daughter-in-law against her mother-in- law; a man's enemies are the men of his own house.	6 In these times sons treat their fathers like fools, daughters oppose their mothers, and young women quarrel with their mothers-in-law; a man's enemies are the members of his own family.
7 But as for me, I watch in hope for the LORD, I wait for God my Savior; my God will hear me.	7 But as for me, I will look to the LORD, I will wait for the God of my salvation; my God will hear me.	7 But I will watch for the LORD; I will wait confidently for God, who will save me. My God will hear me.
19 You will again have compassion on us; you will tread our sins underfoot and hurl all our iniquities into the depths of the sea.	19 He will again have compassion upon us, he will tread our iniquities under foot. Thou wilt cast all our sins into the depths of the sea.	19 You will be merciful to us once again. You will trample our sins underfoot and send them to the bottom of the sea!

Nahum

NIV	RSV	TEV
1:7 The LORD is good, a refuge in times of trouble. He cares for those who trust in him,	1:7 The LORD is good, a stronghold in the day of trouble; he knows those who take refuge in him.	1:7 The LORD is good; he protects his people in times of trouble; he takes care of those who turn to him.
3:1 Woe to the city of blood, full of lies, full of plunder, never without victims!	3:1 Woe to the bloody city, all full of lies and booty— no end to the plunder!	3:1 Doomed is the lying, murderous city, full of wealth to be looted and plundered!

Habakkuk

NIV	RSV	TEV
1:2 How long, O LORD, must I call for help, but you do not listen? Or cry out to you, "Violence!" but you do not save?	1:2 O LORD, how long shall I cry for help, and thou wilt not hear? Or cry to thee "Violence!" and thou wilt not save?	1:2 O LORD, how long must I call for help before you listen, before you save us from vio- lence?
3 Why do you make me look at injustice? Why do you tolerate wrong? Destruction and violence are before me; there is strife, and conflict abounds.	3 Why dost thou make me see wrongs and look upon trouble? Destruction and violence are before me; strife and contention arise.	3 Why do you make me see such trouble? How can you stand to look on such wrongdoing? Destruction and violence are all around me, and there is fighting and quarreling everywhere.
4 Therefore the law is paralyzed, and justice never prevails. The wicked hem in the righteous, so that justice is perverted.	4 So the law is slacked and justice never goes forth. For the wicked surround the righteous, so justice goes forth perverted.	4 The law is weak and useless, and justice is never done. Evil men get the better of the righ- teous, and so justice is perverted.

KJV	NKJV	TLB
12 *Art* thou not from everlasting, O Lord my God, mine Holy One? we shall not die. O Lord, thou hast ordained them for judgment; and, O mighty God, thou hast established them for correction.	12 Are You not from everlasting, O Lord my God, my Holy One? We shall not die. O Lord, You have appointed them for judgment; O Rock, You have marked them for correction.	12 O Lord my God, my Holy One, you who are eternal—is your plan in all of this to wipe us out? Surely not! O God our Rock, you have decreed the rise of these Chaldeans to chasten and correct us for our awful sins.
13 *Thou art* of purer eyes than to behold evil, and canst not look on iniquity: wherefore lookest thou upon them that deal treacherously, *and* holdest thy tongue when the wicked devoureth *the man that is* more righteous than he?	13 *You are* of purer eyes than to behold evil, And cannot look on wickedness. Why do You look on those who deal treacherously, *And* hold Your tongue when the wicked devours *One* more rightous than he?	13 We are wicked, but they far more! Will you, who cannot allow sin in any form, stand idly by while they swallow us up? Should you be silent while the wicked destroy those who are better than they?
2:2 And the Lord answered me, and said, Write the vision, and make *it* plain upon tables, that he may run that readeth it.	2:2 Then the Lord answered me and said: "Write the vision And make *it* plain on tablets, That he may run who reads it.	2:2 And the Lord said to me, "Write my answer on a billboard, large and clear, so that anyone can read it at a glance and rush to tell the others.
3 For the vision *is* yet for an appointed time, but at the end it shall speak, and not lie: though it tarry, wait for it; because it will surely come, it will not tarry.	3 For the vision *is* yet for an appointed time; But at the end it will speak, and it will not lie. Though it tarries, wait for it; Because it will surely come, It will not tarry.	3 But these things I plan won't happen right away. Slowly, steadily, surely, the time approaches when the vision will be fulfilled. If it seems slow, do not despair, for these things will surely come to pass. Just be patient! They will not be overdue a single day!
4 Behold, his soul *which* is lifted up is not upright in him: but the just shall live by his faith.	4 "Behold the proud, His soul is not upright in him; But the just shall live by his faith.	4 "Note this: Wicked men trust themselves alone [as these Chaldeans do], and fail; but the righteous man trusts in me, and lives!
14 For the earth shall be filled with the knowledge of the glory of the Lord, as the waters cover the sea.	14 For the earth will be filled With the knowledge of the glory of the Lord, As the waters cover the sea.	14 ("The time will come when all the earth is filled, as the waters fill the sea, with an awareness of the glory of the Lord.)
3:2 O Lord, I have heard thy speech, *and* was afraid: O Lord, revive thy work in the midst of the years, in the midst of the years make known; in wrath remember mercy.	3:2 O Lord, I have heard your speech *and* was afraid; O Lord, revive Your work in the midst of the years! In the midst of the years make *it* known; In wrath remember mercy.	3:2 O Lord, now I have heard your report, and I worship you in awe for the fearful things you are going to do. In this time of our deep need, begin again to help us, as you did in years gone by. Show us your power to save us. In your wrath, remember mercy.
17 Although the fig tree shall not blossom, neither shall fruit *be* in the vines; the labour of the olive shall fail, and the fields shall yield no meat; the flock shall be cut off from the fold, and *there shall be* no herd in the stalls:	17 Though the fig tree may not blossom, Nor fruit be on the vines; Though the labor of the olive may fail, And the fields yield no food; Though the flock be cut off from the fold, And there be no herd in the stalls—	17 Even though the fig trees are all destroyed, and there is neither blossom left nor fruit, and though the olive crops all fail, and the fields lie barren; even if the flocks die in the fields and the cattle barns are empty,
18 Yet I will rejoice in the Lord, I will joy in the God of my salvation.	18 Yet I will rejoice in the Lord, I will joy in the God of my salvation.	18 yet I will rejoice in the Lord; I will be happy in the God of my salvation.
19 The Lord God *is* my strength, and he will make my feet like hinds' *feet*, and he will make me to walk upon mine high places. To the chief singer on my stringed instruments.	19 The Lord God is my strength; He will make my feet like deer's *feet*, And He will make me walk on my high hills. To the Chief Musician. With my stringed instruments.	19 The Lord God is my Strength, and he will give me the speed of a deer and bring me safely over the mountains.

Zephaniah

1:7 Hold thy peace at the presence of the Lord God: for the day of the Lord *is* at hand: for the Lord hath prepared a sacrifice, he hath bid his guests.	1:7 Be silent in the presence of the Lord God; For the day of the Lord *is* at hand, For the Lord has prepared a sacrifice; He has invited His guests.	1:7 Stand in silence in the presence of the Lord. For the awesome Day of his Judgment has come; he has prepared a great slaughter of his people and has chosen their executioners.
14 The great day of the Lord *is* near, *it is* near, and hasteth greatly, *even* the voice of the day of the Lord: the mighty man shall cry there bitterly.	14 The great day of the Lord *is* near; *It is* near and hastens quickly. The noise of the day of the Lord is bitter; There the mighty men shall cry out.	14 "That terrible day is near. Swiftly it comes—a day when strong men will weep bitterly.

NIV	RSV	TEV
12 O LORD, are you not from everlasting? My God, my Holy One, we will not die. O LORD, you have appointed them to execute judgment; O Rock, you have ordained them to punish.	12 Art thou not from everlasting, O LORD my God, my Holy One? We shall not die. O LORD, thou hast ordained them as a judgment; and thou, O Rock, hast established them for chastisement.	12 LORD, from the very beginning you are God. You are my God, holy and eternal. LORD, my God and protector, you have chosen the Babylonians and made them strong so that they can punish us.
13 Your eyes are too pure to look on evil; you cannot tolerate wrong. Why then do you tolerate the treacherous? Why are you silent while the wicked swallow up those more righteous than themselves?	13 Thou who art of purer eyes than to behold evil and canst not look on wrong, why dost thou look on faithless men, and art silent when the wicked swallows up the man more righteous than he?	13 But how can you stand these treacherous, evil men? Your eyes are too holy to look at evil, and you cannot stand the sight of people doing wrong. So why are you silent while they destroy people who are more righteous than they are?
2:2 Then the LORD replied: "Write down the revelation and make it plain on tablets so that a herald may run with it.	2:2 And the LORD answered me: "Write the vision; make it plain upon tablets, so he may run who reads it.	2:2 The LORD gave me this answer: "Write down clearly on tablets what I reveal to you, so that it can be read at a glance.
3 For the revelation awaits an appointed time; it speaks of the end and will not prove false. Though it linger, wait for it; it will certainly come and will not delay.	3 For still the vision awaits its time; it hastens to the end—it will not lie. If it seem slow, wait for it; it will surely come, it will not delay.	3 Put it in writing, because it is not yet time for it to come true. but the time is coming quickly, and what I show you will come true. It may seem slow in coming, but wait for it; it will certainly take place, and it will not be delayed.
4 "See, he is puffed up; his desires are not upright— but the righteous will live by his faith—	4 Behold, he whose soul is not upright in him shall fail, but the righteous shall live by his faith.	4 And this is the message: 'Those who are evil will not survive, but those who are righteous will live because they are faithful to God.'"
14 For the earth will be filled with the knowledge of the glory of the LORD, as the waters cover the sea.	14 For the earth will be filled with the knowledge of the glory of the LORD, as the waters cover the sea.	14 But the earth will be as full of the knowledge of the LORD's glory as the seas are full of water.
3:2 LORD, I have heard of your fame; I stand in awe of your deeds, O LORD. Renew them in our day, in our time make them known; in wrath remember mercy.	3:2 O LORD, I have heard the report of thee, and thy work, O LORD, do I fear. In the midst of the years renew it; in the midst of the years make it known; in wrath remember mercy.	3:2 O LORD, I have heard of what you have done, and I am filled with awe. Now do again in our times the great deeds you used to do. Be merciful, even when you are angry.
17 Though the fig tree does not bud and there are no grapes on the vines, though the olive crop fails and the fields produce no food, though there are no sheep in the pen and no cattle in the stalls,	17 Though the fig tree do not blossom, nor fruit be on the vines, the produce of the olive fail and the fields yield no food, the flock be cut off from the fold and there be no herd in the stalls,	17 Even though the fig trees have no fruit and no grapes grow on the vines, even though the olive crop fails and the fields produce no grain, even though the sheep all die and the cattle stalls are empty,
18 yet I will rejoice in the LORD, I will be joyful in God my Savior.	18 yet I will rejoice in the LORD, I will joy in the God of my salvation.	18 I will still be joyful and glad, because the LORD God is my savior.
19 The Sovereign LORD is my strength; he makes my feet like the feet of a deer, he enables me to go on the heights. For the director of music. On my stringed instruments.	19 GOD, the Lord, is my strength; he makes my feet like hinds' feet, he makes me tread upon my high places. To the choirmaster: with stringed instruments.	19 The Sovereign LORD gives me strength. He makes me sure-footed as a deer and keeps me safe on the mountains.

Zephaniah

NIV	RSV	TEV
1:7 Be silent before the Sovereign LORD, for the day of the LORD is near. The LORD has prepared a sacrifice; he has consecrated those he has invited.	1:7 Be silent before the Lord GOD! For the day of the LORD is at hand; the LORD has prepared a sacrifice and consecrated his guests.	1:7 The day is near when the LORD will sit in judgment; so be silent in his presence. The LORD is preparing to sacrifice his people and has invited enemies to plunder Judah.
14 "The great day of the LORD is near— near and coming quickly. Listen! The cry on the day of the LORD will be bitter, the shouting of the warrior there.	14 The great day of the LORD is near, near and hastening fast; the sound of the day of the LORD is bitter, the mighty man cries aloud there.	14 The great day of the LORD is near— very near and coming fast! That day will be bitter, for even the bravest soldiers will cry out in despair!

KJV	NKJV	TLB
15 That day *is* a day of wrath, a day of trouble and distress, a day of wasteness and desolation, a day of darkness and gloominess, a day of clouds and thick darkness,	15 That day *is* a day of wrath, A day of trouble and distress, A day of devastation and desolation, A day of darkness and gloominess, A day of clouds and thick darkness,	15 It is a day of the wrath of God poured out; it is a day of terrible distress and anguish, a day of ruin and desolation, of darkness, gloom, clouds, blackness,
16 A day of the trumpet and alarm against the fenced cities, and against the high towers.	16 A day of trumpet and alarm Against the fortified cities And against the high towers.	16 Trumpet calls and battle cries; down go the walled cities and strongest battlements!
17 And I will bring distress upon men, that they shall walk like blind men, because they have sinned against the LORD: and their blood shall be poured out as dust, and their flesh as the dung.	17 "I will bring distress upon men, And they shall walk like blind men, Because they have sinned against the LORD; Their blood shall be poured out like dust, And their flesh like refuse."	17 "I will make you as helpless as a blind man searching for a path, because you have sinned against the Lord; therefore your blood will be poured out into the dust and your bodies will lie there rotting on the ground."
18 Neither their silver nor their gold shall be able to deliver them in the day of the LORD's wrath; but the whole land shall be devoured by the fire of his jealousy: for he shall make even a speedy riddance of all them that dwell in the land.	18 Neither their silver nor their gold Shall be able to deliver them In the day of the LORD's wrath; But the whole land shall be devoured By the fire of His jealousy, For He will make speedy riddance Of all those who dwell in the land.	18 Your silver and gold will be of no use to you in that day of the Lord's wrath. You cannot ransom yourselves from it. For the whole land will be devoured by the fire of his jealousy. He will make a speedy riddance of all the people of Judah.
2:15 This *is* the rejoicing city that dwelt carelessly, that said in her heart, I *am,* and *there is* none beside me: how is she become a desolation, a place for beasts to lie down in! every one that passeth by her shall hiss, *and* wag his hand.	2:15 This is the rejoicing city That dwelt securely, That said in her heart, "I *am* it, and *there is* none besides me." How has she become a desolation, A place for beasts to lie down! Everyone who passes by her Shall hiss and shake his fist.	2:15 This is the fate of that vast, prosperous city that lived in such security, that said to herself, "In all the world there is no city as great as I." But now—see how she has become a place of utter ruins, a place for animals to live! Everyone passing that way will mock, or shake his head in disbelief.
3:1 Woe to her that is filthy and polluted, to the oppressing city!	3:1 Woe to her who is rebellious and polluted, To the oppressing city!	3:1 Woe to filthy, sinful Jerusalem, city of violence and crime.
2 She obeyed not the voice; she received not correction; she trusted not in the LORD; she drew not near to her God.	2 She has not obeyed *His* voice, She has not received correction; She has not trusted in the LORD, She has not drawn near to her God.	2 In her pride she won't listen even to the voice of God. No one can tell her anything; she refuses all correction. She does not trust the Lord, nor seek for God.
3 Her princes within her *are* roaring lions; her judges *are* evening wolves; they gnaw not the bones till the morrow.	3 Her princes in her midst *are* roaring lions; Her judges *are* evening wolves That leave not a bone till morning.	3 Her leaders are like roaring lions hunting for their victims—out for everything that they can get. Her judges are like ravenous wolves at evening time, who by dawn have left no trace of their prey.
4 Her prophets *are* light *and* treacherous persons: her priests have polluted the sanctuary, they have done violence to the law.	4 Her prophets are insolent, treacherous people; Her priests have polluted the sanctuary, They have done violence to the law.	4 Her "prophets" are liars seeking their own gain; her priests defile the Temple by their disobedience to God's laws.
5 The just LORD *is* in the midst thereof; he will not do iniquity: every morning doth he bring his judgment to light, he faileth not; but the unjust knoweth no shame.	5 The LORD *is* righteous, *He is* in her midst, He will do no unrighteousness. Every morning He brings His justice to light; He never fails, But the unjust knows no shame.	5 But the Lord is there within the city, and he does no wrong. Day by day his justice is more evident, but no one heeds—the wicked know no shame.

Haggai

KJV	NKJV	TLB
1:6 Ye have sown much, and bring in little; ye eat, but ye have not enough; ye drink, but ye are not filled with drink; ye clothe you, but there is none warm; and he that earneth wages earneth wages *to put it* into a bag with holes.	1:6 "You have sown much, and bring in little; You eat, but do not have enough; You drink, but you are not filled with drink; You clothe yourselves, but no one is warm; And he who earns wages, Earns wages *to put* into a bag with holes."	1:6 You plant much but harvest little. You have scarcely enough to eat or drink, and not enough clothes to keep you warm. Your income disappears, as though you were putting it into pockets filled with holes!
7 Thus saith the LORD of hosts; Consider your ways.	7 Thus says the LORD of hosts: "Consider your ways!	7 "Think it over," says the Lord of Hosts. "Consider how you have acted, and what has happened as a result!

NIV	RSV	TEV

15 That day will be a day of wrath,
    a day of distress and anguish,
    a day of trouble and ruin,
    a day of darkness and gloom,
    a day of clouds and blackness,
	15 A day of wrath is that day,
	    a day of distress and anguish,
	    a day of ruin and devastation,
	    a day of darkness and gloom,
	    a day of clouds and thick darkness,
		15 It will be a day of fury, a day of trouble and distress, a day of ruin and destruction, a day of darkness and gloom, a black and cloudy day,

16 a day of trumpet and battle cry
    against the fortified cities
    and against the corner towers.
	16 a day of trumpet blast and battle cry
	    against the fortified cities
	    and against the lofty battlements.
		16 a day filled with the sound of war trumpets and the battle cry of soldiers attacking fortified cities and high towers.

17 I will bring distress on the people
    and they will walk like blind men,
    because they have sinned against the
    LORD.
Their blood will be poured out like dust
    and their entrails like filth.
	17 I will bring distress on men,
	    so that they shall walk like the blind,
	    because they have sinned against the
	    LORD;
	    their blood shall be poured out like dust,
	    and their flesh like dung.
		17 The LORD says, "I will bring such disasters on mankind that everyone will grope about like a blind man. They have sinned against me, and now their blood will be poured out like water, and their dead bodies will lie rotting on the ground."

18 Neither their silver nor their gold
    will be able to save them
    on the day of the LORD's wrath.
In the fire of his jealousy
    the whole world will be consumed,
    for he will make a sudden end
    of all who live in the earth."
	18 Neither their silver nor their gold
	    shall be able to deliver them
	    on the day of the wrath of the LORD.
	In the fire of his jealous wrath,
	    all the earth shall be consumed;
	    for a full, yea, sudden end
	    he will make of all the inhabitants of the
	    earth.
		18 On the day when the LORD shows his fury, not even all their silver and gold will save them. The whole earth will be destroyed by the fire of his anger. He will put an end—a sudden end—to everyone who lives on earth.

2:15 This is the carefree city
    that lived in safety.
She said to herself,
    "I am, and there is none besides me."
What a ruin she has become,
    a lair for wild beasts!
All who pass by her scoff
    and shake their fists.
	2:15 This is the exultant city
	    that dwelt secure,
	    that said to herself,
	    "I am and there is none else."
	What a desolation she has become,
	    a lair for wild beasts!
	Every one who passes by her
	    hisses and shakes his fist.
		2:15 That is what will happen to the city that is so proud of its own power and thinks it is safe. Its people think that their city is the greatest in the world. What a desolate place it will become, a place where wild animals will rest! Everyone who passes by will shrink back in horror.

3:1 Woe to the city of oppressors,
    rebellious and defiled!
	3:1 Woe to her that is rebellious and defiled,
	    the oppressing city!
		3:1 Jerusalem is doomed, that corrupt, rebellious city that oppresses its own people.

2 She obeys no one,
    she accepts no correction.
She does not trust in the LORD,
    she does not draw near to her God.
	2 She listens to no voice,
	    she accepts no correction.
	She does not trust in the LORD,
	    she does not draw near to her God.
		2 It has not listened to the LORD or accepted his discipline. It has not put its trust in the LORD or asked for his help.

3 Her officials are roaring lions,
    her rulers are evening wolves,
    who leave nothing for the morning.
	3 Her officials within her
	    are roaring lions;
	    her judges are evening wolves
	    that leave nothing till the morning.
		3 Its officials are like roaring lions; its judges are like hungry wolves, too greedy to leave a bone until morning.

4 Her prophets are arrogant;
    they are treacherous men.
Her priests profane the sanctuary
    and do violence to the law.
	4 Her prophets are wanton,
	    faithless men;
	    her priests profane what is sacred,
	    they do violence to the law.
		4 The prophets are irresponsible and treacherous; the priests defile what is sacred, and twist the law of God to their own advantage.

5 The LORD within her is righteous;
    he does no wrong.
Morning by morning he dispenses his
    justice,
    and every new day he does not fail,
    yet the unrighteous know no shame.
	5 The LORD within her is righteous,
	    he does no wrong;
	    every morning he shows forth his justice,
	    each dawn he does not fail;
	    but the unjust knows no shame.
		5 But the LORD is still in the city; he does what is right and never what is wrong. Every morning without fail, he brings justice to his people. And yet the unrighteous people there keep on doing wrong and are not ashamed.

Haggai

NIV	RSV	TEV
1:6 You have planted much, but have harvested little. You eat, but never have enough. You drink, but never have your fill. You put on clothes, but are not warm. You earn wages, only to put them in a purse with holes in it."	1:6 You have sown much, and harvested little; you eat, but you never have enough; you drink, but you never have your fill; you clothe yourselves, but no one is warm; and he who earns wages earns wages to put them into a bag with holes.	1:6 You have planted much grain, but have harvested very little. You have food to eat, but not enough to make you full. You have wine to drink, but not enough to get drunk on! You have clothing, but not enough to keep you warm. And the working man cannot earn enough to live on.
7 This is what the LORD Almighty says: "Give careful thought to your ways.	7 "Thus says the LORD of hosts: Consider how you have fared.	7 Can't you see why this has happened?

KJV	NKJV	TLB
2:6 For thus saith the LORD of hosts; Yet once, it *is* a little while, and I will shake the heavens, and the earth, and the sea, and the dry *land;*	**2:6** "For thus says the LORD of hosts: "Once more (it *is* a little while) I will shake heaven and earth, the sea and dry land;	**2:6** "For the Lord of Hosts says, 'In just a little while I will begin to shake the heavens and earth—and the oceans, too, and the dry land—
7 And I will shake all nations, and the desire of all nations shall come: and I will find this house with glory, saith the LORD of hosts.	**7** 'and I will shake all nations, and they shall come to the Desire of All Nations, and I will fill this temple with glory,' says the LORD of hosts.	**7** I will shake all nations, and the Desire of All Nations shall come to this Temple, and I will fill this place with my glory,' says the Lord of Hosts.
22 And I will overthrow the throne of kingdoms, and I will destroy the strength of the kingdoms of the heathen; and I will overthrow the chariots, and those that ride in them; and the horses and their riders shall come down, every one by the sword of his brother.	**22** I will overthrow the throne of kingdoms; I will destroy the strength of the Gentile kingdoms. I will overthrow the chariots And those who ride in them; The horses and their riders shall come down, Every one by the sword of his brother.	**22** and to overthrow thrones and destroy the strength of the kingdoms of the nations. I will overthrow their armed might, and brothers and companions will kill each other.
23 In that day, saith the LORD of hosts, will I take thee, O Zerubbabel, my servant, the son of Shealtiel, saith the LORD, and will make thee as a signet: for I have chosen thee, saith the LORD of hosts.	**23** 'In that day,' says the LORD of hosts, 'I will take you, Zerubbabel My servant, the son of Shealtiel,' says the LORD, 'and will make you as a signet *ring;* for I have chosen you,' says the LORD of hosts."	**23** But when that happens, I will take you, O Zerubbabel my servant, and honor you like a signet ring upon my finger; for I have specially chosen you," says the Lord of Hosts.

Zechariah

KJV	NKJV	TLB
2:1 I lifted up mine eyes again, and looked, and behold a man with a measuring line in his hand.	**2:1** Then I raised my eyes and looked, and behold, a man with a measuring line in his hand.	**2:1** When I looked around me again, I saw a man carrying a yardstick in his hand.
2 Then said I, Whither goest thou? And he said unto me, To measure Jerusalem, to see what *is* the breadth thereof, and what *is* the length thereof.	**2** So I said, "Where are you going?" And he said to me, "To measure Jerusalem, to see what *is* its width and what *is* its length."	**2** "Where are you going?" I asked. "To measure Jerusalem," he said. "I want to see whether it is big enough for all the people!"
3 And, behold, the angel that talked with me went forth, and another angel went out to meet him,	**3** And there *was* the angel who talked with me, going out; and another angel was coming out to meet him,	**3** Then the angel who was talking to me went over to meet another angel coming toward him.
4 And said unto him, Run, speak to this young man, saying, Jerusalem shall be inhabited *as* towns without walls for the multitude of men and cattle therein:	**4** who said to him, "Run, speak to this young man, saying: 'Jerusalem shall be inhabited *as* towns without walls, because of the multitude of men and livestock in it.	**4** "Go tell this young man," said the other angel, "that Jerusalem will some day be so full of people that she won't have room enough for all! Many will live outside the city walls, with all their many cattle—and yet they will be safe.
5 For I, saith the LORD, will be unto her a wall of fire round about, and will be the glory in the midst of her.	**5** 'For I,' says the LORD, 'will be a wall of fire all around her, and I will be the glory in her midst.'"	**5** For the Lord himself will be a wall of fire protecting them and all Jerusalem; he will be the glory of the city.
3:8 Hear now, O Joshua the high priest, thou, and thy fellows that sit before thee: for they *are* men wondered at: for, behold, I will bring forth my servant the BRANCH.	**3:8** 'Hear, O Joshua, the high priest, You and your companions who sit before you, For they are a wondrous sign; For behold, I am bringing forth My Servant the BRANCH.	**3:8** Listen to me, O Joshua the High Priest, and all you other priests, you are illustrations of the good things to come. Don't you see?— Joshua represents my servant the Branch whom I will send.
9 For behold the stone that I have laid before Joshua; upon one stone *shall be* seven eyes: behold, I will engrave the graving thereof, saith the LORD of hosts, and I will remove the iniquity of that land in one day.	**9** For behold, the stone That I have laid before Joshua: Upon the stone *are* seven eyes. Behold, I will engrave its inscription,' Says the LORD of hosts, 'And I will remove the iniquity of that land in one day.	**9** He will be the Foundation Stone of the Temple that Joshua is standing beside, and I will engrave this inscription on it seven times: *I will remove the sins of this land in a single day.*
10 In that day, saith the LORD of hosts, shall ye call every man his neighbour under the vine and under the fig tree.	**10** In that day,' says the LORD of hosts, 'Everyone will invite his neighbor Under his vine and under his fig tree.'"	**10** And after that,' the Lord of Hosts declares, 'you will all live in peace and prosperity and each of you will own a home of your own where you can invite your neighbors.'"
4:2 And said unto me, What seest thou? And I said, I have looked, and behold a candlestick all *of* gold, with a bowl upon the top of it, and his seven lamps thereon, and seven pipes to the seven lamps, which *are* upon the top thereof:	**4:2** And he said to me, "What do you see?" So I said, "I am looking, and there *is* a lampstand of solid gold with a bowl on top of it, and on the *stand* seven lamps with seven pipes to the seven lamps.	**4:2** "What do you see now?" he asked. I answered, "I see a golden lampstand holding seven lamps, and at the top there is a reservoir for the olive oil that feeds the lamps, flowing into them through seven tubes.
3 And two olive trees by it, one upon the right *side* of the bowl, and the other upon the left *side* thereof.	**3** "Two olive trees *are* by it, one at the right of the bowl and the other at its left."	**3** And I see two olive trees carved upon the lampstand, one on each side of the reservoir.

NIV	RSV	TEV
2:6 "This is what the LORD Almighty says: 'In a little while I will once more shake the heavens and the earth, the sea and the dry land.	**2:6** For thus says the LORD of hosts: Once again, in a little while, I will shake the heavens and the earth and the sea and the dry land;	**2:6** "Before long I will shake heaven and earth, land and sea.
7 I will shake all nations, and the desired of all nations will come, and I will fill this house with glory,' says the LORD Almighty.	**7** and I will shake all nations, so that the treasures of all nations shall come in, and I will fill this house with splendor, says the LORD of hosts.	**7** I will overthrow all the nations, and their treasures will be brought here, and the Temple will be filled with wealth.
22 I will overturn royal thrones and shatter the power of the foreign kingdoms. I will overthrow chariots and their drivers; horses and their riders will fall, each by the sword of his brother.	**22** and to overthrow the throne of kingdoms; I am about to destroy the strength of the kingdoms of the nations, and overthrow the chariots and their riders; and the horses and their riders shall go down, every one by the sword of his fellow.	**22** and overthrow kingdoms and end their power. I will overturn chariots and their drivers; the horses will die, and their riders will kill one another.
23 "'On that day,' declares the LORD Almighty, 'I will take you, my servant Zerubbabel son of Shealtiel,' declares the LORD, 'and I will make you like my signet ring, for I have chosen you,' declares the LORD Almighty."	**23** On that day, says the LORD of hosts, I will take you, O Zerubbabel my servant, the son of Shealtiel, says the LORD, and make you like a signet ring; for I have chosen you, says the LORD of hosts."	**23** On that day I will take you, Zerubbabel my servant, and I will appoint you to rule in my name. You are the one I have chosen." The LORD Almighty has spoken.

Zechariah

NIV	RSV	TEV
2:1 Then I looked up—and there before me was a man with a measuring line in his hand!	**2:1** And I lifted my eyes and saw, and behold, a man with a measuring line in his hand!	**2:1** In another vision I saw a man with a measuring line in his hand.
2 I asked, "Where are you going?" He answered me, "To measure Jerusalem, to find out how wide and how long it is."	**2** Then I said, "Where are you going?" And he said to me, "To measure Jerusalem, to see what is its breadth and what is its length."	**2** "Where are you going?" I asked. "To measure Jerusalem," he answered, "to see how long and how wide it is."
3 Then the angel who was speaking to me left, and another angel came to meet him	**3** And behold, the angel who talked with me came forward, and another angel came forward to meet him,	**3** Then I saw the angel who had been speaking to me step forward, and another angel came to meet him.
4 and said to him: "Run, tell that young man, 'Jerusalem will be a city without walls because of the great number of men and livestock in it.	**4** and said to him, "Run, say to that young man, 'Jerusalem shall be inhabited as villages without walls, because of the multitude of men and cattle in it.	**4** The first one said to the other, "Run and tell that young man with the measuring line that there are going to be so many people and so much livestock in Jerusalem that it will be too big to have walls.
5 And I myself will be a wall of fire around it,' declares the LORD, 'and I will be its glory within.'	**5** For I will be to her a wall of fire round about, says the LORD, and I will be the glory within her.'"	**5** The LORD has promised that he himself will be a wall of fire around the city to protect it and that he will live there in all his glory."
3:8 "'Listen, O high priest Joshua and your associates seated before you, who are men symbolic of things to come: I am going to bring my servant, the Branch.	**3:8** Hear now, O Joshua the high priest, you and your friends who sit before you, for they are men of good omen: behold, I will bring my servant the Branch.	**3:8** Listen then, Joshua, you who are the High Priest; and listen, you fellow priests of his, you that are the sign of a good future: I will reveal my servant, who is called The Branch!
9 See, the stone I have set in front of Joshua! There are seven eyes on that one stone, and I will engrave an inscription on it,' says the LORD Almighty, 'and I will remove the sin of this land in a single day.	**9** For behold, upon the stone which I have set before Joshua, upon a single stone with seven facets, I will engrave its inscription, says the LORD of hosts, and I will remove the guilt of this land in a single day.	**9** I am placing in front of Joshua a single stone with seven facets. I will engrave an inscription on it, and in a single day I will take away the sin of this land.
10 "'In that day each of you will invite his neighbor to sit under his vine and fig tree,' declares the LORD Almighty."	**10** In that day, says the LORD of hosts, every one of you will invite his neighbor under his vine and under his fig tree."	**10** When that day comes, each of you will invite his neighbor to come and enjoy peace and security, surrounded by your vineyards and fig trees."
4:2 He asked me, "What do you see?" I answered, "I see a solid gold lampstand with a bowl at the top and seven lights on it, with seven channels to the lights.	**4:2** And he said to me, "What do you see?" I said, "I see, and behold, a lampstand all of gold, with a bowl on the top of it, and seven lamps on it, with seven lips on each of the lamps which are on the top of it.	**4:2** "What do you see?" he asked. "A lampstand made of gold," I answered. "At the top is a bowl for the oil. On the lampstand are seven lamps, each one with places for seven wicks.
3 Also there are two olive trees by it, one on the right of the bowl and the other on its left."	**3** And there are two olive trees by it, one on the right of the bowl and the other on its left."	**3** There are two olive trees beside the lampstand, one on each side of it."

KJV	NKJV	TLB
6 Then he answered and spake unto me, saying, This *is* the word of the LORD unto Zerubbabel, saying, Not by might, nor by power, but by my spirit, saith the LORD of hosts.	6 So he answered and said to me: "This *is* the word of the LORD to Zerubbabel: 'Not by might nor by power, but by My Spirit.' Says the LORD of hosts.	6 Then he said, "This is God's message to Zerubbabel: 'Not by might, nor by power, but by my Spirit, says the Lord of Hosts—you will succeed because of my Spirit, though you are few and weak.'
6:12 And speak unto him, saying, Thus speaketh the LORD of hosts, saying, Behold the man whose name *is* The BRANCH; and he shall grow up out of his place, and he shall build the temple of the LORD:	**6:12** "Then speak to him, saying, 'Thus says the LORD of hosts, saying: "Behold, the Man whose name *is* the BRANCH! From His place He shall branch out, And He shall build the temple of the LORD;	**6:12** Tell him that the Lord of Hosts says, 'You represent the Man who will come, whose name is "The Branch"—he will grow up from himself—and will build the Temple of the Lord.
13 Even he shall build the temple of the LORD; and he shall bear the glory, and shall sit and rule upon his throne; and he shall be a priest upon his throne: and the counsel of peace shall be between them both.	13 Yes, He shall build the temple of the LORD. He shall bear the glory, And shall sit and rule on His throne; So He shall be a priest on His throne, And the counsel of peace shall be between them both."'	13 To him belongs the royal title. He will rule both as King and as Priest, with perfect harmony between the two!'
8:20 Thus saith the LORD of hosts; *It shall* yet *come to pass,* that there shall come people, and the inhabitants of many cities:	**8:20** "Thus says the LORD of hosts: 'Peoples shall yet come, Inhabitants of many cities;	**8:20** People from around the world will come on pilgrimages and pour into Jerusalem from many foreign cities to attend these celebrations.
21 And the inhabitants of one *city* shall go to another, saying, Let us go speedily to pray before the LORD, and to seek the LORD of hosts: I will go also.	21 The inhabitants of one *city* shall go to another, saying, "Let us continue to go and pray before the LORD, And seek the LORD of hosts. I myself will go also."	21 People will write their friends in other cities and say, 'Let's go to Jerusalem to ask the Lord to bless us, and be merciful to us. I'm going! Please come with me. Let's go *now!*'
22 Yea, many people and strong nations shall come to seek the LORD of hosts in Jerusalem, and to pray before the LORD.	22 Yes, many peoples and strong nations Shall come to seek the LORD of hosts in Jerusalem, And to pray before the LORD.'	22 Yes, many people, even strong nations, will come to the Lord of Hosts in Jerusalem to ask for his blessing and help.
9:9 Rejoice greatly, O daughter of Zion; shout, O daughter of Jerusalem: behold, thy King cometh unto thee: he *is* just, and having salvation; lowly, and riding upon an ass, and upon a colt the foal of an ass.	**9:9** "Rejoice greatly, O daughter of Zion! Shout, O daughter of Jerusalem! Behold, your King is coming to you; He *is* just and having salvation, Lowly and riding on a donkey, A colt, the foal of a donkey.	**9:9** "Rejoice greatly, O my people! Shout with joy! For look—your King is coming! He is the Righteous One, the Victor! Yet he is lowly, riding on a donkey's colt!
10:10 I will bring them again also out of the land of Egypt, and gather them out of Assyria; and I will bring them into the land of Gilead and Lebanon; and *place* shall not be found for them.	**10:10** I will also bring them back from the land of Egypt, And gather them from Assyria. I will bring them into the land of Gilead and Lebanon, Until no *more room* is found for them.	**10:10** I will bring them back from Egypt and Assyria, and resettle them in Israel—in Gilead and Lebanon; there will scarcely be room for all of them!
11 And he shall pass through the sea with affliction, and shall smite the waves in the sea, and all the deeps of the river shall dry up: and the pride of Assyria shall be brought down, and the sceptre of Egypt shall depart away.	11 He shall pass through the sea with affliction, And strike the waves of the sea: All the depths of the River shall dry up. Then the pride of Assyria shall be brought down, And the scepter of Egypt shall depart.	11 They shall pass safely through the sea of distress, for the waves will be held back. The Nile will become dry—the rule of Assyria and Egypt over my people will end."
12 And I will strengthen them in the LORD; and they shall walk up and down in his name, saith the LORD.	12 "So I will strengthen them in the LORD, And they shall walk up and down in His name," Says the LORD.	12 The Lord says, "I will make my people strong with power from me! They will go wherever they wish, and wherever they go, they will be under my personal care."
12:10 And I will pour upon the house of David, and upon the inhabitants of Jerusalem, the spirit of grace and of supplications: and they shall look upon me whom they have pierced, and they shall mourn for him, as one mourneth for *his* only *son,* and shall be in bitterness for him, as one that is in bitterness for *his* firstborn.	**12:10** "And I will pour on the house of David and on the inhabitants of Jerusalem the Spirit of grace and supplication; then they will look on Me whom they have pierced; they will mourn for Him as one mourns for *his* only *son,* and grieve for Him as one grieves for a firstborn.	**12:10** "Then I will pour out the spirit of grace and prayer on all the people of Jerusalem, and they will look on him they pierced, and mourn for him as for an only son, and grieve bitterly for him as for an oldest child who died.

NIV	RSV	TEV
6 So he said to me, "This is the word of the LORD to Zerubbabel: 'Not by might nor by power, but by my Spirit,' says the LORD Almighty.	6 Then he said to me, "This is the word of the LORD to Zerubbabel: Not by might, nor by power, but by my Spirit, says the LORD of hosts.	6 The angel told me to give Zerubbabel this message from the LORD: "You will succeed, not by military might or by your own strength, but by my spirit.
6:12 Tell him this is what the LORD Almighty says: 'Here is the man whose name is the Branch, and he will branch out from his place and build the temple of the LORD.	6:12 and say to him, 'Thus says the LORD of hosts, "Behold, the man whose name is the Branch: for he shall grow up in his place, and he shall build the temple of the LORD.	6:12 Tell him that the LORD Almighty says, 'The man who is called The Branch will flourish where he is and rebuild the LORD's Temple.
13 It is he who will build the temple of the LORD, and he will be clothed with majesty and will sit and rule on his throne. And he will be a priest on his throne. And there will be harmony between the two.'	13 It is he who shall build the temple of the LORD, and shall bear royal honor, and shall sit and rule upon his throne. And there shall be a priest by his throne, and peaceful understanding shall be between them both.' "	13 He is the one who will build it and receive the honor due a king, and he will rule his people. A priest will stand by his throne, and they will work together in peace and harmony.'
8:20 This is what the LORD Almighty says: "Many peoples and the inhabitants of many cities will yet come,	8:20 "Thus says the LORD of hosts: Peoples shall yet come, even the inhabitants of many cities;	8:20 The LORD Almighty says, "The time is coming when people from many cities will come to Jerusalem.
21 and the inhabitants of one city will go to another and say, 'Let us go at once to entreat the LORD and seek the LORD Almighty. I myself am going.'	21 the inhabitants of one city shall go to another, saying, 'Let us go at once to entreat the favor of the LORD, and to seek the LORD of hosts; I am going.'	21 Those from one city will say to those from another, 'We are going to worship the LORD Almighty and pray for his blessing. Come with us!'
22 And many peoples and powerful nations will come to Jerusalem to seek the LORD Almighty and to entreat him."	22 Many peoples and strong nations shall come to seek the LORD of hosts in Jerusalem, and to entreat the favor of the LORD.	22 Many peoples and powerful nations will come to Jerusalem to worship the LORD Almighty and to pray for his blessing.
9:9 Rejoice greatly, O Daughter of Zion! Shout, Daughter of Jerusalem! See, your king comes to you, righteous and having salvation, gentle and riding on a donkey, on a colt, the foal of a donkey.	9:9 Rejoice greatly, O daughter of Zion! Shout aloud, O daughter of Jerusalem! Lo, your king comes to you; triumphant and victorious is he, humble and riding on an ass, on a colt the foal of an ass.	9:9 Rejoice, rejoice, people of Zion! Shout for joy, you people of Jerusalem! Look, your king is coming to you! He comes triumphant and victorious, but humble and riding on a donkey— on a colt, the foal of a donkey.
10:10 I will bring them back from Egypt and gather them from Assyria. I will bring them to Gilead and Lebanon, and there will not be room enough for them.	10:10 I will bring them home from the land of Egypt, and gather them from Assyria; and I will bring them to the land of Gilead and to Lebanon, till there is not room for them.	10:10 From Egypt and Assyria I will bring them home and settle them in their own country. I will settle them in Gilead and Lebanon also; the whole land will be filled with people.
11 They will pass through the sea of trouble; the surging sea will be subdued and all the depths of the Nile will dry up. Assyria's pride will be brought down and Egypt's scepter will pass away.	11 They shall pass through the sea of Egypt, and the waves of the sea shall be smitten, and all the depths of the Nile dried up. The pride of Assyria shall be laid low, and the scepter of Egypt shall depart.	11 When they pass through their sea of trouble, I, the LORD, will strike the waves, and the depths of the Nile will go dry. Proud Assyria will be humbled, and mighty Egypt will lose her power.
12 I will strengthen them in the LORD and in his name they will walk," declares the LORD.	12 I will make them strong in the LORD. and they shall glory in his name," says the LORD.	12 I will make my people strong; they will worship and obey me." The LORD has spoken.
12:10 "And I will pour out on the house of David and the inhabitants of Jerusalem a spirit of grace and supplication. They will look on me, the one they have pierced, and they will mourn for him as one mourns for an only child, and grieve bitterly for him as one grieves for a first-born son.	12:10 "And I will pour out on the house of David and the inhabitants of Jerusalem a spirit of compassion and supplication, so that, when they look on him whom they have pierced, they shall mourn for him, as one mourns for an only child, and weep bitterly over him, as one weeps over a first-born.	12:10 "I will fill the descendants of David and the other people of Jerusalem with the spirit of mercy and the spirit of prayer. They will look at the one whom they stabbed to death, and they will mourn for him like those who mourn for an only child. They will mourn bitterly, like those who have lost their first-born son.

KJV	NKJV	TLB
13:6 And *one* shall say unto him, What *are* these wounds in thine hands? Then he shall answer, *Those* with which I was wounded *in* the house of my friends.	**13:6** "And *someone* will say to him, 'What are these wounds in your hands?' Then he will answer, *'Those* with which I was wounded in the house of my friends.'	**13:6** "And if someone asks, 'Then what are these scars on your chest and your back?' he will say, 'I got into a brawl at the home of a friend!'
7 Awake, O sword, against my shepherd, and against the man *that is* my fellow, saith the LORD of hosts: smite the shepherd, and the sheep shall be scattered: and I will turn mine hand upon the little ones.	**7** "Awake, O sword, against My Shepherd, Against the Man who is My Companion," Says the LORD of hosts. "Strike the Shepherd, And the sheep will be scattered; then I will turn My hand against the little ones.	**7** "Awake, O sword, against my shepherd, the man who is my associate and equal," says the Lord of Hosts. "Strike down the Shepherd and the sheep will scatter, but I will come back and comfort and care for the lambs.
14:1 Behold, the day of the LORD cometh, and thy spoil shall be divided in the midst of thee.	**14:1** Behold, the day of the LORD is coming, And your spoil will be divided in your midst.	**14:1** Watch, for the day of the Lord is coming soon!
2 For I will gather all nations against Jerusalem to battle; and the city shall be taken, and the houses rifled, and the women ravished; and half of the city shall go forth into captivity, and the residue of the people shall not be cut off from the city.	**2** For I will gather all the nations to battle against Jerusalem; The city shall be taken, The houses rifled, And the women ravished. Half of the city shall go into captivity, But the remnant of the people shall not be cut off from the city.	**2** On that day the Lord will gather together the nations to fight Jerusalem; the city will be taken, the houses rifled, the loot divided, the women raped; half the population will be taken away as slaves, and half will be left in what remains of the city.
3 Then shall the LORD go forth, and fight against those nations, as when he fought in the day of battle.	**3** Then the LORD will go forth And fight against those nations, As He fights in the day of battle.	**3** Then the Lord will go out fully armed for war, to fight against those nations.
4 And his feet shall stand in that day upon the mount of Olives, which *is* before Jerusalem on the east; and the mount of Olives shall cleave in the midst thereof toward the east and toward the west, *and there shall be* a very great valley; and half of the mountain shall remove toward the north, and half of it toward the south.	**4** And in that day His feet will stand on the Mount of Olives, Which faces Jerusalem on the east. And the Mount of Olives shall be split in two, From east to west, *Making* a very large valley; Half of the mountain shall move toward the north And half of it toward the south.	**4** That day his feet will stand upon the Mount of Olives, to the east of Jerusalem, and the Mount of Olives will split apart, making a very wide valley running from east to west, for half the mountain will move toward the north and half toward the south.
8 And it shall be in that day, *that* living waters shall go out from Jerusalem; half of them toward the former sea, and half of them toward the hinder sea: in summer and in winter shall it be.	**8** And in that day it shall be *That* living waters shall flow from Jerusalem, Half of them toward the eastern sea And half of them toward the western sea; In both summer and winter it shall occur.	**8** Life-giving waters will flow out from Jerusalem, half toward the Dead Sea and half towards the Mediterranean, flowing continuously both in winter and in summer.
9 And the LORD shall be king over all the earth: in that day shall there be one LORD, and his name one.	**9** And the LORD shall be the King over all the earth. In that day it shall be— "The LORD *is* one," And His name one.	**9** And the Lord shall be King over all the earth. In that day there shall be one Lord—his name alone will be worshiped.
20 In that day shall there be upon the bells of the horses, HOLINESS UNTO THE LORD; and the pots in the LORD's house shall be like the bowls before the altar.	**20** In that day "HOLINESS TO THE LORD" shall be *engraved* on the bells of the horses. The pots in the LORD's house shall be like the bowls before the altar.	**20** In that day the bells on the horses will have written on them, "These Are Holy Property"; and the trash cans in the Temple of the Lord will be as sacred as the bowls beside the altar.
21 Yea, every pot in Jerusalem and in Judah shall be holiness unto the LORD of hosts: and all they that sacrifice shall come and take of them, and seethe therein: and in that day there shall be no more the Canaanite in the house of the LORD of hosts.	**21** Yes, every pot in Jerusalem and Judah shall be holiness to the LORD of hosts. Everyone who sacrifices shall come and take them and cook in them. In that day there shall no longer be a Canaanite in the house of the LORD of hosts.	**21** In fact, every container in Jerusalem and Judah shall be sacred to the Lord of Hosts; all who come to worship may use any of them free of charge to boil their sacrifices in; there will be no more grasping traders in the Temple of the Lord of Hosts!

Malachi

KJV	NKJV	TLB
1:2 I have loved you, saith the LORD. Yet ye say, Wherein hast thou loved us? *Was* not Esau Jacob's brother? saith the LORD: yet I loved Jacob,	**1:2** "I have loved you," says the LORD. "Yet you say, 'In what way have You loved us?' "*Was* not Esau Jacob's brother?" Says the LORD. "Yet Jacob I have loved;	**1:2** "I have loved you very deeply," says the Lord. But you retort, "Really? When was this?" And the Lord replies, "I showed my love for you by loving your father, Jacob.

NIV	RSV	TEV
13:6 If someone asks him, 'What are these wounds on your body?' he will answer, 'The wounds I was given at the house of my friends.'	**13:6** And if one asks him, 'What are these wounds on your back?' he will say, 'The wounds I received in the house of my friends.'"	**13:6** Then if someone asks him, 'What are those wounds on your chest?' he will answer, 'I got them at a friend's house.'"
7 "Awake, O sword, against my shepherd, against the man who is close to me!" declares the LORD Almighty. "Strike the shepherd, and the sheep will be scattered, and I will turn my hand against the little ones.	**7** "Awake, O sword, against my shepherd, against the man who stands next to me," says the LORD of hosts. "Strike the shepherd, that the sheep may be scattered; I will turn my hand against the little ones.	**7** The LORD Almighty says, "Wake up, sword, and attack the shepherd who works for me! Kill him, and the sheep will be scattered. I will attack my people.
14:1 A day of the LORD is coming when your plunder will be divided among you.	**14:1** Behold, a day of the LORD is coming, when the spoil taken from you will be divided in the midst of you.	**14:1** The day when the LORD will sit in judgment is near. Then Jerusalem will be looted, and the loot will be divided up before your eyes.
2 I will gather all the nations to Jerusalem to fight against it; the city will be captured, the houses ransacked, and the women raped. Half of the city will go into exile, but the rest of the people will not be taken from the city.	**2** For I will gather all the nations against Jerusalem to battle, and the city shall be taken and the houses plundered and the women ravished; half of the city shall go into exile, but the rest of the people shall not be cut off from the city.	**2** The LORD will bring all the nations together to make war on Jerusalem. The city will be taken, the houses looted, and the women raped. Half of the people will go into exile, but the rest of them will not be taken away from the city.
3 Then the LORD will go out and fight against those nations, as he fights in the day of battle.	**3** Then the LORD will go forth and fight against those nations as when he fights on a day of battle.	**3** Then the LORD will go out and fight against those nations, as he has fought in times past.
4 On that day his feet will stand on the Mount of Olives, east of Jerusalem, and the Mount of Olives will be split in two from east to west, forming a great valley, with half of the mountain moving north and half moving south.	**4** On that day his feet shall stand on the Mount of Olives which lies before Jerusalem on the east; and the Mount of Olives shall be split in two from east to west by a very wide valley; so that one half of the Mount shall withdraw northward, and the other half southward.	**4** At that time he will stand on the Mount of Olives, to the east of Jerusalem. Then the Mount of Olives will be split in two from west to east by a large valley. Half of the mountain will move northward, and half of it southward.
8 On that day living water will flow out from Jerusalem, half to the eastern sea and half to the western sea, in summer and in winter.	**8** On that day living waters shall flow out from Jerusalem, half of them to the eastern sea and half of them to the western sea; it shall continue in summer as in winter.	**8** When that day comes, fresh water will flow from Jerusalem, half of it to the Dead Sea and the other half to the Mediterranean. It will flow all year long, in the dry season as well as the wet.
9 The LORD will be king over the whole earth. On that day there will be one LORD, and his name the only name.	**9** And the LORD will become king over all the earth; on that day the LORD will be one and his name one.	**9** Then the LORD will be king over all the earth; everyone will worship him as God and know him by the same name.
20 On that day HOLY TO THE LORD will be inscribed on the bells of the horses, and the cooking pots in the LORD's house will be like the sacred bowls in front of the altar.	**20** And on that day there shall be inscribed on the bells of the horses, "Holy to the LORD." And the pots in the house of the LORD shall be as the bowls before the altar;	**20** At that time even the harness bells of the horses will be inscribed with the words "Dedicated to the LORD." The cooking pots in the Temple will be as sacred as the bowls before the altar.
21 Every pot in Jerusalem and Judah will be holy to the LORD Almighty, and all who come to sacrifice will take some of the pots and cook in them. And on that day there will no longer be a Canaanite in the house of the LORD Almighty.	**21** and every pot in Jerusalem and Judah shall be sacred to the LORD of hosts, so that all who sacrifice may come and take of them and boil the flesh of the sacrifice in them. And there shall no longer be a trader in the house of the LORD of hosts on that day.	**21** Every cooking pot in Jerusalem and in all Judah will be set apart for use in the worship of the LORD Almighty. The people who offer sacrifices will use them for boiling the meat of the sacrifices. When that time comes, there will no longer be any merchant in the Temple of the LORD Almighty.

Malachi

1:2 "I have loved you," says the LORD. "But you ask, 'How have you loved us?' "Was not Esau Jacob's brother?" the LORD says. "Yet I have loved Jacob,	**1:2** "I have loved you," says the LORD. But you say, "How hast thou loved us?" "Is not Esau Jacob's brother?" says the LORD. "Yet I have loved Jacob	**1:2** The LORD says to his people, "I have always loved you." But they reply, "How have you shown your love for us?" The LORD answers, "Esau and Jacob were brothers, but I have loved Jacob and his descendants,

KJV	NKJV	TLB
6 A son honoureth *his* father, and a servant his master: if then I *be* a father, where *is* mine honour? and if I *be* a master, where *is* my fear? saith the LORD of hosts unto you, O priests, that despise my name. And ye say, Wherein have we despised thy name?	6 "A son honors *his* father, And a servant *his* master. If then I am the Father, Where *is* My honor? And if I *am* a Master, Where *is* My reverence? Says the LORD of hosts To you priests who despise My name. Yet you say, 'In what way have we despised Your name?'	6 "A son honors his father, a servant honors his master. I am your Father and Master, yet you don't honor me, O priests, but you despise my name." "Who? Us?" you say. "When did we ever despise your name?"
2:10 Have we not all one father? hath not one God created us? why do we deal treacherously every man against his brother, by profaning the covenant of our fathers?	2:10 Have we not all one Father? Has not one God created us? Why do we deal treacherously with one another By profaning the covenant of the fathers?	2:10 We are children of the same father, Abraham, all created by the same God. And yet we are faithless to each other, violating the covenant of our fathers!
14 Yet we say, Wherefore? Because the LORD hath been witness between thee and the wife of thy youth, against whom thou hast dealt treacherously: yet *is* she thy companion, and the wife of thy covenant.	14 Yet you say, "For what reason?" Because the LORD has been witness Between you and the wife of your youth, With whom you have dealt treacherously; Yet she is your companion And your wife by covenant.	14 "Why has God abandoned us?" you cry. I'll tell you why; it is because the Lord has seen your treachery in divorcing your wives who have been faithful to you through the years, the companions you promised to care for and keep.
17 Ye have wearied the LORD with your words. Yet ye say, Wherein have we wearied *him?* When ye say, Every one that doeth evil *is* good in the sight of the LORD, and he delighteth in them; or, Where *is* the God of judgment?	17 You have wearied the LORD with your words; Yet you say, "In what way have we wearied *Him?*" In that you say, "Everyone who does evil *Is* good in the sight of the LORD, And He delights in them," Or, "Where *is* the God of justice?"	17 You have wearied the Lord with your words. "Wearied him?" you ask in fake surprise. "How have we wearied him?" By saying that evil is good, that it pleases the Lord! Or by saying that God won't punish us—he doesn't care.
3:1 Behold, I will send my messenger, and he shall prepare the way before me: and the Lord, whom ye seek, shall suddenly come to his temple, even the messenger of the covenant, whom ye delight in: behold, he shall come, saith the LORD of hosts.	3:1 "Behold, I send My messenger, And he will prepare the way before Me. And the Lord, whom you seek, Will suddenly come to His temple, Even the Messenger of the covenant, In whom you delight. Behold, He is coming," Says the LORD of hosts.	3:1 "Listen: I will send my messenger befre me to prepare the way. And then the one you are looking for will come suddenly to his Temple— the Messenger of God's promises, to bring you great joy. Yes, he is surely coming," says the Lord of Hosts.
2 But who may abide the day of his coming? and who shall stand when he appeareth? for he *is* like a refiner's fire, and like fullers' soap:	2 "But who can endure the day of His coming? And who can stand when He appears? For He *is* like a refiner's fire And like fuller's soap.	2 "But who can live when he appears? Who can endure his coming? For he is like a blazing fire refining precious metal and he can bleach the dirtiest garments!
3 And he shall sit *as* a refiner and purifier of silver: and he shall purify the sons of Levi, and purge them as gold and silver, that they may offer unto the LORD an offering in righteousness.	3 He will sit as a refiner and a purifier of silver; He will purify the sons of Levi, And purge them as gold and silver, That they may offer to the LORD An offering in righteousness.	3 Like a refiner of silver he will sit and closely watch as the dross is burned away. He will purify the Levites, the ministers of God, refining them like gold or silver, so that they will do their work for God with pure hearts.
8 Will a man rob God? Yet ye have robbed me. But ye say, Wherein have we robbed thee? In tithes and offerings.	8 "Will a man rob God? Yet you have robbed Me! But you say, 'In what way have we robbed You?' In tithes and offerings.	8 "Will a man rob God? Surely not! And yet you have robbed me. "'What do you mean? When did we ever rob you?' "You have robbed me of the tithes and offerings due to me.
16 Then they that feared the LORD spake often one to another: and the LORD hearkened, and heard *it,* and a book of remembrance was written before him for them that feared the LORD, and that thought upon his name.	16 Then those who feared the LORD spoke to one another, And the LORD listened and heard *them;* So a book of remembrance was written before Him For those who fear the LORD And who meditate on His name.	16 Then those who feared and loved the Lord spoke often of him to each other. And he had a Book of Remembrance drawn up in which he recorded the names of those who feared him and loved to think about him.
17 And they shall be mine, saith the LORD of hosts, in that day when I make up my jewels; and I will spare them, as a man spareth his own son that serveth him.	17 "They shall be Mine," says the LORD of hosts, "On the day that I make them My jewels. And I will spare them As a man spares his own son who serves him."	17 "They shall be mine," says the Lord of Hosts, "in that day when I make up my jewels. And I will spare them as a man spares an obedient and dutiful son."

NIV	RSV	TEV
6 "A son honors his father, and a servant his master. If I am a father, where is the honor due me? If I am a master, where is the respect due me?" says the LORD Almighty. "It is you, O priests, who despise my name. "But you ask, 'how have we despised your name?'	6 "A son honors his father, and a servant his master. If then I am a father, where is my honor? And if I am a master, where is my fear? says the LORD of hosts to you, O priests, who despise my name. You say, 'How have we despised thy name?'	6 The LORD Almighty says to the priests, "A son honors his father, and a servant honors his master. I am your father—why don't you honor me? I am your master—why don't you respect me? You despise me, and yet you ask, 'How have we despised you?'
2:10 Have we not all one Father? Did not one God create us? Why do we profane the covenant of our fathers by breaking faith with one another?	2:10 Have we not all one father? Has not one God created us? Why then are we faithless to one another, profaning the covenant of our fathers?	2:10 Don't we all have the same father? Didn't the same God create us all? Then why do we break our promises to one another, and why do we despise the covenant that God made with our ancestors?
14 You ask, "Why?" It is because the LORD is acting as the witness between you and the wife of your youth, because you have broken faith with her, though she is your partner, the wife of your marriage covenant.	14 You ask, "Why does he not?" Because the LORD was witness to the covenant between you and the wife of your youth, to whom you have been faithless, though she is your companion and your wife by covenant.	14 You ask why he no longer accepts them. It is because he knows you have broken your promise to the wife you married when you were young. She was your partner, and you have broken your promise to her, although you promised before God that you would be faithful to her.
17 You have wearied the LORD with your words. "How have we wearied him?" you ask. By saying, "All who do evil are good in the eyes of the LORD, and he is pleased with them" or "Where is the God of justice?"	17 You have wearied the LORD with your words. Yet you say, "How have we wearied him?" By saying, "Every one who does evil is good in the sight of the LORD, and he delights in them." Or by asking, "Where is the God of justice?"	17 You have tired the LORD out with your talk. But you ask, "How have we tired him?" By saying, "The LORD Almighty thinks all evildoers are good; in fact he likes them." Or by asking, "Where is the God who is supposed to be just?"
3:1 "See, I will send my messenger, who will prepare the way before me. Then suddenly the Lord you are seeking will come to his temple; the messenger of the covenant, whom you desire, will come," says the LORD Almighty.	3:1 "Behold, I send my messenger to prepare the way before me, and the Lord whom you seek will suddenly come to his temple; the messenger of the covenant in whom you delight, behold, he is coming, says the LORD of hosts.	3:1 The LORD Almighty answers, "I will send my messenger to prepare the way for me. Then the Lord you are looking for will suddenly come to his temple. The messenger you long to see will come and proclaim my covenant."
2 But who can endure the day of his coming? Who can stand when he appears? For he will be like a refiner's fire or a launderer's soap.	2 But who can endure the day of his coming, and who can stand when he apears? "For he is like a refiner's fire and like fuller's soap;	2 But who will be able to endure the day when he comes? Who will be able to survive when he appears? He will be like strong soap, like a fire that refines metal.
3 He will sit as a refiner and purifier of silver; he will purify the Levites and refine them like gold and silver. Then the LORD will have men who will bring offerings in righteousness,	3 he will sit as a refiner and purifier of silver, and he will purify the sons of Levi and refine them like gold and silver, till they present right offerings to the LORD.	3 He will come to judge like one who refines and purifies silver. As a metal-worker refines silver and gold, so the LORD's messenger will purify the priests, so that they will bring to the LORD the right kind of offerings.
8 "Will a man rob God? Yet you rob me. "But you ask, 'How do we rob you?' "In tithes and offerings.	8 Will man rob God? Yet you are robbing me. But you say, 'How are we robbing thee?' In your tithes and offerings.	8 I ask you, is it right for a person to cheat God? Of course not, yet you are cheating me. 'How?' you ask. In the matter of tithes and offerings.
16 Then those who feared the LORD talked with each other, and the LORD listened and heard. A scroll of remembrance was written in his presence concerning those who feared the LORD and honored his name.	16 Then those who feared the LORD spoke with one another; the LORD heeded and heard them, and a book of remembrance was written before him of those who feared the LORD and thought on his name.	16 Then the people who feared the LORD spoke to one another, and the LORD listened and heard what they said. In his presence, there was written down in a book a record of those who feared the LORD and respected him.
17 "They will be mine," says the LORD Almighty, "in the day when I make up my treasured possession. I will spare them, just as in compassion a man spares his son who serves him.	17 "They shall be mine, says the LORD of hosts, my special possession on the day when I act, and I will spare them as a man spares his son who serves him.	17 "They will be my people," says the LORD Almighty. "On the day when I act, they will be my very own. I will be merciful to them as a father is merciful to the son who serves him.

KEY VERSE COMPARISON CHART

KJV	NKJV	TLB
4:2 But unto you that fear my name shall the Sun of righteousness arise with healing in his wings; and ye shall go forth, and grow up as calves of the stall.	**4:2** But to you who fear My name The Sun of Righteousness shall arise With healing in His wings; And you shall go out And grow fat like stall-fed calves.	**4:2** "But for you who fear my name, the Sun of Righteousness will rise with healing in his wings. And you will go free, leaping with joy like calves let out to pasture.
5 Behold, I will send you Elijah the prophet before the coming of the great and dreadful day of the LORD:	5 Behold, I will send you Elijah the prophet Before the coming of the great and dreadful day of the LORD.	5 "See, I will send you another prophet like Elijah before the coming of the great and dreadful judgment day of God.
6 And he shall turn the heart of the fathers to the children, and the heart of the children to their fathers, lest I come and smite the earth with a curse.	6 And he will turn The hearts of the fathers to the children, And the hearts of the children to their fathers, Lest I come and strike the earth with a curse."	6 His preaching will bring fathers and children together again, to be of one mind and heart, for they will know that if they do not repent, I will come and utterly destroy their land."

NIV	RSV	TEV
4:2 But for you who revere my name, the sun of righteousness will rise with healing in its wings. And you will go out and leap like calves released from the stall.	**4:2** But for you who fear my name the sun of righteousness shall rise, with healing in its wings. You shall go forth leaping like calves from the stall.	**4:2** But for you who obey me, my saving power will rise on you like the sun and bring healing like the sun's rays. You will be as free and happy as calves let out of a stall.
5 "See, I will send you the prophet Elijah before that great and dreadful day of the LORD comes.	5 "Behold, I will send you Elijah the prophet before the great and terrible day of the LORD comes.	5 "But before the great and terrible day of the LORD comes, I will send you the prophet Elijah.
6 He will turn the hearts of the fathers to their children, and the hearts of the children to their fathers; or else I will come and strike the land with a curse."	6 And he will turn the hearts of fathers to their children and the hearts of children to their fathers, lest I come and smite the land with a curse."	6 He will bring fathers and children together again; otherwise I would have to come and destroy your country."

NEW TESTAMENT

KJV	NKJV	TLB

Matthew

KJV	NKJV	TLB
1:21 And she shall bring forth a son, and thou shalt call his name JESUS: for he shall save his people from their sins.	**1:21** "And she will bring forth a Son, and you shall call His name JESUS, for He will save His people from their sins."	**1:21** "And she will have a Son, and you shall name him Jesus (meaning 'Savior'), for he will save his people from their sins.
22 Now all this was done, that it might be fulfilled which was spoken of the Lord by the prophet, saying,	22 Now all this was done that it might be fulfilled which was spoken by the Lord through the prophet, saying:	22 This will fulfill God's message through his prophets—
23 Behold, a virgin shall be with child, and shall bring forth a son, and they shall call his name Emmanuel, which being interpreted is, God with us.	23 "Behold, a virgin shall be with child, and bear a Son, and they shall call His name Immanuel," which is translated, "God with us."	23 'Listen! The virgin shall conceive a child! She shall give birth to a Son, and he shall be called "Emmanuel" (meaning "God is with us").'"
2:1 Now when Jesus was born in Bethlehem of Judæa in the days of Herod the king, behold, there came wise men from the east to Jerusalem.	**2:1** Now after Jesus was born in Bethlehem of Judea in the days of Herod the king, behold, wise men from the East came to Jerusalem,	**2:1** Jesus was born in the town of Bethlehem, in Judea, during the reign of King Herod. At about that time some astrologers from eastern lands arrived in Jerusalem, asking,
2 Saying, Where is he that is born King of the Jews? for we have seen his star in the east, and are come to worship him.	2 saying, "Where is He who has been born King of the Jews? For we have seen His star in the East and have come to worship Him."	2 "Where is the newborn King of the Jews? for we have seen his star in far-off eastern lands, and have come to worship him."
7 Then Herod, when he had privily called the wise men, enquired of them diligently what time the star appeared.	7 Then Herod, when he had secretly called the wise men, determined from them what time the star appeared.	7 Then Herod sent a private message to the astrologers, asking them to come to see him; at this meeting he found out from them the exact time when they first saw the star. Then he told them,
8 And he sent them to Bethlehem, and said, Go and search diligently for the young child; and when ye have found *him,* bring me word again, that I may come and worship him also.	8 And he sent them to Bethlehem and said, "Go and search diligently for the young Child, and when you have found *Him,* bring back word to me, that I may come and worship Him also."	8 "Go to Bethlehem and search for the child. And when you find him, come back and tell me so that I can go and worship him too!"
12 And being warned of God in a dream that they should not return to Herod, they departed into their own country another way.	12 Then, being divinely warned in a dream that they should not return to Herod, they departed for their own country another way.	12 But when they returned to their own land, they didn't go through Jerusalem to report to Herod, for God had warned them in a dream to go home another way.
23 And he came and dwelt in a city called Nazareth: that it might be fulfilled which was spoken by the prophets, He shall be called a Nazarene.	23 And he came and dwelt in a city called Nazareth, that it might be fulfilled which was spoken by the prophets, "He shall be called a Nazarene."	23 and lived in Nazareth. This fulfilled the prediction of the prophets concerning the Messiah, "He shall be called a Nazarene."
3:1 In those days came John the Baptist, preaching in the wilderness of Judæa,	**3:1** In those days John the Baptist came preaching in the wilderness of Judea,	**3:1** While they were living in Nazareth, John the Baptist began preaching out in the Judean wilderness. His constant theme was,
2 And saying, Repent ye: for the kingdom of heaven is at hand.	2 and saying, "Repent, for the kingdom of heaven is at hand!"	2 "Turn from your sins . . . turn to God . . . for the Kingdom of Heaven is coming soon."
13 Then cometh Jesus from Galilee to Jordan unto John, to be baptized of him.	13 Then Jesus came from Galilee to John at the Jordan to be baptized by him.	13 Then Jesus went from Galilee to the Jordan River to be baptized there by John.
14 But John forbad him, saying, I have need to be baptized of thee, and comest thou to me?	14 And John *tried* to prevent Him, saying, "I have need to be baptized by You, and are You coming to me?"	14 John didn't want to do it. "This isn't proper," he said. "I am the one who needs to be baptized by you."
15 And Jesus answering said unto him, Suffer *it to be so* now: for thus it becometh us to fulfil all righteousness. Then he suffered him.	15 But Jesus answered and said to him, "Permit *it to be so* now, for thus it is fitting for us to fulfill all righteousness." Then he allowed Him.	15 But Jesus said, "Please do it, for I must do all that is right." So then John baptized him.
4:3 And when the tempter came to him, he said, If thou be the Son of God, command that these stones be made bread.	**4:3** Now when the tempter came to Him, he said, "If You are the Son of God, command that these stones become bread."	**4:3** Then Satan tempted him to get food by changing stones into loaves of bread. "It will prove you are the Son of God," he said.
4 But he answered and said, It is written, Man shall not live by bread alone, but by every word that proceedeth out of the mouth of God.	4 But He answered and said, "It is written, 'Man shall not live by bread alone, but by every word that proceeds from the mouth of God.'"	4 But Jesus told him, "No! For the Scriptures tell us that bread won't feed men's souls: obedience to every word of God is what we need."

NEW TESTAMENT

Matthew

NIV	RSV	TEV
1:21 She will give birth to a son, and you are to give him the name Jesus, because he will save his people from their sins."	**1:21** she will bear a son, and you shall call his name Jesus, for he will save his people from their sins."	**1:21** She will have a son, and you will name him Jesus—because he will save his people from their sins."
22 All this took place to fulfill what the Lord had said through the prophet:	**22** All this took place to fulfil what the Lord had spoken by the prophet:	**22** Now all this happened in order to make come true what the Lord had said through the prophet,
23 "The virgin will be with child and will give birth to a son, and they will call him Immanuel"—which means, "God with us."	**23** "Behold, a virgin shall conceive and bear a son, and his name shall be called Emmanuel" (which means, God with us).	**23** "A virgin will become pregnant and have a son, and he will be called Immanuel" (which means, "God is with us").
2:1 After Jesus was born in Bethlehem in Judea, during the time of King Herod, Magi from the east came to Jerusalem	**2:1** Now when Jesus was born in Bethlehem of Judea in the days of Herod the king, behold, wise men from the East came to Jerusalem, saying,	**2:1** Jesus was born in the town of Bethlehem in Judea, during the time when Herod was king. Soon afterward, some men who studied the stars came from the East to Jerusalem
2 and asked, "Where is the one who has been born king of the Jews? We saw his star in the east and have come to worship him."	**2** "Where is he who has been born king of the Jews? For we have seen his star in the East, and have come to worship him."	**2** and asked, "Where is the baby born to be the king of the Jews? We saw his star when it came up in the east, and we have come to worship him."
7 Then Herod called the Magi secretly and found out from them the exact time the star had appeared.	**7** Then Herod summoned the wise men secretly and ascertained from them what time the star appeared;	**7** So Herod called the visitors from the East to a secret meeting and found out from them the exact time the star had appeared.
8 He sent them to Bethlehem and said, "Go and make a careful search for the child. As soon as you find him, report to me, so that I too may go and worship him."	**8** and he sent them to Bethlehem, saying, "Go and search diligently for the child, and when you have found him bring me word, that I too may come and worship him."	**8** Then he sent them to Bethlehem with these instructions: "Go and make a careful search for the child; and when you find him, let me know, so that I too may go and worship him."
12 And having been warned in a dream not to go back to Herod, they returned to their country by another route.	**12** And being warned in a dream not to return to Herod, they departed to their own country by another way.	**12** Then they returned to their country by another road, since God had warned them in a dream not to go back to Herod.
23 and he went and lived in a town called Nazareth. So was fulfilled what was said through the prophets: "He will be called a Nazarene."	**23** And he went and dwelt in a city called Nazareth, that what was spoken by the prophets might be fulfilled, "He shall be called a Nazarene."	**23** and made his home in a town named Nazareth. And so what the prophets had said came true: "He will be called a Nazarene."
3:1 In those days John the Baptist came, preaching in the Desert of Judea	**3:1** In those days came John the Baptist preaching in the wilderness of Judea,	**3:1** At that time John the Baptist came to the desert of Judea and started preaching.
2 and saying, "Repent, for the kingdom of heaven is near."	**2** "Repent, for the kingdom of heaven is at hand."	**2** "Turn away from your sins," he said, "because the Kingdom of heaven is near!"
13 Then Jesus came from Galilee to the Jordan to be baptized by John.	**13** Then Jesus came from Galilee to the Jordan to John, to be baptized by him.	**13** At that time Jesus arrived from Galilee and came to John at the Jordan to be baptized by him.
14 But John tried to deter him, saying, "I need to be baptized by you, and do you come to me?"	**14** John would have prevented him, saying, "I need to be baptized by you, and do you come to me?"	**14** But John tried to make him change his mind. "I ought to be baptized by you," John said, "and yet you have come to me!"
15 Jesus replied, "Let it be so now; it is proper for us to do this to fulfill all righteousness." Then John consented.	**15** But Jesus answered him, "Let it be so now; for thus it is fitting for us to fulfil all righteousness." Then he consented.	**15** But Jesus answered him, "Let it be so for now. For in this way we shall do all that God requires." So John agreed.
4:3 The tempter came to him and said, "If you are the Son of God, tell these stones to become bread."	**4:3** And the tempter came and said to him, "If you are the Son of God, command these stones to become loaves of bread."	**4:3** Then the Devil came to him and said, "If you are God's Son, order these stones to turn into bread."
4 Jesus answered, "It is written: 'Man does not live on bread alone, but on every word that comes from the mouth of God.'"	**4** But he answered, "It is written, 'Man shall not live by bread alone, but by every word that proceeds from the mouth of God.'"	**4** But Jesus answered, "The scripture says, 'Man cannot live on bread alone, but needs every word that God speaks.'"

KJV	NKJV	TLB
7 Jesus said unto him, It is written again. Thou shalt not tempt the Lord thy God.	7 Jesus said to him, "It is written again, 'You shall not tempt the LORD your God.'"	7 Jesus retorted, "It also says not to put the Lord your God to a foolish test!"
10 Then saith Jesus unto him, Get thee hence, Satan: for it is written, Thou shalt worship the Lord thy God, and him only shalt thou serve.	10 Then Jesus said to him, "Away with you, Satan! For it is written, 'You shall worship the LORD your God, and Him only you shall serve.'"	10 "Get out of here, Satan," Jesus told him. "The Scriptures say, 'Worship only the Lord God. Obey only him.'"
5:3 Blessed *are* the poor in spirit: for theirs is the kingdom of heaven.	5:3 "Blessed *are* the poor in spirit, For theirs is the kingdom of heaven.	5:3 "Humble men are very fortunate!" he told them, "for the Kingdom of Heaven is given to them.
4 Blessed *are* they that mourn: for they shall be comforted.	4 Blessed *are* those who mourn, For they shall be comforted.	4 Those who mourn are fortunate! for they shall be comforted.
5 Blessed *are* the meek: for they shall inherit the earth.	5 Blessed *are* the meek, For they shall inherit the earth.	5 The meek and lowly are fortunate! for the whole wide world belongs to them.
6 Blessed *are* they which do hunger and thirst after righteousness: for they shall be filled.	6 Blessed *are* those who hunger and thirst for righteousness, For they shall be filled.	6 "Happy are those who long to be just and good, for they shall be completely satisfied.
7 Blessed *are* the merciful: for they shall obtain mercy.	7 Blessed *are* the merciful, For they shall obtain mercy.	7 Happy are the kind and merciful, for they shall be shown mercy.
8 Blessed *are* the pure in heart: for they shall see God.	8 Blessed *are* the pure in heart, For they shall see God.	8 Happy are those whose hearts are pure, for they shall see God.
9 Blessed *are* the peacemakers: for they shall be called the children of God.	9 Blessed *are* the peacemakers, For they shall be called sons of God.	9 Happy are those who strive for peace—they shall be called the sons of God.
10 Blessed *are* they which are persecuted for righteousness' sake: for theirs is the kingdom of heaven.	10 Blessed are those who are persecuted for righteousness' sake, For theirs is the kingdom of heaven.	10 Happy are those who are persecuted because they are good, for the Kingdom of Heaven is theirs.
13 Ye are the salt of the earth: but if the salt have lost his savour, wherewith shall it be salted? it is thenceforth good for nothing, but to be cast out, and to be trodden under foot of men.	13 "You are the salt of the earth; but if the salt loses its flavor, how shall it be seasoned? It is then good for nothing but to be thrown out and trampled under foot by men.	13 "You are the world's seasoning, to make it tolerable. If you lose your flavor, what will happen to the world? And you yourselves will be thrown out and trampled underfoot as worthless.
14 Ye are the light of the world. A city that is set on an hill cannot be hid.	14 "You are the light of the world. A city that is set on a hill cannot be hidden.	14 You are the world's light—a city on a hill, glowing in the night for all to see.
15 Neither do men light a candle, and put it under a bushel, but on a candlestick; and it giveth light unto all that are in the house.	15 "Nor do they light a lamp and put it under a basket, but on a lampstand, and it gives light to all *who are* in the house.	15 Don't hide your light!
16 Let your light so shine before men, that they may see your good works, and glorify your Father which is in heaven.	16 "Let your light so shine before men, that they may see your good works and glorify your Father in heaven.	16 Let it shine for all; let your good deeds glow for all to see, so that they will praise your heavenly Father.
22 But I say unto you, That whosoever is angry with his brother without a cause shall be in danger of the judgment: and whosoever shall say to his brother, Raca, shall be in danger of the council: but whosoever shall say, Thou fool, shall be in danger of hell fire.	22 "But I say to you that whoever is angry with his brother without a cause shall be in danger of the judgment. And whoever says to his brother, 'Raca!' shall be in danger of the council. But whoever says, 'You fool!' shall be in danger of hell fire.	22 But I have added to that rule, and tell you that if you are only *angry*, even in your own home, you are in danger of judgment! If you call your friend an idiot, you are in danger of being brought before the court. And if you curse him, you are in danger of the fires of hell.
31 It hath been said, Whosoever shall put away his wife, let him give her a writing of divorcement:	31 "Furthermore it has been said, 'Whoever divorces his wife, let him give her a certificate of divorce.'	31 "The law of Moses says, 'If anyone wants to be rid of his wife, he can divorce her merely by giving her a letter of dismissal.'
32 But I say unto you, That whosoever shall put away his wife, saving for the cause of fornication, causeth her to commit adultery: and whosoever shall marry her that is divorced committeth adultery.	32 "But I say to you that whoever divorces his wife for any reason except sexual immorality causes her to commit adultery; and whoever marries a woman who is divorced commits adultery.	32 But I say that a man who divorces his wife, except for fornication, causes her to commit adultery if she marries again. And he who marries her commits adultery.
44 But I say unto you, Love your enemies, bless them that curse you, do good to them that hate you, and pray for them which despitefully use you, and persecute you;	44 "But I say to you, love your enemies, bless those who curse you, do good to those who hate you, and pray for those who spitefully use you and persecute you,	44 But I say: Love your *enemies!* Pray for those who *persecute* you!
6:3 But when thou doest alms, let not thy left hand know what thy right hand doeth:	6:3 "But when you do a charitable deed, do not let your left hand know what your right hand is doing,	6:3 But when you do a kindness to someone, do it secretly—don't tell your left hand what your right hand is doing.

NIV	RSV	TEV
7 Jesus answered him, "It is also written: 'Do not put the Lord your God to the test.'"	7 Jesus said to him, "Again it is written, 'You shall not tempt the Lord your God.'"	7 Jesus answered, "But the scripture also says, 'Do not put the Lord your God to the test.'"
10 Jesus said to him, "Away from me, Satan! For it is written: 'Worship the Lord your God, and serve him only.'"	10 Then Jesus said to him, "Begone, Satan! for it is written, 'You shall worship the Lord your God and him only shall you serve.'"	10 Then Jesus answered, "Go away, Satan! The scripture says, 'Worship the Lord your God and serve only him!'"
5:3 "Blessed are the poor in spirit, for theirs is the kingdom of heaven.	5:3 "Blessed are the poor in spirit, for theirs is the kingdom of heaven.	5:3 "Happy are those who know they are spiritually poor; the Kingdom of heaven belongs to them!
4 Blessed are those who mourn, for they will be comforted.	4 "Blessed are those who mourn, for they shall be comforted.	4 "Happy are those who mourn; God will comfort them!
5 Blessed are the meek, for they will inherit the earth.	5 "Blessed are the meek, for they shall inherit the earth.	5 "Happy are those who are humble; they will receive what God has promised!
6 Blessed are those who hunger and thirst for righteousness, for they will be filled.	6 "Blessed are those who hunger and thirst for righteousness, for they shall be satisfied.	6 "Happy are those whose greatest desire is to do what God requires; God will satisfy them fully!
7 Blessed are the merciful, for they will be shown mercy.	7 "Blessed are the merciful, for they shall obtain mercy.	7 "Happy are those who are merciful to others; God will be merciful to them!
8 Blessed are the pure in heart, for they will see God.	8 "Blessed are the pure in heart, for they shall see God.	8 "Happy are the pure in heart; they will see God!
9 Blessed are the peacemakers, for they will be called sons of God.	9 "Blessed are the peacemakers, for they shall be called sons of God.	9 "Happy are those who work for peace; God will call them his children!
10 Blessed are those who are persecuted because of righteousness, for theirs is the kingdom of heaven,	10 "Blessed are those who are persecuted for righteousness' sake, for theirs is the kingdom of heaven.	10 "Happy are those who are persecuted because they do what God requires; the Kingdom of heaven belongs to them!
13 "You are the salt of the earth. But if the salt loses its saltiness, how can it be made salty again? It is no longer good for anything, except to be thrown out and trampled by men.	13 "You are the salt of the earth; but if salt has lost its taste, how shall its saltness be restored? It is no longer good for anything except to be thrown out and trodden under foot by men.	13 "You are like salt for all mankind. But if salt loses its saltiness, there is no way to make it salty again. It has become worthless, so it is thrown out and people trample on it.
14 "You are the light of the world. A city on a hill cannot be hidden.	14 "You are the light of the world. A city set on a hill cannot be hid.	14 "You are like light for the whole world. A city built on a hill cannot be hid.
15 Neither do people light a lamp and put it under a bowl. Instead they put it on its stand, and it gives light to everyone in the house.	15 Nor do men light a lamp and put it under a bushel, but on a stand, and it gives light to all in the house.	15 No one lights a lamp and puts it under a bowl; instead he puts it on the lampstand, where it gives light for everyone in the house.
16 In the same way, let your light shine before men, that they may see your good deeds and praise your Father in heaven.	16 Let your light so shine before men, that they may see your good works and give glory to your Father who is in heaven.	16 In the same way your light must shine before people, so that they will see the good things you do and praise your Father in heaven.
22 But I tell you that anyone who is angry with his brother will be subject to judgment. Again, anyone who says to his brother, 'Raca,' is answerable to the Sanhedrin. But anyone who says, 'You fool!' will be in danger of the fire of hell.	22 But I say to you that every one who is angry with his brother shall be liable to judgment; whoever insults his brother shall be liable to the council, and whoever says, 'You fool!' shall be liable to the hell of fire.	22 But now I tell you: whoever is angry with his brother will be brought to trial, whoever calls his brother 'You good-for-nothing!' will be brought before the Council, and whoever calls his brother a worthless fool will be in danger of going to the fire of hell.
31 "It has been said, 'Anyone who divorces his wife must give her a certificate of divorce.'	31 "It was also said, 'Whoever divorces his wife, let him give her a certificate of divorce.'	31 "It was also said, 'Anyone who divorces his wife must give her a written notice of divorce.'
32 But I tell you that anyone who divorces his wife, except for marital unfaithfulness, causes her to commit adultery, and anyone who marries a woman so divorced commits adultery.	32 But I say to you that every one who divorces his wife, except on the ground of unchastity, makes her an adulteress; and whoever marries a divorced woman commits adultery.	32 But now I tell you: if a man divorces his wife for any cause other than her unfaithfulness, then he is guilty of making her commit adultery if she marries again; and the man who marries her commits adultery also.
44 But I tell you: Love your enemies and pray for those who persecute you,	44 But I say to you, Love your enemies and pray for those who persecute you,	44 But now I tell you: love your enemies and pray for those who persecute you,
6:3 But when you give to the needy, do not let your left hand know what your right hand is doing,	6:3 But when you give alms, do not let your left hand know what your right hand is doing,	6:3 But when you help a needy person, do it in such a way that even your closest friend will not know about it.

KJV	NKJV	TLB
4 That thine alms may be in secret: and thy Father which seeth in secret himself shall reward thee openly.	4 "that your charitable deed may be in secret; and your Father who sees in secret will Himself reward you openly.	4 And your Father who knows all secrets will reward you.
6 But thou, when thou prayest, enter into thy closet, and when thou hast shut thy door, pray to thy Father which is in secret; and thy Father which seeth in secret shall reward thee openly.	6 "But you, when you pray, go into your room, and when you have shut your door, pray to your Father who is in the secret place; and your Father who sees in secret will reward you openly.	6 But when you pray, go away by yourself, all alone, and shut the door behind you and pray to your Father secretly, and your Father, who knows your secrets, will reward you.
9 After this manner therefore pray ye: Our Father which art in heaven, Hallowed be thy name.	9 "In this manner, therefore, pray: Our Father in heaven, Hallowed be Your name.	9 "Pray along these lines: 'Our Father in heaven, we honor your holy name.
10 Thy kingdom come. Thy will be done in earth, as it is in heaven.	10 Your kingdom come. Your will be done On earth as it is in heaven.	10 We ask that your kingdom will come now. May your will be done here on earth, just as it is in heaven.
11 Give us this day our daily bread.	11 Give us this day our daily bread.	11 Give us our food again today, as usual,
12 And forgive us our debts, as we forgive our debtors.	12 And forgive us our debts, As we forgive our debtors.	12 and forgive us our sins, just as we have forgiven those who have sinned against us.
13 And lead us not into temptation, but deliver us from evil: For thine is the kingdom, and the power, and the glory, for ever. Amen.	13 And do not lead us into temptation, But deliver us from the evil one. For Yours is the kingdom and the power and the glory forever. Amen.	13 Don't bring us into temptation, but deliver us from the Evil One, Amen.'
20 But lay up for yourselves treasures in heaven, where neither moth nor rust doth corrupt, and where thieves do not break through nor steal:	20 "but lay up for yourselves treasures in heaven, where neither moth nor rust destroys and where thieves do not break in and steal.	20 Store them in heaven where they will never lose their value, and are safe from thieves.
21 For where your treasure is, there will your heart be also.	21 "For where your treasure is, there your heart will be also.	21 If your profits are in heaven your heart will be there too.
25 Therefore I say unto you, Take no thought for your life, what ye shall eat, or what ye shall drink; nor yet for your body, what ye shall put on. Is not the life more than meat, and the body than raiment?	25 "Therefore I say to you, do not worry about your life, what you will eat or what you will drink; nor about your body, what you will put on. Is not life more than food and the body more than clothing?	25 "So my counsel is: Don't worry about things—food, drink, and clothes. For you already have life and a body—and they are far more important than what to eat and wear.
33 But seek ye first the kingdom of God, and his righteousness; and all these things shall be added unto you.	33 "But seek first the kingdom of God and His righteousness, and all these things shall be added to you.	33 and he will give them to you if you give him first place in your life and live as he wants you to.
7:7 Ask, and it shall be given you; seek, and ye shall find; knock, and it shall be opened unto you:	7:7 "Ask, and it will be given to you; seek, and you will find; knock, and it will be opened to you.	7:7 "Ask, and you will be given what you ask for. Seek, and you will find. Knock, and the door will be opened.
12 Therefore all things whatsoever ye would that men should do to you, do ye even so to them: for this is the law and the prophets.	12 "Therefore, whatever you want men to do to you, do also to them, for this is the Law and the Prophets.	12 "Do for others what you want them to do for you. This is the teaching of the laws of Moses in a nutshell.
13 Enter ye in at the strait gate: for wide is the gate, and broad is the way, that leadeth to destruction, and many there be which go in thereat:	13 "Enter by the narrow gate; for wide is the gate and broad is the way that leads to destruction, and there are many who go in by it.	13 "Heaven can be entered only through the narrow gate! The highway to hell is broad, and its gate is wide enough for all the multitudes who choose its easy way.
14 Because strait is the gate, and narrow is the way, which leadeth unto life, and few there be that find it.	14 "Because narrow is the gate and difficult is the way which leads to life, and there are few who find it.	14 But the Gateway to Life is small, and the road is narrow, and only a few ever find it.
21 Not every one that saith unto me, Lord, Lord, shall enter into the kingdom of heaven; but he that doeth the will of my Father which is in heaven.	21 "Not everyone who says to Me, 'Lord, Lord,' shall enter the kingdom of heaven, but he who does the will of My Father in heaven.	21 "Not all who sound religious are really godly people. They may refer to me as 'Lord,' but still won't get to heaven. For the decisive question is whether they obey my Father in heaven.
9:12 But when Jesus heard that, he said unto them, They that be whole need not a physician, but they that are sick.	9:12 But when Jesus heard that, He said to them, "Those who are well have no need of a physician, but those who are sick.	9:12 "Because people who are well don't need a doctor! It's the sick people who do!" was Jesus' reply.
13 But go ye and learn what that meaneth, I will have mercy, and not sacrifice: for I am not come to call the righteous, but sinners to repentance.	13 "But go and learn what this means: 'I desire mercy and not sacrifice.' For I did not come to call the righteous, but sinners, to repentance."	13 Then he added, "Now go away and learn the meaning of this verse of Scripture, 'It isn't your sacrifices and your gifts I want—I want you to be merciful.' For I have come to urge sinners, not the self-righteous, back to God."
20 And, behold, a woman, which was diseased with an issue of blood twelve years, came behind him, and touched the hem of his garment.	20 And suddenly, a woman who had a flow of blood for twelve years came from behind and touched the hem of His garment;	20 a woman who had been sick for twelve years with internal bleeding came up behind him and touched a tassel of his robe,

NIV	RSV	TEV
4 so that your giving may be in secret. Then your Father, who sees what is done in secret, will reward you.	4 so that your alms may be in secret; and your Father who sees in secret will reward you.	4 Then it will be a private matter. And your Father, who sees what you do in private, will reward you.
6 When you pray, go into your room, close the door and pray to your Father, who is unseen. Then your Father, who sees what is done in secret, will reward you.	6 But when you pray, go into your room and shut the door and pray to your Father who is in secret; and your Father who sees in secret will reward you.	6 But when you pray, go to your room, close the door, and pray to your Father, who is unseen. And your Father, who sees what you do in private, will reward you.
9 "This is how you should pray: "'Our Father in heaven, hallowed be your name,	9 Pray then like this: Our Father who art in heaven, Hallowed be thy name.	9 This, then is how you should pray: 'Our Father in heaven: May your holy name be honored;
10 your kingdom come, your will be done on earth as it is in heaven.	10 Thy kingdom come, Thy will be done, On earth as it is in heaven.	10 may your Kingdom come; may your will be done on earth as it is in heaven.
11 Give us today our daily bread.	11 Give us this day our daily bread;	11 Give us today the food we need.
12 Forgive us our debts, as we also have forgiven our debtors.	12 And forgive us our debts, As we also have forgiven our debtors;	12 Forgive us the wrongs we have done, as we forgive the wrongs that others have done to us.
13 And lead us not into temptation, but deliver us from the evil one.	13 And lead us not into temptation, But deliver us from evil.	13 Do not bring us to hard testing, but keep us safe from the Evil One.'
20 But store up for yourselves treasures in heaven, where moth and rust do not destroy, and where thieves do no break in and steal.	20 but lay up for yourselves treasures in heaven, where neither moth nor rust consumes and where thieves do not break in and steal.	20 Instead, store up riches for yourselves in heaven, where moths and rust cannot destroy, and robbers cannot break in and steal.
21 For where your treasure is, there your heart will be also.	21 For where your treasure is, there will your heart be also.	21 For your heart will always be where your riches are.
25 "Therefore I tell you, do not worry about your life, what you will eat or drink; or about your body, what you will wear. Is not life more important than food, and the body more important than clothes?	25 "Therefore I tell you, do not be anxious about your life, what you shall eat or what you shall drink, nor about your body, what you shall put on. Is not life more than food, and the body more than clothing?	25 "This is why I tell you: do not be worried about the food and drink you need in order to stay alive, or about clothes for your body. After all, isn't life worth more than food? And isn't the body worth more than clothes?
33 But seek first his kingdom and his righteousness, and all these things will be given to you as well.	33 But seek first his kingdom and his righteousness, and all these things shall be yours as well.	33 Instead, be concerned above everything else with the Kingdom of God and with what he requires of you, and he will provide you with all these other things.
7:7 "Ask and it will be given to you; seek and you will find; knock and the door will be opened to you.	7:7 "Ask, and it will be given you; seek, and you will find; knock, and it will be opened to you.	7:7 "Ask, and you will receive; seek, and you will find; knock, and the door will be opened to you.
12 In everything, do to others what you would have them do to you, for this sums up the Law and the Prophets.	12 So whatever you wish that men would do to you, do so to them; for this is the law and the prophets.	12 "Do for others what you want them to do for you: this is the meaning of the Law of Moses and of the teachings of the prophets.
13 "Enter through the narrow gate. For wide is the gate and broad is the road that leads to destruction, and many enter through it.	13 "Enter by the narrow gate; for the gate is wide and the way is easy, that leads to destruction, and those who enter by it are many.	13 "Go in through the narrow gate, because the gate to hell is wide and the road that leads to it is easy, and there are many who travel it.
14 But small is the gate and narrow the road that leads to life, and only a few find it.	14 For the gate is narrow and the way is hard, that leads to life, and those who find it are few.	14 But the gate to life is narrow and the way that leads to it is hard, and there are few people who find it.
21 "Not everyone who says to me, 'Lord, Lord,' will enter the kingdom of heaven, but only he who does the will of my Father who is in heaven.	21 "Not every one who says to me, 'Lord, Lord,' shall enter the kingdom of heaven, but he who does the will of my Father who is in heaven.	21 "Not everyone who calls me 'Lord, Lord' will enter the Kingdom of heaven, but only those who do what my Father in heaven wants them to do.
9:12 On hearing this, Jesus said, "It is not the healthy who need a doctor, but the sick.	9:12 But when he heard it, he said, "Those who are well have no need of a physician, but those who are sick.	9:12 Jesus heard them and answered, "People who are well do not need a doctor, but only those who are sick.
13 But go and learn what this means: 'I desire mercy, not sacrifice.' For I have not come to call the righteous, but sinners."	13 Go and learn what this means, 'I desire mercy, and not sacrifice.' For I came not to call the righteous, but sinners."	13 Go and find out what is meant by the scripture that says: 'It is kindness that I want, not animal sacrifices.' I have not come to call respectable people, but outcasts."
20 Just then a woman who had been subject to bleeding for twelve years came up behind him and touched the edge of his cloak.	20 And behold, a woman who had suffered from a hemorrhage for twelve years came up behind him and touched the fringe of his garment;	20 A woman who had suffered from severe bleeding for twelve years came up behind Jesus and touched the edge of his cloak.

164   Matthew 9:21
         Matthew 13:18
         KEY VERSE COMPARISON CHART

KJV	NKJV	TLB
21 For she said within herself, If I may but touch his garment, I shall be whole.	21 for she said to herself, "If only I may touch His garment, I shall be made well."	21 for she thought, "If I only touch him, I will be healed."
22 But Jesus turned him about, and when he saw her, he said, Daughter, be of good comfort; thy faith hath made thee whole. And the woman was made whole from that hour.	22 But Jesus turned around, and when He saw her He said, "Be of good cheer, daughter; your faith has made you well." And the woman was made well from that hour.	22 Jesus turned around and spoke to her. "Daughter," he said, "all is well! Your faith has healed you." And the woman was well from that moment.
37 Then saith he unto his disciples, The harvest truly *is* plenteous, but the labourers *are* few;	37 Then He said to His disciples, "The harvest truly *is* plentiful, but the laborers *are* few.	37 "The harvest is so great, and the workers are so few," he told his disciples.
38 Pray ye therefore the Lord of the harvest, that he will send forth labourers into his harvest.	38 "Therefore pray the Lord of the harvest to send out laborers into His harvest."	38 "So pray to the one in charge of the harvesting, and ask him to recruit more workers for his harvest fields."
10:32 Whosoever therefore shall confess me before men, him will I confess also before my Father which is in heaven.	10:32 "Therefore whoever confesses Me before men, him I will also confess before My Father who is in heaven.	10:32 "If anyone publicly acknowledges me as his friend, I will openly acknowledge him as my friend before my Father in heaven.
33 But whosoever shall deny me before men, him will I also deny before my Father which is in heaven.	33 "But whoever denies Me before men, him I will also deny before My Father who is in heaven.	33 But if anyone publicly denies me, I will openly deny him before my Father in heaven.
11:25 At that time Jesus answered and said, I thank thee, O Father, Lord of heaven and earth, because thou hast hid these things from the wise and prudent, and hast revealed them unto babes.	11:25 At that time Jesus answered and said, "I thank You, Father, Lord of heaven and earth, because You have hidden these things from the wise and prudent and have revealed them to babes.	11:25 And Jesus prayed this prayer: "O Father, Lord of heaven and earth, thank you for hiding the truth from those who think themselves so wise, and for revealing it to little children.
28 Come unto me, all *ye* that labour and are heavy laden, and I will give you rest.	28 "Come to Me, all *you* who labor and are heavy laden, and I will give you rest.	28 Come to me and I will give you rest—all of you who work so hard beneath a heavy yoke.
29 Take my yoke upon you, and learn of me; for I am meek and lowly in heart: and ye shall find rest unto your souls.	29 "Take My yoke upon you and learn from Me, for I am gentle and lowly in heart, and you will find rest for your souls.	29 Wear my yoke—for it fits perfectly—and let me teach you; for I am gentle and humble, and you shall find rest for your souls;
30 For my yoke *is* easy, and my burden is light.	30 "For My yoke *is* easy and My burden is light."	30 for I give you only light burdens."
12:28 But if I cast out devils by the Spirit of God, then the kingdom of God is come unto you.	12:28 "But if I cast out demons by the Spirit of God, surely the kingdom of God has come upon you.	12:28 But if I am casting out demons by the Spirit of God, then the Kingdom of God has arrived among you.
41 The men of Nineveh shall rise in judgment with this generation, and shall condemn it: because they repented at the preaching of Jonas; and, behold, a greater than Jonas *is* here.	41 "The men of Nineveh will rise in the judgment with this generation and condemn it, because they repented at the preaching of Jonah; and indeed a greater than Jonah *is* here.	41 The men of Nineveh shall arise against this nation at the judgment and condemn you. For when Jonah preached to them, they repented and turned to God from all their evil ways. And now a greater than Jonah is here—and you refuse to believe him.
42 The queen of the south shall rise up in the judgment with this generation, and shall condemn it: for she came from the uttermost parts of the earth to hear the wisdom of Solomon; and, behold, a greater than Solomon *is* here.	42 "The queen of the South will rise up in the judgment with this generation and condemn it, for she came from the ends of the earth to hear the wisdom of Solomon; and indeed a greater than Solomon *is* here.	42 The Queen of Sheba shall rise against this nation in the judgment, and condemn it; for she came from a distant land to hear the wisdom of Solomon; and now a greater than Solomon is here—and you refuse to believe him.
50 For whosoever shall do the will of my Father which is in heaven, the same is my brother, and sister, and mother.	50 "For whoever does the will of My Father in heaven is My brother and sister and mother."	50 Then he added, "Anyone who obeys my Father in heaven is my brother, sister and mother!"

13:14 And in them is fulfilled the prophecy of Esaias, which saith, By hearing ye shall hear, and shall not understand; and seeing ye shall see, and shall not perceive:	13:14 "And in them the prophecy of Isaiah is fulfilled, which says:
	'Hearing you will hear
	   and shall not understand,
	And seeing you will see
	   and not perceive;
		13:14 "This fulfills the prophecy of Isaiah; 'They hear, but don't understand; they look, but don't see!

15 For this people's heart is waxed gross, and *their* ears are dull of hearing, and their eyes they have closed; lest at any time they should see with *their* eyes, and hear with *their* ears, and should understand with *their* heart, and should be converted, and I should heal them.	15 For the heart of this people has grown dull.
	Their ears are hard of hearing,
	And their eyes they have closed,
	Lest they should see with *their* eyes and
	   hear with *their* ears,
	Lest they should understand with *their*
	   heart and turn,
	So that I should heal them.'
		15 For their hearts are fat and heavy, and their ears are dull, and they have closed their eyes in sleep,

18 Hear ye therefore the parable of the sower.	18 "Therefore hear the parable of the sower:	18 "Now here is the explanation of the story I told about the farmer planting grain:

NIV	RSV	TEV
21 She said to herself, "If I only touch his cloak, I will be healed."	21 for she said to herself, "If I only touch his garment, I shall be made well."	21 She said to herself, "If only I touch his cloak, I will get well."
22 Jesus turned and saw her. "Take heart, daughter," he said, "your faith has healed you." And the woman was healed from that moment.	22 Jesus turned, and seeing her he said, "Take heart, daughter; your faith has made you well." And instantly the woman was made well.	22 Jesus turned around and saw her, and said, "Courage, my daughter! Your faith has made you well." At that very moment the woman became well.
37 Then he said to his disciples, "The harvest is plentiful but the workers are few.	37 Then he said to his disciples, "The harvest is plentiful, but the laborers are few;	37 So he said to his disciples, "The harvest is large, but there are few workers to gather it in.
38 Ask the Lord of the harvest, therefore, to send out workers into his harvest field."	38 pray therefore the Lord of the harvest to send out laborers into his harvest."	38 Pray to the owner of the harvest that he will send out workers to gather in his harvest."
10:32 "Whoever acknowledges me before men, I will also acknowledge him before my Father in heaven.	**10:32** So every one who acknowledges me before men, I also will acknowledge before my Father who is in heaven;	**10:32** "If anyone declares publicly that he belongs to me, I will do the same for him before my Father in heaven.
33 But whoever disowns me before men, I will disown him before my Father in heaven.	33 but whoever denies me before men, I also will deny before my Father who is in heaven.	33 But if anyone rejects me publicly, I will reject him before my Father in heaven.
11:25 At that time Jesus said, "I praise you, Father, Lord of heaven and earth, because you have hidden these things from the wise and learned, and revealed them to little children.	**11:25** At that time Jesus declared, "I thank thee, Father, Lord of heaven and earth, that thou hast hidden these things from the wise and understanding and revealed them to babes;	**11:25** At that time Jesus said, "Father, Lord of heaven and earth! I thank you because you have shown to the unlearned what you have hidden from the wise and learned.
28 "Come to me, all you who are weary and burdened, and I will give you rest.	28 Come to me, all who labor and are heavy laden, and I will give you rest.	28 "Come to me, all of you who are tired from carrying heavy loads, and I will give you rest.
29 Take my yoke upon you and learn from me, for I am gentle and humble in heart, and you will find rest for your souls.	29 Take my yoke upon you, and learn from me; for I am gentle and lowly in heart, and you will find rest for your souls.	29 Take my yoke and put it on you, and learn from me, because I am gentle and humble in spirit; and you will find rest.
30 For my yoke is easy and my burden is light."	30 For my yoke is easy, and my burden is light."	30 For the yoke I will give you is easy, and the load I will put on you is light."
12:28 But if I drive out demons by the Spirit of God, then the kingdom of God has come upon you.	**12:28** But if it is by the Spirit of God that I cast out demons, then the kingdom of God has come upon you.	**12:28** No, it is not Beelzebul, but God's Spirit, who gives me the power to drive out demons, which proves that the Kingdom of God has already come upon you.
41 The men of Nineveh will stand up at the judgment with this generation and condemn it; for they repented at the preaching of Jonah, and now one greater than Jonah is here.	41 The men of Nineveh will arise at the judgment with this generation and condemn it; for they repented at the preaching of Jonah, and behold, something greater than Jonah is here.	41 On the Judgment Day the people of Nineveh will stand up and accuse you, because they turned from their sins when they heard Jonah preach; and I tell you that there is something here greater than Jonah!
42 The Queen of the South will rise at the judgment with this generation and condemn it; for she came from the ends of the earth to listen to Solomon's wisdom, and now one greater than Solomon is here.	42 The queen of the South will arise at the judgment with this generation and condemn it; for she came from the ends of the earth to hear the wisdom of Solomon, and behold, something greater than Solomon is here.	42 On the Judgment Day the Queen of Sheba will stand up and accuse you, because she traveled all the way from her country to listen to King Solomon's wise teaching; and I assure you that there is something here greater than Solomon!
50 For whoever does the will of my Father in heaven is my brother and sister and mother."	50 For whoever does the will of my Father in heaven is my brother, and sister, and mother."	50 Whoever does what my Father in heaven wants him to do is my brother, my sister, and my mother."
13:14 In them is fulfilled the prophecy of Isaiah: "'You will be ever hearing but never understanding; you will be ever seeing but never perceiving.	**13:14** With them indeed is fulfilled the prophecy of Isaiah which says: 'You shall indeed hear but never understand, and you shall indeed see but never perceive.	**13:14** So the prophecy of Isaiah applies to them: 'This people will listen and listen, but not understand; they will look and look, but not see,
15 For this people's heart has become calloused; they hardly hear with their ears, and they have closed their eyes. Otherwise they might see with their eyes, hear with their ears, understand with their hearts and turn, and I would heal them.'	15 For this people's heart has grown dull, and their ears are heavy of hearing, and their eyes they have closed, lest they should perceive with their eyes, and hear with their ears, and understand with their heart, and turn for me to heal them.'	15 because their minds are dull, and they have stopped up their ears and have closed their eyes. Otherwise, their eyes would see, their ears would hear, their minds would understand, and they would turn to me, says God, and I would heal them.'
18 "Listen then to what the parable of the sower means:	18 "Hear then the parable of the sower.	18 "Listen, then, and learn what the parable of the sower means.

KJV	NKJV	TLB
19 When any one heareth the word of the kingdom, and understandeth *it* not, then cometh the wicked *one*, and catcheth away that which was sown in his heart. This is he which received seed by the way side.	19 "When anyone hears the word of the kingdom, and does not understand *it*, then the wicked *one* comes and snatches away what was sown in his heart. This is he who received seed by the wayside.	19 The hard path where some of the seeds fell represents the heart of a person who hears the Good News about the Kingdom and doesn't understand it; then Satan comes and snatches away the seeds from his heart.
20 But he that received the seed into stony places, the same is he that heareth the word, and anon with joy receiveth it;	20 "But he who received the seed on stony places, this is he who hears the word and immediately receives it with joy;	20 The shallow, rocky soil represents the heart of a man who hears the message and receives it with real joy,
21 Yet hath he not root in himself, but dureth for a while: for when tribulation or persecution ariseth because of the word, by and by he is offended.	21 "yet he has no root in himself, but endures only for a while. For when tribulation or persecution arises because of the word, immediately he stumbles.	21 but he doesn't have much depth in his life, and the seeds don't root very deeply, and after a while when trouble comes, or persecution begins because of his beliefs, his enthusiasm fades, and he drops out.
22 He also that received seed among the throns is he that heareth the word; and the care of this world, and the deceitfulness of riches, choke the word, and he becometh unfruitful.	22 "Now he who received seed among the thorns is he who hears the word, and the cares of this world and the deceitfulness of riches choke the word, and he becomes unfruitful.	22 The ground covered with thistles represents a man who hears the message, but the cares of this life and his longing for money choke out God's Word, and he does less and less for God.
23 But he that received seed into the good ground is he that heareth the word, and understandeth *it;* which also beareth fruit, and bringeth forth, some an hundredfold, some sixty, some thirty.	23 "But he who received seed on the good ground is he who hears the word and understands *it,* who indeed bears fruit and produces: some a hundredfold, some sixty, some thirty."	23 The good ground represents the heart of a man who listens to the message and understands it and goes out and brings thirty, sixty, or even a hundred others into the Kingdom."
44 Again, the kingdom of heaven is like unto treasure hid in a field; the which when a man hath found, he hideth, and for joy thereof goeth and selleth all that he hath, and buyeth that field.	44 "Again, the kingdom of heaven is like treasure hidden in a field, which a man found and hid; and for joy over it he goes and sells all that he has and buys that field.	44 "The Kingdom of Heaven is like a treasure a man discovered in a field. In his excitement, he sold everything he owned to get enough money to buy the field—and get the treasure, too!
45 Again, the kingdom of heaven is like unto a merchant man, seeking goodly pearls:	45 "Again, the kingdom of heaven is like a merchant seeking beautiful pearls,	45 "Again, the Kingdom of Heaven is like a pearl merchant on the lookout for choice pearls.
46 Who, when he had found one pearl of great price, went and sold all that he had, and brought it.	46 "who, when he had found one pearl of great price, went and sold all that he had and bought it.	46 He discovered a real bargain—a pearl of great value—and sold everything he owned to purchase it!
15:7 *Ye* hypocrites, well did Esaias prophesy of you, saying,	15:7 "Hypocrites! Well did Isaiah prophesy about you, saying:	15:7 You hypocrites! Well did Isaiah prophesy of you,
8 This people draweth nigh unto me with their mouth, and honoureth me with *their* lips; but their heart is far from me.	8 'These people draw near to Me with their mouth, And honor Me with *their* lips, But their heart is far from Me.	8 'These people say they honor me, but their hearts are far away.
9 But in vain they do worship me, teaching *for* doctrines the commandments of men.	9 And in vain they *worship* Me, Teaching *as* doctrines the commandments of men.'"	9 Their worship is worthless, for they teach their man-made laws instead of those from God.'"
16:15 He saith unto them, But whom say ye that I am?	16:15 He said to them, "But who do you say that I am?"	16:15 Then he asked them, "Who do *you* think I am?"
16 And Simon Peter answered and said, Thou art the Christ, the Son of the living God.	16 And Simon Peter answered and said, "You are the Christ, the Son of the living God."	16 Simon Peter answered, "The Christ, the Messiah, the Son of the living God."
18 And I say also unto thee, That thou art Peter, and upon this rock I will build my church; and the gates of hell shall not prevail against it.	18 "And I also say to you that you are Peter, and on this rock I will build My church, and the gates of Hades shall not prevail against it.	18 You are Peter, a stone; and upon this rock I will build my church; and all the powers of hell shall not prevail against it.
19 And I will give you unto thee the keys of the kingdom of heaven: and whatsoever thou shalt bind on earth shall be bound in heaven: and whatsoever thou shalt loose on earth shall be loosed in heaven.	19 "And I will give you the keys of the kingdom of heaven, and whatever you bind on earth will be bound in heaven, and whatever you loose on earth will be loosed in heaven."	19 And I will give you the keys of the Kingdom of Heaven; whatever doors you lock on earth shall be locked in heaven; and whatever doors you open on earth shall be open in heaven!"
24 Then said Jesus unto his disciples, If any *man* will come after me, let him deny himself, and take up his cross, and follow me.	24 Then Jesus said to His disciples, "If anyone desires to come after Me, let him deny himself, and take up his cross, and follow Me.	24 Then Jesus said to the disciples, "If anyone wants to be a follower of mine, let him deny himself and take up his cross and follow me.
25 For whosoever will save his life shall lose it: and whosoever will lose his life for my sake shall find it.	25 "For whoever desires to save his life will lose it, and whoever loses his life for My sake will find it.	25 For anyone who keeps his life for himself shall lose it; and anyone who loses his life for me shall find it again.
26 For what is a man profited, if he shall gain the whole world, and lose his own soul? or what shall a man give in exchange for his soul?	26 "For what is a man profited if he gains the whole world, and loses his own soul? Or what will a man give in exchange for his soul?	26 What profit is there if you gain the whole world—and lose eternal life? What can be compared with the value of eternal life?
18:11 For the Son of man is come to save that which was lost.	18:11 "For the Son of Man has come to save that which was lost.	18:11 And I, the Messiah, came to save the lost.

NIV	RSV	TEV
19 When anyone hears the message about the kingdom and does not understand it, the evil one comes and snatches away what was sown in his heart. This is the seed sown along the path.	19 When any one hears the word of the kingdom and does not understand it, the evil one comes and snatches away what is sown in his heart; this is what was sown along the path.	19 Those who hear the message about the Kingdom but do not understand it are like the seeds that fell along the path. The Evil One comes and snatches away what was sown in them.
20 What was sown on rocky places is the man who hears the word and at once receives it with joy.	20 As for what was sown on rocky ground, this is he who hears the word and immediately receives it with joy;	20 The seeds that fell on rocky ground stand for those who receive the message gladly as soon as they hear it.
21 But since he has no root, he lasts only a short time. When trouble or persecution comes because of the word, he quickly falls away.	21 yet he has no root in himself, but endures for a while, and when tribulation or persecution arises on account of the word, immediately he falls away.	21 But it does not sink deep into them, and they don't last long. So when trouble or persecution comes because of the message, they give up at once.
22 What was sown among the thorns is the man who hears the word, but the worries of this life and the deceitfulness of wealth choke it, making it unfruitful.	22 As for what was sown among thorns, this is he who hears the word, but the cares of the world and the delight in riches choke the word, and it proves unfruitful.	22 The seeds that fell among thorn bushes stand for those who hear the message; but the worries about this life and the love for riches choke the message, and they don't bear fruit.
23 But what was sown on good soil is the man who hears the word and understands it. He produces a crop, yielding a hundred, sixty or thirty times what was sown."	23 As for what was sown on good soil, this is he who hears the word and understands it; he indeed bears fruit, and yields, in one case a hundredfold, in another sixty, and in another thirty."	23 And the seeds sown in the good soil stand for those who hear the message and understand it: they bear fruit, some as much as one hundred, others sixty, and others thirty."
44 "The kingdom of heaven is like treasure hidden in a field. When a man found it, he hid it again, and then in his joy went and sold all he had and bought that field.	44 "The kingdom of heaven is like treasure hidden in a field, which a man found and covered up; then in his joy he goes and sells all that he has and buys that field.	44 "The Kingdom of heaven is like this. A man happens to find a treasure hidden in a field. He covers it up again, and is so happy that he goes and sells everything he has, and then goes back and buys that field.
45 "Again, the kingdom of heaven is like a merchant looking for fine pearls.	45 "Again, the kingdom of heaven is like a merchant in search of fine pearls,	45 "Also, the Kingdom of heaven is like this. A man is looking for fine pearls,
46 When he found one of great value, he went away and sold everything he had and bought it.	46 who, on finding one pearl of great value, went and sold all that he had and bought it.	46 and when he finds one that is unusually fine, he goes and sells everything he has, and buys that pearl.
15:7 You hypocrites! Isaiah was right when he prophesied about you:	15:7 You hypocrites! Well did Isaiah prophesy of you, when he said:	15:7 You hypocrites! How right Isaiah was when he prophesied about you!
8 "'These people honor me with their lips, but their hearts are far from me.	8 'This people honors me with their lips, but their heart is far from me;	8 'These people, says God, honor me with their words, but their heart is really far away from me.
9 They worship me in vain; their teachings are but rules taught by men.'"	9 in vain do they worship me, teaching as doctrines the precepts of men.'"	9 It is no use for them to worship me, because they teach man-made rules as though they were my laws!'"
16:15 "But what about you?" he asked. "Who do you say I am?"	16:15 He said to them, "But who do you say that I am?"	16:15 "What about you?" he asked them. "Who do you say I am?"
16 Simon Peter answered, "You are the Christ, the Son of the living God."	16 Simon Peter replied, "You are the Christ, the Son of the living God."	16 Simon Peter answered, "You are the Messiah, the Son of the living God."
18 And I tell you that you are Peter, and on this rock I will build my church, and the gates of Hades will not overcome it.	18 And I tell you, you are Peter, and on this rock I will build my church, and the powers of death shall not prevail against it.	18 And so I tell you, Peter: you are a rock, and on this rock foundation I will build my church, and not even death will ever be able to overcome it.
19 I will give you the keys of the kingdom of heaven; whatever you bind on earth will be bound in heaven, and whatever you loose on earth will be loosed in heaven."	19 I will give you the keys of the kingdom of heaven, and whatever you bind on earth shall be bound in heaven, and whatever you loose on earth shall be loosed in heaven."	19 I will give you the keys of the Kingdom of heaven; what you prohibit on earth will be prohibited in heaven, and what you permit on earth will be permitted in heaven."
24 Then Jesus said to his disciples, "If anyone would come after me, he must deny himself and take up his cross and follow me.	24 Then Jesus told his disciples, "If any man would come after me, let him deny himself and take up his cross and follow me.	24 Then Jesus said to his disciples, "If anyone wants to come with me, he must forget himself, carry his cross, and follow me.
25 For whoever wants to save his life will lose it, but whoever loses his life for me will find it.	25 For whoever would save his life will lose it, and whoever loses his life for my sake will find it.	25 For whoever wants to save his own life will lose it; but whoever loses his life for my sake will find it.
26 What good will it be for a man if he gains the whole world, yet forfeits his soul? Or what can a man give in exchange for his soul?	26 For what will it profit a man, if he gains the whole world and forfeits his life? Or what shall a man give in return for his life?	26 Will a person gain anything if he wins the whole world but loses his life? Of course not! There is nothing he can give to regain his life.
(omitted)	(omitted)	(omitted)

KJV	NKJV	TLB
12 How think ye? if a man have an hundred sheep, and one of them be gone astray, doth he not leave the ninety and nine, and goeth into the mountains, and seeketh that which is gone astray?	12 "What do you think? If a man has a hundred sheep, and one of them goes astray, does he not leave the ninety-nine and go to the mountains to seek the one that is straying?	12 "If a man has a hundred sheep, and one wanders away and is lost, what will he do? Won't he leave the ninety-nine others and go out into the hills to search for the lost one?
19 Again I say unto you, That if two of you shall agree on earth as touching any thing that they shall ask, it shall be done for them of my Father which is in heaven.	19 "Again I say to you that if two of you agree on earth concerning anything that they ask, it will be done for them by My Father in heaven.	19 "I also tell you this—if two of you agree down here on earth concerning anything you ask for, my Father in heaven will do it for you.
20 For where two or three are gathered together in my name, there am I in the midst of them.	20 "For where two or three are gathered together in My name, I am there in the midst of them."	20 For where two or three gather together because they are mine, I will be right there among them."
19:4 And he answered and said unto them, Have ye not read, that he which made *them* at the beginning made them male and female,	19:4 And He answered and said to them, "Have you not read that He who made *them* at the beginning 'made them male and female.'	19:4 "Don't you read the Scriptures?" he replied. "In them it is written that at the beginning God created man and woman,
5 And said, For this cause shall a man leave father and mother, and shall cleave to his wife: and they twain shall be one flesh?	5 "and said, 'For this reason a man shall leave his father and mother and be joined to his wife and the two shall become one flesh'?	5 and that a man should leave his father and mother, and be forever united to his wife. The two shall become one—
6 Wherefore they are no more twain, but one flesh. What therefore God hath joined together, let not man put asunder.	6 "So then, they are no longer two but one flesh. Therefore what God has joined together, let not man separate."	6 no longer two, but one! And no man may divorce what God has joined together."
14 But Jesus said, Suffer little children, and forbid them not, to come unto me: for of such is the kingdom of heaven.	14 But Jesus said, "Let the little children come to Me, and do not forbid them; for of such is the kingdom of heaven."	14 But Jesus said, "Let the little children come to me, and don't prevent them. For of such is the Kingdom of Heaven."
29 And every one that hath forsaken houses, or brethren, or sisters, or father, or mother, or wife, or children, or lands, for my name's sake, shall receive an hundredfold, and shall inherit everlasting life.	29 "And everyone who has left houses or brothers or sisters or father or mother or wife or children or lands, for My name's sake, shall receive a hundredfold, and inherit everlasting life.	29 And anyone who gives up his home, brothers, sisters, father, mother, wife, children, or property, to follow me, shall receive a hundred times as much in return, and shall have eternal life.
20:27 And whosoever will be chief among you, let him be your servant:	20:27 "And whoever desires to be first among you, let him be your slave—	20:27 And if you want to be right at the top, you must serve like a slave.
28 Even as the Son of man came not to be ministered unto, but to minister, and to give his life a ransom for many.	28 "just as the Son of Man did not come to be served, but to serve, and to give His life a ransom for many."	28 Your attitude must be like my own, for I, the Messiah, did not come to be served, but to serve, and to give my life as a ransom for many."
21:28 But what think ye? A *certain* man had two sons; and he came to the first, and said, Son, go work to day in my vineyard.	21:28 "But what do you think? A man had two sons, and he came to the first and said, 'Son, go, work today in my vineyard.'	21:28 "But what do you think about this? A man with two sons told the older boy, 'Son, go out and work on the farm today.'
29 He answered and said, I will not: but afterward he repented, and went.	29 "He answered and said, 'I will not,' but afterward he regretted it and went.	29 'I won't,' he answered, but later he changed his mind and went.
30 And he came to the second, and said likewise. And he answered and said, I *go,* sir: and went not.	30 "Then he came to the second and said likewise. And he answered and said, 'I *go,* sir,' but he did not go.	30 Then the father told the youngest, 'You go!' and he said, 'Yes, sir, I will.' But he didn't.
31 Whether of them twain did the will of *his* father? They say unto him, The first. Jesus saith unto them, Verily I say unto you, That the publicans and the harlots go into the kingdom of God before you.	31 "Which of the two did the will of *his* father?" They said to Him, "The first." Jesus said to them, "Assuredly, I say to you that tax collectors and harlots enter the kingdom of God before you.	31 Which of the two was obeying his father?" They replied, "The first, of course." Then Jesus explained his meaning: "Surely evil men and prostitutes will get into the Kingdom before you do.
22:37 Jesus said unto him, Thou shalt love the Lord thy God with all thy heart, and with all thy soul, and with all thy mind.	22:37 Jesus said to him, " 'You shall love the LORD your God with all your heart, with all your soul, and with all your mind.'	22:37 Jesus replied, " 'Love the Lord your God with all your heart, soul, and mind.'
38 This is the first and great commandment.	38 "This is *the* first and great commandment.	38 This is the first and greatest commandment.
39 And the second *is* like unto it, Thou shalt love thy neighbour as thyself.	39 "And *the* second *is* like it: 'You shall love your neighbor as yourself.'	39 The second most important is similar: 'Love your neighbor as much as you love yourself.'
40 On these two commandments hang all the law and the prophets.	40 "On these two commandments hang all the Law and the Prophets."	40 All the other commandments and all the demands of the prophets stem from these two laws and are fulfilled if you obey them. Keep only these and you will find that you are obeying all the others."

NIV	RSV	TEV
12 "What do you think? If a man owns a hundred sheep, and one of them wanders away, will he not leave the ninety-nine on the hills and go to look for the one that wandered off?	12 What do you think? If a man has a hundred sheep, and one of them has gone astray, does he not leave the ninety-nine on the mountains and go in search of the one that went astray?	12 "What do you think a man does who has one hundred sheep and one of them gets lost? He will leave the other ninety-nine grazing on the hillside and go and look for the lost sheep.
19 "Again, I tell you that if two of you on earth agree about anything you ask for, it will be done for you by my Father in heaven.	19 Again I say to you, if two of you agree on earth about anything they ask, it will be done for them by my Father in heaven.	19 "And I tell you more: whenever two of you on earth agree about anything you pray for, it will be done for you by my Father in heaven.
20 For where two or three come together in my name, there am I with them."	20 For where two or three are gathered in my name, there am I in the midst of them."	20 For where two or three come together in my name, I am there with them."
19:4 "Haven't you read," he replied, "that at the beginning the Creator 'made them male and female,'	19:4 He answered, "Have you not read that he who made them from the beginning made them male and female,	19:4 Jesus answered, "Haven't you read the scripture that says that in the beginning the Creator made people male and female?
5 and said, 'For this reason a man will leave his father and mother and be united to his wife, and the two will become one flesh'?	5 and said, 'For this reason a man shall leave his father and mother and be joined to his wife, and the two shall become one flesh'?	5 And God said, 'For this reason a man will leave his father and mother and unite with his wife, and the two will become one.'
6 So they are no longer two, but one. Therefore what God has joined together, let man not separate."	6 So they are no longer two but one flesh. What therefore God has joined together, let not man put asunder."	6 So they are no longer two, but one. Man must not separate, then, what God has joined together."
14 Jesus said, "Let the little children come to me, and do not hinder them, for the kingdom of heaven belongs to such as these."	14 but Jesus said, "Let the children come to me, and do not hinder them; for to such belongs the kingdom of heaven."	14 Jesus said, "Let the children come to me and do not stop them, because the Kingdom of heaven belongs to such as these."
29 And everyone who has left houses or brothers or sisters or father or mother or children or fields for my sake will receive a hundred times as much and will inherit eternal life.	29 And every one who has left houses or brothers or sisters or father or mother or children or lands, for my name's sake, will receive a hundredfold, and inherit eternal life.	29 And everyone who has left houses or brothers or sisters or father or mother or children or fields for my sake, will receive a hundred times more and will be given eternal life.
20:27 and whoever wants to be first must be your slave—	20:27 and whoever would be first among you must be your slave;	20:27 and if one of you wants to be first, he must be your slave—
28 just as the Son of Man did not come to be served, but to serve, and to give his life as a ransom for many."	28 even as the Son of man came not to be served but to serve, and to give his life as a ransom for many."	28 like the Son of Man, who did not come to be served, but to serve and to give his life to redeem many people."
21:28 "What do you think? There was a man who had two sons. He went to the first and said, 'Son, go and work today in the vineyard.'	21:28 "What do you think? A man had two sons; and he went to the first and said, 'Son, go and work in the vineyard today.'	21:28 "Now, what do you think? There was once a man who had two sons. He went to the older one and said, 'Son, go and work in the vineyard today.'
29 "'I will not,' he answered, but later he changed his mind and went.	29 And he answered, 'I will not'; but afterward he repented and went.	29 'I don't want to,' he answered, but later he changed his mind and went.
30 "Then the father went to the other son and said the same thing. He answered, 'I will, sir,' but he did not go.	30 And he went to the second and said the same; and he answered, 'I go, sir,' but did not go.	30 Then the father went to the other son and said the same thing. 'Yes sir,' he answered, but he did not go.
31 "Which of the two did what his father wanted?" "The first," they answered. Jesus said to them, "I tell you the truth, the tax collectors and the prostitutes are entering the kingdom of God ahead of you.	31 Which of the two did the will of his father?" They said, "The first." Jesus said to them, "Truly, I say to you, the tax collectors and the harlots go into the kingdom of God before you.	31 Which one of the two did what his father wanted?" "The older one," they answered. So Jesus said to them, "I tell you: the tax collectors and the prostitutes are going into the Kingdom of God ahead of you.
22:37 Jesus replied: "'Love the Lord your God with all your heart and with all your soul and with all your mind.'	22:37 And he said to him, 'You shall love the Lord your God with all your heart, and with all your soul, and with all your mind.	22:37 Jesus answered, "'Love the Lord your God with all your heart, with all your soul, and with all your mind.'
38 This is the first and greatest commandment.	38 This is the great and first commandment.	38 This is the greatest and the most important commandment.
39 And the second is like it: 'Love your neighbor as yourself.'	39 And a second is like it, You shall love your neighbor as yourself.	39 The second most important commandment is like it: 'Love your neighbor as you love yourself.'
40 All the Law and the Prophets hang on these two commandments."	40 On these two commandments depend all the law and the prophets."	40 The whole Law of Moses and the teachings of the prophets depend on these two commandments."

170   Matthew 23:23
       Matthew 25:46
              KEY VERSE COMPARISON CHART

KJV	NKJV	TLB
23:23 Woe unto you, scribes and Pharisees, hypocrites! for ye pay tithe of mint and anise and cummin, and have omitted the weightier *matters* of the law, judgment, mercy, and faith: these ought ye to have done, and not to leave the other undone.	**23:23** "Woe to you, scribes and Pharisees, hypocrites! For you pay tithe of mint and anise and cumin, and have neglected the weightier *matters* of the law: justice and mercy and faith. These you ought to have done, without leaving the others undone.	**23:23** "Yes, woe upon you, Pharisees, and you other religious leaders—hypocrites! For you tithe down to the last mint leaf in your garden, but ignore the important things—justice and mercy and faith. Yes, you should tithe, but you shouldn't leave the more important things undone.
28 Even so ye also outwardly appear righteous unto men, but within ye are full of hypocrisy and iniquity.	**28** "Even so you also outwardly appear righteous to men, but inside you are full of hypocrisy and lawlessness.	**28** You try to look like saintly men, but underneath those pious robes of yours are hearts besmirched with every sort of hypocrisy and sin.
37 O Jerusalem, Jerusalem, *thou* that killest the prophets, and stonest them which are sent unto thee, how often would I have gathered thy children together, even as a hen gathereth her chickens under *her* wings, and ye would not!	**37** "O Jerusalem, Jerusalem, the one who kills the prophets and stones those who are sent to her! How often I wanted to gather your children together, as a hen gathers her chicks under *her* wings, but you were not willing!	**37** "O Jerusalem, Jerusalem, the city that kills the prophets, and stones all those God sends to her! How often I have wanted to gather your children together as a hen gathers her chicks beneath her wings, but you wouldn't let me.
38 Behold, your house is left unto you desolate.	**38** "See! Your house is left to you desolate;	**38** And now your house is left to you, desolate.
24:14 And this gospel of the kingdom shall be preached in all the world for a witness unto all nations; and then shall the end come.	**24:14** "And this gospel of the kingdom will be preached in all the world as a witness to all the nations, and then the end will come.	**24:14** "And the Good News about the Kingdom will be preached throughout the whole world, so that all nations will hear it, and then, finally, the end will come.
27 For as the lightning cometh out of the east, and shineth even unto the west; so shall also the coming of the Son of man be.	**27** "For as the lightning comes from the east and flashes to the west, so also will the coming of the Son of Man be.	**27** For as the lightning flashes across the sky from east to west, so shall my coming be, when I, the Messiah, return.
30 And then shall appear the sign of the Son of man in heaven: and then shall all the tribes of the earth mourn, and they shall see the Son of man coming in the clouds of heaven with power and great glory.	**30** "Then the sign of the Son of Man will appear in heaven, and then all the tribes of the earth will mourn, and they will see the Son of Man coming on the clouds of heaven with power and great glory.	**30** "And then at last the signal of my coming will appear in the heavens and there will be deep mourning all around the earth. And the nations of the world will see me arrive in the clouds of heaven, with power and great glory.
42 Watch therefore: for ye know not what hour your Lord doth come.	**42** "Watch therefore, for you do not know what hour your Lord is coming.	**42** "So be prepared, for you don't know what day your Lord is coming.
25:21 His lord said unto him, Well done, *thou* good and faithful servant: thou hast been faithful over a few things, I will make thee ruler over many things: enter thou into the joy of thy lord.	**25:21** "His lord said to him, 'Well *done*, good and faithful servant; you were faithful over a few things, I will make you ruler over many things. Enter into the joy of your lord.'	**25:21** "His master praised him for good work. 'You have been faithful in handling this small amount,' he told him, 'so now I will give you many more responsibilities. Begin the joyous tasks I have assigned to you.'
33 And he shall set the sheep on his right hand, but the goats on the left.	**33** "And He will set the sheep on His right hand, but the goats on the left.	**33** and place the sheep at my right hand, and the goats at my left.
34 Then shall the King say unto them on his right hand, Come, ye blessed of my Father, inherit the kingdom prepared for you from the foundation of the world:	**34** "Then the King will say to those on His right hand, 'Come, you blessed of My Father, inherit the kingdom prepared for you from the foundation of the world:	**34** "Then I, the King, shall say to those at my right, 'Come, blessed of my Father, into the Kingdom prepared for you from the founding of the world.
35 For I was an hungred, and ye gave me meat: I was thirsty, and ye gave me drink: I was a stranger, and ye took me in:	**35** 'for I was hungry and you gave Me food; I was thirsty and you gave Me drink; I was a stranger and you took Me in;	**35** For I was hungry and you fed me; I was thirsty and you gave me water; I was a stranger and you invited me into your homes;
36 Naked, and ye clothed me: I was sick, and ye visited me: I was in prison, and ye came unto me.	**36** 'I *was* naked and you clothed Me; I was sick and you visited Me; I was in prison and you came to Me.'	**36** naked and you clothed me; sick and in prison, and you visited me.'
41 Then shall he say also unto them on the left hand, Depart from me, ye cursed, into everlasting fire, prepared for the devil and his angels:	**41** "Then He will also say to those on the left hand, 'Depart from Me, you cursed, into the everlasting fire prepared for the devil and his angels:	**41** Then I will turn to those on my left and say, 'Away with you, you cursed ones, into the eternal fire prepared for the devil and his demons.
42 For I was an hungred, and ye gave me no meat: I was thirsty, and ye gave me no drink:	**42** 'for I was hungry and you gave Me no food; I was thirsty and you gave Me no drink;	**42** For I was hungry and you wouldn't feed me; thirsty, and you wouldn't give me anything to drink;
43 I was a stranger, and ye took me not in: naked, and ye clothed me not: sick, and in prison, and ye visited me not.	**43** 'I was a stranger and you did not take Me in, naked and you did not clothe Me, sick and in prison and you did not visit Me.'	**43** a stranger, and you refused me hospitality; naked, and you wouldn't clothe me; sick, and in prison, and you didn't visit me.'
46 And these shall go away into everlasting punishment: but the righteous into life eternal.	**46** "And these will go away into everlasting punishment, but the righteous into eternal life."	**46** "And they shall go away into eternal punishment; but the righteous into everlasting life."

NIV	RSV	TEV
23:23 "Woe to you, teachers of the law and Pharisees, you hypocrites! You give a tenth of your spices—mint, dill and cummin. But you have neglected the more important matters of the law—justice, mercy and faithfulness. You should have practiced the latter, without neglecting the former.	**23:23** "Woe to you, scribes and Pharisees, hypocrites! for you tithe mint and dill and cummin, and have neglected the weightier matters of the law, justice and mercy and faith; these you ought to have done, without neglecting the others.	**23:23** "How terrible for you, teachers of the Law and Pharisees! You hypocrites! You give to God one tenth even of the seasoning herbs, such as mint, dill, and cumin, but you neglect to obey the really important teachings of the Law, such as justice and mercy and honesty. These you should practice, without neglecting the others.
28 In the same way, on the outside you appear to people as righteous but on the inside you are full of hypocrisy and wickedness.	**28** So you also outwardly appear righteous to men, but within you are full of hypocrisy and iniquity.	**28** In the same way, on the outside you appear good to everybody, but inside you are full of hypocrisy and sins.
37 "O Jerusalem, Jerusalem, you who kill the prophets and stone those sent to you, how often I have longed to gather your children together, as a hen gathers her chicks under her wings, but you were not willing.	**37** "O Jerusalem, Jerusalem, killing the prophets and stoning those who are sent to you! How often would I have gathered your children together as a hen gathers her brood under her wings, and you would not!	**37** "Jerusalem, Jerusalem! You kill the prophets and stone the messengers God has sent you! How many times I wanted to put my arms around all your people, just as a hen gathers her chicks under her wings, but you would not let me!
38 Look, your house is left to you desolate.	**38** Behold, your house is forsaken and desolate.	**38** And so your Temple will be abandoned and empty.
24:14 And this gospel of the kingdom will be preached in the whole world as a testimony to all nations, and then the end will come.	**24:14** And this gospel of the kingdom will be preached throughout the whole world, as a testimony to all nations; and then the end will come.	**24:14** And this Good News about the Kingdom will be preached through all the world for a witness to all mankind; and then the end will come.
27 For as the lightning comes from the east and flashes to the west, so will be the coming of the Son of Man.	**27** For as the lightning comes from the east and shines as far as the west, so will be the coming of the Son of man.	**27** For the Son of Man will come like the lightning which flashes across the whole sky from the east to the west.
30 "At that time the sign of the Son of Man will appear in the sky, and all the nations of the earth will mourn. They will see the Son of Man coming on the clouds of the sky, with power and great glory.	**30** then will appear the sign of the Son of man in heaven, and then all the tribes of the earth will mourn, and they will see the Son of man coming on the clouds of heaven with power and great glory;	**30** Then the sign of the Son of Man will appear in the sky; and all the peoples of earth will weep as they see the Son of Man coming on the clouds of heaven with power and great glory.
42 "Therefore keep watch, because you do not know on what day your Lord will come.	**42** Watch therefore, for you do not know on what day your Lord is coming.	**42** Watch out, then, because you do not know what day your Lord will come.
25:21 "His master replied, 'Well done, good and faithful servant! You have been faithful with a few things; I will put you in charge of many things. Come and share your master's happiness!'	**25:21** His master said to him, 'Well done, good and faithful servant; you have been faithful over a little, I will set you over much; enter into the joy of your master.'	**25:21** 'Well done, you good and faithful servant!' said his master. 'You have been faithful in managing small amounts, so I will put you in charge of large amounts. Come on in and share my happiness!'
33 He will put the sheep on his right and the goats on his left.	**33** and he will place the sheep at his right hand, but the goats at the left.	**33** He will put the righteous people at his right and the others at his left.
34 "Then the King will say to those on his right, 'Come, you who are blessed by my Father; take your inheritance, the kingdom prepared for you since the creation of the world.	**34** Then the King will say to those at his right hand, 'Come, O blessed of my Father, inherit the kingdom prepared for you from the foundation of the world;	**34** Then the King will say to the people on his right, 'Come, you that are blessed by my Father! Come and possess the kingdom which has been prepared for you ever since the creation of the world.
35 For I was hungry and you gave me something to eat, I was thirsty and you gave me something to drink, I was a stranger and you invited me in,	**35** for I was hungry and you gave me food, I was thirsty and you gave me drink, I was a stranger and you welcomed me,	**35** I was hungry and you fed me, thirsty and you gave me a drink; I was a stranger and you received me in your homes,
36 I needed clothes and you clothed me, I was sick and you looked after me, I was in prison and you came to visit me.'	**36** I was naked and you clothed me, I was sick and you visited me, I was in prison and you came to me.'	**36** naked and you clothed me; I was sick and you took care of me, in prison and you visited me.'
41 "Then he will say to those on his left, 'Depart from me, you who are cursed, into the eternal fire prepared for the devil and his angels.	**41** Then he will say to those at his left hand, 'Depart from me, you cursed, into the eternal fire prepared for the devil and his angels;	**41** "Then he will say to those on his left, 'Away from me, you that are under God's curse! Away to the eternal fire which has been prepared for the Devil and his angels!
42 For I was hungry and you gave me nothing to eat, I was thirsty and you gave me nothing to drink,	**42** for I was hungry and you gave me no food, I was thirsty and you gave me no drink,	**42** I was hungry but you would not feed me, thirsty but you would not give me a drink;
43 I was a stranger and you did not invite me in, I needed clothes and you did not clothe me, I was sick and in prison and you did not look after me.'	**43** I was a stranger and you did not welcome me, naked and you did not clothe me, sick and in prison and you did not visit me.'	**43** I was a stranger but you would not welcome me in your homes, naked but you would not clothe me; I was sick and in prison but you would not take care of me.'
46 "Then they will go away to eternal punishment, but the righteous to eternal life."	**46** And they will go away into eternal punishment, but the righteous into eternal life."	**46** These, then, will be sent off to eternal punishment, but the righteous will go to eternal life."

KJV	NKJV	TLB
26:26 And as they were eating, Jesus took bread, and blessed *it*, and brake *it*, and gave *it* to the disciples, and said, Take, eat; this is my body.	**26:26** And as they were eating, Jesus took bread, blessed *it* and broke *it*, and gave *it* to the disciples and said, "Take, eat; this is My body."	**26:26** As they were eating, Jesus took a small loaf of bread and blessed it and broke it apart and gave it to the disciples and said, "Take it and eat it, for this is my body."
27 And he took the cup, and gave thanks, and gave *it* to them, saying, Drink ye all of it;	27 Then He took the cup, and gave thanks, and gave *it* to them, saying, "Drink from it, all of you.	27 And he took a cup of wine and gave thanks for it and gave it to them and said, "Each one drink from it,
28 For this is my blood of the new testament, which is shed for many for the remission of sins.	28 "For this is My blood of the new covenant, which is shed for many for the remission of sins.	28 for this is my blood, sealing the New Covenant. It is poured out to forgive the sins of multitudes.
27:35 And they crucified him, and parted his garments, casting lots: that it might be fulfilled which was spoken by the prophet, They parted my garments among them, and upon my vesture did they cast lots.	**27:35** Then they crucified Him, and divided His garments, casting lots, that it might be fulfilled which was spoken by the prophet: "They divided My garments among them, And for My clothing they cast lots."	**27:35** After the crucifixion, the soldiers threw dice to divide up his clothes among themselves.
50 Jesus, when he had cried again with a loud voice, yielded up the ghost.	50 Jesus, when He had cried out again with a loud voice, yielded up His spirit.	50 Then Jesus shouted out again, dismissed his spirit, and died.
51 And, behold, the vail of the temple was rent in twain from the top to the bottom; and the earth did quake, and the rocks rent;	51 And behold, the veil of the temple was torn in two from top to bottom; and the earth quaked, and the rocks were split,	51 And look! The curtain secluding the Holiest Place in the Temple was split apart from top to bottom; and the earth shook, and rocks broke,
54 Now when the centurion, and they that were with him, watching Jesus, saw the earthquake, and those things that were done, they feared greatly, saying, Truly this was the Son of God.	54 Now when the centurion and those with him, who were guarding Jesus, saw the earthquake and the things that had happened, they feared greatly, saying, "Truly this was the Son of God!"	54 The soldiers at the crucifixion and their sergeant were terribly frightened by the earthquake and all that happened. They exclaimed, "Surely this was God's Son."
28:5 And the angel answered and said unto the women, Fear not ye: for I know that ye seek Jesus, which was crucified.	**28:5** But the angel answered and said to the women, "Do not be afraid, for I know that you seek Jesus who was crucified.	**28:5** Then the angel spoke to the women. "Don't be frightened!" he said. "I know you are looking for Jesus, who was crucified,
6 He is not here: for he is risen, as he said. Come, see the place where the Lord lay.	6 "He is not here; for He is risen, as He said. Come, see the place where the Lord lay.	6 but he isn't here! For he has come back to life again, just as he said he would. Come in and see where his body was lying. . . .
18 And Jesus came and spake unto them, saying, All power is given unto me in heaven and in earth.	18 Then Jesus came and spoke to them, saying, "All authority has been given to Me in heaven and on earth.	18 He told his disciples, "I have been given all authority in heaven and earth.
19 Go ye therefore, and teach all nations, baptizing them in the name of the Father, and of the Son, and of the Holy Ghost:	19 "Go therefore and make disciples of all the nations, baptizing them in the name of the Father and of the Son and of the Holy Spirit,	19 Therefore go and make disciples in all the nations, baptizing them into the name of the Father and of the Son and of the Holy Spirit,
20 Teaching them to observe all things whatsoever I have commanded you: and, lo, I am with you always, *even* unto the end of the world. Amen.	20 "teaching them to observe all things that I have commanded you; and lo, I am with you always, *even* to the end of the age." Amen.	20 and then teach these new disciples to obey all the commands I have given you; and be sure of this—that I am with you always, even to the end of the world."

Mark

1:1 The beginning of the gospel of Jesus Christ, the Son of God;	**1:1** The beginning of the gospel of Jesus Christ, the Son of God.	**1:1** Here begins the wonderful story of Jesus the Messiah, the Son of God.
2 As it is written in the prophets, Behold, I send my messenger before thy face, which shall prepare thy way before thee.	2 As it is written in the Prophets: "Behold, I send My messenger before Your face, Who will prepare Your way before You."	2 In the book written by the prophet Isaiah, God announced that he would send his Son to earth, and that a special messenger would arrive first to prepare the world for his coming.
3 The voice of one crying in the wilderness, Prepare ye the way of the Lord, make his paths straight.	3 "The voice of one crying in the wilderness: 'Prepare the way of the LORD, Make His paths straight.'"	3 "This messenger will live out in the barren wilderness," Isaiah said, "and will proclaim that everyone must straighten out his life to be ready for the Lord's arrival."
14 Now after that John was put in prison, Jesus came into Galilee, preaching the gospel of the kingdom of God,	14 Now after John was put in prison, Jesus came to Galilee, preaching the gospel of the kingdom of God,	14 Later on, after John was arrested by King Herod, Jesus went to Galilee to preach God's Good News.
15 And saying, The time is fulfilled, and the kingdom of God is at hand: repent ye, and believe the gospel.	15 and saying, "The time is fulfilled, and the kingdom of God is at hand. Repent, and believe in the gospel."	15 "At last the time has come!" he announced. "God's Kingdom is near! Turn from your sins and act on this glorious news!"
2:21 No man also seweth a piece of new cloth on an old garment: else the new piece that filled it up taketh away from the old, and the rent is made worse.	**2:21** "No one sews a piece of unshrunk cloth on an old garment; or else the new piece pulls away from the old, and the tear is made worse.	**2:21** [Besides, going without food is part of the old way of doing things.] It is like patching an old garment with unshrunk cloth! What happens? The patch pulls away and leaves the hole worse than before.

NIV	RSV	TEV
26:26 While they were eating, Jesus took bread, gave thanks and broke it, and gave it to his disciples, saying, "Take and eat; this is my body."	**26:26** Now as they were eating, Jesus took bread, and blessed, and broke it, and gave it to the disciples and said, "Take, eat; this is my body."	**26:26** While they were eating, Jesus took a piece of bread, gave a prayer of thanks, broke it, and gave it to his disciples. "Take and eat it," he said; "this is my body."
27 Then he took the cup, gave thanks and offered it to them, saying, "Drink from it, all of you.	27 And he took a cup, and when he had given thanks he gave it to them, saying, "Drink of it, all of you;	27 Then he took a cup, gave thanks to God, and gave it to them. "Drink it, all of you," he said;
28 This is my blood of the covenant, which is poured out for many for the forgiveness of sins.	28 for this is my blood of the covenant, which is poured out for many for the forgiveness of sins.	28 "this is my blood, which seals God's covenant, my blood poured out for many for the forgiveness of sins.
27:35 When they had crucified him, they divided up his clothes by casting lots.	**27:35** And when they had crucified him, they divided his garments among them by casting lots;	**27:35** They crucified him and then divided his clothes among them by throwing dice.
50 And when Jesus had cried out again in a loud voice, he gave up his spirit.	50 And Jesus cried again with a loud voice and yielded up his spirit.	50 Jesus again gave a loud cry and breathed his last.
51 At that moment the curtain of the temple was torn in two from top to bottom. The earth shook and the rocks split.	51 And behold, the curtain of the temple was torn in two, from top to bottom; and the earth shook, and the rocks were split;	51 Then the curtain hanging in the Temple was torn in two from top to bottom. The earth shook, the rocks split apart,
54 When the centurion and those with him who were guarding Jesus saw the earthquake and all that had happened, they were terrified, and exclaimed, "Surely he was the Son of God!"	54 When the centurion and those who were with him, keeping watch over Jesus, saw the earthquake and what took place, they were filled with awe, and said, "Truly this was the Son of God!"	54 When the army officer and the soldiers with him who were watching Jesus saw the earthquake and everything else that happened, they were terrified and said, "He really was the Son of God!"
28:5 The angel said to the women, "Do not be afraid, for I know that you are looking for Jesus, who was crucified.	**28:5** But the angel said to the women, "Do not be afraid; for I know that you seek Jesus who was crucified.	**28:5** The angel spoke to the women. "You must not be afraid," he said. "I know you are looking for Jesus, who was crucified.
6 He is not here; he has risen, just as he said. Come and see the place where he lay.	6 He is not here; for he has risen, as he said. Come, see the place where he lay.	6 He is not here; he has been raised, just as he said. Come here and see the place where he was lying.
18 Then Jesus came to them and said, "All authority in heaven and on earth has been given to me.	18 And Jesus came and said to them, "All authority in heaven and on earth has been given to me.	18 Jesus drew near and said to them, "I have been given all authority in heaven and on earth.
19 Therefore go and make disciples of all nations, baptizing them in the name of the Father and of the Son and of the Holy Spirit,	19 Go therefore and make disciples of all nations, baptizing them in the name of the Father and of the Son and of the Holy Spirit,	19 Go, then, to all peoples everywhere and make them my disciples: baptize them in the name of the Father, the Son, and the Holy Spirit,
20 and teaching them to obey everything I have commanded you. And surely I will be with you always, to the very end of the age."	20 teaching them to observe all that I have commanded you; and lo, I am with you always, to the close of the age."	20 and teach them to obey everything I have commanded you. And I will be with you always, to the end of the age."

Mark

NIV	RSV	TEV
1:1 The beginning of the gospel about Jesus Christ, the Son of God.	**1:1** The beginning of the gospel of Jesus Christ, the Son of God.	**1:1** This is the Good News about Jesus Christ, the Son of God.
2 It is written in Isaiah the prophet: "I will send my messenger ahead of you, 　who will prepare your way"—	2 As it is written in Isaiah the prophet, "Behold, I send my messenger before thy face, 　who shall prepare thy way;	2 It began as the prophet Isaiah had written: "God said, 'I will send my messenger ahead of you 　to open the way for you.'
3 "a voice of one calling in the desert, 　'Prepare the way for the Lord, 　　make straight paths for him.'"	3 the voice of one crying in the wilderness: 　Prepare the way of the Lord, 　　make his paths straight—"	3 Someone is shouting in the desert, 　'Get the road ready for the Lord; 　　make a straight path for him to travel!'"
14 After John was put in prison, Jesus went into Galilee, proclaiming the good news of God.	14 Now after John was arrested, Jesus came into Galilee, preaching the gospel of God,	14 After John had been put in prison, Jesus went to Galilee and preached the Good News from God.
15 "The time has come," he said, "The kingdom of God is near. Repent and believe the good news!"	15 and saying, "The time is fulfilled, and the kingdom of God is at hand; repent, and believe in the gospel."	15 "The right time has come," he said, "and the Kingdom of God is near! Turn away from your sins and believe the Good News!"
2:21 "No one sews a patch of unshrunk cloth on an old garment. If he does, the new piece will pull away from the old, making the tear worse.	**2:21** No one sews a piece of unshrunk cloth on an old garment; if he does, the patch tears away from it, the new from the old, and a worse tear is made.	**2:21** "No one uses a piece of new cloth to patch up an old coat, because the new patch will shrink and tear off some of the old cloth, making an even bigger hole.

KJV	NKJV	TLB
22 And no man putteth new wine into old bottles: else the new wine doth burst the bottles, and the wine is spilled, and the bottles will be marred: but new wine must be put into new bottles.	22 "And no one puts new wine into old wineskins; or else the new wine bursts the wineskins, the wine is spilled, and the wineskins are ruined. But new wine must be put into new wineskins."	22 You know better than to put new wine into old wineskins. They would burst. The wine would be spilled out and the wineskins ruined. New wine needs fresh wineskins."
6:4 But Jesus said unto them, A prophet is not without honour, but in his own country, and among his own kin, and in his own house.	6:4 But Jesus said to them, "A prophet is not without honor except in his own country, among his own relatives, and in his own house."	6:4 Then Jesus told them, "A prophet is honored everywhere except in his home town and among his relatives and by his own family."
8:34 And when he had called the people *unto him* with his disciples also, he said unto them, Whosoever will come after me, let him deny himself, and take up his cross, and follow me.	8:34 And when He had called the people *to Him,* with His disciples also, He said to them, "Whoever desires to come after Me, let him deny himself, and take up his cross, and follow Me.	8:34 Then he called his disciples and the crowds to come over and listen. "If any of you wants to be my follower," he told them, "you must put aside your own pleasures and shoulder your cross, and follow me closely.
35 For whosoever will save his life shall lose it; but whosoever shall lose his life for my sake and the gospel's, the same shall save it.	35 "For whoever desires to save his life will lose it, but whoever loses his life for My sake and the gospel's will save it.	35 If you insist on saving your life, you will lose it. Only those who throw away their lives for my sake and for the sake of the Good News will ever know what it means to really live.
10:6 But from the beginning of the creation God made them male and female.	10:6 "But from the beginning of the creation, God 'made them male and female.'	10:6 But it certainly isn't God's way. For from the very first he made man and woman
7 For this cause shall a man leave his father and mother, and cleave to his wife;	7 'For this reason a man shall leave his father and mother and be joined to his wife,	7 to be joined together permanently in marriage; therefore a man is to leave his father and mother,
8 And they twain shall be one flesh: so then they are no more twain, but one flesh.	8 and the two shall become one flesh'; so then they are no longer two, but one flesh.	8 and he and his wife are united so that they are no longer two, but one.
9 What therefore God hath joined together, let not man put asunder.	9 "Therefore what God has joined together, let not man separate."	9 And no man may separate what God has joined together."
29 And Jesus answered and said, Verily I say unto you, There is no man that hath left house, or brethren, or sisters, or father, or mother, or wife, or children, or lands, for my sake, and the gospel's,	29 So Jesus answered and said, "Assuredly, I say to you, there is no one who has left house or brothers or sisters or father or mother or wife or children or lands, for My sake and the gospel's,	29 And Jesus replied, "Let me assure you that no one has ever given up anything—home, brothers, sisters, mother, father, children, or property—for love of me and to tell others the Good News,
30 But he shall receive an hundredfold now in this time, houses, and brethren, and sisters, and mothers, and children, and lands, with persecutions; and in the world to come eternal life.	30 "who shall not receive a hundredfold now in this time—houses and brothers and sisters and mothers and children and lands, with persecutions—and in the age to come, eternal life.	30 who won't be given back, a hundred times over, homes, brothers, sisters, mothers, children, and land—with persecutions! "All these will be his here on earth, and in the world to come he shall have eternal life.
11:24 Therefore I say unto you, What things soever ye desire, when you pray, believe that ye receive *them,* and ye shall have *them.*	11:24 "Therefore I say to you, whatever things you ask when you pray, believe that you receive *them,* and you will have *them.*	11:24 Listen to me! You can pray for *anything,* and *if you believe, you have it;* it's yours!
25 And when ye stand praying, forgive, if ye have ought against any: that your Father also which is in heaven may forgive you your trespasses.	25 "And whenever you stand praying, if you have anything against anyone, forgive him, that your Father in heaven may also forgive you your trespasses.	25 But when you are praying, first forgive anyone you are holding a grudge against, so that your Father in heaven will forgive you your sins too."
12:29 And Jesus answered him, The first of all the commandments *is,* Hear, O Israel; The Lord our God is one Lord:	12:29 Jesus answered him, "The first of all the commandments *is:* 'Hear, O Israel, the LORD our God, the LORD is one.	12:29 Jesus replied, "The one that says, 'Hear, O Israel! The Lord our God is the one and only God.
30 And thou shalt love the Lord thy God with all thy heart, and with all thy soul, and with all thy mind, and with all thy strength: this *is* the first commandment.	30 'And you shall love the LORD your God with all your heart, with all your soul, with all your mind, and with all your strength.' This *is* the first commandment.	30 And you must love him with all your heart and soul and mind and strength.'
31 And the second *is* like, *namely* this, Thou shalt love thy neighbour as thyself. There is none other commandment greater than these.	31 "And the second, like *it, is* this: 'You shall love your neighbor as yourself.' There is no other commandment great than these."	31 "The second is: 'You must love others as much as yourself.' No other commandments are greater than these."
13:31 Heaven and earth shall pass away: but my words shall not pass away.	13:31 "Heaven and earth will pass away, but My words will by no means pass away.	13:31 Heaven and earth shall disappear, but my words stand sure forever.
32 But of that day and *that* hour knoweth no man, no, not the angels which are in heaven, neither the Son, but the Father.	32 "But of that day and hour no one knows, neither the angels in heaven, nor the Son, but only the Father.	32 "However, no one, not even the angels in heaven, nor I myself, knows the day or hour when these things will happen; only the Father knows.
33 Take ye heed, watch and pray: for ye know not when the time is.	33 "Take heed, watch and pray; for you do not know when the time is.	33 And since you don't know when it will happen, stay alert. Be on the watch [for my return].

NIV	RSV	TEV
22 And no one pours new wine into old wineskins. If he does, the wine will burst the skins, and both the wine and the wineskins will be ruined. No, he pours new wine into new wineskins."	22 And no one puts new wine into old wineskins; if he does, the wine will burst the skins, and the wine is lost, and so are the skins; but new wine is for fresh skins."	22 Nor does anyone pour new wine into used wineskins, because the wine will burst the skins, and both the wine and the skins will be ruined. Instead, new wine must be poured into fresh wineskins."
6:4 Jesus said to them, "Only in his home town, among his relatives and in his own house is a prophet without honor."	6:4 And Jesus said to them, "A prophet is not without honor, except in his own country, and among his own kin, and in his own house."	6:4 Jesus said to them, "A prophet is respected everywhere except in his own home town and by his relatives and his family."
8:34 Then he called the crowd to him along with his disciples and said: "If anyone would come after me, he must deny himself and take up his cross and follow me.	8:34 And he called to him the multitude with his disciples, and said to them, "If any man would come after me, let him deny himself and take up his cross and follow me.	8:34 Then Jesus called the crowd and his disciples to him. "If anyone wants to come with me," he told them, "he must forget himself, carry his cross, and follow me.
35 For whoever wants to save his life will lose it, but whoever loses his life for me and for the gospel will save it.	35 For whoever would save his life will lose it; and whoever loses his life for my sake and the gospel's will save it.	35 For whoever wants to save his own life will lose it; but whoever loses his life for me and for the gospel will save it.
10:6 "But at the beginning of creation God 'made them male and female.'	10:6 But from the beginning of creation, 'God made them male and female.'	10:6 But in the beginning, at the time of creation, 'God made them male and female,' as the scripture says.
7 'For this reason a man will leave his father and mother and be united to his wife,	7 'For this reason a man shall leave his father and mother and be joined to his wife,	7 'And for this reason a man will leave his father and mother and unite with his wife,
8 and the two will become one flesh.' So they are no longer two, but one.	8 and the two shall become one flesh.' So they are no longer two but one flesh.	8 and the two will become one.' So they are no longer two, but one.
9 Therefore what God has joined together, let man not separate."	9 What therefore God has joined together, let not man put asunder."	9 Man must not separate, then, what God has joined together."
29 "I tell you the truth," Jesus replied, "no one who has left home or brothers or sisters or mother or father or children or fields for me and the gospel	29 Jesus said, "Truly, I say to you, there is no one who has left house or brothers or sisters or mother or father or children or lands, for my sake and for the gospel,	29 "Yes," Jesus said to them, "and I tell you that anyone who leaves home or brothers or sisters or mother or father or children or fields for me and for the gospel,
30 will fail to receive a hundred times as much in this present age (homes, brothers, sisters, mothers, children and fields—and with them, persecutions) and in the age to come, eternal life.	30 who will not receive a hundredfold now in this time, houses and brothers and sisters and mothers and children and lands, with persecutions, and in the age to come eternal life.	30 will receive much more in this present age. He will receive a hundred times more houses, brothers, sisters, mothers, children, and fields—and persecutions as well; and in the age to come he will receive eternal life.
11:24 Therefore I tell you, whatever you ask for in prayer, believe that you have received it, and it will be yours.	11:24 Therefore I tell you, whatever you ask in prayer, believe that you have received it, and it will be yours.	11:24 For this reason I tell you: When you pray and ask for something, believe that you have received it, and you will be given whatever you ask for.
25 And when you stand praying, if you hold anything against anyone, forgive him, so that your Father in heaven may forgive you your sins."	25 And whenever you stand praying, forgive, if you have anything against any one; so that your Father also who is in heaven may forgive you your trespasses."	25 And when you stand and pray, forgive anything you may have against anyone, so that your Father in heaven will forgive the wrongs you have done."
12:29 "The most important one," answered Jesus, "is this: 'Hear, O Israel, the Lord our God, the Lord is one.	12:29 Jesus answered, "The first is, 'Hear, O Israel: The Lord our God, the Lord is one;	12:29 Jesus replied, "The most important one is this: 'Listen, Israel! The Lord our God is the only Lord.
30 Love the Lord your God with all your heart and with all your soul and with all your mind and with all your strength.'	30 and you shall love the Lord your God with all your heart, and with all your soul, and with all your mind, and with all your strength.'	30 Love the Lord your God with all your heart, with all your soul, with all your mind, and with all your strength.'
31 The second is this: 'Love your neighbor as yourself.' There is no commandment greater than these."	31 The second is this, 'You shall love your neighbor as yourself.' There is no other commandment greater than these."	31 The second most important commandment is this: 'Love your neighbor as you love yourself.' There is no other commandment more important than these two."
13:31 Heaven and earth will pass away, but my words will never pass away.	13:31 Heaven and earth will pass away, but my words will not pass away.	13:31 Heaven and earth will pass away, but my words will never pass away.
32 "No one knows about that day or hour, not even the angels in heaven, nor the Son, but only the Father.	32 "But of that day or that hour no one knows, not even the angels in heaven, nor the Son, but only the Father.	32 "No one knows, however, when that day or hour will come—neither the angels in heaven, nor the Son; only the Father knows.
33 Be on guard! Be alert! You do not know when that time will come.	33 Take heed, watch; for you do not know when the time will come.	33 Be on watch, be alert, for you do not know when the time will come.

KJV	NKJV	TLB
14:62 And Jesus said, I am: and ye shall see the Son of man sitting on the right hand of power, and coming in the clouds of heaven.	**14:62** And Jesus said, "I am. And you will see the Son of Man sitting at the right hand of the Power, and coming with the clouds of heaven."	**14:62** Jesus said, "I am, and you will see me sitting at the right hand of God, and returning to earth in the clouds of heaven."
15:22 And they bring him unto the place Golgotha, which is, being interpreted, The place of a skull.	**15:22** And they brought Him to the place Golgotha, which is translated, Place of a Skull.	**15:22** And they brought Jesus to a place called Golgotha. (Golgotha means skull.)
23 And they gave him to drink wine mingled with myrrh: but he received *it* not.	23 Then they gave Him wine mingled with myrrh to drink, but He did not take *it*.	23 Wine drugged with bitter herbs was offered to him there, but he refused it.
24 And when they had crucified him, they parted his garments, casting lots upon them, what every man should take.	24 And when they crucified Him, they divided His garments, casting lots for them to determine what every man should take.	24 And then they crucified him—and threw dice for his clothes.
34 And at the ninth hour Jesus cried with a loud voice, saying, Eloi, Eloi, lama sabachthani? which is, being interpreted, My God, my God, why hast thou forsaken me?	34 And at the ninth hour Jesus cried out with a loud voice, saying, "Eloi, Eloi, lama sabachthani?" which is translated, "My God, My God, why have You forsaken Me?"	34 Then Jesus called out with a loud voice, "Eli, Eli, lama sabachthani?" ("My God, my God, why have you deserted me?")
16:5 And entering into the sepulchre, they saw a young man sitting on the right side, clothed in a long white garment; and they were affrighted.	**16:5** And entering the tomb, they saw a young man clothed in a long white robe sitting on the right side; and they were alarmed.	**16:5** So they entered the tomb—and there on the right sat a young man clothed in white. The women were startled,
6 And he saith unto them, Be not affrighted: Ye seek Jesus of Nazareth, which was crucified: he is risen; he is not here: behold the place where they laid him.	6 But he said to them, "Do not be alarmed. You seek Jesus of Nazareth, who was crucified. He is risen! He is not here. See the place where they laid Him.	6 but the angel said, "Don't be so surprised. Aren't you looking for Jesus, the Nazarene who was crucified? He isn't here! He has come back to life! Look, that's where his body was lying.
7 But go your way, tell his disciples and Peter that he goeth before you into Galilee: there shall ye see him, as he said unto you.	7 "But go *and* tell His disciples—and Peter—that He is going before you into Galilee; there you will see Him, as He said to you."	7 Now go and give this message to his disciples including Peter: "'Jesus is going ahead of you to Galilee. You will see him there, just as he told you before he died!'"
15 And he said unto them, Go ye into all the world, and preach the gospel to every creature.	15 And He said to them, "Go into all the world and preach the gospel to every creature.	15 And then he told them, "You are to go into all the world and preach the Good News to everyone, everywhere.
16 He that believeth and is baptized shall be saved; but he that believeth not shall be damned.	16 "He who believes and is baptized will be saved; but he who does not believe will be condemned.	16 Those who believe and are baptized will be saved. But those who refuse to believe will be condemned.

Luke

KJV	NKJV	TLB
1:30 And the angel said unto her, Fear not, Mary: for thou hast found favour with God.	**1:30** Then the angel said to her, "Do not be afraid, Mary, for you have found favor with God.	**1:30** "Don't be frightened, Mary," the angel told her, "for God has decided to wonderfully bless you!
31 And, behold, thou shalt conceive in thy womb, and bring forth a son, and shalt call his name JESUS.	31 "And behold, you will conceive in your womb and bring forth a Son, and shall call His name JESUS.	31 Very soon now, you will become pregnant and have a baby boy, and you are to name him 'Jesus.'
32 He shall be great, and shall be called the Son of the Highest: and the Lord God shall give unto him the throne of his father David:	32 "He will be great, and will be called the Son of the Highest; and the Lord God will give Him the throne of His father David.	32 He shall be very great and shall be called the Son of God. And the Lord God shall give him the throne of his ancestor David.
33 And he shall reign over the house of Jacob for ever; and of his kingdom there shall be no end.	33 "And He will reign over the house of Jacob forever, and of His kingdom there will be no end."	33 And he shall reign over Israel forever; his Kingdom shall never end!"
2:1 And it came to pass in those days, that there went out a decree from Cæsar Augustus, that all the world should be taxed.	**2:1** And it came to pass in those days *that* a decree went out from Caesar Augustus that all the world should be registered.	**2:1** About this time Caesar Augustus, the Roman Emperor, decreed that a census should be taken throughout the nation.
2 (*And* this taxing was first made when Cyrenius was governor of Syria.)	2 This census first took place while Quirinius was governing Syria.	2 (This census was taken when Quirinius was governor of Syria.)
3 And all went to be taxed, every one into his own city.	3 So all went to be registered, everyone to his own city.	3 Everyone was required to return to his ancestral home for this registration.
4 And Joseph also went up from Galilee, out of the city of Nazareth, into Judæa, unto the city of David, which is called Bethlehem; (because he was of the house and lineage of David:)	4 And Joseph also went up from Galilee, out of the city of Nazareth, to Judea, to the city of David, which is called Bethlehem, because he was of the house and lineage of David,	4 And because Joseph was a member of the royal line, he had to go to Bethlehem in Judea, King David's ancient home—journeying there from the Galilean village of Nazareth.
5 To be taxed with Mary his espoused wife, being great with child.	5 to be registered with Mary, his betrothed wife, who was with child.	5 He took with him Mary, his fiancée, who was obviously pregnant by this time.

NIV	RSV	TEV
14:62 "I am," said Jesus. "And you will see the Son of Man sitting at the right hand of the Mighty One and coming on the clouds of heaven."	**14:62** And Jesus said, "I am; and you will see the Son of man seated at the right hand of Power, and coming with the clouds of heaven."	**14:62** "I am," answered Jesus, "and you will all see the Son of Man seated at the right side of the Almighty and coming with the clouds of heaven!"
15:22 They brought Jesus to the place called Golgotha (which means The Place of the Skull).	**15:22** And they brought him to the place called Golgotha (which means the place of a skull).	**15:22** They took Jesus to a place called Golgotha, which means "The Place of the Skull."
23 Then they offered him wine mixed with myrrh, but he did not take it.	**23** And they offered him wine mingled with myrrh; but he did not take it.	**23** There they tried to give him wine mixed with a drug called myrrh, but Jesus would not drink it.
24 And they crucified him. Dividing up his clothes, they cast lots to see what each would get.	**24** And they crucified him, and divided his garments among them, casting lots for them, to decide what each should take.	**24** Then they crucified him and divided his clothes among themselves, throwing dice to see who would get which piece of clothing.
34 And at the ninth hour Jesus cried out in a loud voice, "*Eloi, Eloi, lama sabachthani?*"—which means, "My God, my God, why have you forsaken me?"	**34** And at the ninth hour Jesus cried with a loud voice, "Eloi, Eloi, lama sabachthani?"—which means, "My God, my God, why hast thou forsaken me?"	**34** At three o'clock Jesus cried out with a loud shout, "*Eloi, Eloi, lema sabachthani?*" which means, "My God, my God, why did you abandon me?"
16:5 As they entered the tomb, they saw a young man dressed in a white robe sitting on the right side, and they were alarmed.	**16:5** And entering the tomb, they saw a young man sitting on the right side, dressed in a white robe; and they were amazed.	**16:5** So they entered the tomb, where they saw a young man sitting at the right, wearing a white robe—and they were alarmed.
6 "Don't be alarmed," he said. "You are looking for Jesus the Nazarene, who was crucified. He has risen! He is not here. See the place where they laid him.	**6** And he said to them, "Do not be amazed; you seek Jesus of Nazareth, who was crucified. He has risen, he is not here; see the place where they laid him.	**6** "Don't be alarmed," he said. "I know you are looking for Jesus of Nazareth, who was crucified. He is not here—he has been raised! Look, here is the place where he was placed.
7 But go, tell his disciples and Peter, 'He is going ahead of you into Galilee. There you will see him, just as he told you.'"	**7** But go, tell his disciples and Peter that he is going before you to Galilee; there you will see him, as he told you."	**7** Now go and give this message to his disciples, including Peter: 'He is going to Galilee ahead of you; there you will see him, just as he told you.'"
15 He said to them, "Go into all the world and preach the good news to all creation.	**15** And he said to them, "Go into all the world and preach the gospel to the whole creation.	**15** He said to them, "Go throughout the whole world and preach the gospel to all mankind.
16 Whoever believes and is baptized will be saved, but whoever does not believe will be condemned.	**16** He who believes and is baptized will be saved; but he who does not believe will be condemned.	**16** Whoever believes and is baptized will be saved; whoever does not believe will be condemned.

Luke

NIV	RSV	TEV
1:30 But the angel said to her, "Do not be afraid, Mary, you have found favor with God.	**1:30** And the angel said to her, "Do not be afraid, Mary, for you have found favor with God.	**1:30** The angel said to her, "Don't be afraid, Mary; God has been gracious to you.
31 You will be with child and give birth to a son, and you are to give him the name Jesus.	**31** And behold, you will conceive in your womb and bear a son, and you shall call his name Jesus.	**31** You will become pregnant and give birth to a son, and you will name him Jesus.
32 He will be great and will be called the Son of the Most High. The Lord God will give him the throne of his father David,	**32** He will be great, and will be called the Son of the Most High; and the Lord God will give to him the throne of his father David,	**32** He will be great and will be called the Son of the Most High God. The Lord God will make him a king, as his ancestor David was,
33 and he will reign over the house of Jacob forever; his kingdom will never end."	**33** and he will reign over the house of Jacob for ever; and of his kingdom there will be no end."	**33** and he will be the king of the descendants of Jacob forever; his kingdom will never end!"
2:1 In those days Caesar Augustus issued a decree that a census should be taken of the entire Roman world.	**2:1** In those days a decree went out from Caesar Augustus that all the world should be enrolled.	**2:1** At that time Emperor Augustus ordered a census to be taken throughout the Roman Empire.
2 (This was the first census that took place while Quirinius was governor of Syria.)	**2** This was the first enrollment, when Quirinius was governor of Syria.	**2** When this first census took place, Quirinius was the governor of Syria.
3 And everyone went to his own town to register.	**3** And all went to be enrolled, each to his own city.	**3** Everyone, then, went to register himself, each to his own hometown.
4 So Joseph also went up from the town of Nazareth in Galilee to Judea, to Bethlehem the town of David, because he belonged to the house and line of David.	**4** And Joseph also went up from Galilee, from the city of Nazareth, to Judea, to the city of David, which is called Bethlehem, because he was of the house and lineage of David.	**4** Joseph went from the town of Nazareth in Galilee to the town of Bethlehem in Judea, the birthplace of King David. Joseph went there because he was a descendant of David.
5 He went there to register with Mary, who was pledged to be married to him and was expecting a child.	**5** to be enrolled with Mary his betrothed, who was with child.	**5** He went to register with Mary, who was promised in marriage to him. She was pregnant.

KJV	NKJV	TLB
6 And so it was, that, while they were there, the days were accomplished that she should be delivered.	6 So it was, that while they were there, the days were completed for her to be delivered.	6 And while they were there, the time came for her baby to be born;
7 And she brought forth her firstborn son, and wrapped him in swaddling cloths, and laid him in a manger; because there was no room for them in the inn.	7 And she brought forth her firstborn Son, and wrapped Him in swaddling cloths, and laid Him in a manger, because there was no room for them in the inn.	7 and she gave birth to her first child, a son. She wrapped him in a blanket and laid him in a manger, because there was no room for them in the village inn.
10 And the angel said unto them, Fear not: for, behold, I bring you good tidings of great joy, which shall be to all people.	10 Then the angel said to them, "Do not be afraid, for behold, I bring you good tidings of great joy which will be to all people.	10 but the angel reassured them. "Don't be afraid!" he said. "I bring you the most joyful news ever announced, and it is for everyone!
11 For unto you is born this day in the city of David a Saviour, which is Christ the Lord.	11 "For there is born to you this day in the city of David a Savior, who is Christ the Lord.	11 The Savior—yes, the Messiah, the Lord—has been born tonight in Bethlehem!
12 And this *shall be* a sign unto you; Ye shall find the babe wrapped in swaddling clothes, lying in a manger.	12 "And this *will be* the sign to you: You will find a Babe wrapped in swaddling cloths, lying in a manger."	12 How will you recognize him? You will find a baby wrapped in a blanket, lying in a manger!"
13 And suddenly there was with the angel a multitude of the heavenly host praising God, and saying,	13 And suddenly there was with the angel a multitude of the heavenly host praising God and saying:	13 Suddenly, the angel was joined by a vast host of others—the armies of heaven—praising God:
14 Glory to God in the highest, and on earth peace, good will toward men.	14 "Glory to God in the highest, And on earth peace, good will toward men!"	14 "Glory to God in the highest heaven," they sang, "and peace on earth for all those pleasing him."
3:16 John answered, saying unto *them* all, I indeed baptize you with water; but one mightier than I cometh, the latchet of whose shoes I am not worthy to unloose: he shall baptize you with the Holy Ghost and with fire:	3:16 John answered, saying to *them* all, "I indeed baptize you with water; but One mightier than I is coming, whose sandal strap I am not worthy to loose. He will baptize you with the Holy Spirit and with fire.	3:16 John answered the question by saying, "I baptize only with water; but someone is coming soon who has far higher authority than mine; in fact, I am not even worthy of being his slave. He will baptize you with fire—with the Holy Spirit.
21 Now when all the people were baptized, it came to pass, that Jesus also being baptized, and praying, the heaven was opened,	21 Now when all the people were baptized, it came to pass that Jesus also was baptized; and while He prayed, the heaven was opened.	21 Then one day, after the crowds had been baptized, Jesus himself was baptized; and as he was praying, the heavens opened,
22 And the Holy Ghost descended in a bodily shape like a dove upon him, and a voice came from heaven, which said, Thou art my beloved Son; in thee I am well pleased.	22 And the Holy Spirit descended in bodily form like a dove upon Him, and a voice came from heaven which said, "You are My beloved Son; in You I am well pleased."	22 and the Holy Spirit in the form of a dove settled upon him, and a voice from heaven said, "You are my much loved Son, yes, my delight."
4:18 The Spirit of the Lord *is* upon me, because he hath anointed me to preach the gospel to the poor; he hath sent me to heal the brokenhearted, to preach deliverance to the captives, and recovering of sight to the blind, to set at liberty them that are bruised,	4:18 "The Spirit of the LORD *is* upon Me, Because He has anointed Me to preach the gospel to *the poor.* He has sent Me to heal the brokenhearted, To preach deliverance to *the captives* And recovery of sight to *the blind,* To set at liberty those who are oppressed,	4:18 "The Spirit of the Lord is upon me; he has appointed me to preach Good News to the poor; he has sent me to heal the brokenhearted and to announce that captives shall be released and the blind shall see, that the downtrodden shall be freed from their oppressors,
19 To preach the acceptable year of the Lord.	19 To preach the acceptable year of the LORD."	19 and that God is ready to give blessings to all who come to him."
5:8 When Simon Peter saw *it,* he fell down at Jesus' knees, saying, Depart from me; for I am a sinful man, O Lord.	5:8 When Simon Peter saw *it,* he fell down at Jesus' knees, saying, "Depart from me, for I am a sinful man, O Lord!"	5:8 When Simon Peter realized what had happened, he fell to his knees before Jesus and said, "Oh, sir, please leave us—I'm too much of a sinner for you to have around."
31 And Jesus answering said unto them, They that are whole need not a physician; but they that are sick.	31 And Jesus answered and said to them, "Those who are well do not need a physician, but those who are sick.	31 Jesus answered them, "It is the sick who need a doctor, not those in good health.
32 I came not to call the righteous, but sinners to repentance.	32 "I have not come to call *the* righteous, but sinners, to repentance."	32 My purpose is to invite sinners to turn from their sins, not to spend my time with those who think themselves already good enough."
6:37 Judge not, and ye shall not be judged: condemn not, and ye shall not be condemned: forgive, and ye shall be forgiven:	6:37 "Judge not, and you shall not be judged. Condemn not, and you shall not be condemned. Forgive, and you will be forgiven.	6:37 Never criticize or condemn—or it will all come back on you. Go easy on others; then they will do the same for you.
38 Give, and it shall be given unto you; good measure, pressed down, and shaken together, and running over, shall men give into your bosom. For with the same measure that ye mete withal it shall be measured to you again.	38 "Give, and it will be given to you: good measure, pressed down, shaken together, and running over will be put into your bosom. For with the same measure that you use, it will be measured back to you."	38 For if you give, you will get! Your gift will return to you in full and overflowing measure, pressed down, shaken together to make room for more, and running over. Whatever measure you use to give—large or small—will be used to measure what is given back to you."
8:11 Now the parable is this: The seed is the word of God.	8:11 "Now the parable is this: The seed is the word of God.	8:11 "This is its meaning: The seed is God's message to men.

NIV	RSV	TEV
6 While they were there, the time came for the baby to be born,	6 And while they were there, the time came for her to be delivered.	6 and while they were in Bethlehem, the time came for her to have her baby.
7 and she gave birth to her firstborn, a son. She wrapped him in cloths and placed him in a manger, because there was no room for them in the inn.	7 And she gave birth to her first-born son and wrapped him in swaddling cloths, and laid him in a manger, because there was no place for them in the inn.	7 She gave birth to her first son, wrapped him in cloths and laid him in a manger—there was no room for them to stay in the inn.
10 But the angel said to them, "Do not be afraid. I bring you good news of great joy that will be for all the people.	10 And the angel said to them, "Be not afraid; for behold, I bring you good news of a great joy which will come to all the people;	10 but the angel said to them, "Don't be afraid! I am here with good news for you, which will bring great joy to all the people.
11 Today in the town of David a Savior has been born to you; he is Christ the Lord.	11 for to you is born this day in the city of David a Savior, who is Christ the Lord.	11 This very day in David's town your Savior was born—Christ the Lord!
12 This will be a sign to you: You will find a baby wrapped in cloths and lying in a manger."	12 And this will be a sign for you: you will find a babe wrapped in swaddling cloths and lying in a manger."	12 And this is what will prove it to you: you will find a baby wrapped in cloths and lying in a manger."
13 Suddenly a great company of the heavenly host appeared with the angel, praising God and saying,	13 And suddenly there was with the angel a multitude of the heavenly host praising God and saying,	13 Suddenly a great army of heaven's angels appeared with the angel, singing praises to God:
14 "Glory to God in the highest, and on earth peace to men on whom his favor rests."	14 "Glory to God in the highest, and on earth peace among men with whom he is pleased!"	14 "Glory to God in the highest heaven, and peace on earth to those with whom he is pleased!"
3:16 John answered them all, "I baptize you with water. But one more powerful than I will come, the thongs of whose sandals I am not worthy to untie. He will baptize you with the Holy Spirit and with fire.	3:16 John answered them all, "I baptize you with water; but he who is mightier than I is coming, the thong of whose sandals I am not worthy to untie; he will baptize you with the Holy Spirit and with fire.	3:16 So John said to all of them, "I baptize you with water, but someone is coming who is much greater than I am. I am not good enough even to untie his sandals. He will baptize you with the Holy Spirit and fire.
21 When all the people were being baptized, Jesus was baptized too. And as he was praying, heaven was opened	21 Now when all the people were baptized, and when Jesus also had been baptized and was praying, the heaven was opened,	21 After all the people had been baptized, Jesus also was baptized. While he was praying, heaven was opened,
22 and the Holy Spirit descended on him in bodily form like a dove. And a voice came from heaven: "You are my Son, whom I love; with you I am well pleased."	22 and the Holy Spirit descended upon him in bodily form, as a dove, and a voice came from heaven, "Thou art my beloved Son; with thee I am well pleased."	22 and the Holy Spirit came down upon him in bodily form like a dove. And a voice came from heaven, "You are my own dear Son. I am pleased with you."
4:18 "The Spirit of the Lord is on me, because he has anointed me to preach good news to the poor. He has sent me to proclaim freedom for the prisoners and recovery of sight for the blind, to release the oppressed,	4:18 "The Spirit of the Lord is upon me, because he has anointed me to preach good news to the poor. He has sent me to proclaim release to the captives and recovering of sight to the blind, to set at liberty those who are oppressed,	4:18 "The Spirit of the Lord is upon me, because he has chosen me to bring good news to the poor. He has sent me to proclaim liberty to the captives and recovery of sight to the blind, to set free the oppressed
19 to proclaim the year of the Lord's favor."	19 to proclaim the acceptable year of the Lord."	19 and announce that the time has come when the Lord will save his people."
5:8 When Simon Peter saw this, he fell at Jesus' knees and said, "Go away from me, Lord; I am a sinful man!"	5:8 But when Simon Peter saw it, he fell down at Jesus' knees, saying, "Depart from me, for I am a sinful man, O Lord."	5:8 When Simon Peter saw what had happened, he fell on his knees before Jesus and said, "Go away from me, Lord! I am a sinful man!"
31 Jesus answered them, "It is not the healthy who need a doctor, but the sick.	31 And Jesus answered them, "Those who are well have no need of a physician, but those who are sick;	31 Jesus answered them, "People who are well do not need a doctor, but only those who are sick.
32 I have not come to call the righteous, but sinners to repentance."	32 I have not come to call the righteous, but sinners to repentance."	32 I have not come to call respectable people to repent, but outcasts."
6:37 "Do not judge, and you will not be judged. Do not condemn, and you will not be condemned. Forgive, and you will be forgiven.	6:37 "Judge not, and you will not be judged; condemn not, and you will not be condemned; forgive, and you will be forgiven;	6:37 "Do not judge others, and God will not judge you; do not condemn others, and God will not condemn you; forgive others, and God will forgive you.
38 Give, and it will be given to you. A good measure, pressed down, shaken together and running over, will be poured into your lap. For with the measure you use, it will be measured to you."	38 give, and it will be given to you; good measure, pressed down, shaken together, running over, will be put into your lap. For the measure you give will be the measure you get back."	38 Give to others, and God will give to you. Indeed, you will receive a full measure, a generous helping, poured into your hands—all that you can hold. The measure you use for others is the one that God will use for you."
8:11 "This is the meaning of the parable: The seed is the word of God.	8:11 Now the parable is this: The seed is the word of God.	8:11 "This is what the parable means: the seed is the word of God.

KJV	NKJV	TLB
12 Those by the way side are they that hear; then cometh the devil, and taketh away the word out of their hearts, lest they should believe and be saved.	12 "Those by the wayside are the ones who hear; then the devil comes and takes away the word out of their hearts, lest they should believe and be saved.	12 The hard path where some seed fell represents the hard hearts of those who hear the words of God, but then the devil comes and steals the words away and prevents people from believing and being saved.
13 They on the rock *are they*, which, when they hear, receive the word with joy; and these have no root, which for a while believe, and in time of temptation fall away.	13 "But the ones on the rock *are those* who, when they hear, receive the word with joy; and these have no root, who believe for a while and in time of temptation fall away.	13 The stony ground represents those who enjoy listening to sermons, but somehow the message never really gets through to them and doesn't take root and grow. They know the message is true, and sort of believe for awhile; but when the hot winds of persecution blow, they lose interest.
14 And that which fell among thorns are they, which, when they have heard, go forth, and are choked with cares and riches and pleasures of *this* life, and bring no fruit to perfection.	14 "And the ones *that* fell among thorns are those who, when they have heard, go out and are choked with cares, riches, and pleasures of life, and bring no fruit to maturity.	14 The seed among the thorns represents those who listen and believe God's words but whose faith afterwards is choked out by worry and riches and the responsibilities and pleasures of life. And so they are never able to help anyone else to believe the Good News.
15 But that on the good ground are they, which in an honest and good heart, having heard the word, keep *it*, and bring forth fruit with patience.	15 "But the ones *that* fell on the good ground are those who, having heard the word with a noble and good heart, keep *it* and bear fruit with patience.	15 "But the good soil represents honest, good-hearted people. They listen to God's words and cling to them and steadily spread them to others who also soon believe."
9:23 And he said to *them* all, If any *man* will come after me, let him deny himself, and take up his cross daily, and follow me.	9:23 Then He said to *them* all, "If anyone desires to come after Me, let him deny himself, and take up his cross daily, and follow Me.	9:23 Then he said to all, "Anyone who wants to follow me must put aside his own desires and conveniences and carry his cross with me every day and *keep close to me!*
24 For whosoever will save his life shall lose it: but whosoever will lose his life for my sake, the same shall save it.	24 "For whoever desires to save his life will lose it, but whoever loses his life for My sake will save it.	24 Whoever loses his life for my sake will save it, but whoever insists on keeping his life will lose it;
10:30 And Jesus answering said, A certain *man* went down from Jerusalem to Jericho, and fell among thieves, which stripped him of his raiment, and wounded *him,* and departed, leaving *him* half dead.	10:30 Then Jesus answered and said: "A certain *man* went down from Jerusalem to Jericho, and fell among thieves, who stripped him of his clothing, wounded *him,* and departed, leaving *him* half dead.	10:30 Jesus replied with an illustration: "A Jew going on a trip from Jerusalem to Jericho was attacked by bandits. They stripped him of his clothes and money and beat him up and left him lying half dead beside the road.
31 And by chance there came down a certain priest that way: and when he saw him, he passed by on the other side.	31 "Now by chance a certain priest came down that road. And when he saw him, he passed by on the other side.	31 "By chance a Jewish priest came along; and when he saw the man lying there, he crossed to the other side of the road and passed him by.
32 And likewise a Levite, when he was at the place, came and looked *on him,* and passed by on the other side.	32 "Likewise a Levite, when he arrived at the place, came and looked, and passed by on the other side.	32 A Jewish Temple-assistant walked over and looked at him lying there, but then went on.
33 But a certain Samaritan, as he journeyed, came where he was: and when he saw him, he had compassion *on him.*	33 "But a certain Samaritan, as he journeyed, came where he was. And when he saw him, he had compassion *on him,*	33 "But a despised Samaritan came along, and when he saw him, he felt deep pity.
34 And went to *him,* and bound up his wounds, pouring in oil and wine, and set him on his own beast, and brought him to an inn, and took care of him.	34 "and went to *him* and bandaged his wounds, pouring on oil and wine; and he set him on his own animal, brought him to an inn, and took care of him.	34 Kneeling beside him the Samaritan soothed his wounds with medicine and bandaged them. Then he put the man on his donkey and walked along beside him till they came to an inn, where he nursed him through the night.
35 And on the morrow when he departed, he took out two pence, and gave *them* to the host, and said unto him, Take care of him; and whatsoever thou spendest more, when I come again, I will repay thee.	35 "On the next day, when he departed, he took out two denarii, gave *them* to the innkeeper, and said to him, 'Take care of him; and whatever more you spend, when I come again, I will repay you.'	35 The next day he handed the innkeeper two twenty-dollar bills and told him to take care of the man. 'If his bill runs higher than that,' he said, 'I'll pay the difference the next time I am here.'
36 Which now of these three, thinkest thou, was neighbour unto him that fell among the thieves?	36 "So which of these three do you think was neighbor to him who fell among the thieves?"	36 "Now which of these three would you say was a neighbor to the bandits' victim?"
37 And he said, He that shewed mercy on him. Then said Jesus unto him, Go, and do thou likewise.	37 And he said, "He who showed mercy on him." Then Jesus said to him, "Go and do likewise."	37 The man replied, "The one who showed him some pity." Then Jesus said, "Yes, now go and do the same."
11:2 And he said unto them, When ye pray, say, Our Father which art in heaven, Hallowed be thy name. Thy kingdom come. Thy will be done, as in heaven, so in earth.	11:2 So He said to them, "When you pray, say: Our Father in heaven, Hallowed be Your name. Your kingdom come. Your will be done On earth as *it is* in heaven.	11:2 And this is the prayer he taught them: "Father, may your name be honored for its holiness; send your Kingdom soon.
3 Give us day by day our daily bread.	3 Give us day by day our daily bread.	3 Give us our food day by day.

NIV	RSV	TEV
12 Those along the path are the ones who hear, and then the devil comes and takes away the word from their hearts, so that they cannot believe and be saved.	12 The ones along the path are those who have heard; then the devil comes and takes away the word from their hearts, that they may not believe and be saved.	12 The seeds that fell along the path stand for those who hear; but the Devil comes and takes the message away from their hearts in order to keep them from believing and being saved.
13 Those on the rock are the ones who receive the word with joy when they hear it, but they have no root. They believe for a while, but in the time of testing they fall away.	13 And the ones on the rock are those who, when they hear the word, receive it with joy; but these have no root, they believe for a while and in time of temptation fall away.	13 The seeds that fell on rocky ground stand for those who hear the message and receive it gladly. But it does not sink deep into them; they believe only for a while but when the time of testing comes, they fall away.
14 The seed that fell among thorns stands for those who hear, but as they go on their way they are choked by life's worries, riches and pleasures, and they do not mature.	14 And as for what fell among the thorns, they are those who hear, but as they go on their way they are choked by the cares and riches and pleasures of life, and their fruit does not mature.	14 The seeds that fell among thorn bushes stand for those who hear; but the worries and riches and pleasures of this life crowd in and choke them, and their fruit never ripens.
15 But the seed on good soil stands for those with a noble and good heart, who hear the word, retain it, and by persevering produce a crop.	15 And as for that in the good soil, they are those who, hearing the word, hold it fast in an honest and good heart, and bring forth fruit with patience.	15 The seeds that fell in good soil stand for those who hear the message and retain it in a good and obedient heart, and they persist until they bear fruit.
9:23 Then he said to them all: "If anyone would come after me, he must deny himself and take up his cross daily and follow me.	9:23 And he said to all, "If any man would come after me, let him deny himself and take up his cross daily and follow me.	9:23 And he said to them all, "If anyone wants to come with me, he must forget himself, take up his cross every day, and follow me.
24 For whoever wants to save his life will lose it, but whoever loses his life for me will save it.	24 For whoever would save his life will lose it; and whoever loses his life for my sake, he will save it.	24 For whoever wants to save his own life will lose it, but whoever loses his life for my sake will save it.
10:30 In reply Jesus said: "A man was going down from Jerusalem to Jericho, when he fell into the hands of robbers. They stripped him of his clothes, beat him and went away, leaving him half dead.	10:30 Jesus replied, "A man was going down from Jerusalem to Jericho, and he fell among robbers, who stripped him and beat him, and departed, leaving him half dead.	10:30 Jesus answered, "There was once a man who was going down from Jerusalem to Jericho when robbers attacked him, stripped him, and beat him up, leaving him half dead.
31 A priest happened to be going down the same road, and when he saw the man, he passed by on the other side.	31 Now by chance a priest was going down that road; and when he saw him he passed by on the other side.	31 It so happened that a priest was going down that road; but when he saw the man, he walked on by on the other side.
32 So too, a Levite, when he came to the place and saw him, passed by on the other side.	32 So likewise a Levite, when he came to the place and saw him, passed by on the other side.	32 In the same way a Levite also came there, went over and looked at the man, and then walked on by on the other side.
33 But a Samaritan, as he traveled, came where the man was; and when he saw him, he took pity on him.	33 But a Samaritan, as he journeyed, came to where he was; and when he saw him, he had compassion,	33 But a Samaritan who was traveling that way came upon the man, and when he saw him, his heart was filled with pity.
34 He went to him and bandaged his wounds, pouring on oil and wine. Then he put the man on his own donkey, took him to an inn and took care of him.	34 and went to him and bound up his wounds, pouring on oil and wine; then he set him on his own beast and brought him to an inn, and took care of him.	34 He went over to him, poured oil and wine on his wounds and bandaged them; then he put the man on his own animal and took him to an inn, where he took care of him.
35 The next day he took out two silver coins and gave them to the innkeeper. 'Look after him,' he said, 'and when I return, I will reimburse you for any extra expense you may have.'	35 And the next day he took out two denarii and gave them to the innkeeper, saying, 'Take care of him; and whatever more you spend, I will repay you when I come back.'	35 The next day he took out two silver coins and gave them to the innkeeper. 'Take care of him,' he told the innkeeper, 'and when I come back this way, I will pay you whatever else you spend on him.'"
36 "Which of these three do you think was a neighbor to the man who fell into the hands of robbers?"	36 Which of these three, do you think, proved neighbor to the man who fell among the robbers?"	36 And Jesus concluded, "In your opinion, which one of these three acted like a neighbor toward the man attacked by the robbers?"
37 The expert in the law replied, "The one who had mercy on him." Jesus told him, "Go and do likewise."	37 He said, "The one who showed mercy on him." And Jesus said to him, "Go and do likewise."	37 The teacher of the Law answered, "The one who was kind to him." Jesus replied, "You go, then, and do the same."
11:2 He said to them, "When you pray, say: "'Father, hallowed be your name, your kingdom come.	11:2 And he said to them, "When you pray, say: "Father, hallowed be thy name. Thy kingdom come.	11:2 Jesus said to them, "When you pray, say this: 'Father: May your holy name be honored; may your Kingdom come.
3 Give us each day our daily bread.	3 Give us each day our daily bread;	3 Give us day by day the food we need.

KEY VERSE COMPARISON CHART

KJV	NKJV	TLB
4 And forgive us our sins; for we also forgive every one that is indebted to us. And lead us not into temptation; but deliver us from evil.	4 And forgive us our sins, For we also forgive everyone who is indebted to us. And do not lead us into temptation, But deliver us from the evil one."	4 And forgive our sins—for we have forgiven those who sinned against us. And don't allow us to be tempted."
12:8 Also I say unto you, Whosoever shall confess me before men, him shall the Son of man also confess before the angels of God:	12:8 "Also I say to you, whoever confesses Me before men, him the Son of Man also will confess before the angels of God.	12:8 "And I assure you of this: I, the Messiah, will publicly honor you in the presence of God's angels if you publicly acknowledge me here on earth as your Friend.
9 But he that denieth me before men shall be denied before the angels of God.	9 "But he who denies Me before men will be denied before the angels of God.	9 But I will deny before the angels those who deny me here among men.
13:34 O Jerusalem, Jerusalem, which killest the prophets, and stonest them that are sent unto thee; how often would I have gathered thy children together, as a hen *doth gather* her brood under *her* wings, and ye would not!	13:34 "O Jerusalem, Jerusalem, the one who kills the prophets and stones those who are sent to her! How often I wanted to gather your children together, as a hen *gathers* her brood under *her* wings, but you were not willing!	13:34 "O Jerusalem, Jerusalem! The city that murders the prophets. The city that stones those sent to help her. How often I have wanted to gather your children together even as a hen protects her brood under her wings, but you wouldn't let me.
35 Behold, your house is left unto you desolate: and verily I say unto you, Ye shall not see me, until *the time* come when ye shall say, Blessed *is* he that cometh in the name of the Lord.	35 "See! Your house is left to you desolate; and assuredly, I say to you, you shall not see Me until *the time* comes when you say, 'Blessed is He who comes in the name of the LORD!'"	35 And now—now your house is left desolate. And you will never again see me until you say, 'Welcome to him who comes in the name of the Lord.'"
14:13 But when thou makest a feast, call the poor, the maimed, the lame, the blind:	14:13 "But when you give a feast, invite *the* poor, *the* maimed, *the* lame, *the* blind.	14:13 Instead, invite the poor, the crippled, the lame, and the blind.
14 And thou shalt be blessed; for they cannot recompense thee: for thou shalt be recompensed at the resurrection of the just.	14 "And you will be blessed, because they cannot repay you; for you shall be repaid at the resurrection of the just."	14 Then at the resurrection of the godly, God will reward you for inviting those who can't repay you."
15:20 And he arose, and came to his father. But when he was yet a great way off, his father saw him, and had compassion, and ran, and fell on his neck, and kissed him.	15:20 "And he arose and came to his father. But when he was still a great way off, his father saw him and had compassion, and ran and fell on his neck and kissed him.	15:20 "So he returned home to his father. And while he was still a long distance away, his father saw him coming, and was filled with loving pity and ran and embraced him and kissed him.
21 And the son said unto him, Father, I have sinned against heaven, and in thy sight, and am no more worthy to be called thy son.	21 "And the son said to him, 'Father, I have sinned against heaven and in your sight, and am no longer worthy to be called your son.'	21 "His son said to him, 'Father, I have sinned against heaven and you, and am not worthy of being called your son—'
22 But the father said to his servants, Bring forth the best robe, and put *it* on him; and put a ring on his hand, and shoes on *his* feet:	22 "But the father said to his servants, 'Bring out the best robe and put *it* on him, and put a ring on his hand and sandals on *his* feet.	22 "But his father said to the slaves, 'Quick! Bring the finest robe in the house and put it on him. And a jeweled ring for his finger; and shoes!
23 And bring hither the fatted calf, and kill *it;* and let us eat, and be merry:	23 'And bring the fatted calf here and kill *it,* and let us eat and be merry;	23 And kill the calf we have in the fattening pen. We must celebrate with a feast,
24 For this my son was dead, and is alive again; he was lost, and is found. And they began to be merry.	24 'for this my son was dead and is alive again; he was lost and is found.' And they began to be merry.	24 for this son of mine was dead and has returned to life. He was lost and is found.' So the party began.
16:30 And he said, Nay, father Abraham: but if one went unto them from the dead, they will repent.	16:30 "And he said, 'No, father Abraham; but if one goes to them from the dead, they will repent.'	16:30 "The rich man replied, 'No, Father Abraham, they won't bother to read them. But if someone is sent to them from the dead, then they will turn from their sins.'
31 And he said unto him, If they hear not Moses and the prophets, neither will they be persuaded, though one rose from the dead.	31 "But he said to him, 'If they do not hear Moses and the prophets, neither will they be persuaded though one rise from the dead.'"	31 "But Abraham said, 'If they won't listen to Moses and the prophets, they won't listen even though someone rises from the dead.'"
18:1 And he spake a parable unto them *to this end,* that men ought always to pray, and not to faint;	18:1 Then He spoke a parable to them, that men always ought to pray and not lose heart,	18:1 One day Jesus told his disciples a story to illustrate their need for constant prayer and to show them that they must keep praying until the answer comes.
13 And the publican, standing afar off, would not lift up so much as *his* eyes unto heaven, but smote upon his breast, saying, God be merciful to me a sinner.	13 "And the tax collector, standing afar off, would not so much as raise *his* eyes to heaven, but beat his breast, saying, 'God be merciful to me a sinner!'	13 "But the corrupt tax collector stood at a distance and dared not even lift his eyes to heaven as he prayed, but beat upon his chest in sorrow, exclaiming, 'God, be merciful to me, a sinner.'
14 I tell you, this man went down to his house justified *rather* than the other: for every one that exalteth himself shall be abased; and he that humbleth himself shall be exalted.	14 "I tell you, this man went down to his house justified *rather* than the other; for everyone who exalts himself will be abased, and he who humbles himself will be exalted."	14 I tell you, this sinner, not the Pharisee, returned home forgiven! For the proud shall be humbled, but the humble shall be honored."
19:10 For the Son of man is come to seek and to save that which was lost.	19:10 "for the Son of Man has come to seek and to save that which was lost."	19:10 and I, the Messiah, have come to search for and to save such souls as his."

NIV	RSV	TEV
4 Forgive us our sins, for we also forgive everyone who sins against us. And lead us not into temptation.'"	4 and forgive us our sins, for we ourselves forgive every one who is indebted to us; and lead us not into temptation."	4 Forgive us our sins, for we forgive everyone who does us wrong. And do not bring us to hard testing.'"
12:8 "I tell you, whoever acknowledges me before men, the Son of Man will also acknowledge him before the angels of God.	12:8 "And I tell you, every one who acknowledges me before men, the Son of man also will acknowledge before the angels of God;	12:8 "I assure you that whoever declares publicly that he belongs to me, the Son of Man will do the same for him before the angels of God.
9 But he who disowns me before men will be disowned before the angels of God.	9 but he who denies me before men will be denied before the angels of God.	9 But whoever rejects me publicly, the Son of Man will also reject him before the angels of God.
13:34 "O Jerusalem, Jerusalem, you who kill the prophets and stone those sent to you, how often I have longed to gather your children together, as a hen gathers her chicks under her wings, but you were not willing!	13:34 O Jerusalem, Jerusalem, killing the prophets and stoning those who are sent to you! How often would I have gathered your children together as a hen gathers her brood under her wings, and you would not!	13:34 "Jerusalem, Jerusalem! You kill the prophets, you stone the messengers God has sent you! How many times I wanted to put my arms around all your people, just as a hen gathers her chicks under her wings, but you would not let me!
35 Look, your house is left to you desolate. I tell you, you will not see me again until you say, 'Blessed is he who comes in the name of the Lord.'"	35 Behold, your house is forsaken. And I tell you, you will not see me until you say, 'Blessed is he who comes in the name of the Lord!'"	35 And so your Temple will be abandoned. I assure you that you will not see me until the time comes when you say, 'God bless him who comes in the name of the Lord.'"
14:13 But when you give a banquet, invite the poor, the crippled, the lame, the blind,	14:13 But when you give a feast, invite the poor, the maimed, the lame, the blind,	14:13 When you give a feast, invite the poor, the crippled, the lame, and the blind;
14 and you will be blessed. Although they cannot repay you, you will be repaid at the resurrection of the righteous."	14 and you will be blessed, because they cannot repay you. You will be repaid at the resurrection of the just."	14 and you will be blessed, because they are not able to pay you back. God will repay you on the day the good people rise from death."
15:20 So he got up and went to his father. "But while he was still a long way off, his father saw him and was filled with compassion for him; he ran to his son, threw his arms around him and kissed him.	15:20 And he arose and came to his father. But while he was yet at a distance, his father saw him and had compassion, and ran and embraced him and kissed him.	15:20 So he got up and started back to his father. "He was still a long way from home when his father saw him; his heart was filled with pity, and he ran, threw his arms around his son, and kissed him.
21 "The son said to him, 'Father, I have sinned against heaven and against you. I am no longer worthy to be called your son.'	21 And the son said to him, 'Father, I have sinned against heaven and before you; I am no longer worthy to be called your son.'	21 'Father,' the son said, 'I have sinned against God and against you. I am no longer fit to be called your son.'
22 "But the father said to his servants, 'Quick! Bring the best robe and put it on him. Put a ring on his finger and sandals on his feet.	22 But the father said to his servants, 'Bring quickly the best robe, and put it on him; and put a ring on his hand, and shoes on his feet;	22 But the father called to his servants. 'Hurry!' he said. 'Bring the best robe and put it on him. Put a ring on his finger and shoes on his feet.
23 Bring the fattened calf and kill it. Let's have a feast and celebrate.	23 and bring the fatted calf and kill it, and let us eat and make merry;	23 Then go and get the prize calf and kill it, and let us celebrate with a feast!
24 For this son of mine was dead and is alive again; he was lost and is found.' So they began to celebrate.	24 for this my son was dead, and is alive again; he was lost, and is found.' And they began to make merry.	24 For this son of mine was dead, but now he is alive; he was lost, but now he has been found.' And so the feasting began.
16:30 "'No, father Abraham,' he said, 'but if someone from the dead goes to them, they will repent.'	16:30 And he said, 'No, father Abraham; but if some one goes to them from the dead, they will repent.'	16:30 The rich man answered, 'That is not enough, father Abraham! But if someone were to rise from death and go to them, then they would turn from their sins.'
31 "He said to him, 'If they do not listen to Moses and the Prophets, they will not be convinced even if someone rises from the dead.'"	31 He said to him, 'If they do not hear Moses and the prophets, neither will they be convinced if some one should rise from the dead.'"	31 But Abraham said, 'If they will not listen to Moses and the prophets, they will not be convinced even if someone were to rise from death.'"
18:1 Then Jesus told his disciples a parable to show them that they should always pray and not give up.	18:1 And he told them a parable, to the effect that they ought always to pray and not lose heart.	18:1 Then Jesus told his disciples a parable to teach them that they should always pray and never become discouraged.
13 "But the tax collector stood at a distance. He would not even look up to heaven, but beat his breast and said, 'God, have mercy on me, a sinner.'	13 But the tax collector, standing far off, would not even lift up his eyes to heaven, but beat his breast, saying, 'God, be merciful to me a sinner!'	13 But the tax collector stood at a distance and would not even raise his face to heaven, but beat on his breast and said, 'God, have pity on me, a sinner!'
14 "I tell you that this man, rather than the other, went home justified before God. For everyone who exalts himself will be humbled, and he who humbles himself will be exalted."	14 I tell you, this man went down to his house justified rather than the other; for every one who exalts himself will be humbled, but he who humbles himself will be exalted."	14 I tell you," said Jesus, "the tax collector, and not the Pharisee, was in the right with God when he went home. For everyone who makes himself great will be humbled, and everyone who humbles himself will be made great."
19:10 For the Son of Man came to seek and to save what was lost."	19:10 For the Son of man came to seek and to save the lost."	19:10 The Son of Man came to seek and to save the lost."

KJV	NKJV	TLB
20:25 And he said unto them, Render therefore unto Cæsar the things which be Cæsar's, and unto God the things which be God's.	**20:25** And He said to them, "Render therefore to Caesar the things that are Caesar's, and to God the things that are God's."	**20:25** He said, "Then give the emperor all that is his—and give to God all that is his!"
42 And David himself saith in the book of Psalms, The LORD said unto my Lord, Sit thou on my right hand,	42 "Now David himself said in the Book of Psalms, 'The LORD said to my Lord, "Sit at My right hand,	42 For David himself wrote in the book of Psalms: 'God said to my Lord, the Messiah, "Sit at my right hand
43 Till I make thine enemies thy footstool.	43 Till I make Your enemies Your footstool."'	43 until I place your enemies beneath your feet."'
22:31 And the Lord said, Simon, Simon, behold, Satan hath desired to *have* you, that he may sift *you* as wheat:	**22:31** And the Lord said, "Simon, Simon! Indeed, Satan has asked for you, that he may sift *you* as wheat.	**22:31** "Simon, Simon, Satan has asked to have you, to sift you like wheat,
32 But I have prayed for thee, that thy faith fail not: and when thou art converted, strengthen thy brethren.	32 "But I have prayed for you, that your faith should not fail; and when you have returned to *Me,* strengthen your brethren."	32 but I have pleaded in prayer for you that your faith should not completely fail. So when you have repented and turned to me again, strengthen and build up the faith of your brothers."
33 And he said unto him, Lord, I am ready to go with thee, both into prison, and to death.	33 But he said to Him, "Lord, I am ready to go with You, both to prison and to death."	33 Simon said, "Lord, I am ready to go to jail with you, and even to die with you."
34 And he said, I tell thee, Peter, the cock shall not crow this day, before that thou shalt thrice deny that thou knowest me.	34 Then He said, "I tell you, Peter, the rooster will not crow this day before you will deny three times that you know Me."	34 But Jesus said, "Peter, let me tell you something. Between now and tomorrow morning when the rooster crows, you will deny me three times, declaring that you don't even know me."
23:43 And Jesus said unto him, Verily I say unto thee, To day shalt thou be with me in paradise.	**23:43** And Jesus said to him, "Assuredly, I say to you, today you will be with Me in Paradise."	**23:43** And Jesus replied, "Today you will be with me in Paradise. This is a solemn promise."
24:46 And said unto them, Thus it is written, and thus it behoved Christ to suffer, and to rise from the dead the third day:	**24:46** Then He said to them, "Thus it is written, and thus it was necessary for the Christ to suffer and to rise from the dead the third day,	**24:46** And he said, "Yes, it was written long ago that the Messiah must suffer and die and rise again from the dead on the third day;
47 And that repentance and remission of sins should be preached in his name among all nations, beginning at Jerusalem.	47 "and that repentance and remission of sins should be preached in His name to all nations, beginning at Jerusalem.	47 and that this message of salvation should be taken from Jerusalem to all the nations: *There is forgiveness of sins for all who turn to me.*
48 And ye are witnesses of these things.	48 "And you are witnesses of these things.	48 You have seen these prophecies come true.

John

1:1 In the beginning was the Word, and the Word was with God, and the Word was God.	**1:1** In the beginning was the Word, and the Word was with God, and the Word was God.	**1:1–2** Before anything else existed, there was Christ, with God. He has always been alive and is himself God.
2 The same was in the beginning with God.	2 He was in the beginning with God.	
3 All things were made by him; and without him was not any thing made that was made.	3 All things were made through Him, and without Him nothing was made that was made.	3 He created everything there is—nothing exists that he didn't make.
12 But as many as received him, to them gave he power to become the sons of God, *even* to them that believe on his name:	12 But as many as received Him, to them He gave the right to become children of God, *even* to those who believe in His name:	12 But to all who received him, he gave the right to become children of God. All they needed to do was to trust him to save them.
14 And the Word was made flesh, and dwelt among us, (and we beheld his glory, the glory as of the only begotten of the Father,) full of grace and truth.	14 And the Word became flesh and dwelt among us, and we beheld His glory, the glory of the only begotten of the Father, full of grace and truth.	14 And Christ became a human being and lived here on earth among us and was full of loving forgiveness and truth. And some of us have seen his glory—the glory of the only Son of the heavenly Father!
3:3 Jesus answered and said unto him, Verily, verily, I say unto thee, Except a man be born again, he cannot see the kingdom of God.	**3:3** Jesus answered and said to him, "Most assuredly, I say to you, unless one is born again, he cannot see the kingdom of God."	**3:3** Jesus replied, "With all the earnestness I possess I tell you this: Unless you are born again, you can never get into the Kingdom of God."
16 For God so loved the world, that he gave his only begotten Son, that whosoever believeth in him should not perish, but have everlasting life.	16 "For God so loved the world that He gave His only begotten Son, that whoever believes in Him should not perish but have everlasting life.	16 For God loved the world so much that he gave his only Son so that anyone who believes in him shall not perish but have eternal life.
17 For God sent not his Son into the world to condemn the world; but that the world through him might be saved.	17 "For God did not send His Son into the world to condemn the world, but that the world through Him might be saved.	17 God did not send his Son into the world to condemn it, but to save it.
18 He that believeth on him is not condemned: but he that believeth not is condemned already, because he hath not believed in the name of the only begotten Son of God.	18 "He who believes in Him is not condemned; but he who does not believe is condemned already, because he has not believed in the name of the only begotten Son of God.	18 "There is no eternal doom awaiting those who trust him to save them. But those who don't trust him have already been tried and condemned for not believing in the only Son of God.

NIV	RSV	TEV
20:25 "Caesar's," they replied. He said to them, "Then give to Caesar what is Caesar's, and to God what is God's."	**20:25** He said to them, "Then render to Caesar the things that are Caesar's, and to God the things that are God's."	**20:25** So Jesus said, "Well, then, pay to the Emperor what belongs to the Emperor, and pay to God what belongs to God."
42 David himself declares in the Book of Psalms: "'The Lord said to my Lord: "Sit at my right hand	**42** For David himself says in the Book of Psalms, 'The Lord said to my Lord, Sit at my right hand,	**42** For David himself says in the book of Psalms, 'The Lord said to my Lord: Sit here at my right side
43 until I make your enemies a footstool for your feet.'"	**43** till I make thy enemies a stool for thy feet.'	**43** until I put your enemies as a footstool under your feet.'
22:31 "Simon, Simon, Satan has asked to sift you as wheat.	**22:31** "Simon, Simon, behold, Satan demanded to have you, that he might sift you like wheat,	**22:31** "Simon, Simon! Listen! Satan has received permission to test all of you, to separate the good from the bad, as a farmer separates the wheat from the chaff.
32 But I have prayed for you, Simon, that your faith may not fail. And when you have turned back, strengthen your brothers."	**32** but I have prayed for you that your faith may not fail; and when you have turned again, strengthen your brethren."	**32** But I have prayed for you, Simon, that your faith will not fail. And when you turn back to me, you must strengthen your brothers."
33 But he replied, "Lord, I am ready to go with you to prison and to death."	**33** And he said to him, "Lord, I am ready to go with you to prison and to death."	**33** Peter answered, "Lord, I am ready to go to prison with you and to die with you!"
34 Jesus answered, "I tell you, Peter, before the rooster crows today, you will deny three times that you know me."	**34** He said, "I tell you, Peter, the cock will not crow this day, until you three times deny that you know me."	**34** "I tell you, Peter," Jesus said, "the rooster will not crow tonight until you have said three times that you do not know me."
23:43 Jesus answered him, "I tell you the truth, today you will be with me in paradise."	**23:43** And he said to him, "Truly, I say to you, today you will be with me in Paradise."	**23:43** Jesus said to him, "I promise you that today you will be in Paradise with me."
24:46 He told them, "This is what is written: The Christ will suffer and rise from the dead on the third day,	**24:46** and said to them, "Thus it is written, that the Christ should suffer and on the third day rise from the dead,	**24:46** and said to them, "This is what is written: the Messiah must suffer and must rise from death three days later,
47 and repentance and forgiveness of sins will be preached in his name to all nations, beginning at Jerusalem.	**47** and that repentance and forgiveness of sins should be preached in his name to all nations, beginning from Jerusalem.	**47** and in his name the message about repentance and the forgiveness of sins must be preached to all nations, beginning in Jerusalem.
48 You are witnesses of these things.	**48** You are witnesses of these things.	**48** You are witnesses of these things.

John

NIV	RSV	TEV
1:1 In the beginning was the Word, and the Word was with God, and the Word was God.	**1:1** In the beginning was the Word, and the Word was with God, and the Word was God.	**1:1** Before the world was created, the Word already existed; he was with God, and he was the same as God.
2 He was with God in the beginning.	**2** He was in the beginning with God;	**2** From the very beginning the Word was with God.
3 Through him all things were made; without him nothing was made that has been made.	**3** all things were made through him, and without him was not anything made that was made.	**3** Through him God made all things; not one thing in all creation was made without him.
12 Yet to all who received him, to those who believed in his name, he gave the right to become children of God—	**12** But to all who received him, who believed in his name, he gave power to become children of God;	**12** Some, however, did receive him and believed in him; so he gave them the right to become God's children.
14 The Word became flesh and lived for a while among us. We have seen his glory, the glory of the one and only Son who came from the Father, full of grace and truth.	**14** And the Word became flesh and dwelt among us, full of grace and truth; we have beheld his glory, glory as of the only Son from the Father.	**14** The Word became a human being and, full of grace and truth, lived among us. We saw his glory, the glory which he received as the Father's only Son.
3:3 In reply Jesus declared, "I tell you the truth, unless a man is born again, he cannot see the kingdom of God."	**3:3** Jesus answered him, "Truly, truly, I say to you, unless one is born anew, he cannot see the kingdom of God."	**3:3** Jesus answered, "I am telling you the truth: no one can see the Kingdom of God unless he is born again."
16 "For God so loved the world that he gave his one and only Son, that whoever believes in him shall not perish but have eternal life.	**16** For God so loved the world that he gave his only Son, that whoever believes in him should not perish but have eternal life.	**16** For God loved the world so much that he gave his only Son, so that everyone who believes in him may not die but have eternal life.
17 For God did not send his Son into the world to condemn the world, but to save the world through him.	**17** For God sent the Son into the world, not to condemn the world, but that the world might be saved through him.	**17** For God did not send his Son into the world to be its judge, but to be its savior.
18 Whoever believes in him is not condemned, but whoever does not believe stands condemned already because he has not believed in the name of God's one and only Son.	**18** He who believes in him is not condemned; he who does not believe is condemned already, because he has not believed in the name of the only Son of God.	**18** Whoever believes in the Son is not judged; but whoever does not believe has already been judged, because he has not believed in God's only Son.

KJV	NKJV	TLB
4:14 But whosoever drinketh of the water that I shall give him shall never thirst; but the water that I shall give him shall be in him a well of water springing up into everlasting life.	**4:14** "but whoever drinks of the water that I shall give him will never thirst. But the water that I shall give him will become in him a fountain of water springing up into everlasting life."	**4:14** "But the water I give them," he said, "becomes a perpetual spring within them, watering them forever with eternal life."
5:24 Verily, verily, I say unto you, He that heareth my word, and believeth on him that sent me, hath everlasting life, and shall not come into condemnation; but is passed from death unto life.	**5:24** "Most assuredly, I say to you, he who hears My word and believes in Him who sent Me has everlasting life, and shall not come into judgment, but has passed from death into life.	**5:24** "I say emphatically that anyone who listens to my message and believes in God who sent me has eternal life, and will never be damned for his sins, but has already passed out of death into life.
28 Marvel not at this: for the hour is coming, in the which all that are in the graves shall hear his voice,	**28** "Do not marvel at this; for the hour is coming in which all who are in the graves will hear His voice	**28** Don't be so surprised! Indeed the time is coming when all the dead in their graves shall hear the voice of God's Son,
29 And shall come forth; they that have done good, unto the resurrection of life; and they that have done evil, unto the resurrection of damnation.	**29** "and come forth—those who have done good, to the resurrection of life, and those who have done evil, to the resurrection of condemnation.	**29** and shall rise again—those who have done good, to eternal life; and those who have continued in evil, to judgment.
39 Search the scriptures; for in them ye think ye have eternal life: and they are they which testify of me.	**39** "You search the Scriptures, for in them you think you have eternal life; and these are they which testify of Me.	**39** "You search the Scriptures, for you believe they give you eternal life. And the Scriptures point to me!
6:27 Labour not for the meat which perisheth, but for that meat which endureth unto everlasting life, which the Son of man shall give unto you: for him hath God the Father sealed.	**6:27** "Do not labor for the food which perishes, but for the food which endures to everlasting life, which the Son of Man will give you, because God the Father has set His seal on Him."	**6:27** But you shouldn't be so concerned about perishable things like food. No, spend your energy seeking the eternal life that I, the Messiah, can give you. For God the Father has sent me for this very purpose."
35 And Jesus said unto them, I am the bread of life: he that cometh to me shall never hunger; and he that believeth on me shall never thirst.	**35** And Jesus said to them, "I am the bread of life. He who comes to Me shall never hunger, and he who believes in Me shall never thirst.	**35** Jesus replied, "I am the Bread of Life. No one coming to me will ever be hungry again. Those believing in me will never thirst.
37 All that the Father giveth me shall come to me; and him that cometh to me I will in no wise cast out.	**37** "All that the Father gives Me will come to Me, and the one who comes to Me I will by no means cast out.	**37** But some will come to me—those the Father has given me—and I will never, never reject them.
47 Verily, verily, I say unto you, He that believeth on me hath everlasting life.	**47** "Most assuredly, I say to you, he who believes in Me has everlasting life.	**47** "How earnestly I tell you this—anyone who believes in me already has eternal life!
51 I am the living bread which came down from heaven: if any man eat of this bread, he shall live for ever: and the bread that I will give is my flesh, which I will give for the life of the world.	**51** "I am the living bread which came down from heaven. If anyone eats of this bread, he will live forever; and the bread that I shall give is My flesh, which I shall give for the life of the world."	**51** I am that Living Bread that came down out of heaven. Anyone eating this Bread shall live forever; this Bread is my flesh given to redeem humanity."
54 Whoso eateth my flesh, and drinketh my blood, hath eternal life; and I will raise him up at the last day.	**54** "Whoever eats My flesh and drinks My blood has eternal life, and I will raise him up at the last day.	**54** But anyone who does eat my flesh and drink my blood has eternal life, and I will raise him at the Last Day.
7:17 If any man will do his will, he shall know of the doctrine, whether it be of God, or *whether* I speak of myself.	**7:17** "If anyone wants to do His will, he shall know concerning the doctrine, whether it is from God or *whether* I speak on My own *authority*.	**7:17** If any of you really determines to do God's will, then you will certainly know whether my teaching is from God or is merely my own.
8:12 Then spake Jesus again unto them, saying, I am the light of the world: he that followeth me shall not walk in darkness, but shall have the light of life.	**8:12** Then Jesus spoke to them again, saying, "I am the light of the world. He who follows Me shall not walk in darkness, but have the light of life."	**8:12** Later, in one of his talks, Jesus said to the people, "I am the Light of the world. So if you follow me, you won't be stumbling through the darkness, for living light will flood your path."
31 Then said Jesus to those Jews which believed on him, If ye continue in my word, *then* are ye my disciples indeed;	**31** Then Jesus said to those Jews who believed Him, "If you abide in My word, you are My disciples indeed.	**31** Jesus said to them, "You are truly my disciples if you live as I tell you to,
32 And ye shall know the truth, and the truth shall make you free.	**32** "And you shall know the truth, and the truth shall make you free."	**32** and you will know the truth, and the truth will set you free."
10:27 My sheep hear my voice, and I know them, and they follow me:	**10:27** "My sheep hear My voice, and I know them, and they follow Me.	**10:27** My sheep recognize my voice, and I know them, and they follow me.
28 And I give unto them eternal life; and they shall never perish, neither shall any *man* pluck them out of my hand.	**28** "And I give them eternal life, and they shall never perish; neither shall anyone snatch them out of My hand.	**28** I give them eternal life and they shall never perish. No one shall snatch them away from me,
29 My Father, which gave *them* me, is greater than all; and no *man* is able to pluck *them* out of my Father's hand.	**29** "My Father, who has given *them* to Me, is greater than all; and no one is able to snatch *them* out of My Father's hand.	**29** for my Father has given them to me, and he is more powerful than anyone else, so no one can kidnap them from me.
11:25 Jesus said unto her, I am the resurrection, and the life: he that believeth in me, though he were dead, yet shall he live:	**11:25** Jesus said to her, "I am the resurrection and the life. He who believes in Me, though he may die, he shall live.	**11:25** Jesus told her, "I am the one who raises the dead and gives them life again. Anyone who believes in me, even though he dies like anyone else, shall live again.

NIV	RSV	TEV
4:14 but whoever drinks the water I give him will never thirst. Indeed, the water I give him will become in him a spring of water welling up to eternal life."	**4:14** but whoever drinks of the water that I shall give him will never thirst; the water that I shall give him will become in him a spring of water welling up to eternal life."	**4:14** but whoever drinks the water that I will give him will never be thirsty again. The water that I will give him will become in him a spring which will provide him with lifegiving water and give him eternal life."
5:24 "I tell you the truth, whoever hears my word and believes him who sent me has eternal life and will not be condemned; he has crossed over from death to life.	**5:24** Truly, truly, I say to you, he who hears my word and believes him who sent me, has eternal life; he does not come into judgment, but has passed from death to life.	**5:24** "I am telling you the truth: whoever hears my words and believes in him who sent me has eternal life. He will not be judged, but has already passed from death to life.
28 "Do not be amazed at this, for a time is coming when all who are in their graves will hear his voice	**28** Do not marvel at this; for the hour is coming when all who are in the tombs will hear his voice	**28** Do not be surprised at this; the time is coming when all the dead will hear his voice
29 and come out—those who have done good will rise to live, and those who have done evil will rise to be condemned.	**29** and come forth, those who have done good, to the resurrection of life, and those who have done evil, to the resurrection of judgment.	**29** and come out of their graves: those who have done good will rise and live, and those who have done evil will rise and be condemned.
39 You diligently study the Scriptures because you think that by them you possess eternal life. These are the Scriptures that testify about me,	**39** You search the scriptures, because you think that in them you have eternal life; and it is they that bear witness to me;	**39** You study the Scriptures, because you think that in them you will find eternal life. And these very Scriptures speak about me!
6:27 Do not work for food that spoils, but for food that endures to eternal life, which the Son of Man will give you. On him God the Father has placed his seal of approval."	**6:27** Do not labor for the food which perishes, but for the food which endures to eternal life, which the Son of man will give to you; for on him has God the Father set his seal."	**6:27** Do not work for food that spoils; instead, work for the food that lasts for eternal life. This is the food which the Son of Man will give you, because God, the Father, has put his mark of approval on him."
35 Then Jesus declared, "I am the bread of life. He who comes to me will never go hungry, and he who believes in me will never be thirsty.	**35** Jesus said to them, "I am the bread of life; he who comes to me shall not hunger, and he who believes in me shall never thirst.	**35** "I am the bread of life," Jesus told them. "He who comes to me will never be hungry; he who believes in me will never be thirsty.
37 All that the Father gives me will come to me, and whoever comes to me I will never drive away.	**37** All that the Father gives me will come to me; and him who comes to me I will not cast out.	**37** Everyone whom my Father gives me will come to me. I will never turn away anyone who comes to me,
47 I tell you the truth, he who believes has everlasting life.	**47** Truly, truly, I say to you, he who believes has eternal life.	**47** I am telling you the truth: he who believes has eternal life.
51 I am the living bread that came down from heaven. If a man eats of this bread, he will live forever. This bread is my flesh, which I will give for the life of the world."	**51** I am the living bread which came down from heaven; if any one eats of this bread, he will live for ever; and the bread which I shall give for the life of the world is my flesh."	**51** I am the living bread that came down from heaven. If anyone eats this bread, he will live forever. The bread that I will give him is my flesh, which I give so that the world may live."
54 Whoever eats my flesh and drinks my blood has eternal life, and I will raise him up at the last day.	**54** he who eats my flesh and drinks my blood has eternal life, and I will raise him up at the last day.	**54** Whoever eats my flesh and drinks my blood has eternal life, and I will raise him to life on the last day.
7:17 If any one chooses to do God's will, he will find out whether my teaching comes from God or whether I speak on my own.	**7:17** if any man's will is to do his will, he shall know whether the teaching is from God or whether I am speaking on my own authority.	**7:17** Whoever is willing to do what God wants will know whether what I teach comes from God or whether I speak on my own authority.
8:12 When Jesus spoke again to the people, he said, "I am the light of the world. Whoever follows me will never walk in darkness, but will have the light of life."	**8:12** Again Jesus spoke to them, saying, "I am the light of the world; he who follows me will not walk in darkness, but will have the light of life."	**8:12** Jesus spoke to the Pharisees again. "I am the light of the world," he said. "Whoever follows me will have the light of life and will never walk in darkness."
31 To the Jews who had believed him, Jesus said, "If you hold to my teaching, you are really my disciples.	**31** Jesus then said to the Jews who had believed in him, "If you continue in my word, you are truly my disciples,	**31** So Jesus said to those who believed in him, "If you obey my teaching, you are really my disciples;
32 Then you will know the truth, and the truth will set you free."	**32** and you will know the truth, and the truth will make you free."	**32** you will know the truth, and the truth will set you free."
10:27 My sheep listen to my voice; I know them, and they follow me.	**10:27** My sheep hear my voice, and I know them, and they follow me;	**10:27** My sheep listen to my voice; I know them, and they follow me.
28 I give them eternal life, and they shall never perish; no one can snatch them out of my hand.	**28** and I give them eternal life, and they shall never perish, and no one shall snatch them out of my hand.	**28** I give them eternal life, and they shall never die. No one can snatch them away from me.
29 My Father, who has given them to me, is greater than all; no one can snatch them out of my Father's hand.	**29** My Father, who has given them to me, is greater than all, and no one is able to snatch them out of the Father's hand.	**29** What my Father has given me is greater than everything, and no one can snatch them away from the Father's care.
11:25 Jesus said to her, "I am the resurrection and the life. He who believes in me will live, even though he dies;	**11:25** Jesus said to her, "I am the resurrection and the life; he who believes in me, though he die, yet shall he live,	**11:25** Jesus said to her, "I am the resurrection and the life. Whoever believes in me will live, even though he dies;

KJV	NKJV	TLB
26 And whosoever liveth and believeth in me shall never die. Believest thou this?	26 "And whoever lives and believes in Me shall never die. Do you believe this?"	26 He is given eternal life for believing in me and shall never perish. Do you believe this, Martha?"
12:32 And I, if I be lifted up from the earth, will draw all *men* unto me.	12:32 "And I, if I am lifted up from the earth, will draw all *peoples* to Myself."	12:32 And when I am lifted up [on the cross], I will draw everyone to me."
48 He that rejecteth me, and receiveth not my words, hath one that judgeth him: the word that I have spoken, the same shall judge him in the last day.	48 "He who rejects Me, and does not receive My words, has that which judges him—the word that I have spoken will judge him in the last day.	48 But all who reject me and my message will be judged at the Day of Judgment by the truths I have spoken.
49 For I have not spoken of myself; but the Father which sent me, he gave me a commandment, what I should say, and what I should speak.	49 "For I have not spoken on My own *authority;* but the Father who sent Me gave Me a command, what I should say and what I should speak.	49 For these are not my own ideas, but I have told you what the Father said to tell you.
50 And I know that his commandment is life everlasting: whatsoever I speak therefore, even as the Father said unto me, so I speak.	50 "And I know that His command is everlasting life. Therefore, whatever I speak, just as the Father has told Me, so I speak."	50 And I know his instructions lead to eternal life; so whatever he tells me to say, I say!"
13:17 If ye know these things, happy are ye if ye do them.	13:17 "If you know these things, happy are you if you do them.	13:17 You know these things—now do them! That is the path of blessing.
34 A new commandment I give unto you, That ye love one another; as I have loved you, that ye also love one another.	34 "A new commandment I give to you, that you love one another; as I have loved you, that you also love one another.	34 "And so I am giving a new commandment to you now—love each other just as much as I love you.
35 By this shall all *men* know that ye are my disciples, if ye have love one to another.	35 "By this all will know that you are My disciples, if you have love for one another."	35 Your strong love for each other will prove to the world that you are my disciples."
14:1 Let not your heart be troubled: ye believe in God, believe also in me.	14:1 "Let not your heart be troubled; you believe in God, believe also in Me.	14:1 "Let not your heart be troubled. You are trusting God, now trust in me.
2 In my Father's house are many mansions: if *it were* not *so*, I would have told you. I go to prepare a place for you.	2 "In My Father's house are many mansions; if *it were* not *so*, I would have told you. I go to prepare a place for you.	2 There are many homes up there where my Father lives, and I am going to prepare them for your coming. If this weren't so, I would tell you plainly.
3 And if I go and prepare a place for you, I will come again, and receive you unto myself; that where I am, *there* ye may be also.	3 "And if I go and prepare a place for you, I will come again and receive you to Myself; that where I am, *there* you may be also.	3 When everything is ready, then I will come and get you, so that you can always be with me where I am.
12 Verily, verily, I say unto you, He that believeth on me, the works that I do shall he do also; and gather *works* than these shall he do; because I go unto my Father.	12 "Most assuredly, I say to you, he who believes in Me, the works that I do he will do also; and greater *works* than these he will do, because I go to My Father.	12 "In solemn truth I tell you, anyone believing in me shall do the same miracles I have done, and even greater ones, because I am going to be with the Father.
13 And whatsoever ye shall ask in my name, that will I do, that the Father may be glorified in the Son.	13 "And whatever you ask in My name, that I will do, that the Father may be glorified in the Son.	13 You can ask him for *anything*, using my name, and I will do it, for this will bring praise to the Father because of what I, the Son, will do for you.
15 If ye love me, keep my commandments.	15 "If you love Me, keep My commandments.	15 "If you love me, obey me;
16 And I will pray the Father, and he shall give you another Comforter, that he may abide with you for ever;	16 "And I will pray the Father, and He will give you another Helper, that He may abide with you forever,	16 and I will ask the Father and he will give you another Comforter, and he will never leave you.
27 Peace I leave with you, my peace I give unto you: not as the world giveth, give I unto you. Let not your heart be troubled, neither let it be afraid.	27 "Peace I leave with you, My peace I give to you; not as the world gives do I give to you. Let not your heart be troubled, neither let it be afraid.	27 "I am leaving you with a gift—peace of mind and heart! And the peace I give isn't fragile like the peace the world gives. So don't be troubled or afraid.
15:1 I am the true vine, and my Father is the husbandman.	15:1 "I am the true vine, and My Father is the vinedresser.	15:1 "I am the true Vine, and my Father is the Gardener.
2 Every branch in me that beareth not fruit he taketh away: and every *branch* that beareth fruit, he purgeth it, that it may bring forth more fruit.	2 "Every branch in Me that does not bear fruit He takes away; and every *branch* that bears fruit He prunes, that it may bear more fruit.	2 He lops off every branch that doesn't produce. And he prunes those branches that bear fruit for even larger crops.
5 I am the vine, ye *are* the branches: He that abideth in me, and I in him, the same bringeth forth much fruit: for without me ye can do nothing.	5 "I am the vine, you *are* the branches. He who abides in Me, and I in him, bears much fruit; for without Me you can do nothing.	5 "Yes, I am the Vine; you are the branches. Whoever lives in me and I in him shall produce a large crop of fruit. For apart from me you can't do a thing.
7 If ye abide in me, and my words abide in you, ye shall ask what ye will, and it shall be done unto you.	7 "If you abide in Me, and My words abide in you, you will ask what you desire, and it shall be done for you.	7 But if you stay in me and obey my commands, you may ask any request you like, and it will be granted!
11 These things have I spoken unto you, that my joy might remain in you, and *that* your joy might be full.	11 "These things I have spoken to you, that My joy may remain in you, and *that* your joy may be full.	11 I have told you this so that you will be filled with my joy. Yes, your cup of joy will overflow!

NIV	RSV	TEV
26 and whoever lives and believes in me will never die. Do you believe this?"	26 and whoever lives and believes in me shall never die. Do you believe this?"	26 and whoever lives and believes in me will never die. Do you believe this?"
12:32 But I, when I am lifted up from the earth, will draw all men to myself."	**12:32** and I, when I am lifted up from the earth, will draw all men to myself."	**12:32** When I am lifted up from the earth, I will draw everyone to me."
48 There is a judge for the one who rejects me and does not accept my words; that very word which I spoke will condemn him at the last day.	48 He who rejects me and does not receive my sayings has a judge; the word that I have spoken will be his judge on the last day.	48 Whoever rejects me and does not accept my message has one who will judge him. The words I have spoken will be his judge on the last day!
49 For I did not speak of my own accord, but the Father who sent me commanded me what to say and how to say it.	49 For I have not spoken on my own authority; the Father who sent me has himself given me commandment what to say and what to speak.	49 This is true, because I have not spoken on my own authority, but the Father who sent me has commanded me what I must say and speak.
50 I know that his command leads to eternal life. So whatever I say is just what the Father has told me to say."	50 And I know that his commandment is eternal life. What I say, therefore, I say as the Father has bidden me."	50 And I know that his command brings eternal life. What I say, then, is what the Father has told me to say."
13:17 Now that you know these things, you will be blessed if you do them.	**13:17** If you know these things, blessed are you if you do them.	**13:17** Now that you know this truth, how happy you will be if you put it into practice!
34 "A new command I give you: Love one another. As I have loved you, so you must love one another.	34 A new commandment I give to you, that you love one another; even as I have loved you, that you also love one another.	34 And now I give you a new commandment: love one another. As I have loved you, so you must love one another.
35 All men will know that you are my disciples if you love one another."	35 By this all men will know that you are my disciples, if you have love for one another."	35 If you have love for one another, then everyone will know that you are my disciples."
14:1 "Do not let your hearts be troubled. Trust in God; trust also in me.	**14:1** "Let not your hearts be troubled; believe in God, believe also in me.	**14:1** "Do not be worried and upset," Jesus told them. "Believe in God and believe also in me.
2 In my Father's house are many rooms; if it were not so, I would have told you. I am going there to prepare a place for you.	2 In my Father's house are many rooms; if it were not so, would I have told you that I go to prepare a place for you?	2 There are many rooms in my Father's house, and I am going to prepare a place for you. I would not tell you this if it were not so.
3 And if I go and prepare a place for you, I will come back and take you to be with me that you also may be where I am.	3 And when I go and prepare a place for you, I will come again and will take you to myself, that where I am you may be also.	3 And after I go and prepare a place for you, I will come back and take you to myself, so that you will be where I am.
12 I tell you the truth, anyone who has faith in me will do what I have been doing. He will do even greater things than these, because I am going to the Father.	12 "Truly, truly, I say to you, he who believes in me will also do the works that I do; and greater works than these will he do, because I go to the Father.	12 I am telling you the truth: whoever believes in me will do what I do—yes, he will do even greater things, because I am going to the Father.
13 And I will do whatever you ask in my name, so that the Son may bring glory to the Father.	13 Whatever you ask in my name, I will do it, that the Father may be glorified in the Son;	13 And I will do whatever you ask for in my name, so that the Father's glory will be shown through the Son.
15 "If you love me, you will obey what I command.	15 "If you love me, you will keep my commandments.	15 "If you love me, you will obey my commandments.
16 And I will ask the Father, and he will give you another Counselor to be with you forever—	16 And I will pray the Father, and he will give you another Counselor, to be with you for ever,	16 I will ask the Father, and he will give you another Helper, who will stay with you forever.
27 Peace I leave with you; my peace I give you. I do not give to you as the world gives. Do not let your hearts be troubled and do not be afraid.	27 Peace I leave with you; my peace I give to you; not as the world gives do I give to you. Let not your hearts be troubled, neither let them be afraid.	27 "Peace is what I leave with you; it is my own peace that I give you. I do not give it as the world does. Do not be worried and upset; do not be afraid.
15:1 "I am the true vine and my Father is the gardener.	**15:1** "I am the true vine, and my Father is the vinedresser.	**15:1** "I am the real vine, and my Father is the gardener.
2 He cuts off every branch in me that bears no fruit, while every branch that does bear fruit he trims clean so that it will be even more fruitful.	2 Every branch of mine that bears no fruit, he takes away, and every branch that does bear fruit he prunes, that it may bear more fruit.	2 He breaks off every branch in me that does not bear fruit, and he prunes every branch that does bear fruit, so that it will be clean and bear more fruit.
5 "I am the vine; you are the branches. If a man remains in me and I in him, he will bear much fruit; apart from me you can do nothing.	5 I am the vine, you are the branches. He who abides in me, and I in him, he it is that bears much fruit, for apart from me you can do nothing.	5 "I am the vine, and you are the branches. Whoever remains in me, and I in him, will bear much fruit: for you can do nothing without me.
7 If you remain in me and my words remain in you, ask whatever you wish, and it will be given you.	7 If you abide in me, and my words abide in you, ask whatever you will, and it shall be done for you.	7 If you remain in me and my words remain in you, then you will ask for anything you wish, and you shall have it.
11 I have told you this so that my joy may be in you and that your joy may be complete.	11 These things I have spoken to you, that my joy may be in you, and that your joy may be full.	11 "I have told you this so that my joy may be in you and that your joy may be complete.

KJV	NKJV	TLB
12 This is my commandment, That ye love one another, as I have loved you.	12 "This is My commandment, that you love one another as I have loved you.	12 I demand that you love each other as much as I love you.
13 Greater love hath no man than this, that a man lay down his life for his friends.	13 "Greater love has no one than this, than to lay down one's life for his friends.	13 And here is how to measure it—the greatest love is shown when a person lays down his life for his friends;
16:7 Nevertheless I tell you the truth; It is expedient for you that I go away: for if I go not away, the Comforter will not come unto you; but if I depart, I will send him unto you.	16:7 "Nevertheless I tell you the truth. It is to your advantage that I go away; for if I do not go away, the Helper will not come to you; but if I depart, I will send Him to you.	16:7 But the fact of the matter is that it is best for you that I go away, for if I don't, the Comforter won't come. If I do, he will—for I will send him to you.
8 And when he is come, he will reprove the world of sin, and of righteousness, and of judgment:	8 "And when He has come, He will convict the world of sin, and of righteousness, and of judgment:	8 "And when he has come he will convince the world of its sin, and of the availability of God's goodness, and of deliverance from judgment.
9 Of sin, because they believe not on me;	9 "of sin, because they do not believe in Me;	9 The world's sin is unbelief in me;
10 Of righteousness, because I go to my Father, and ye see me no more;	10 "of righteousness, because I go to My Father and you see Me no more;	10 there is righteousness available because I go to the Father and you shall see me no more;
11 Of judgment, because the prince of this world is judged.	11 "of judgment, because the ruler of this world is judged.	11 there is deliverance from judgment because the prince of this world has already been judged.
13 Howbeit when he, the Spirit of truth, is come, he will guide you into all truth: for he shall not speak of himself; but whatsoever he shall hear, that shall he speak: and he will shew you things to come.	13 "However, when He, the Spirit of truth, has come, He will guide you into all truth; for He will not speak on His own authority, but whatever He hears He will speak; and He will tell you things to come.	13 When the Holy Spirit, who is truth, comes, he shall guide you into all truth, for he will not be presenting his own ideas, but will be passing on to you what he has heard. He will tell you about the future.
33 These things I have spoken unto you, that in me ye might have peace. In the world ye shall have tribulation: but be of good cheer; I have overcome the world.	33 "These things I have spoken to you, that in Me you may have peace. In the world you will have tribulation; but be of good cheer, I have overcome the world."	33 I have told you all this so that you will have peace of heart and mind. Here on earth you will have many trials and sorrows; but cheer up, for I have overcome the world."
19:30 When Jesus therefore had received the vinegar, he said, It is finished: and he bowed his head, and gave up the ghost.	19:30 So when Jesus had received the sour wine, He said, "It is finished!" And bowing His head, He gave up His spirit.	19:30 When Jesus had tasted it, he said, "It is finished," and bowed his head and dismissed his spirit.
20:30 And many other signs truly did Jesus in the presence of his disciples, which are not written in this book:	20:30 And truly Jesus did many other signs in the presence of His disciples, which are not written in this book;	20:30 Jesus' disciples saw him do many other miracles besides the ones told about in this book,
31 But these are written, that ye might believe that Jesus is the Christ, the Son of God; and that believing ye might have life through his name.	31 but these are written that you may believe that Jesus is the Christ, the Son of God, and that believing you may have life in His name.	31 but these are recorded so that you will believe that he is the Messiah, the Son of God, and that believing in him you will have life.

Acts

KJV	NKJV	TLB
1:8 But ye shall receive power, after that the Holy Ghost is come upon you: and ye shall be witnesses unto me both in Jerusalem, and in all Judaea, and in Samaria, and unto the uttermost part of the earth.	1:8 "But you shall receive power when the Holy Spirit has come upon you; and you shall be witnesses to Me in Jerusalem, and in all Judea and Samaria, and to the end of the earth."	1:8 But when the Holy Spirit has come upon you, you will receive power to testify about me with great effect, to the people in Jerusalem, throughout Judea, in Samaria, and to the ends of the earth, about my death and resurrection."
11 Which also said, Ye men of Galilee, why stand ye gazing up into heaven? this same Jesus, which is taken up from you into heaven, shall so come in like manner as ye have seen him go into heaven.	11 who also said, "Men of Galilee, why do you stand gazing up into heaven? This same Jesus, who was taken up from you into heaven, will so come in like manner as you saw Him go into heaven."	11 and said, "Men of Galilee, why are you standing here staring at the sky? Jesus has gone away to heaven, and some day, just as he went, he will return!"
2:4 And they were all filled with the Holy Ghost, and began to speak with other tongues, as the Spirit gave them utterance.	2:4 And they were all filled with the Holy Spirit and began to speak with other tongues, as the Spirit gave them utterance.	2:4 And everyone present was filled with the Holy Spirit and began speaking in languages they didn't know, for the Holy Spirit gave them this ability.
21 And it shall come to pass, that whosoever shall call on the name of the Lord shall be saved.	21 And it shall come to pass that whoever calls on the name of the LORD shall be saved.'	21 But anyone who asks for mercy from the Lord shall have it and shall be saved.'
38 Then Peter said unto them, Repent, and be baptized every one of you in the name of Jesus Christ for the remission of sins, and ye shall receive the gift of the Holy Ghost.	38 Then Peter said to them, "Repent, and let every one of you be baptized in the name of Jesus Christ for the remission of sins; and you shall receive the gift of the Holy Spirit.	38 And Peter replied, "Each one of you must turn from sin, return to God, and be baptized in the name of Jesus Christ for the forgiveness of your sins; then you also shall receive this gift, the Holy Spirit.

NIV	RSV	TEV
12 My command is this: Love each other as I have loved you.	12 "This is my commandment, that you love one another as I have loved you.	12 My commandment is this: love one another, just as I love you.
13 Greater love has no one than this, that one lay down his life for his friends.	13 Greater love has no man than this, that a man lay down his life for his friends.	13 The greatest love a person can have for his friends is to give his life for them.
16:7 But I tell you the truth: It is for your good that I am going away. Unless I go away, the Counselor will not come to you; but if I go, I will send him to you.	16:7 Nevertheless I tell you the truth: it is to your advantage that I go away, for if I do not go away, the Counselor will not come to you; but if I go, I will send him to you.	16:7 But I am telling you the truth: it is better for you that I go away, because if I do not go, the Helper will not come to you. But if I do go away, then I will send him to you.
8 When he comes, he will convict the world of guilt in regard to sin and righteousness and judgment:	8 And when he comes, he will convince the world concerning sin and righteousness and judgment:	8 And when he comes, he will prove to the people of the world that they are wrong about sin and about what is right and about God's judgment.
9 in regard to sin, because men do not believe in me;	9 concerning sin, because they do not believe in me;	9 They are wrong about sin, because they do not believe in me;
10 in regard to righteousness, because I am going to the Father, where you can see me no longer;	10 concerning righteousness, because I go to the Father, and you will see me no more;	10 they are wrong about what is right, because I am going to the Father and you will not see me any more;
11 and in regard to judgment, because the prince of this world now stands condemned.	11 concerning judgment, because the ruler of this world is judged.	11 and they are wrong about judgment, because the ruler of this world has already been judged.
13 But when he, the Spirit of truth, comes, he will guide you into all truth. He will not speak on his own; he will speak only what he hears, and he will tell you what is yet to come.	13 When the Spirit of truth comes, he will guide you into all the truth; for he will not speak on his own authority, but whatever he hears he will speak, and he will declare to you the things that are to come.	13 When, however, the Spirit comes, who reveals the truth about God, he will lead you into all the truth. He will not speak on his own authority, but he will speak of what he hears and will tell you of things to come.
33 "I have told you these things, so that in me you may have peace. In this world you will have trouble. But take heart! I have overcome the world."	33 I have said this to you, that in me you may have peace. In the world you have tribulation; but be of good cheer, I have overcome the world."	33 I have told you this so that you will have peace by being united to me. The world will make you suffer. But be brave! I have defeated the world!"
19:30 When he had received the drink, Jesus said, "It is finished." With that, he bowed his head and gave up his spirit.	19:30 When Jesus had received the vinegar, he said, "It is finished"; and he bowed his head and gave up his spirit.	19:30 Jesus drank the wine and said, "It is finished!" Then he bowed his head and gave up his spirit.
20:30 Jesus did many other miraculous signs in the presence of his disciples, which are not recorded in this book.	20:30 Now Jesus did many other signs in the presence of the disciples, which are not written in this book;	20:30 In his disciples' presence Jesus performed many other miracles which are not written down in this book.
31 But these are written that you may believe that Jesus is the Christ, the Son of God, and that by believing you may have life in his name.	31 but these are written that you may believe that Jesus is the Christ, the Son of God, and that believing you may have life in his name.	31 But these have been written in order that you may believe that Jesus is the Messiah, the Son of God, and that through your faith in him you may have life.

Acts

NIV	RSV	TEV
1:8 But you will receive power when the Holy Spirit comes on you; and you will be my witnesses in Jerusalem, and in all Judea and Samaria, and to the ends of the earth."	1:8 But you shall receive power when the Holy Spirit has come upon you; and you shall be my witnesses in Jerusalem and in all Judea and Samaria and to the end of the earth."	1:8 But when the Holy Spirit comes upon you, you will be filled with power, and you will be witnesses for me in Jerusalem, in all of Judea and Samaria, and to the ends of the earth."
11 "Men of Galilee," they said, "why do you stand here looking into the sky? This same Jesus, who has been taken from you into heaven, will come back in the same way you have seen him go into heaven."	11 and said, "Men of Galilee, why do you stand looking into heaven? This Jesus, who was taken up from you into heaven, will come in the same way as you saw him go into heaven."	11 and said, "Galileans, why are you standing there looking up at the sky? This Jesus, who was taken from you into heaven, will come back in the same way that you saw him go to heaven."
2:4 All of them were filled with the Holy Spirit and began to speak in other tongues as the Spirit enabled them.	2:4 And they were all filled with the Holy Spirit and began to speak in other tongues, as the Spirit gave them utterance.	2:4 They were all filled with the Holy Spirit and began to talk in other languages, as the Spirit enabled them to speak.
21 And everyone who calls on the name of the Lord will be saved.'	21 And it shall be that whoever calls on the name of the Lord shall be saved.'	21 And then, whoever calls out to the Lord for help will be saved.'
38 Peter replied, "Repent and be baptized, every one of you, in the name of Jesus Christ so that your sins may be forgiven. And you will receive the gift of the Holy Spirit.	38 And Peter said to them, "Repent, and be baptized every one of you in the name of Jesus Christ for the forgiveness of your sins; and you shall receive the gift of the Holy Spirit.	38 Peter said to them, "Each one of you must turn away from his sins and be baptized in the name of Jesus Christ, so that your sins will be forgiven; and you will receive God's gift, the Holy Spirit.

KJV	NKJV	TLB
3:19 Repent ye therefore, and be converted, that your sins may be blotted out, when the times of refreshing shall come from the presence of the Lord;	**3:19** "Repent therefore and be converted, that your sins may be blotted out, so that times of refreshing may come from the presence of the Lord,	**3:19** Now change your mind and attitude to God and turn to him so he can cleanse away your sins and send you wonderful times of refreshment from the presence of the Lord
4:32 And the multitude of them that believed were of one heart and of one soul: neither said any *of them* that ought of the things which he possessed was his own; but they had all things common.	**4:32** Now the multitude of those who believed were of one heart and one soul; neither did anyone say that any of the things he possessed was his own, but they had all things in common.	**4:32** All the believers were of one heart and mind, and no one felt that what he owned was his own; everyone was sharing.
5:31 Him hath God exalted with his right hand *to be* a Prince and a Saviour, for to give repentance to Israel, and forgiveness of sins.	**5:31** "Him God has exalted to His right hand *to be* Prince and Savior, to give repentance to Israel and forgiveness of sins.	**5:31** Then, with mighty power, God exalted him to be a Prince and Savior, so that the people of Israel would have an opportunity for repentance, and for their sins to be forgiven.
7:55 But he, being full of the Holy Ghost, looked up stedfastly into heaven, and saw the glory of God, and Jesus standing on the right hand of God,	**7:55** But he, being full of the Holy Spirit, gazed into heaven and saw the glory of God, and Jesus standing at the right hand of God,	**7:55** But Stephen, full of the Holy Spirit, gazed steadily upward into heaven and saw the glory of God and Jesus standing at God's right hand.
56 And said, Behold, I see the heavens opened, and the Son of man standing on the right hand of God.	**56** and said, "Look! I see the heavens opened and the Son of Man standing at the right hand of God!"	**56** And he told them, "Look, I see the heavens opened and Jesus the Messiah standing beside God, at his right hand!"
8:37 And Philip said, If thou believest with all thine heart, thou mayest. And he answered and said, I believe that Jesus Christ is the Son of God.	**8:37** Then Philip said, "If you believe with all your heart, you may." And he answered and said, "I believe that Jesus Christ is the Son of God."	**8:37** "You can," Philip answered, "if you believe with all your heart." And the eunuch replied, "I believe that Jesus Christ is the Son of God."
9:4 And he fell to the earth, and heard a voice saying unto him, Saul, Saul, why persecutest thou me?	**9:4** Then he fell to the ground, and heard a voice saying to him, "Saul, Saul, why are you persecuting Me?"	**9:4** He fell to the ground and heard a voice saying to him, "Paul! Paul! Why are you persecuting me?"
5 And he said, Who art thou, Lord? And the Lord said, I am Jesus whom thou persecutest: *it is* hard for thee to kick against the pricks.	**5** And he said, "Who are You, Lord?" And the Lord said, "I am Jesus, whom you are persecuting. *It is* hard for you to kick against the goads."	**5** "Who is speaking, sir?" Paul asked. And the voice replied, "I am Jesus, the one you are persecuting!
31 Then had the churches rest throughout all Judæa and Galilee and Samaria, and were edified; and walking in the fear of the Lord, and in the comfort of the Holy Ghost, were multiplied.	**31** Then the churches throughout all Judea, Galilee, and Samaria had peace and were edified. And walking in the fear of the Lord and in the comfort of the Holy Spirit, they were multiplied.	**31** Meanwhile, the church had peace throughout Judea, Galilee and Samaria, and grew in strength and numbers. The believers learned how to walk in the fear of the Lord and in the comfort of the Holy Spirit.
13:38 Be it known unto you therefore, men *and* brethren, that through this man is preached unto you the forgiveness of sins:	**13:38** "Therefore let it be known to you, brethren, that through this Man is preached to you the forgiveness of sins;	**13:38** "Brothers! Listen! In this man Jesus, there is forgiveness for your sins!
39 And by him all that believe are justified from all things, from which ye could not be justified by the law of Moses.	**39** "and by Him everyone who believes is justified from all things from which you could not be justified by the law of Moses.	**39** Everyone who trusts in him is freed from all guilt and declared righteous—something the Jewish law could never do.
15:11 But we believe that through the grace of the Lord Jesus Christ we shall be saved, even as they.	**15:11** "But we believe that through the grace of the Lord Jesus Christ we shall be saved in the same manner as they."	**15:11** Don't you believe that all are saved the same way, by the free gift of the Lord Jesus?"
16:29 Then he called for a light, and sprang in, and came trembling, and fell down before Paul and Silas,	**16:29** Then he called for a light, ran in, and fell down trembling before Paul and Silas.	**16:29** Trembling with fear, the jailer called for lights and ran to the dungeon and fell down before Paul and Silas.
30 And brought them out, and said, Sirs, what must I do to be saved?	**30** And he brought them out and said, "Sirs, what must I do to be saved?"	**30** He brought them out and begged them, "Sirs, what must I do to be saved?"
31 And they said, Believe on the Lord Jesus Christ, and thou shalt be saved, and thy house.	**31** So they said, "Believe on the Lord Jesus Christ, and you will be saved, you and your household."	**31** They replied, "Believe on the Lord Jesus and you will be saved, and your entire household."
17:30 And the times of this ignorance God winked at; but now commandeth all men every where to repent:	**17:30** "Truly, these times of ignorance God overlooked, but now commands all men everywhere to repent,	**17:30** God tolerated man's past ignorance about these things, but now he commands everyone to put away idols and worship only him.
31 Because he hath appointed a day, in the which he will judge the world in righteousness by *that* man whom he hath ordained; *whereof* he hath given assurance unto all *men*, in that he hath raised him from the dead.	**31** "because He has appointed a day on which He will judge the world in righteousness by the Man whom He has ordained. He has given assurance of this to all, by raising Him from the dead."	**31** For he has set a day for justly judging the world by the man he has appointed, and has pointed him out by bringing him back to life again."
20:27 For I have not shunned to declare unto you all the counsel of God.	**20:27** "For I have not shunned to declare to you the whole counsel of God.	**20:27** for I didn't shrink from declaring all God's message to you.

NIV	RSV	TEV
3:19 Repent, then, and turn to God, so that your sins may be wiped out, that times of refreshing may come from the Lord,	**3:19** Repent therefore, and turn again, that your sins may be blotted out, that times of refreshing may come from the presence of the Lord,	**3:19** Repent, then, and turn to God, so that he will forgive your sins. If you do,
4:32 All the believers were one in heart and mind. No one claimed that any of his possessions was his own, but they shared everything they had.	**4:32** Now the company of those who believed were of one heart and soul, and no one said that any of the things which he possessed was his own, but they had everything in common.	**4:32** The group of believers was one in mind and heart. No one said that any of his belongings was his own, but they all shared with one another everything they had.
5:31 God exalted him to his own right hand as Prince and Savior that he might give repentance and forgiveness of sins to Israel.	**5:31** God exalted him at his right hand as Leader and Savior, to give repentance to Israel and forgiveness of sins.	**5:31** God raised him to his right side as Leader and Savior, to give the people of Israel the opportunity to repent and have their sins forgiven.
7:55 But Stephen, full of the Holy Spirit, looked up to heaven and saw the glory of God, and Jesus standing at the right hand of God.	**7:55** But he, full of the Holy Spirit, gazed into heaven and saw the glory of God, and Jesus standing at the right hand of God;	**7:55** But Stephen, full of the Holy Spirit, looked up to heaven and saw God's glory and Jesus standing at the right side of God.
56 "Look," he said, "I see heaven open and the Son of Man standing at the right hand of God."	**56** and he said, "Behold, I see the heavens opened, and the Son of man standing at the right hand of God."	**56** "Look!" he said. "I see heaven opened and the Son of Man standing at the right side of God!"
(omitted)	(omitted)	(omitted)
9:4 He fell to the ground and heard a voice say to him, "Saul, Saul, why do you persecute me?"	**9:4** And he fell to the ground and heard a voice saying to him, "Saul, Saul, why do you persecute me?"	**9:4** He fell to the ground and heard a voice saying to him, "Saul, Saul! Why do you persecute me?"
5 "Who are you, Lord?" Saul asked. "I am Jesus, whom you are persecuting," he replied.	**5** And he said, "Who are you, Lord?" And he said, "I am Jesus, whom you are persecuting;	**5** "Who are you, Lord?" he asked. "I am Jesus, whom you persecute," the voice said.
31 Then the church throughout Judea, Galilee and Samaria enjoyed a time of peace. It was strengthened; and encouraged by the Holy Spirit, it grew in numbers, living in the fear of the Lord.	**31** So the church throughout all Judea and Galilee and Samaria had peace and was built up; and walking in the fear of the Lord and in the comfort of the Holy Spirit it was multiplied.	**31** And so it was that the church throughout Judea, Galilee, and Samaria had a time of peace. Through the help of the Holy Spirit it was strengthened and grew in numbers, as it lived in reverence for the Lord.
13:38 "Therefore, my brothers, I want you to know that through Jesus the forgiveness of sins is proclaimed to you.	**13:38** Let it be known to you therefore, brethren, that through this man forgiveness of sins is proclaimed to you,	**13:38–39** All of you, my fellow Israelites, are to know for sure that it is through Jesus that the message about forgiveness of sins is preached to you; you are to know that everyone who believes in him is set free from all the sins from which the Law of Moses could not set you free.
39 Through him everyone who believes is justified from everything you could not be justified from by the law of Moses.	**39** and by him every one that believes is freed from everything from which you could not be freed by the law of Moses.	
15:11 No! We believe it is through the grace of our Lord Jesus that we are saved, just as they are."	**15:11** But we believe that we shall be saved through the grace of the Lord Jesus, just as they will."	**15:11** No! We believe and are saved by the grace of the Lord Jesus, just as they are."
16:29 The jailer called for lights, rushed in and fell trembling before Paul and Silas.	**16:29** And he called for lights and rushed in, and trembling with fear he fell down before Paul and Silas,	**16:29** The jailer called for a light, rushed in, and fell trembling at the feet of Paul and Silas.
30 He then brought them out and asked, "Sirs, what must I do to be saved?"	**30** and brought them out and said, "Men, what must I do to be saved?"	**30** Then he led them out and asked, "Sirs, what must I do to be saved?"
31 They replied, "Believe in the Lord Jesus, and you will be saved—you and your household."	**31** And they said, "Believe in the Lord Jesus, and you will be saved, you and your household."	**31** They answered, "Believe in the Lord Jesus, and you will be saved—you and your family."
17:30 In the past God overlooked such ignorance, but now he commands all people everywhere to repent.	**17:30** The times of ignorance God overlooked, but now he commands all men everywhere to repent,	**17:30** God has overlooked the times when people did not know him, but now he commands all of them everywhere to turn away from their evil ways.
31 For he has set a day when he will judge the world with justice by the man he has appointed. He has given proof of this to all men by raising him from the dead."	**31** because he has fixed a day on which he will judge the world in righteousness by a man whom he has appointed, and of this he has given assurance to all men by raising him from the dead."	**31** For he has fixed a day in which he will judge the whole world with justice by means of a man he has chosen. He has given proof of this to everyone by raising that man from death!"
20:27 For I have not hesitated to proclaim to you the whole will of God.	**20:27** for I did not shrink from declaring to you the whole counsel of God.	**20:27** For I have not held back from announcing to you the whole purpose of God.

KJV	NKJV	TLB
35 I have shewed you all things, how that so labouring ye ought to support the weak, and to remember the words of the Lord Jesus, how he said, It is more blessed to give than to receive.	35 "I have shown you in every way, by laboring like this, that you must support the weak. And remember the words of the Lord Jesus, that He said, 'It is more blessed to give than to receive.'"	35 And I was a constant example to you in helping the poor; for I remembered the words of the Lord Jesus, 'It is more blessed to give than to receive.'"

Romans

KJV	NKJV	TLB
1:16 For I am not ashamed of the gospel of Christ: for it is the power of God unto salvation to every one that believeth; to the Jew first, and also to the Greek.	1:16 For I am not ashamed of the gospel of Christ, for it is the power of God to salvation for everyone who believes, for the Jew first and also for the Greek.	1:16 For I am not ashamed of this Good News about Christ. It is God's powerful method of bringing all who believe it to heaven. This message was preached first to the Jews alone, but now everyone is invited to come to God in this same way.
17 For therein is the righteousness of God revealed from faith to faith: as it is written, The just shall live by faith.	17 For in it the righteousness of God is revealed from faith to faith; as it is written, "The just shall live by faith."	17 This Good News tells us that God makes us ready for heaven—makes us right in God's sight—when we put our faith and trust in Christ to save us. This is accomplished from start to finish by faith. As the Scripture says it, "The man who finds life will find it through trusting God."
18 For the wrath of God is revealed from heaven against all ungodliness and unrighteousness of men, who hold the truth in unrighteousness;	18 For the wrath of God is revealed from heaven against all ungodliness and unrighteousness of men, who suppress the truth in unrighteousness,	18 But God shows his anger from heaven against all sinful, evil men who push away the truth from them.
21 Because that, when they knew God, they glorified him not as God, neither were thankful; but became vain in their imaginations, and their foolish heart was darkened.	21 because, although they knew God, they did not glorify Him as God, nor were thankful, but became futile in their thoughts, and their foolish hearts were darkened.	21 Yes, they knew about him all right, but they wouldn't admit it or worship him or even thank him for all his daily care. And after awhile they began to think up silly ideas of what God was like and what he wanted them to do. The result was that their foolish minds became dark and confused.
24 Wherefore God also gave them up to uncleanness through the lusts of their own hearts, to dishonour their own bodies between themselves:	24 Therefore God also gave them up to uncleanness, in the lusts of their hearts, to dishonor their bodies among themselves,	24 So God let them go ahead into every sort of sex sin, and do whatever they wanted to—yes, vile and sinful things with each other's bodies.
25 Who changed the truth of God into a lie, and worshipped and served the creature more than the Creator, who is blessed for ever. Amen.	25 who exchanged the truth of God for the lie, and worshiped and served the creature rather than the Creator, who is blessed forever. Amen.	25 Instead of believing what they knew was the truth about God, they deliberately chose to believe lies. So they prayed to the things God made, but wouldn't obey the blessed God who made these things.
2:15 Which shew the work of the law written in their hearts, their conscience also bearing witness, and their thoughts the mean while accusing or else excusing one another;)	2:15 who show the work of the law written in their hearts, their conscience also bearing witness, and between themselves their thoughts accusing or else excusing them)	2:15 God's laws are written within them; their own conscience accuses them, or sometimes excuses them.
3:10 As it is written, There is none righteous, no, not one:	3:10 As it is written: "There is none righteous, no, not one;	3:10 As the Scriptures say, "No one is good—no one in all the world is innocent."
11 There is none that understandeth, there is none that seeketh after God.	11 There is none who understands; There is none who seeks after God.	11 No one has ever really followed God's paths, or even truly wanted to.
12 They are all gone out of the way, they are together become unprofitable; there is none that doeth good, no, no one.	12 They have all gone out of the way; They have together become unprofitable; There is none who does good, no, not one."	12 Every one has turned away; all have gone wrong. No one anywhere has kept on doing what is right; not one.
23 For all have sinned, and come short of the glory of God;	23 for all have sinned and fall short of the glory of God,	23 Yes, all have sinned; all fall short of God's glorious ideal;
24 Being justified freely by his grace through the redemption that is in Christ Jesus:	24 being justified freely by His grace through the redemption that is in Christ Jesus,	24 yet now God declares us "not guilty" of offending him if we trust in Jesus Christ, who in his kindness freely takes away our sins.
5:1 Therefore being justified by faith, we have peace with God through our Lord Jesus Christ:	5:1 Therefore, having been justified by faith, we have peace with God through our Lord Jesus Christ,	5:1 So now, since we have been made right in God's sight by faith in his promises, we can have real peace with him because of what Jesus Christ our Lord has done for us.
3 And not only so, but we glory in tribulations also: knowing that tribulation worketh patience;	3 And not only that, but we also glory in tribulations, knowing that tribulation produces perseverance;	3 We can rejoice, too, when we run into problems and trials for we know that they are good for us—they help us learn to be patient.
4 And patience, experience; and experience, hope:	4 and perseverance, character; and character, hope.	4 And patience develops strength of character in us and helps us trust God more each time we use it until finally our hope and faith are strong and steady.
5 And hope maketh not ashamed; because the love of God is shed abroad in our hearts by the Holy Ghost which is given unto us.	5 Now hope does not disappoint, because the love of God has been poured out in our hearts by the Holy Spirit who was given to us.	5 Then, when that happens, we are able to hold our heads high no matter what happens and know that all is well, for we know how dearly God loves us, and we feel this warm love everywhere within us because God has given us the Holy Spirit to fill our hearts with his love.

NIV	RSV	TEV
35 In everything I did, I showed you that by this kind of hard work we must help the weak, remembering the words the Lord Jesus himself said: 'It is more blessed to give than to receive.'"	35 In all things I have shown you that by so toiling one must help the weak, remembering the words of the Lord Jesus, how he said, 'It is more blessed to give than to receive.'"	35 I have shown you in all things that by working hard in this way we must help the weak, remembering the words that the Lord Jesus himself said, 'There is more happiness in giving than in receiving.'"

Romans

NIV	RSV	TEV
1:16 I am not ashamed of the gospel, because it is the power of God for the salvation of everyone who believes: first for the Jew, then for the Gentile.	1:16 For I am not ashamed of the gospel: it is the power of God for salvation to every one who has faith, to the Jew first and also to the Greek.	1:16 I have complete confidence in the gospel; it is God's power to save all who believe, first the Jews and also the Gentiles.
17 For in the gospel a righteousness from God is revealed, a righteousness that is by faith from first to last, just as it is written: "The righteous will live by faith."	17 For in it the righteousness of God is revealed through faith for faith; as it is written, "He who through faith is righteous shall live."	17 For the gospel reveals how God puts people right with himself: it is through faith from beginning to end. As the scripture says, "The person who is put right with God through faith shall live."
18 The wrath of God is being revealed from heaven against all the godlessness and wickedness of men who suppress the truth by their wickedness,	18 For the wrath of God is revealed from heaven against all ungodliness and wickedness of men who by their wickedness suppress the truth.	18 God's anger is revealed from heaven against all the sin and evil of the people whose evil ways prevent the truth from being known.
21 For although they knew God, they neither glorified him as God nor gave thanks to him, but their thinking became futile and their foolish hearts were darkened.	21 for although they knew God they did not honor him as God or give thanks to him, but they became futile in their thinking and their senseless minds were darkened.	21 They know God, but they do not give him the honor that belongs to him, nor do they thank him. Instead, their thoughts have become complete nonsense, and their empty minds are filled with darkness.
24 Therefore God gave them over in the sinful desires of their hearts to sexual impurity for the degrading of their bodies with one another.	24 Therefore God gave them up in the lusts of their hearts to impurity, to the dishonoring of their bodies among themselves,	24 And so God has given those people over to do the filthy things their hearts desire, and they do shameful things with each other.
25 They exchanged the truth of God for a lie, and worshiped and served created things rather than the Creator—who is forever praised. Amen.	25 because they exchanged the truth about God for a lie and worshiped and served the creature rather than the Creator, who is blessed for ever! Amen.	25 They exchange the truth about God for a lie; they worship and serve what God has created instead of the Creator himself, who is to be praised forever! Amen.
2:15 since they show that the requirements of the law are written on their hearts, their consciences also bearing witness, and their thoughts now accusing, now even defending them.)	2:15 They show that what the law requires is written on their hearts, while their conscience also bears witness and their conflicting thoughts accuse or perhaps excuse them.	2:15 Their conduct shows that what the Law commands is written in their hearts. Their consciences also show that this is true, since their thoughts sometimes accuse them and sometimes defend them.

3:10 As it is written:
    "There is no one righteous, not even one;
	3:10 as it is written:
	    "None is righteous, no, not one;
		3:10 As the Scriptures say:
		    "There is no one who is righteous,

11 there is no one who understands,
    no one who seeks God.
	11 no one understands, no one seeks for God.	11 no one who is wise
		    or who worships God.

12 All have turned away,
    they have together become worthless;
    there is no one who does good,
    not even one."
	12 All have turned aside, together they have
	    gone wrong;
	    no one does good, not even one."
		12 All have turned away from God;
		    they have all gone wrong;
		    no one does what is right, not even one.

23 for all have sinned and fall short of the glory of God,	23 since all have sinned and fall short of the glory of God,	23 everyone has sinned and is far away from God's saving presence.
24 and are justified freely by his grace through the redemption that came by Christ Jesus.	24 they are justified by his grace as a gift, through the redemption which is in Christ Jesus,	24 But by the free gift of God's grace all are put right with him through Christ Jesus, who sets them free.
5:1 Therefore, since we have been justified through faith, we have peace with God through our Lord Jesus Christ,	5:1 Therefore, since we are justified by faith, we have peace with God through our Lord Jesus Christ.	5:1 Now that we have been put right with God through faith, we have peace with God through our Lord Jesus Christ.
3 Not only so, but we also rejoice in our sufferings, because we know that suffering produces perseverance;	3 More than that, we rejoice in our sufferings, knowing that suffering produces endurance,	3 We also boast of our troubles, because we know that trouble produces endurance,
4 perseverance, character; and character, hope.	4 and endurance produces character, and character produces hope,	4 endurance brings God's approval, and his approval creates hope.
5 And hope does not disappoint us, because God has poured out his love into our hearts by the Holy Spirit, whom he has given us.	5 and hope does not disappoint us, because God's love has been poured into our hearts through the Holy Spirit which has been given to us.	5 This hope does not disappoint us, for God has poured out his love into our hearts by means of the Holy Spirit, who is God's gift to us.

KJV	NKJV	TLB
6 For when we were yet without strength, in due time Christ died for the ungodly.	6 For when we were still without strength, in due time Christ died for the ungodly.	6 When we were utterly helpless with no way of escape, Christ came at just the right time and died for us sinners who had no use for him.
7 For scarcely for a righteous man will one die: yet peradventure for a good man some would even dare to die.	7 For scarcely for a righteous man will one die; yet perhaps for a good man someone would even dare to die.	7 Even if we were good, we really wouldn't expect anyone to die for us, though, of course, that might be barely possible.
8 But God commendeth his love toward us, in that, while we were yet sinners, Christ died for us.	8 But God demonstrates His own love toward us, in that while we were still sinners, Christ died for us.	8 But God showed his great love for us by sending Christ to die for us while we were still sinners.
19 For as by one man's disobedience many were made sinners, so by the obedience of one shall many be made righteous.	19 For as by one man's disobedience many were made sinners, so also by one Man's obedience many will be made righteous.	19 Adam caused many to be sinners because he *disobeyed* God, and Christ caused many to be made acceptable to God because he *obeyed*.
6:6 Knowing this, that our old man is crucified with *him,* that the body of sin might be destroyed, that henceforth we should not serve sin.	6:6 knowing this, that our old man was crucified with *Him,* that the body of sin might be done away with, that we should no longer be slaves of sin.	6:6 Your old evil desires were nailed to the cross with him; that part of you that loves to sin was crushed and fatally wounded, so that your sin-loving body is no longer under sin's control, no longer needs to be a slave to sin;
14 For sin shall not have dominion over you: for ye are not under the law, but under grace.	14 For sin shall not have dominion over you, for you are not under law but under grace.	14 Sin need never again be your master, for now you are no longer tied to the law where sin enslaves you, but you are free under God's favor and mercy.
23 For the wages of sin *is* death; but the gift of God *is* eternal life through Jesus Christ our Lord.	23 For the wages of sin *is* death, but the gift of God is eternal life in Christ Jesus our Lord.	23 For the wages of sin is death, but the free gift of God is eternal life through Jesus Christ our Lord.
7:24 O wretched man that I am! who shall deliver me from the body of this death?	7:24 O wretched man that I am! Who will deliver me from this body of death?	7:24 Oh, what a terrible predicament I'm in! Who will free me from my slavery to this deadly lower nature?
25 I thank God through Jesus Christ our Lord. So then with the mind I myself serve the law of God; but with the flesh the law of sin.	25 I thank God—through Jesus Christ our Lord! So then, with the mind I myself serve the law of God, but with the flesh the law of sin.	25 Thank God! It has been done by Jesus Christ our Lord. He has set me free. So you see how it is: my new life tells me to do right, but the old nature that is still inside me loves to sin.
8:1 *There is* therefore now no condemnation to them which are in Christ Jesus, who walk not after the flesh, but after the Spirit.	8:1 *There is* therefore now no condemnation to those who are in Christ Jesus, who do not walk according to the flesh, but according to the Spirit.	8:1 So there is now no condemnation awaiting those who belong to Christ Jesus.
11 But if the Spirit of him that raised up Jesus from the dead dwell in you, he that raised up Christ from the dead shall also quicken your mortal bodies by his Spirit that dwelleth in you.	11 But if the Spirit of Him who raised Jesus from the dead dwells in you, He who raised Christ from the dead will also give life to your mortal bodies through His Spirit who dwells in you.	11 And if the Spirit of God, who raised up Jesus from the dead, lives in you, he will make your dying bodies live again after you die, by means of this same Holy Spirit living within you.
14 For as many as are led by the Spirit of God, they are the sons of God.	14 For as many as are led by the Spirit of God, these are sons of God.	14 For all who are led by the Spirit of God are sons of God.
15 For ye have not received the spirit of bondage again to fear; but ye have received the Spirit of adoption, whereby we cry, Abba, Father.	15 For you did not receive the spirit of bondage again to fear, but you received the Spirit of adoption by whom we cry out, "Abba, Father."	15 And so we should not be like cringing, fearful slaves, but we should behave like God's very own children, adopted into the bosom of his family, and calling to him, "Father, Father."
16 The Spirit itself beareth witness with our spirit, that we are the children of God:	16 The Spirit Himself bears witness with our spirit that we are children of God,	16 For his Holy Spirit speaks to us deep in our hearts, and tells us that we really are God's children.
26 Likewise the Spirit also helpeth our infirmities: for we know not what we should pray for as we ought: but the Spirit itself maketh intercession for us with groanings which cannot be uttered.	26 Likewise the Spirit also helps in our weaknesses. For we do not know what we should pray for as we ought, but the Spirit Himself makes intercession for us with groanings which cannot be uttered.	26 And in the same way—by our faith—the Holy Spirit helps us with our daily problems and in our praying. For we don't even know what we should pray for, nor how to pray as we should; but the Holy Spirit prays for us with such feeling that it cannot be expressed in words.
28 And we know that all things work together for good to them that love God, to them who are the called according to *his* purpose.	28 And we know that all things work together for good to those who love God, to those who are the called according to *His* purpose.	28 And we know that all that happens to us is working for our good if we love God and are fitting into his plans.
29 For whom he did foreknow, he also did predestinate *to be* conformed to the image of his Son, that he might be the firstborn among many brethren.	29 For whom He foreknew, He also predestined *to be* conformed to the image of His Son, that He might be the firstborn among many brethren.	29 For from the very beginning God decided that those who came to him—and all along he knew who would—should become like his Son, so that his Son would be the First, with many brothers.
30 Moreover whom he did predestinate, them he also called: and whom he called, them he also justified: and whom he justified, them he also glorified.	30 Moreover whom He predestined, these He also called; whom He called, these He also justified; and whom He justified, these He also glorified.	30 And having chosen us, he called us to come to him; and when we came, he declared us "not guilty," filled us with Christ's goodness, gave us right standing with himself, and promised us his glory.

NIV	RSV	TEV
6 You see, at just the right time, when we were still powerless, Christ died for the ungodly.	6 While we were still weak, at the right time Christ died for the ungodly.	6 For when we were still helpless, Christ died for the wicked at the time that God chose.
7 Very rarely will anyone die for a righteous man, though for a good man someone might possibly dare to die.	7 Why, one will hardly die for a righteous man—though perhaps for a good man one will dare even to die.	7 It is a difficult thing for someone to die for a righteous person. It may even be that someone might dare to die for a good person.
8 But God demonstrates his own love for us in this: While we were still sinners, Christ died for us.	8 But God shows his love for us in that while we were yet sinners Christ died for us.	8 But God has shown us how much he loves us—it was while we were still sinners that Christ died for us!
19 For just as through the disobedience of the one man the many were made sinners, so also through the obedience of the one man the many will be made righteous.	19 For as by one man's disobedience many were made sinners, so by one man's obedience many will be made righteous.	19 And just as all people were made sinners as the result of the disobedience of one man, in the same way they will all be put right with God as the result of the obedience of the one man.
6:6 For we know that our old self was crucified with him so that the body of sin might be rendered powerless, that we should no longer be slaves to sin—	6:6 We know that our old self was crucified with him so that the sinful body might be destroyed, and we might no longer be enslaved to sin.	6:6 And we know that our old being has been put to death with Christ on his cross, in order that the power of the sinful self might be destroyed, so that we should no longer be the slaves of sin.
14 For sin shall not be your master, because you are not under law, but under grace.	14 For sin will have no dominion over you, since you are not under law but under grace.	14 Sin must not be your master; for you do not live under law but under God's grace.
23 For the wages of sin is death, but the gift of God is eternal life in Christ Jesus our Lord.	23 For the wages of sin is death, but the free gift of God is eternal life in Christ Jesus our Lord.	23 For sin pays its wage—death; but God's free gift is eternal life in union with Christ Jesus our Lord.
7:24 What a wretched man I am! Who will rescue me from this body of death?	7:24 Wretched man that I am! Who will deliver me from this body of death?	7:24 What an unhappy man I am! Who will rescue me from this body that is taking me to death?
25 Thanks be to God—through Jesus Christ our Lord! So then, I myself in my mind am a slave to God's law, but in the sinful nature a slave to the law of sin.	25 Thanks be to God through Jesus Christ our Lord! So then, I of myself serve the law of God with my mind, but with my flesh I serve the law of sin.	25 Thanks be to God, who does this through our Lord Jesus Christ! This, then, is my condition: on my own I can serve God's law only with my mind, while my human nature serves the law of sin.
8:1 Therefore, there is now no condemnation for those who are in Christ Jesus,	8:1 There is therefore now no condemnation for those who are in Christ Jesus.	8:1 There is no condemnation now for those who live in union with Christ Jesus.
11 And if the Spirit of him who raised Jesus from the dead is living in you, he who raised Christ from the dead will also give life to your mortal bodies through his Spirit, who lives in you.	11 If the Spirit of him who raised Jesus from the dead dwells in you, he who raised Christ Jesus from the dead will give life to your mortal bodies also through his Spirit which dwells in you.	11 If the Spirit of God, who raised Jesus from death, lives in you, then he who raised Christ from death will also give life to your mortal bodies by the presence of his Spirit in you.
14 because those who are led by the Spirit of God are sons of God.	14 For all who are led by the Spirit of God are sons of God.	14 Those who are led by God's Spirit are God's sons.
15 For you did not receive a spirit that makes you a slave again to fear, but you received the Spirit of sonship. And by him we cry, "Abba, Father."	15 For you did not receive the spirit of slavery to fall back into fear, but you have received the spirit of sonship. When we cry, "Abba! Father!"	15 For the Spirit that God has given you does not make you slaves and cause you to be afraid; instead, the Spirit makes you God's children, and by the Spirit's power we cry out to God, "Father! my Father!"
16 The Spirit himself testifies with our spirit that we are God's children.	16 it is the Spirit himself bearing witness with our spirit that we are children of God,	16 God's Spirit joins himself to our spirits to declare that we are God's children.
26 In the same way, the Spirit helps us in our weakness. We do not know what we ought to pray, but the Spirit himself intercedes for us with groans that words cannot express.	26 Likewise the Spirit helps us in our weakness; for we do not know how to pray as we ought, but the Spirit himself intercedes for us with sighs too deep for words.	26 In the same way the Spirit also comes to help us, weak as we are. For we do not know how we ought to pray; the Spirit himself pleads with God for us in groans that words cannot express.
28 And we know that in all things God works for the good of those who love him, who have been called according to his purpose.	28 We know that in everything God works for good with those who love him, who are called according to his purpose.	28 We know that in all things God works for good with those who love him, those whom he has called according to his purpose.
29 For those God foreknew he also predestined to be conformed to the likeness of his Son, that he might be the firstborn among many brothers.	29 For those whom he foreknew he also predestined to be conformed to the image of his Son, in order that he might be the first-born among many brethren.	29 Those whom God had already chosen he also set apart to become like his Son, so that the Son would be the first among many brothers.
30 And those he predestined, he also called; those he called, he also justified; those he justified, he also glorified.	30 And those whom he predestined he also called; and those whom he called he also justified; and those whom he justified he also glorified.	30 And so those whom God set apart, he called; and those he called, he put right with himself, and he shared his glory with them.

KJV	NKJV	TLB
31 What shall we then say to these things? If God *be* for us, who *can be* against us?	31 What then shall we say to these things? If God *is* for us, who *can be* against us?	31 What can we ever say to such wonderful things as these? If God is on our side, who can ever be against us?
32 He that spared not his own Son, but delivered him up for us all, how shall he not with him also freely give us all things?	32 He who did not spare His own Son, but delivered Him up for us all, how shall He not with Him also freely give us all things?	32 Since he did not spare even his own Son for us but gave him up for us all, won't he also surely give us everything else?
33 Who shall lay any thing to the charge of God's elect? *It is* God that justifieth.	33 Who shall bring a charge against God's elect? *It is* God who justifies.	33 Who dares accuse us whom God has chosen for his own? Will God? No! He is the one who has forgiven us and given us right standing with himself.
34 Who *is* he that condemneth? *It is* Christ that died, yea rather, that is risen again, who is even at the right hand of God, who also maketh intercession for us.	34 Who *is* he who condemns? *It is* Christ who died, and furthermore is also risen, who is even at the right hand of God, who also makes intercession for us.	34 Who then will condemn us? Will Christ? No! For he is the one who died for us and came back to life again for us and is sitting at the place of highest honor next to God, pleading for us there in heaven.
35 Who shall separate us from the love of Christ? *shall* tribulation, or distress, or persecution, or famine, or nakedness, or peril, or sword?	35 Who shall separate us from the love of Christ? *Shall* tribulation, or distress, or persecution, or famine, or nakedness, or peril, or sword?	35 Who then can ever keep Christ's love from us? When we have trouble or calamity, when we are hunted down or destroyed, is it because he doesn't love us anymore? And if we are hungry, or penniless, or in danger, or threatened with death, has God deserted us?
36 As it is written, For thy sake we are killed all the day long; we are accounted as sheep for the slaughter.	36 As it is written: "For Your sake we are killed all day long; We are accounted as sheep for the slaughter."	36 No, for the Scriptures tell us that for his sake we must be ready to face death at every moment of the day—we are like sheep awaiting slaughter;
37 Nay, in all these things we are more than conquerors through him that loved us.	37 Yet in all these things we are more than conquerors through Him who loved us.	37 but despite all this, overwhelming victory is ours through Christ who loved us enough to die for us.
38 For I am persuaded, that neither death, nor life, nor angels, nor principalities, nor powers, nor things present, nor things to come,	38 For I am persuaded that neither death nor life, nor angels nor principalities nor powers, nor things present nor things to come,	38 For I am convinced that nothing can ever separate us from his love. Death can't, and life can't. The angels won't, and all the powers of hell itself cannot keep God's love away. Our fears for today, our worries about tomorrow,
39 Nor height, nor depth, nor any other creature, shall be able to separate us from the love of God, which is in Christ Jesus our Lord.	39 nor height nor depth, nor any other created thing, shall be able to separate us from the love of God which is in Christ Jesus our Lord.	39 or where we are—high above the sky, or in the deepest ocean—nothing will ever be able to separate us from the love of God demonstrated by our Lord Jesus Christ when he died for us.
9:30 What shall we say then? That the Gentiles, which followed not after righteousness, have attained to righteousness, even the righteousness which is of faith.	9:30 What shall we say then? That Gentiles, who did not pursue righteousness, have attained to righteousness, even the righteousness of faith;	9:30 Well then, what shall we say about these things? Just this, that God has given the Gentiles the opportunity to be acquitted by faith, even though they had not been really seeking God.
31 But Israel, which followed after the law of righteousness, hath not attained to the law of righteousness.	31 but Israel, pursuing the law of righteousness, has not attained to the law of righteousness.	31 But the Jews, who tried so hard to get right with God by keeping his laws, never succeeded.
32 Wherefore? Because *they sought it* not by faith, but as it were by the works of the law. For they stumbled at that stumblingstone;	32 Why? Because *they did* not *seek it* by faith, but as it were, by the works of the law. For they stumbled at that stumbling stone.	32 Why not? Because they were trying to be saved by keeping the law and being good instead of by depending on faith. They have stumbled over the great stumbling stone.
33 As it is written, Behold, I lay in Sion a stumblingstone and rock of offence: and whosoever believeth on him shall not be ashamed.	33 As it is written: "Behold, I lay in Zion a stumbling stone and rock of offense, And whoever believes on Him will not be put to shame."	33 God warned them of this in the Scriptures when he said, "I have put a Rock in the path of the Jews, and many will stumble over him (Jesus). Those who believe in him will never be disappointed."
10:9 That if thou shalt confess with thy mouth the Lord Jesus, and shalt believe in thine heart that God hath raised him from the dead, thou shalt be saved.	10:9 that if you confess with your mouth the Lord Jesus and believe in your heart that God has raised Him from the dead, you will be saved.	10:9 For if you tell others with your own mouth that Jesus Christ is your Lord, and believe in your own heart that God has raised him from the dead, you will be saved.
10 For with the heart man believeth unto righteousness; and with the mouth confession is made unto salvation.	10 For with the heart one believes to righteousness, and with the mouth confession is made to salvation.	10 For it is by believing in his heart that a man becomes right with God; and with his mouth he tells others of his faith, confirming his salvation.
11 For the scripture saith, Whosoever believeth on him shall not be ashamed.	11 For the Scripture says, "Whoever believes on Him will not be put to shame."	11 For the Scriptures tell us that no one who believes in Christ will ever be disappointed.
13 For whosoever shall call upon the name of the Lord shall be saved.	13 For "whoever calls upon the name of the LORD shall be saved."	13 Anyone who calls upon the name of the Lord will be saved.
17 So then faith *cometh* by hearing, and hearing by the word of God.	17 So then faith *comes* by hearing, and hearing by the word of God.	17 Yet faith comes from listening to this Good News—the Good News about Christ.

NIV	RSV	TEV
31 What, then, shall we say in response to this? If God is for us, who can be against us?	31 What then shall we say to this? If God is for us, who is against us?	31 In view of all this, what can we say? If God is for us, who can be against us?
32 He who did not spare his own Son, but gave him up for us all—how will he not also, along with him, graciously give us all things?	32 He who did not spare his own Son but gave him up for us all, will he not also give us all things with him?	32 Certainly not God, who did not even keep back his own Son, but offered him for us all! He gave us his Son—will he not also freely give us all things?
33 Who will bring any charge against those whom God has chosen? It is God who justifies.	33 Who shall bring any charge against God's elect? It is God who justifies;	33 Who will accuse God's chosen people? God himself declares them not guilty!
34 Who is he that condemns? Christ Jesus, who died—more than that, who was raised to life—is at the right hand of God and is also interceding for us.	34 who is to condemn? Is it Christ Jesus, who died, yes, who was raised from the dead, who is at the right hand of God, who indeed intercedes for us?	34 Who, then, will condemn them? Not Christ Jesus, who died, or rather, who was raised to life and is at the right side of God, pleading with him for us!
35 Who shall separate us from the love of Christ? Shall trouble or hardship or persecution or famine or nakedness or danger or sword?	35 Who shall separate us from the love of Christ? Shall tribulation, or distress, or persecution, or famine, or nakedness, or peril, or sword?	35 Who, then, can separate us from the love of Christ? Can trouble do it, or hardship or persecution or hunger or poverty or danger or death?

36 As it is written:
 	
"For your sake we face death all day long;
  we are considered as sheep to be slaughtered."
	36 As it is written,
	"For thy sake we are being killed all the day long;
	  we are regarded as sheep to be slaughtered."
		36 As the scripture says,
		"For your sake we are in danger of death at all times;
		  we are treated like sheep that are going to be slaughtered."

37 No, in all these things we are more than conquerors through him who loved us.	37 No, in all these things we are more than conquerors through him who loved us.	37 No, in all these things we have complete victory through him who loved us!
38 For I am convinced that neither death nor life, neither angels nor demons, neither the present nor the future, nor any powers,	38 For I am sure that neither death, nor life, nor angels, nor principalities, nor things present, nor things to come, nor powers,	38 For I am certain that nothing can separate us from his love: neither death nor life, neither angels nor other heavenly rulers or powers, neither the present nor the future,
39 neither height nor depth, nor anything else in all creation, will be able to separate us from the love of God that is in Christ Jesus our Lord.	39 nor height, nor depth, nor anything else in all creation, will be able to separate us from the love of God in Christ Jesus our Lord.	39 neither the world above nor the world below—there is nothing in all creation that will ever be able to separate us from the love of God which is ours through Christ Jesus our Lord.
9:30 What then shall we say? That the Gentiles, who did not pursue righteousness, have obtained it, a righteousness that is by faith;	9:30 What shall we say, then? That Gentiles who did not pursue righteousness have attained it, that is, righteousness through faith;	9:30 So we say that the Gentiles, who were not trying to put themselves right with God, were put right with him through faith;
31 but Israel, who pursued a law of righteousness, has not attained it.	31 but that Israel who pursued the righteousness which is based on law did not succeed in fulfilling that law.	31 while God's people, who were seeking a law that would put them right with God, did not find it.
32 Why not? Because they pursued it not by faith but as if it were by works. They stumbled over the "stumbling stone."	32 Why? Because they did not pursue it through faith, but as if it were based on works. They have stumbled over the stumbling stone,	32 And why not? Because they did not depend on faith but on what they did. And so they stumbled over the "stumbling stone"

33 As it is written:
 	
"See, I lay in Zion a stone that causes men to stumble
  and a rock that makes them fall,
  and the one who trusts in him will never be put to shame."
	33 as it is written,
	"Behold, I am laying in Zion a stone that will make men stumble,
	a rock that will make them fall;
	and he who believes in him will not be put to shame."
		33 that the scripture speaks of:
		"Look, I place in Zion a stone
		  that will make people stumble,
		a rock that will make them fall.
		But whoever believes in him will not be disappointed."

10:9 That if you confess with your mouth, "Jesus is Lord," and believe in your heart that God raised him from the dead, you will be saved.	10:9 because, if you confess with your lips that Jesus is Lord and believe in your heart that God raised him from the dead, you will be saved.	10:9 If you confess that Jesus is Lord and believe that God raised him from death, you will be saved.
10 For it is with your heart that you believe and are justified, and it is with your mouth that you confess and are saved.	10 For man believes with his heart and so is justified, and he confesses with his lips and so is saved.	10 For it is by our faith that we are put right with God; it is by our confession that we are saved.
11 As the Scripture says, "Everyone who trusts in him will never be put to shame."	11 The scripture says, "No one who believes in him will be put to shame."	11 The scripture says, "Whoever believes in him will not be disappointed."
13 for, "Everyone who calls on the name of the Lord will be saved."	13 For, "every one who calls upon the name of the Lord will be saved."	13 As the scripture says, "Everyone who calls out to the Lord for help will be saved."
17 Consequently, faith comes from hearing the message, and the message is heard through the word of Christ.	17 So faith comes from what is heard, and what is heard comes by the preaching of Christ.	17 So then, faith comes from hearing the message, and the message comes through preaching Christ.

KJV	NKJV	TLB
11:26 And so all Israel shall be saved: as it is written, There shall come out of Sion the Deliverer, and shall turn away ungodliness from Jacob.	**11:26** And so all Israel will be saved, as it is written: "The Deliverer will come out of Zion, And He will turn away ungodliness from Jacob:	**11:26** And then all Israel will be saved. Do you remember what the prophets said about this? "There shall come out of Zion a Deliverer, and he shall turn the Jews from all ungodliness.
27 For this *is* my covenant unto them, when I shall take away their sins.	27 For this *is* My covenant with them, When I take away their sins."	27 At that time I will take away their sins, just as I promised."
12:1 I beseech you therefore, brethren, by the mercies of God, that ye present your bodies a living sacrifice, holy, acceptable unto God, *which is* your reasonable service.	**12:1** I beseech you therefore, brethren, by the mercies of God, that you present your bodies a living sacrifice, holy, acceptable to God, *which is* your reasonable service.	**12:1** And so, dear brothers, I plead with you to give your bodies to God. Let them be a living sacrifice, holy—the kind he can accept. When you think of what he has done for you, is this too much to ask?
2 And be not conformed to this world: but be ye transformed by the renewing of your mind, that ye may prove what *is* that good, and acceptable, and perfect, will of God.	2 And do not be conformed to this world, but be transformed by the renewing of your mind, that you may prove what *is* that good and acceptable and perfect will of God.	2 Don't copy the behavior and customs of this world, but be a new and different person with a fresh newness in all you do and think. Then you will learn from your own experience how his ways will really satisfy you.
5 So we, *being* many, are one body in Christ, and every one members one of another.	5 so we, *being* many, are one body in Christ, and individually members of one another.	5 so it is with Christ's body. We are all parts of it, and it takes every one of us to make it complete. So we belong to each other, and each needs all the others.
15 Rejoice with them that do rejoice, and weep with them that weep.	15 Rejoice with those who rejoice, and weep with those who weep.	15 When others are happy, be happy with them. If they are sad, share their sorrow.
21 Be not overcome of evil, but overcome evil with good.	21 Do not be overcome by evil, but overcome evil with good.	21 Don't let evil get the upper hand but conquer evil by doing good.
13:8 Owe no man any thing, but to love one another: for he that loveth another hath fulfilled the law.	**13:8** Owe no one anything except to love one another, for he who loves another has fulfilled the law.	**13:8** Pay all your debts except the debt of love for others—never finish paying that! For if you love them, you will be obeying all of God's laws, fulfilling all his requirements.
9 For this, Thou shalt not commit adultery, Thou shalt not kill, Thou shalt not steal, Thou shalt not bear false witness, Thou shalt not covet; and if *there be* any other commandment, it is briefly comprehended in this saying, namely, Thou shalt love thy neighbour as thyself.	9 For the commandments, "You shall not commit adultery," "You shall not murder," "You shall not steal," "You shall not bear false witness," "You shall not covet," and if *there is* any other commandment, are *all* summed up in this saying, namely, "You shall love your neighbor as yourself."	9 If you love your neighbor as much as you love yourself you will not want to harm or cheat him, or kill him or steal from him. And you won't sin with his wife or want what is his, or do anything else the Ten Commandments say is wrong. All ten are wrapped up in this one, to love your neighbor as you love yourself.
10 Love worketh no ill to his neighbour: therefore love *is* the fulfilling of the law.	10 Love does no harm to a neighbor; therefore love *is* the fulfillment of the law.	10 Love does no wrong to anyone. That's why it fully satisfies all of God's requirements. It is the only law you need.
14:7 For none of us liveth to himself, and no man dieth to himself.	**14:7** For none of us lives to himself, and no one dies to himself.	**14:7** We are not our own bosses to live or die as we ourselves might choose.
8 For whether we live, we live unto the Lord; and whether we die, we die unto the Lord: whether we live therefore, or die, we are the Lord's.	8 For if we live, we live to the Lord; and if we die, we die to the Lord. Therefore, whether we live or die, we are the Lord's.	8 Living or dying we follow the Lord. Either way we are his.
17 For the kingdom of God is not meat and drink; but righteousness, and peace, and joy in the Holy Ghost.	17 for the kingdom of God is not food and drink, but righteousness and peace and joy in the Holy Spirit.	17 For, after all, the important thing for us as Christians is not what we eat or drink but stirring up goodness and peace and joy from the Holy Spirit.
15:1 We then that are strong ought to bear the infirmities of the weak, and not to please ourselves.	**15:1** We then who are strong ought to bear with the scruples of the weak, and not to please ourselves.	**15:1** Even if we believe that it makes no difference to the Lord whether we do these things, still we cannot just go ahead and do them to please ourselves; for we must bear the "burden" of being considerate of the doubts and fears of others—of those who feel*
2 Let every one of us please *his* neighbour for *his* good to edification.	2 Let each of us please *his* neighbor for *his* good, leading to edification.	2 Let's please the other fellow, not ourselves, and do what is for his good and thus build him up in the Lord.
3 For even Christ pleased not himself; but, as it is written, The reproaches of them that reproached thee fell on me.	3 For even Christ did not please Himself; but as it is written, "The reproaches of those who reproached You fell on Me."	3 Christ didn't please himself. As the Psalmist said, "He came for the very purpose of suffering under the insults of those who were against the Lord."
4 For whatsoever things were written aforetime were written for our learning, that we through patience and comfort of the scriptures might have hope.	4 For whatever things were written before were written for our learning, that we through the patience and comfort of the Scriptures might have hope.	4 These things that were written in the Scriptures so long ago are to teach us patience and to encourage us, so that we will look forward expectantly to the time when God will conquer sin and death.
16:20 And the God of peace shall bruise Satan under your feet shortly. The grace of our Lord Jesus Christ *be* with you. Amen.	**16:20** And the God of peace will crush Satan under your feet shortly. The grace of our Lord Jesus Christ *be* with you. Amen.	**16:20** The God of peace will soon crush Satan under your feet. The blessings from our Lord Jesus Christ be upon you.

*these things are wrong.

NIV	RSV	TEV

11:26 And so all Israel will be saved, as it is written:
"The deliverer will come from Zion;
  he will turn godlessness away from Jacob.
	11:26 and so all Israel will be saved; as it is written,
	"The Deliverer will come from Zion, he will
	  banish ungodliness from Jacob":
		11:26 And this is how all Israel will be saved.
		As the scripture says,
		"The Savior will come from Zion
		  and remove all wickedness from the
		  descendants of Jacob.

27 And this is my covenant with them
  when I take away their sins."
	27 "and this will be my covenant with them
	  when I take away their sins."
		27 I will make this covenant with them
		  when I take away their sins."

12:1 Therefore, I urge you, brothers, in view of God's mercy, to offer your bodies as living sacrifices, holy and pleasing to God— which is your spiritual worship.	**12:1** I appeal to you therefore, brethren, by the mercies of God, to present your bodies as a living sacrifice, holy and acceptable to God, which is your spiritual worship.	**12:1** So then, my brothers, because of God's great mercy to us I appeal to you: Offer yourselves as a living sacrifice to God, dedicated to his service and pleasing to him. This is the true worship that you should offer.
2 Do not conform any longer to the pattern of this world, but be transformed by the renewing of your mind. Then you will be able to test and approve what God's will is—his good, pleasing and perfect will.	**2** Do not be conformed to this world but be transformed by the renewal of your mind, that you may prove what is the will of God, what is good and acceptable and perfect.	**2** Do not conform yourselves to the standards of this world, but let God transform you inwardly by a complete change of your mind. Then you will be able to know the will of God— what is good and is pleasing to him and is perfect.
5 so in Christ we who are many form one body, and each member belongs to all the others.	**5** so we, though many, are one body in Christ, and individually members one of another.	**5** In the same way, though we are many, we are one body in union with Christ, and we are all joined to each other as different parts of one body.
15 Rejoice with those who rejoice; mourn with those who mourn.	**15** Rejoice with those who rejoice, weep with those who weep.	**15** Be happy with those who are happy, weep with those who weep.
21 Do not be overcome by evil, but overcome evil with good.	**21** Do not be overcome by evil, but overcome evil with good.	**21** Do not let evil defeat you; instead, conquer evil with good.
13:8 Let no debt remain outstanding, except the continuing debt to love one another, for he who loves his fellow man has fulfilled the law.	**13:8** Owe no one anything, except to love one another; for he who loves his neighbor has fulfilled the law.	**13:8** Be under obligation to no one—the only obligation you have is to love one another. Whoever does this has obeyed the Law.
9 The commandments, "Do not commit adultery," "Do not murder," "Do not steal," "Do not covet," and whatever other commandment there may be, are summed up in this one rule: "Love your neighbor as yourself."	**9** The commandments, "You shall not commit adultery, You shall not kill, You shall not steal, You shall not covet," and any other commandment, are summed up in this sentence, "You shall love your neighbor as yourself."	**9** The commandments, "Do not commit adultery; do not commit murder; do not steal; do not desire what belongs to someone else"—all these, and any others besides, are summed up in the one command, "Love your neighbor as you love yourself."
10 Love does no harm to its neighbor. Therefore love is the fulfillment of the law.	**10** Love does no wrong to a neighbor; therefore love is the fulfilling of the law.	**10** If you love someone, you will never do him wrong; to love, then, is to obey the whole Law.
14:7 For none of us lives to himself alone and none of us dies to himself alone.	**14:7** None of us lives to himself, and none of us dies to himself.	**14:7** None of us lives for himself only, none of us dies for himself only.
8 If we live, we live to the Lord; and if we die, we die to the Lord. So, whether we live or die, we belong to the Lord.	**8** If we live, we live to the Lord, and if we die, we die to the Lord; so then, whether we live or whether we die, we are the Lord's.	**8** If we live, it is the Lord that we live, and if we die, it is for the Lord that we die. So whether we live or die, we belong to the Lord.
17 For the kingdom of God is not a matter of eating and drinking, but of righteousness, peace and joy in the Holy Spirit.	**17** For the kingdom of God is not food and drink but righteousness and peace and joy in the Holy Spirit;	**17** For God's Kingdom is not a matter of eating and drinking, but of the righteousness, peace, and joy which the Holy Spirit gives.
15:1 We who are strong ought to bear with the failings of the weak and not to please ourselves.	**15:1** We who are strong ought to bear with the failings of the weak, and not to please ourselves;	**15:1** We who are strong in the faith ought to help the weak to carry their burdens. We should not please ourselves.
2 Each of us should please his neighbor for his good, to build him up.	**2** let each of us please his neighbor for his good, to edify him.	**2** Instead, we should all please our brothers for their own good, in order to build them up in the faith.
3 For even Christ did not please himself but, as it is written: "The insults of those who insult you have fallen on me."	**3** For Christ did not please himself; but, as it is written, "The reproaches of those who reproached thee fell on me."	**3** For Christ did not please himself. Instead, as the scripture says, "The insults which are hurled at you have fallen on me."
4 For everything that was written in the past was written to teach us, so that through endurance and the encouragement of the Scriptures we might have hope.	**4** For whatever was written in former days was written for our instruction, that by steadfastness and by the encouragement of the scriptures we might have hope.	**4** Everything written in the Scriptures was written to teach us, in order that we might have hope through the patience and encouragement which the Scriptures give us.
16:20 The God of peace will soon crush Satan under your feet. The grace of our Lord Jesus be with you.	**16:20** then the God of peace will soon crush Satan under your feet. The grace of our Lord Jesus Christ be with you.	**16:20** And God, our source of peace, will soon crush Satan under your feet. The grace of our Lord Jesus be with you.

KJV	NKJV	TLB

First Corinthians

KJV	NKJV	TLB
1:30 But of him are ye in Christ Jesus, who of God is made unto us wisdom, and righteousness, and sanctification, and redemption;	**1:30** But of Him you are in Christ Jesus, who became for us wisdom from God—and righteousness and sanctification and redemption—	**1:30** For it is from God alone that you have your life through Christ Jesus. He showed us God's plan of salvation; he was the one who made us acceptable to God; he made us pure and holy and gave himself to purchase our salvation.
2:9 But as it is written, Eye hath not seen, nor ear heard, neither have entered into the heart of man, the things which God hath prepared for them that love him.	**2:9** But as it is written: "Eye has not seen, nor ear heard, Nor have entered into the heart of man The things which God has prepared for those who love Him."	**2:9** That is what is meant by the Scriptures which say that no mere man has ever seen, heard or even imagined what wonderful things God has ready for those who love the Lord.
14 But the natural man receiveth not the things of the Spirit of God: for they are foolishness unto him: neither can he know *them,* because they are spiritually discerned.	**14** But the natural man does not receive the things of the Spirit of God, for they are foolishness to him; nor can he know *them,* because they are spiritually discerned.	**14** But the man who isn't a Christian can't understand and can't accept these thoughts from God, which the Holy Spirit teaches us. They sound foolish to him, because only those who have the Holy Spirit within them can understand what the Holy Spirit means. Others just can't take it in.
3:22 Whether Paul, or Apollos, or Cephas, or the world, or life, or death, or things present, or things to come; all are yours:	**3:22** whether Paul or Apollos or Cephas, or the world or life or death, or things present or things to come—all are yours.	**3:22** He has given you Paul and Apollos and Peter as your helpers. He has given you the whole world to use, and life and even death are your servants. He has given you all of the present and all of the future. All are yours,
23 And ye are Christ's; and Christ *is* God's.	**23** And you *are* Christ's, and Christ *is* God's.	**23** and you belong to Christ, and Christ is God's.
6:11 And such were some of you: but ye are washed, but ye are sanctified, but ye are justified in the name of the Lord Jesus, and by the Spirit of our God.	**6:11** And such were some of you. But you were washed, but you were sanctified, but you were justified in the name of the Lord Jesus and by the Spirit of our God.	**6:11** There was a time when some of you were just like that but now your sins are washed away, and you are set apart for God, and he has accepted you because of what the Lord Jesus Christ and the Spirit of our God have done for you.
7:10 And unto the married I command, *yet* not I, but the Lord, Let not the wife depart from *her* husband:	**7:10** Now to the married I command, *yet* not I but the Lord: A wife is not to depart from *her* husband.	**7:10** Now, for those who are married I have a command, not just a suggestion. And it is not a command from me, for this is what the Lord himself has said: A wife must not leave her husband.
11 But and if she depart, let her remain unmarried, or be reconciled to *her* husband: and let not the husband put away *his* wife.	**11** But even if she does depart, let her remain unmarried or be reconciled to *her* husband. And a husband is not to divorce *his* wife.	**11** But if she is separated from him, let her remain single or else go back to him. And the husband must not divorce his wife.
8:3 But if any man love God, the same is known of him.	**8:3** But if anyone loves God, this one is known by Him.	**8:3** But the person who truly loves God is the one who is open to God's knowledge.
10:13 There hath no temptation taken you but such as is common to man: but God *is* faithful, who will not suffer you to be tempted above that ye are able; but will with the temptation also make a way to escape, that ye may be able to bear *it.*	**10:13** No temptation has overtaken you except such as is common to man; but God *is* faithful, who will not allow you to be tempted beyond what you are able, but with the temptation will also make the way of escape, that you may be able to bear *it.*	**10:13** But remember this—the wrong desires that come into your life aren't anything new and different. Many others have faced exactly the same problems before you. And no temptation is irresistible. You can trust God to keep the temptation from becoming so strong that you can't stand up against it, for he has promised this and will do what he says. He will show you how to escape temptation's power so that you can bear up patiently against it.
11:26 For as often as ye eat this bread, and drink this cup, ye do shew the Lord's death till he come.	**11:26** For as often as you eat this bread and drink this cup, you proclaim the Lord's death till He comes.	**11:26** For every time you eat this bread and drink this cup you are re-telling the message of the Lord's death, that he has died for you. Do this until he comes again.
13:13 And now abideth faith, hope, charity, these three; but the greatest of these *is* charity.	**13:13** And now abide faith, hope, love, these three; but the greatest of these *is* love.	**13:13** There are three things that remain—faith, hope, and love—and the greatest of these is love.
14:33 For God is not the *author* of confusion, but of peace, as in all churches of the saints.	**14:33** For God is not the *author* of confusion but of peace, as in all the churches of the saints.	**14:33** God is not one who likes things to be disorderly and upset. He likes harmony, and he finds it in all the other churches.
15:3 For I delivered unto you first of all that which I also received, how that Christ died for our sins according to the scriptures;	**15:3** For I delivered to you first of all that which I also received: that Christ died for our sins according to the Scriptures,	**15:3** I passed on to you right from the first what had been told to me, that Christ died for our sins just as the Scriptures said he would,
4 And that he was buried, and that he rose again the third day according to the scriptures:	**4** and that He was buried, and that He rose again the third day according to the Scriptures,	**4** and that he was buried, and that three days afterwards he arose from the grave just as the prophets foretold.
21 For since by man *came* death, by man *came* also the resurrection of the dead.	**21** For since by man *came* death, by Man also *came* the resurrection of the dead.	**21** Death came into the world because of what one man (Adam) did, and it is because of this other man (Christ) has done that now there is the resurrection from the dead.

NIV   RSV   TEV

First Corinthians

1:30 It is because of him that you are in Christ Jesus, who has become for us wisdom from God—that is, our righteousness, holiness and redemption.

1:30 He is the source of your life in Christ Jesus, whom God made our wisdom, our righteousness and sanctification and redemption;

1:30 But God has brought you into union with Christ Jesus, and God has made Christ to be our wisdom. By him we are put right with God; we become God's holy people and are set free.

2:9 However, as it is written:

"No eye has seen,
  no ear has heard,
no mind has conceived
  what God has prepared for those who love
  him"

2:9 But, as it is written,
  "What no eye has seen, nor ear heard,
  nor the heart of man conceived,
  what God has prepared for those who
  love him,"

2:9 However, as the scripture says,
"What no one ever saw or heard,
  what no one ever thought could happen,
  is the very thing God prepared for those
  who love him."

14 The man without the Spirit does not accept the things that come from the Spirit of God, for they are foolishness to him, and he cannot understand them, because they are spiritually discerned.

14 The unspiritual man does not receive the gifts of the Spirit of God, for they are folly to him, and he is not able to understand them because they are spiritually discerned.

14 Whoever does not have the Spirit cannot receive the gifts that come from God's Spirit. Such a person really does not understand them; they are nonsense to him, because their value can be judged only on a spiritual basis.

3:22 whether Paul or Apollos or Cephas or the world or life or death or the present or the future—all are yours,

3:22 whether Paul or Apollos or Cephas or the world or life or death or the present or the future, all are yours;

3:22 Paul, Apollos, and Peter; this world, life and death, the present and the future—all these are yours,

23 and you are of Christ, and Christ is of God.

23 and you are Christ's; and Christ is God's.

23 and you belong to Christ, and Christ belongs to God.

6:11 And that is what some of you were. But you were washed, you were sanctified, you were justified in the name of the Lord Jesus Christ and by the Spirit of our God.

6:11 And such were some of you. But you were washed, you were sanctified, you were justified in the name of the Lord Jesus Christ and in the Spirit of our God.

6:11 Some of you were like that. But you have been purified from sin; you have been dedicated to God; you have been put right with God by the Lord Jesus Christ and by the Spirit of our God.

7:10 To the married I give this command (not I, but the Lord): A wife must not separate from her husband.

7:10 To the married I give charge, not I but the Lord, that the wife should not separate from her husband

7:10 For married people I have a command which is not my own but the Lord's: a wife must not leave her husband;

11 But if she does, she must remain unmarried or else be reconciled to her husband. And a husband must not divorce his wife.

11 (but if she does, let her remain single or else be reconciled to her husband)—and that the husband should not divorce his wife.

11 but if she does, she must remain single or else be reconciled to her husband; and a husband must not divorce his wife.

8:3 But the man who loves God is known by God.

8:3 But if one loves God, one is known by him.

8:3 But the person who loves God is known by him.

10:13 No temptation has seized you except what is common to man. And God is faithful; he will not let you be tempted beyond what you can bear. But when you are tempted, he will also provide a way out so that you can stand up under it.

10:13 No temptation has overtaken you that is not common to man. God is faithful, and he will not let you be tempted beyond your strength, but with the temptation will also provide the way of escape, that you may be able to endure it.

10:13 Every test that you have experienced is the kind that normally comes to people. But God keeps his promise, and he will not allow you to be tested beyond your power to remain firm; at the time you are put to the test, he will give you the strength to endure it, and so provide you with a way out.

11:26 For whenever you eat this bread and drink this cup, you proclaim the Lord's death until he comes.

11:26 For as often as you eat this bread and drink the cup, you proclaim the Lord's death until he comes.

11:26 This means that every time you eat this bread and drink from this cup you proclaim the Lord's death until he comes.

13:13 And now these three remain: faith, hope and love. But the greatest of these is love.

13:13 So faith, hope, love abide, these three; but the greatest of these is love.

13:13 Meanwhile these three remain: faith, hope, and love; and the greatest of these is love.

14:33 For God is not a God of disorder but of peace.
As in all the congregations of the saints,

14:33 For God is not a God of confusion but of peace.
As in all the churches of the saints,

14:33 because God does not want us to be in disorder but in harmony and peace.
As in all the churches of God's people,

15:3 For what I received I passed on to you as of first importance: that Christ died for our sins according to the Scriptures.

15:3 For I delivered to you as of first importance what I also received, that Christ died for our sins in accordance with the scriptures,

15:3 I passed on to you what I received, which is of the greatest importance: that Christ died for our sins, as written in the Scriptures;

4 that he was buried, that he was raised on the third day according to the Scriptures,

4 that he was buried, that he was raised on the third day in accordance with the scriptures,

4 that he was buried and that he was raised to life three days later, as written in the Scriptures;

21 For since death came through a man, the resurrection of the dead comes also through a man.

21 For as by a man came death, by a man has come also the resurrection of the dead.

21 For just as death came by means of a man, in the same way the rising from death comes by means of a man.

KJV	NKJV	TLB
51 Behold, I shew you a mystery; We shall not all sleep, but we shall all be changed,	51 Behold, I tell you a mystery: We shall not all sleep, but we shall all be changed—	51 But I am telling you this strange and wonderful secret: we shall not all die, but we shall all be given new bodies!
52 In a moment, in the twinkling of an eye, at the last trump: for the trumpet shall sound, and the dead shall be raised incorruptible, and we shall be changed.	52 in a moment, in the twinkling of an eye, at the last trumpet. For the trumpet will sound, and the dead will be raised incorruptible, and we shall be changed.	52 It will all happen in a moment, in the twinkling of an eye, when the last trumpet is blown. For there will be a trumpet blast from the sky and all the Christians who have died will suddenly become alive, with new bodies that will never, never die; and then we who are still alive shall suddenly have new bodies too.
55 O death, where is thy sting? O grave, where is thy victory?	55 "O Death, where is your sting? O Hades, where is your victory?"	55 O death, where then your victory? Where then your sting?
56 The sting of death is sin; and the strength of sin is the law.	56 The sting of death is sin, and the strength of sin is the law.	56 For sin—the sting that causes death—will all be gone; and the law, which reveals our sins, will no longer be our judge.
57 But thanks be to God, which giveth us the victory through our Lord Jesus Christ.	57 But thanks be to God, who gives us the victory through our Lord Jesus Christ.	57 How we thank God for all of this! It is he who makes us victorious through Jesus Christ our Lord!

Second Corinthians

KJV	NKJV	TLB
1:3 Blessed be God, even the Father of our Lord Jesus Christ, the Father of mercies, and the God of all comfort;	1:3 Blessed be the God and Father of our Lord Jesus Christ, the Father of mercies and God of all comfort,	1:3 What a wonderful God we have—he is the Father of our Lord Jesus Christ, the source of every mercy, and the one who so wonderfully comforts and strengthens us in our hardships and trials.
4 Who comforteth us in all our tribulation, that we may be able to comfort them which are in any trouble, by the comfort wherewith we ourselves are comforted of God.	4 who comforts us in all our tribulation, that we may be able to comfort those who are in any trouble, with the comfort with which we ourselves are comforted by God.	4 And why does he do this? So that when others are troubled, needing our sympathy and encouragement, we can pass on to them this same help and comfort God has given us.
21 Now he which stablisheth us with you in Christ, and hath anointed us, is God;	21 Now He who establishes us with you in Christ and has anointed us is God,	21 It is this God who has made you and me into faithful Christians and commissioned us apostles to preach the Good News.
22 Who hath also sealed us, and given the earnest of the Spirit in our hearts.	22 who also has sealed us and given us the Spirit in our hearts as a deposit.	22 He has put his brand upon us—his mark of ownership—and given us his Holy Spirit in our hearts as guarantee that we belong to him, and as the first installment of all that he is going to give us.
4:4 In whom the god of this world hath blinded the minds of them which believe not, lest the light of the glorious gospel of Christ, who is the image of God, should shine unto them.	4:4 whose minds the god of this age has blinded, who do not believe, lest the light of the gospel of the glory of Christ, who is the image of God, should shine on them.	4:4 Satan, who is the god of this evil world, has made him blind, unable to see the glorious light of the Gospel that is shining upon him, or to understand the amazing message we preach about the glory of Christ, who is God.
6 For God, who commanded the light to shine out of darkness, hath shined in our hearts, to give the light of the knowledge of the glory of God in the face of Jesus Christ.	6 For it is the God who commanded light to shine out of darkness, who has shone in our hearts to give the light of the knowledge of the glory of God in the face of Jesus Christ.	6 For God, who said, "Let there be light in the darkness," has made us understand that it is the brightness of his glory that is seen in the face of Jesus Christ.
17 For our light affliction, which is but for a moment, worketh for us a far more exceeding and eternal weight of glory;	17 For our light affliction, which is but for a moment, is working for us a far more exceeding and eternal weight of glory,	17 These troubles and sufferings of ours are, after all, quite small and won't last very long. Yet this short time of distress will result in God's richest blessing upon us forever and ever!
18 While we look not at the things which are seen, but at the things which are not seen: for the things which are seen are temporal; but the things which are not seen are eternal.	18 while we do not look at the things which are seen, but at the things which are not seen. For the things which are seen are temporary, but the things which are not seen are eternal.	18 So we do not look at what we can see right now, the troubles all around us, but we look forward to the joys in heaven which we have not yet seen. The troubles will soon be over, but the joys to come will last forever.
5:1 For we know that if our earthly house of this tabernacle were dissolved, we have a building of God, an house not made with hands, eternal in the heavens.	5:1 For we know that if our earthly house, this tent, is destroyed, we have a building from God, a house not made with hands, eternal in the heavens.	5:1 For we know that when this tent we live in now is taken down—when we die and leave these bodies—we will have wonderful new bodies in heaven, homes that will be ours forevermore, made for us by God himself, and not by human hands.
20 Now then we are ambassadors for Christ, as though God did beseech you by us: we pray you in Christ's stead, be ye reconciled to God.	20 Therefore we are ambassadors for Christ, as though God were pleading through us: we implore you on Christ's behalf, be reconciled to God.	20 We are Christ's ambassadors. God is using us to speak to you: we beg you, as though Christ himself were here pleading with you, receive the love he offers you—be reconciled to God.
21 For he hath made him to be sin for us, who knew no sin; that we might be made the righteousness of God in him.	21 For He made Him who knew no sin to be sin for us, that we might become the righteousness of God in Him.	21 For God took the sinless Christ and poured into him our sins. Then, in exchange, he poured God's goodness into us!
7:9 Now I rejoice, not that ye were made sorry, but that ye sorrowed to repentance: for ye were made sorry after a godly manner, that ye might receive damage by us in nothing.	7:9 Now I rejoice, not that you were made sorry, but that your sorrow led to repentance. For you were made sorry in a godly manner, that you might suffer loss from us in nothing.	7:9 Now I am glad I sent it, not because it hurt you, but because the pain turned you to God. It was a good kind of sorrow you felt, the kind of sorrow God wants his people to have, so that I need not come to you with harshness.

NIV	RSV	TEV
51 Listen, I tell you a mystery: We will not all sleep, but we will all be changed—	51 Lo! I tell you a mystery. We shall not all sleep, but we shall all be changed,	51–52 Listen to this secret truth: we shall not all die, but when the last trumpet sounds, we shall all be changed in an instant, as quickly as the blinking of an eye. For when the trumpet sounds, the dead will be raised, never to die again, and we shall all be changed.
52 in a flash, in the twinkling of an eye, at the last trumpet. For the trumpet will sound, the dead will be raised imperishable, and we will be changed.	52 in a moment, in the twinkling of an eye, at the last trumpet. For the trumpet will sound, and the dead will be raised imperishable, and we shall be changed.	
55 "Where, O death, is your victory? Where, O death, is your sting?"	55 "O death, where is thy victory? O death, where is thy sting?"	55 "Where, Death, is your victory? Where, Death, is your power to hurt?"
56 The sting of death is sin, and the power of sin is the law.	56 The sting of death is sin, and the power of sin is the law.	56 Death gets its power to hurt from sin, and sin gets its power from the Law.
57 But thanks be to God! He gives us the victory through our Lord Jesus Christ.	57 But thanks be to God, who gives us the victory through our Lord Jesus Christ.	57 But thanks be to God who gives us the victory through our Lord Jesus Christ!

Second Corinthians

NIV	RSV	TEV
1:3 Praise be to the God and Father of our Lord Jesus Christ, the Father of compassion and the God of all comfort,	1:3 Blessed be the God and Father of our Lord Jesus Christ, the Father of mercies and God of all comfort,	1:3 Let us give thanks to the God and Father of our Lord Jesus Christ, the merciful Father, the God from whom all help comes!
4 who comforts us in all our troubles, so that we can comfort those in any trouble with the comfort we ourselves have received from God.	4 who comforts us in all our affliction, so that we may be able to comfort those who are in any affliction, with the comfort with which we ourselves are comforted by God.	4 He helps us in all our troubles, so that we are able to help others who have all kinds of troubles, using the same help that we ourselves have received from God.
21 Now it is God who makes both us and you stand firm in Christ. He anointed us,	21 But it is God who establishes us with you in Christ, and has commissioned us;	21 It is God himself who makes us, together with you, sure of our life in union with Christ; it is God himself who has set us apart,
22 sets his seal of ownership on us, and put his Spirit in our hearts as a deposit, guaranteeing what is to come.	22 he has put his seal upon us and given us his Spirit in our hearts as a guarantee.	22 who has placed his mark of ownership upon us, and who has given us the Holy Spirit in our hearts as the guarantee of all that he has in store for us.
4:4 The god of this age has blinded the minds of unbelievers, so that they cannot see the light of the gospel of the glory of Christ, who is the image of God.	4:4 In their case the god of this world has blinded the minds of the unbelievers, to keep them from seeing the light of the gospel of the glory of Christ, who is the likeness of God.	4:4 They do not believe, because their minds have been kept in the dark by the evil god of this world. He keeps them from seeing the light shining on them, the light that comes from the Good News about the glory of Christ, who is the exact likeness of God.
6 For God, who said, "Let light shine out of darkness," made his light shine in our hearts to give us the light of the knowledge of the glory of God in the face of Christ.	6 For it is the God who said, "Let light shine out of darkness," who has shone in our hearts to give the light of the knowledge of the glory of God in the face of Christ.	6 The God who said, "Out of darkness the light shall shine!" is the same God who made his light shine in our hearts, to bring us the knowledge of God's glory shining in the face of Christ.
17 For our light and momentary troubles are achieving for us an eternal glory that far outweighs them all.	17 For this slight momentary affliction is preparing for us an eternal weight of glory beyond all comparison.	17 And this small and temporary trouble we suffer will bring us a tremendous and eternal glory, much greater than the trouble.
18 So we fix our eyes not on what is seen, but on what is unseen. For what is seen is temporary, but what is unseen is eternal.	18 because we look not to the things that are seen but to the things that are unseen; for the things that are seen are transient, but the things that are unseen are eternal.	18 For we fix our attention, not on things that are seen, but on things that are unseen. What can be seen lasts only for a time, but what cannot be seen lasts forever.
5:1 Now we know that if the earthly tent we live in is destroyed, we have a building from God, an eternal house in heaven, not built by human hands.	5:1 For we know that if the earthly tent we live in is destroyed, we have a building from God, a house not made with hands, eternal in the heavens.	5:1 For we know that when this tent we live in—our body here on earth—is torn down, God will have a house in heaven for us to live in, a home he himself has made, which will last forever.
20 We are therefore Christ's ambassadors, as though God were making his appeal through us. We implore you on Christ's behalf: Be reconciled to God.	20 So we are ambassadors for Christ, God making his appeal through us. We beseech you on behalf of Christ, be reconciled to God.	20 Here we are, then, speaking for Christ, as though God himself were making his appeal through us. We plead on Christ's behalf: let God change you from enemies into his friends!
21 God made him who had no sin to be sin for us, so that in him we might become the righteousness of God.	21 For our sake he made him to be sin who knew no sin, so that in him we might become the righteousness of God.	21 Christ was without sin, but for our sake God made him share our sin in order that in union with him we might share the righteousness of God.
7:9 yet now I am happy, not because you were made sorry, but because your sorrow led you to repentance. For you became sorrowful as God intended and so were not harmed in any way by us.	7:9 As it is, I rejoice, not because you were grieved, but because you were grieved into repenting; for you felt a godly grief, so that you suffered no loss through us.	7:9 But now I am happy—not because I made you sad, but because your sadness made you change your ways. That sadness was used by God, and so we caused you no harm.

KJV	NKJV	TLB
9:6 But this *I say,* He which soweth sparingly shall reap also sparingly; and he which soweth bountifully shall reap also bountifully.	**9:6** But this *I say:* He who sows sparingly will also reap sparingly, and he who sows bountifully will also reap bountifully.	**9:6** But remember this—if you give little, you will get little. A farmer who plants just a few seeds will get only a small crop, but if he plants much, he will reap much.
7 Every man according as he purposeth in his heart, *so let him give;* not grudgingly, or of necessity: for God loveth a cheerful giver.	**7** *So let* each one *give* as he purposes in his heart, not grudgingly or of necessity; for God loves a cheerful giver.	**7** Every one must make up his own mind as to how much he should give. Don't force anyone to give more than he really wants to, for cheerful givers are the ones God prizes.
10:5 Casting down imaginations, and every high thing that exalteth itself against the knowledge of God, and bringing into captivity every thought to the obedience of Christ;	**10:5** casting down arguments and every high thing that exalts itself against the knowledge of God, bringing every thought into captivity to the obedience of Christ,	**10:5** These weapons can break down every proud argument against God and every wall that can be built to keep men from finding him. With these weapons I can capture rebels and bring them back to God, and change them into men whose hearts' desire is obedience to Christ.
12:9 And he said unto me, My grace is sufficient for thee: for my strength is made perfect in weakness. Most gladly therefore will I rather glory in my infirmities, that the power of Christ may rest upon me.	**12:9** And He said to me, "My grace is sufficient for you, for My strength is made perfect in weakness." Therefore most gladly I will rather boast in my infirmities, that the power of Christ may rest upon me.	**12:9** Each time he said, "No. But I am with you; that is all you need. My power shows up best in weak people." Now I am glad to boast about how weak I am; I am glad to be a living demonstration of Christ's power, instead of showing off my own power and abilities.

Galatians

2:16 Knowing that a man is not justified by the works of the law, but by the faith of Jesus Christ, even we have believed in Jesus Christ, that we might be justified by the faith of Christ, and not by the works of the law: for by the works of the law shall no flesh be justified.	**2:16** "knowing that a man is not justified by the works of the law but by faith in Jesus Christ, even we have believed in Christ Jesus, that we might be justified by faith in Christ and not by the works of the law; for by the works of the law no flesh shall be justified.	**2:16** and yet we Jewish Christians know very well that we cannot become right with God by obeying our Jewish laws, but only by faith in Jesus Christ to take away our sins. And so we, too, have trusted Jesus Christ, that we might be accepted by God because of faith—and not because we have obeyed the Jewish laws. For no one will ever be saved by obeying them."
3:24 Wherefore the law was our schoolmaster *to bring us* unto Christ, that we might be justified by faith.	**3:24** Therefore the law was our tutor *to bring us* to Christ, that we might be justified by faith.	**3:24** Let me put it another way. The Jewish laws were our teacher and guide until Christ came to give us right standing with God through our faith.
4:4 But when the fulness of the time was come, God sent forth his Son, made of a woman, made under the law,	**4:4** But when the fullness of the time had come, God sent forth His Son, born of a woman, born under the law,	**4:4** But when the right time came, the time God decided on, he sent his Son, born of a woman, born as a Jew,
5 To redeem them that were under the law, that we might receive the adoption of sons.	**5** to redeem those who were under the law, that we might receive the adoption as sons.	**5** to buy freedom for us who were slaves to the law so that he could adopt us as his very own sons.
5:16 *This* I say then, Walk in the Spirit, and ye shall not fulfil the lust of the flesh.	**5:16** I say then: Walk in the Spirit, and you shall not fulfill the lust of the flesh.	**5:16** I advise you to obey only the Holy Spirit's instructions. He will tell you where to go and what to do, and then you won't always be doing the wrong things your evil nature wants you to.
6:2 Bear ye one another's burdens, and so fulfil the law of Christ.	**6:2** Bear one another's burdens, and so fulfill the law of Christ.	**6:2** Share each other's troubles and problems, and so obey our Lord's command.
9 And let us not be weary in well doing: for in due season we shall reap, if we faint not.	**9** And let us not grow weary while doing good, for in due season we shall reap if we do not lose heart.	**9** And let us not get tired of doing what is right, for after a while we will reap a harvest of blessing if we don't get discouraged and give up.
14 But God forbid that I should glory, save in the cross of our Lord Jesus Christ, by whom the world is crucified unto me, and I unto the world.	**14** But God forbid that I should glory except in the cross of our Lord Jesus Christ, by whom the world has been crucified to me, and I to the world.	**14** As for me, God forbid that I should boast about anything except the cross of our Lord Jesus Christ. Because of that cross my interest in all the attractive things of the world was killed long ago, and the world's interest in me is also long dead.

Ephesians

1:3 Blessed *be* the God and Father of our Lord Jesus Christ, who hath blessed us with all spiritual blessings in heavenly *places* in Christ:	**1:3** Blessed *be* the God and Father of our Lord Jesus Christ, who has blessed us with every spiritual blessing in the heavenly *places* in Christ,	**1:3** How we praise God, the Father of our Lord Jesus Christ, who has blessed us with every blessing in heaven because we belong to Christ.
4 According as he hath chosen us in him before the foundation of the world, that we should be holy and without blame before him in love:	**4** just as He chose us in Him before the foundation of the world, that we should be holy and without blame before Him in love,	**4** Long ago, even before he made the world, God chose us to be his very own, through what Christ would do for us; he decided then to make us holy in his eyes, without a single fault—we who stand before him covered with his love.
5 Having predestinated us unto the adoption of children by Jesus Christ to himself, according to the good pleasure of his will,	**5** having predestined us to adoption as sons by Jesus Christ to Himself, according to the good pleasure of His will,	**5** His unchanging plan has always been to adopt us into his own family by sending Jesus Christ to die for us. And he did this because he wanted to!

NIV	RSV	TEV
9:6 Remember this: Whoever sows sparingly will also reap sparingly, and whoever sows generously will also reap generously.	**9:6** The point is this: he who sows sparingly will also reap sparingly, and he who sows bountifully will also reap bountifully.	**9:6** Remember that the person who plants few seeds will have a small crop; the one who plants many seeds will have a large crop.
7 Each man should give what he has decided in his heart to give, not reluctantly or under compulsion, for God loves a cheerful giver.	**7** Each one must do as he has made up his mind, not reluctantly or under compulsion, for God loves a cheerful giver.	**7** Each one should give, then, as he has decided, not with regret or out of a sense of duty; for God loves the one who gives gladly.
10:5 We demolish arguments and every pretension that sets itself up against the knowledge of God, and we take captive every thought to make it obedient to Christ.	**10:5** We destroy arguments and every proud obstacle to the knowledge of God, and take every thought captive to obey Christ,	**10:5** we pull down every proud obstacle that is raised against the knowledge of God; we take every thought captive and make it obey Christ.
12:9 But he said to me, "My grace is sufficient for you, for my power is made perfect in weakness." Therefore I will boast all the more gladly about my weaknesses, so that Christ's power may rest on me.	**12:9** but he said to me, "My grace is sufficient for you, for my power is made perfect in weakness." I will all the more gladly boast of my weaknesses, that the power of Christ may rest upon me.	**12:9** But his answer was: "My grace is all you need, for my power is greatest when you are weak." I am most happy, then, to be proud of my weaknesses, in order to feel the protection of Christ's power over me.

Galatians

NIV	RSV	TEV
2:16 know that a man is not justified by observing the law, but by faith in Jesus Christ. So we, too, have put our faith in Christ Jesus that we may be justified by faith in Christ and not by observing the law, because by observing the law no one will be justified.	**2:16** yet who know that a man is not justified by works of the law but through faith in Jesus Christ, even we have believed in Christ Jesus, in order to be justified by faith in Christ, and not by works of the law, because by works of the law shall no one be justified.	**2:16** Yet we know that a person is put right with God only through faith in Jesus Christ, never by doing what the Law requires. We, too, have believed in Christ Jesus in order to be put right with God through our faith in Christ, and not by doing what the Law requires. For no one is put right with God by doing what the Law requires.
3:24 So the law was put in charge to lead us to Christ that we might be justified by faith.	**3:24** So that the law was our custodian until Christ came, that we might be justified by faith.	**3:24** And so the Law was in charge of us until Christ came, in order that we might then be put right with God through faith.
4:4 But when the time had fully come, God sent his Son, born of a woman, born under law,	**4:4** But when the time had fully come, God sent forth his Son, born of woman, born under the law,	**4:4** But when the right time finally came, God sent his own Son. He came as the son of a human mother and lived under the Jewish Law,
5 to redeem those under law, that we might receive the full rights of sons.	**5** to redeem those who were under the law, so that we might receive adoption as sons.	**5** to redeem those who were under the Law, so that we might become God's sons.
5:16 So I say, live by the Spirit, and you will not gratify the desires of the sinful nature.	**5:16** But I say, walk by the Spirit, and do not gratify the desires of the flesh.	**5:16** What I say is this: let the Spirit direct your lives, and you will not satisfy the desires of the human nature.
6:2 Carry each other's burdens, and in this way you will fulfill the law of Christ.	**6:2** Bear one another's burdens, and so fulfil the law of Christ.	**6:2** Help carry one another's burdens, and in this way you will obey the law of Christ.
9 Let us not become weary in doing good, for at the proper time we will reap a harvest if we do not give up.	**9** And let us not grow weary in well-doing, for in due season we shall reap, if we do not lose heart.	**9** So let us not become tired of doing good; for if we do not give up, the time will come when we will reap the harvest.
14 May I never boast except in the cross of our Lord Jesus Christ, through which the world has been crucified to me, and I to the world.	**14** But far be it from me to glory except in the cross of our Lord Jesus Christ, by which the world has been crucified to me, and I to the world.	**14** As for me, however, I will boast only about the cross of our Lord Jesus Christ; for by means of his cross the world is dead to me, and I am dead to the world.

Ephesians

NIV	RSV	TEV
1:3 Praise be to the God and Father of our Lord Jesus Christ, who has blessed us in the heavenly realms with every spiritual blessing in Christ.	**1:3** Blessed be the God and Father of our Lord Jesus Christ, who has blessed us in Christ with every spiritual blessing in the heavenly places,	**1:3** Let us give thanks to the God and Father of our Lord Jesus Christ! For in our union with Christ he has blessed us by giving us every spiritual blessing in the heavenly world.
4 For he chose us in him before the creation of the world to be holy and blameless in his sight. In love.	**4** even as he chose us in him before the foundation of the world, that we should be holy and blameless before him.	**4** Even before the world was made, God had already chosen us to be his through our union with Christ, so that we would be holy and without fault before him. Because of his love
5 he predestined us to be adopted as his sons through Jesus Christ, in accordance with his pleasure and will—	**5** He destined us in love to be his sons through Jesus Christ, according to the purpose of his will,	**5** God had already decided that through Jesus Christ he would make us his sons—this was his pleasure and purpose.

KJV	NKJV	TLB
2:8 For by grace are ye saved through faith; and that not of yourselves: *it is* the gift of God:	**2:8** for by grace you have been saved through faith, and that not of yourselves; *it is* the gift of God,	**2:8** Because of his kindness you have been saved through trusting Christ. And even trusting is not of yourselves; it too is a gift from God.
9 Not of works, lest any man should boast.	9 not of works, lest anyone should boast.	9 Savlation is not a reward for the good we have done, so none of us can take any credit for it.
10 For we are his workmanship, created in Christ Jesus unto good works, which God hath before ordained that we should walk in them.	10 For we are His workmanship, created in Christ Jesus for good works, which God prepared beforehand that we should walk in them.	10 It is God himself who has made us what we are and given us new lives from Christ Jesus; and long ages ago he planned that we should spend these lives in helping others.
3:20 Now unto him that is able to do exceeding abundantly above all that we ask or think, according to the power that worketh in us,	**3:20** Now to Him who is able to do exceedingly abundantly above all that we ask or think, according to the power that works in us,	3:20 Now glory be to God who by his mighty power at work within us is able to do far more than we would ever dare to ask or even dream of—infinitely beyond our highest prayers, desires, thoughts, or hopes.
21 Unto him *be* glory in the church by Christ Jesus throughout all ages, world without end. Amen.	21 to Him *be* glory in the church by Christ Jesus throughout all ages, world without end. Amen.	21 May he be given glory forever and ever through endless ages because of his master plan of salvation for the church through Jesus Christ.
4:11 And he gave some, apostles; and some, prophets; and some, evangelists; and some, pastors and teachers;	**4:11** And He Himself gave some *to be* apostles, some prophets, some evangelists, and some pastors and teachers,	4:11 Some of us have been given special ability as apostles; to others he has given the gift of being able to preach well; some have special ability in winning people to Christ, helping them to trust him as their Savior; still others have a gift for caring for God's people as a shepherd does his sheep, leading and teaching them in the ways of God.
12 For the perfecting of the saints, for the work of the ministry, for the edifying of the body of Christ:	12 for the equipping of the saints for the work of ministry, for the edifying of the body of Christ,	12 Why is it that he gives us these special abilities to do certain things best? It is that God's people will be equipped to do better work for him, building up the church, the body of Christ, to a position of strength and maturity;
13 Till we all come in the unity of the faith, and of the knowledge of the Son of God, unto a perfect man, unto the measure of the stature of the fulness of Christ:	13 till we all come to the unity of the faith and the knowledge of the Son of God, to a perfect man, to the measure of the stature of the fullness of Christ;	13 until finally we all believe alike about our salvation and about our Savior, God's Son, and all become full-grown in the Lord—yes, to the point of being filled full with Christ.
26 Be ye angry, and sin not: let not the sun go down upon your wrath:	26 "Be angry, and do not sin": do not let the sun go down on your wrath,	26 If you are angry, don't sin by nursing your grudge. Don't let the sun go down with you still angry—get over it quickly;
32 And be ye kind one to another, tenderhearted, forgiving one another, even as God for Christ's sake hath forgiven you.	32 And be kind to one another, tenderhearted, forgiving one another, just as God in Christ also forgave you.	32 Instead, be kind to each other, tenderhearted, forgiving one another, just as God has forgiven you because you belong to Christ.
5:2 And walk in love, as Christ also hath loved us, and hath given himself for us an offering and a sacrifice to God for a sweetsmelling savour.	**5:2** And walk in love, as Christ also has loved us and given Himself for us, an offering and a sacrifice to God for a sweetsmelling aroma.	5:2 Be full of love for others, following the example of Christ who loved you and gave himself to God as a sacrifice to take away your sins. And God was pleased, for Christ's love for you was like sweet perfume to him.
6 Let no man deceive you with vain words: for because of these things cometh the wrath of God upon the children of disobedience.	6 Let no one deceive you with empty words, for because of these things the wrath of God comes upon the sons of disobedience.	6 Don't be fooled by those who try to excuse these sins, for the terrible wrath of God is upon all those who do them.
33 Nevertheless let every one of you in particular so love his wife even as himself; and the wife *see* that she reverence *her* husband.	33 Nevertheless let each one of you in particular so love his own wife as himself, and let the wife *see* that she respects *her* husband.	33 So again I say, a man must love his wife as a part of himself; and the wife must see to it that she deeply respects her husband—obeying, praising and honoring him.
6:2 Honour thy father and mother; which is the first commandment with promise;	**6:2** "Honour your father and mother," which is the first commandment with promise:	**6:2** Honor your father and mother. This is the first of God's Ten Commandments that ends with a promise.
3 That it may be well with thee, and thou mayest live long on the earth.	3 "that it may be well with you and you may live long on the earth."	3 And this is the promise: that if you honor your father and mother, yours will be a long life, full of blessing.
10 Finally, my brethren, be strong in the Lord, and in the power of his might.	10 Finally, my brethren, be strong in the Lord and in the power of His might.	10 Last of all I want to remind you that your strength must come from the Lord's mighty power within you.
11 Put on the whole armour of God, that ye may be able to stand against the wiles of the devil.	11 Put on the whole armor of God, that you may be able to stand against the wiles of the devil.	11 Put on all of God's armor so that you will be able to stand safe against all strategies and tricks of Satan.
12 For we wrestle not against flesh and blood, but against principalities, against powers, against the rulers of the darkness of this world, against spiritual wickedness in high *places*.	12 For we do not wrestle against flesh and blood, but against principalities, against powers, against the rulers of the darkness of this age, against spiritual *hosts* of wickedness in the heavenly *places*.	12 For we are not fighting against people made of flesh and blood, but against persons without bodies—the evil rulers of the unseen world, those mighty satanic beings and great evil princes of darkness who rule this world; and against huge numbers of wicked spirits in the spirit world.

Philippians

1:6 Being confident of this very thing, that he which hath begun a good work in you will perform *it* until the day of Jesus Christ:	**1:6** being confident of this very thing, that He who has begun a good work in you will complete *it* until the day of Jesus Christ;	1:6 And I am sure that God who began the good work within you will keep right on helping you grow in his grace until his task within you is finally finished on that day when Jesus Christ returns.

NIV	RSV	TEV
2:8 For it is by grace you have been saved, through faith—and this not from yourselves, it is the gift of God—	2:8 For by grace you have been saved through faith; and this is not your own doing, it is the gift of God—	2:8–9 For it is by God's grace that you have been saved through faith. It is not the result of your own efforts, but God's gift, so that no one can boast about it.
9 not by works, so that no one can boast.	9 not because of works, lest any man should boast.	
10 For we are God's workmanship, created in Christ Jesus to do good works, which God prepared in advance for us to do.	10 For we are his workmanship, created in Christ Jesus for good works, which God prepared beforehand, that we should walk in them.	10 God has made us what we are, and in our union with Christ Jesus he has created us for a life of good deeds, which he has already prepared for us to do.
3:20 Now to him who is able to do immeasurably more than all we ask or imagine, according to his power that is at work within us,	3:20 Now to him who by the power at work within us is able to do far more abundantly than all that we ask or think,	3:20 To him who by means of his power working in us is able to do so much more than we can ever ask for, or even think of:
21 to him be glory in the church and in Christ Jesus throughout all generations, for ever and ever! Amen.	21 to him be glory in the church and in Christ Jesus to all generations, for ever and ever. Amen.	21 to God be the glory in the church and in Christ Jesus for all time, forever and ever! Amen.
4:11 It was he who gave some to be apostles, some to be prophets, some to be evangelists, and some to be pastors and teachers,	4:11 And his gifts were that some should be apostles, some prophets, some evangelists, some pastors and teachers,	4:11 It was he who "gave gifts to mankind"; he appointed some to be apostles, others to be prophets, others to be evangelists, others to be pastors and teachers.
12 to prepare God's people for works of service, so that the body of Christ may be built up	12 to equip the saints for the work of ministry, for building up the body of Christ,	12 He did this to prepare all God's people for the work of Christian service, in order to build up the body of Christ.
13 until we all reach unity in the faith and in the knowledge of the Son of God and become mature, attaining to the whole measure of the fullness of Christ.	13 until we all attain to the unity of the faith and of the knowledge of the Son of God, to mature manhood, to the measure of the stature of the fulness of Christ;	13 And so we shall all come together to that oneness in our faith and in our knowledge of the Son of God; we shall become mature people, reaching to the very height of Christ's full stature.
26 "In your anger do not sin": Do no let the sun go down while you are still angry,	26 Be angry but do not sin; do not let the sun go down on your anger,	26 If you become angry, do not let your anger lead you into sin, and do not stay angry all day.
32 Be kind and compassionate to one another, forgiving each other, just as in Christ God forgave you.	32 and be kind to one another, tenderhearted, forgiving one another, as God in Christ forgave you.	32 Instead, be kind and tender-hearted to one another, and forgive one another, as God has forgiven you through Christ.
5:2 and live a life of love, just as Christ loved us and gave himself up for us as a fragrant offering and sacrifice to God.	5:2 And walk in love, as Christ loved us and gave himself up for us, a fragrant offering and sacrifice to God.	5:2 Your life must be controlled by love, just as Christ loved us and gave his life for us as a sweet-smelling offering and sacrifice that pleases God.
6 Let no one deceive you with empty words, for because of such things God's wrath comes on those who are disobedient.	6 Let no one deceive you with empty words, for it is because of these things that the wrath of God comes upon the sons of disobedience.	6 Do not let anyone deceive you with foolish words; it is because of these very things that God's anger will come upon those who do not obey him.
33 However, each one of you also must love his wife as he loves himself, and the wife must respect her husband.	33 however, let each one of you love his wife as himself, and let the wife see that she respects her husband.	33 But it also applies to you: every husband must love his wife as himself, and every wife must respect her husband.
6:2 "Honor your father and mother"—which is the first commandment with a promise—	6:2 "Honor your father and mother" (this is the first commandment with a promise),	6:2 "Respect your father and mother" is the first commandment that has a promise added:
3 "that it may go well with you and that you may enjoy long life on the earth."	3 "that it may be well with you and that you may live long on the earth."	3 "so that all may go well with you, and you may live a long time in the land."
10 Finally, be strong in the Lord and in his mighty power.	10 Finally, be strong in the Lord and in the strength of his might.	10 Finally, build up your strength in union with the Lord and by means of his mighty power.
11 Put on the full armor of God so that you can take your stand against the devil's schemes.	11 Put on the whole armor of God, that you may be able to stand against the wiles of the devil.	11 Put on all the armor that God gives you, so that you will be able to stand up against the Devil's evil tricks.
12 For our struggle is not against flesh and blood, but against the rulers, against the authorities, against the powers of this dark world and against the spiritual forces of evil in the heavenly realms.	12 For we are not contending against flesh and blood, but against the principalities, against the powers, against the world rulers of this present darkness, against the spiritual hosts of wickedness in the heavenly places.	12 For we are not fighting against human beings but against the wicked spiritual forces in the heavenly world, the rulers, authorities, and cosmic powers of this dark age.

Philippians

NIV	RSV	TEV
1:6 being confident of this, that he who began a good work in you will carry it on to completion until the day of Christ Jesus.	1:6 And I am sure that he who began a good work in you will bring it to completion at the day of Jesus Christ.	1:6 And so I am sure that God, who began this good work in you, will carry it on until it is finished on the Day of Christ Jesus.

KJV	NKJV	TLB
21 For to me to live *is* Christ, and to die *is* gain.	21 For to me, to live *is* Christ, and to die *is* gain.	21 For to me, living means opportunities for Christ, and dying—well, that's better yet!
29 For unto you it is given in the behalf of Christ, not only to believe on him, but also to suffer for his sake;	29 For to you it has been granted on behalf of Christ, not only to believe in Him, but also to suffer for His sake,	29 For to you has been given the privilege not only of trusting him but also of suffering for him.
2:5 Let this mind be in you, which was also in Christ Jesus:	2:5 Let this mind be in you which was also in Christ Jesus,	2:5 Your attitude should be the kind that was shown us by Jesus Christ,
6 Who, being in the form of God, thought it not robbery to be equal with God:	6 who, being in the form of God, did not consider it robbery to be equal with God,	6 who, though he was God, did not demand and cling to his rights as God,
7 But made himself of no reputation, and took upon him the form of a servant, and was made in the likeness of men:	7 but made Himself of no reputation, taking the form of a servant, *and* coming in the likeness of men.	7 but laid aside his mighty power and glory, taking the disguise of a slave and becoming like men.
8 And being found in fashion as a man, he humbled himself, and became obedient unto death, even the death of the cross.	8 And being found in appearance as a man, He humbled Himself and became obedient to *the point of* death, even the death of the cross.	8 And he humbled himself even further, going so far as actually to die a criminal's death on a cross.
9 Wherefore God also hath highly exalted him, and given him a name which is above every name:	9 Therefore God also has highly exalted Him and given Him the name which is above every name,	9 Yet it was because of this that God raised him up to the heights of heaven and gave him a name which is above every other name,
10 That at the name of Jesus every knee should bow, of *things* in heaven, and *things* in earth, and *things* under the earth;	10 that at the name of Jesus every knee should bow, of those in heaven, and of those on earth, and of those under the earth,	10 that at the name of Jesus every knee shall bow in heaven and on earth and under the earth,
11 And *that* every tongue should confess that Jesus Christ *is* Lord, to the glory of God the Father.	11 and *that* every tongue should confess that Jesus Christ *is* Lord, to the glory of God the Father.	11 and every tongue shall confess that Jesus Christ is Lord, to the glory of God the Father.
3:8 Yea doubtless, and I count all things *but* loss for the excellency of the knowledge of Christ Jesus my Lord: for whom I have suffered the loss of all things, and do count them *but* dung, that I may win Christ,	3:8 But indeed I also count all things loss for the excellence of the knowledge of Christ Jesus my Lord, for whom I have suffered the loss of all things, and count them as rubbish, that I may gain Christ	3:8 Yes, everything else is worthless when compared with the priceless gain of knowing Christ Jesus my Lord. I have put aside all else, counting it worth less than nothing, in order that I can have Christ,
9 And be found in him, not having mine own righteousness, which is of the law, but that which is through the faith of Christ, the righteousness which is of God by faith:	9 and be found in Him, not having my own righteousness, which *is* from the law, but that which *is* through faith in Christ, the righteousness which is from God by faith;	9 and become one with him, no longer counting on being saved by being good enough or by obeying God's laws, but by trusting Christ to save me; for God's way of making us right with himself depends on faith—counting on Christ alone.
4:6 Be careful for nothing; but in every thing by prayer and supplication with thanksgiving let your requests be made known unto God.	4:6 Be anxious for nothing, but in everything by prayer and supplication, with thanksgiving, let your requests be made known to God;	4:6 Don't worry about anything; instead, pray about everything; tell God your needs and don't forget to thank him for his answers.
7 And the peace of God, which passeth all understanding, shall keep your hearts and minds through Christ Jesus.	7 and the peace of God, which surpasses all understanding, will guard your hearts and minds through Christ Jesus.	7 If you do this you will experience God's peace, which is far more wonderful than the human mind can understand. His peace will keep your thoughts and your hearts quiet and at rest as you trust in Christ Jesus.
8 Finally, brethren, whatsoever things are true, whatsoever things *are* honest, whatsoever things *are* just, whatsoever things *are* pure, whatsoever things *are* lovely, whatsoever things *are* of good report; if *there be* any virtue, and if *there be* any praise, think on these things.	8 Finally, brethren, whatever things are true, whatever things are noble, whatever things *are* just, whatever things *are* pure, whatever things *are* lovely, whatever things *are* of good report, if *there is* any virtue and if *there is* anything praiseworthy—meditate on these things.	8 And now, brothers, as I close this letter let me say this one more thing: Fix your thoughts on what is true and good and right. Think about things that are pure and lovely, and dwell on the fine, good things in others. Think about all you can praise God for and be glad about.
13 I can do all things through Christ which strengtheneth me.	13 I can do all things through Christ who strengthens me.	13 for I can do everything God asks me to with the help of Christ who gives me the strength and power.
19 But my God shall supply all your need according to his riches in glory by Christ Jesus.	19 And my God shall supply all your need according to His riches in glory by Christ Jesus.	19 And it is he who will supply all your needs from his riches in glory, because of what Christ Jesus has done for us.

Colossians

1:13 Who hath delivered us from the power of darkness, and hath translated *us* into the kingdom of his dear Son:	1:13 He has delivered us from the power of darkness and translated *us* into the kingdom of the Son of His love,	1:13 For he has rescued us out of the darkness and gloom of Satan's kingdom and brought us into the kingdom of his dear Son,

NIV	RSV	TEV
21 For to me, to live is Christ and to die is gain.	21 For to me to live is Christ, and to die is gain.	21 For what is life? To me, it is Christ. Death, then, will bring more.
29 For it has been granted to you on behalf of Christ not only to believe on him, but also to suffer for him,	29 For it has been granted to you that for the sake of Christ you should not only believe in him but also suffer for his sake,	29 For you have been given the privilege of serving Christ, not only by believing in him, but also by suffering for him.
2:5 Your attitude should be the same as that of Christ Jesus:	**2:5** Have this mind among yourselves, which is yours in Christ Jesus,	**2:5** The attitude you should have is the one that Christ Jesus had:
6 Who, being in very nature God, did not consider equality with God something to be grasped,	6 who, though he was in the form of God, did not count equality with God a thing to be grasped,	6 He always had the nature of God, but he did not think that by force he should try to become equal with God.
7 but made himself nothing, taking the very nature of a servant, being made in human likeness.	7 but emptied himself, taking the form of a servant, being born in the likeness of men.	7 Instead of this, of his own free will he gave up all he had, and took the nature of a servant. He became like man and appeared in human likeness.
8 And being found in appearance as a man, he humbled himself and became obedient to death—even death on a cross!	8 And being found in human form he humbled himself and became obedient unto death, even death on a cross.	8 He was humble and walked the path of obedience all the way to death— his death on the cross.
9 Therefore God exalted him to the highest place and gave him the name that is above every name,	9 Therefore God has highly exalted him and bestowed on him the name which is above every name,	9 For this reason God raised him to the highest place above and gave him the name that is greater than any other name.
10 that at the name of Jesus every knee should bow, in heaven and on earth and under the earth,	10 that at the name of Jesus every knee should bow, in heaven and on earth and under the earth,	10 And so, in honor of the name of Jesus all beings in heaven, on earth, and in the world below will fall on their knees,
11 and every tongue confess that Jesus Christ is Lord, to the glory of God the Father.	11 and every tongue confess that Jesus Christ is Lord, to the glory of God the Father.	11 and all will openly proclaim that Jesus Christ is Lord, to the glory of God the Father.
3:8 What is more, I consider everything a loss compared to the surpassing greatness of knowing Christ Jesus my Lord, for whose sake I have lost all things. I consider them rubbish, that I may gain Christ	**3:8** Indeed I count everything as loss because of the surpassing worth of knowing Christ Jesus my Lord. For his sake I have suffered the loss of all things, and count them as refuse, in order that I may gain Christ	**3:8** Not only those things; I reckon everything as complete loss for the sake of what is so much more valuable, the knowledge of Christ Jesus my Lord. For his sake I have thrown everything away; I consider it all as mere garbage, so that I may gain Christ
9 and be found in him, not having a righteousness of my own that comes from the law, but that which is through faith in Christ—the righteousness that comes from God and is by faith.	9 and be found in him, not having a righteousness of my own, based on law, but that which is through faith in Christ, the righteousness from God that depends on faith;	9 and be completely united with him. I no longer have a righteousness of my own, the kind that is gained by obeying the Law. I now have the righteousness that is given through faith in Christ, the righteousness that comes from God and is based on faith.
4:6 Do not be anxious about anything, but in everything, by prayer and petition, with thanksgiving, present your requests to God.	**4:6** Have no anxiety about anything, but in everything by prayer and supplication with thanksgiving let your requests be made known to God.	**4:6** Don't worry about anything, but in all your prayers ask God for what you need, always asking him with a thankful heart.
7 And the peace of God, which transcends all understanding, will guard your hearts and your minds in Christ Jesus.	7 And the peace of God, which passes all understanding, will keep your hearts and your minds in Christ Jesus.	7 And God's peace, which is far beyond human understanding, will keep your hearts and minds safe in union with Christ Jesus.
8 Finally, brothers, whatever is true, whatever is noble, whatever is right, whatever is pure, whatever is lovely, whatever is admirable—if anything is excellent or praiseworthy—think about such things.	8 Finally, brethren, whatever is true, whatever is honorable, whatever is just, whatever is pure, whatever is lovely, whatever is gracious, if there is any excellence, if there is anything worthy of praise, think about these things.	8 In conclusion, my brothers, fill your minds with those things that are good and that deserve praise: things that are true, noble, right, pure, lovely, and honorable.
13 I can do everything through him who gives me strength.	13 I can do all things in him who strengthens me.	13 I have the strength to face all conditions by the power that Christ gives me.
19 And my God will meet all your needs according to his glorious riches in Christ Jesus.	19 And my God will supply every need of yours according to his riches in glory in Christ Jesus.	19 And with all his abundant wealth through Christ Jesus, my God will supply all your needs.

Colossians

NIV	RSV	TEV
1:13 For he has rescued us from the dominion of darkness and brought us into the kingdom of the Son he loves,	**1:13** He has delivered us from the dominion of darkness and transferred us to the kingdom of his beloved Son,	**1:13** He rescued us from the power of darkness and brought us safe into the kingdom of his dear Son,

KJV	NKJV	TLB
14 In whom we have redemption through his blood, *even* the forgiveness of sins:	14 in whom we have redemption through His blood, the forgiveness of sins.	14 who bought our freedom with his blood and forgave us all our sins.
18 And he is the head of the body, the church: who is the beginning, the first-born from the dead; that in all *things* he might have the preeminence.	18 And He is the head of the body, the church, who is the beginning, the first-born from the dead, that in all things He may have the preeminence.	18 He is the Head of the body made up of his people—that is, his church—which he began; and he is the Leader of all those who arise from the dead, so that he is first in everything;
2:9 For in him dwelleth all the fulness of the Godhead bodily.	2:9 For in Him dwells all the fullness of the Godhead bodily;	2:9 For in Christ there is all of God in a human body;
10 And ye are complete in him, which is the head of all principality and power:	10 and you are complete in Him, who is the head of all principality and power.	10 *so you have everything when you have Christ,* and you are filled with God through your union with Christ. He is the highest Ruler, with authority over every other power.
13 And you, being dead in your sins and the uncircumcision of your flesh, hath he quickened together with him, having forgiven you all trespasses;	13 And you, being dead in your trespasses and the uncircumcision of your flesh, He has made alive together with Him, having forgiven you all trespasses,	13 You were dead in sins, and your sinful desires were not yet cut away. Then he gave you a share in the very life of Christ, for he forgave all your sins,
3:4 When Christ, *who is* our life, shall appear, then shall ye also appear with him in glory.	3:4 When Christ *who is* our life appears, then you also will appear with Him in glory.	3:4 And when Christ who is our real life comes back again, you will shine with him and share in all his glories.
5 Mortify therefore your members which are upon the earth; fornication, uncleanness, inordinate affection, evil concupiscence, and covetousness, which is idolatry:	5 Therefore put to death your members which are on the earth: fornication, uncleanness, passion, evil desire, and covetousness, which is idolatry.	5 Away then with sinful, earthly things; deaden the evil desires lurking within you; have nothing to do with sexual sin, impurity, lust and shameful desires; don't worship the good things of life, for that is idolatry.
6 For which things' sake the wrath of God cometh on the children of disobedience:	6 Because of these things the wrath of God is coming upon the sons of disobedience,	6 God's terrible anger is upon those who do such things.
14 And above all these things *put on* charity, which is the bond of perfectness.	14 But above all these things put on love, which is the bond of perfection.	14 Most of all, let love guide your life, for then the whole church will stay together in perfect harmony.
15 And let the peace of God rule in your hearts, to the which also ye are called in one body; and be ye thankful.	15 And let the peace of God rule in your hearts, to which also you were called in one body; and be thankful.	15 Let the peace of heart which comes from Christ be always present in your hearts and lives, for this is your responsibility and privilege as members of his body. And always be thankful.
16 Let the word of Christ dwell in you richly in all wisdom; teaching and admonishing one another in psalms and hymns and spiritual songs, singing with grace in your hearts to the Lord.	16 Let the word of Christ dwell in you richly in all wisdom, teaching and admonishing one another in psalms and hymns and spiritual songs, singing with grace in your hearts to the Lord.	16 Remember what Christ taught and let his words enrich your lives and make you wise; teach them to each other and sing them out in psalms and hymns and spiritual songs, singing to the Lord with thankful hearts.
17 And whatsoever ye do in word or deed, *do* all in the name of the Lord Jesus, giving thanks to God and the Father by him.	17 And *whatever* you do in word or deed, *do* all in the name of the Lord Jesus, giving thanks to God the Father through Him.	17 And whatever you do or say, let it be as a representative of the Lord Jesus, and come with him into the presence of God the Father to give him your thanks.
4:1 Masters, give unto *your* servants that which is just and equal; knowing that ye also have a Master in heaven.	4:1 Masters, give your servants what is just and fair, knowing that you also have a Master in heaven.	4:1 You slave owners must be just and fair to all your slaves. Always remember that you, too, have a Master in heaven who is closely watching you.

First Thessalonians

KJV	NKJV	TLB
1:5 For our gospel came not unto you in word only, but also in power, and in the Holy Ghost, and in much assurance; as ye know what manner of men we were among you for your sake.	1:5 For our gospel did not come to you in word only, but also in power, and in the Holy Spirit and in much assurance, as you know what kind of men we were among you for your sake.	1:5 For when we brought you the Good News, it was not just meaningless chatter to you; no, you listened with great interest. What we told you produced a powerful effect upon you, for the Holy Spirit gave you great and full assurance that what we said was true. And you know how our very lives were further proof to you of the truth of our message.
2:10 Ye *are* witnesses, and God *also*, how holily and justly and unblameably we behaved ourselves among you that believe:	2:10 You *are* witnesses, and God *also*, how devoutly and justly and blamelessly we behaved ourselves among you who believe;	2:10 You yourselves are our witnesses—as is God—that we have been pure and honest and faultless toward every one of you.
19 For what *is* our hope, or joy, or crown of rejoicing? *Are* not even ye in the presence of our Lord Jesus Christ at his coming?	19 For what *is* our hope, or joy, or crown of rejoicing? *Is it* not even you in the presence of our Lord Jesus Christ at His coming?	19 For what is it we live for, that gives us hope and joy and is our proud reward and crown? It is you! Yes, you will bring us much joy as we stand together before our Lord Jesus Christ when he comes back again.
3:12 And the Lord make you to increase and abound in love one toward another, and toward all *men*, even as we *do* toward you:	3:12 And may the Lord make you increase and abound in love to one another and to all, just as we *do* to you,	3:12 And may the Lord make your love to grow and overflow to each other and to everyone else, just as our love does toward you.
4:15 For this we say unto you by the word of the Lord, that we which are alive *and* remain unto the coming of the Lord shall not prevent them which are asleep.	4:15 For this we say to you by the word of the Lord, that we who are alive *and* remain until the coming of the Lord will by no means precede those who are asleep.	4:15 I can tell you this directly from the Lord: that we who are still living when the Lord returns will not rise to meet him ahead of those who are in their graves.

NIV	RSV	TEV
14 in whom we have redemption, the forgiveness of sins.	14 in whom we have redemption, the forgiveness of sins.	14 by whom we are set free, that is, our sins are forgiven.
18 And he is the head of the body, the church; he is the beginning and the firstborn from among the dead, so that in everything he might have the supremacy.	18 He is the head of the body, the church; he is the beginning, the first-born from the dead, that in everything he might be pre-eminent.	18 He is the head of his body, the church; he is the source of the body's life. He is the first-born Son, who was raised from death, in order that he alone might have the first place in all things.
2:9 For in Christ all the fullness of the Deity lives in bodily form,	2:9 For in him the whole fulness of deity dwells bodily,	2:9 For the full content of divine nature lives in Christ, in his humanity,
10 and you have been given fullness in Christ, who is the head over every power and authority.	10 and you have come to fulness of life in him, who is the head of all rule and authority.	10 and you have been given full life in union with him. He is supreme over every spiritual ruler and authority.
13 When you were dead in your sins and in the uncircumcision of your sinful nature, God made you alive with Christ. He forgave us all our sins,	13 And you, who were dead in trespasses and the uncircumcision of your flesh, God made alive together with him, having forgiven us all our trespasses,	13 You were at one time spiritually dead because of your sins and because you were Gentiles without the Law. But God has now brought you to life with Christ. God forgave us all our sins;
3:4 When Christ, who is your life, appears, then you also will appear with him in glory.	3:4 When Christ who is our life appears, then you also will appear with him in glory.	3:4 Your real life is Christ and when he appears, then you too will appear with him and share his glory!
5 Put to death, therefore, whatever belongs to your earthly nature: sexual immorality, impurity, lust, evil desires and greed, which is idolatry.	5 Put to death therefore what is earthly in you: fornication, impurity, passion, evil desire, and covetousness, which is idolatry.	5 You must put to death, then, the earthly desires at work in you, such as sexual immorality, indecency, lust, evil passions, and greed (for greed is a form of idolatry).
6 Because of these, the wrath of God is coming.	6 On account of these the wrath of God is coming.	6 Because of such things God's anger will come upon those who do not obey him.
14 And over all these virtues put on love, which binds them all together in perfect unity.	14 And above all these put on love, which binds everything together in perfect harmony.	14 And to all these qualities add love, which binds all things together in perfect unity.
15 Let the peace of Christ rule in your hearts, since as members of one body you were called to peace. And be thankful.	15 And let the peace of Christ rule in your hearts, to which indeed you were called in the one body. And be thankful.	15 The peace that Christ gives is to guide you in the decisions you make; for it is to this peace that God has called you together in the one body. And be thankful.
16 Let the word of Christ dwell in you richly as you teach and admonish one another with all wisdom, and as you sing psalms, hymns and spiritual songs with gratitude in your hearts to God.	16 Let the word of Christ dwell in you richly, teach and admonish one another in all wisdom, and sing psalms and hymns and spiritual songs with thankfulness in your hearts to God.	16 Christ's message in all its richness must live in your hearts. Teach and instruct one another with all wisdom. Sing psalms, hymns, and sacred songs; sing to God with thanksgiving in your hearts.
17 And whatever you do, whether in word or deed, do it all in the name of the Lord Jesus, giving thanks to God the Father through him.	17 And whatever you do, in word or deed, do everything in the name of the Lord Jesus, giving thanks to God the Father through him.	17 Everything you do or say, then, should be done in the name of the Lord Jesus, as you give thanks through him to God the Father.
4:1 Masters, provide your slaves with what is right and fair, because you know that you also have a Master in heaven.	4:1 Masters, treat your slaves justly and fairly, knowing that you also have a Master in heaven.	4:1 Masters, be fair and just in the way you treat your slaves. Remember that you too have a Master in heaven.

First Thessalonians

NIV	RSV	TEV
1:5 because our gospel came to you not simply with words, but also with power, with the Holy Spirit and with deep conviction. You know how we live among you for your sake.	1:5 for our gospel came to you not only in word, but also in power and in the Holy Spirit and with full conviction. You know what kind of men we proved to be among you for your sake.	1:5 For we brought the Good News to you, not with words only, but also with power and the Holy Spirit, and with complete conviction of its truth. You know how we live when we were with you; it was for your own good.
2:10 You are witnesses, and so is God, of how holy, righteous and blameless we were among you who believed.	2:10 You are witnesses, and God also, how holy and righteous and blameless was our behavior to you believers;	2:10 You are our witnesses, and so is God, that our conduct toward you who believe was pure, right, and without fault.
19 For what is our hope, our joy, or the crown in which we will glory in the presence of our Lord Jesus when he comes? Is it not you?	19 For what is our hope or joy or crown of boasting before our Lord Jesus at his coming? Is it not you?	19 After all, it is you—you, no less than others!—who are our hope, our joy, and our reason for boasting of our victory in the presence of our Lord Jesus when he comes.
3:12 May the Lord make your love increase and overflow for each other and for everyone else, just as ours does for you.	3:12 and may the Lord make you increase and abound in love to one another and to all men, as we do to you,	3:12 May the Lord make your love for one another and for all people grow more and more and become as great as our love for you.
4:15 According to the Lord's own word, we tell you that we who are still alive, who are left till the coming of the Lord, will certainly not precede those who have fallen asleep.	4:15 For this we declare to you by the word of the Lord, that we who are alive, who are left until the coming of the Lord, shall not precede those who have fallen asleep.	4:15 What we are teaching you now is the Lord's teaching: we who are alive on the day the Lord comes will not go ahead of those who have died.

KJV	NKJV	TLB
16 For the Lord himself shall descend from heaven with a shout, with the voice of the archangel, and with the trump of God: and the dead in Christ shall rise first:	16 For the Lord Himself will descend from heaven with a shout, with the voice of an archangel, and with the trumpet of God. And the dead in Christ will rise first.	16 For the Lord himself will come down from heaven with a mighty shout and with the soul-stirring cry of the archangel and the great trumpet-call of God. And the believers who are dead will be the first to rise to meet the Lord.
17 Then we which are alive *and* remain shall be caught up together with them in the clouds to meet the Lord in the air: and so shall we ever be with the Lord.	17 Then we who are alive *and* remain shall be caught up together with them in the clouds to meet the Lord in the air. And thus we shall always be with the Lord.	17 Then we who are still alive and remain on the earth will be caught up with them in the clouds to meet the Lord in the air and remain with him forever.
5:9 For God hath not appointed us to wrath, but to obtain salvation by our Lord Jesus Christ,	5:9 For God did not appoint us to wrath, but to obtain salvation through our Lord Jesus Christ,	5:9 For God has not chosen to pour out his anger upon us, but to save us through our Lord Jesus Christ;
10 Who died for us, that, whether we wake or sleep, we should live together with him.	10 who died for us, that whether we wake or sleep, we should live together with Him.	10 he died for us so that we can live with him forever, whether we are dead or alive at the time of his return.
15 See that none render evil for evil unto any *man;* but ever follow that which is good, both among yourselves, and to all *men.*	15 See that no one renders evil for evil to anyone, but always pursue what is good both for yourselves and for all.	15 See that no one pays back evil for evil, but always try to do good to each other and to everyone else.
16 Rejoice evermore.	16 Rejoice always,	16 Always be joyful.
17 Pray without ceasing.	17 pray without ceasing,	17 Always keep on praying.
18 In every thing give thanks: for this is the will of God in Christ Jesus concerning you.	18 in everything give thanks; for this is the will of God in Christ Jesus for you.	18 No matter what happens, always be thankful, for this is God's will for you who belong to Christ Jesus.
19 Quench not the Spirit.	19 Do not quench the Spirit.	19 Do not smother the Holy Spirit.
20 Despise not prophesyings.	20 Do not despise prophecies.	20 Do not scoff at those who prophesy,
21 Prove all things; hold fast that which is good.	21 Test all things; hold fast what is good.	21 but test everything that is said to be sure it is true, and if it is, then accept it.
22 Abstain from all appearance of evil.	22 Abstain from every form of evil.	22 Keep away from every kind of evil.
23 And the very God of peace sanctify you wholly; and *I pray God* your whole spirit and soul and body be preserved blameless unto the coming of our Lord Jesus Christ.	23 Now may the God of peace Himself sanctify you completely; and may your whole spirit, soul, and body be preserved blameless at the coming of our Lord Jesus Christ.	23 May the God of peace himself make you entirely pure and devoted to God; and may your spirit and soul and body be kept strong and blameless until that day when our Lord Jesus Christ comes back again.
24 Faithful *is* he that calleth you, who also will do *it.*	24 He who calls you *is* faithful, who also will do *it.*	24 God, who called you to become his child, will do all this for you, just as he promised.

Second Thessalonians

KJV	NKJV	TLB
1:3 We are bound to thank God always for you, brethren, as it is meet, because that your faith groweth exceedingly, and the charity of every one of you all toward each other aboundeth;	1:3 We are bound to thank God always for you, brethren, as it is fitting, because that your faith grows exceedingly, and the love of every one of you all abounds toward each other,	1:3 Dear brothers, giving thanks to God for you is not only the right thing to do, but it is our duty to God, because of the really wonderful way your faith has grown, and because of your growing love for each other.
4 So that we ourselves glory in you in the churches of God for your patience and faith in all your persecutions and tribulations that ye endure:	4 so that we ourselves boast of you among the churches of God for your patience and faith in all your persecutions and tribulations that you endure,	4 We are happy to tell other churches about your patience and complete faith in God, in spite of all the crushing troubles and hardships you are going through.
2:1 Now we beseech you, brethren, by the coming of our Lord Jesus Christ, and *by* our gathering together unto him,	2:1 Now, brethren, concerning the coming of our Lord Jesus Christ and our gathering together to Him, we ask you,	2:1 And now, what about the coming again of our Lord Jesus Christ, and our being gathered together to meet him? Please
2 That ye be not soon shaken in mind, or be troubled, neither by spirit, nor by word, nor by letter as from us, as that the day of Christ is at hand.	2 not to be soon shaken in mind or troubled, either by spirit or by word or by letter, as if from us, as though the day of Christ had come.	2 don't be upset and excited, dear brothers, by the rumor that this day of the Lord has already begun. If you hear of people having visions and special messages from God about this, or letters that are supposed to have come from me, don't believe them.
3 Let no man deceive you by any means: for *that day shall not come,* except there come a falling away first, and that man of sin be revealed, the son of perdition;	3 Let no one deceive you by any means; for *that Day will not come* unless the falling away comes first, and the man of sin is revealed, the son of perdition,	3 Don't be carried away and deceived regardless of what they say. For that day will not come until two things happen: first, there will be a time of great rebellion against God, and then the man of rebellion will come—the son of hell.
4 Who opposeth and exalteth himself above all that is called God, or that is worshipped; so that he as God sitteth in the temple of God, shewing himself that he is God.	4 who opposes and exalts himself above all that is called God or that is worshiped, so that he sits as God in the temple of God, showing himself that he is God.	4 He will defy every god there is, and tear down every other object of adoration and worship. He will go in and sit as God in the temple of God, claiming that he himself is God.

NIV	RSV	TEV
16 For the Lord himself will come down from heaven, with a loud command, with the voice of the archangel and with the trumpet call of God, and the dead in Christ will rise first.	16 For the Lord himself will descend from heaven with a cry of command, with the archangel's call, and with the sound of the trumpet of God. And the dead in Christ will rise first;	16 There will be the shout of command, the archangel's voice, the sound of God's trumpet, and the Lord himself will come down from heaven. Those who have died believing in Christ will rise to life first;
17 After that, we who are still alive and are left will be caught up with them in the clouds to meet the Lord in the air. And so we will be with the Lord forever.	17 then we who are alive, who are left, shall be caught up together with them in the clouds to meet the Lord in the air; and so we shall always be with the Lord.	17 then we who are living at that time will be gathered up along with them in the clouds to meet the Lord in the air. And so we will always be with the Lord.
5:9 For God did not appoint us to suffer wrath but to receive salvation through our Lord Jesus Christ.	5:9 For God has not destined us for wrath, but to obtain salvation through our Lord Jesus Christ,	5:9 God did not choose us to suffer his anger, but to possess salvation through our Lord Jesus Christ,
10 He died for us so that, whether we are awake or asleep, we may live together with him.	10 who died for us so that whether we wake or sleep we might live with him.	10 who died for us in order that we might live together with him, whether we are alive or dead when he comes.
15 Make sure that nobody pays back wrong for wrong, but always try to be kind to each other and to everyone else.	15 See that none of you repays evil for evil, but always seek to do good to one another and to all.	15 See that no one pays back wrong for wrong, but at all times make it your aim to do good to one another and to all people.
16 Be joyful always;	16 Rejoice always,	16 Be joyful always,
17 pray continually;	17 pray constantly,	17 pray at all times,
18 give thanks in all circumstances, for this is God's will for you in Christ Jesus.	18 give thanks in all circumstances; for this is the will of God in Christ Jesus for you.	18 be thankful in all circumstances. This is what God wants from you in your life in union with Christ Jesus.
19 Do not put out the Spirit's fire;	19 Do not quench the Spirit,	19 Do not restrain the Holy Spirit;
20 do not treat prophecies with contempt.	20 do not despise prophesying,	20 do not despise inspired messages.
21 Test everything. Hold on to the good.	21 but test everything; hold fast what is good,	21 Put all things to the test: keep what is good
22 Avoid every kind of evil.	22 abstain from every form of evil.	22 and avoid every kind of evil.
23 May God himself, the God of peace, sanctify you through and through. May your whole spirit, soul and body be kept blameless at the coming of our Lord Jesus Christ.	23 May the God of peace himself sanctify you wholly; and may your spirit and soul and body be kept sound and blameless at the coming of our Lord Jesus Christ.	23 May the God who gives us peace make you holy in every way and keep your whole being—spirit, soul, and body—free from every fault at the coming of our Lord Jesus Christ.
24 The one who calls you is faithful and he will do it.	24 He who calls you is faithful, and he will do it.	24 He who calls you will do it, because he is faithful.

Second Thessalonians

1:3 We ought always to thank God for you, brothers, and rightly so, because your faith is growing more and more, and the love every one of you has for each other is increasing.	1:3 We are bound to give thanks to God always for you, brethren, as is fitting, because your faith is growing abundantly, and the love of every one of you for one another is increasing.	1:3 Our brothers, we must thank God at all times for you. It is right for us to do so, because your faith is growing so much and the love each of you has for the others is becoming greater.
4 Therefore, among God's churches we boast about your perseverance and faith in all the persecutions and trials you are enduring.	4 Therefore we ourselves boast of you in the churches of God for your steadfastness and faith in all your persecutions and in the afflictions which you are enduring.	4 That is why we ourselves boast about you in the churches of God. We boast about the way you continue to endure and believe through all the persecutions and sufferings you are experiencing.
2:1 Concerning the coming of our Lord Jesus Christ and our being gathered to him, we ask you, brothers,	2:1 Now concerning the coming of our Lord Jesus Christ and our assembling to meet him, we beg you, brethren,	2:1 Concerning the coming of our Lord Jesus Christ and our being gathered together to be with him: I beg you, my brothers,
2 not to become easily unsettled or alarmed by some prophecy, report or letter supposed to have come from us, saying that the day of the Lord has already come.	2 not to be quickly shaken in mind or excited, either by spirit or by word, or by letter purporting to be from us, to the effect that the day of the Lord has come.	2 not to be so easily confused in your thinking or upset by the claim that the Day of the Lord has come. Perhaps it is thought that we said this while prophesying or preaching, or that we wrote it in a letter.
3 Don't let anyone deceive you in any way, for that day will not come until the rebellion occurs and the man of lawlessness is revealed, the man doomed to destruction.	3 Let no one deceive you in any way; for that day will not come, unless the rebellion comes first, and the man of lawlessness is revealed, the son of perdition,	3 Do not let anyone deceive you in any way. For the Day will not come until the final Rebellion takes place and the Wicked One appears, who is destined to hell.
4 He opposes and exalts himself over everything that is called God or is worshiped, and even sets himself up in God's temple, proclaiming himself to be God.	4 who opposes and exalts himself against every so-called god or object of worship, so that he takes his seat in the temple of God, proclaiming himself to be God.	4 He will oppose every so-called god or object of worship and will put himself above them all. He will even go in and sit down in God's Temple and claim to be God.

KJV	NKJV	TLB
8 And then shall that Wicked be revealed, whom the Lord shall consume with the spirit of his mouth, and shall destroy with the brightness of his coming:	8 And then the lawless one will be revealed, whom the Lord will consume with the breath of His mouth and destroy with the brightness of His coming.	8 Then this wicked one will appear, whom the Lord Jesus will burn up with the breath of his mouth and destroy by his presence when he returns.
13 But we are bound to give thanks alway to God for you, brethren beloved of the Lord, because God hath from the beginning chosen you to salvation through sanctification of the Spirit and belief of the truth:	13 But we are bound to give thanks to God always for you, brethren beloved by the Lord, because God from the beginning chose you for salvation through sanctification by the Spirit and belief in the truth,	13 But we must forever give thanks to God for you, our brothers loved by the Lord, because God chose from the very first to give you salvation, cleansing you by the work of the Holy Spirit and by your trusting in the Truth.
3:3 But the Lord is faithful, who shall stablish you, and keep *you* from evil.	3:3 But the Lord is faithful, who will establish you and guard *you* from the evil one.	3:3 But the Lord is faithful; he will make you strong and guard you from satanic attacks of every kind.
7 For yourselves know how ye ought to follow us: for we behaved not ourselves disorderly among you;	7 For you yourselves know how you ought to follow us, for we were not disorderly among you;	7 For you well know that you ought to follow our example: you never saw us loafing;
8 Neither did we eat any man's bread for nought; but wrought with labour and travail night and day, that we might not be chargeable to any of you:	8 nor did we eat anyone's bread free of charge, but worked with labor and toil night and day, that we might not be a burden to any of you,	8 we never accepted food from anyone without buying it; we worked hard day and night for the money we needed to live on, in order that we would not be a burden to any of you.
9 Not because we have not power, but to make ourselves an ensample unto you to follow us.	9 not because we do not have authority, but to make ourselves an example of how you should follow us.	9 It wasn't that we didn't have the right to ask you to feed us, but we wanted to show you, firsthand, how you should work for your living.
10 For even when we were with you, this we commanded you, that if any would not work, neither should he eat.	10 For even when we were with you, we commanded you this: If anyone will not work, neither shall he eat.	10 Even while we were still there with you we gave you this rule: "He who does not work shall not eat."
13 But ye, brethren, be not weary in well doing.	13 But *as for* you, brethren, do not grow weary *in* doing good.	13 And to the rest of you I say, dear brothers, never be tired of doing right.

First Timothy

KJV	NKJV	TLB
1:5 This *is* a faithful saying, and worthy of all acceptation, that Christ Jesus came into the world to save sinners; of whom I am chief.	1:15 This *is* a faithful saying and worthy of all acceptance, that Christ Jesus came into the world to save sinners, of whom I am chief.	1:15 How true it is, and how I long that everyone should know it, that Christ Jesus came into the world to save sinners—and I was the greatest of them all.
3:1 This *is* a true saying, If a man desire the office of a bishop, he desireth a good work.	3:1 This *is* a faithful saying: If a man desires the position of a bishop, he desires a good work.	3:1 It is a true saying that if a man wants to be a pastor he has a good ambition.
16 And without controversy great is the mystery of godliness: God was manifest in the flesh, justified in the Spirit, seen of angels, preached unto the Gentiles, believed on in the world, received up into glory.	16 And without controversy great is the mystery of godliness: God was manifested in the flesh, Justified in the Spirit, Seen by angels, Preached among the Gentiles, Believed on in the world, Received up in glory.	16 It is quite true that the way to live a godly life is not an easy matter. But the answer lies in Christ, who came to earth as a man, was proved spotless and pure in his Spirit, was served by angels, was preached among the nations, was accepted by men everywhere and was received up again to his glory in heaven.
4:12 Let no man despise thy youth; but be thou an example of the believers, in word, in conversation, in charity, in spirit, in faith, in purity.	4:12 Let no one despise your youth, but be an example to the believers in word, in conduct, in love, in spirit, in faith, in purity.	4:12 Don't let anyone think little of you because you are young. Be their ideal; let them follow the way you teach and live; be a pattern for them in your love, your faith, and your clean thoughts.
5:4 But if any widow have children or nephews, let them learn first to shew piety at home, and to requite their parents: for that is good and acceptable before God.	5:4 But if any widow has children or grandchildren, let them first learn to show piety at home and to repay their parents; for this is good and acceptable before God.	5:4 But if they have children or grandchildren, these are the ones who should take the responsibility, for kindness should begin at home, supporting needy parents. This is something that pleases God very much.
8 But if any provide not for his own, and specially for those of his own house, he hath denied the faith, and is worse than an infidel.	8 But if anyone does not provide for his own, and especially for those of his household, he has denied the faith and is worse than an unbeliever.	8 But anyone who won't care for his own relatives when they need help, especially those living in his own family, has no right to say he is a Christian. Such a person is worse than the heathen.
6:6 But godliness with contentment is great gain.	6:6 But godliness with contentment is great gain.	6:6 Do you want to be truly rich? You already are if you are happy and good.
7 For we brought nothing into *this* world, *and it is* certain we can carry nothing out.	7 For we brought nothing into *this* world, *and it is* certain we can carry nothing out.	7 After all, we didn't bring any money with us when we came into the world, and we can't carry away a single penny when we die.
8 And having food and raiment let us be therewith content.	8 And having food and clothing, with these we shall be content.	8 So we should be well satisfied without money if we have enough food and clothing.

NIV	RSV	TEV
8 And then the lawless one will be revealed, whom the Lord Jesus will overthrow with the breath of his mouth and destroy by the splendor of his coming.	8 And then the lawless one will be revealed, and the Lord Jesus will slay him with the breath of his mouth and destroy him by his appearing and his coming.	8 Then the Wicked One will be revealed, but when the Lord Jesus comes, he will kill him with the breath from his mouth and destroy him with his dazzling presence.
13 But we ought always to thank God for you, brothers loved by the Lord, because from the beginning God chose you to be saved through the sanctifying work of the Spirit and through belief in the truth.	13 But we are bound to give thanks to God always for you, brethren beloved by the Lord, because God chose you from the beginning to be saved through sanctification by the Spirit and belief in the truth.	13 We must thank God at all times for you, brothers, you whom the Lord loves. For God chose you as the first to be saved by the Spirit's power to make you his holy people and by your faith in the truth.
3:3 But the Lord is faithful, and he will strengthen and protect you from the evil one.	3:3 But the Lord is faithful; he will strengthen you and guard you from evil.	3:3 But the Lord is faithful, and he will strengthen you and keep you safe from the Evil One.
7 For you yourselves know how you ought to follow our example. We were not idle when we were with you,	7 For you yourselves know how you ought to imitate us; we were not idle when we were with you,	7 You yourselves know very well that you should do just what we did. We were not lazy when we were with you.
8 nor did we eat anyone's food without paying for it. On the contrary, we worked night and day, laboring and toiling so that we would not be a burden to any of you.	8 we did not eat any one's bread without paying, but with toil and labor we worked night and day, that we might not burden any of you.	8 We did not accept anyone's support without paying for it. Instead, we worked and toiled; we kept working day and night so as not to be an expense to any of you.
9 We did this, not because we do not have the right to such help, but in order to make ourselves a model for you to follow.	9 It was not because we have not that right, but to give you in our conduct an example to imitate.	9 We did this, not because we do not have the right to demand our support; we did it to be an example for you to follow.
10 For even when we were with you, we gave you this rule: "If a man will not work, he shall not eat."	10 For even when we were with you, we gave you this command: If any one will not work, let him not eat.	10 While we were with you, we used to tell you, "Whoever refuses to work is not allowed to eat."
13 And as for you, brothers, never tire of doing what is right.	13 Brethren, do not be weary in well-doing.	13 But you, brothers, must not become tired of doing good.

First Timothy

NIV	RSV	TEV
1:15 Here is a trustworthy saying that deserves full acceptance: Christ Jesus came into the world to save sinners—of whom I am the worst.	1:15 The saying is sure and worthy of full acceptance, that Christ Jesus came into the world to save sinners. And I am the foremost of sinners;	1:15 This is a true saying, to be completely accepted and believed: Christ Jesus came into the world to save sinners. I am the worst of them.
3:1 Here is a trustworthy saying: If anyone sets his heart on being an overseer, he desires a noble task.	3:1 The saying is sure: If any one aspires to the office of bishop, he desires a noble task.	3:1 This is a true saying: If a man is eager to be a church leader, he desires an excellent work.
16 Beyond all question, the mystery of godliness is great: He appeared in a body, was vindicated by the Spirit, was seen by angels, was preached among the nations, was believed on in the world, was taken up in glory.	16 Great indeed, we confess, is the mystery of our religion: He was manifested in the flesh, vindicated in the Spirit, seen by angels, preached among the nations, believed on in the world, taken up in glory.	16 No one can deny how great is the secret of our religion: He appeared in human form, was shown to be right by the Spirit, and was seen by angels. He was preached among the nations, was believed in throughout the world, and was taken up to heaven.
4:12 Don't let anyone look down on you because you are young, but set an example for the believers in speech, in life, in love, in faith and in purity.	4:12 Let no one despise your youth, but set the believers an example in speech and conduct, in love, in faith, in purity.	4:12 Do not let anyone look down on you because you are young, but be an example for the believers in your speech, your conduct, your love, faith, and purity.
5:4 But if a widow has children or grandchildren, these should learn first of all to put their religion into practice by caring for their own family and so repaying their parents and grandparents, for this is pleasing to God.	5:4 If a widow has children or grandchildren, let them first learn their religious duty to their own family and make some return to their parents; for this is acceptable in the sight of God.	5:4 But if a widow has children or grandchildren, they should learn first to carry out their religious duties toward their own family and in this way repay their parents and grandparents, because that is what pleases God.
8 If anyone does not provide for his relatives, and especially for his immediate family, he has denied the faith and is worse than an unbeliever.	8 If any one does not provide for his relatives, and especially for his own family, he has disowned the faith and is worse than an unbeliever.	8 But if anyone does not take care of his relatives, especially the members of his own family, he has denied the faith and is worse than an unbeliever.
6:6 But godliness with contentment is great gain.	6:6 There is great gain in godliness with contentment;	6:6 Well, religion does make a person very rich, if he is satisfied with what he has.
7 For we brought nothing into the world, and we can take nothing out of it.	7 for we brought nothing into the world, and we cannot take anything out of the world;	7 What did we bring into the world? Nothing! What can we take out of the world? Nothing!
8 But if we have food and clothing, we will be content with that.	8 but if we have food and clothing, with these we shall be content.	8 So then, if we have food and clothes, that should be enough for us.

KJV	NKJV	TLB
9 But they that will be rich fall into temptation and a snare, and *into* many foolish and hurtful lusts, which drown men in destruction and perdition.	9 But those who desire to be rich fall into temptation and a snare, and *into* many foolish and harmful lusts which drown men in destruction and perdition.	9 But people who long to be rich soon begin to do all kinds of wrong things to get money, things that hurt them and make them evil-minded and finally send them to hell itself.
10 For the love of money is the root of all evil: which while some coveted after, they have erred from the faith, and pierced themselves through with many sorrows.	10 For the love of money is a root of all *kinds of* evil, for which some have strayed from the faith in their greediness, and pierced themselves through with many sorrows.	10 For the love of money is the first step toward all kinds of sin. Some people have even turned away from God because of their love for it, and as a result have pierced themselves with many sorrows.

Second Timothy

KJV	NKJV	TLB
1:7 For God hath not given us the spirit of fear; but of power, and of love, and of a sound mind.	1:7 For God has not given us a spirit of fear, but of power and of love and of a sound mind.	1:7 For the Holy Spirit, God's gift, does not want you to be afraid of people, but to be wise and strong, and to love them and enjoy being with them.
2:13 If we believe not, *yet* he abideth faithful: he cannot deny himself.	2:13 If we are faithless, He remains faithful; He cannot deny Himself.	2:13 Even when we are too weak to have any faith left, he remains faithful to us and will help us, for he cannot disown us who are part of himself, and he will always carry out his promises to us.
19 Nevertheless the foundation of God standeth sure, having this seal, The Lord knoweth them that are his. And, Let every one that nameth the name of Christ depart from iniquity.	19 Nevertheless the solid foundation of God stands, having this seal: "The Lord knows those who are His," and, "Let everyone who names the name of Christ depart from iniquity."	19 But God's truth stands firm like a great rock, and nothing can shake it. It is a foundation stone with these words written on it: "The Lord knows those who are really his," and "A person who calls himself a Christian should not be doing things that are wrong."
24 And the servant of the Lord must not strive; but be gentle unto all *men*, apt to teach, patient,	24 And a servant of the Lord must not quarrel but be gentle to all, able to teach, patient,	24 God's people must not be quarrelsome; they must be gentle, patient teachers of those who are wrong.
25 In meekness instructing those that oppose themselves; if God peradventure will give them repentance to the acknowledging of the truth;	25 in humility correcting those who are in opposition, if God perhaps will grant them repentance, so that they may know the truth,	25 Be humble when you are trying to teach those who are mixed up concerning the truth. For if you talk meekly and courteously to them they are more likely, with God's help, to turn away from their wrong ideas and believe what is true.
26 And *that* they may recover themselves out of the snare of the devil, who are taken captive by him at his will.	26 and *that* they may come to their senses *and escape* the snare of the devil, having been taken captive by him to *do* his will.	26 Then they will come to their senses and escape from Satan's trap of slavery to sin which he uses to catch them whenever he likes, and then they can begin doing the will of God.
3:16 All scripture *is* given by inspiration of God, and *is* profitable for doctrine, for reproof, for correction, for instruction in righteousness:	3:16 All Scripture *is* given by inspiration of God, and *is* profitable for doctrine, for reproof, for correction, for instruction in righteousness,	3:16 The whole Bible was given to us by inspiration from God and is useful to teach us what is true and to make us realize what is wrong in our lives; it straightens us out and helps us do what is right.
17 That the man of God may be perfect, throughly furnished unto all good works.	17 that the man of God may be complete, thoroughly equipped for every good work.	17 It is God's way of making us well prepared at every point, fully equipped to do good to everyone.
4:7 I have fought a good fight, I have finished *my* course, I have kept the faith:	4:7 I have fought the good fight, I have finished the race, I have kept the faith.	4:7 I have fought long and hard for my Lord, and through it all I have kept true to him. And now the time has come for me to stop fighting and rest.
8 Henceforth there is laid up for me a crown of righteousness, which the Lord, the righteous judge, shall give me at that day: and not to me only, but unto all them also that love his appearing.	8 Finally, there is laid up for me the crown of righteousness, which the Lord, the righteous Judge, will give to me on that Day, and not to me only but also to all who have loved His appearing.	8 In heaven a crown is waiting for me which the Lord, the righteous Judge, will give me on that great day of his return. And not just to me, but to all those whose lives show that they are eagerly looking forward to his coming back again.

Titus

KJV	NKJV	TLB
1:15 Unto the pure all things *are* pure: but unto them that are defiled and unbelieving *is* nothing pure; but even their mind and conscience is defiled.	1:15 To the pure all things are pure, but to those who are defiled and unbelieving nothing is pure; but even their mind and conscience are defiled.	1:15 A person who is pure of heart sees goodness and purity in everything; but a person whose own heart is evil and untrusting finds evil in everything, for his dirty mind and rebellious heart color all he sees and hears.
2:11 For the grace of God that bringeth salvation hath appeared to all men,	2:11 For the grace of God that brings slavation has appeared to all men,	2:11 For the free gift of eternal salvation is now being offered to everyone;
12 Teaching us that, denying ungodliness and worldly lusts, we should live soberly, righteously, and godly, in this present world;	12 teaching us that, denying ungodliness and worldy lusts, we should live soberly, righteously, and godly in the present age,	12 and along with this gift comes the realization that God wants us to turn from godless living and sinful pleasures and to live good, God-fearing lives day after day,
13 Looking for that blessed hope, and the glorious appearing of the great God and our Saviour Jesus Christ;	13 looking for the blessed hope and glorious appearing of our great God and Savior Jesus Christ,	13 looking forward to that wonderful time we've been expecting, when his glory shall be seen—the glory of our great God and Savior Jesus Christ.

NIV	RSV	TEV
9 People who want to get rich fall into temptation and a trap and into many foolish and harmful desires that plunge men into ruin and destruction.	9 But those who desire to be rich fall into temptation, into a snare, into many senseless and hurtful desires that plunge men into ruin and destruction.	9 But those who want to get rich fall into temptation and are caught in the trap of many foolish and harmful desires, which pull them down to ruin and destruction.
10 For the love of money is a root of all kinds of evil. Some people, eager for money, have wandered from the faith and pierced themselves with many griefs.	10 For the love of money is the root of all evils; it is through this craving that some have wandered away from the faith and pierced their hearts with many pangs.	10 For the love of money is a source of all kinds of evil. Some have been so eager to have it that they have wandered away from the faith and have broken their hearts with many sorrows.

Second Timothy

NIV	RSV	TEV
1:7 For God did not give us a spirit of timidity, but a spirit of power, of love and of self-discipline.	**1:7** for God did not give us a spirit of timidity but a spirit of power and love and self-control.	**1:7** For the Spirit that God has given us does not make us timid; instead, his Spirit fills us with power, love, and self-control.
2:13 if we are faithless, he will remain faithful, for he cannot disown himself.	**2:13** if we are faithless, he remains faithful— for he cannot deny himself.	**2:13** If we are not faithful, he remains faithful, because he cannot be false to himself."
19 Nevertheless, God's solid foundation stands firm, sealed with this inscription: "The Lord knows those who are his," and, "Everyone who confesses the name of the Lord must turn away from wickedness."	19 But God's firm foundation stands, bearing this seal: "The Lord knows those who are his," and, "Let every one who names the name of the Lord depart from iniquity."	19 But the solid foundation that God has laid cannot be shaken; and on it are written these words: "The Lord knows those who are his" and "Whoever says that he belongs to the Lord must turn away from wrongdoing."
24 And the Lord's servant must not quarrel; instead, he must be kind to everyone, able to teach, not resentful.	24 And the Lord's servant must not be quarrelsome but kindly to every one, an apt teacher, forbearing,	24 The Lord's servant must not quarrel. He must be kind toward all, a good and patient teacher,
25 Those who oppose him he must gently instruct, in the hope that God will grant them repentance leading them to a knowledge of the truth,	25 correcting his opponents with gentleness. God may perhaps grant that they will repent and come to know the truth,	25 who is gentle as he corrects his opponents, for it may be that God will give them the opportunity to repent and come to know the truth.
26 and that they will come to their senses and escape from the trap of the devil, who has taken them captive to do his will.	26 and they may escape from the snare of the devil, after being captured by him to do his will.	26 And then they will come to their senses and escape from the trap of the Devil, who had caught them and made them obey his will.
3:16 All Scripture is God-breathed and is useful for teaching, rebuking, correcting and training in righteousness,	**3:16** All scripture is inspired by God and profitable for teaching, for reproof, for correction, and for training in righteousness,	**3:16** All Scripture is inspired by God and is useful for teaching the truth, rebuking error, correcting faults, and giving instruction for right living,
17 so that the man of God may be thoroughly equipped for every good work.	17 that the man of God may be complete, equipped for every good work.	17 so that the person who serves God may be fully qualified and equipped to do every kind of good deed.
4:7 I have fought the good fight, I have finished the race, I have kept the faith.	**4:7** I have fought the good fight, I have finished the race, I have kept the faith.	**4:7** I have done my best in the race, I have run the full distance, and I have kept the faith.
8 Now there is in store for me the crown of righteousness, which the Lord, the righteous Judge, will award to me on that day—and not only to me, but also to all who have longed for his appearing.	8 Henceforth there is laid up for me the crown of righteousness, which the Lord, the righteous judge, will award to me on that Day, and not only to me but also to all who have loved his appearing.	8 And now there is waiting for me the prize of victory awarded for a righteous life, the prize which the Lord, the righteous Judge, will give me on that Day—and not only to me, but to all those who wait with love for him to appear.

Titus

NIV	RSV	TEV
1:15 To the pure, all things are pure, but to those who are corrupted and do not believe, nothing is pure. In fact, both their minds and consciences are corrupted.	**1:15** To the pure all things are pure, but to the corrupt and unbelieving nothing is pure; their very minds and consciences are corrupted.	**1:15** Everything is pure to those who are themselves pure; but nothing is pure to those who are defiled and unbelieving, for their minds and consciences have been defiled.
2:11 For the grace of God that brings salvation has appeared to all men.	**2:11** For the grace of God has appeared for the salvation of all men,	**2:11** For God has revealed his grace for the salvation of all mankind.
12 It teaches us to say "No" to ungodliness and worldly passions, and to live self-controlled, upright and godly lives in this present age,	12 training us to renounce irreligion and worldly passions, and to live sober, upright, and godly lives in this world,	12 That grace instructs us to give up ungodly living and worldly passions, and to live self-controlled, upright, and godly lives in this world,
13 while we wait for the blessed hope—the glorious appearing of our great God and Savior, Jesus Christ,	13 awaiting our blessed hope, the appearing of the glory of our great God and Savior Jesus Christ,	13 as we wait for the blessed Day we hope for, when the glory of our great God and Savior Jesus Christ will appear.

KJV	NKJV	TLB
14 Who gave himself for us, that he might redeem us from all iniquity, and purify unto himself a peculiar people, zealous of good works.	14 who gave Himself for us, that He might redeem us from every lawless deed and purify for Himself *His* own special people, zealous for good works.	14 He died under God's judgment against our sins, so that he could rescue us from constant falling into sin and make us his very own people, with cleansed hearts and real enthusiasm for doing kind things for others.
3:5 Not by works of righteousness which we have done, but according to his mercy he saved us, by the washing of regeneration, and renewing of the Holy Ghost;	3:5 not by works of righteousness which we have done, but according to His mercy He saved us, through the washing of regeneration and renewing of the Holy Spirit,	3:5 then he saved us—not because we were good enough to be saved, but because of his kindness and pity—by washing away our sins and giving us the new joy of the indwelling Holy Spirit

Philemon

10 I beseech thee for my son Onesimus, whom I have begotten in my bonds:	10 I appeal to you for my son Onesimus, whom I have begotten *while* in my chains,	10 My plea is that you show kindness to my child Onesimus, whom I won to the Lord while here in my chains.
15 For perhaps he therefore departed for a season, that thou shouldest receive him for ever;	15 For perhaps he departed for a while for this *purpose,* that you might receive him forever,	15 Perhaps you could think of it this way: that he ran away from you for a little while so that now he can be yours forever,
16 Not now as a servant, but above a servant, a brother beloved, specially to me, but how much more unto thee, both in the flesh, and in the Lord?	16 no longer as a slave but more than a slave, *as* a beloved brother, especially to me but how much more to you, both in the flesh and in the Lord.	16 no longer only a slave, but something much better—a beloved brother, especially to me. Now he will mean much more to you too, because he is not only a servant but also your brother in Christ.

Hebrews

1:1 God, who at sundry times and in divers manners spake in time past unto the fathers by the prophets,	1:1 God, who at various times and in different ways spoke in time past to the fathers by the prophets,	1:1 Long ago God spoke in many different ways to our fathers through the prophets [in visions, dreams, and even face to face], telling them little by little about his plans.
2 Hath in these last days spoken unto us by *his* Son, whom he hath appointed heir of all things, by whom also he made the worlds;	2 has in these last days spoken to us by *His* Son, whom He has appointed heir of all things, through whom also He made the worlds;	2 But now in these days he has spoken to us through his Son to whom he has given everything, and through whom he made the world and everything there is.
2:9 But we see Jesus, who was made a little lower than the angels for the suffering of death, crowned with glory and honour; that he by the grace of God should taste death for every man.	2:9 But we see Jesus, who was made a little lower than the angels, for the suffering of death crowned with glory and honor, that He, by the grace of God, might taste death for everyone.	2:9 but we do see Jesus—who for awhile was a little lower than the angels—crowned now by God with glory and honor because of God's great kindness, Jesus tasted death for everyone in all the world.
18 For in that he himself hath suffered being tempted, he is able to succour them that are tempted.	18 For in that He Himself has suffered, being tempted, He is able to aid those who are tempted.	18 For since he himself has now been through suffering and temptation, he knows what it is like when we suffer and are tempted, and he is wonderfully able to help us.
4:9 There remaineth therefore a rest to the people of God.	4:9 There remains therefore a rest for the people of God.	4:9 So there is a full complete rest *still waiting* for the people of God.
10 For he that is entered into his rest, he also hath ceased from his own works, as God *did* from his.	10 For he who has entered His rest has himself also ceased from his works as God *did* from His.	10 Christ has already entered there. He is resting from his work, just as God did after the creation.
12 For the word of God *is* quick, and powerful, and sharper than any twoedged sword, piercing even to the dividing asunder of soul and spirit, and of the joints and marrow, and *is* a discerner of the thoughts and intents of the heart.	12 For the word of God *is* living and powerful, and sharper than any twoedged sword, piercing even to the division of soul and spirit, and of joints and marrow, and is a discerner of the thoughts and intents of the heart.	12 For whatever God says to us is full of living power: it is sharper than the sharpest dagger, cutting swift and deep into our innermost thoughts and desires with all their parts, exposing us for what we really are.
15 For we have not an high priest which cannot be touched with the feeling of our infirmities; but was in all points tempted like as *we are,* yet without sin.	15 For we do not have a High Priest who cannot sympathize with our weaknesses, but was in all *points* tempted as *we are,* yet without sin.	15 This High Priest of ours understands our weaknesses, since he had the same temptations we do, though he never once gave way to them and sinned.
16 Let us therefore come boldly unto the throne of grace, that we may obtain mercy, and find grace to help in time of need.	16 Let us therefore come boldly to the throne of grace, that we may obtain mercy and find grace to help in time of need.	16 So let us come boldly to the very throne of God and stay there to receive his mercy and to find grace to help us in our times of need.
5:12 For when for the time ye ought to be teachers, ye have need that one teach you again which *be* the first principles of the oracles of God; and are become such as have need of milk, and not of strong meat.	5:12 For though by this time you ought to be teachers, you need *someone* to teach you again the first principles of the oracles of God; and you have come to need milk and not solid food.	5:12 You have been Christians a long time now, and you ought to be teaching others, but instead you have dropped back to the place where you need someone to teach you all over again the very first principles in God's Word. You are like babies who can drink only milk, not old enough for solid food.

NIV	RSV	TEV
14 who gave himself for us to redeem us from all wickedness and to purify for himself a people that are his very own, eager to do what is good.	14 who gave himself for us to redeem us from all iniquity and to purify for himself a people of his own who are zealous for good deeds.	14 He gave himself for us, to rescue us from all wickedness and to make us a pure people who belong to him alone and are eager to do good.
3:5 he saved us, not because of righteous things we had done, but because of his mercy. He saved us through the washing of rebirth and renewal by the Holy Spirit,	3:5 he saved us, not because of deeds done by us in righteousness, but in virtue of his own mercy, by the washing of regeneration and renewal in the Holy Spirit,	3:5 he saved us. It was not because of any good deeds that we ourselves had done, but because of his own mercy that he saved us, through the Holy Spirit, who gives us new birth and new life by washing us.

Philemon

NIV	RSV	TEV
10 I appeal to you for my son Onesimus, who became my son while I was in chains.	10 I appeal to you for my child, Onesimus, whose father I have become in my imprisonment.	10 So I make a request to you on behalf of Onesimus, who is my own son in Christ; for while in prison I have become his spiritual father.
15 Perhaps the reason he was separated from you for a little while was that you might have him back for good—	15 Perhaps this is why he was parted from you for a while, that you might have him back for ever,	15 It may be that Onesimus was away from you for a short time so that you might have him back for all time.
16 no longer as a slave, but better than a slave, as a dear brother. He is very dear to me but even dearer to you, both as a man and as a brother in the Lord.	16 no longer as a slave but more than a slave, as a beloved brother, especially to me but how much more to you, both in the flesh and in the Lord.	16 And now he is not just a slave, but much more than a slave: he is a dear brother in Christ. How much he means to me! And how much more he will mean to you, both as a slave and as a brother in the Lord!

Hebrews

NIV	RSV	TEV
1:1 In the past God spoke to our forefathers through the prophets at many times and in various ways,	1:1 In many and various ways God spoke of old to our fathers by the prophets;	1:1 In the past God spoke to our ancestors many times and in many ways through the prophets,
2 but in these last days he has spoken to us by his Son, whom he appointed heir of all things, and through whom he made the universe.	2 but in these last days he has spoken to us by a Son, whom he appointed the heir of all things, through whom also he created the world.	2 but in these last days he has spoken to us through his Son. He is the one through whom God created the universe, the one whom God has chosen to possess all things at the end.
2:9 But we see Jesus, who was made a little lower than the angels, now crowned with glory and honor because he suffered death, so that by the grace of God he might taste death for everyone.	2:9 But we see Jesus, who for a little while was made lower than the angels, crowned with glory and honor because of the suffering of death, so that by the grace of God he might taste death for every one.	2:9 But we do see Jesus, who for a little while was made lower than the angels, so that through God's grace he should die for everyone. We see him now crowned with glory and honor because of the death he suffered.
18 Because he himself suffered when he was tempted, he is able to help those who are being tempted.	18 For because he himself has suffered and been tempted, he is able to help those who are tempted.	18 And now he can help those who are tempted, because he himself was tempted and suffered.
4:9 There remains, then, a Sabbath-rest for the people of God;	4:9 So then, there remains a sabbath rest for the people of God;	4:9 As it is, however, there still remains for God's people a rest like God's resting on the seventh day.
10 for anyone who enters God's rest also rests from his own work, just as God did from his.	10 for whoever enters God's rest also ceases from his labors as God did from his.	10 For whoever receives that rest which God promised will rest from his own work, just as God rested from his.
12 For the word of God is living and active. Sharper than any double-edged sword, it penetrates even to dividing soul and spirit, joints and marrow; it judges the thoughts and attitudes of the heart.	12 For the word of God is living and active, sharper than any two-edged sword, piercing to the division of soul and spirit, of joints and marrow, and discerning the thoughts and intentions of the heart.	12 The word of God is alive and active, sharper than any double-edged sword. It cuts all the way through, to where soul and spirit meet, to where joints and marrow come together. It judges the desires and thoughts of man's heart.
15 For we do not have a high priest who is unable to sympathize with our weaknesses, but we have one who has been tempted in every way, just as we are—yet was without sin.	15 For we have not a high priest who is unable to sympathize with our weaknesses, but one who in every respect has been tempted as we are, yet without sin.	15 Our High Priest is not one who cannot feel sympathy for our weaknesses. On the contrary, we have a High Priest who was tempted in every way that we are, but did not sin.
16 Let us then approach the throne of grace with confidence, so that we may receive mercy and find grace to help us in our time of need.	16 Let us then with confidence draw near to the throne of grace, that we may receive mercy and find grace to help in time of need.	16 Let us have confidence, then, and approach God's throne, where there is grace. There we will receive mercy and find grace to help us just when we need it.
5:12 In fact, though by this time you ought to be teachers, you need someone to teach you the elementary truths of God's word all over again. You need milk, not solid food!	5:12 For though by this time you ought to be teachers, you need some one to teach you again the first principles of God's word. You need milk, not solid-food;	5:12 There has been enough time for you to be teachers—yet you still need someone to teach you the first lessons of God's message. Instead of eating solid food, you still have to drink milk.

KJV	NKJV	TLB
6:11 And we desire that every one of you do shew the same diligence to the full assurance of hope unto the end:	**6:11** And we desire that each one of you show the same diligence to the full assurance of hope until the end,	**6:11** And we are anxious that you keep right on loving others as long as life lasts, so that you will get your full reward.
12 That ye be not slothful, but followers of them who through faith and patience inherit the promises.	12 that you do not become sluggish, but imitate those who through faith and patience inherit the promises.	12 Then, knowing what lies ahead for you, you won't become bored with being a Christian, nor become spiritually dull and indifferent, but you will be anxious to follow the example of those who receive all that God has promised them because of their strong faith and patience.
7:21 (For those priests were made without an oath; but this with an oath by him that said unto him, The Lord sware and will not repent, Thou *art* a priest for ever after the order of Melchisedec:)	**7:21** (for they have become priests without an oath, but He with an oath by Him who said to Him: "The LORD has sworn And will not relent, 'You *are* a priest forever According to the order of Melchizedek' "),	**7:21** although he never said that of other priests. Only to Christ he said, "The Lord has sworn and will never change his mind: You are a Priest forever, with the rank of Melchizedek."
9:15 And for this cause he is the mediator of the new testament, that by means of death, for the redemption of the transgressions *that were* under the first testament, they which are called might receive the promise of eternal inheritance.	**9:15** And for this reason He is the Mediator of the new covenant, by means of death, for the redemption of the transgressions under the first covenant, that those who are called may receive the promise of the eternal inheritance.	**9:15** Christ came with this new agreement so that all who are invited may come and have forever all the wonders God has promised them. For Christ died to rescue them from the penalty of the sins they had committed while still under that old system.
28 So Christ was once offered to bear the sins of many; and unto them that look for him shall he appear the second time without sin unto salvation.	28 so Christ was offered once to bear the sins of many. To those who eagerly wait for Him He will appear a second time, apart from sin, for salvation.	28 so also Christ died only once as an offering for the sins of many people; and he will come again, but not to deal again with our sins. This time he will come bringing salvation to all those who are eagerly and patiently waiting for him.
10:16 This *is* the covenant that I will make with them after those days, saith the Lord, I will put my laws into their hearts, and in their minds will I write them;	**10:16** "This *is* the covenant that I will make with them after those days, says the LORD: I will put My laws into their hearts, and in their minds I will write them,"	**10:16** "This is the agreement I will make with the people of Israel, though they broke their first agreement: I will write my laws into their minds so that they will always know my will, and I will put my laws in their hearts so that they will want to obey them."
17 And their sins and iniquities will I remember no more.	17 then *He adds,* "Their sins and their lawless deeds I will remember no more."	17 And then he adds, "I will never again remember their sins and lawless deeds."
30 For we know him that hath said, Vengeance *belongeth* unto me, I will recompense, saith the Lord. And again, The Lord shall judge his people.	30 For we know Him who said, "Vengeance is Mine; I will repay, says the Lord." And again, "The LORD will judge His people."	30 For we know him who said, "Justice belongs to me; I will repay them"; who also said, "The Lord himself will handle these cases."
38 Now the just shall live by faith: but if *any man* draw back, my soul shall have no pleasure in him.	38 Now the just shall live by faith; But if anyone draws back, My soul has no pleasure in him."	38 And those whose faith has made them good in God's sight must live by faith, trusting him in everything. Otherwise, if they shrink back, God will have no pleasure in them.
11:1 Now faith is the substance of things hoped for, the evidence of things not seen.	**11:1** Now faith is the substance of things hoped for, the evidence of things not seen.	**11:1** What is faith? It is the confident assurance that something we want is going to happen. It is the certainty that what we hope for is waiting for us, even though we cannot see it up ahead.
16 But now they desire a better *country,* that is, an heavenly: wherefore God is not ashamed to be called their God: for he hath prepared for them a city.	16 But now they desire a better, that is, a heavenly *country.* Therefore God is not ashamed to be called their God, for He has prepared a city for them.	16 But they didn't want to. They were living for heaven. And now God is not ashamed to be called their God, for he has made a heavenly city for them.
12:1 Wherefore seeing we also are compassed about with so great a cloud of witnesses, let us lay aside every weight, and the sin which doth so easily beset *us,* and let us run with patience the race that is set before us,	**12:1** Therefore we also, since we are surrounded by so great a cloud of witnesses, lay aside every weight, and the sin which so easily ensnares *us,* and let us run with endurance the race that is set before us,	**12:1** Since we have such a huge crowd of men of faith watching us from the grandstands, let us strip off anything that slows us down or holds us back, and especially those sins that wrap themselves so tightly around our feet and trip us up; and let us run with patience the particular race that God has set before us.
2 Looking unto Jesus the author and finisher of *our* faith; who for the joy that was set before him endured the cross, despising the shame, and is set down at the right hand of the throne of God.	2 looking unto Jesus, the author and finisher of *our* faith, who for the joy that was set before Him endured the cross, despising the shame, and has sat down at the right hand of the throne of God.	2 Keep your eyes on Jesus, our leader and instructor. He was willing to die a shameful death on the cross because of the joy he knew would be his afterwards; and now he sits in the place of honor by the throne of God.
6 For whom the Lord loveth he chasteneth, and scourgeth every son whom he receiveth.	6 For whom the LORD loves He chastens, And scourges every son whom He receives."	6 For when he punishes you, it proves that he loves you. When he whips you it proves you are really his child."

NIV	RSV	TEV
6:11 We want each of you to show this same diligence to the very end, in order to make your hope sure.	**6:11** And we desire each one of you to show the same earnestness in realizing the full assurance of hope until the end,	**6:11** Our great desire is that each of you keep up his eagerness to the end, so that the things you hope for will come true.
12 We do not want you to become lazy, but to imitate those who through faith and patience inherit what has been promised.	12 so that you may not be sluggish, but imitators of those who through faith and patience inherit the promises.	12 We do not want you to become lazy, but to be like those who believe and are patient, and so receive what God has promised.

7:21 but he became a priest with an oath when God said to him:
"The Lord has sworn
  and will not change his mind:
'You are a priest forever.'"
	7:21 Those who formerly became priests took their office without an oath, but this one was addressed with an oath,
	"The Lord has sworn
	  and will not change his mind,
	'Thou art a priest for ever.'"
		7:21 But Jesus became a priest by means of a vow when God said to him,
		"The Lord has made a solemn promise
		  and will not take it back:
		'You will be a priest forever.'"

9:15 For this reason Christ is the mediator of a new covenant, that those who are called may receive the promised eternal inheritance—now that he has died as a ransom to set them free from the sins committed under the first covenant.	**9:15** Therefore he is the mediator of a new covenant, so that those who are called may receive the promised eternal inheritance, since a death has occurred which redeems them from the transgressions under the first covenant.	**9:15** For this reason Christ is the one who arranges a new covenant, so that those who have been called by God may receive the eternal blessings that God has promised. This can be done because there has been a death which sets people free from the wrongs they did while the first covenant was in effect.
28 so Christ was sacrificed once to take away the sins of many people; and he will appear a second time, not to bear sin, but to bring salvation to those who are waiting for him.	28 so Christ, having been offered once to bear the sins of many, will appear a second time, not to deal with sin but to save those who are eagerly waiting for him.	28 In the same manner Christ also was offered in sacrifice once to take away the sins of many. He will appear a second time, not to deal with sin, but to save those who are waiting for him.

10:16 "This is the covenant I will make with them
  after that time, says the Lord.
I will put my laws in their hearts,
  and I will write them on their minds."
	10:16 "This is the covenant that I will make with them
	  after those days, says the Lord:
	I will put my laws on their hearts,
	  and write them on their minds,"
		10:16 "This is the covenant that I will make with them
		  in the days to come, says the Lord:
		I will put my laws in their hearts
		  and write them on their minds."

17 Then he adds:
"Their sins and lawless acts
  I will remember no more."
	17 then he adds,
	"I will remember their sins and their
	  misdeeds no more."
		17 And then he says, "I will not remember their sins and evil deeds any longer."

30 For we know him who said, "It is mine to avenge; I will repay," and again, "The Lord will judge his people."	30 For we know him who said, "Vengeance is mine, I will repay." And again, "The Lord will judge his people."	30 For we know who said, "I will take revenge, I will repay"; and who also said, "The Lord will judge his people."

38 But my righteous one will live by faith.
  And if he shrinks back,
  I will not be pleased with him."
	38 but my righteous one shall live by faith,
	  and if he shrinks back,
	  my soul has no pleasure in him."
		38 My righteous people, however, will believe
		  and live;
		  but if any of them turns back,
		  I will not be pleased with him."

11:1 Now faith is being sure of what we hope for and certain of what we do not see.	**11:1** Now faith is the assurance of things hoped for, the conviction of things not seen.	**11:1** To have faith is to be sure of the things we hope for, to be certain of the things we cannot see.
16 Instead, they were longing for a better country—a heavenly one. Therefore God is not ashamed to be called their God, for he has prepared a city for them.	16 But as it is, they desire a better country, that is, a heavenly one. Therefore God is not ashamed to be called their God, for he has prepared for them a city.	16 Instead, it was a better country they longed for, the heavenly country. And so God is not ashamed for them to call him their God, because he has prepared a city for them.
12:1 Therefore, since we are surrounded by such a great cloud of witnesses, let us throw off everything that hinders and the sin that so easily entangles, and let us run with perseverance the race marked out for us.	**12:1** Therefore, since we are surrounded by so great a cloud of witnesses, let us also lay aside every weight, and sin which clings so closely, and let us run with perseverance the race that is set before us,	**12:1** As for us, we have this large crowd of witnesses around us. So then, let us rid ourselves of everything that gets in the way, and of the sin which holds on to us so tightly, and let us run with determination the race that lies before us.
2 Let us fix our eyes on Jesus, the author and perfecter of our faith, who for the joy set before him endured the cross, scorning its shame, and sat down at the right hand of the throne of God.	2 looking to Jesus the pioneer and perfecter of our faith, who for the joy that was set before him endured the cross, despising the shame, and is seated at the right hand of the throne of God.	2 Let us keep our eyes fixed on Jesus, on whom our faith depends from beginning to end. He did not give up because of the cross! On the contrary, because of the joy that was waiting for him, he thought nothing of the disgrace of dying on the cross, and he is now seated at the right side of God's throne.

6 because the Lord disciplines those he loves,
  and he punishes everyone he accepts as a
  son."
	6 For the Lord disciplines him whom he
	  loves,
	  and chastises every son whom he receives."
		6 Because the Lord corrects everyone he
		  loves,
		  and punishes everyone he accepts as a
		  son."

KJV	NKJV	TLB
7 If ye endure chastening, God dealeth with you as with sons; for what son is he whom the father chasteneth not?	7 If you endure chastening, God deals with you as with sons; for what son is there whom a father does not chasten?	7 Let God train you, for he is doing what any loving father does for his children. Whoever heard of a son who was never corrected?
13:5 *Let your* conversation *be* without covetousness; *and be* content with such things as ye have: for he hath said, I will never leave thee, nor forsake thee.	13:5 *Let your* conduct *be* without covetousness, *and be* content with such things as you have. For He Himself has said, "I will never leave you nor forsake you."	13:5 Stay away from the love of money; be satisfied with what you have. For God has said, "I will never, *never* fail you nor forsake you."
17 Obey them that have the rule over you, and submit yourselves: for they watch for your souls, as they that must give account, that they may do it with joy, and not with grief: for that *is* unprofitable for you.	17 Obey those who rule over you, and be submissive, for they watch out for your souls, as those who must give account. Let them do so with joy and not with grief, for that would be unprofitable for you.	17 Obey your spiritual leaders and be willing to do what they say. For their work is to watch over your souls, and God will judge them on how well they do this. Give them reason to report joyfully about you to the Lord and not with sorrow, for then you will suffer for it too.

James

KJV	NKJV	TLB
1:2 My brethren, count it all joy when ye fall into divers temptations;	1:2 My brethren, count it all joy when you fall into various trials,	1:2 Dear brothers, is your life full of difficulties and temptations? Then be happy,
3 Knowing *this*, that the trying of your faith worketh patience.	3 knowing that the testing of your faith produces patience.	3 for when the way is rough, your patience has a chance to grow.
4 But let patience have *her* perfect work, that ye may be perfect and entire, wanting nothing.	4 But let patience have *its* perfect work, that you may be perfect and complete, lacking nothing.	4 So let it grow, and don't try to squirm out of your problems. For when your patience is finally in full bloom, then you will be ready for anything, strong in character, full and complete.
5 If any of you lack wisdom, let him ask of God, that giveth to all *men* liberally, and upbradieth not; and it shall be given him.	5 If any of you lacks wisdom, let him ask of God, who gives to all liberally and without reproach, and it will be given to him.	5 If you want to know what God wants you to do, ask him, and he will gladly tell you, for he is always ready to give a bountiful supply of wisdom to all who ask him; he will not resent it.
12 Blessed *is* the man that endureth temptation: for when he is tried, he shall receive the crown of life, which the Lord hath promised to them that love him.	12 Blessed *is* the man who endures temptation; for when he has been proved, he will receive the crown of life which the Lord has promised to those who love Him.	12 Happy is the man who doesn't give in and do wrong when he is tempted, for afterwards he will get as his reward the crown of life that God has promised those who love him.
13 Let no man say when he is tempted, I am tempted of God: for God cannot be tempted with evil, neither tempteth he any man:	13 Let no one say when he is tempted, "I am tempted by God"; for God cannot be tempted by evil, nor does He Himself tempt anyone.	13 And remember, when someone wants to do wrong it is never God who is tempting him, for God never wants to do wrong and never tempts anyone else to do it.
14 But every man is tempted, when he is drawn away of his own lust, and enticed.	14 But each one is tempted when he is drawn away by his own desires and enticed.	14 Temptation is the pull of man's own evil thoughts and wishes.
19 Wherefore, my beloved brethren, let every man be swift to hear, slow to speak, slow to wrath:	19 Therefore, my beloved brethren, let every man be swift to hear, slow to speak, slow to wrath;	19 Dear brothers, don't ever forget that it is best to listen much, speak little, and not become angry;
20 For the wrath of man worketh not the righteousness of God.	20 for the wrath of man does not produce the righteousness of God.	20 for anger doesn't make us good, as God demands that we must be.
21 Wherefore lay apart all filthiness and superfluity of naughtiness, and receive with meekness the engrafted word, which is able to save your souls.	21 Therefore lay aside all filthiness and overflow of wickedness, and receive with meekness the implanted word, which is able to save your souls.	21 So get rid of all that is wrong in your life, both inside and outside, and humbly be glad for the wonderful message we have received, for it is able to save our souls as it takes hold of our hearts.
25 But whoso looketh into the perfect law of liberty, and continueth *therein*, he being not a forgetful hearer, but a doer of the work, this man shall be blessed in his deed.	25 But he who looks into the perfect law of liberty and continues *in it*, and is not a forgetful hearer but a doer of the work, this one will be blessed in what he does.	25 But if anyone keeps looking steadily into God's law for free men, he will not only remember it but he will do what it says, and God will greatly bless him in everything he does.
27 Pure religion and undefiled before God and the Father is this, To visit the fatherless and widows in their affliction, *and* to keep himself unspotted from the world.	27 Pure and undefiled religion before God and the Father is this: to visit orphans and widows in their trouble, *and* to keep oneself unspotted from the world.	27 The Christian who is pure and without fault, from God the Father's point of view, is the one who takes care of orphans and widows, and who remains true to the Lord—not soiled and dirtied by his contacts with the world.
2:5 Hearken, my beloved brethren, Hath not God chosen the poor of this world rich in faith, and heirs of the kingdom which he hath promised to them that love him?	2:5 Listen, my beloved brethren: Has God not chosen the poor of this world *to be* rich in faith and heirs of the kingdom which He promised to those who love Him?	2:5 Listen to me, dear brothers: God has chosen poor people to be rich in faith, and the Kingdom of Heaven is theirs, for that is the gift God has promised to all those who love him.
15 If a brother or sister be naked, and destitute of daily food,	15 If a brother or sister is naked and destitute of daily food,	15 If you have a friend who is in need of food and clothing,

NIV	RSV	TEV
7 Endure hardship as discipline; God is treating you as sons. For what son is not disciplined by his father?	7 It is for discipline that you have to endure. God is treating you as sons; for what son is there whom his father does not discipline?	7 Endure what you suffer as being a father's punishment; your suffering shows that God is treating you as his sons. Was there ever a son who was not punished by his father?
13:5 Keep your lives free from the love of money and be content with what you have, because God has said, "Never will I leave you; never will I forsake you."	13:5 Keep your life free from love of money, and be content with what you have; for he has said, "I will never fail you nor forsake you."	13:5 Keep your lives free from the love of money, and be satisfied with what you have. For God has said, "I will never leave you; I will never abandon you."
17 Obey your leaders and submit to their authority. They keep watch over you as men who must give an account. Obey them so that their work will be a joy, not a burden, for that would be of no advantage to you.	17 Obey your leaders and submit to them; for they are keeping watch over your souls, as men who will have to give account. Let them do this joyfully, and not sadly, for that would be of no advantage to you.	17 Obey your leaders and follow their orders. They watch over your souls without resting, since they must give to God an account of their service. If you obey them, they will do their work gladly; if not, they will do it with sadness, and that would be of no help to you.

James

NIV	RSV	TEV
1:2 Consider it pure joy, my brothers, whenever you face trials of many kinds,	1:2 Count it all joy, my brethren, when you meet various trials,	1:2 My brothers, consider yourselves fortunate when all kinds of trials come your way,
3 because you know that the testing of your faith develops perseverance.	3 for you know that the testing of your faith produces steadfastness.	3 for you know that when your faith succeeds in facing such trials, the result is the ability to endure.
4 Perseverance must finish its work so that you may be mature and complete, not lacking anything.	4 And let steadfastness have its full effect, that you may be perfect and complete, lacking in nothing.	4 Make sure that your endurance carries you all the way without failing, so that you may be perfect and complete, lacking nothing.
5 If any of you lacks wisdom, he should ask God, who gives generously to all without finding fault, and it will be given to him.	5 If any of you lacks wisdom, let him ask God, who gives to all men generously and without reproaching, and it will be given to him.	5 But if any of you lacks wisdom, he should pray to God, who will give it to him; because God gives generously and graciously to all.
12 Blessed is the man who perseveres under trial, because when he has stood the test, he will receive the crown of life that God has promised to those who love him.	12 Blessed is the man who endures trial, for when he has stood the test he will receive the crown of life which God has promised to those who love him.	12 Happy is the person who remains faithful under trials, because when he succeeds in passing such a test, he will receive as his reward the life which God has promised to those who love him.
13 When tempted, no one should say, "God is tempting me." For God cannot be tempted by evil, nor does he tempt anyone;	13 Let no one say when he is tempted, "I am tempted by God"; for God cannot be tempted with evil and he himself tempts no one;	13 If a person is tempted by such trials, he must not say, "This temptation comes from God." For God cannot be tempted by evil, and he himself tempts no one.
14 but each one is tempted when, by his own evil desire, he is dragged away and enticed.	14 but each person is tempted when he is lured and enticed by his own desire.	14 But a person is tempted when he is drawn away and trapped by his own evil desire.
19 My dear brothers, take note of this: Everyone should be quick to listen, slow to speak and slow to become angry,	19 Know this, my beloved brethren. Let every man be quick to hear, slow to speak, slow to anger,	19 Remember this, my dear brothers! Everyone must be quick to listen, but slow to speak and slow to become angry.
20 for man's anger does not bring about the righteous life that God desires.	20 for the anger of man does not work the righteousness of God.	20 Man's anger does not achieve God's righteous purpose.
21 Therefore, get rid of all moral filth and the evil that is so prevalent, and humbly accept the word planted in you, which can save you.	21 Therefore put away all filthiness and rank growth of wickedness and receive with meekness the implanted word, which is able to save your souls.	21 So get rid of every filthy habit and all wicked conduct. Submit to God and accept the word that he plants in your hearts, which is able to save you.
25 But the man who looks intently into the perfect law that gives freedom, and continues to do this, not forgetting what he has heard, but doing it—he will be blessed in what he does.	25 But he who looks into the perfect law, the law of liberty, and perseveres, being no hearer that forgets but a doer that acts, he shall be blessed in his doing.	25 But whoever looks closely into the perfect law that sets people free, who keeps on paying attention to it and does not simply listen and then forget it, but puts it into practice—that person will be blessed by God in what he does.
27 Religion that God our Father accepts as pure and faultless is this: to look after orphans and widows in their distress and to keep oneself from being polluted by the world.	27 Religion that is pure and undefiled before God and the Father is this: to visit orphans and widows in their affliction, and to keep oneself unstained from the world.	27 What God the Father considers to be pure and genuine religion is this: to take care of orphans and widows in their suffering and to keep oneself from being corrupted by the world.
2:5 Listen, my dear brothers: Has not God chosen those who are poor in the eyes of the world to be rich in faith and to inherit the kingdom he promised those who love him?	2:5 Listen, my beloved brethren. Has not God chosen those who are poor in the world to be rich in faith and heirs of the kingdom which he has promised to those who love him?	2:5 Listen, my dear brothers! God chose the poor people of this world to be rich in faith and to possess the kingdom which he promised to those who love him.
15 Suppose a brother or sister is without clothes and daily food.	15 If a brother or sister is ill-clad and in lack of daily food,	15 Suppose there are brothers or sisters who need clothes and don't have enough to eat.

KJV	NKJV	TLB
16 And one of you say unto them, Depart in peace, be ye warmed and filled; notwithstanding ye give them not those things which are needful to the body; what *doth it* profit?	16 and one of you says to them, "Depart in peace, be warmed and filled," but you do not give them the things which are needed for the body, what *does it* profit?	16 and you say to him, "Well, good-bye and God bless you; stay warm and eat hearty," and then don't give him clothes or food, what good does that do?
17 Even so faith, if it hath not works, is dead, being alone.	17 Thus also faith by itself, if it does not have works, is dead.	17 So you see, it isn't enough just to have faith. You must also do good to prove that you have it. Faith that doesn't show itself by good works is no faith at all—it is dead and useless.
21 Was not Abraham our father justified by works, when he had offered Isaac his son upon the altar?	21 Was not Abraham our father justified by works when he offered Isaac his son on the altar?	21 Don't you remember that even our father Abraham was declared good because of what he *did*, when he was willing to obey God, even if it meant offering his son Isaac to die on the altar?
22 Seest thou how faith wrought with his works, and by works was faith made perfect?	22 Do you see that faith was working together with his works, and by works faith was made perfect?	22 You see, he was trusting God so much that he was willing to do whatever God told him to; his faith made complete by what he did, by his actions, his good deeds.
3:17 But the wisdom that is from above is first pure, then peaceable, gentle, *and* easy to be intreated, full of mercy and good fruits, without partiality, and without hypocrisy.	3:17 But the wisdom that is from above is first pure, then peaceable, gentle, willing to yield, full of mercy and good fruits, without partiality and without hypocrisy.	3:17 But the wisdom that comes from heaven is first of all pure and full of quiet gentleness. Then it is peace-loving and courteous. It allows discussion and is willing to yield to others; it is full of mercy and good deeds. It is wholehearted and straightforward and sincere.
4:6 But he giveth more grace. Wherefore he saith, God resisteth the proud, but giveth grace unto the humble.	4:6 But He gives more grace. Therefore He says: "God resists the proud, But gives grace to the humble."	4:6 But he gives us more and more strength to stand against all such evil longings. As the Scripture says, God gives strength to the humble, but sets himself against the proud and haughty.
7 Submit yourselves therefore to God. Resist the devil, and he will flee from you.	7 Therefore submit to God. Resist the devil and he will flee from you.	7 So give yourselves humbly to God. Resist the devil and he will flee from you.
8 Draw nigh to God, and he will draw nigh to you. Cleanse *your* hands, *ye* sinners; and purify *your* hearts, *ye* double minded.	8 Draw near to God and He will draw near to you. Cleanse *your* hands, *you* sinners; and purify *your* hearts, *you* double-minded.	8 And when you draw close to God, God will draw close to you. Wash your hands, you sinners, and let your hearts be filled with God alone to make them pure and true to him.
5:8 Be ye also patient; stablish your hearts: for the coming of the Lord draweth nigh.	5:8 You also be patient. Establish your hearts, for the coming of the Lord is at hand.	5:8 Yes, be patient. And take courage, for the coming of the Lord is near.
13 Is any among you afflicted? let him pray. Is any merry? let him sing psalms.	13 Is anyone among you suffering? Let him pray. Is anyone cheerful? Let him sing psalms.	13 Is anyone among you suffering? He should keep on praying about it. And those who have reason to be thankful should continually be singing praises to the Lord.
14 Is any sick among you? let him call for the elders of the church; and let them pray over him, anointing him with oil in the name of the Lord:	14 Is anyone among you sick? Let him call for the elders of the church, and let them pray over him, anointing him with oil in the name of the Lord.	14 Is anyone sick? He should call for the elders of the church and they should pray over him and pour a little oil upon him, calling on the Lord to heal him.
15 And the prayer of faith shall save the sick, and the Lord shall raise him up; and if he have committed sins, they shall be forgiven him.	15 And the prayer of faith will save the sick, and the Lord will raise him up. And if he has committed sins, he will be forgiven.	15 And their prayer, if offered in faith, will heal him, for the Lord will make him well; and if his sickness was caused by some sin, the Lord will forgive him.
16 Confess *your* faults one to another, and pray one for another, that ye may be healed. The effectual fervent prayer of a righteous man availeth much.	16 Confess *your* trespasses to one another, and pray for one another, that you may be healed. The effective, fervent prayer of a righteous man avails much.	16 Admit your faults to one another and pray for each other so that you may be healed. The earnest prayer of a righteous man has great power and wonderful results.

First Peter

KJV	NKJV	TLB
1:3 Blessed *be* the God and Father of our Lord Jesus Christ, which according to his abundant mercy hath begotten us again unto a lively hope by the resurrection of Jesus Christ from the dead.	1:3 Blessed *be* the God and Father of our Lord Jesus Christ, who according to His abundant mercy has begotten us again to a living hope through the resurrection of Jesus Christ from the dead,	1:3 All honor to God, the God and Father of our Lord Jesus Christ; for it is his boundless mercy that has given us the privilege of being born again, so that we are now members of God's own family. Now we live in the hope of eternal life because Christ rose again from the dead.
4 To an inheritance incorruptible and undefiled, and that fadeth not away, reserved in heaven for you,	4 to an inheritance incorruptible and undefiled and that does not fade away, reserved in heaven for you.	4 And God has reserved for his children the priceless gift of eternal life; it is kept in heaven for you, pure and undefiled, beyond the reach of change and decay.
5 Who are kept by the power of God through faith unto salvation ready to be revealed in the last time.	5 who are kept by the power of God through faith for salvation ready to be revealed in the last time.	5 And God, in his mighty power, will make sure that you get there safely to receive it, because you are trusting him. It will be yours in that coming last day for all to see.
6 Wherein ye greatly rejoice, though now for a season, if need be, ye are in heaviness through manifold temptations:	6 In this you greatly rejoice, though now for a little while, if need be, you have been grieved by various trials,	6 So be truly glad! There is wonderful joy ahead, even though the going is rough for a while down here.

NIV	RSV	TEV
16 If one of you says to him, "Go, I wish you well; keep warm and well fed," but does nothing about his physical needs, what good is it?	16 and one of you says to them, "Go in peace, be warmed and filled," without giving them the things needed for the body, what does it profit?	16 What good is there in your saying to them, "God bless you! Keep warm and eat well!"—if you don't give them the necessities of life?
17 In the same way, faith by itself, if it is not accompanied by action, is dead.	17 So faith by itself, if it has no works, is dead.	17 So it is with faith: if it is alone and includes no actions, then it is dead.
21 Was not our ancestor Abraham considered righteous for what he did when he offered his son Isaac on the altar?	21 Was not Abraham our father justified by works, when he offered his son Isaac upon the altar?	21 How was our ancestor Abraham put right with God? It was through his actions, when he offered his son Isaac on the alter.
22 You see that his faith and his actions were working together, and his faith was made complete by what he did.	22 You see that faith was active along with his works, and faith was completed by works,	22 Can't you see? His faith and his actions worked together; his faith was made perfect through his actions.
3:17 But the wisdom that comes from heaven is first of all pure; then peace loving, considerate, submissive, full of mercy and good fruit, impartial and sincere.	3:17 But the wisdom from above is first pure, then peaceable, gentle, open to reason, full of mercy and good fruits, without uncertainty or insincerity.	3:17 But the wisdom from above is pure first of all; it is also peaceful, gentle, and friendly; it is full of compassion and produces a harvest of good deeds; it is free from prejudice and hypocrisy.
4:6 but he gives us more grace? That is why Scripture says: "God opposes the proud but gives grace to the humble."	4:6 But he gives more grace; therefore it says, "God opposes the proud, but gives grace to the humble."	4:6 But the grace that God gives is even stronger. As the scripture says, "God resists the proud, but gives grace to the humble."
7 Submit yourselves, then, to God. Resist the devil, and he will flee from you.	7 Submit yourselves therefore to God. Resist the devil and he will flee from you.	7 So then, submit yourselves to God. Resist the Devil, and he will run away from you.
8 Come near to God and he will come near to you. Wash you hands, you sinners, and purify your hearts, you double-minded.	8 Draw near to God and he will draw near to you. Cleanse your hands, you sinners, and purify your hearts, you men of double mind.	8 Come near to God, and he will come near to you. Wash your hands, you sinners! Purify your hearts, you hypocrites!
5:8 You too, be patient and stand firm, because the Lord's coming is near.	5:8 You also be patient. Establish your hearts, for the coming of the Lord is at hand.	5:8 You also must be patient. Keep your hopes high, for the day of the Lord's coming is near.
13 Is any one of you in trouble? He should pray. Is anyone happy? Let him sing songs of praise.	13 Is any one among you suffering? Let him pray. Is any cheerful? Let him sing praise.	13 Is anyone among you in trouble? He should pray. Is anyone happy? He should sing praises.
14 Is any one of you sick? He should call the elders of the church to pray over him and anoint him with oil in the name of the Lord.	14 Is any among you sick? Let him call for the elders of the church, and let them pray over him, anointing him with oil in the name of the Lord;	14 Is there anyone who is sick? He should send for the church elders, who will pray for him and rub olive oil on him in the name of the Lord.
15 And the prayer offered in faith will make the sick person well; the Lord will raise him up. If he has sinned, he will be forgiven.	15 and the prayer of faith will save the sick man, and the Lord will raise him up; and if he has committed sins, he will be forgiven.	15 This prayer made in faith will heal the sick person; the Lord will restore him to health, and the sins he has committed will be forgiven.
16 Therefore confess your sins to each other and pray for each other so that you may be healed. The prayer of a righteous man is powerful and effective.	16 Therefore confess your sins to one another, and pray for one another, that you may be healed. The prayer of a righteous man has great power in its effects.	16 So then, confess your sins to one another and pray for one another, so that you will be healed. The prayer of a good person has a powerful effect.

First Peter

NIV	RSV	TEV
1:3 Praise be to the God and Father of our Lord Jesus Christ! In his great mercy he has given us new birth into a living hope through the resurrection of Jesus Christ from the dead,	1:3 Blessed be the God and Father of our Lord Jesus Christ! By his great mercy we have been born anew to a living hope through the resurrection of Jesus Christ from the dead,	1:3 Let us give thanks to the God and Father of our Lord Jesus Christ! Because of his great mercy he gave us new life by raising Jesus Christ from death. This fills us with a living hope,
4 and into an inheritance that can never perish, spoil or fade—kept in heaven for you,	4 and to an inheritance which is imperishable, undefiled, and unfading, kept in heaven for you,	4 and so we look forward to possessing the rich blessings that God keeps for his people. He keeps them for you in heaven, where they cannot decay or spoil or fade away.
5 who through faith are shielded by God's power until the coming of the salvation that is ready to be revealed in the last time.	5 who by God's power are guarded through faith for a salvation ready to be revealed in the last time.	5 They are for you, who through faith are kept safe by God's power for the salvation which is ready to be revealed at the end of time.
6 In this you greatly rejoice, though now for a little while you may have had to suffer grief in all kinds of trials.	6 In this you rejoice, though now for a little while you may have to suffer various trials,	6 Be glad about this, even though it may now be necessary for you to be sad for a while because of the many kinds of trials you suffer.

KJV	NKJV	TLB
7 That the trial of your faith, being much more precious than of gold that perisheth, though it be tried with fire, might be found unto praise and honour and glory at the appearing of Jesus Christ:	7 that the genuineness of your faith, *being* much more precious than gold that perishes, though it is tested by fire, may be found to praise, honor, and glory at the revelation of Jesus Christ,	7 These trials are only to test your faith, to see whether or not it is strong and pure. It is being tested as fire tests gold and purifies it—and your faith is far more precious to God than mere gold; so if your faith remains strong after being tried in the test tube of fiery trials, it will bring you much praise and glory and honor on the day of his return.
8 Whom having not seen, ye love; in whom, though now ye see *him* not, yet believing, ye rejoice with joy unspeakable and full of glory:	8 whom having not seen you love. Though now you do not see *Him,* yet believing, you rejoice with joy inexpressible and full of glory,	8 You love him even though you have never seen him; though not seeing him, you trust him; and even now you are happy with the inexpressible joy that comes from heaven itself.
9 Receiving the end of your faith, *even* the salvation of *your* souls.	9 receiving the end of your faith—the salvation of *your* souls.	9 And your further reward for trusting him will be the salvation of your souls.
15 But as he which hath called you is holy, so be ye holy in all manner of conversation;	15 but as He who called you *is* holy, you also be holy in all *your* conduct,	15 But be holy now in everything you do, just as the Lord is holy, who invited you to be his child.
16 Because it is written, Be ye holy; for I am holy.	16 because it is written, "Be holy, for I am holy."	16 He himself has said, "You must be holy, for I am holy."
23 Being born again, not of corruptible seed, but of incorruptible, by the word of God, which liveth and abideth for ever.	23 having been born again, not of corruptible seed but incorruptible, through the word of God which lives and abides forever,	23 For you have a new life. It was not passed on to you from your parents, for the life they gave you will fade away. This new one will last forever, for it comes from Christ, God's ever-living Message to men.
24 For all flesh *is* as grass, and all the glory of man as the flower of grass. The grass withereth, and the flower thereof falleth away:	24 because "All flesh *is* as grass, And all the glory of man as the flower of the grass. The grass withers, And its flower falls away,	24 Yes, our natural lives will fade as grass does when it becomes all brown and dry. All our greatness is like a flower that droops and falls;
25 But the word of the Lord endureth for ever. And this is the word which by the gospel is preached unto you.	25 But the word of the Lord endures forever." Now this is the word which by the gospel was preached to you.	25 but the Word of the Lord will last forever. And his message is the Good News that was preached to you.
2:4 To whom coming, *as unto* a living stone, disallowed indeed of men, but chosen of God, *and* precious,	2:4 Coming to Him *as to* a living stone, rejected indeed by men, but chosen by God *and* precious,	2:4 Come to Christ, who is the living Foundation of Rock upon which God builds; though men have spurned him, he is very precious to God who has chosen him above all others.
5 Ye also, as lively stones, are built up a spiritual house, an holy priesthood, to offer up spiritual sacrifices, acceptable to God by Jesus Christ.	5 you also, as living stones, are being built up a spiritual house, a holy priesthood, to offer up spiritual sacrifices acceptable to God through Jesus Christ.	5 And now you have become living building-stones for God's use in building his house. What's more, you are his holy priests; so come to him—[you who are acceptable to him because of Jesus Christ]—and offer to God those things that please him.
9 But ye *are* a chosen generation, a royal priesthood, an holy nation, a peculiar people; that ye should shew forth the praises of him who hath called you out of darkness into his marvellous light:	9 But you *are* a chosen generation, a royal priesthood, a holy nation, His own special people, that you may proclaim the praises of him who called you out of darkness into His marvelous light;	9 But you are not like that, for you have been chosen by God himself—you are priests of the King, you are holy and pure, you are God's very own—all this so that you may show to others how God called you out of the darkness into his wonderful light.
13 Submit yourselves to every ordinance of man for the Lord's sake: whether it be to the king, as supreme;	13 Therefore submit yourselves to every ordinance of man for the Lord's sake, whether to the king as supreme,	13 For the Lord's sake, obey every law of your government: those of the king as head of the state,
14 Or unto governors, as unto them that are sent by him for the punishment of evildoers, and for the praise of them that do well.	14 or to governors, as to those who are sent by him for the punishment of evildoers and *for the* praise of those who do good.	14 and those of the king's officers, for he has sent them to punish all who do wrong, and to honor those who do right.
15 For so is the will of God, that with well doing ye may put to silence the ignorance of foolish men:	15 For this is the will of God, that by doing good you may put to silence the ignorance of foolish men—	15 It is God's will that your good lives should silence those who foolishly condemn the Gospel without knowing what it can do for them, having never experienced its power.
24 Who his own self bare our sins in his own body on the tree, that we, being dead to sins, should live unto righteousness: by whose stripes ye were healed.	24 who Himself bore our sins in His own body on the tree, that we, having died to sins, might live for righteousness—by whose stripes you were healed.	24 He personally carried the load of our sins in his own body when he died on the cross, so that we can be finished with sin and live a good life from now on. For his wounds have healed ours!
25 For ye were as sheep going astray; but are now returned unto the Shepherd and Bishop of your souls.	25 For you were like sheep going astray, but have now returned to the Shepherd and Overseer of your souls.	25 Like sheep you wandered away from God, but now you have returned to your Shepherd, the Guardian of your souls who keeps you safe from all attacks.
3:1 Likewise, ye wives, *be* in subjection to your own husbands; that, if any obey not the word, they also may without the word be won by the conversation of the wives;	3:1 Likewise *you* wives, *be* submissive to your own husbands, that even if some do not obey the word, they, without a word, may be won by the conduct of their wives,	3:1 Wives, fit in with your husbands' plans; for then if they refuse to listen when you talk to them about the Lord, they will be won by your respectful, pure behavior. Your godly lives will speak to them better than any words.

NIV	RSV	TEV
7 These have come so that your faith—of greater worth than gold, which perishes even though refined by fire—may be proved genuine and may result in praise, glory and honor when Jesus Christ is revealed.	7 so that the genuineness of your faith, more precious than gold which though perishable is tested by fire, may redound to praise and glory and honor at the revelation of Jesus Christ.	7 Their purpose is to prove that your faith is genuine. Even gold, which can be destroyed, is tested by fire; and so your faith, which is much more precious than gold, must also be tested, so that it may endure. Then you will receive praise and glory and honor on the Day when Jesus Christ is revealed.
8 Though you have not seen him, you love him; and even though you do not see him now, you believe in him and are filled with an inexpressible and glorious joy,	8 Without having seen him you love him; though you do not now see him you believe in him and rejoice with unutterable and exalted joy.	8 You love him, although you have not seen him, and you believe in him, although you do not now see him. So you rejoice with a great and glorious joy which words cannot express,
9 for you are receiving the goal of your faith, the salvation of your souls.	9 As the outcome of your faith you obtain the salvation of your souls.	9 because you are receiving the salvation of your souls, which is the purpose of your faith in him.
15 But just as he who called you is holy, so be holy in all you do;	15 but as he who called you is holy, be holy yourselves in all your conduct;	15 Instead, be holy in all that you do, just as God who called you is holy.
16 for it is written: "Be holy, because I am holy."	16 since it is written, "You shall be holy, for I am holy."	16 The scripture says, "Be holy because I am holy."
23 For you have been born again, not of perishable seed, but of imperishable, through the living and enduring word of God.	23 You have been born anew, not of perishable seed but of imperishable, through the living and abiding word of God;	23 For through the living and eternal word of God you have been born again as the children of a parent who is immortal, not mortal.
24 For, "All men are like grass, and all their glory is like the flowers of the field; the grass withers and the flowers fall,"	24 for "All flesh is like grass and all its glory like the flower of grass. The grass withers, and the flower falls,	24 As the scripture says, "All mankind are like grass, and all their glory is like wild flowers. The grass withers, and the flowers fall,
25 but the word of the Lord stands forever." And this is the word that was preached to you.	25 but the word of the Lord abides for ever." That word is the good news which was preached to you.	25 but the word of the Lord remains forever." This word is the Good News that was proclaimed to you.
2:4 As you come to him, the living Stone—rejected by men but chosen by God and precious to him—	2:4 Come to him, to that living stone, rejected by men but in God's sight chosen and precious;	2:4 Come to the Lord, the living stone rejected by man as worthless but chosen by God as valuable.
5 you also, like living stones, are being built into a spiritual house to be a holy priesthood, offering spiritual sacrifices acceptable to God through Jesus Christ.	5 and like living stones be yourselves built into a spiritual house, to be a holy priesthood, to offer spiritual sacrifices acceptable to God through Jesus Christ.	5 Come as living stones, and let yourselves be used in building the spiritual temple, where you will serve as holy priests to offer spiritual and acceptable sacrifices to God through Jesus Christ.
9 But you are a chosen people, a royal priesthood, a holy nation, a people belonging to God, that you may declare the praises of him who called you out of darkness into his wonderful light.	9 But you are a chosen race, a royal priesthood, a holy nation, God's own people, that you may declare the wonderful deeds of him who called you out of darkness into his marvelous light.	9 But you are the chosen race, the King's priests, the holy nation, God's own people, chosen to proclaim the wonderful acts of God, who called you out of darkness into his own marvelous light.
13 Submit yourselves for the Lord's sake to every authority instituted among men: whether to the king, as the supreme authority,	13 Be subject for the Lord's sake to every human institution, whether it be to the emperor as supreme,	13 For the sake of the Lord submit yourselves to every human authority: to the Emperor, who is the supreme authority,
14 or to governors, who are sent by him to punish those who do wrong and to commend those who do right.	14 or to governors as sent by him to punish those who do wrong and to praise those who do right.	14 and to the governors, who have been appointed by him to punish the evildoers and to praise those who do good.
15 For it is God's will that by doing good you should silence the ignorant talk of foolish men.	15 For it is God's will that by doing right you should put to silence the ignorance of foolish men.	15 For God wants you to silence the ignorant talk of foolish people by the good things you do.
24 He himself bore our sins in his body on the tree, so that we might die to sins and live for righteousness; by his wounds you have been healed.	24 He himself bore our sins in his body on the tree, that we might die to sin and live to righteousness. By his wounds you have been healed.	24 Christ himself carried our sins in his body to the cross, so that we might die to sin and live for righteousness. It is by his wounds that you have been healed.
25 For you were like sheep going astray, but now you have returned to the Shepherd and Overseer of your souls.	25 For you were straying like sheep, but have now returned to the Shepherd and Guardian of your souls.	25 You were like sheep that had lost their way, but now you have been brought back to follow the Shepherd and Keeper of your souls.
3:1 Wives, in the same way be submissive to your husbands so that, if any of them do not believe the word, they may be won over without talk by the behavior of their wives,	3:1 Likewise you wives, be submissive to your husbands, so that some, though they do not obey the word, may be won without a word by the behavior of their wives,	3:1 In the same way you wives must submit yourselves to your husbands, so that if any of them do not believe God's word, your conduct will win them over to believe. It will not be necessary for you to say a word,

KJV	NKJV	TLB
7 Likewise, ye husbands, dwell with *them* according to knowledge, giving honour unto the wife, as unto the weaker vessel, and as being heirs together of the grace of life; that your prayers be not hindered.	7 Likewise *you* husbands, dwell with *them* with understanding, giving honor to the wife, as to the weaker vessel, and as *being* heirs together of the grace of life, that your prayers may not be hindered.	7 You husbands must be careful of your wives, being thoughtful of their needs and honoring them as the weaker sex. Remember that you and your wife are partners in receiving God's blessings, and if you don't treat her as you should, your prayers will not get ready answers.
15 But sanctify the Lord God in your hearts: and *be* ready always to *give* an answer to every man that asketh you a reason of the hope that is in you with meekness and fear:	15 But sanctify the Lord God in your hearts, and always *be* ready to *give* a defense to everyone who asks you a reason for the hope that is in you, with meekness and fear	15 Quietly trust yourself to Christ your Lord and if anybody asks why you believe as you do, be ready to tell him, and do it in a gentle and respectful way.
4:12 Beloved, think it not strange concerning the fiery trial which is to try you, as though some strange thing happened unto you:	4:12 Beloved, do not think it strange concerning the fiery trial which is to try you, as though some strange thing happened to you;	4:12 Dear friends, don't be bewildered or surprised when you go through the fiery trials ahead, for this is no strange, unusual thing that is going to happen to you.
13 But rejoice, inasmuch as ye are partakers of Christ's sufferings; that, when his glory shall be revealed, ye may be glad also with exceeding joy.	13 but rejoice to the extent that you partake of Christ's sufferings, that when His glory is revealed, you may also be glad with exceeding joy.	13 Instead, be really glad—because these trials will make you partners with Christ in his suffering, and afterwards you will have the wonderful joy of sharing his glory in that coming day when it will be displayed.
5:6 Humble yourselves therefore under the mighty hand of God, that he may exalt you in due time:	5:6 Therefore humble yourselves under the mighty hand of God, that He may exalt you in due time,	5:6 If you will humble yourselves under the mighty hand of God, in his good time he will lift you up.
7 Casting all your care upon him; for he careth for you.	7 casting all your care upon Him, for He cares for you.	7 Let him have all your worries and cares, for he is always thinking about you and watching everything that concerns you.
8 Be sober, be vigilant; because your adversary the devil, as a roaring lion, walketh about, seeking whom he may devour:	8 Be sober, be vigilant; because your adversary the devil walks about like a roaring lion, seeking whom he may devour.	8 Be careful—watch out for attacks from Satan, your great enemy. He prowls around like a hungry, roaring lion, looking for some victim to tear apart.
9 Whom resist stedfast in the faith, knowing that the same afflictions are accomplished in your brethren that are in the world.	9 Resist him, steadfast in the faith, knowing that the same sufferings are experienced by your brotherhood in the world.	9 Stand firm when he attacks. Trust the Lord; and remember that other Christians all around the world are going through these sufferings too.

Second Peter

KJV	NKJV	TLB
1:5 And beside this, giving all diligence, add to your faith virtue; and to virtue knowledge;	1:5 But also for this very reason, giving all diligence, add to your faith virtue, to virtue knowledge,	1:5 But to obtain these gifts, you need more than faith; you must also work hard to be good, and even that is not enough. For then you must learn to know God better and discover what he wants you to do.
6 And to knowledge temperance; and to temperance patience; and to patience godliness;	6 to knowledge self-control, to self-control perseverance, to perseverance godliness,	6 Next, learn to put aside your own desires so that you will become patient and godly, gladly letting God have his way with you.
7 And to godliness brotherly kindness; and to brotherly kindness charity.	7 to godliness brotherly kindness, and to brotherly kindness love.	7 This will make possible the next step, which is for you to enjoy other people and to like them, and finally you will grow to love them deeply.
8 For if these things be in you, and abound, they make *you that ye shall* neither *be* barren nor unfruitful in the knowledge of our Lord Jesus Christ.	8 For if these things are yours and abound, *you will be* neither barren nor unfruitful in the knowledge of our Lord Jesus Christ.	8 The more you go on in this way, the more you will grow strong spiritually and become fruitful and useful to our Lord Jesus Christ.
20 Knowing this first, that no prophecy of the scripture is of any private interpretation.	20 knowing this first, that no prophecy of Scripture is of any private interpretation,	20 For no prophecy recorded in Scripture was ever thought up by the prophet himself.
21 For the prophecy came not in old time by the will of man: but holy men of God spake *as they were* moved by the Holy Ghost.	21 for prophecy never came by the will of man, but holy men of God spoke *as they were* moved by the Holy Spirit.	21 It was the Holy Spirit within these godly men who gave them true messages from God.
2:20 For if after they have escaped the pollutions of the world through the knowledge of the Lord and Saviour Jesus Christ, they are again entangled therein, and overcome, the latter end is worse with them than the beginning.	2:20 For if, after they have escaped the pollutions of the world through the knowledge of the Lord and Savior Jesus Christ, they are again entangled in them and overcome, the latter end is worse for them than the beginning.	2:20 And when a person has escaped from the wicked ways of the world by learning about our Lord and Savior Jesus Christ, and then gets tangled up with sin and becomes its slave again, he is worse off than he was before.
21 For it had been better for them not to have known the way of righteousness, than, after they have known *it,* to turn from the holy commandment delivered unto them.	21 For it would have been better for them not to have known the way of righteousness, than having known *it,* to turn from the holy commandment delivered to them.	21 It would be better if he had never known about Christ at all than to learn of him and then afterwards turn his back on the holy commandments that were given to him.

NIV	RSV	TEV
7 Husbands, in the same way be considerate as you live with your wives, and treat them with respect as the weaker partner and as heirs with you of the gracious gift of life, so that nothing will hinder your prayers.	7 Likewise you husbands, live considerately with your wives, bestowing honor on the woman as the weaker sex, since you are joint heirs of the grace of life, in order that your prayers may not be hindered.	7 In the same way you husbands must live with your wives with the proper understanding that they are the weaker sex. Treat them with respect, because they also will receive, together with you, God's gift of life. Do this so that nothing will interfere with your prayers.
15 But in your hearts set apart Christ as Lord. Always be prepared to give an answer to everyone who asks you to give the reason for the hope that you have. But do this with gentleness and respect,	15 but in your hearts reverence Christ as Lord. Always be prepared to make a defense to any one who calls you to account for the hope that is in you, yet do it with gentleness and reverence;	15 But have reverence for Christ in your hearts, and honor him as Lord. Be ready at all times to answer anyone who asks you to explain the hope you have in you,
4:12 Dear friends, do not be surprised at the painful trial you are suffering, as though something strange were happening to you.	4:12 Beloved, do not be surprised at the fiery ordeal which comes upon you to prove you, as though something strange were happening to you.	4:12 My dear friends, do not be surprised at the painful test you are suffering, as though something unusual were happening to you.
13 But rejoice that you participate in the sufferings of Christ, so that you may be overjoyed when his glory is revealed.	13 But rejoice in so far as you share Christ's sufferings, that you may also rejoice and be glad when his glory is revealed.	13 Rather be glad that you are sharing Christ's sufferings, so that you may be full of joy when his glory is revealed.
5:6 Humble yourselves, therefore, under God's mighty hand, that he may lift you up in due time.	5:6 Humble yourselves therefore under the mighty hand of God, that in due time he may exalt you.	5:6 Humble yourselves, then, under God's mighty hand, so that he will lift you up in his own good time.
7 Cast all your anxiety on him because he cares for you.	7 Cast all your anxieties on him, for he cares about you.	7 Leave all your worries with him, because he cares for you.
8 Be self-controlled and alert. Your enemy the devil prowls around like a roaring lion looking for someone to devour.	8 Be sober, be watchful. Your adversary the devil prowls around like a roaring lion, seeking some one to devour.	8 Be alert, be on watch! Your enemy, the Devil, roams around like a roaring lion, looking for someone to devour.
9 Resist him, standing firm in the faith, because you know that your brothers throughout the world are undergoing the same kind of sufferings.	9 Resist him, firm in your faith, knowing that the same experience of suffering is required of your brotherhood throughout the world.	9 Be firm in your faith and resist him, because you know that your fellow believers in all the world are going through the same kind of sufferings.

Second Peter

1:5 For this very reason, make every effort to add to your faith goodness; and to goodness, knowledge;	1:5 For this very reason make every effort to supplement your faith with virtue, and virtue with knowledge,	1:5 For this very reason do your best to add goodness to your faith; to your goodness add knowledge;
6 and to knowledge, self-control; and to self-control, perseverance; and to perseverance, godliness;	6 and knowledge with self-control, and self-control with steadfastness, and steadfastness with godliness,	6 to your knowledge add self-control; to your self-control add endurance; to your endurance add godliness;
7 and to godliness, brotherly kindness; and to brotherly kindness, love.	7 and godliness with brotherly affection, and brotherly affection with love.	7 to your godliness add brotherly affection; and to your brotherly affection add love.
8 For if you possess these qualities in increasing measure, they will keep you from being ineffective and unproductive in your knowledge of our Lord Jesus Christ.	8 For if these things are yours and abound, they keep you from being ineffective or unfruitful in the knowledge of our Lord Jesus Christ.	8 These are the qualities you need, and if you have them in abundance, they will make you active and effective in your knowledge of our Lord Jesus Christ.
20 Above all, you must understand that no prophecy of Scripture came about by the prophet's own interpretation.	20 First of all you must understand this, that no prophecy of scripture is a matter of one's own interpretation,	20 Above all else, however, remember that no one can explain by himself a prophecy in the Scriptures.
21 For prophecy never had its origin in the will of man, but men spoke from God as they were carried along by the Holy Spirit.	21 because no prophecy ever came by the impulse of man, but men moved by the Holy Spirit spoke from God.	21 For no prophetic message ever came just from the will of man, but men were under the control of the Holy Spirit as they spoke the message that came from God.
2:20 If they have escaped the corruption of the world by knowing our Lord and Savior Jesus Christ and are again entangled in it and overcome, they are worse off at the end than they were at the beginning.	2:20 For if, after they have escaped the defilements of the world through the knowledge of our Lord and Savior Jesus Christ, they are again entangled in them and overpowered, the last state has become worse for them than the first.	2:20 If people have escaped from the corrupting forces of the world through their knowledge of our Lord and Savior Jesus Christ, and then are again caught and conquered by them, such people are in worse condition at the end than they were at the beginning.
21 It would have been better for them not to have known the way of righteousness, than to have known it and then to turn their backs on the sacred commandment that was passed on to them.	21 For it would have been better for them never to have known the way of righteousness than after knowing it to turn back from the holy commandment delivered to them.	21 It would have been much better for them never to have known the way of righteousness than to know it and then turn away from the sacred command that was given them.

KJV	NKJV	TLB
22 But it is happened unto them according to the true proverb, The dog *is* turned to his own vomit again; and the sow that was washed to her wallowing in the mire.	22 But it has happened to them according to the true proverb: "A dog returns to his own vomit," and, "a sow, having washed, to her wallowing in the mire."	22 There is an old saying that "A dog comes back to what he has vomited, and a pig is washed only to come back and wallow in the mud again." That is the way it is with those who turn again to their sin.
3:9 The Lord is not slack concerning his promise, as some men count slackness; but is longsuffering to us-ward, not willing that any should perish, but that all should come to repentance.	3:9 The Lord is not slack concerning *His* promise, as some count slackness, but is longsuffering toward us, not willing that any should perish but that all should come to repentance.	3:9 He isn't really being slow about his promised return, even though it sometimes seems that way. But he is waiting, for the good reason that he is not willing that any should perish, and he is giving more time for sinners to repent.
10 But the day of the Lord will come as a thief in the night; in the which the heavens shall pass away with a great noise, and the elements shall melt with fervent heat, the earth also and the works that are therein shall be burned up.	10 But the day of the Lord will come as a thief in the night, in which the heavens will pass away with a great noise, and the elements will melt with fervent heat; both the earth and the works that are in it will be burned up.	10 The day of the Lord is surely coming, as unexpectedly as a thief, and then the heavens will pass away with a terrible noise, and the heavenly bodies will disappear in fire, and the earth and everything on it will be burned up.
12 Looking for and hasting unto the coming of the day of God, wherein the heavens being on fire shall be dissolved, and the elements shall melt with fervent heat?	12 looking for and hastening the coming of the day of God, because of which the heavens will be dissolved being on fire, and the elements will melt with fervent heat?	12 You should look forward to that day and hurry it along—the day when God will set the heavens on fire, and the heavenly bodies will melt and disappear in flames.

First John

KJV	NKJV	TLB
1:1 That which was from the beginning, which we have heard, which we have seen with our eyes, which we have looked upon, and our hands have handled, of the Word of life;	1:1 That which was from the beginning, which we have heard, which we have seen with our eyes, which we have looked upon, and our hands have handled, concerning the Word of life—	1:1 Christ was alive when the world began, yet I myself have seen him with my own eyes and listened to him speak. I have touched him with my own hands. He is God's message of Life.
2 (For the life was manifested, and we have seen *it*, and bear witness, and shew unto you that eternal life, which was with the Father, and was manifested unto us;)	2 the life was manifested, and we have seen, and bear witness, and declare to you that eternal life which was with the Father and was manifested to us—	2 This one who is Life from God has been shown to us and we guarantee that we have seen him; I am speaking of Christ, who is eternal Life. He was with the Father and then was shown to us.
3 That which we have seen and heard declare we unto you, that ye also may have fellowship with us: and truly our fellowship *is* with the Father, and with his Son Jesus Christ.	3 that which we have seen and heard we declare to you, that you also may have fellowship with us; and truly our fellowship *is* with the Father and with His Son Jesus Christ.	3 Again I say, we are telling you about what we ourselves have actually seen and heard, so that you may share the fellowship and the joys we have with the Father and with Jesus Christ his Son.
4 And these things write we unto you, that your joy may be full.	4 And these things we write to you that your joy may be full.	4 And if you do as I say in this letter, then you, too, will be full of joy, and so will we.
7 But if we walk in the light, as he is in the light, we have fellowship one with another, and the blood of Jesus Christ his Son cleanseth us from all sin.	7 But if we walk in the light as He is in the light, we have fellowship with one another, and the blood of Jesus Christ His Son cleanses us from all sin.	7 But if we are living in the light of God's presence, just as Christ does, then we have wonderful fellowship and joy with each other, and the blood of Jesus his Son cleanses us from every sin.
8 If we say that we have no sin, we deceive ourselves, and the truth is not in us.	8 If we say that we have no sin, we deceive ourselves, and the truth is not in us.	8 If we say that we have no sin, we are only fooling ourselves, and refusing to accept the truth.
9 If we confess our sins, he is faithful and just to forgive us *our* sins, and to cleanse us from all unrighteousness.	9 If we confess our sins, He is faithful and just to forgive us *our* sins and to cleanse us from all unrighteousness.	9 But if we confess our sins to him, he can be depended on to forgive us and to cleanse us from every wrong. [And it is perfectly proper for God to do this for us because Christ died to wash away our sins.]
2:3 And hereby we do know that we know him, if we keep his commandments.	2:3 Now by this we know that we know Him, if we keep His commandments.	2:3 And how can we be sure that we belong to him? By looking within ourselves: are we really trying to do what he wants us to?
4 He that saith, I know him, and keepeth not his commandments, is a liar, and the truth is not in him.	4 He who says, "I know Him," and does not keep His commandments, is a liar, and the truth is not in him.	4 Someone may say, "I am a Christian; I am on my way to heaven; I belong to Christ." But if he doesn't do what Christ tells him to, he is a liar.
10 He that loveth his brother abideth in the light, and there is none occasion of stumbling in him.	10 He who loves his brother abides in the light, and there is no cause for stumbling in him.	10 But whoever loves his fellow man is "walking in the light" and can see his way without stumbling around in darkness and sin.
25 And this is the promise that he hath promised us, *even* eternal life.	25 And this is the promise that He has promised us—eternal life.	25 And he himself has promised us this: *eternal life.*
3:1 Behold, what manner of love the Father hath bestowed upon us, that we should be called the sons of God: therefore the world knoweth us not, because it knew him not.	3:1 Behold what manner of love the Father has bestowed on us, that we should be called children of God! Therefore the world does not know us, because it did not know Him.	3:1 See how very much our heavenly Father loves us, for he allows us to be called his children—think of it—and we really *are!* But since most people don't know God, naturally they don't understand that we are his children.
2 Beloved, now are we the sons of God, and it doth not yet appear what we shall be: but we know that, when he shall appear, we shall be like him; for we shall see him as he is.	2 Beloved, now we are children of God; and it has not yet been revealed what we shall be, but we know that when He is revealed, we shall be like Him, for we shall see Him as He is.	2 Yes, dear friends, we are already God's children, right now, and we can't even imagine what it is going to be like later on. But we do know this, that when he comes we will be like him, as a result of seeing him as he really is.

NIV	RSV	TEV
22 Of them the proverbs are true: "A dog returns to its vomit," and, "A sow that is washed goes back to her wallowing in the mud."	22 It has happened to them according to the true proverb, The dog turns back to his own vomit, and the sow is washed only to wallow in the mire.	22 What happened to them shows that the proverbs are true: "A dog goes back to what it has vomited" and "A pig that has been washed goes back to roll in the mud."
3:9 The Lord is not slow in keeping his promise, as some understand slowness. He is patient with you, not wanting anyone to perish, but everyone to come to repentance.	3:9 The Lord is not slow about his promise as some count slowness, but is forbearing toward you, not wishing that any should perish, but that all should reach repentance.	3:9 The Lord is not slow to do what he has promised, as some think. Instead, he is patient with you, because he does not want anyone to be destroyed, but wants all to turn away from their sins.
10 But the day of the Lord will come like a thief. The heavens will disappear with a roar; the elements will be destroyed by fire, and the earth and everything in it will be laid bare.	10 But the day of the Lord will come like a thief, and then the heavens will pass away with a loud noise, and the elements will be dissolved with fire, and the earth and the works that are upon it will be burned up.	10 But the Day of the Lord will come like a thief. On that Day the heavens will disappear with a shrill noise, the heavenly bodies will burn up and be destroyed, and the earth with everything in it will vanish.
12 as you look forward to the day of God and speed its coming. That day will bring about the destruction of the heavens by fire, and the elements will melt in the heat.	12 waiting for and hastening the coming of the day of God, because of which the heavens will be kindled and dissolved, and the elements will melt with fire!	12 as you wait for the Day of God and do your best to make it come soon—the Day when the heavens will burn up and be destroyed, and the heavenly bodies will be melted by the heat.

First John

1:1 That which was from the beginning, which we have heard, which we have seen with our eyes, which we have looked at and our hands have touched—this we proclaim concerning the Word of life.	1:1 That which was from the beginning, which we have heard, which we have seen with our eyes, which we have looked upon and touched with our hands, concerning the word of life—	1:1 We write to you about the Word of life, which has existed from the very beginning. We have heard it, and we have seen it with our eyes; yes, we have seen it, and our hands have touched it.
2 The life appeared; we have seen it and testify to it, and we proclaim to you the eternal life, which was with the Father and has appeared to us.	2 the life was made manifest, and we saw it, and testify to it, and proclaim to you the eternal life which was with the Father and was made manifest to us—	2 When this life became visible, we saw it; so we speak of it and tell you about the eternal life which was with the Father and was made known to us.
3 We proclaim to you what we have seen and heard, so that you also may have fellowship with us. And our fellowship is with the Father and with his Son, Jesus Christ.	3 that which we have seen and heard we proclaim also to you, so that you may have fellowship with us; and our fellowship is with the Father and with his Son Jesus Christ.	3 What we have seen and heard we announce to you also, so that you will join with us in the fellowship that we have with the Father and with his Son Jesus Christ.
4 We write this to make our joy complete.	4 And we are writing this that our joy may be complete.	4 We write this in order that our joy may be complete.
7 But if we walk in the light, as he is in the light, we have fellowship with one another, and the blood of Jesus, his Son, purifies us from all sin.	7 but if we walk in the light, as he is in the light, we have fellowship with one another, and the blood of Jesus his Son cleanses us from all sin.	7 But if we live in the light—just as he is in the light—then we have fellowship with one another, and the blood of Jesus, his Son, purifies us from every sin.
8 If we claim to be without sin, we deceive ourselves and the truth is not in us.	8 If we say we have no sin, we deceive ourselves, and the truth is not in us.	8 If we say that we have no sin, we deceive ourselves, and there is no truth in us.
9 If we confess our sins, he is faithful and just and will forgive us our sins and purify us from all unrighteousness.	9 If we confess our sins, he is faithful and just, and will forgive our sins and cleanse us from all unrighteousness.	9 But if we confess our sins to God, he will keep his promise and do what is right: he will forgive us our sins and purify us from all our wrongdoing.
2:3 We know that we have come to know him if we obey his commands.	2:3 And by this we may be sure that we know him, if we keep his commandments.	2:3 If we obey God's commands, then we are sure that we know him.
4 The man who says, "I know him," but does not do what he commands is a liar, and the truth is not in him.	4 He who says "I know him" but disobeys his commandments is a liar, and the truth is not in him;	4 If someone says that he knows him, but does not obey his commands, such a person is a liar and there is no truth in him.
10 Whoever loves his brother lives in the light, and there is nothing in him to make him stumble.	10 He who loves his brother abides in the light, and in it there is no cause for stumbling.	10 Whoever loves his brother lives in the light, and so there is nothing in him that will cause someone else to sin.
25 And this is what he promised us—even eternal life.	25 And this is what he has promised us, eternal life.	25 And this is what Christ himself promised to give us—eternal life.
3:1 How great is the love the Father has lavished on us, that we should be called children of God! And that is what we are! The reason the world does not know us is that it did not know him.	3:1 See what love the Father has given us, that we should be called children of God; and so we are. The reason why the world does not know us is that it did not know him.	3:1 See how much the Father has loved us! His love is so great that we are called God's children—and so, in fact, we are. This is why the world does not know us: it has not known God.
2 Dear friends, now we are children of God, and what we will be has not yet been made known. But we know that when he appears, we shall be like him, for we shall see him as he is.	2 Beloved, we are God's children now; it does not yet appear what we shall be, but we know that when he appears we shall be like him, for we shall see him as he is.	2 My dear friends, we are now God's children, but it is not yet clear what we shall become. But we know that when Christ appears, we shall be like him, because we shall see him as he really is.

KJV	NKJV	TLB
16 Hereby perceive we the love *of God,* because he laid down his life for us: and we ought to lay down *our* lives for the brethren.	16 By this we know love, because He laid down His life for us. And we also ought to lay down *our* lives for the brethren.	16 We know what real love is from Christ's example in dying for us. And so we also ought to lay down our lives for our Christian brothers.
17 But whoso hath this world's good, and seeth his brother have need, and shutteth up his bowels *of compassion* from him, how dwelleth the love of God in him?	17 But whoever has this world's goods, and sees his brother in need, and shuts up his heart from him, how does the love of God abide in him?	17 But if someone who is supposed to be a Christian has money enough to live well, and sees a brother in need, and won't help him—how can God's love be within *him?*
18 My little children, let us not love in word, neither in tongue; but in deed and in truth.	18 My little children, let us not love in word or in tongue, but in deed and in truth.	18 Little children, let us stop just *saying* we love people; let us *really* love them, and *show it* by our *actions.*
19 And hereby we know that we are of the truth, and shall assure our hearts before him.	19 And by this we know that we are of the truth, and shall assure our hearts before Him.	19 Then we will know for sure, by our actions, that we are on God's side, and our consciences will be clear, even when we stand before the Lord.
20 For if our heart condemn us, God is greater than our heart, and knoweth all things.	20 For if our heart condemns us, God is greater than our heart, and knows all things.	20 But if we have bad consciences and feel that we have done wrong, the Lord will surely feel it even more, for he knows everything we do.
4:4 Ye are of God, little children, and have overcome them: because greater is he that is in you, than he that is in the world.	4:4 You are of God, little children, and have overcome them, because He who is in you is greater than he who is in the world.	4:4 Dear young friends, you belong to God and have already won your fight with those who are against Christ, because there is someone in your hearts who is stronger than any evil teacher in this wicked world.
7 Beloved, let us love one another: for love is of God; and every one that loveth is born of God, and knoweth God.	7 Beloved, let us love one another, for love is of God; and everyone who loves is born of God and knows God.	7 Dear friends, let us practice loving each other, for love comes from God and those who are loving and kind show that they are the children of God, and that they are getting to know him better.
8 He that loveth not knoweth not God; for God is love.	8 He who does not love does not know God, for God is love.	8 But if a person isn't loving and kind, it shows that he doesn't know God—for God is love.
10 Herein is love, not that we loved God, but that he loved us, and sent his Son *to be* the propitiation for our sins.	10 In this is love, not that we loved God, but that He loved us and sent His Son *to be* the propitiation for our sins.	10 In this act we see what real love is: it is not our love for God, but his love for us when he sent his Son to satisfy God's anger against our sins.
11 Beloved, if God so loved us, we ought also to love one another.	11 Beloved, if God so loved us, we also ought to love one another.	11 Dear friends, since God loved us as much as that, we surely ought to love each other too.
16 And we have known and believed the love that God hath to us. God is love; and he that dwelleth in love dwelleth in God, and God in him.	16 And we have known and believed the love that God has for us. God is love, and he who abides in love abides in God, and God in him.	16 We know how much God loves us because we have felt his love and because we believe him when he tells us that he loves us dearly. God is love, and anyone who lives in love is living with God and God is living in him.
18 There is no fear in love; but perfect love casteth out fear: because fear hath torment. He that feareth is not made perfect in love.	18 There is no fear in love; but perfect love casts out fear, because fear involves torment. But he who fears has not been made perfect in love.	18 We need have no fear of someone who loves us perfectly; his perfect love for us eliminates all dread of what he might do to us. If we are afraid, it is for fear of what he might do to us, and shows that we are not fully convinced that he really loves us.
19 We love him, because he first loved us.	19 We love Him because He first loved us.	19 So you see, our love for him comes as a*
5:4 For whatsoever is born of God overcometh the world: and this is the victory that overcometh the world, *even* our faith.	5:4 For whatever is born of God overcomes the world. And this is the victory that has overcome the world—our faith.	5:4 for every child of God can obey him, defeating sin and evil pleasure by trusting Christ to help him.
5 Who is he that overcometh the world, but he that believeth that Jesus is the Son of God?	5 Who is he who overcomes the world, but he who believes that Jesus is the Son of God?	5 But who could possibly fight and win this battle except by believing that Jesus is truly the Son of God?
10 He that believeth on the Son of God hath the witness in himself: he that believeth not God hath made him a liar; because he believeth not the record that God gave of his Son.	10 He who believes in the Son of God has the witness in himself; he who does not believe God has made Him a liar, because he has not believed the testimony that God has given of His Son.	10 All who believe this know in their hearts that it is true. If anyone doesn't believe this, he is actually calling God a liar, because he doesn't believe what God has said about his Son.
11 And this is the record, that God hath given to us eternal life, and this life is in his Son.	11 And this is the testimony: that God has given us eternal life, and this life is in His Son.	11 And what is it that God has said? That he has given us eternal life, and that this life is in his Son.
12 He that hath the Son hath life; *and* he that hath not the Son of God hath not life.	12 He who has the Son has life; he who does not have the Son of God does not have life.	12 So whoever has God's Son has life; whoever does not have his Son, does not have life.
13 These things have I written unto you that believe on the name of the Son of God; that ye may know that ye have eternal life, and that ye may believe on the name of the Son of God.	13 These things I have written to you who believe in the name of the Son of God, that you may know that you have eternal life, and that you may *continue to* believe in the name of the Son of God.	13 I have written this to you who believe in the Son of God so that you may know you have eternal life.

*result of his loving us first.

NIV	RSV	TEV
16 This is how we know what love is: Jesus Christ laid down his life for us. And we ought to lay down our lives for our brothers.	16 By this we know love, that he laid down his life for us; and we ought to lay down our lives for the brethren.	16 This is how we know what love is: Christ gave his life for us. We too, then, ought to give our lives for our brothers!
17 If anyone has material possessions and sees his brother in need but has no pity on him, how can the love of God be in him?	17 But if any one has the world's goods and sees his brother in need, yet closes his heart against him, how does God's love abide in him?	17 If a rich person sees his brother in need, yet closes his heart against his brother, how can he claim that he loves God?
18 Dear children, let us not love with words or tongue but with actions and in truth.	18 Little children, let us not love in word or speech but in deed and in truth.	18 My children, our love should not be just words and talk; it must be true love, which shows itself in action.
19 This then is how we know that we belong to the truth, and how we set our hearts at rest in his presence	19 By this we shall know that we are of the truth, and reassure our hearts before him	19 This, then, is how we will know that we belong to the truth; this is how we will be confident in God's presence.
20 whenever our hearts condemn us. For God is greater than our hearts, and he knows everything.	20 whenever our hearts condemn us; for God is greater than our hearts, and he knows everything.	20 If our conscience condmens us, we know that God is greater than our conscience and that he knows everything.
4:4 You, dear children, are from God and have overcome them, because the one who is in you is greater than the one who is in the world.	4:4 Little children, you are of God, and have overcome them; for he who is in you is greater than he who is in the world.	4:4 But you belong to God, my children, and have defeated the false prophets, because the Spirit who is in you is more powerful than the spirit in those who belong to the world.
7 Dear friends, let us love one another, for love comes from God. Everyone who loves has been born of God and knows God.	7 Beloved, let us love one another; for love is of God, and he who loves is born of God and knows God.	7 Dear friends, let us love one another, because love comes from God. Whoever loves is a child of God and knows God.
8 Whoever does not love does not know God, because God is love.	8 He who does not love does not know God; for God is love.	8 Whoever does not love does not know God, for God is love.
10 This is love: not that we loved God, but that he loved us and sent his Son as an atoning sacrifice for our sins.	10 In this is love, not that we loved God but that he loved us and sent his Son to be the expiation for our sins.	10 This is what love is: it is not that we have loved God, but that he loved us and sent his Son to be the means by which our sins are forgiven.
11 Dear friends, since God so loved us, we also ought to love one another.	11 Beloved, if God so loved us, we also ought to love one another.	11 Dear friends, if this is how God loved us, then we should love one another.
16 And so we know and rely on the love God has for us. God is love. Whoever lives in love lives in God, and God in him.	16 So we know and believe the love God has for us. God is love, and he who abides in love abides in God, and God abides in him.	16 And we ourselves know and believe the love which God has for us. God is love, and whoever lives in love lives in union with God and God lives in union with him.
18 There is no fear in love. But perfect love drives out fear, because fear has to do with punishment. The man who fears is not made perfect in love.	18 There is no fear in love, but perfect love casts out fear. For fear has to do with punishment, and he who fears is not perfected in love.	18 There is no fear in love; perfect love drives out all fear. So then, love has not been made perfect in anyone who is afraid, because fear has to do with punishment.
19 We love because he first loved us.	19 We love, because he first loved us.	19 We love because God first loved us.
5:4 for everyone born of God overcomes the world. This is the victory that has overcome the world, even our faith.	5:4 For whatever is born of God overcomes the world; and this is the victory that overcomes the world, our faith.	5:4 because every child of God is able to defeat the world. And we win the victory over the world by means of our faith.
5 Who is it that overcomes the world? Only he who believes that Jesus is the Son of God.	5 Who is it that overcomes the world but he who believes that Jesus is the Son of God?	5 Who can defeat the world? Only the person who believes that Jesus is the Son of God.
10 Anyone who believes in the Son of God has this testimony in his heart. Anyone who does not believe God has made him out to be a liar, because he has not believed the testimony God has given about his Son.	10 He who believes in the Son of God has the testimony in himself. He who does not believe God has made him a liar, because he has not believed in the testimony that God has borne to his Son.	10 So whoever believes in the Son of God has this testimony in his own heart; but whoever does not believe God, has made a liar of him, because he has not believed what God has said about his Son.
11 And this is the testimony: God has given us eternal life, and this life is in his Son.	11 And this is the testimony, that God gave us eternal life, and this life is in his Son.	11 The testimony is this: God has given us eternal life, and this life has its source in his Son.
12 He who has the Son has life; he who does not have the Son of God does not have life.	12 He who has the Son has life; he who has not the Son of God has not life.	12 Whoever has the Son has this life; whoever does not have the Son of God does not have life.
13 I write these things to you who believe in the name of the Son of God so that you may know that you have eternal life.	13 I write this to you who believe in the name of the Son of God, that you may know that you have eternal life.	13 I am writing this to you so that you may know that you have eternal life—you that believe in the Son of God.

KJV	NKJV	TLB
20 And we know that the Son of God is come, and hath given us an understanding, that we may know him that is true, and we are in him that is true, *even* in his Son Jesus Christ. This is the true God, and eternal life.	20 And we know that the Son of God has come and has given us an understanding, that we may know Him who is true; and we are in Him who is true, in His Son Jesus Christ. This is the true God and eternal life.	20 And we know that Christ, God's Son, has come to help us understand and find the true God. And now we are in God because we are in Jesus Christ his Son, who is the only true God; and he is eternal Life.

Second John

5 And now I beseech thee, lady, not as though I wrote a new commandment unto thee, but that which we had from the beginning, that we love one another.	5 And now I plead with you, lady, not as though I wrote a new commandment to you, but that which we have had from the beginning: that we love one another.	5 And now I want to urgently remind you, dear friends, of the old rule God gave us right from the beginning, that Christians should love one another.
7 For many deceivers are entered into the world, who confess not that Jesus Christ is come in the flesh. This is a deceiver and an antichrist.	7 For many deceivers have gone out into the world who do not confess Jesus Christ *as* coming in the flesh. This is a deceiver and an antichrist.	7 Watch out for the false leaders—and there are many of them around—who don't believe that Jesus Christ came to earth as a human being with a body like ours. Such people are against the truth and against Christ.

Third John

2 Beloved, I wish above all things that thou mayest prosper and be in health, even as thy soul prospereth.	2 Beloved, I pray that you may prosper in all things and be in health, just as your soul prospers.	2 Dear friend, I am praying that all is well with you and that your body is as healthy as I know your soul is.
3 For I rejoiced greatly, when the brethren came and testified of the truth that is in thee, even as thou walkest in the truth.	3 For I rejoiced greatly when brethren came and testified of the truth *that is* in you, just as you walk in the truth.	3 Some of the brothers traveling by have made me very happy by telling me that your life stays clean and true, and that you are living by the standards of the Gospel.
11 Beloved, follow not that which is evil, but that which is good. He that doeth good is of God: but he that doeth evil hath not seen God.	11 Beloved, do not imitate what is evil, but what is good. He who does good is of God, but he who does evil has not seen God.	11 Dear friend, don't let this bad example influence you. Follow only what is good. Remember that those who do what is right prove that they are God's children; and those who continue in evil prove that they are far from God.

Jude

11 Woe unto them! for they have gone in the way of Cain, and ran greedily after the error of Balaam for reward, and perished in the gainsaying of Core.	11 Woe to them! For they have gone in the way of Cain, have run greedily in the error of Balaam for profit, and perished in the rebellion of Korah.	11 Woe upon them! For they follow the example of Cain who killed his brother; and, like Balaam, they will do anything for money; and like Korah, they have disobeyed God and will die under his curse.
20 But ye, beloved, building up yourselves on your most holy faith, praying in the Holy Ghost,	20 But you, beloved, building yourselves up on your most holy faith, praying in the Holy Spirit,	20 But you, dear friends, must build up your lives ever more strongly upon the foundation of our holy faith, learning to pray in the power and strength of the Holy Spirit.
21 Keep yourselves in the love of God, looking for the mercy of our Lord Jesus Christ unto eternal life.	21 keep yourselves in the love of God, looking for the mercy of our Lord Jesus Christ unto eternal life.	21 Stay always within the boundaries where God's love can reach and bless you. Wait patiently for the eternal life that our Lord Jesus Christ in his mercy is going to give you.
24 Now unto him that is able to keep you from falling, and to present *you* faultless before the presence of his glory with exceeding joy,	24 Now to Him who is able to keep you from stumbling, And to present *you* faultless Before the presence of His glory with exceeding joy,	24 And he is able to keep you from slipping and falling away, and to bring you, sinless and perfect, into his glorious presence with mighty shouts of everlasting joy.
25 To the only wise God our Saviour, *be* glory and majesty, dominion and power, both now and ever. Amen.	25 To God our Savior, Who alone is wise, *Be* glory and majesty, Dominion and power, Both now and forever. Amen.	25 And now—all glory to him who alone is God, who saves us through Jesus Christ our Lord; yes, splendor and majesty, all power and authority are his from the beginning; his they are and his they evermore shall be. Amen.

Revelation

1:1 The Revelation of Jesus Christ, which God gave unto him, to shew unto his servants things which must shortly come to pass; and he sent and signified *it* by his angel unto his servant John:	1:1 The Revelation of Jesus Christ, which God gave Him to show His servants—things which must shortly take place. And He sent and signified *it* by His angel to His servant John,	1:1 This book unveils some of the future activities soon to occur in the life of Jesus Christ. God permitted him to reveal these things to his servant John in a vision; and then an angel was sent from heaven to explain the vision's meaning.

NIV	RSV	TEV
20 We know also that the Son of God has come and has given us understanding, so that we may know him who is true. And we are in him who is true—even in his Son Jesus Christ. He is the true God and eternal life.	20 And we know that the Son of God has come and has given us understanding, to know him who is true; and we are in him who is true, in his Son Jesus Christ. This is the true God and eternal life.	20 We know that the Son of God has come and has given us understanding, so that we know the true God. We live in union with the true God—in union with his Son Jesus Christ. This is the true God, and this is eternal life.

Second John

NIV	RSV	TEV
5 And now, dear lady, I am not writing you a new command but one we have had from the beginning. I ask that we love one another.	5 And now I beg you, lady, not as though I were writing you a new commandment, but the one we have had from the beginning, that we love one another.	5 And so I ask you, dear Lady: let us all love one another. This is no new command I am writing you; it is the command which we have had from the beginning.
7 Many deceivers, who do not acknowledge Jesus Christ as coming in the flesh, have gone out into the world. Any such person is the deceiver and the antichrist.	7 For many deceivers have gone out into the world, men who will not acknowledge the coming of Jesus Christ in the flesh; such a one is the deceiver and the antichrist.	7 Many deceivers have gone out over the world, people who do not acknowledge that Jesus Christ came as a human being. Such a person is a deceiver and the Enemy of Christ.

Third John

NIV	RSV	TEV
2 Dear friend, I pray that you may enjoy good health and that all may go well with you, even as your soul is getting along well.	2 Beloved, I pray that all may go well with you and that you may be in health; I know that it is well with your soul.	2 My dear friend, I pray that everything may go well with you and that you may be in good health—as I know you are well in spirit.
3 It gave me great joy to have some brothers come and tell about your faithfulness to the truth and how you continue to walk in the truth.	3 For I greatly rejoiced when some of the brethren arrived and testified to the truth of your life, as indeed you do follow the truth.	3 I was so happy when some Christian brothers arrived and told me how faithful you are to the truth—just as you always live in the truth.
11 Dear friend, do not imitate what is evil but what is good. Anyone who does what is good is from God. Anyone who does what is evil has not seen God.	11 Beloved, do not imitate evil but imitate good. He who does good is of God; he who does evil has not seen God.	11 My dear friend, do not imitate what is bad, but imitate what is good. Whoever does good belongs to God; whoever does what is bad has not seen God.

Jude

NIV	RSV	TEV
11 Woe to them! They have taken the way of Cain; they have rushed for profit into Balaam's error; they have been destroyed in Korah's rebellion.	11 Woe to them! For they walk in the way of Cain, and abandon themselves for the sake of gain to Balaam's error, and perish in Korah's rebellion.	11 How terrible for them! They have followed the way that Cain took. For the sake of money they have given themselves over to the error that Balaam committed. They have rebelled as Korah rebelled, and like him they are destroyed.
20 But you, dear friends, build yourselves up in your most holy faith and pray in the Holy Spirit.	20 But you, beloved, build yourselves up on your most holy faith; pray in the Holy Spirit;	20 But you, my friends, keep on building yourselves up on your most sacred faith. Pray in the power of the Holy Spirit,
21 Keep yourselves in God's love as you wait for the mercy of our Lord Jesus Christ to bring you to eternal life.	21 keep yourselves in the love of God; wait for the mercy of our Lord Jesus Christ unto eternal life.	21 and keep yourselves in the love of God, as you wait for our Lord Jesus Christ in his mercy to give you eternal life.
24 To him who is able to keep you from falling and to present you before his glorious presence without fault and with great joy—	24 Now to him who is able to keep you from falling and to present you without blemish before the presence of his glory with rejoicing,	24 To him who is able to keep you from falling and to bring you faultless and joyful before his glorious presence—
25 to the only God our Savior be glory, majesty, power and authority, through Jesus Christ our Lord, before all ages, now and forevermore! Amen.	25 to the only God, our Savior through Jesus Christ our Lord, be glory, majesty, dominion, and authority, before all time and now and for ever. Amen.	25 to the only God our Savior, through Jesus Christ our Lord, be glory, majesty, might, and authority, from all ages past, and now, and forever and ever! Amen.

Revelation

NIV	RSV	TEV
1:1 The revelation of Jesus Christ, which God gave him to show his servants what must soon take place. He made it known by sending his angel to his servant John,	1:1 The revelation of Jesus Christ, which God gave him to show to his servants what must soon take place; and he made it known by sending his angel to his servant John,	1:1 This book is the record of the events that Jesus Christ revealed. God gave him this revelation in order to show to his servants what must happen very soon. Christ made these things known to his servant John by sending his angel to him,

KJV	NKJV	TLB
3 Blessed *is* he that readeth, and they that hear the words of this prophecy, and keep those things which are written therein: for the time *is* at hand.	3 Blessed *is* he who reads and those who hear the words of this prophecy, and keep those things which are written in it; for the time *is* near.	3 If you read this prophecy aloud to the church, you will receive a special blessing from the Lord. Those who listen to it being read and do what it says will also be blessed. For the time is near when these things will all come true.
7 Behold, he cometh with clouds; and every eye shall see him, and they *also* which pierced him: and all kindreds of the earth shall wail because of him. Even so, Amen.	7 Behold, He is coming with clouds, and every eye will see Him, and they *also* who pierced Him. And all the tribes of the earth will mourn because of Him. Even so, Amen.	7 See! He is arriving, surrounded by clouds; and every eye shall see him—yes, and those who pierced him. And the nations will weep in sorrow and in terror when he comes. Yes! Amen! Let it be so!
8 I am Alpha and Omega, the beginning and the ending, saith the Lord, which is, and which was, and which is to come, the Almighty.	8 "I am the Alpha and the Omega, *the* Beginning and *the* End," says the Lord, "who is and who was and who is to come, the Almighty."	8 "I am the A and the Z, the Beginning and the Ending of all things," says God, who is the Lord, the All Powerful One who is, and was, and is coming again!
2:7 He that hath an ear, let him hear what the Spirit saith unto the churches; To him that overcometh will I give to eat of the tree of life, which is in the midst of the paradise of God.	2:7 "He who has an ear, let him hear what the Spirit says to the churches. To him who overcomes I will give to eat from the tree of life, which is in the midst of the Paradise of God."'	2:7 "Let this message sink into the ears of anyone who listens to what the Spirit is saying to the churches: To everyone who is victorious, I will give fruit from the Tree of Life in the Paradise of God.
11 He that hath an ear, let him hear what the Spirit saith unto the churches; He that overcometh shall not be hurt of the second death.	11 "He who has an ear, let him hear what the Spirit says to the churches. He who overcomes shall not be hurt by the second death."'	11 Let everyone who can hear, listen to what the Spirit is saying to the churches: He who is victorious shall not be hurt by the Second Death.
17 He that hath an ear, let him hear what the Spirit saith unto the churches; To him that overcometh will I give to eat of the hidden manna, and will give him a white stone, and in the stone a new name written, which no man knoweth saving he that receiveth *it*.	17 "He who has an ear, let him hear what the Spirit says to the churches. To him who overcomes I will give some of the hidden manna to eat. And I will give him a white stone, and on the stone a new name written which no one knows except him who receives *it*."'	17 "Let everyone who can hear, listen to what the Spirit is saying to the churches: Every one who is victorious shall eat of the hidden manna, the secret nourishment from heaven; and I will give to each a white stone, and on the stone will be engraved a new name that no one else knows except the one receiving it.
26 And he that overcometh, and keepeth my works unto the end, to him will I give power over the nations:	26 "And he who overcomes, and keeps My works until the end, to him I will give power over the nations—	26 "To every one who overcomes—who to the very end keeps on doing things that please me—I will give power over the nations.
27 And he shall rule them with a rod of iron; as the vessels of a potter shall they be broken to shivers: even as I recieved of my Father.	27 'He shall rule them with a rod of iron; As the potter's vessels shall be broken to pieces'— as I also have received from My Father;	27 You will rule them with a rod of iron just as my Father gave me the authority to rule them; they will be shattered like a pot of clay that is broken into tiny pieces.
28 And I will give him the morning star.	28 "and I will give him the morning star.	28 And I will give you the Morning Star!
3:5 He that overcometh, the same shall be clothed in white raiment; and I will not blot out his name out of the book of life, but I will confess his name before my Father, and before his angels.	3:5 "He who overcomes shall be clothed in white garments, and I will not blot out his name from the Book of Life; but I will confess his name before My Father and before His angels.	3:5 Everyone who conquers will be clothed in white, and I will not erase his name from the Book of Life, but I will announce before my Father and his angels that he is mine.
12 Him that overcometh will I make a pillar in the temple of my God, and he shall go no more out: and I will write upon him the name of my God, and the name of the city of my God, *which is* new Jerusalem, which cometh down out of heaven from my God: and *I will write upon him* my new name.	12 "He who overcomes, I will make him a pillar in the temple of My God, and he shall go out no more. And I will write on him the name of My God and the name of the city of My God, the New Jerusalem, which comes down out of heaven from My God. And *I will write on him* My new name.	12 "As for the one who conquers, I will make him a pillar in the temple of my God; he will be secure, and will go out no more; and I will write my God's Name on him, and he will be a citizen in the city of my God—the New Jerusalem, coming down from heaven from my God; and he will have my new Name inscribed upon him.
21 To him that overcometh will I grant to sit with me in my throne, even as I also overcame, and am set down with my Father in his throne.	21 "To him who overcomes I will grant to sit with Me on My throne, as I also overcame and sat down with My Father on His throne.	21 I will let every one who conquers sit beside me on my throne, just as I took my place with my Father on his throne when I had conquered.
4:2 And immediately I was in the spirit: and, behold, a throne was set in heaven, and *one* sat on the throne.	4:2 Immediately I was in the Spirit; and behold, a throne set in heaven, and *One* sat on the throne.	4:2 And instantly I was, in spirit, there in heaven and saw—oh, the glory of it!—a throne and someone sitting on it!
3 And he that sat was to look upon like a jasper and a sardine stone: and *there was* a rainbow round about the throne, in sight like unto an emerald.	3 And He who sat there was like a jasper and a sardius stone in appearance; and *there was* a rainbow around the throne, in appearance like an emerald.	3 Great bursts of light flashed forth from him as from a glittering diamond, or from a shining ruby, and a rainbow glowing iike an emerald encircled his throne.
5:5 And one of the elders saith unto me, Weep not: behold, the Lion of the tribe of Juda, the Root of David, hath prevailed to open the book, and to loose the seven seals thereof.	5:5 But one of the elders said to me, "Do not weep. Behold, the Lion of the tribe of Judah, the Root of David, has prevailed to open the scroll and to loose its seven seals."	5:5 But one of the twenty-four Elders said to me, "Stop crying, for look! The Lion of the tribe of Judah, the Root of David, has conquered, and proved himself worthy to open the scroll and to break its seven seals."

NIV	RSV	TEV
3 Blessed is the one who reads the words of this prophecy, and blessed are those who hear it and take to heart what is written in it, because the time is near.	3 Blessed is he who reads aloud the words of the prophecy, and blessed are those who hear, and who keep what is written therein; for the time is near.	3 Happy is the one who reads this book, and happy are those who listen to the words of this prophetic message and obey what is written in this book! For the time is near when all these things will happen.

7 Look, he is coming with the clouds,
    and every eye will see him,
even those who pierced him;
    and all the peoples of the earth will
        mourn because of him.
                So shall it be! Amen.
	7 Behold, he is coming with the clouds, and every eye will see him, every one who pierced him; and all tribes of the earth will wail on account of him. Even so. Amen.	7 Look, he is coming on the clouds! Everyone will see him, including those who pierced him. All peoples on earth will mourn over him. So shall it be!

8 "I am the Alpha and the Omega," says the Lord God, "who is, and who was, and who is to come, the Almighty."	8 "I am the Alpha and the Omega," says the Lord God, who is and who was and who is to come, the Almighty.	8 "I am the first and the last," says the Lord God Almighty, who is, who was, and who is to come.
2:7 He who has an ear, let him hear what the Spirit says to the churches. To him who overcomes, I will give the right to eat from the tree of life, which is in the paradise of God.	2:7 He who has an ear, let him hear what the Spirit says to the churches. To him who conquers I will grant to eat of the tree of life, which is in the paradise of God.'	2:7 "If you have ears, then, listen to what the Spirit says to the churches! "To those who win the victory I will give the right to eat the fruit of the tree of life that grows in the Garden of God.
11 He who has an ear, let him hear what the Spirit says to the churches. He who overcomes will not be hurt at all by the second death.	11 He who has an ear, let him hear what the Spirit says to the churches. He who conquers shall not be hurt by the second death.'	11 "If you have ears, then, listen to what the Spirit says to the churches! "Those who win the victory will not be hurt by the second death.
17 He who has an ear, let him hear what the Spirit says to the churches. To him who overcomes, I will give some of the hidden manna. I will also give him a white stone with a new name written on it, known only to him who receives it.	17 He who has an ear, let him hear what the Spirit says to the churches. To him who conquers I will give some of the hidden manna, and I will give him a white stone, with a new name written on the stone which no one knows except him who receives it.'	17 "If you have ears, then, listen to what the Spirit says to the churches! "To those who win the victory I will give some of the hidden manna. I will also give each of them a white stone on which is written a new name that no one knows except the one who receives it.
26 To him who overcomes and does my will to the end, I will give authority over the nations—	26 He who conquers and who keeps my works until the end, I will give him power over the nations,	26–28 To those who win the victory, who continue to the end to do what I want, I will give the same authority that I received from my Father: I will give them authority over the nations, to rule them with an iron rod and to break them to pieces like clay pots. I will also give them the morning star.
27 'He will rule them with an iron scepter; he will dash them to pieces like pottery' just as I have received authority from my Father.	27 and he shall rule them with a rod of iron, as when earthen pots are broken in pieces, even as I myself have received power from my Father;	
28 I will also give him the morning star.	28 and I will give him the morning star.	
3:5 He who overcomes will, like them, be dressed in white. I will never erase his name from the book of life, but will acknowledge his name before my Father and his angels.	3:5 He who conquers shall be clad thus in white garments, and I will not blot his name out of the book of life; I will confess his name before my Father and before his angels.	3:5 Those who win the victory will be clothed like this in white, and I will not remove their names from the book of the living. In the presence of my Father and of his angels I will declare openly that they belong to me.
12 Him who overcomes I will make a pillar in the temple of my God. Never again will he leave it. I will write on him the name of my God and the name of the city of my God, the new Jerusalem, which is coming down out of heaven from my God; and I will also write on him my new name.	12 He who conquers, I will make him a pillar in the temple of my God; never shall he go out of it, and I will write on him the name of my God, and the name of the city of my God, the new Jerusalem which comes down from my God out of heaven, and my own new name.	12 I will make him who is victorious a pillar in the temple of my God, and he will never leave it. I will write on him the name of my God and the name of the city of my God, the new Jerusalem, which will come down out of heaven from my God. I will also write on him my new name.
21 To him who overcomes, I will give the right to sit with me on my throne, just as I overcame and sat down with my Father on his throne.	21 He who conquers, I will grant him to sit with me on my throne, as I myself conquered and sat down with my Father on his throne.	21 To those who win the victory I will give the right to sit beside me on my throne, just as I have been victorious and now sit by my Father on his throne.
4:2 At once I was in the Spirit, and there before me was a throne in heaven with someone sitting on it.	4:2 At once I was in the Spirit, and lo, a throne stood in heaven, with one seated on the throne!	4:2 At once the Spirit took control of me. There in heaven was a throne with someone sitting on it.
3 And the one who sat there had the appearance of jasper and carnelian. A rainbow, resembling an emerald, encircled the throne.	3 And he who sat there appeared like jasper and carnelian, and round the throne was a rainbow that looked like an emerald.	3 His face gleamed like such precious stones as jasper and carnelian, and all around the throne there was a rainbow the color of an emerald.
5:5 Then one of the elders said to me, "Do not weep! See, the Lion of the tribe of Judah, the Root of David, has triumphed. He is able to open the scroll and its seven seals."	5:5 Then one of the elders said to me, "Weep not; lo, the Lion of the tribe of Judah, the Root of David, has conquered, so that he can open the scroll and its seven seals."	5:5 Then one of the elders said to me, "Don't cry. Look! The Lion from Judah's tribe, the great descendant of David, has won the victory, and he can break the seven seals and open the scroll."

KJV	NKJV	TLB
6 And I beheld, and, lo, in the midst of the throne and of the four beasts, and in the midst of the elders, stood a Lamb as it had been slain, having seven horns and seven eyes, which are the seven Spirits of God sent forth into all the earth.	6 And I looked, and behold, in the midst of the throne and of the four living creatures, and in the midst of the elders, stood a Lamb as though it had been slain, having seven horns and seven eyes, which are the seven Spirits of God sent out into all the earth.	6 I looked and saw a Lamb standing there before the twenty-four Elders, in front of the throne and the Living Beings, and on the Lamb were wounds that once had caused his death. He had seven horns and seven eyes, which represent the seven-fold Spirit of God, sent out into every part of the world.
9 And they sung a new song, saying, Thou art worthy to take the book, and to open the seals thereof: for thou wast slain, and hast redeemed us to God by thy blood out of every kindred, and tongue, and people, and nation;	9 And they sang a new song, saying: "You are worthy to take the scroll, And to open its seals; For You were slain, And have redeemed us to God by Your blood Out of every tribe and tongue and people and nation,	9 They were singing him a new song with these words: "You are worthy to take the scroll and break its seals and open it; for you were slain, and your blood has bought people from every nation as gifts for God.
10 And hast made us unto our God kings and priests: and we shall reign on the earth.	10 And have made us kings and priests to our God; And we shall reign on the earth."	10 And you have gathered them into a kingdom and made them priests of our God; they shall reign upon the earth."
6:14 And the heaven departed as a scroll when it is rolled together, and every mountain and island were moved out of their places.	**6:14** Then the sky receded as a scroll when it is rolled up, and every mountain and island was moved out of its place.	**6:14** And the starry heavens disappeared as though rolled up like a scroll and taken away; and every mountain and island shook and shifted.
15 And the kings of the earth, and the great men, and the rich men, and the chief captains, and the mighty men, and every bondman, and every free man, hid themselves in the dens and in the rocks of the mountains;	15 And the kings of the earth, the great men, the rich men, the commanders, the mighty men, every slave and every free man, hid themselves in the caves and in the rocks of the mountains,	15 The kings of the earth, and world leaders and rich men, and high-ranking military officers, and all men great and small, slave and free, hid themselves in the caves and rocks of the mountains,
7:15 Therefore are they before the throne of God, and serve him day and night in his temple: and he that sitteth on the throne shall dwell among them.	**7:15** "Therefore they are before the throne of God, and serve Him day and night in His temple. And He who sits on the throne will dwell among them.	**7:15** That is why they are here before the throne of God, serving him day and night in his temple. The one sitting on the throne will shelter them;
16 They shall hunger no more, neither thirst any more; neither shall the sun light on them, nor any heat.	16 "They shall neither hunger anymore nor thirst anymore; the sun shall not strike them, nor any heat;	16 they will never be hungry again, nor thirsty, and they will be fully protected from the scorching noontime heat.
12:10 And I heard a loud voice saying in heaven, Now is come salvation, and strength, and the kingdom of our God, and the power of his Christ: for the accuser of our brethren is cast down, which accused them before our God day and night.	**12:10** Then I heard a loud voice saying in heaven, "Now salvation, and strength, and the kingdom of our God, and the power of His Christ have come, for the accuser of our brethren, who accused them before our God day and night, has been cast down.	**12:10** Then I heard a loud voice shouting across the heavens, "It has happened at last! God's salvation and the power and the rule, and the authority of his Christ are finally here; for the Accuser of our brothers has been thrown down from heaven onto earth—he accused them day and night before our God.
11 And they overcame him by the blood of the Lamb, and by the word of their testimony; and they loved not their lives unto the death.	11 "And they overcame him by the blood of the Lamb and by the word of their testimony, and they did not love their lives to the death.	11 They defeated him by the blood of the Lamb, and by their testimony; for they did not love their lives but laid them down for him.
14:9 And the third angel followed them, saying with a loud voice, If any man worship the beast and his image, and receive *his* mark in his forehead, or in his hand,	**14:9** Then a third angel followed them, saying with a loud voice, "If anyone worships the beast and his image, and receives *his* mark on his forehead or on his hand,	**14:9** Then a third angel followed them shouting, "Anyone worshiping the Creature from the sea and his statue and accepting his mark on the forehead or the hand,
10 The same shall drink of the wine of the wrath of God, which is poured out without mixture into the cup of his indignation; and he shall be tormented with fire and brimstone in the presence of the holy angels, and in the presence of the Lamb:	10 "he himself shall also drink of the wine of the wrath of God, which is poured out full strength into the cup of His indignation. And he shall be tormented with fire and brimstone in the presence of the holy angels and in the presence of the Lamb.	10 must drink the wine of the anger of God; it is poured out undiluted into God's cup of wrath. And they will be tormented with fire and burning sulphur in the presence of the holy angels and the Lamb.
18:2 And he cried mightily with a strong voice, saying, Babylon the great is fallen, is fallen, and is become the habitation of devils, and the hold of every foul spirit, and a cage of every unclean and hateful bird.	**18:2** And he cried mightily with a loud voice, saying, "Babylon the great is fallen, is fallen, and has become a habitation of demons, a prison for every foul spirit, and a cage for every unclean and hated bird!	**18:2** He gave a mighty shout, "Babylon the Great is fallen, is fallen; she has become a den of demons, a haunt of devils and every kind of evil spirit.

NIV	RSV	TEV
6 Then I saw a Lamb, looking as if it had been slain, standing in the center of the throne, encircled by the four living creatures and the elders. He had seven horns and seven eyes, which are the seven spirits of God sent out into all the earth.	6 And between the throne and the four living creatures and among the elders, I saw a Lamb standing, as though it had been slain, with seven horns and with seven eyes, which are the seven spirits of God sent out into all the earth;	6 Then I saw a Lamb standing in the center of the throne, surrounded by the four living creatures and the elders. The Lamb appeared to have been killed. It had seven horns and seven eyes, which are the seven spirits of God that have been sent through the whole earth.

9 And they sang a new song:
 	
"You are worthy to take the scroll
  and to open its seals,
because you were slain,
  and with your blood you purchased men
    for God
  from every tribe and language and people
    and nation.
	9 and they sang a new song, saying,
	"Worthy art thou to take the scroll and to
	  open its seals,
	for thou wast slain and by thy blood didst
	  ransom men for God
	from every tribe and tongue and people and
	  nation,
		9 They sang a new song:
		"You are worthy to take the scroll
		  and to break open its seals.
		For you were killed, and by your sacrificial
		  death you bought for God
		people from every tribe, language, nation,
		  and race.

10 You have made them to be a kingdom and
  priests to serve our God,
  and they will reign on the earth."
	10 and hast made them a kingdom and priests
	  to our God,
	  and they shall reign on earth."
		10 You have made them a kingdom of priests
		  to serve our God,
		  and they shall rule on earth."

6:14 The sky receded like a scroll, rolling up, and every mountain and island was removed from its place.	6:14 the sky vanished like a scroll that is rolled up, and every mountain and island was removed from its place.	6:14 The sky disappeared like a scroll being rolled up, and every mountain and island was moved from its place.
15 Then the kings of the earth, the princes, the generals, the rich, the mighty, and every slave and every free man hid in caves and among the rocks of the mountains.	15 Then the kings of the earth and the great men and the generals and the rich and the strong, and every one, slave and free, hid in the caves and among the rocks of the mountains,	15 Then the kings of the earth, the rulers and the military chiefs, the rich and the powerful, and all other men, slave and free, hid themselves in caves and under rocks on the mountains.

7:15 Therefore,
 	
"they are before the throne of God
  and serve him day and night in his
    temple;
  and he who sits on the throne will
    spread his tent over them.
	7:15 Therefore are they before the throne of
	  God,
	  and serve him day and night within his
	    temple;
	  and he who sits upon the throne will
	    shelter them with his presence.
		7:15 That is why they stand before God's throne and serve him day and night in his temple. He who sits on the throne will protect them with his presence.

16 Never again will they hunger;
  never again will they thirst.
The sun will not beat upon them,
  nor any scorching heat.
	16 They shall hunger no more, neither thirst
	  any more;
	the sun shall not strike them, nor any
	  scorching heat.
		16 Never again will they hunger or thirst; neither sun nor any scorching heat will burn them,

12:10 Then I heard a loud voice in heaven say:
 	
"Now have come the salvation and the power
  and the kingdom of our God,
  and the authority of his Christ.
For the accuser of our brothers,
  who accuses them before our God day and
    night,
  has been hurled down.
	12:10 And I heard a loud voice in heaven, saying, "Now the salvation and the power and the kingdom of our God and the authority of his Christ have come, for the accuser of our brethren has been thrown down, who accuses them day and night before our God.	12:10 Then I heard a loud voice in heaven saying, "Now God's salvation has come! Now God has shown his power as King! Now his Messiah has shown his authority! For the one who stood before our God and accused our brothers day and night has been thrown out of heaven.

11 They overcame him
  by the blood of the Lamb
  and by the word of their testimony;
they did not love their lives so much
  as to shrink from death.
	11 And they have conquered him by the blood of the Lamb and by the word of their testimony, for they loved not their lives even unto death.	11 Our brothers won the victory over him by the blood of the Lamb and by the truth which they proclaimed; and they were willing to give up their lives and die.

14:9 A third angel followed them and said in a loud voice: "If anyone worships the beast and his image and receives his mark on the forehead or on the hand,	14:9 And another angel, a third, followed them, saying with a loud voice, "If any one worships the beast and its image, and receives a mark on his forehead or on his hand,	14:9 A third angel followed the first two, saying in a loud voice, "Whoever worships the beast and its image and receives the mark on his forehead or on his hand
10 he, too, will drink of the wine of God's fury, which has been poured full strength into the cup of his wrath. He will be tormented with burning sulfur in the presence of the holy angels and of the Lamb.	10 he also shall drink the wine of God's wrath, poured unmixed into the cup of his anger, and he shall be tormented with fire and sulphur in the presence of the holy angels and in the presence of the Lamb.	10 will himself drink God's wine, the wine of his fury, which he has poured at full strength into the cup of his anger! All who do this will be tormented in fire and sulfur before the holy angels and the Lamb.

18:2 With a mighty voice he shouted:
 	
"Fallen! Fallen is Babylon the Great!
  She has become a home for demons
and a haunt for every evil spirit,
  a haunt for every unclean and detestable
    bird.
	18:2 And he called out with a mighty voice,
	"Fallen, fallen is Babylon the great!
	  It has become a dwelling place of demons,
	  a haunt of every foul spirit,
	  a haunt of every foul and hateful bird;
		18:2 He cried out in a loud voice: "She has fallen! Great Babylon has fallen! She is now haunted by demons and unclean spirits; all kinds of filthy and hateful birds live in her.

KJV	NKJV	TLB
19:11 And I saw heaven opened, and behold a white horse; and he that sat upon him *was* called Faithful and True, and in righteousness he doth judge and make war.	**19:11** Then I saw heaven opened, and behold, a white horse. And He who sat on him *was* called Faithful and True, and in righteousness He judges and makes war.	**19:11** Then I saw heaven opened and a white horse standing there; and the one sitting on the horse was named "Faithful and True"—the one who justly punishes and makes war.

16 And he hath on *his* vesture and on his thigh a name written, KING OF KINGS, AND LORD OF LORDS.	16 And He has on *His* robe and on His thigh a name written:
	
	    KING OF KINGS
	   AND LORD OF LORDS.
		16 On his robe and thigh was written this title: "King of Kings and Lord of Lords."

20:4 And I saw thrones, and they sat upon them, and judgment was given unto them: and *I saw* the souls of them that were beheaded for the witness of Jesus, and for the word of God, and which had not worshipped the beast, neither his image, neither had received *his* mark upon their foreheads, or in their hands; and they lived and reigned with Christ a thousand years.	**20:4** And I saw thrones, and they sat on them, and judgment was committed to them. And *I saw* the souls of those who had been beheaded for their witness to Jesus and for the word of God, who had not worshiped the beast or his image, and had not received *his* mark on their foreheads or on their hands. And they lived and reigned with Christ for a thousand years.	**20:4** Then I saw thrones, and sitting on them were those who had been given the right to judge. And I saw the souls of those who had been beheaded for their testimony about Jesus, for proclaiming the Word of God, and who had not worshiped the Creature or his statue, nor accepted his mark on their foreheads or their hands. They had come to life again and now they reigned with Christ for a thousand years.
21:1 And I saw a new heaven and a new earth: for the first heaven and the first earth were passed away; and there was no more sea.	**21:1** And I saw a new heaven and a new earth, for the first heaven and the first earth had passed away. Also there was no more sea.	**21:1** Then I saw a new earth (with no oceans!) and a new sky, for the present earth and sky had disappeared.
2 And I John saw the holy city, new Jerusalem, coming down from God out of heaven, prepared as a bride adorned for her husband.	2 Then I, John, saw the holy city, New Jerusalem, coming down out of heaven from God, prepared as a bride adorned for her husband.	2 And I, John, saw the Holy City, the new Jerusalem, coming down from God out of heaven. It was a glorious sight, beautiful as a bride at her wedding.
4 And God shall wipe away all tears from their eyes; and there shall be no more death, neither sorrow, nor crying, neither shall there be any more pain: for the former things are passed away.	4 "And God will wipe away every tear from their eyes; there shall be no more death, nor sorrow, nor crying; and there shall be no more pain, for the former things have passed away."	4 He will wipe away all tears from their eyes, and there shall be no more death, nor sorrow, nor crying, nor pain. All of that has gone forever."
7 He that overcometh shall inherit all things; and I will be his God, and he shall be my son.	7 "He who overcomes shall inherit all things, and I will be his God and he shall be My son.	7 Everyone who conquers will inherit all these blessings, and I will be his God and he will be my son.
22 And I saw no temple therein: for the Lord God Almighty and the Lamb are the temple of it.	22 But I saw no temple in it, for the Lord God Almighty and the Lamb are its temple.	22 No temple could be seen in the city, for the Lord God Almighty and the Lamb are worshiped in it everywhere.
22:12 And, behold, I come quickly; and my reward *is* with me, to give every man according as his work shall be.	**22:12** "And behold, I am coming quickly, and My reward *is* with Me, to give to every one according to his work.	**22:12** "See, I am coming soon, and my reward is with me, to repay everyone according to the deeds he has done.
13 I am Alpha and Omega, the beginning and the end, the first and the last.	13 "I am the Alpha and the Omega, *the* Beginning and *the* End, the First and the Last."	13 I am the A and the Z, the Beginning and the End, the First and Last.
20 He which testifieth these things saith, Surely I come quickly. Amen. Even so, come, Lord Jesus.	20 He who testifies to these things says, "Surely I am coming quickly." Amen. Even so, come, Lord Jesus!	20 "He who has said all these things declares: Yes, I am coming soon!" Amen! Come, Lord Jesus!

NIV	RSV	TEV
19:11 I saw heaven standing open and there before me was a white horse, whose rider is called Faithful and True. With justice he judges and makes war.	**19:11** Then I saw heaven opened, and behold, a white horse! He who sat upon it is called Faithful and True, and in righteousness he judges and makes war.	**19:11** Then I saw heaven open, and there was a white horse. Its rider is called Faithful and True; it is with justice that he judges and fights his battles.
16 On his robe and on his thigh he has this name written: KING OF KINGS AND LORD OF LORDS.	16 On his robe and on his thigh he has a name inscribed, King of kings and Lord of lords.	16 On his robe and on his thigh was written the name: "King of kings and Lord of lords."
20:4 I saw thrones on which were seated those who had been given authority to judge. And I saw the souls of those who had been beheaded because of their testimony for Jesus and because of the word of God. They had not worshiped the beast or his image and had not received his mark on their foreheads or their hands. They came to life and reigned with Christ a thousand years.	**20:4** Then I saw thrones, and seated on them were those to whom judgment was committed. Also I saw the souls of those who had been beheaded for their testimony to Jesus and for the word of God, and who had not worshiped the beast or its image and had not received its mark on their foreheads or their hands. They came to life, and reigned with Christ a thousand years.	**20:4** Then I saw thrones, and those who sat on them were given the power to judge. I also saw the souls of those who had been executed because they had proclaimed the truth that Jesus revealed and the word of God. They had not worshiped the beast or its image, nor had they received the mark of the beast on their foreheads or their hands. They came to life and ruled as kings with Christ for a thousand years.
21:1 Then I saw a new heaven and a new earth, for the first heaven and the first earth had passed away, and there was no longer any sea.	**21:1** Then I saw a new heaven and a new earth; for the first heaven and the first earth had passed away, and the sea was no more.	**21:1** Then I saw a new heaven and a new earth. The first heaven and the first earth disappeared, and the sea vanished.
2 I saw the Holy City, the new Jerusalem, coming down out of heaven from God, prepared as a bride beautifully dressed for her husband.	2 And I saw the holy city, new Jerusalem, coming down out of heaven from God, prepared as a bride adorned for her husband;	2 And I saw the Holy City, the new Jerusalem, coming down out of heaven from God, prepared and ready, like a bride dressed to meet her husband.
4 He will wipe every tear from their eyes. There will be no more death or mourning or crying or pain, for the old order of things has passed away."	4 he will wipe away every tear from their eyes, and death shall be no more, neither shall there be mourning nor crying nor pain any more, for the former things have passed away."	4 He will wipe away all tears from their eyes. There will be no more death, no more grief or crying or pain. The old things have disappeared."
7 He who overcomes will inherit all this, and I will be his God and he will be my son.	7 He who conquers shall have this heritage, and I will be his God and he shall be my son.	7 Whoever wins the victory will receive this from me: I will be his God, and he will be my son.
22 I did not see a temple in the city, because the Lord God Almighty and the Lamb are its temple.	22 And I saw no temple in the city, for its temple is the Lord God the Almighty and the Lamb.	22 I did not see a temple in the city, because its temple is the Lord God Almighty and the Lamb.
22:12 "Behold, I am coming soon! My reward is with me, and I will give to everyone according to what he has done.	**22:12** "Behold, I am coming soon, bringing my recompense, to repay every one for what he has done.	**22:12** "Listen!" says Jesus. "I am coming soon! I will bring my rewards with me, to give to each one according to what he has done.
13 I am the Alpha and the Omega, the First and the Last, the Beginning and the End.	13 I am the Alpha and the Omega, the first and the last, the beginning and the end."	13 I am the first and the last, the beginning and the end."
20 He who testifies to these things says, "Yes, I am coming soon." Amen. Come, Lord Jesus.	20 He who testifies to these things says, "Surely I am coming soon." Amen. Come, Lord Jesus!	20 He who gives his testimony to all this says, "Yes indeed! I am coming soon! So be it. Come, Lord Jesus!